MW00565642

An exploratory human services program from Goodheart-Willcox

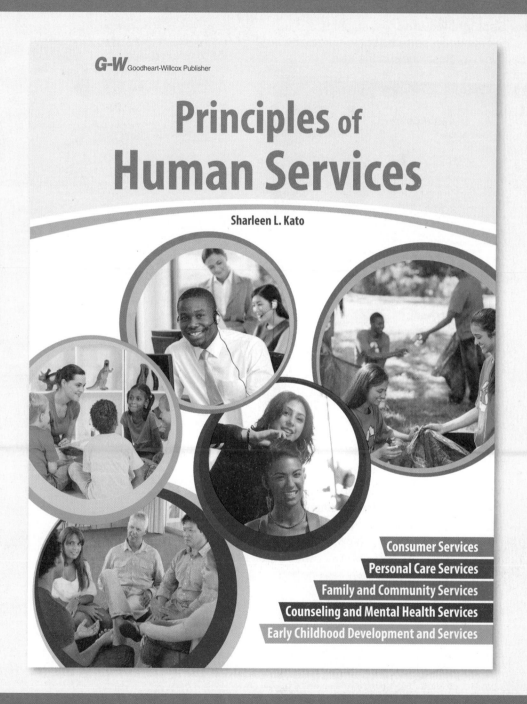

G-W Goodheart-Willcox Publisher

Principles of Human Services

Sharleen L. Kato

Consumer Services
Personal Care Services
Family and Community Services
Counseling and Mental Health Services
Early Childhood Development and Services

introduces students to all five human services career pathways

Spotlights diverse careers for students to consider

Career Spotlight features give students a closer look at human services careers from the perspective of professionals in the field.

Copyright Goodheart-Willcox Co., Inc.

Career Spotlight

Certified Hospital Child Life Specialist

Madeline Caryl Wion

My job is to prepare children for procedures and medical care to reduce stress and anxiety in the hospital environment. Preparation can come in many forms. Typically, however, it involves teaching children in developmentally appropriate terms about what is going to happen to them. I often describe procedures in terms of senses: what they will smell, see, feel, hear, and taste. I also work with the children and families to discover and implement coping skills that will be beneficial throughout the procedure, illness, and hospital stay.

Every morning, our staff gets a census that has the name, age, diagnosis, and additional psychosocial and medical information necessary to work with the patient and family. My job revolves around family-centered care. This means that we treat not only the patient, but the whole family. I prioritize my patients for the day and work accordingly. Procedures, such as surgeries and IV placement, and new diagnoses often take priority in the day.

Play is also a very important part of child life. Play is often how a child communicates and processes information. Providing play opportunities allows us to normalize the hospital environment, as well as get an insight into how the child is coping with hospitalization.

In the PICU (pediatric intensive care unit), I work with children and their families in very high-stress situations. Much of my work in the PICU deals with end-of-life issues. This means that the child is actively dying. We focus on preparing siblings and parents for what to expect and how to cope. I also do "memory making" for the family to have handprints/footprints and molds, as well as a clipping of hair and other mementos, to aid in the grieving process. I believe it is a great honor when a family allows you to be involved in their child's end-of-life process.

I love being a child life specialist! Although it can be emotionally taxing at times, I believe there is so much reward in helping a child and family in the hospital. Sickness is the reality for many families. My goal is to help reduce the stress and fear as much as possible.

Research Activity

Conduct online research to learn more about the different human services careers in the healthcare field. Choose one occupation that sounds appealing to you. Research the requirements for that type of position. Be sure to find out the education requirements, what kind of previous experience is needed, and what skills and personal qualities a person with that occupation should have. Research the salary ranges and typical job duties for your chosen occupation. After completing your research, determine whether or not you would be interested in pursuing this as a career. Why or why not?

Photo courtesy of Madeline Caryl Wion

Copyright Goodheart-Willcox Co., Inc.

Career Spotlight

Curriculum Director

Curtis Larkins

I have always loved working with children. Throughout high school, I babysat for several families to earn spending money. In college, I found that working as a nanny for a professional working family was both rewarding and allowed me the flexibility to earn a living while attending school. Through these experiences, I learned how important my work was in the lives of young children. Because I found the children to be utterly amazing, I quickly changed my major to early childhood education.

To add more practical experience to my education, I did an internship as part of my studies with an early childhood education center. During my internship, I learned about child-directed learning, the role of the teacher as a learning facilitator, and how to document childhood learning activities. I gained insight into the logistical and business aspects of the business of early childhood education. This is where I found my home and knew that this was the field in which I wanted to have a career.

After graduation, I first worked as an assistant teacher and then as a lead teacher. At our center, we take a whole family approach, involving children and their families in the joy of learning through play. Our classrooms are designed to feel like home with soft textures, warm lighting, plenty of art supplies, and opportunities for play and exploration. The children even have their own family photos displayed. We rely on natural and reused materials for artistic play, such as rocks, beans, and interesting recycled goods. The children paint, sculpt, draw, sing, and dance on a daily basis as a way of expressing their thoughts and ideas. We try to spend time outdoors each day, whenever possible. I take lots of photographs and record their intellectual, emotional, and social growth so I can share with and support their parents in facilitating their holistic growth.

Last year, I became the Curriculum Director for the center. This means that I lead teacher training, keeping them updated in the newest research about how young children learn. We brainstorm together about ways that we can best meet the needs of our children.

I know that this has been the right career path for me and that I am making a difference in the lives of young children. Someone once asked me, "What is it that you are really good at?" It seemed like a difficult question at the time, but now I know. I am good at creating learning environments where children can learn through play and discovery.

Research Activity

Conduct online research about different careers that would allow you to work with children. What common aptitudes, abilities, and skills are needed? What are the educational requirements? Would you be interested in this type of career?

eurobanks/Shutterstock.com

Copyright Goodheart-Willcox Co., Inc.

111

Succinct tables list relevant occupations in each pathway, including future trends and projected growth.

Figure 8.1 There are many different careers in consumer services. Which area of consumer services interests you most?

Examples of Consumer Services Careers	
Consumer advocacy	• Community consumer educator • Community organizer • Consumer advocate • Consumer journalist • Consumer litigation attorney • Consumer lobbyist • Nonprofit foundation manager • Policy analyst
Financial services	• Budget analyst • Credit counselor • Financial advisor • Financial analyst • Financial manager • Insurance sales agent • Insurance underwriter
Customer service	• Computer support specialist • Customer service representative • Retail sales manager • Retail sales worker • Sales manager • Sales worker
Buying	• Buyer • Purchasing agent • Purchasing manager • Retail buyer • Supply chain manager

Copyright Goodheart-Willcox Co., Inc.

Future Trends for Consumer Services Careers				
Occupation	**Projected Growth (2014–2024)**	**Projected Job Openings (2014–2024)**	**Median Wages (2014)**	**Education**
Budget analyst	Slower than average (2–4%)	16,700	$71,220	Bachelor's degree
Community consumer educator	Decline (–2% or lower)	800	$63,390	Master's degree
Computer support specialist	Faster than average (9–13%)	150,500	$47,610	Bachelor's degree
Consumer journalist	Decline (–2% or lower)	15,900	$36,000	Bachelor's degree
Consumer litigation attorney	Average (5–8%)	157,700	$114,970	Doctoral degree
Credit counselor	Much faster than average (14% or higher)	10,500	$42,110	Bachelor's degree
Customer service representative	Faster than average (9–13%)	888,700	$31,200	High school diploma
Financial advisor	Much faster than average (14% or higher)	136,400	$81,060	Bachelor's degree
Financial analyst	Faster than average (9–13%)	89,400	$78,620	Bachelor's degree
Financial manager	Average (5–8%)	169,300	$115,320	Bachelor's degree
Insurance sales agent	Faster than average (9–13%)	165,800	$47,860	Bachelor's degree
Insurance underwriter	Decline (–2% or lower)	19,500	$64,220	Bachelor's degree
Nonprofit foundation manager	Average (5–8%)	27,100	$101,510	Bachelor's degree
Policy analyst	Average (5–8%)	7,000	$95,710	Doctoral degree
Purchasing agent	Little or no change (–1–1%)	82,700	$60,980	Bachelor's degree
Purchasing manager	Little or no change (–1–1%)	17,900	$106,090	Bachelor's degree
Retail buyer	Average (5–8%)	49,100	$52,270	Bachelor's degree
Retail sales manager	Slower than average (2–4%)	411,300	$37,860	High school diploma
Retail sales worker	Average (5–8%)	1,917,200	$21,390	High school diploma
Sales manager	Average (5–8%)	108,000	$110,660	Bachelor's degree
Supply chain manager	Slower than average (2–4%)	255,400	$105,060	Bachelor's degree

Sources: O*NET and the Occupational Outlook Handbook

Figure 8.20 Learning as much as possible about careers can help you make informed career decisions. According to the information in this chart, which consumer services careers are predicted to have the highest projected growth?

Copyright Goodheart-Willcox Co., Inc.

Copyright Goodheart-Willcox Co., Inc.

Presents new terms to expand students' vocabulary

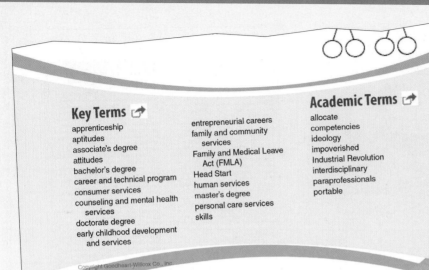

Key Terms enhance students' understanding of content vocabulary. **Academic Terms** build students' everyday vocabulary.

Key Terms

apprenticeship
aptitudes
associate's degree
attitudes
bachelor's degree
career and technical program
consumer services
counseling and mental health services
doctorate degree
early childhood development and services

entrepreneurial careers
family and community services
Family and Medical Leave Act (FMLA)
Head Start
human services
master's degree
personal care services
skills

Academic Terms

allocate
competencies
ideology
impoverished
Industrial Revolution
interdisciplinary
paraprofessionals
portable

5

Copyright Goodheart-Willcox Co., Inc.

Key Terms appear in bold, highlighted type in the text where they are defined. **Academic Terms** are shown in blue, italic type.

Counseling and Mental Health Services

The **counseling and mental health services** field involves helping people maintain healthy, productive lives. This is achieved through therapy, counseling, and education or training. Common counseling and mental health services positions include counselors, psychologists, and other *paraprofessionals* (trained workers who assist qualified professionals).

Counseling and mental health services workers work in settings that include clinics, research labs, schools, group homes, and hospitals. They also work in corporate settings, promoting positive relationships among employees. Counseling and mental health services workers know about human behavior. They frequently work with mental health issues, substance abuse, eating disorders, special needs, family relationships, and career and life counseling.

Vocabulary Activities invite students to apply their knowledge at the end of every chapter.

Vocabulary Activities

13. **Key terms** In teams, create categories for the following terms and classify as many of the terms as possible. Then, share your ideas with the remainder of the class.

behaviorism
classical conditioning
cognitive theories
developmental theories
expansion mode
human development
operant conditioning

psychoanalytic theories
recession mode
recovery mode
resources
social cognitive theory
standard of living

Copyright Goodheart-Willcox Co., Inc.

Review and Assessment

14. **Academic terms** Work with a partner to write the definitions of the following terms based on your current understanding before reading the chapter. Then, pair up with another partner to discuss your definitions and any discrepancies. Finally, discuss the definitions with the class. Ask your instructor for necessary correction or clarification.

elements
environment
esteem
heredity

hierarchy
inferiority
moral issues
self-actualization

Copyright Goodheart-Willcox Co., Inc.

Engages students with high-interest features

Pathway to Success hands-on activities provide opportunities for students to build skills and learn best practices they can apply to their everyday lives now and in the future.

Pathway to Success

Portable Skills in the Twenty-First Century

You hear the buzz word "portable skills" when people talk about résumés and look for a job. What are portable skills? How can you find out if you have any? *Portable skills* are skills you learn at one job that you can use in different work situations—even in a different industry. These might also be skills you develop through volunteer work, hobbies, sports, or other life experiences.

Some of the basic portable skills that almost everyone has include decision-making, communication (both written and verbal), problem-solving, and leadership skills. Other portable skills that employers look for may include

- meeting deadlines;
- having the ability to plan and delegate;
- accepting responsibility;
- instructing others;
- using good time management skills;
- being open to learning new skills; and
- showing how you can increase sales or productivity.

Now that you know what portable skills include, you can work on your own list of personal portable skills. Some easy steps to help figure out what portable skills you have include

- making a list of your experiences on and off campus;
- developing an inventory of skills;
- highlighting your research experiences;
- describing how you make a decision;
- listing leadership roles; and
- explaining how well you function in a group setting.

The portable skills you develop now will help shape the professional you will become. While you are still in school, you are able to work on your creativity, learn how to ask for help, and build your personal credibility. Volunteer opportunities will enable you to meet new people and network. Remember the old adage, "it's not what you know, but who you know."

Create a Personal Skills and Job Chart

Using the steps above, make a list of skills you possess, as well as skills you are learning. Update this list throughout the year. Remember to also keep a list of any volunteer and work experiences, including the duties you perform. These lists come in handy to remind you of your accomplishments. You can add them to your résumé or talk about them during a job interview.

After gathering this information, put it into a chart. You can do this in many ways. One way is to list the job in one column and the skills learned in a second column. Another way is to break down the skills into areas in one column (such as communication skills, decision making, problem solving, and leadership) and list examples in the second column. Be creative as you make your own list and chart. Use this information to help you determine which portable skills you can start developing now.

Copyright Goodheart-Willcox Co., Inc.

Case Study   *Making a Difference*

Amelia learned about four-year-old Michael several months ago. When neighbors reported concerns about his safety, the state's child protective services became involved. He had not been physically abused. It appeared, however, that Michael was often left without proper supervision.

Neglect is hard to prove. It took several months to build a case for removing Michael from his home and placing him in foster care. Amelia was sure that Michael's mother had a desire to care for him. Her lack of family support and struggle with substance abuse, however, make it difficult for her to care for Michael. Amelia and her colleagues at the foster care agency provide emotional support for Michael's mother. They hope that she will get her life under control so she can properly care for her son.

A neighbor found Michael alone, hungry, and dirty this afternoon. When his mother could not be found, the local police stepped in. Later that evening, a social worker called Amelia to take Michael. As the human services case manager, Amelia had to quickly find a place for Michael to live.

Amelia knew Michael would be well taken care of in this emergency foster home. For now, Amelia would rest easy. Tomorrow would hold a new day for Michael, his mother, and his foster parents. It could be filled with fear, grief and loss, and dismay. She hoped

it would also hold a sense of warmth and stability for Michael.

Amelia has a career in human services. People are drawn to human services careers for different reasons. Like most Americans living with basic needs met, watching news reports of children in need profoundly affected Amelia. During Amelia's high school years, her town was affected by a severe rainstorm that caused flash floods and evacuations. During that event, Amelia's passion grew for helping people, especially displaced children.

Sometimes it takes a big event like Amelia's to jolt a person into meaningful life choices. Sometimes it is a gradual realization that helping others is what gives meaning to life. For Amelia, helping others means helping foster children find safe, temporary homes.

Personally, Amelia had no experience with foster care. She grew up in a privileged urban home. During her teen years, she lived with her mother after her parents divorced. Even so, she maintained a strong relationship with both of her parents. Education was highly esteemed in Amelia's family. She had many strong role models. She was considered a high achiever throughout high school and college, both in academics and in extracurricular leadership activities. Human services proved to be the career track that allowed Amelia to combine her drive for excellence and her leadership skills with her passion to make a difference in the world.

EBPhoto/Shutterstock.com

For Discussion

1. What are three specific ways that Amelia helped make Michael's life better?
2. List two ways that Amelia could help Michael's mother better parent him.
3. What appeals to Amelia about her career in human services?
4. Do you share any common interests or traits with Amelia? If so, which one(s)?

Copyright Goodheart-Willcox Co., Inc.

Case Studies capture students' interest with real-life scenarios and follow-up questions to involve students in class discussion.

Law and Ethics   *Using Technology In Human Services*

In recent decades, technology has changed virtually all aspects of society and continues to do so. Human services is no exception. While computers were originally developed for use by business and government, their application to other areas, including human services, quickly became apparent. Other related forms of technology soon followed.

Many human services careers involve keeping track of and using numerous types of factual information, or data, for future use. Computers are particularly suited to simplifying those tasks.

Keeping accurate records is essential for many human services workers. Each time a human services worker meets with a client, he or she must record and save the information for future use. At the end of a service period, human services workers must calculate costs and provide billing information. Electronic programs can greatly simplify this process. Any files including confidential information should be password protected.

Electronic spreadsheet programs, such as Excel™, allow information to be adapted for different uses. For example, a human services worker might set up a basic spreadsheet with a list of clients and services provided. This same spreadsheet could also be adapted to keep track of each client's progress toward meeting specific class goals or any other need. Various types of reports could be generated based on the data in a particular spreadsheet.

There are countless other ways that human services workers can use technology to boost their productivity. For example, a human services worker might send a weekly or monthly newsletter to clients. After developing the newsletter template, the human services worker can simply add new information as needed. Using an electronic contact list could speed the process of sending the newsletter electronically or printing labels for

mailing. Many human services workers also have their own professional websites.

Technology offers human services workers exciting options for presenting information in diverse ways that can bring learning to life. It takes effort, imagination, and a willingness to learn new skills. Some options require more sophisticated technology than others. Even with limited equipment, however, human services workers can add variety to the services they provide.

Although technology offers tremendous advantages, it also offers challenges in a field that is so personal and people oriented. A tremendous amount of confidential information may be shared between clients and the care provider. Private financial, medical, and employment information, along with information about family relationships, drug use or addictions, abuse or other violence, and criminal activities, may be recorded. Human services workers must be extra vigilant in using secure technology tools to store, communicate, and retrieve this information. They must take precautions to ensure that privacy is maintained at all times and that all confidentiality laws and requirements are observed.

Writing Activity

Keep a log for a week of all the types of technology you use to transmit information to others. Write an essay in response to the following questions:

1. What information would you not want conveyed to the general public without your knowledge? Why?
2. What harm might come from personal information being shared with others?
3. How might you ensure that the information you have shared is not passed on to other unintended receivers?

Law and Ethics features deliver thought-provoking information and topics to keep students attentive and interested.

Copyright Goodheart-Willcox Co., Inc.

Improves comprehension with study aids

Reading Strategies

Before reading, skim the chapter and consider what each concept you learn might teach you about yourself. Write a list of these ideas, placing a star beside any concepts that especially interest you. As you are reading, take notes about information relating to these concepts. After reading this chapter, pick three of the ideas and write a few paragraphs reflecting on how these concepts have helped or will help you understand yourself.

Mapping Concepts

In the middle circle of a chart like the one shown, write *My Personal Brand*. Then, as you read this chapter and complete the activities of self-reflection, write your unique qualities in the surrounding boxes. After you have filled in the boxes, consider your personal brand. Next to each box, write any areas you would like to change or qualities you would like to develop.

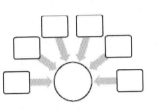

Reading Strategies and **Mapping Concepts** activities enhance students' reading and note-taking skills.

Reading Recall questions throughout each chapter check students' understanding of main concepts.

Reading Recall

1. Give five examples of human services careers.
2. What do consumer services workers do?
3. Who are *paraprofessionals*?
4. Human services workers in _____ understand and meet the needs of infants, toddlers, and young children.
5. Which broad employment category in the field of human services includes emergency and relief workers and social workers?
6. List three jobs in personal care services.
7. People who pursue entrepreneurial careers are called _____.
8. Human services workers may provide related services in which three areas?

Core Skills

23. **Reading and writing** Find a nonfiction book to read about one of the following historical events: the Industrial Revolution, World War I, the Great Depression, or World War II. Create a time line of important events and dates discussed in the book. Share your findings with the class.
24. **Reading and math** Reread the Case Study, *Making a Difference*, in this chapter to find out why Amelia chose to become a human services worker. What are some other reasons people might be drawn to human services careers? As a class, create a survey to poll human services workers to find out why they entered the field of human services. Tally the survey results and post them in class.
25. **Listening, writing, and speaking** Arrange to interview a human services worker to learn more about his or her job. Before the interview, write a list of 10 questions that you intend to ask during the interview. After the interview, write a summary detailing what you learned from this experience. Share your summaries with the rest of the class.

26

Critical Thinking

15. **Make inferences** Based on the last 100 years of growth in the field of human services, what do you predict will happen with jobs in these fields over the next 50 years?
16. **Cause and effect** During the Industrial Revolution, the needs of the impoverished could no longer be ignored. What caused this shift in thinking and what effect did it have on society?
17. **Draw conclusions** There is a quote in the chapter by Jane Addams. What do you think this quote meant at the time it was said? Do you think this quote holds true today?

25

End-of-chapter reviews are built-in opportunities for discussion, higher-order thinking, and collaborative learning.

Review and Reflect

1. What is the primary focus of the human services profession?
2. Summarize how the events of World War I, the Great Depression, and World War II changed how society viewed poverty.
3. Describe two programs that have resulted from the HHS.
4. Identify the broad employment categories in the field of human services and give an example of an occupation within each of these categories.

Copyright Goodheart-Willcox Co., Inc.

Targets professional development and community involvement

College and Career Portfolio activities guide students through developing their own portfolio and collecting meaningful samples of their work.

College and Career Portfolio

Portfolio Checklist

Now that you know the purpose of and how you will organize your portfolio, consider what items you want to include. Having a checklist of components to include in your portfolio can help keep you organized. Your instructor may provide you with or guide you in developing a checklist. Make sure to create a checklist that works best for you and for the purpose of your portfolio.

After you create your checklist, identify *where* you will acquire these items. Also determine *how* you will acquire them and *what resources* you will need. Identify any items on your checklist which you will need outside help to acquire. Identifying these items early will enable you to obtain them in a timely manner.

Complete the following steps to create your portfolio checklist:
1. Compile a checklist of items to include in your portfolio. If you need guidance, talk to your teacher or to a college or career counselor.
2. Determine how you will acquire the items on your checklist. Make note of any outside help you may need.
3. Save your checklist to an easy-to-access location in your e-Portfolio. Also, print a copy for easy reference.

Copyright Goodheart-Willcox Co., Inc.

Lend a Hand

Volunteering: Where to Start?

Doing volunteer work and community service is a great way to get involved and give back to your local and global communities. There are opportunities to help others everywhere you look. Getting started with a service project can seem daunting, however, if you do not know where to start.

First, determine what type of project you want to do. What needs exist in your community? What are your personal interests? What skills do you have to offer? Think about your service goals. What effect do you want your volunteer work to have? How much time are you willing or able to commit to your service project? Would you prefer to start a new project or join in someone else's efforts?

Next, do your research. Find out what resources are available in your area. One way to do this is to conduct an online search for local volunteer opportunities. Some websites, such as VolunteerMatch, can help you identify opportunities in your area. Searching for volunteer networks and resources and looking at nonprofit databases online are other ways to identify possible volunteer opportunities.

In addition to searching online, you might also want to contact different organizations, nonprofit agencies, and local businesses to assess their needs. Places like food banks, animal shelters, soup kitchens, and hospitals work with volunteers often and are easy to join.

To get started on your path toward volunteering, complete the following:
1. Brainstorm a list of volunteer ideas that interest you. Think about your skills and what you might enjoy doing. Narrow your list to about five options.
2. Using your list of volunteer ideas, research how you can make a difference in your community. Search online to find out about volunteer opportunities. Contact different businesses or organizations to learn more about ways you can help.

Lend a Hand activities provide opportunities for students to get involved, help others, and give back to their local and global communities.

Copyright Goodheart-Willcox Co., Inc.

Copyright Goodheart-Willcox Co., Inc.

A complete program for students and teachers

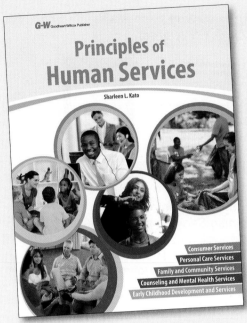

Student Textbook— Print or Online
The student edition of *Principles of Human Services* is available as a printed textbook or as an interactive online text. Simply choose the format that works best for your students.
www.g-wonlinetextbooks.com

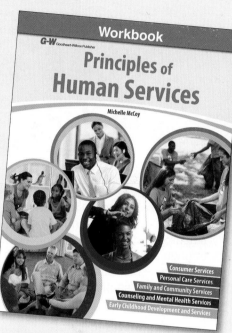

Student Workbook— Print or Online
Workbook activities reinforce material presented in the textbook, offering students a hands-on learning experience.

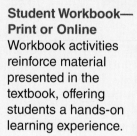

ExamView® Assessment Suite
Quickly and easily prepare and print tests with the ExamView® Assessment Suite. You can choose which questions to include in each test, create multiple versions of a single test, and automatically generate answer keys.

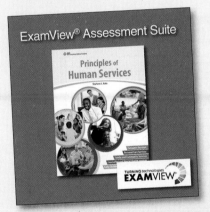

Instructor's Resource CD
Includes lesson plans, answer keys, and grading rubrics.

Instructor's Presentations for PowerPoint®
Visually reinforce key concepts with prepared lectures. Integrated review questions make the presentations interactive.

Copyright Goodheart-Willcox Co., Inc.

G-W integrated learning solution

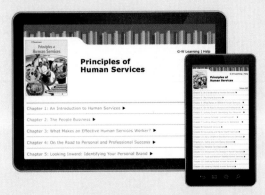

The **G-W Integrated Learning Solution** offers easy-to-use resources for both instructors and students. Both digital and blended (print + digital) teaching and learning content can be accessed through any Internet-enabled device, such as a computer, smartphone, or tablet. From the following options, choose the ones that work best for you and your students.

The **G-W Learning Companion Website** for *Principles of Human Services* accompanies the **Student Textbook** and provides content to help students build skills and knowledge, extend textbook content, and reinforce learning. The website complements textbook chapters and is available to students at no charge.

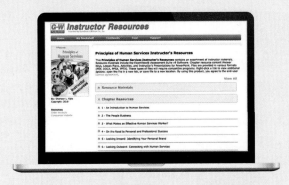

The **Online Learning Suite** for *Principles of Human Services* is available as a classroom subscription. It includes the online student text, the companion website content, and the digital workbook.

The **Online Instructor Resources** provide extensive support for instructors. Included in the online resources are Answer Keys, Lesson Plans, Instructor's Presentations for PowerPoint®, ExamView® Assessment Suite, and much more. These resources are available as a subscription and can be accessed at school or at home. They are also available on CDs.

Looking for a **Blended Solution**? G-W offers the Online Learning Suite bundled with the printed textbook in one easy-to-access package for school districts and instructors seeking a combination of print and digital tools. With this option, individual students and instructors have the flexibility of using solely print, solely digital, or a combination of print and digital versions of the *Principles of Human Services* educational materials to best meet their particular learning and teaching styles.

Copyright Goodheart-Willcox Co., Inc.

Principles of
Human Services

by

Sharleen L. Kato, EdD, CFCS-HDFS
Professor and Director
Department of Family and Consumer Sciences
Seattle Pacific University
Seattle, Washington

Pedagogy Developer
Michelle McCoy
Family and Consumer Sciences Instructor
Hendrickson High School
Pflugerville, Texas

Publisher
The Goodheart-Willcox Company, Inc.
Tinley Park, IL
www.g-w.com

Copyright © 2018
by
The Goodheart-Willcox Company, Inc.

All rights reserved. No part of this work may be reproduced, stored, or
transmitted in any form or by any electronic or mechanical means, including
information storage and retrieval systems, without the prior written permission of
The Goodheart-Willcox Company, Inc.

Manufactured in the United States of America.

ISBN 978-1-63126-531-0

4 5 6 7 8 9 – 18 – 22 21 20 19 18

The Goodheart-Willcox Company, Inc. Brand Disclaimer: Brand names, company names, and illustrations for products
and services included in this text are provided for educational purposes only and do not represent or imply endorsement or
recommendation by the author or the publisher.

The Goodheart-Willcox Company, Inc. Safety Notice: The reader is expressly advised to carefully read, understand, and apply
all safety precautions and warnings described in this book or that might also be indicated in undertaking the activities and
exercises described herein to minimize risk of personal injury or injury to others. Common sense and good judgment should also
be exercised and applied to help avoid all potential hazards. The reader should always refer to the appropriate manufacturer's
technical information, directions, and recommendations; then proceed with care to follow specific equipment operating
instructions. The reader should understand these notices and cautions are not exhaustive.

The publisher makes no warranty or representation whatsoever, either expressed or implied, including but not limited to
equipment, procedures, and applications described or referred to herein, their quality, performance, merchantability, or fitness for
a particular purpose. The publisher assumes no responsibility for any changes, errors, or omissions in this book. The publisher
specifically disclaims any liability whatsoever, including any direct, indirect, incidental, consequential, special, or exemplary
damages resulting, in whole or in part, from the reader's use or reliance upon the information, instructions, procedures, warnings,
cautions, applications, or other matter contained in this book. The publisher assumes no responsibility for the activities of the
reader.

The Goodheart-Willcox Company, Inc. Internet Disclaimer: The Internet resources and listings in this Goodheart-Willcox
Publisher product are provided solely as a convenience to you. These resources and listings were reviewed at the time of
publication to provide you with accurate, safe, and appropriate information. Goodheart-Willcox Publisher has no control over
the referenced websites and, due to the dynamic nature of the Internet, is not responsible or liable for the content, products, or
performance of links to other websites or resources. Goodheart-Willcox Publisher makes no representation, either expressed or
implied, regarding the content of these websites, and such references do not constitute an endorsement or recommendation of the
information or content presented. It is your responsibility to take all protective measures to guard against inappropriate content,
viruses, or other destructive elements.

Front cover images (clockwise from left with classroom being the farthest left):
michaeljung/Shutterstock.com, ©iStock.com/omgimages, wavebreakmedia/Shutterstock.com,
bikeriderlondon/Shutterstock.com, Monkey Business Images/Shutterstock.com

Back cover image: Monkey Business Images/Shutterstock.com

Lend a Hand image: wavebreakmedia/Shutterstock.com

About the Author

Sharleen L. Kato, *EdD, CFCS-HDFS*

Professor and Director
Department of Family and Consumer Sciences
Seattle Pacific University
Seattle, Washington

Sharleen L. Kato loves teaching as well as learning. She is a Professor at Seattle Pacific University where she encourages students to become creative problem solvers and to make a positive impact in their communities. Dr. Kato has taught undergraduate students for over 25 years, and currently serves as the Family and Consumer Sciences Department Director. She holds a Doctorate in Education, a Master's in Human Ecology, and an undergraduate degree in Home Economics. Dr. Kato has served on the Bellevue Christian Schools Education Committee and Board of Directors, Hilltop Children's Center Board of Directors, the Health and Wellness Advisory Committee for Seattle Public Schools, and education committees and task forces for Washington State Public Schools.

Dr. Kato has published many books and articles, and has presented papers in the education field. She travels extensively—spending at least two weeks each year serving in an orphanage, school, teen home, and prenatal clinic in the Philippines. Dr. Kato is passionate about inspiring others to take on the challenge of improving the quality of life of those around them.

Copyright Goodheart-Willcox Co., Inc.

Reviewers

Goodheart-Willcox Publisher and the author would like to thank the following instructors who reviewed selected manuscript chapters and provided valuable input into the development of this textbook program.

Melessa Barbknecht
Family Consumer Science Teacher
Celina High School
Celina, TX

Amber Beasley
FCS Teacher
Pflugerville High School
Pflugerville, TX

Denise Bourdeau
Family and Consumer Sciences Teacher
Shaker High School
Latham, NY

Lyn Bratten
FCS Teacher, CTE Dept. Chair
Byron Nelson High School, Northwest High School
Trophy Club, TX; Justin, TX

Nicholle Caruthers
FCS Teacher
Alvarado High School
Alvarado, TX

Jean Clarke
Family and Consumer Sciences Instructor
Bridgewater-Emery High School
Emery, SD

Anne Cornell
Consumer and Family Studies Instructor
John H. Pitman High School
Turlock, CA

Jill Duvall
Teacher
C. E. King High School
Houston, TX

Marcia Elizandro
Family and Consumer Science Teacher
Arlington High School
Arlington, TX

Amy Flick
Family and Consumer Sciences Instructor
Naaman Forest High School
Garland, TX

Sylvia Franze
Family and Consumer Sciences Instructor
Mansfield High School
Mansfield, TX

Sheryl Garofano
Family and Consumer Sciences Instructor
Cicero-North Syracuse High School
Cicero, NY

Copyright Goodheart-Willcox Co., Inc.

Jennifer Gorell
Family & Consumer Science Teacher
Kaufman High School
Kaufman, TX

Diane Jensen
Family and Consumer Sciences Teacher
Terre Haute North High School
Terre Haute, IN

Judy King
Family and Consumer Sciences Instructor
Deer Park High School
Deer Park, TX

Jennifer Lee
Family & Consumer Sciences Teacher
Harker Heights High School
Harker Heights, TX

Holly Mann
Family and Consumer Sciences Teacher
Whitehouse High School
Whitehouse, TX

Michelle McCoy
Family and Consumer Sciences Instructor
Hendrickson High School
Pflugerville, TX

Cindy Nichols
FCS Teacher
Martinsville ISD
Martinsville, TX

Wendy Shepard-Tuten
Family and Consumer Science Teacher
Duncanville High School
Duncanville, TX

Lana Shuck
Family & Consumer Science Teacher
Terre Haute South Vigo High School
Terre Haute, IN

Jelena Skaro-Soots
Teacher
Clay High School
South Bend, IN

Mary Testerman
Family and Consumer Sciences/Human
    Services Instructor
Mingo Central High School
Delbarton, WV

Kristina Wuergler
Career & Technical Education Teacher
La Porte High School
La Porte, TX

Lynette Yevak
Family and Consumer Sciences Instructor
Emporia High School
Emporia, KS

Copyright Goodheart-Willcox Co., Inc.

Brief Contents

Copyright Goodheart-Willcox Co., Inc.

Contents

Copyright Goodheart-Willcox Co., Inc.

Unit 2   Preparing for Career Success

Copyright Goodheart-Willcox Co., Inc.

Unit 3   Investigating Career Pathways in Human Services

Copyright Goodheart-Willcox Co., Inc.

Unit 4   Exploring Human Services Related Careers

Copyright Goodheart-Willcox Co., Inc.

Features

Pathway to Success

Case Study

Copyright Goodheart-Willcox Co., Inc.

Law and Ethics

Career Spotlight

College and Career Portfolio

Lend a Hand

Copyright Goodheart-Willcox Co., Inc.

To the Student

Do you want to have a career that focuses on people? If so, the field of human services may be for you. Human services workers are those ready to offer a helping hand to people struggling with life's countless obstacles. They do their best to help others meet their own needs. They understand and appreciate the human condition, and for those who enjoy working with people, human services careers can provide ample opportunity.

People are drawn to human services careers for different reasons. For those who enjoy working with people and value helping others, these careers are ideal. From child care workers and educators to financial counselors, from marriage and family therapists to housing specialists, these jobs can be found wherever people have needs, which, of course, is everywhere. The five different career pathways in human services include *consumer services, counseling and mental health services, early childhood development and services, family and community services*, and *personal care services*. Human services careers are not limited to these pathways, however. In this book, you will learn about the broad range of jobs that exist in human services.

The human services field can offer you an opportunity to work with diverse clients, including infants, children, teens, and adults. Human services workers interact with older adults; the homeless; and people with mental illnesses, disabilities, and addictions. In doing so, they may provide housing assistance for low-income individuals, offer financial education and assistance to single parents, provide counseling to those in grief, or offer after-school activities for young teens. They may also provide day care for older adults, nutrition advice for young parents, or supply temporary housing for people in transition. Daily tasks may be highly varied, requiring workers to employ a wide range of skills, knowledge, creativity, and resources.

Will you be prepared to enter the human services field when you finish this book? *No.* This book will, however, inspire you and provide a road map for your exploration of the human services field. Remember, helping people requires action. Begin to take action toward your human services career today!

Copyright Goodheart-Willcox Co., Inc.

Unit 1

Learning About Human Services

america365/Shutterstock.com

Certified Hospital Child Life Specialist

Madeline Caryl Wion

My job is to prepare children for procedures and medical care to reduce stress and anxiety in the hospital environment. Preparation can come in many forms. Typically, however, it involves teaching children in developmentally appropriate terms about what is going to happen to them. I often describe procedures in terms of senses: what they will smell, see, feel, hear, and taste. I also work with the children and families to discover and implement coping skills that will be beneficial throughout the procedure, illness, and hospital stay.

Every morning, our staff gets a census that has the name, age, diagnosis, and additional psychosocial and medical information necessary to work with the patient and family. My job revolves around family-centered care. This means that we treat not only the patient, but the whole family. I prioritize my patients for the day and work accordingly. Procedures, such as surgeries and IV placement, and new diagnoses often take priority in the day.

Photo courtesy of Madeline Caryl Wion

Play is also a very important part of child life. Play is often how a child communicates and processes information. Providing play opportunities allows us to normalize the hospital environment, as well as get an insight into how the child is coping with hospitalization.

In the PICU (pediatric intensive care unit), I work with children and their families in very high-stress situations. Much of my work in the PICU deals with end-of-life issues. This means that the child is actively dying. We focus on preparing siblings and parents for what to expect and how to cope. I also do "memory making" for the family to have handprints/footprints and molds, as well as a clipping of hair and other mementos, to aid in the grieving process. I believe it is a great honor when a family allows you to be involved in their child's end-of-life process.

I love being a child life specialist! Although it can be emotionally taxing at times, I believe there is so much reward in helping a child and family in the hospital. Sickness is the reality for many families. My goal is to help reduce the stress and fear as much as possible.

Research Activity

Conduct online research to learn more about the different human services careers in the healthcare field. Choose one occupation that sounds appealing to you. Research the requirements for that type of position. Be sure to find out the education requirements, what kind of previous experience is needed, and what skills and personal qualities a person with that occupation should have. Research the salary ranges and typical job duties for your chosen occupation. After completing your research, determine whether or not you would be interested in pursuing this as a career. Why or why not?

Copyright Goodheart-Willcox Co., Inc.

An Introduction to Human Services

While studying, look for the activity icon 📲 to

- **practice** key and academic terms with e-flash cards and matching activities;
- **assess** what you learn by completing self-assessment quizzes; and
- **reinforce** what you learn by mapping concepts and completing review and reflect questions.

www.g-wlearning.com/humanservices/

©iStock.com/Steve Debenport

After studying this chapter, you will be able to

- **explain** the historical beginnings and growth of the human services field;
- **identify** the broad employment categories in the field of human services;
- **give examples** of career opportunities for human services workers within each of the broad employment categories;
- **recognize** common aptitudes, attitudes, and skills of human services workers;
- **summarize** key education, training, and experience expectations for human services careers;
- **identify** common challenges and rewards in human services careers; and
- **describe** the job outlook for careers in human services.

Reading Strategies

Before reading, write the learning outcomes for this chapter on a separate piece of paper. Then, rewrite each outcome as a question. As you are reading this chapter, take notes about information relating to these learning outcomes. After reading, write a two- to three-sentence answer for each of the questions you wrote. If necessary, refer to your notes as you respond to the questions.

Mapping Concepts

As you read this chapter, use a tree diagram like the one shown to organize information about the field of human services. Write *An Introduction to Human Services* in the top circle and then record major categories and specific activities and notes in the circles below.

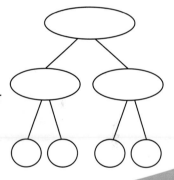

Key Terms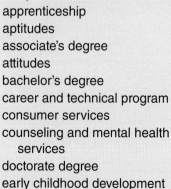

apprenticeship
aptitudes
associate's degree
attitudes
bachelor's degree
career and technical program
consumer services
counseling and mental health services
doctorate degree
early childhood development and services

entrepreneurial careers
family and community services
Family and Medical Leave Act (FMLA)
Head Start
human services
master's degree
personal care services
skills

Academic Terms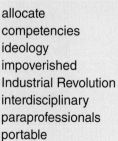

allocate
competencies
ideology
impoverished
Industrial Revolution
interdisciplinary
paraprofessionals
portable

What is *human services*? Human services is a field of work and study that focuses on meeting the needs of people and improving their quality of life. It focuses on helping people prevent and solve problems. Using applied knowledge and skills, human services workers make a positive impact on their clients, families, and communities.

In this chapter, you will learn about the history of human services and current careers in human services. You will also learn about the common aptitudes, attitudes, and skills needed in human services. In addition, this chapter will answer basic questions about education, training, and experience. You will find out about common challenges and rewards of working in the field. You will also find out about the job outlook in human services.

What Is Human Services?

Human services is a generic term that describes a career field providing for the needs of people. In human services, the primary focus is on improving people's quality of life by helping to provide needed services (**Figure 1.1**). Solving and preventing problems are also important focuses in this field. Human services workers achieve these goals through the use of a wide range of skills, knowledge, and resources.

Human services care providers is a term that refers to the agencies and organizations serving the needs of people at all stages of life.

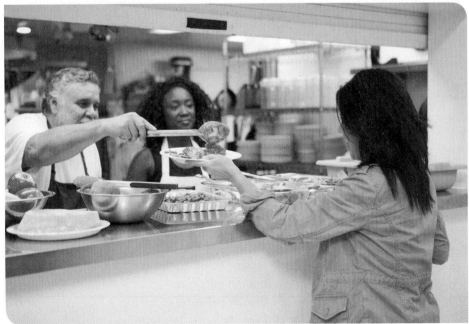

Monkey Business Images/Shutterstock.com

Figure 1.1 Human services workers provide a variety of services for people in need. *When have you volunteered to help someone in need?*

Copyright Goodheart-Willcox Co., Inc.

These care providers offer a wide variety of services. For example, some agencies provide housing assistance for people with low income. Some offer financial education and assistance to single parents. Other agencies provide counseling to those in grief. Some offer after-school activities for young teens and day care for older adults. Still others offer nutrition advice for young parents or supply temporary housing for people in transition. For every identified personal need, there is usually a provider that can *allocate* (distribute) the resources to meet the need.

Human services care providers employ *human services workers* to coordinate access to services, helping to simplify complex problems people face. People who receive services range from the very young to the very old. Human services workers serve those who have few emotional resources and those who have many. They serve the underprivileged and sometimes the very privileged. They serve the unskilled and the skilled. They serve the dependent and the independent. They also serve those who need assistance and those who can help themselves (**Figure 1.2**). Sometimes they serve people struggling with addictions.

Human services workers are ready to offer a helping hand to people struggling with life's countless obstacles. They do their best to help others meet their own needs. They understand and appreciate the human condition. For those who enjoy working with people, human services careers can provide ample opportunity.

JPC-PROD/Shutterstock.com

Figure 1.2 Some human services workers assist older adults with daily living tasks, transportation, and simple companionship. *Why do you think compassion for others is an important personal trait for human services workers?*

Reading Recall

1. What is *human services*?
2. Name one common goal of human services professionals.
3. List three types of services provided by human services care providers.
4. What does the term *allocate* mean?
5. Describe the type of people human services workers serve.

Copyright Goodheart-Willcox Co., Inc.

The History of Human Services

People always have had and always will have needs. Even so, human services is a relatively new career field that has only been around for the past 100 years or so. This does not mean that needs did not exist. Rather, it represents a cultural shift in *ideology* about who is responsible to meet needs and how to meet them. *Ideology* is a system of beliefs and ideals important to a society. Before this cultural shift, people living in poverty or with special needs were often thought of as deserving of their circumstances. At best, they were a responsibility of family members. This was especially true in more developed areas of the world, where taking care of those in need was a part of community life.

In the United States and much of Europe, tending to people's needs was not about charity. Instead, it often came more from a concern about keeping the social order and preventing diseases. Hospitals and temporary shelters were used to quarantine the sick (**Figure 1.3**). It was not until around the *Industrial Revolution* (time in history of rapid industrial growth) that a shift in thought began to occur as families came together in urban areas. Urban density was an issue. Along with the density, came the need for affordable housing, food, and other necessities, including medical care. People could no longer ignore the needs of the *impoverished* (poor).

At the dawn of the twentieth century, group homes were built to care for older adults who had no family to care for them. Orphanages housed

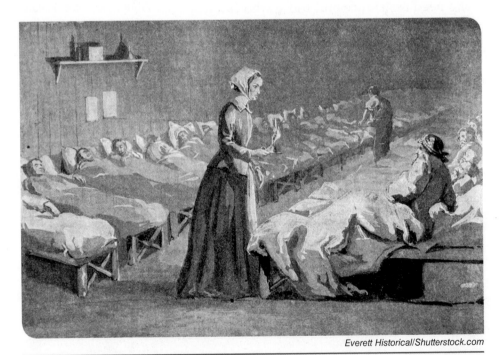

Everett Historical/Shutterstock.com

Figure 1.3 Sick people were often kept in hospitals or encampments to treat them and quarantine them from others. *In what ways is this hospital different from hospitals today?*

Copyright Goodheart-Willcox Co., Inc.

infants and youth who did not have families to care for them. The Social Work field expanded. Many charitable organizations, including places of worship, stepped up to care for those in need.

Mary Richmond began the *Charitable Organization Society* (COS). This society offered care for the needy. Jane Addams founded the *US Settlement House Movement*. This movement led the crusade toward not just providing charity, but also looking at the causes of poverty and initiating change. At the same time, the modern field of psychology developed. This resulted in a greater understanding of the concept that people could be helped in ways beyond just meeting the basic needs of food, clothing, and shelter.

As culture ideologies began to change, world events continued. World War I, and later the Great Depression of the 1930s, resulted in many Americans being displaced, disabled, unemployed, homeless, or widowed without financial support. This led President Franklin D. Roosevelt to initiate the New Deal. The New Deal focused on offering relief for those in need and recovery from the current crisis. It also focused on reforming systems so an economic depression such as was currently being felt would not be experienced again.

Around this time, the US government passed the *Social Security Act of 1935*. This act provided for the retired elderly and widows and dependent children of deceased workers. It eventually included those with special needs. Other government programs provided employment for youth and assistance to those with special needs (such as blindness). Hospitals specializing in mental health care were also formed.

World War II followed the Great Depression. Economic recovery eventually came from manufacturing. Postwar life in the US made the American Dream of financial independence real for many families. The ideological changes of the early part of the century, however, had changed the way many Americans viewed poverty and needs within their communities. Ideas shifted from care being a responsibility of the family and places of worship to being a responsibility of the government and private or corporate service providers. As a result, career opportunities in the human services field expanded at a rapid pace.

During the latter part of the twentieth century and into the present time, government within the US continued to expand services. The *Department of Health and Human Services (HHS)* is part of the federal government that administers and oversees programs and services concerning health and welfare. Programs such as *Head Start* and the *Family and Medical Leave Act* are just a couple of the services that have resulted from the HHS. **Head Start** is a government-funded preschool program that focuses on preparing disadvantaged children for school. The **Family and Medical Leave Act (FMLA)** allows full-time employees to take unpaid job-protected leave for family transitions involving close family members, such as spouses, children, and parents.

Copyright Goodheart-Willcox Co., Inc.

Expert Insight

"Social advance depends as much upon the process through which it is secured as upon the result itself."

Jane Addams, pioneer social worker

Law and Ethics   *FMLA Eligibility*

Do workers have the right to take time off work to care for family members? It depends. They always have the choice, of course. The right to not be terminated in the event of taking a leave for family reasons, however, varies.

In the US, the Family and Medical Leave Act (FMLA) enables employees to take job-protected leave to care for family members in need. Family members that the law covers involve close family members, such as spouses, children, and parents. FMLA became law in 1993. This act gave many families the flexibility to care for their loved ones in times of need. In 2008, the law was expanded to include care for military family members, especially when returning from deployment.

Examples of circumstances when the FMLA could provide coverage include

- the birth and care of the newborn child of the employee, for both mothers and fathers;
- the placement with the employee of a son or daughter for adoption or foster care, for both mothers and fathers;
- care for an immediate family member (spouse, child, or parent) with a serious health condition; and
- medical leave when the employee is unable to work because of a serious health condition.

Not all employers are required to comply. Generally, however, government, public education, and companies employing 50 people or more are included. Eligible employees are those who have worked for a covered employer for at least 12 months. During this time, they must also have worked at least 1,250 hours. They must also work at a location where the employer has at least 50 employees within a 75-mile radius.

Qualified employers must grant an eligible employee a total of up to 12 workweeks of unpaid leave during any 12-month period. Even so, work and family issues require thought, planning, and flexibility.

Writing Activity

Write a one- to two-page scenario in story form about a fictional family that qualifies for taking leave under the FMLA. When writing your story, consider the following:
- How might taking a leave affect the employee positively? negatively?
- How might taking a leave affect the employer and coworkers positively? negatively?
- In what specific ways might taking a leave under the FMLA positively affect the family?

Today, human services professionals work in government, private businesses, places of worship, hospitals, schools, and throughout communities. New programs continue to be developed to help meet people's needs.

Reading Recall

1. Define the term *ideology*.
2. Identify two factors that influenced the formation of human services.
3. How did Mary Richmond's philosophy of helping the poor differ from Jane Addams' philosophy?
4. Name three world events that helped shape human services in the US.
5. How did the New Deal impact human services?
6. Which part of the federal government administers and oversees programs and services concerning health and welfare?

Copyright Goodheart-Willcox Co., Inc.

Current Careers in Human Services

Human services workers can be employed wherever there are people. Today, there are many positions available in the field of human services. Common human services careers include case managers, counselors, therapists, and social workers. This is just a beginning list of opportunities in human services, however. At the administrative level, program directors, development directors, and executive directors lead human services agencies. **Figure 1.4** shows some examples of human services careers. Keep in mind that hundreds of human services careers exist that this chapter or even this book cannot begin to cover.

Human services career settings vary greatly (**Figure 1.5**). For example, agencies provide client services in offices, schools, government offices, and clinics or hospitals. Day treatment programs, correctional institutions, group homes, shelters, and clients' homes are other settings. Within each setting, human services workers serve diverse clients. This includes infants, older adults, people with special needs, addicts, and the homeless. Because of this diversity, workers' job titles and daily tasks

Examples of Human Services Careers

4-H youth development specialist	Curriculum specialist	Patient advocate
Agency administrator	Daycare center director	Personal financial advisor
Business family and consumer scientist	Early childhood intervention specialist	Public relations specialist
Caseworker	Early childhood program director	Recreation therapist
Child advocate	Education advisor	Rehabilitation counselor
Child care consultant	Extension specialist	Residence life coordinator
Child care worker	Family and consumer science researcher	Residential counselor
Child life specialist	Family finances consultant	Sales representative
Child protective services caseworker	Family life specialist	School counselor
Child recreation specialist	Family planning counselor	School social worker
Child support case officer	Foster care social worker	Social services program coordinator
Community organizer	Head Start program director	Social worker substance abuse counselor
Consultant to child-related industry	Health educator	Teacher of English as a second language
Consumer advocate	Hospital child life specialist	Teacher—preschool, elementary, secondary
Consumer credit counselor	Hospital education/trainer	Victim advocate
Consumer educator	Life coach	Volunteer coordinator
County extension agent	Mental health counselor	Youth organizer
Crisis counselor	Nanny	
	Parent education specialist	

Figure 1.4 This chart shows some examples of human services careers. *Which of these careers are the most appealing to you?*

Copyright Goodheart-Willcox Co., Inc.

Examples of Where Human Services Careers May Be Found

Adoption agencies	Elementary schools	Nursing homes
Child abuse centers	Family advocacy services	Peace Corp
Children's homes	Family and children's services	Places of worship
Civic groups	agencies	Planned Parenthood
Consumer credit agencies	Federal/state governments	Public or private schools
Cooperative extension agencies	Food assistance programs	Publishers, educational
Correctional facilities	Foster care agencies	materials
Crisis centers	Halfway houses	Residential homes
Day care centers	Hospitals	School boards
Early childhood programs	Intervention programs	Shelters
Economic opportunity corps	Neighborhood youth corps	Social Security offices
Elder services	Nursery schools/preschools	Trade organizations

Figure 1.5 Human services careers may be found in many different settings. *What other examples would you add to this chart?*

may be very different from one place to the next. These differences make tracking statistics about specific career opportunities in human services rather difficult.

Depending on your education and career goals, there are a range of human services careers from which you can choose. Most human services careers fall under one or more of the following broad employment categories:

- consumer services
- counseling and mental health services
- early childhood development and services
- family and community services
- personal care services
- entrepreneurial careers
- related services in food, clothing, and housing

Consumer Services

In **consumer services**, workers help people budget, solve financial problems, and make good consumer decisions. Examples of careers in consumer services include consumer credit counselors, consumer advocates, financial advisors, customer service representatives, and sales consultants. Consumer services workers are often employed in places such as financial institutions, investment firms, credit bureaus, hospitals, and insurance companies (**Figure 1.6**).

Consumer services workers educate their clients on how to invest, save, spend wisely, plan financially, and overall make sound financial

Copyright Goodheart-Willcox Co., Inc.

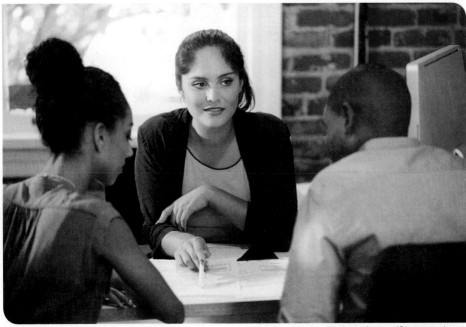

Monkey Business Images/Shutterstock.com

Figure 1.6 This consumer services worker helps families manage their finances and make sound financial decisions. *Do you think you would enjoy a career in consumer services?*

decisions. They help people objectively evaluate consumer media, including marketing and sales. They work with clients to solve consumer issues. They can also help people plan their education, career, and financial goals.

Counseling and Mental Health Services

The **counseling and mental health services** field involves helping people maintain healthy, productive lives. This is achieved through therapy, counseling, and education or training. Common counseling and mental health services positions include counselors, psychologists, and other *paraprofessionals* (trained workers who assist qualified professionals).

Counseling and mental health services workers work in settings that include clinics, research labs, schools, group homes, and hospitals. They also work in corporate settings, promoting positive relationships among employees. Counseling and mental health services workers know about human behavior. They frequently work with mental health issues, substance abuse, eating disorders, special needs, family relationships, and career and life counseling.

Early Childhood Development and Services

Early childhood development and services workers understand and meet the needs of infants, toddlers, and young children. Common

Case Study   *Making a Difference*

Amelia learned about four-year-old Michael several months ago. When neighbors reported concerns about his safety, the state's child protective services became involved. He had not been physically abused. It appeared, however, that Michael was often left without proper supervision.

Neglect is hard to prove. It took several months to build a case for removing Michael from his home and placing him in foster care. Amelia was sure that Michael's mother had a desire to care for him. Her lack of family support and struggle with substance abuse, however, make it difficult for her to care for Michael. Amelia and her colleagues at the foster care agency provide emotional support for Michael's mother. They hope that she will get her life under control so she can properly care for her son.

A neighbor found Michael alone, hungry, and dirty this afternoon. When his mother could not be found, the local police stepped in. Later that evening, a social worker called Amelia to take Michael. As the human services case manager, Amelia had to quickly find a place for Michael to live.

Amelia knew Michael would be well taken care of in this emergency foster home. For now, Amelia would rest easy. Tomorrow would hold a new day for Michael, his mother, and his foster parents. It could be filled with fear, grief and loss, and dismay. She hoped it would also hold a sense of warmth and stability for Michael.

Amelia has a career in human services. People are drawn to human services careers for different reasons. Like most Americans living with basic needs met, watching news reports of children in need profoundly affected Amelia. During Amelia's high school years, her town was affected by a severe rainstorm that caused flash floods and evacuations. During that event, Amelia's passion grew for helping people, especially displaced children.

Sometimes it takes a big event like Amelia's to jolt a person into meaningful life choices. Sometimes it is a gradual realization that helping others is what gives meaning to life. For Amelia, helping others means helping foster children find safe, temporary homes.

Personally, Amelia had no experience with foster care. She grew up in a privileged urban home. During her teen years, she lived with her mother after her parents divorced. Even so, she maintained a strong relationship with both of her parents. Education was highly esteemed in Amelia's family. She had many strong role models. She was considered a high achiever throughout high school and college, both in academics and in extracurricular leadership activities. Human services proved to be the career track that allowed Amelia to combine her drive for excellence and her leadership skills with her passion to make a difference in the world.

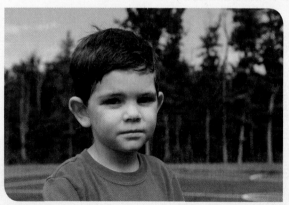

EBPhoto/Shutterstock.com

For Discussion

1. What are three specific ways that Amelia helped make Michael's life better?

2. List two ways that Amelia could help Michael's mother better parent him.

3. What appeals to Amelia about her career in human services?

4. Do you share any common interests or traits with Amelia? If so, which one(s)?

Copyright Goodheart-Willcox Co., Inc.

careers in this field include nannies, child care workers, teachers, and administrators. Early childhood development and services workers may work in family homes and early childhood education programs. They may also work in community centers and corporate or medical child care centers.

Effective early childhood development and services workers and educators know about how children develop and grow. They apply this knowledge through the use of age-appropriate activities and teaching methods. They consider each child's strengths, interests, and culture, while respecting the milestones of the young children in their care.

Family and Community Services

Family and community services workers are a central part of the human services industry. They offer advice and assistance to people at all stages of life. Positions available in family and community services include emergency and relief workers, adult day care workers, and social workers. *Social workers*, in particular, have a high level of specialized education and experience.

Family and community services workers work with people directly in the field. They help people cope with and resolve personal issues. They teach people how to maintain healthy relationships, deal with crises, or become sober. They assist people following natural disasters or other crises. Family and community services workers work in schools, communities, family services, foster care, adoption services, older adult care, and family health clinics.

Personal Care Services

In **personal care services** careers, workers provide personal services for people. Personal care services workers include cosmetologists, massage therapists, funeral services workers, and personal and home care aides. Personal care services workers may work in hair salons, spas, funeral homes, and people's private homes.

Personal care services workers have a lot of one-on-one interaction with clients. They provide personal services, such as hair care, nail care, and skin care. Funeral services workers help people deal with the death of a loved one. Personal and home care aides help people with daily living skills, such as feeding, bathing, cooking, or shopping. Sometimes personal and home care aides simply provide companionship. These services can occur in the home or be brought to the home, group homes, or community centers.

Entrepreneurial Careers

Entrepreneurial careers offer people an opportunity to establish and run their own businesses. People who start their own businesses are called *entrepreneurs*. Entrepreneurs decide which services or goods to

Copyright Goodheart-Willcox Co., Inc.

provide, how to provide them, when to provide them, and at what cost. Establishing a new business requires a lot of work. Entrepreneurs assume the responsibilities and risks for their own businesses. Entrepreneurs also enjoy the flexibly of being one's own boss.

In the human services field, people can start all kinds of businesses, from a hair salon to child care to counseling. Personal services, such as in-home care, are particularly well-suited to self-run businesses (**Figure 1.7**).

Related Services in Food, Clothing, and Housing

Human services workers come in many forms and provide many different kinds of services—sometimes in unexpected ways. For example, related services workers help people meet their needs for food, clothing, and shelter. They assist people in making decisions, purchasing, using, and maintaining products and services in these industries.

Food brokers, growers and retailers, product developers, designers, and housing specialists are a few examples of related services workers. They work as farmers and ranchers, food chemists, nutritionists, and grocers. They also work as apparel designers, manufacturers, interior designers, and real estate agents and brokers. They are found in agriculture, small manufacturers, corporations, and throughout communities.

Alexander Raths/Shutterstock.com

Figure 1.7 Some entrepreneurs in human services might choose to establish a business that provides in-home care. *What other types of services might be well-suited to self-run businesses?*

Copyright Goodheart-Willcox Co., Inc.

Reading Recall

1. Give five examples of human services careers.
2. What do consumer services workers do?
3. Who are *paraprofessionals*?
4. Human services workers in _____ understand and meet the needs of infants, toddlers, and young children.
5. Which broad employment category in the field of human services includes emergency and relief workers and social workers?
6. List three jobs in personal care services.
7. People who pursue entrepreneurial careers are called _____.
8. Human services workers may provide related services in which three areas?

Common Aptitudes, Attitudes, and Skills

Aptitudes (natural abilities), **attitudes** (set ways of thinking or feeling about someone or something), and **skills** (developed talents or abilities) of human services workers vary by occupation. In general, human services workers share a common desire to help people. They tend to be socially perceptive, compassionate, caring, and patient. Human services workers typically possess good communication, problem-solving, and time management skills. They can work well with others, in teams, and when necessary, independently. All of these skills and abilities are *portable*, meaning they are easily transferrable from one job to another.

Along with the common aptitudes, attitudes, and skills, people in human services share a common core of *competencies* (abilities; skills). These competencies include the following:

1. Understanding of human development. This includes knowledge of physical, cognitive, social, emotional, and spiritual development.
2. Awareness of social and societal interactions. This includes group dynamics and organizational structures.
3. Knowledge of how national policy is set and how public policy is used to solve human problems.
4. Consideration of, and respect for, personal values, client values, and corporate culture.
5. Understanding of what people need to live healthy lives and maintain healthy relationships.
6. Knowledge of conditions that promote or limit optimal healthy living and relationships.
7. Belief that for people with the right resources and support, quality of life can be enhanced.
8. Awareness of resources that can promote healthy functioning.

Copyright Goodheart-Willcox Co., Inc.

Pathway to Success

Portable Skills in the Twenty-First Century

You hear the buzz word "portable skills" when people talk about résumés and look for a job. What are portable skills? How can you find out if you have any? *Portable skills* are skills you learn at one job that you can use in different work situations—even in a different industry. These might also be skills you develop through volunteer work, hobbies, sports, or other life experiences.

Some of the basic portable skills that almost everyone has include decision-making, communication (both written and verbal), problem-solving, and leadership skills. Other portable skills that employers look for may include

- meeting deadlines;
- having the ability to plan and delegate;
- accepting responsibility;
- instructing others;
- using good time management skills;
- being open to learning new skills; and
- showing how you can increase sales or productivity.

Now that you know what portable skills include, you can work on your own list of personal portable skills. Some easy steps to help figure out what portable skills you have include

- making a list of your experiences on and off campus;
- developing an inventory of skills;
- highlighting your research experiences;
- describing how you make a decision;
- listing leadership roles; and
- explaining how well you function in a group setting.

The portable skills you develop now will help shape the professional you will become. While you are still in school, you are able to work on your creativity, learn how to ask for help, and build your personal credibility. Volunteer opportunities will enable you to meet new people and network. Remember the old adage, "it's not what you know, but who you know."

Create a Personal Skills and Job Chart

Using the steps above, make a list of skills you possess, as well as skills you are learning. Update this list throughout the year. Remember to also keep a list of any volunteer and work experiences, including the duties you perform. These lists come in handy to remind you of your accomplishments. You can add them to your résumé or talk about them during a job interview.

After gathering this information, put it into a chart. You can do this in many ways. One

way is to list the job in one column and the skills learned in a second column. Another way is to break down the skills into areas in one column (such as communication skills, decision making, problem solving, and leadership) and list examples in the second column. Be creative as you make your own list and chart. Use this information to help you determine which portable skills you can start developing now.

Copyright Goodheart-Willcox Co., Inc.

Reading Recall

1. List common aptitudes, attitudes, and skills of human services workers.
2. Define the term *competencies*.
3. Identify four core competencies people in human services occupations share.

Education, Training, and Experience

Students in human services learn knowledge and practical skills that prepare them to help people and meet their needs. Sometimes this learning can occur through a career and technical program. Apprenticeships or *postsecondary* (beyond high school) training are other learning opportunities.

A **career and technical program** is a course of study that prepares students for careers in specific trades and occupations that need skilled workers. Career and technical programs are available for high school and college students, as well as adults. These programs combine academics and job-specific skills.

An **apprenticeship** involves working for a qualified professional to learn a skilled trade. With an apprenticeship, workers earn a salary while learning important skills they need to succeed in a high-demand career. Apprenticeships vary in how long they last. Some may last for a year while others can last for four years.

Postsecondary educational requirements vary by occupation or specific career field. A four-year degree is commonly needed, however, for many jobs today. Human services occupations often require experience, too. It is important to gain skill in working with people beyond book knowledge (**Figure 1.8**). Many human services careers provide on-the-job training so workers can learn about the specific job duties and responsibilities.

When preparing for careers in human services, educational requirements may include

- an **associate's degree**—a two-year degree earned through community colleges;
- a **bachelor's degree**—a four-year degree earned through colleges and universities;
- a **master's degree**—earned after completing at least one year of study beyond a bachelor's degree; and
- a **doctorate degree**—the highest degree a person can earn (also called a *PhD*).

Many colleges and universities offer a bachelor's degree in human services, early childhood education, and family and consumer sciences. Students can also obtain bachelor's degrees in social work, counseling,

Copyright Goodheart-Willcox Co., Inc.

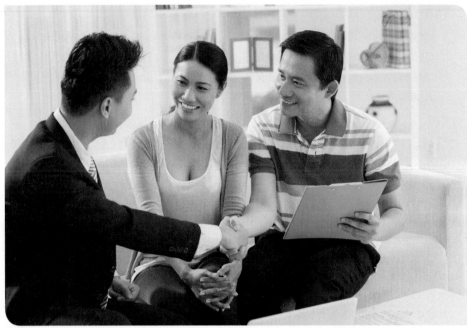

Dragon Images/Shutterstock.com

Figure 1.8 Skills in working with people are important in many human services careers. *Do you have experience working with people?*

family advocacy, child life, and other related programs. Programs like these that are *interdisciplinary* (relating to more than one branch of knowledge) broadly prepare students for careers in human services. For human services careers requiring either a master's or doctorate degree to advance, related graduate degrees may be found in marriage and family therapy, psychology, school counseling, social work, or education, among others (**Figure 1.9**).

In addition to a degree, some human services careers also require state licensure, certifications, or professional registration. Sometimes these additional requirements are earned through hours in practice, a qualifying exam, or a combination of both. In the end, the fact remains that even some postsecondary education can add thousands of dollars to personal income over a lifetime.

Reading Recall

1. What does *postsecondary* mean?
2. Differentiate between a *career and technical program* and an *apprenticeship*.
3. Although postsecondary educational requirements vary by occupation or specific career field, which degree is commonly required for many jobs today?
4. Define the term *interdisciplinary*.
5. Besides a degree, what are three other requirements of some human services occupations? How might these additional requirements be earned?

Copyright Goodheart-Willcox Co., Inc.

Sample Graduate Degrees for Human Services Careers

Master's in counseling (MS, MA, MEd, MAEd)

Master's in marriage and family therapy (MFT)

Master's in school psychology (MS)

Master's in social work (MSW)

Master's or doctorate in industrial-organizational psychology (MA, MS, PhD)

Doctorate in counseling and/or counselor education (PhD, EdD)

Doctorate in (general) psychology (PhD)

Doctorate in counseling psychology (PhD)

Doctorate in clinical psychology (PhD)

Doctor of psychology (PsyD)

Doctorate in social work (PhD, DSW)

Medical doctor (psychiatrist) (MD)

©iStock.com/Steve Debenport

Figure 1.9 There are many options for graduate degrees for careers in human services. For example, a human services worker might want to pursue a graduate degree in school counseling. *What other human services careers require advanced degrees?*

Common Challenges and Rewards

Careers in human services can be both challenging and rewarding. Human services workers deal with people in times of crisis and need. This can be challenging and emotionally taxing. Great resourcefulness is often required to bring together sometimes scarce resources needed to solve a client's given problem. Sometimes clients do not want to change, and their quality of life remains at a standstill. In some human services careers, the hours can be long, and the pay can be relatively low.

On the other hand, there are many rewards in helping people achieve their goals, secure needed resources, and maintain healthy relationships. Human services workers see positive stories of renewal and change unfold before their eyes. Knowing that they played a part in providing necessary services is gratifying. They continually enhance their skills, aptitudes, and resources. They often work with diverse clients and develop meaningful relationships. In many skilled human services careers, the hours can be flexible, and the pay can be very competitive with other professional career salaries.

Reading Recall

1. Name three potential challenges from a career in human services.

2. Name three potential rewards from a career in human services.

Copyright Goodheart-Willcox Co., Inc.

Job Outlook for Human Services

The job outlook for human services careers is bright. Employment of human services workers is expected to grow much faster than the average for most occupations in the coming decades. Later in this text, you will learn more about future trends and projected job growth for various careers within each of the pathways in the field of human services.

People need the "human touch," especially as technology becomes more and more a part of our lives (**Figure 1.10**). People will always have needs. Human services workers are the ones to provide these resources. As the population grows, so does the need for human services workers.

Although basic human needs remain the same, careers in human services may ebb and flow in relation to what is happening in the overall economy. For example, in times of economic hardship, emphasis is placed on basic needs of providing food and housing resources. In times of economic plenty, more emphasis is placed on personal exploration. In good times and in bad times, however, people need help navigating their interpersonal relationships. Likewise, the need for child care services continues to grow, as both numbers and expectations for preschool education increases.

Paul Vasarhelyi/Shutterstock.com

Figure 1.10 As advancements in technology continue to occur, many people, especially older adults, need help in learning how to use technological devices and programs. *Are there any classes available in your community to teach older adults how to use the computer?*

Copyright Goodheart-Willcox Co., Inc.

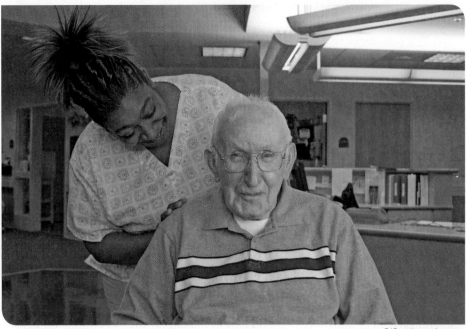

©iStock.com/agentry

Figure 1.11 Human services workers are needed in facilities, such as nursing homes, to help care for the aging population. *In what ways do you think this type of career would be rewarding?*

The expected human lifespan continues to lengthen, now well into the eighties. With extended life expectancy comes a greater need for human services workers to provide care in nursing homes, adult day care centers, assisted care, and resource allocation (**Figure 1.11**). A growing need for more care for those living with mental illness or substance abuse exists in group homes and residential care facilities as well. If you love caring for and helping people, a human services career might be right for you.

Reading Recall

1. Describe the job outlook for human services careers.
2. What does *ebb and flow* mean?
3. List four areas that may experience an increased demand for human services workers as the expected human lifespan continues to lengthen.

Copyright Goodheart-Willcox Co., Inc.

Summary

- In human services, the primary focus is on meeting people's needs and improving their quality of life. Human services jobs can be found wherever people have needs, which, of course, is everywhere.

- In the last 100 years or so, the field of human services has expanded and evolved to meet the changing needs of society and offer new services when they are needed.

- Human services careers fall under the following broad employment categories: consumer services, counseling and mental health services, early childhood development and services, family and community services, personal care services, entrepreneurial careers, and related services in food, clothing, and housing.

- The aptitudes, attitudes, and skills of human services workers vary by occupation. Human services workers, however, share a common core of competencies.

- Qualifications for occupations in human services vary, but a four-year degree is commonly required for many jobs today. Some human services careers also require state licensure, certifications, professional registration, and on-the-job experience.

- Human services workers deal with people in times of crisis and need, which can be challenging and emotionally taxing. On the other hand, there are many rewards in helping people achieve their goals and maintain healthy relationships.

- Employment of human services workers is expected to grow much faster than the average for most occupations in the coming decades. Careers in human services may ebb and flow in relation to what is happening in the overall economy. The need for child care services and older adult care will continue to grow.

College and Career Portfolio

Portfolio Foundations

When you apply for college admission, a job, or a community service position, you may need to tell others about your qualifications. A portfolio is a selection of related materials that you collect and organize to showcase your strengths and experience. These materials show your qualifications, skills, and talents. For example, a certificate that shows you have completed CPR and first-aid training could help you get a job working with children or older adults. A research paper about effective teaching strategies could show that you are serious about working with children. It might help you get a tutor position at an after-school program. A transcript of your school grades also shows your qualifications to a potential college.

Two types of portfolios are commonly used: print portfolios and electronic portfolios (e-Portfolios). An e-Portfolio is also known as a *digital portfolio*. To learn more about each type of portfolio, complete the following activities:

1. Use the Internet to search for *print portfolio* and *e-Portfolio*. Read articles about each type of portfolio. In your own words, briefly describe each type.

2. You will be creating a portfolio in this class. Based on your reading, which portfolio type would you prefer to create? Write a paragraph describing the type of portfolio you would like to create.

Copyright Goodheart-Willcox Co., Inc.

Review and Reflect

1. What is the primary focus of the human services profession?
2. Summarize how the events of World War I, the Great Depression, and World War II changed how society viewed poverty.
3. Describe two programs that have resulted from the HHS.
4. Identify the broad employment categories in the field of human services and give an example of an occupation within each of these categories.
5. Compare and contrast *early childhood development and services* and *personal care services*.
6. How would you describe what is involved in working in the counseling and mental health services field?
7. What is the goal of having a personal home care aide?
8. Give an example of an entrepreneurial opportunity in human services.
9. Why should human services workers understand human life stage development?
10. What kinds of resources should human services workers be aware of when serving their clients?
11. Paraphrase the differences between *associate's*, *bachelor's*, *master's*, and *doctorate* degrees.
12. Give an example of how careers in human services may ebb and flow in relation to what is happening in the overall economy.

Vocabulary Activities

13. **Key terms** Write each of the following terms on a separate sheet of paper. For each term, quickly write a word you think relates to the term. In small groups, exchange papers. Have each person in the group explain a term on the list. Take turns until all terms have been explained.

apprenticeship
aptitudes
associate's degree
attitudes
bachelor's degree
career and technical program
consumer services
counseling and mental health services
doctorate degree
early childhood development and services
entrepreneurial careers
family and community services
Family and Medical Leave Act (FMLA)
Head Start
human services
master's degree
personal care services
skills

14. **Academic terms** Read the text passages that contain each of the following terms. Then, write the definition of each term in your own words. Double-check your definitions by rereading the text and using the text glossary.

allocate
competencies
ideology
impoverished
Industrial Revolution
interdisciplinary
paraprofessionals
portable

Self-Assessment Quiz

Complete the self-assessment quiz online to help you practice and expand your knowledge and skills.

Critical Thinking

15. **Make inferences** Based on the last 100 years of growth in the field of human services, what do you predict will happen with jobs in these fields over the next 50 years?
16. **Cause and effect** During the Industrial Revolution, the needs of the impoverished could no longer be ignored. What caused this shift in thinking and what effect did it have on society?
17. **Draw conclusions** There is a quote in the chapter by Jane Addams. What do you think this quote meant at the time it was said? Do you think this quote holds true today?

18. **Analyze**   Examine your aptitudes, attitudes, and skills. How do they match up with those of people working in human services careers?
19. **Identify**   Identify how an interdisciplinary program broadly prepares students for careers in human services.
20. **Evaluate**   Find information from five colleges or universities that offer degrees in a human services career that interests you. List the advantages and disadvantages of each school based on information you gather and on your personal wants and needs.
21. **Compare and contrast**   In teams, compare and contrast the challenges and rewards of working with people in times of crisis and need.
22. **Determine**   After reading this chapter, what is your opinion of careers in the human services field? Are you still interested in a career in human services? Why or why not?

Core Skills

23. **Reading and writing**   Find a nonfiction book to read about one of the following historical events: the Industrial Revolution, World War I, the Great Depression, or World War II. Create a time line of important events and dates discussed in the book. Share your findings with the class.
24. **Reading and math**   Reread the Case Study, *Making a Difference*, in this chapter to find out why Amelia chose to become a human services worker. What are some other reasons people might be drawn to human services careers? As a class, create a survey to poll human services workers to find out why they entered the field of human services. Tally the survey results and post them in class.
25. **Listening, writing, and speaking**   Arrange to interview a human services worker to learn more about his or her job. Before the interview, write a list of 10 questions that you intend to ask during the interview. After the interview, write a summary detailing what you learned from this experience. Share your summaries with the rest of the class.

26. **Math and speaking**   Choose an occupation in the field of human services that interests you. Using online sources, such as the *Occupational Outlook Handbook* website, research the median pay per year and per hour for workers in this occupation. Share your findings with the class and justify whether or not you could live on that salary and pay your utilities and required bills.
27. **Research and technology**   Research human services agencies and organizations in your local area. Identify contact information, what services they provide, and hours of operation. Use desktop publishing software to create a professional-looking pamphlet or handout that includes the results of your research. Share your completed project with local elementary, middle, and high schools in your area to be given out to families in need. Identify other places within the community you might also use to circulate the pamphlet or handout.
28. **Writing and speaking**   Make a list of your portable skills. With a partner, discuss each other's lists. How are your lists similar? How are they different? Are there skills on your partner's list that you could add to your list?
29. **Speaking, writing, and listening**   Working in small groups, brainstorm common challenges and rewards associated with careers in human services. Create a T-chart to organize the results of your group's brainstorming session. Then, as a class, compare and discuss each group's charts and ideas.
30. **Research and technology**   Use online or print resources to research the job duties, educational requirements, and job outlook for one career in each of the broad employment categories in the field of human services as discussed in this chapter. Create an electronic slide show to present your findings to the class.
31. **CTE career readiness practice**   Select two human services careers to research on O*NET. Read the summary reports for these careers, especially the knowledge, skills, abilities, and interests required to do the work. Analyze whether your personal

Copyright Goodheart-Willcox Co., Inc.

interests, skills, and abilities are a logical fit with one or both careers. Write a summary explaining why you think you are well suited for either career.

32. **CTE career readiness practice**   In human services careers, you will come into contact with many different types of people. You may have been taught to treat others how *you* would like to be treated. This is often referred to as the *golden rule*. Productively working with others who have a background different from yours may require that you learn to treat others as *they* wish to be treated. Conduct research on the Internet about cultural differences related to personal space, time, gestures, body language, and views of authority figures. List four differences and how you would approach each.

Lend a Hand

Volunteering: Where to Start?

Doing volunteer work and community service is a great way to get involved and give back to your local and global communities. There are opportunities to help others everywhere you look. Getting started with a service project can seem daunting, however, if you do not know where to start.

First, determine what type of project you want to do. What needs exist in your community? What are your personal interests? What skills do you have to offer? Think about your service goals. What effect do you want your volunteer work to have? How much time are you willing or able to commit to your service project? Would you prefer to start a new project or join in someone else's efforts?

Next, do your research. Find out what resources are available in your area. One way to do this is to conduct an online search for local volunteer opportunities. Some websites, such as VolunteerMatch, can help you identify opportunities in your area. Searching for volunteer networks and resources and looking at nonprofit databases online are other ways to identify possible volunteer opportunities.

In addition to searching online, you might also want to contact different organizations, nonprofit agencies, and local businesses to assess their needs. Places like food banks, animal shelters, soup kitchens, and hospitals work with volunteers often and are easy to join.

To get started on your path toward volunteering, complete the following:

1. Brainstorm a list of volunteer ideas that interest you. Think about your skills and what you might enjoy doing. Narrow your list to about five options.
2. Using your list of volunteer ideas, research how you can make a difference in your community. Search online to find out about volunteer opportunities. Contact different businesses or organizations to learn more about ways you can help.

Chapter 2

The People Business

G-WLEARNING.com

While studying, look for the activity icon  to

- **practice** key and academic terms with e-flash cards and matching activities;
- **assess** what you learn by completing self-assessment quizzes; and
- **reinforce** what you learn by mapping concepts and completing review and reflect questions.

www.g-wlearning.com/humanservices/

Rob Marmion/Shutterstock.com

Learning Outcomes

After studying this chapter, you will be able to

- **explain** the principles and theories of human development;
- **describe** Abraham Maslow's *hierarchy of human needs* and give an example of how human services workers use this information when working with people;
- **assess** resources people use to meet their needs; and
- **describe** how economic and employment changes can affect how people meet their needs.

Reading Strategies

Before reading, scan this chapter's captions and caption questions. On a separate piece of paper, answer each of the caption questions based on your current knowledge. As you are reading the chapter, notice how the captions and caption questions relate to the content being presented. After you finish reading the chapter, look at your answers to each of the caption questions. Based on what you learned, would you change any of your responses?

Mapping Concepts

In a chart like the one shown, write the main headings of this chapter. As you read, take notes and organize them by heading. Draw a star beside any words or concepts you do not yet understand.

Human Development
What Every Human Needs
How People Meet Their Needs

Key Terms

behaviorism
classical conditioning
cognitive theories
developmental theories
expansion mode
human development
operant conditioning
psychoanalytic theories

recession mode
recovery mode
resources
social cognitive theory
standard of living

Academic Terms

elements
environment
esteem
heredity
hierarchy
inferiority
moral issues
self-actualization

The human services profession is often referred to as "the people business." This is because human services workers share a common goal of helping people. Human services workers help people of all ages and from all walks of life. People who need human services represent every race, gender, ethnicity, and nationality. They come from all family types and share the same basic needs of food, clothing, shelter, and relationships with others. They have strengths, weaknesses, hopes, and dreams.

To effectively help people, human services workers need to understand human development and people's basic human needs throughout the lifespan. Sometimes these needs are quite simple. At other times, people's needs can be quite complex. Typically, people use and manage resources to meet their needs. Human services workers find resources for people who are not able to meet their own basic needs.

Human Development

People are all unique. Of course, people are similar to one another in some ways, but very different from one another in other ways (**Figure 2.1**). An example of a similarity among people is how they grow and change throughout their lives. This process, called **human development**, is an amazing, gradual process in which people change from birth through

Rawpixel/Shutterstock.com

Figure 2.1 Although they are similar in many ways, each person in this group is unique. *Think about your family or your group of friends. In what ways are you similar? How are you different?*

Copyright Goodheart-Willcox Co., Inc.

adulthood. Over their lifespan, people change
and develop in the following major ways:

- *Physical development* involves the changes in
  size, body composition, chemical make-up,
  and height that occur from birth through
  adulthood. With these physical changes
  also come differences in physical abilities.
  Individually, people differ in balance,
  strength, coordination, and energy levels.

- *Cognitive development* refers to the ways
  in which people change and grow in
  how they think over the stages of life.
  Throughout the lifespan, cognitive abilities
  change due to both social interaction
  and brain development. Part of cognitive
  development involves *moral development*.
  As people develop, moral issues become
  more prevalent. *Moral issues* deal with what
  a person judges to be right or wrong. Moral
  decision making is included under the
  category of cognitive development because
  it involves problem solving and reasoning.

- *Social-emotional development* refers to changes
  in the ways in which people's social
  relationships, feelings, social skills, and ways
  of coping with situations change over time
  (**Figure 2.2**).

michaeljung/Shutterstock.com

Figure 2.2 Social-emotional development in children
is affected by relationships with familiar adults, such
as parents or other caregivers. *Why do you think these
relationships are so important?*

There is a lot that is known about the ways in which humans
grow and change. At the same time, there is much that is still
unknown. The details of what people know about human
development, however, will continue to change and increase.
Current principles and theories of human development help human
services workers better understand the capabilities, motivations, and
expectations of the clients they serve.

Principles of Human Development

When considering principles of human development, four basic
guidelines can be established. That is, these are ideas believed to be true
about how people develop. These four guidelines are as follows:

1. Human development is relatively orderly. Development occurs in an
   orderly manner. For example, children learn their alphabet before they
   can read. They learn to walk before they run. They learn to ride a bike
   before driving a car. Although not everyone proceeds in exactly the

Copyright Goodheart-Willcox Co., Inc.

Zhao jian kang/Shutterstock.com

Figure 2.3 This baby must learn to walk before he can run. *How might this child build on the skills of walking and running as his body continues to grow and develop?*

same manner, as people develop, their abilities build on each other in an orderly way (**Figure 2.3**).

2. Human development takes place gradually. While some changes occur within minutes, most changes take weeks, months, or even years to complete. Consider height as an example. The physical changes that occur from birth through adolescence are astounding. A growth spurt might occur over a few months or a year, but for the most part, these changes are gradual.

3. Human development is interrelated. Physical, cognitive, and social-emotional development occur together and are interdependent of one another. In other words, they are mutually dependent and supporting. Development in one area coincides with development in another area. For example, a young child behind in physical coordination is often behind in cognitive and social-emotional development. If the same child is helped with physical coordination, then cognitive and social-emotional development are often enhanced, too.

4. Human development varies among individuals. Although development is orderly and predictable, the outcomes and rate of development vary by individual. Many different factors cause these differences.

First, genetics and *heredity* (traits people are born with) are different for everyone. Next, a person's experiences and *environment* (all of a person's surroundings and the people in them) are not exactly the same. Because both heredity and environment influence development, and because no one is exactly alike, individual variations in developmental characteristics can be expected. There are differences in the ages when people experience events that will influence their development (**Figure 2.4**). The bottom line is that everyone grows and changes at a different rate and on a different time schedule.

Theories of Human Development

People have opinions about why others act the way they do. Researchers and scientists explore the many ways in which humans grow and develop. They are motivated by the intrigue of understanding how humans develop. They observe people, perform experiments,

Copyright Goodheart-Willcox Co., Inc.

Monkey Business Images/Shutterstock.com

Figure 2.4 During puberty, people experience many changes, both physical and emotional. Different people may experience puberty at different ages and may develop at different rates. *Why is it important to remember that everyone is different?*

and draw conclusions based on their studies and earlier studies by others. As a result of observation and experimentation, scientists and researchers formulate developmental theories. **Developmental theories** are comprehensive explanations about why people act and behave the way they do and how they change over time.

Psychoanalytic Theory

Many theorists have held different ideas about how and why humans develop and change the way they do. Some theorists believe that much development happens at an unconscious level and is buried in emotions. These ideas are called **psychoanalytic theories**. Psychoanalytic theorists analyze the symbolic meaning behind behaviors. They often believe that early life experiences are important in development. Two such psychoanalytic theorists were Sigmund Freud and Erik Erikson.

Freud's Theory

Sigmund Freud was a pioneer in applying psychoanalytic theory (**Figure 2.5**). With the goal of restoring psychological health, he helped his patients talk through their issues. As he

Miscellaneous Items in High Demand, Prints & Photographs Division, Library of Congress, LC-USZ62-139124

Figure 2.5 In many ways, Sigmund Freud's theory paved the way for further studies of human development. He is often called the father of psychoanalysis. *What else do you know about Freud?*

Copyright Goodheart-Willcox Co., Inc.

talked with more and more patients, he began to create a theory that focused on early life experiences. He believed that what happens early in life affects a person for years to come. Although his theory is not considered scientifically sound today, he opened the door to a new way of understanding development.

Erikson's Psychosocial Theory

Erik Erikson appreciated Freud's work, but believed that both early and later life experiences affect development. Erikson felt that people are always changing and developing and that development occurs throughout people's lives. He also believed that development is a social process. People are motivated by their desire to connect with other people.

Erikson theorized that all humans develop in eight *psychosocial development stages*. In each stage, people must successfully resolve a psychological and/or social conflict (**Figure 2.6**). If they do not, their failure to do so will affect future stages of development. According to Erikson, personality can develop in ways that are healthy or unhealthy.

Erikson's Psychosocial Developmental Stages		
Stage	**Age**	**Description**
Trust versus mistrust	Infancy (birth to 1 year)	Babies learn about trust from their caregivers who meet their needs, including food, attention, physical contact, interaction, and safety. When needs are not met, babies do not learn to trust others and the world is perceived as unpredictable.
Autonomy versus shame and doubt	Toddlerhood (1 to 3 years)	Toddlers learn how to control their physical bodies by feeding, toileting, dressing and undressing, and making strides in physical development. As toddlers learn new skills, they become self-confident. A lack of control or independence can make them feel like failures and cause shame and doubt. Often, this is caused by caregivers punishing them for not doing things right.
Initiative versus guilt	Early childhood (3 to 6 years)	Through discovery and exploration, young children learn about the world and their place in it. They learn what is real and what is imaginary. They learn to take initiative. Criticism and punishment can result in guilt for their own actions.
Industry versus inferiority	Middle childhood (6 to 13 years)	Children develop competencies both at school and at home. They develop a sense of self and confidence by becoming competent in the outside world. If they or others compare them negatively against others, feelings of inferiority can surface.

(Continued)

Figure 2.6 There are eight psychosocial development stages in Erikson's theory. *Review the stages in this chart. What stage are you in? Does the description match actual conflicts in your life? Why or why not?*

Copyright Goodheart-Willcox Co., Inc.

Erikson's Psychosocial Developmental Stages (*Continued*)		
Stage	**Age**	**Description**
Identity versus identity confusion	Adolescence (13 to 19 years or older)	Preteens and teens begin to understand and experiment with a number of different roles. A task during this stage is to integrate multiple roles such as sister, daughter, student, athlete, friend, and employee into one consistent role. If a central or core identity is not established, role confusion exists.
Intimacy versus isolation	Early adulthood (19 to 40 years)	During later adolescence and early adulthood, intimate relationships form. These relationships should involve sharing one's self emotionally. Success in this stage is based on success in earlier stages. Failure to establish intimacy results in emotional or psychological isolation.
Generativity versus stagnation	Middle adulthood (40 to 66 years)	Adults in midlife begin to place emphasis on assisting others through sharing culture with the next generation. This can be done in many ways, including rearing children, teaching others in the workplace or community, or passing on cultural values. A lack of generativity leads to stagnation.
Integrity versus despair	Older adulthood (66 years and older)	In the last stage of life, adults review their life and reflect on its meaning. If people are satisfied with the meaning of their life and involvement, there is a sense of integrity. Without it, despair emerges at the end of their life.

Cognitive Theory

Ideas about how people process information, think, and learn are called **cognitive theories**. Cognitive researchers seek to explain the differences in how people think throughout the stages of life. They look for explanations of how cognition changes throughout the lifespan. The most well-known researcher was Jean Piaget. Other cognitive theorists include Lev Vygotsky and Lawrence Kohlberg.

Piaget's Cognitive Theory

Piaget recognized that children do not think like adults. He also realized that babies are alike in how they think. Children are alike in how they think. Teens are alike in how they think. Lastly, adults are alike in how they think. In **Figure 2.7**, you will see that Piaget described the stages of cognitive development in four stages.

So why do young children think differently from teens? Piaget believed young children base their thinking on what they know. When children think the moon is following them or that babies are delivered at the front door, their beliefs make sense to them based on their limited experiences. As they gain more experience, their way of thinking will change and adapt.

Copyright Goodheart-Willcox Co., Inc.

Piaget's Stages of Cognitive Development		
Stage	**Age**	**Description**
Sensorimotor	Birth to 2 years	Babies begin to learn about the world through exploring with their mouths, grasping objects, and using other senses. Learning relies on reflexes, but moves to more sophisticated behaviors.
Preoperational	2 to 7 years	Toddlers and young children begin to learn to communicate through language or other symbols. They do not make broad generalizations about things they learn, but rather learn specific knowledge. As they progress through this stage, they begin to understand concepts such as reversibility and consequences.
Concrete operational	7 to 11 years	Children in this stage can make generalizations and understand reversibility and consequences. They understand that an action or behavior can cause a chain of events resulting in a different result. They can group, subgroup, and make classification hierarchies. They become more logical during this stage.
Formal operational	11 years and older	Individuals become more logical, concrete, and can process abstract thoughts during this stage. They can make predictions about cause and effect, use analogies and metaphors, and entertain "what if" questions. Objects do not need to be seen to be considered.

Figure 2.7 Piaget's four stages of cognitive development describe how people think in different life stages. *In which stage do children begin to understand concepts such as reversibility and consequences?*

Although many researchers have added to people's understanding of how thinking occurs, Piaget's stages of development remain important. His theory helps people understand how children are active in their own development and learning. They need a lot of exposure to experimentation, discovery, and firsthand experiences.

Vygotsky's Sociocultural Theory

Piaget theorized that all humans develop through experimentation with objects. Lev Vygotsky had a different theory. He theorized that the social and cultural environment shapes human cognitive development. Cognitive development does not just happen, but occurs because humans interact with other people, not just objects. Vygotsky believed that children are social beings. They develop their minds through interactions with parents, teachers, and other informed people.

Kohlberg's Theory of Moral Development

Imagine that you really need a medication, but do not have enough money to pay the pharmacy. Would you steal the medicine from the pharmacy? What if having the medicine is a matter of life and death?

Expert Insight

"Through others we become ourselves."

Lev Vygotsky, psychologist

Copyright Goodheart-Willcox Co., Inc.

Lawrence Kohlberg asked a similar question to children, teens, and adults. How do people decide what is right and what is wrong? In doing his research, Kohlberg identified three different levels of thinking that people go through in making moral decisions. *Moral decisions* are personal decisions that evaluate what is right and what is wrong.

In the first level, people make decisions based on whether or not they will be punished or rewarded. All children are in this level. In the second level, people's moral decisions are motivated by laws and how they might be perceived. Some older children and many youth are in this level. In the third level, some teens and many adults make moral decisions based on principles such as justice.

Kohlberg observed men and boys to develop his theory. Carol Gilligan expanded on his theory by considering how women and girls make moral decisions. She believed that the idea of justice was typical of males, but less typical of females. She felt that many women used the idea of care for others as a motivating factor in making moral decisions.

Behaviorism

Behaviorism is the belief that people's behavior is determined by forces in the environment that are beyond their control (**Figure 2.8**). Ivan Pavlov demonstrated the idea of behaviorism through his infamous experiment with a dog.

©iStock.com/MachineHeadz

Figure 2.8 According to behaviorists, how people behave depends solely on what they are taught, not what they are born with. *Why do you think Kevin fights with others on the playground? Does this behavior occur because he was modeled aggressive behavior at home?*

Copyright Goodheart-Willcox Co., Inc.

Expert Insight

"The way positive reinforcement is carried out is more important than the amount."

B.F. Skinner,
psychologist

The dog, which had a natural innate tendency to salivate when in the sight of food, learned to salivate at the sound of a bell. This happened after a training period when a bell would ring each time the dog was to be served food. After awhile, food was no longer needed for the dog to salivate—only the sound of the bell. Since that time, this has been termed **classical conditioning** (behaviors associated with emotional responses).

B.F. Skinner was well-known for identifying the basic principle of **operant conditioning**, which is the repetition of behaviors when reinforced. People tend to repeat behaviors that have a positive effect. Skinner saw that to make the behavior stick, the reinforcement must be gradually removed following an unpredictable pattern. Sometimes reinforcement occurs, whereas other times it does not. Skinner believed that these stages were crucial to learning.

Behaviorism in the form of operant conditioning became quite popular in American education. Children would receive continuous positive reinforcement when a new skill or behavior is learned. Then, gradual removal of the reinforcement would occur. This process is believed to result in a permanent behavioral change. Negative reinforcement, or punishment, is also believed to be very important.

Social Cognitive Theory

Is behaviorism really that simple? If simple positive reinforcement and punishment is all that is necessary, why do children not learn and behave the way people want them to? Also, if behaviorism really works, why can people not use behaviorism to control behaviors in adults?

Albert Bandura argued that people are very different from Pavlov's dog. They are much more complex. He argued that people watch and imitate other people's behaviors, despite whether or not there are rewards and punishments involved. People are affected by rewards and punishments, but their reactions to them are filtered by their own perceptions, thoughts, and motivations. He called this **social cognitive theory**.

Social cognitive theorists believe that a child who observes a kind act may later imitate the same act toward a sibling or classmate (**Figure 2.9**). Another learns how to swear or eat healthy by imitating other people's actions. The same experiences, however, will not have the same result on every person.

How a person responds is based on personal reaction and how he or she processes the information. A child who observes aggressive behavior may become aggressive or a person who avoids conflict. The result all depends on how the person processes the information and his or her cognitive abilities.

Which Theory Is Correct?

There are hundreds of theories about the ways humans develop. This chapter covers just a few. Which theory is the most correct? No one theory should be regarded as the absolute truth. Humans are much too complex to describe using simplistic theory.

Copyright Goodheart-Willcox Co., Inc.

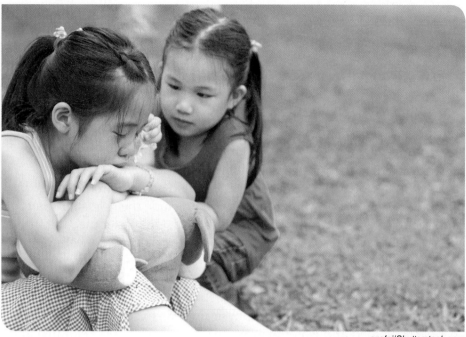

szefei/Shutterstock.com

Figure 2.9 A child who observes an adult comforting another person may imitate that behavior later toward a sibling or classmate. *What other kind acts might children imitate?*

Although there are many different, and sometimes conflicting, ways to explain human development, most are valid to some extent. Some theories may fit better than others. Sometimes theories may conflict. The conflict between two theories, however, often leads to more valid insights.

Human services workers can benefit from understanding several approaches to development and applying them to clients of all ages. Throughout life there will always be more theories that emerge as knowledge about human development grows. This makes working in the people business exciting.

Reading Recall

1. List the major ways people change and develop over their lifespan.
2. Name two factors that cause differences in the outcomes and rate of development among individuals.
3. What do psychoanalytic theorists analyze? What do they often believe?
4. Name two psychoanalytic theorists.
5. What are *cognitive theories*? Identify three cognitive theorists.
6. Define the terms *behaviorism* and *classical conditioning*.
7. Which theorist was well-known for identifying the basic principle of operant conditioning?
8. Explain Albert Bandura's social cognitive theory.

Copyright Goodheart-Willcox Co., Inc.

What Every Human Needs

Human psychologist Abraham Maslow theorized that all people have the same basic needs to survive. People need air to breathe, food to eat, water to drink, and a safe place to sleep. They need to feel love and acceptance from others. Maslow's theory identifies people's needs in a *hierarchy*, which he called the *Hierarchy of Human Needs* (**Figure 2.10**). *Hierarchy* is an arrangement of something according to importance.

In Maslow's theory, people's most basic needs (physical needs) are the first priority. These needs are indicated at the bottom of the pyramid. Other needs Maslow recognized include the needs for safety and security, love and acceptance, and esteem. Only after meeting the needs of one level to some extent can people work toward meeting their higher-level needs.

Physical Needs

Everyone has the same basic physical needs to survive. For example, people need food and water to grow and thrive. They need clothing and shelter to protect them from the *elements* (weather conditions). People need plenty of sleep each night to function properly the next day. Physical needs also include adequate medical and dental care.

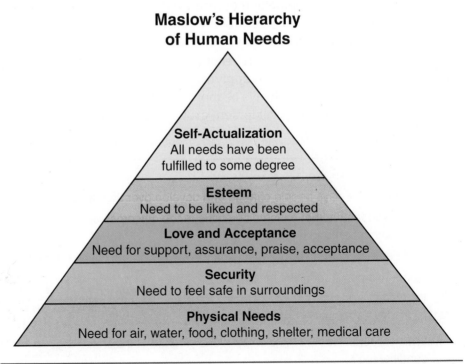

Maslow's Hierarchy of Human Needs

Self-Actualization
All needs have been fulfilled to some degree

Esteem
Need to be liked and respected

Love and Acceptance
Need for support, assurance, praise, acceptance

Security
Need to feel safe in surroundings

Physical Needs
Need for air, water, food, clothing, shelter, medical care

Figure 2.10 Maslow sees two kinds of needs in all humans—basic and higher-level needs. *According to Maslow, when can people work toward meeting their higher-level needs?*

Copyright Goodheart-Willcox Co., Inc.

Meeting these basic physical needs is critical to a person's health and well-being. Because children cannot meet their basic needs independently, adults are responsible for meeting their needs. Adults also need to effectively meet their own basic needs. Once people fulfill these basic needs, they can realize other needs.

Safety and Security

All people have a need to feel safe and secure. If people must constantly worry about their safety, they are unable to focus on other needs. Both children and adults need to feel safe in their environments. This includes their homes, schools, workplaces, and communities (**Figure 2.11**). For children to feel safe, they must know that adults will be able to protect them from harmful people, objects, and situations. Adults need to feel protected as well.

Security comes from stability, and stability gives people a sense of comfort. People need to experience a sense of stability in their daily schedules and activities. Structured routines, such as set times for specific activities and rest, help people know what to expect from life. Too many changes can disrupt a sense of stability for a child or an adult. This can result in feelings of insecurity. If a person has to invest too much energy into creating a sense of stability, other basic needs may not be met.

imtmphoto/Shutterstock.com

Figure 2.11 Adults can help children feel safe and secure. *What might happen if a person has to invest too much energy into creating a sense of stability?*

Copyright Goodheart-Willcox Co., Inc.

Love and Acceptance

From babies to older adults, everyone needs to feel the love and acceptance of others. Parents and caregivers show babies physical affection by cuddling and comforting them. In turn, children feel loved and also learn about positive interactions. These interactions are important because young children learn how to develop relationships with others by modeling their caregivers' behaviors.

Older children, teens, and adults all need physical affection, too. This promotes emotional and social health. By developing encouraging and supportive relationships with family members and friends, people fulfill their needs for love and acceptance (**Figure 2.12**). They become part of a secure community. Being part of a community is important to social and emotional health. It even affects people's cognitive and physical health.

Esteem

The need for *esteem* (respect; admiration) involves a person's need to feel respected and valued. People need to feel that others view them as worthy and important. When people feel the respect of others, they develop confidence in their abilities. This helps them establish good self-esteem and self-respect. People who do not feel valued often struggle with feelings of self-doubt and inferiority. *Inferiority* is a person's belief that he or she is not as good as other people.

Vibe Images/Shutterstock.com

Figure 2.12 A close friendship is one way to meet the needs of love and acceptance. *How are your needs for love and acceptance being met?*

Copyright Goodheart-Willcox Co., Inc.

Case Study *A Family of Five*

Jesse thought about her day, which had been fulfilling, exhausting, and frustrating all at the same time. She had seen a dozen clients—some dealing with addiction, major health concerns, and domestic abuse. The day had started, however, with her first clients who presented a scenario that pulled at her heartstrings. Their situation motivated her to help them find resources to care for and raise their young family well.

Jesse's first clients of the day were Matt and Julie, both in their early 20s. They have been together for four years. They have two children—Jordan, age 3, and Taylor, 18 months. Recently, they learned that Julie is pregnant.

Both Matt and Julie are high school graduates with some college experience, a little less than two years each. Matt feels fortunate to have a full-time job making double the minimum wage. He works from 7:00 a.m. to 4:00 p.m. Monday through Friday. Julie works part-time at a neighborhood floral shop. She works about 15 hours per week, 10 hours during weekdays and 5 hours on weekends. Julie earns minimum wage.

Currently, the couple lives with Matt's mother, Donna, and her husband, Bill. Donna and Bill provide child care when both Matt and Julie are working. Because Donna and Bill have been experiencing long-term unemployment, their mortgage payments have not been made regularly. Their house is now in foreclosure, so they have decided to relocate to a state with a lower cost of living. Now, Matt and Julie must find a new place to live. They are barely making ends meet.

What will happen to Matt and Julie without housing? How are they going to support another baby? Will Julie be able to continue working throughout her pregnancy? Where should they live? How much can they afford? Should they pursue further education to prepare them for higher paying jobs? If so, when and how might they do this? Should they both continue to work? Would it be more affordable if one parent stayed home to care for their young children, at least for the next 5 years? Where would they like to be in 10 years?

Matt and Julie need help finding affordable housing and child care. They need help making decisions about their future. Jesse worked with her clients to determine their needs. She helped them focus on decisions they need to make. She also connected them with community resources that could help meet their basic needs. It was a lot to cover, but by the end of their session, Jesse felt that Matt and Julie had made some important decisions and connections.

Vibe Images/Shutterstock.com

For Discussion

1. Who is (are) Jesse's clients?
2. What are the three top needs of her clients?
3. If you were Jesse, which issue would you help them with first? Why?
4. Is it Jesse's responsibility to help Donna and Bill? Why or why not?

Copyright Goodheart-Willcox Co., Inc.

Showing respect is important to help people develop healthy esteem throughout life. Interaction with caregivers is especially critical to the development of young children's self-esteem. Being positive and praising school-age children as they learn new skills can help them feel good about themselves and their accomplishments. This helps them develop healthy self-esteem. Positive interactions with teens and adults let them know they are cared for and valued.

Self-Actualization

Expert Insight

"What a man can be, he must be. This need we call self-actualization."
Abraham Maslow, psychologist

The need for *self-actualization*, to fully realize one's own potential, is a lifelong process. According to Maslow, people cannot begin to reach this higher-level need until at least partially fulfilling other needs.

At this level, people have self-awareness and are confident in themselves and their abilities. They are concerned about creative personal growth and the fulfillment of purpose in life. They focus on and find solutions to problems in the world. They strive to reach their full potential and become the best they can be.

Reading Recall

1. List people's needs in order of priority as described in Abraham Maslow's *Hierarchy of Human Needs*.
2. Identify three physical needs of every human.
3. Describe how security comes from stability.
4. How can people fulfill their need for love and acceptance throughout the lifespan?
5. Give an example of how caregivers can help school-age children develop healthy self-esteem.
6. What is *self-actualization*? Why is self-actualization a lifelong process?

How People Meet Their Needs

To meet their basic needs, people use and manage **resources** (a supply of assets that can be used when needed). Money is an important resource people use to help meet their needs. Personal knowledge, skills, time, and energy are important resources people use to meet needs. Other people, such as family members, friends, community members, and coworkers, can also be a valuable resource for meeting needs.

Many times, people are able to meet their own needs and their families' needs by combining their resources. Some people, however, may have insufficient resources and lack the support of others, thereby preventing them from meeting their basic needs. These people may

Copyright Goodheart-Willcox Co., Inc.

Pathway to Success

Money Management Tips

How many times have you heard the phrase "Money doesn't grow on trees"? Money is an important resource. It requires careful managing to meet needs, satisfy wants, and still be able to save for the future.

Following are some easy tips to help you manage your money wisely:

- Write down your goals. When you have a goal in mind it is easier to spend less knowing you will use that money to get something you really want.

- Track your spending. Record your spending to see where your money goes. You might be surprised to see how much you actually spend. Use this information to adjust your spending habits accordingly.

- Use a money register. Record deposits and withdrawals in a money/check register to keep up with the balance in your account. This will help you avoid overcharges or overdrafts. *Overcharges* occur when companies charge you too much. *Overdrafts*

are a result of not having enough money in your account to cover an expense.

- Save a set amount each month. Earmark a set amount from your earnings to save each month. This will get you in the habit of saving for the future.

- Write a budget. Look at your spending record and categorize your expenses. Total your expenses for each category. This will give you a basic budget you can change and adapt whenever necessary. Be careful that your spending does not exceed your income.

- Get organized. Set up a bill paying system to ensure you pay all your bills on time. You might create a spreadsheet to keep track of your bills. Maybe you would rather set up automatic bill pay through your bank. Using file folders is another way to keep track of your bills. You may have to try several systems to find what works for you. When you do find a system that works, stick with it.

Create a Budget

As a class, poll high school students with jobs to find out their hourly wages. Average the wages and use the amount as the monthly income for this activity.

For the next two weeks, keep track of the money you spend. Then, double this amount to figure what you spend in a month. If there are some expenses you do not pay, such as for a cell phone or car insurance, find out how much your portion of the bill would be. Next, as a class, identify the types of bills to pay in this activity, such as *cell phone, car payment,*

car insurance and gas, school supplies, snacks, dates, and *clothing.*

Now you are ready to write your budget. Categorize your bills according to the bill types identified by the class. Then, rank in order the bills to be paid first to last. (This helps when you need to trim expenses because you do not have enough to pay for something.) Finally, create a word document or spreadsheet listing each bill, the amount you owe, and the date due. Subtract the total payments from the monthly income identified at the beginning of this activity.

Copyright Goodheart-Willcox Co., Inc.

be unable to provide food, clothing, or shelter for themselves or their families. In cases such as these, human services workers often help people meet their needs by finding the necessary resources, such as nutritious food or warm clothing. Human services workers also work with people to help them develop and manage their resources. This enables them to have the tools to successfully meet their own needs.

Although everyone needs resources to be able to meet their needs, people have different amounts of resources available to them. Some people have plenty of resources. Other people have very few. People today live in a money-driven society and must work to provide financial stability for themselves and their families. The work people choose to do will affect their standard of living.

A person or family's **standard of living** is a measure of the wealth, comforts, and material goods available to them. Most people have a standard of living they aspire to meet. This could be the same as their current level of living.

Many people aspire to a higher standard of living. That is, they want to be able to buy better quality items. They may want to have a higher status in the community. Perhaps they want to buy a bigger house or purchase more consumer goods. If this standard is out of reach, stress, frustration, and unhappiness can result. At times, economic and employment changes can cause people to struggle financially, resulting in an inability to meet their needs.

Economic Changes

As the economy grows or falters, personal spending, unemployment rates, and prices of *consumer goods* (products and services people buy) rise and fall. These changes affect how people meet their needs. Economic changes generally fall into three categories: *recession*, *recovery*, and *expansion*.

When the economy is in a **recession mode**, there is a slowing and decline in the economy. Families tend to carefully monitor their spending and savings. Rather than hiring people, companies are more likely to let workers go. More people access food banks and subsidized government programs. **Figure 2.13** shows several national and federal assistance programs that help economically disadvantaged people meet their food and housing needs.

When the economy is in a **recovery mode**, things again start to look hopeful. Consumer spending on goods and services increases. People still tend to be more conservative in their spending, however.

When the economy is in an **expansion mode**, unemployment rates are usually lower. Many people who seek employment can find jobs. There is a feeling of prosperity. Simply put, financial resources give people more choices they would not have otherwise.

Copyright Goodheart-Willcox Co., Inc.

National and Federal Assistance Programs	
Food Purchasing Assistance Programs	
Program	**Description**
Supplemental Nutritional Assistance Program (SNAP)	Formerly known as *Food Stamps*, this program offers families financial assistance for purchasing foods. Supervised by US Social Security.
Special Supplemental Program for Women, Infants, and Children (WIC)	Program provides food assistance to infants, children through 4 years of age, and pregnant and lactating women.
Commodity Supplemental Food Program (CSFP)	This program provides nutritional foods to community locations as dietary supplements for women during pregnancy and postpartum stage, infants and children through 6 years of age, and adults 60 years and older. Program is operated by the US Food and Nutrition Service.
WIC and Senior Farmers' Market Nutrition Program (FMNP)	Two separate programs that offer supplemental food from farmer's markets and roadside stands. WIC FMNP is for infants, children through 4 years of age, and pregnant and lactating women. The senior program (SFMNP) is for adults 60 years and older.
Federal Housing Assistance Programs	
Program	**Description**
Public Housing Program	Program offers affordable housing to low-income families, older adults, and individuals with disabilities. Housing agencies manage housing units and charge rent on a sliding scale based on income.
Housing Choice Voucher Program	Through this program, vouchers are given to eligible low-income families, older adults, and individuals with disabilities. Families can select eligible housing and use vouchers to help pay rent.
Supportive Housing for the Elderly Program	This program helps low-income adults 62 years of age and older with rent assistance for housing that offers support and caregiving services.
Supportive Housing for Persons with Disabilities	Program offers low-income individuals with disabilities rental assistance for housing that provides specialized support and caregiving services.
Rural Renting Housing Loans	Government administers property loans to individuals or organizations to provide affordable rent to low-income families, older adults, and those with disabilities in rural areas.

Figure 2.13 There are national and federal assistance programs available to help people meet their basic needs. *How might these programs help people work toward meeting their higher-level needs?*

Copyright Goodheart-Willcox Co., Inc.

Ways in which the economy influences people are complex. Some people do not have the choice to spend or save more, even when the economy is in an expansion mode. They may be struggling financially due to personal issues. Likewise, some people at the upper end of the economic scale may hardly feel the effects of a changing economy.

Employment Changes

Paid work helps provide financial security. It supports the meeting of both client needs and desires. As people work, improve their skills, and advance in their careers, they earn higher pay, which provides financial stability (**Figure 2.14**).

Unfortunately, sometimes jobs are lost involuntarily. The loss of a job, especially the main income for a family, can cause much stress on all family members. Work contributes to the family's financial health, as well as its sense of identity. When income is lost, people have a much more difficult time trying to meet their needs.

Preparing for a job market and finding a new job can be challenging. This is especially true if the person has not recently conducted a job search, or if the search lasts for an extended time. Many adults report that looking for a job can affect a person's self-esteem or self-worth. In a tough job market, unemployment not only affects financial stability, but a person's sense of place in the community. Work, whether paid or not,

Michaelpuche/Shutterstock.com

Figure 2.14 Working can give people a sense of fulfillment, financial stability, and new skills. *How does employment help people meet their needs?*

Copyright Goodheart-Willcox Co., Inc.

gives a sense of purpose and is important to adult development. Human services workers help their clients with many types of transitions related to employment.

Reading Recall

1. Name three resources that human services workers help their clients manage.
2. What is meant by the term *standard of living*?
3. Describe how fluctuations in the economy affect how people meet their needs.
4. Describe how employment changes affect how people meet their needs.

Law and Ethics / Unemployment Compensation

The Social Security Act of 1935 created the federal-state unemployment compensation (UC) program, which serves as the first economic line of defense against the ripple effects of unemployment. By offering temporary, partial wage replacement, this program ensures that unemployed workers are able to pay for some of the necessities of life, such as food, shelter, and clothing. The UC program helps stabilize the economy when people lose their jobs by ensuring that those people still have *purchasing power*, or the financial ability to buy goods and services. The UC program is a social insurance program. It provides benefits to many out-of-work individuals that have lost their jobs involuntarily while they search for a new job.

To qualify for unemployment benefits, jobless workers must have worked for a certain amount of time (called the *base period*) and must be able to work and are available for work. The base period varies by state, but in most states, it is a 12- to 18-month period. Most states also have an earnings requirement for the base period. The earnings requirement measures the minimum earnings a worker must have earned during the base period to be eligible for unemployment benefits. In most cases, jobless workers can collect unemployment benefits for up to 6 months. In some cases, however, benefits can be extended. Unemployed workers apply to receive unemployment benefits in their state.

Research and Writing Activity

Use online or print resources to learn about your state's unemployment benefits. As you conduct your research, consider the following questions:
- What are the eligibility requirements for collecting unemployment benefits?
- Is there anything that would disqualify a jobless worker from collecting unemployment benefits? Explain.
- What different types of assistance does the government offer to unemployed individuals?
- What is the application process for receiving unemployment benefits in your state?
- What can a person do if his or her claim for benefits is denied?

Then, write a reflection about what you have learned. Think about how this information might be useful to you in the future. Include your thoughts on the UC program. What do you think could happen to the nation's economy if this program was not in place?

Summary

- To effectively help people, human services workers need to have an understanding of human development principles and theories. By understanding several approaches to development, human services workers can apply this knowledge to helping clients of all ages with whom they serve.

- Four basic guidelines when considering principles of human development include the following: human development is relatively orderly, human development takes place gradually, human development is interrelated, and human development varies among individuals.

- Researchers and scientists explore the many ways in which humans grow and develop. Through observation and experimentation, they formulate developmental theories. *Developmental theories* are comprehensive explanations about why people act and behave the way they do and how they change over time.

- According to Maslow's *Hierarchy of Human Needs*, people's most basic needs are their physical needs. Other needs include the needs for safety and security, love and acceptance, esteem, and self-actualization. Only after meeting the needs of one level to some extent can people work toward meeting their higher-level needs.

- To meet their basic needs, people use and manage resources, such as money, personal knowledge, skills, time, energy, and other people. Economic and employment changes can cause people to struggle financially, resulting in an inability to meet their needs.

- Human services workers often help disadvantaged individuals meet their needs by finding the necessary resources. They also help their clients develop and manage their resources so they can have the tools to successfully meet their own needs.

College and Career Portfolio

Portfolio Objective

Before you begin collecting information for your portfolio, write a portfolio objective. A *portfolio objective* is a complete sentence or two that states what you want to accomplish by creating a portfolio.

The language you use for your objective should be clear, specific, detailed, and measurable. For instance, "I will create a portfolio for my future education" is too general. A better, more detailed objective might read: "I will work with my teacher and spend at least three hours per week creating, editing, and compiling items which will help me get into a college child care program."

A clear objective is a good starting point for building a portfolio. As you think about building your portfolio, complete the following:

1. Decide on the purpose of your portfolio—temporary or short-term employment, career, and/or college application.
2. Use online or print resources to find articles about writing objectives. Also, look for articles containing sample objectives.
3. Write an objective for your portfolio.

Copyright Goodheart-Willcox Co., Inc.

Review and Reflect ↗

1. The human services profession is referred to as the "people business." In your own words, explain what this means.

2. Which category of development includes moral decision making? Why?

3. There are four ideas that are believed to be true about human development. In your own words, define and interpret these four ideas to a person who has never read this textbook.

4. Using Figure 2.6, summarize Erik Erikson's eight psychosocial stages of development.

5. What are the three levels of thinking that people go through when making a moral decision?

6. Draw and label Maslow's *Hierarchy of Needs*. On each level, list how it is used by human services workers when working with people.

7. What happens when a person's need for esteem is not met?

8. What does *inferiority* mean?

9. What are *resources*? Explain how human services workers help disadvantaged individuals meet their needs.

10. What does *standard of living* mean?

11. List the three categories of economic changes.

12. When the economy is in an expansion mode, are unemployment rates usually higher or lower?

Vocabulary Activities

13. **Key terms** In teams, create categories for the following terms and classify as many of the terms as possible. Then, share your ideas with the remainder of the class.

behaviorism
classical
   conditioning
cognitive theories
developmental
   theories
expansion mode
human development
operant conditioning

psychoanalytic
   theories
recession mode
recovery mode
resources
social cognitive
   theory
standard of living

14. **Academic terms** Work with a partner to write the definitions of the following terms based on your current understanding before reading the chapter. Then, pair up with another partner to discuss your definitions and any discrepancies. Finally, discuss the definitions with the class. Ask your instructor for necessary correction or clarification.

elements
environment
esteem
heredity

hierarchy
inferiority
moral issues
self-actualization

Self-Assessment Quiz ↗

Complete the self-assessment quiz online to help you practice and expand your knowledge and skills.

Critical Thinking

15. **Evaluate** In teams, evaluate the two psychoanalytic theories of Sigmund Freud and Erik Erikson. How are they similar? How are they different?

16. **Compare and contrast** Using a graphic organizer, such as a Venn-Diagram, compare and contrast cognitive theories and developmental theories.

17. **Draw conclusions** How would you apply what you have learned about the behavioral theory to train a new puppy?

18. **Analyze** Analyze the differences between behavioral theories and social cognitive theories. Which theory do you think is correct about learning desired behaviors? Explain.

19. **Determine** At the top of Maslow's *Hierarchy of Needs* is the term *self-actualization*. How will you determine in your own life when you have reached this level? What activities will you complete to show you are at this level in your life?

20. **Make inferences** Think about all of the resources you currently possess. How will your current resources impact your ability to meet your needs? Are there resources you would like to develop? How can you develop these resources? What services in your local area are available to help you develop your resources?

21. **Identify**   Using Figure 2.13, identify which of these programs are available in your area. Are there any prerequisites to getting help?
22. **Cause and effect**   Imagine a local factory in your community shut down and hundreds of workers became unemployed. Now, almost a year later, many of these workers are still unemployed. What might the effects of unemployment be on physical and mental health? What effects might this have on the local economy?

Core Skills

23. **Listening and speaking**   Arrange to interview an older adult about how both heredity and environment influenced his or her development through the lifespan. What traits did he or she inherit? What events had a great influence on development? Prepare a list of questions to ask prior to the interview. After the interview, create a scrapbook to record the interview questions and responses.
24. **Reading and writing**   Read a biography about someone's life. How has this person grown and changed over his or her lifetime? What factors may have affected these changes in growth and development? Write an essay discussing your findings.
25. **Listening and speaking**   Working in groups, use Figure 2.7 to create a handout to present in class explaining Piaget's theory and the different stages of cognitive development. Give examples for each of the stages.
26. **Listening, speaking, and technology**   As a class, brainstorm a list of ethical-related dilemmas. Working in small groups, choose one of the dilemmas on the list, debate the topic, and solve the dilemma. Create a five-minute video presentation outlining the group's view on the dilemma. Share your presentations with the rest of the class. As a class, discuss each group's presentation.
27. **Research and writing**   To meet their basic needs, people use and manage a variety of resources. Conduct online research to determine what technology is available to manage your finances at home. Do you have to pay for this technology or is it free? Can you create your own software programs to manage

your finances or do you have to pay someone to do them for you? If you pay for someone to manage your finances, what do they charge and what do their services include? Using your research, create a chart showing the various resources available, including the pros and cons of each type.
28. **Writing**   Using the list you came up with for number 21, write the script you would use when calling the different agencies in your area to find out their location, what services they have available, the cost, and who to contact. You should have a list of at least 10 questions to ask.
29. **Research and writing**   Using Figure 2.13, choose two of the programs to research. Write a one-page paper explaining each of these programs, requirements for enrollment, how the programs can help people, and where people can go locally to get enrolled in these programs.
30. **Math**   Use a checkbook register (or similar form) to keep track of your checkbook or debit card transactions for one month. After recording your expenditures for the month, evaluate your spending habits. Are there spending categories you could cut if you needed to save money for an upcoming event?
31. **Speaking and math**   Talk to a local human resources worker at a nonprofit agency about the types and costs of services the agency provides for disadvantaged families. Find out where the agency's funding comes from and how often the agency has fundraisers to meet budgetary needs. Using the information you obtain, create a budget for an imaginary nonprofit you would like to open in your local area. In your budget, include costs for an office, staff members' salaries, marketing, and other services you will provide.
32. **CTE career readiness practice**   Choose a moral dilemma that many people face. Analyze and describe what each pressure source might say to a person. Pressure sources might include peer groups, religious beliefs, cultural values, and moral standards of parents, teachers, institutions, or youth leaders. Explain why the dilemma requires difficult decision making. For instance, are people getting mixed messages or are one or more pressure sources silent on an issue?

Copyright Goodheart-Willcox Co., Inc.

Lend a Hand

Why Volunteer?

People who volunteer cite many different reasons for making volunteering a regular part of their lives. Following are some of the common reasons people often give for volunteering:

- to feel needed;
- to be a part of the community;
- to make a difference;
- for academic credit;
- to learn more about a career or add an experience to a résumé;
- because someone asked for help;
- because of personal experience with a particular cause or problem;
- to remain active and be a part of a team; and
- for recognition.

Although people give many reasons for volunteering, one of the primary reasons is to have a chance to help others. In this way, volunteering is much like "the people business." Through volunteering, people are helping those who are in need and less fortunate. In return, they feel a sense of purpose or accomplishment as a result of their work. In fact, studies have shown that there is a positive relationship between volunteering and happiness. The more time you spend volunteering, the more potential there is to gain happiness and fulfillment from helping others.

Volunteering presents many social opportunities to give you a feeling of happiness. Through volunteering, you will be exposed to a more diverse group of people. You will meet people who care about the same issues that interest you. This can be an excellent way for making new friends. If you are shy or have a hard time meeting people, volunteering can be a good way to meet likeminded people. You can even improve your social skills in the process.

Volunteering can also help you connect with family and friends. As you work together to help others, you have a chance to spend time together and talk. You share a common goal and work as a team. Adult family members can set an example of community service for younger family members. There are many benefits to volunteering with family and friends.

To discover the ways in which volunteering can benefit you and your family and friends, complete the following:

1. With your classmates, brainstorm a list of possible social benefits of volunteering. Which benefits are the most important to you? Why?
2. Choose one or two possible benefits of volunteering. Locate volunteer opportunities that would provide you with those benefits. Find out how to apply for the volunteer opportunities you locate. Then, write a practice application for one of the positions.

Copyright Goodheart-Willcox Co., Inc.

Chapter 3

What Makes an Effective Human Services Worker?

While studying, look for the activity icon ⤴ **to**

- **practice** key and academic terms with e-flash cards and matching activities;
- **assess** what you learn by completing self-assessment quizzes; and
- **reinforce** what you learn by mapping concepts and completing review and reflect questions.

www.g-wlearning.com/humanservices/

Andresr/Shutterstock.com

Learning Outcomes

After studying this chapter, you will be able to

- **describe** two key components of effective communication;
- **apply** the decision-making process to make a responsible decision consistent with personal needs, wants, values, and priorities;
- **summarize** the steps of the problem-solving process and explain the importance of critical thinking during this process;
- **give examples** of measurable short- and long-term goals;
- **use** constructive conflict management to resolve a conflict; and
- **explain** and recognize the value of effective collaboration and leadership skills in human services.

Reading Strategies

Before reading, scan the pages of the chapter and note the main headings. Compare these headings to the learning outcomes. Based on this information, write a list of the items that you think are important to note while reading. As you are reading, analyze how the author presents these concepts. After you finish reading the chapter, summarize what you learned.

Mapping Concepts

Write each of the six learning outcomes for this chapter on index cards. Arrange these cards near you as you read the chapter. On each index card, take notes about the appropriate learning outcome. Exchange your index cards with a partner. Discuss how your notes are similar or different.

Carolyn Franks/Shutterstock.com

Key Terms

active listening
aggressive communicators
assertive communicators
Career and Technical Student
    Organization (CTSO)
constructive conflict
    management
critical thinking
decision-making process
empathy

leadership
long-term goals
mediation
mediator
mixed message
passive communicators
problem-solving process
receiver
sender
short-term goals

Academic Terms

collaborate
concessions
diverse
impulsively
priorities
Standard English
validate
values

Copyright Goodheart-Willcox Co., Inc.

What makes an effective human services worker? If you put a group of highly effective human services workers together in a room, you might be surprised by their obvious differences. They would, for example, vary in personality. By looking deeper, however, you would find they have much in common.

Effective human services workers possess strong *interpersonal skills*. These are the skills people use to interact and work with others (**Figure 3.1**). Human services workers know how to communicate effectively with others. They demonstrate good decision-making, problem-solving, and conflict resolution skills. They also exhibit strong collaboration and leadership skills.

You, like every person thinking of becoming a human services worker, want to be a great one. Perhaps you were inspired by a wonderful human services worker who made a real difference in your life or the life of someone you know. This chapter will help you learn more about the essential skills you need to become that great human services worker. As you read, think about how you can develop the skills you will need to have a positive impact on your clients' lives.

Communication Skills

At the core of virtually every aspect of human services is *communication*. Human services workers must communicate effectively

Rawpixel/Shutterstock.com

Figure 3.1 Effective human services workers can interact well with both coworkers and clients. *Why is it important for human services workers to have strong interpersonal skills?*

Copyright Goodheart-Willcox Co., Inc.

with their clients, clients' families, coworkers, and other human services providers. Communicating effectively can enhance human services. Communication is, however, complex. There are many ways in which communication can break down.

People communicate continually, even when they are not aware they are doing so. Think about your interactions with others today. What messages were you communicating? What messages were others communicating to you? Every word a person speaks and every gesture, action, and facial expression he or she conveys sends a message that the other person interprets (**Figure 3.2**). In communication, the person who transmits a message or messages is called the **sender**. The **receiver** is the person who accepts a message from the sender. Normally, communication involves being both a sender and a receiver.

To communicate effectively, the words the sender speaks and the nonverbal messages he or she conveys must match. The nonverbal messages may come from a person's posture, tone of voice, facial expressions, eye contact (or lack thereof), and many other factors.

When a difference between the sender's verbal and nonverbal messages occurs, the receiver gets a **mixed message**. For example, a counselor who grimaces while verbally encouraging a client who is attempting to perform a difficult task is sending a mixed message. Mixed messages confuse receivers and can cause communication to break down.

While there are many components of effective communication, this chapter will explore two key components. First, communication

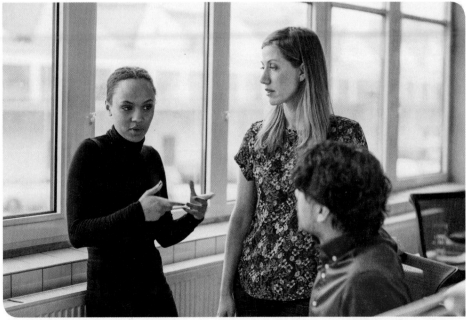

Jacob Lund/Shutterstock.com

Figure 3.2 Gestures and facial expressions are considered nonverbal communication. *What happens when the words a sender speaks do not match her nonverbal messages?*

Copyright Goodheart-Willcox Co., Inc.

must occur in the context of positive relationships. Second, each form of communication—verbal, nonverbal, written, and electronic—depends on specific, but related skills.

Creating Positive Relationships

Negative relationships create barriers that interfere with effective communication. Therefore, good communication begins with positive relationships. Several factors go into building positive relationships. These include

- taking ownership in the relationship;

- being an active listener; and

- using assertive communication.

Taking Ownership in the Relationship

When a person takes ownership in a relationship, he or she is taking responsibility for his or her own feelings and behaviors rather than blaming others. Events may influence a person's feelings. Another person does not cause them.

Human services workers understand this difference. They realize that, although they can influence others, they cannot control the feelings or behaviors of others. For example, a substance abuse counselor can encourage an alcoholic to stop drinking, but cannot force the person to want to quit (**Figure 3.3**). If the person does drink, the human services worker who takes ownership in the relationship may say, "I feel disappointed." The counselor does not blame the client and say, "You

Figure 3.3 A substance abuse counselor can provide encouragement and guidance to a client, but the person must *want* to quit. *Why is it important for human services workers to understand that they cannot control the feelings or behaviors of others?*

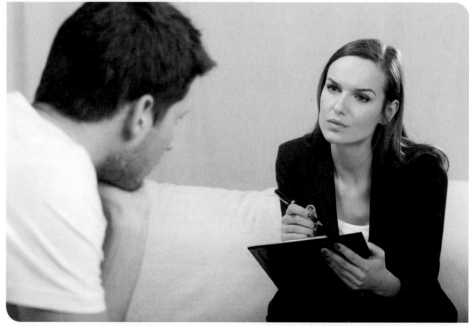

©iStock.com/ KatarzynaBialasiewicz

Copyright Goodheart-Willcox Co., Inc.

disappoint me." Rewards, encouragement, or punishments may influence a person toward a particular behavioral goal. The motivation, however, must come from the person.

Being an Active Listener

Active listening involves asking questions and restating ideas to discover the true message of the sender. Being an active listener requires the receiver to focus on the message the sender is conveying. By giving verbal feedback, the receiver is letting the sender know that he or she is listening to and understanding the message. Active listening helps increase the exchange of clear communication.

Active listening skills are highly important in the field of human services. Effective human services workers actively listen to their clients to help them solve their problems. **Figure 3.4** shows tips for developing effective active listening skills.

Using Assertive Communication

Good communicators realize that *how* they say something is just as important as *what* they say. To be a good communicator, effective human services workers use assertive communication. **Assertive communicators** freely express their thoughts, ideas, and feelings respectfully and allow others to do the same. The receiver is more likely to hear and understand the messages as the sender intends them because assertive communication is straightforward. It avoids hidden meanings or agendas.

Becoming an Active Listener

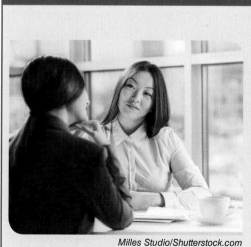

Milles Studio/Shutterstock.com

- Pay attention to what the other person is saying. Avoid thinking about something else while the person is talking. External distractions, such as other people's conversations or a television show playing in the background, should also be avoided. Tune in to the conversation and focus on the speaker.
- Show the speaker you are listening. Nonverbal cues, such as maintaining eye contact or leaning toward the speaker, help encourage the speaker to continue talking.
- Do not interrupt the speaker or assume to know what the speaker will say next.
- After the speaker finishes talking, restate the speaker's ideas and ask questions to make sure the message is clearly understood.
- Acknowledge the speaker's feelings and be empathetic.

Figure 3.4 Active listening is an important skill for a human services worker. *What does active listening involve?*

Copyright Goodheart-Willcox Co., Inc.

Other methods of communication include using aggressive and passive communication. These methods, however, do not encourage good communication. For example, **aggressive communicators** aim to hurt or put down other people and show disrespect. Aggressive communication hinders understanding, as the receiver may feel offended, hurt, or frightened. These emotional states can cloud or filter both understanding and responses to the message sender.

Passive communicators are the opposite of aggressive communicators. **Passive communicators** are unwilling to say what they feel, think, or desire and want to avoid all conflict. In passive communication, messages are not sent clearly. As a result, they are often difficult to decipher. Receivers may be confused or respond inappropriately.

Both aggressive and passive communication styles make good, clear communication difficult for senders and receivers. Assertive communication, on the other hand, gives the best chance for messages to be understood.

Improving Communication Skills

Effective human services workers rely on exceptional communication skills. They are able to communicate verbal messages clearly. Their nonverbal messages are consistent with what they say. They also use written and electronic communication to their advantage.

Verbal Communication

Even though effective human services workers are good listeners, the many aspects of serving clients involve a great deal of speaking. Unlike casual conversation, human services workers must speak with thought, empathy, care, and purpose. **Empathy** is the ability to identify with and share another person's feelings. Empathy is not the same as sympathy. Sympathy is feeling compassion for a person or cause. Empathy occurs when one is able to understand another person's feelings by imagining him- or herself in the person's situation.

Effective speaking requires tailoring the message to a particular audience or client. To do this, human services workers consider their clients' needs and interests. They think about what motivates them and keeps their attention. Human services workers consider how their messages will affect listeners.

Human services workers also remember that simplicity and clarity are important, as is their choice of words. When they must use unfamiliar words, they briefly explain the meanings of these words to ensure their clients understand. As human services workers are speaking, they are also checking for signs that their clients are actively listening to the message they are conveying.

The old saying "Think twice before you speak" is a wise one. Words are powerful. Once a person speaks them, these words can never be

Copyright Goodheart-Willcox Co., Inc.

Expert Insight

"Think twice before you speak, because your words and influence will plant the seed of either success or failure in the mind of another."

Napoleon Hill, author, *Think and Grow Rich*

Pathway to Success

Verbal Presentation Skills

Verbal presentations include any presentation given to a group. They can vary in length, as well as include a question and answer session. There are several steps in presenting a speech. These include choosing a topic, writing an outline, and practicing repeatedly.

Once you have chosen a topic for your presentation, you need to identify the purpose and analyze the audience. Are you passing on information? Responding to questions and/or requests? Directing others? Persuading others? Think about your audience and what will interest them about the topic. For example, you would not want to discuss going to a rock concert when you are trying to convince someone to buy a violin.

To prepare your presentation, you need to do some research, gather information, and then organize it. Your presentation has several sections to put it together. These include an introduction, a body, and a conclusion.

1 In the *introduction*, you will introduce the topic, preview the main points, and draw the listener into the presentation. This is usually done by using an attention-getting device.

2 The *body* of the presentation is where you make the main points. This needs to be done in a logical order. Normally, you will have three main points with three supporting facts.

3 The *conclusion* should relate to the purpose of the presentation and summarize the entire presentation.

After preparing your presentation, the next step is to practice, practice, practice. Several do's and don'ts for presenting include

- maintaining eye contact with the audience;

- being specific when using facts;

- using humor to engage the audience;

- adjusting your volume to project your voice throughout the room;

- dressing appropriately;

- not reading your presentation word for word;

- not trying to recall information completely from memory; and

- not altering data.

Give a Persuasive Speech

Using the above information, prepare a verbal presentation to give in class. First, select a common digital product, such as a smartphone, tablet, iPod, or video game console. The purpose of your speech is to persuade the audience to purchase the product.

Create an outline for a 5-minute presentation that includes a visual aid. Be sure to write an introduction, body, and conclusion for your speech. Practice giving the speech so you feel comfortable with what you are saying. Present the speech to the class using your visual aid to help get your point across. Ask classmates to evaluate your performance and provide feedback. How persuasive were you?

Copyright Goodheart-Willcox Co., Inc.

taken back. Therefore, thinking about what to say before speaking is very important. Making a habit of pausing for a few seconds before saying something is a simple step in the communication process that can help avoid conflicts. It can also save people much embarrassment and hurt feelings.

Nonverbal Communication

While words can be powerful, so are other aspects of communication. Even when a person is not speaking, his or her body is communicating a message. The nonverbal messages a person sends can reinforce or take away from the importance of what he or she is verbally communicating. Facial expressions, body posture and movements, and tone of voice are all forms of nonverbal communication.

Another form of nonverbal communication involves a person's dress and appearance. The way a person looks and dresses sends a message to others. Being well-groomed and wearing clean, well-maintained clothing communicates a positive message and makes a good impression on others. Wearing appropriate clothing for the occasion is also important in communicating a positive, nonverbal message (**Figure 3.5**). Effective human services workers try to look their best and dress appropriately for their job. They seek to make a good impression at all times.

Nonverbal communication has the power to confuse the listener. Especially when a person's nonverbal and verbal messages are in conflict with one another. In fact, nonverbal cues account for a major part of miscommunication and often cause stress in relationships. For example, a facial expression may communicate anger, even when a person's words do not. A smile may mask a message of seriousness. By being aware of nonverbal cues, human services workers can communicate effectively with their clients and others.

Tyler Olson/Shutterstock.com

Figure 3.5 This outfit is appropriate for a job in a child care center, but may not be appropriate for a school counselor. *In what ways does the occasion for which you are dressing dictate your clothing choices?*

Written Communication

In these days of dashing off text messages, formal writing may seem too time-consuming. Important information, however, particularly in human services, is still conveyed in writing. Filling out forms, completing applications, and maintaining records are common day-to-day tasks. Paperwork in the form of recordkeeping is frequently required for the purpose of

Copyright Goodheart-Willcox Co., Inc.

reporting client progress or problems. Recordkeeping provides a way to document progress and record services provided. It is also a way to collect information about changes in circumstances, events, or personal dynamics.

Overall, recordkeeping can work to *validate* (confirm) the work that human services workers are providing. In some ways, it offers a safety net in recording services offered and actions taken. Although not always the favorite part of the job, recordkeeping is a necessary and important part of the human services field. Therefore, being able to write well is an essential skill of effective human services workers.

Most of the guidelines for speaking effectively also apply to writing effectively. A few additional important points to remember include the following:

- Write objectively. Good writers stick to the facts. They avoid expressing personal opinions through their writing.

- Avoid trying to impress people with complicated words and long sentences. Sometimes people think that complex writing full of difficult or trendy terms will make them seem more intelligent. Actually, this type of writing can frustrate readers. It can make them feel as if the writer is trying to put them down. Effective human services workers understand their audience. They remember to convey their messages clearly and concisely and consider their tone.

- Organize writing effectively. People who organize their writing effectively clearly state their main points. They move logically from one topic to another. If what they write is long, they use headings to divide sections and provide a brief summary. **Figure 3.6** shows some tips for organizing writing effectively.

- Check spelling, grammar, and punctuation. Good writers never rely on their computer's spelling- and grammar-checking features. These features often miss problems or suggest incorrect solutions. Instead, they learn the rules of good grammar. They keep a grammar reference at hand. They proofread what they write (preferably more than once) before submitting their work to someone else.

- Avoid the use of slang or texting abbreviations. Writing effectively involves the use of formal *Standard English* (most widely accepted form of the English language). Effective human services workers understand that slang and texting abbreviations are inappropriate in professional writing.

- Realize that any written work may be permanent. Effective human services workers think carefully about what they put in writing. They make sure their work represents themselves and their organizations professionally.

Copyright Goodheart-Willcox Co., Inc.

Tips for Organizing Writing Effectively
Start with an *introduction* or "say what you are going to say." Introductions help to organize the whole written statement, report, paper, or memo. Consider   • putting the big idea into a single sentence;   • presenting an outline of what you will cover in your writing;   • beginning with something that will grab readers' attention and give them a sense of what is coming;   • expressing the purpose and goals for the paper; and   • assuring readers that the topic is important.
Organize the *body* of the written statement, report, paper, or memo in a logical way. Consider presenting the content by   • describing the sequential order of events;   • ordering information from the most important to the least important;   • defining the big idea followed by the details;   • describing the arrangement of the topic from top to bottom;   • comparing two ideas by describing the characteristics of one idea and then the other idea;   • describing the process or necessary steps in a procedure;   • using a topic sentence for each paragraph that, if read alone, would tell the message;   • including headings and subheadings to visually organize material; and   • connecting paragraphs logically by using transitions, such as *for example*, *however*, *therefore*, *in addition*, and *but*.
Draw the message to a *conclusion*. Conclusions help to summarize the whole written statement, report, paper, or memo. Generally, conclusions do not include new information. Depending on the type of writing, consider   • proposing an action;   • making a prediction, forecast, or expectation;   • posing a question about what to do next;   • restating the main points and then providing a brief summary; and   • using the transition *finally* to make the last statement.

Figure 3.6 This chart provides some tips for organizing writing effectively. *Which of these tips do you already use in your writing? How do you plan to incorporate the tips that are new to you?*

Electronic Communication

Communicating via e-mail or text messages enables people to quickly translate their thoughts and feelings into words and hit the Send button. Electronic communication has enormous benefits for human services workers. It allows them to stay in touch with clients or customers and can be a great link to coworkers. Communicating electronically, however, comes with additional potential pitfalls.

E-mailing and text messaging may seem like private forms of conversation. The problem is that, once messages are sent, people no longer have control over what happens to their messages. E-mail and other electronic forms of communication can easily be sent to unintended receivers. Electronic messages can be copied or forwarded inappropriately without the sender's permission.

Copyright Goodheart-Willcox Co., Inc.

Law and Ethics   *Using Technology In Human Services*

In recent decades, technology has changed virtually all aspects of society and continues to do so. Human services is no exception. While computers were originally developed for use by business and government, their application to other areas, including human services, quickly became apparent. Other related forms of technology soon followed.

Many human services careers involve keeping track of and using numerous types of factual information, or data, for future use. Computers are particularly suited to simplifying those tasks.

Keeping accurate records is essential for many human services workers. Each time a human services worker meets with a client, he or she must record and save the information for future use. At the end of a service period, human services workers must calculate costs and provide billing information. Electronic programs can greatly simplify this process. Any files including confidential information should be password protected.

Electronic spreadsheet programs, such as Excel™, allow information to be adapted for different uses. For example, a human services worker might set up a basic spreadsheet with a list of clients and services provided. This same spreadsheet could also be adapted to keep track of each client's progress toward meeting specific class goals or any other need. Various types of reports could be generated based on the data in a particular spreadsheet.

There are countless other ways that human services workers can use technology to boost their productivity. For example, a human services worker might send a weekly or monthly newsletter to clients. After developing the newsletter template, the human services worker can simply add new information as needed. Using an electronic contact list could speed the process of sending the newsletter electronically or printing labels for mailing. Many human services workers also have their own professional websites.

Technology offers human services workers exciting options for presenting information in diverse ways that can bring learning to life. It takes effort, imagination, and a willingness to learn new skills. Some options require more sophisticated technology than others. Even with limited equipment, however, human services workers can add variety to the services they provide.

Although technology offers tremendous advantages, it also offers challenges in a field that is so personal and people oriented. A tremendous amount of confidential information may be shared between clients and the care provider. Private financial, medical, and employment information, along with information about family relationships, drug use or addictions, abuse or other violence, and criminal activities, may be recorded. Human services workers must be extra vigilant in using secure technology tools to store, communicate, and retrieve this information. They must take precautions to ensure that privacy is maintained at all times and that all confidentiality laws and requirements are observed.

Writing Activity

Keep a log for a week of all the types of technology you use to transmit information to others. Write an essay in response to the following questions:

1. What information would you not want conveyed to the general public without your knowledge? Why?
2. What harm might come from personal information being shared with others?
3. How might you ensure that the information you have shared is not passed on to other unintended receivers?

Human services workers deal with clients' private, sensitive information. Imagine the problems that might arise from this information ending up in the wrong person's hands. Therefore, human services workers avoid sending through electronic means any sensitive information. This is information that could potentially cause harm to their

Copyright Goodheart-Willcox Co., Inc.

clients, clients' families, or communities. Human services workers take great precautions to protect their clients' privacy.

Reading Recall

1. What are *interpersonal skills*? Give an example of an interpersonal skill.
2. What happens when a difference between the sender's verbal and nonverbal messages occurs?
3. What happens when a person takes ownership in a relationship?
4. Define *active listening*.
5. To be a good communicator, effective human services workers use _____ communication.
6. Why is it important to think about what to say before speaking?
7. List four forms of nonverbal communication. Give an example of how nonverbal and verbal messages can contradict one another.
8. List four tips for effective written communication.

Decision-Making Skills

People make many decisions every day. Some decisions are routine and do not require much thought. What to eat for breakfast or what clothes to wear to work are routine decisions. Other decisions, however, can be quite complex. These decisions must require careful consideration. For example, deciding on a career field is a major decision. You would not want to make this kind of decision *impulsively* (acting without thinking something through).

People's needs, wants, values, and priorities often affect the decisions they make. Although people have the same basic needs, their wants, values, and priorities are often very different. A person's *values* are those things that are considered to be important in life. Examples of values may include family, education, health, religion, happiness, love, or money. Values help determine a person's wants and *priorities*, or the things that are most important to him or her.

Decision-making skills are necessary at any level in the field of human services, from entry-level to management positions. Human services workers must make their own decisions. They are also tasked with helping clients make decisions. Using the **decision-making process** (a step-by-step approach) can help people make responsible decisions based on their needs, wants, values, and priorities.

The steps of the decision-making process include the following:

1. State the decision to be made. Determine if the issue is a problem, opportunity, or goal.
2. Identify alternatives (options). Usually, there is more than one possible way to address a decision.

Copyright Goodheart-Willcox Co., Inc.

Case Study / *Paper Trails*

As a college summer intern working in the office of a team of personal financial advisors, Salim was learning a lot. More and more, he believed this was a career field he would enjoy. He liked helping others. He could see how the services provided in this office helped clients make solid and sound financial decisions. He saw the joy and relief (and sometimes concern) on the clients' faces as they left the office after a consultation with a financial advisor.

As an intern, Salim spent a lot of time making photocopies, transmitting information electronically, and mailing billing invoices to clients. He also filed numerous items containing clients' personal information throughout the day. Salim understood the importance of keeping this information confidential. He was always extremely careful to follow the company's confidentiality guidelines. As Salim gained experience, his boss trusted him to handle more and more sensitive data from their clients' personal records. This included clients' financial statements and bank account information.

After a busy day of handling and processing clients' records, Salim left the office in a hurry.

He was anxious to meet friends at a summer baseball game. While at the game, Salim mentally reviewed the day's activities. He had a sinking feeling that, in his haste to meet his friends, he left some sensitive paperwork on the copy machine.

Salim felt conflicted about how he should handle this dilemma. He could try to just forget about it and enjoy the game. That didn't feel right, however. He knew he could not get back in the office tonight or in the morning to correct his mistake without others knowing. Finally, Salim decided to take the direct approach.

Salim called his boss and shared his concerns. His boss thanked him for his straightforward approach. He also reminded Salim that, indeed, this could be a breach of confidentiality. He then told Salim that he had seen the exposed paperwork prior to leaving the office himself and had filed it away for safekeeping. Salim breathed a sigh of relief, grateful for the learning experience. He also appreciated the solid relationship he had built with his boss through open communication, and the end result.

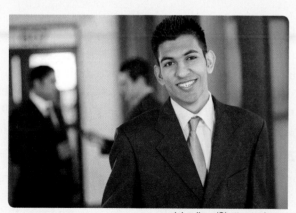

michaeljung/Shutterstock.com

For Discussion

1. What problems may have arisen from Salim's mistake?
2. How might Salim avoid making this mistake in the future?
3. Did Salim make the right decision to call his boss? Why or why not?
4. How did the trusting relationship between Salim and his boss help in this situation?
5. What might have been some alternative responses to Salim's dilemma?

3. Consider each alternative. This may include thinking through the best- and worst-case scenarios.

4. Choose the best alternative. After careful evaluation of each alternative, make the choice that seems best for the given situation.

5. Take action to follow through on the decision. Carry through with the alternative selected.

Copyright Goodheart-Willcox Co., Inc.

Expert Insight

"In the long run, we shape our lives, and we shape ourselves. The process never ends until we die. And, the choices we make are ultimately our own responsibility."

Eleanor Roosevelt, first lady and author, *You Learn by Living*

6. Evaluate the results of the decision. Determine whether or not this was the best choice. Could the situation be handled differently next time?

The goal of human services workers is to help their clients make responsible decisions for themselves. Accepting responsibility for decisions, whether the results are positive or negative, is part of becoming independent. You may have heard the phrase, "people who are accountable." People who are accountable acknowledge, accept, and make decisions or actions in regard to themselves or a given topic. When a negative outcome occurs, they accept the consequences. They create a new plan to fix or better address the issue. They accept that their actions affect others and act accordingly for the best outcome.

Human services workers help their clients at all stages of decision making, including helping them to accept negative outcomes. They also help their clients make new plans and become self-aware of the effect of their decisions on others.

Reading Recall

1. Differentiate between a person's *values* and *priorities*.

2. Why do human services workers need to practice good decision making?

3. Give an example of a responsible decision you made using the decision-making process. Explain how this decision is consistent with your needs, wants, values, and priorities.

4. What does it mean to be accountable in decision making?

Problem-Solving Skills

In addition to helping their clients make decisions, human services workers also help their clients solve problems to improve their quality of life. In doing so, they employ the **problem-solving process**. This includes defining and analyzing the problem, setting and implementing goals, and monitoring and evaluating the plan.

Defining and Analyzing the Problem

The first step in the problem-solving process is to define the problem. Often, people experience a situation and think they can identify the problem. Many times, however, people are only recognizing an issue that is contributing to the real problem. For example, an immediate issue, such as a client not showing up for work consistently, may be the symptom of a bigger issue, which is unreliable transportation. Skilled human services workers help their clients identify the real problem. They also help them recognize the underlying factors contributing to the problem situation.

Once the problem is identified, human services workers then help clients think about their problem from different perspectives. For example, the client who consistently misses work may need help

Copyright Goodheart-Willcox Co., Inc.

navigating public transportation, rather than using an unreliable car. Human services workers evaluate how the problem is affecting their clients personally, as well as those around them. Will the additional time needed to access public transportation negatively affect the client's child care options? They teach their clients to think critically about their problems. **Critical thinking** involves looking closely at a situation and weighing possible outcomes before determining a solution.

Setting and Implementing Goals

Setting and implementing goals are crucial steps in the problem-solving process. Human services workers teach their clients how to set both short- and long-term goals to help solve their problems. **Short-term goals** are achievable in the immediate to near future. **Long-term goals** are major goals that may take months or even years to achieve.

Short-term goals are often set to help meet a long-term goal. For example, a client may set a long-term goal to pay off credit card debt in the next two years. To meet the long-term goal, the client sets a short-term goal to pay an additional $20 each month toward the debt. Before the long-term goal is achieved, other short-term goals may need to be set along the way. Human services workers help their clients write specific, measurable, attainable, relevant, and time-bound (S.M.A.R.T.) goals (**Figure 3.7**).

After establishing realistic short- and long-term goals, the next step is to implement them. This involves forming a plan of action and then carrying out that plan. During this process, people may choose to implement their goals in a number of different ways. How people implement their goals often depends on the human, nonhuman, and community resources they have available to them.

Human resources are resources that come from oneself or other people. Examples include knowledge, time, energy, and abilities. Friends and family are valuable human resources. *Nonhuman resources* include material items, such as money, books, and other objects. Amounts of nonhuman resources vary from person to person. *Community resources* are shared with others and may include places such as libraries, parks, stores, or museums. Helping clients to access community resources is an important role human services workers play.

Monitoring and Evaluating the Plan

The final steps of the problem-solving process are to monitor the implementation of the plan and to evaluate the plan's effectiveness. Human services workers help their clients consider whether or not the plan is addressing or solving the identified problem. If it is not, they reevaluate and adjust the plan accordingly.

The problem-solving process is cyclical in nature. In other words, unless the problem is eliminated or solved, a problem may need "tweaking." This involves defining and analyzing, planning,

Expert Insight

"To raise new questions, new possibilities, to regard old problems from a new angle, requires creative imagination and marks real advance in science."

Albert Einstein, theoretical physicist

Copyright Goodheart-Willcox Co., Inc.

Example of S.M.A.R.T. Goals Used When Working with Client		
S.M.A.R.T. Stands for…	**Simple Goals Expressed by Client**	**S.M.A.R.T. Goals**
Specific: Well-defined using the three "W's" of *who*, *why*, and *what*	Find child care in my community that I feel good about.	Find affordable, safe child care for my two- and five-year-olds.
Measurable: How attainment will be measured	When a child care provider is selected.	I will find acceptable child care for my two children and enroll them to start attending on the first of next month.
Attainable: Realistic	Ask around for child care options and then select.	I will look on my community child care website tomorrow and will select 10 possibilities that are within my price range, + 10%. I will visit each of these child care sites within the next two weeks.
Relevant: Pertinent to long-term goals	I want to make sure that my children are settled for a while.	The child care I choose will be flexible so that my oldest child may continue after-school care once he begins kindergarten.
Time-oriented: Goal can be achieved within a framework	I want to have child care before my new job starts.	During this month, I will spend two days researching child care options, two weeks visiting the sites, and one week selecting and enrolling my children in child care that will begin on the first of next month.

Figure 3.7 Using the S.M.A.R.T. acronym, human services workers can help their clients transform simple goals into S.M.A.R.T. goals. *Why do you think S.M.A.R.T. goals are more effective than simple goals?*

implementing, and monitoring. Problem solving, especially when it involves emotional or personal challenges, is not easy. Human services workers provide emotional support to their clients as they work through the difficult task of problem solving.

Reading Recall

1. What are the steps of the problem-solving process?
2. Define the term *critical thinking*.
3. How do short- and long-term goals differ?
4. What are *S.M.A.R.T. goals*?
5. Knowledge, time, and energy are all examples of which type of resources?
6. Describe how the problem-solving process is cyclical in nature.

Conflict Resolution Skills

Conflict is inevitable in any active relationship. People simply have different ideas, beliefs, and priorities. When they communicate, these differences may easily surface. People also react to conflict in different ways.

Copyright Goodheart-Willcox Co., Inc.

Some people view all disagreements as negative and try to avoid them. Others find conflict positive and enriching.

Certain situations increase the likelihood of conflict. For example, conflict is often common in close relationships (**Figure 3.8**). This is especially true when one person is comfortable communicating (especially communicating feelings) and the other is not. Conflict is also common when people are under stress. During stressful times, people are more likely to say things to someone that they later regret.

Human services workers often work with people who are under stress. They may routinely encounter situations in which disagreements or miscommunications lead to conflict. Effective human services workers can help those involved deal with their differences in positive ways.

When two (or more) people work through a conflict in a constructive way, the result is greater understanding and relationship growth. Conflict that is not handled constructively can lead to continued conflict and broken relationships. One effective approach human services workers often use to resolve conflict is **constructive conflict management** (step-by-step method to resolve a disagreement). The steps in the constructive conflict management process include the following:

1. Clarify the issue. The process begins with identifying the problem. Remember that when two people are in conflict, they often identify the problem differently. Each person must honestly and clearly state the problem from his or her perspective. Each must also listen carefully to the other person.

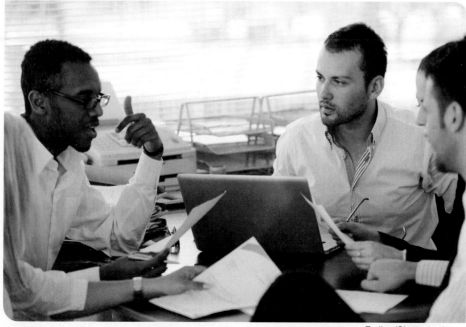

Zurijeta/Shutterstock.com

Figure 3.8 Conflict occurs even between coworkers who get along well. *What is one way to resolve a conflict?*

Copyright Goodheart-Willcox Co., Inc.

2. Find out what each person wants. Each person in the conflict must identify and express what he or she wants or needs as a desired outcome to the situation.

3. Identify various alternatives. The next step in the process is to identify various ways to resolve the conflict. In constructive conflict resolution, both parties are open to suggestions and are willing to brainstorm creative solutions. They try to focus on finding a solution together, not just on meeting their own needs.

4. Decide how to negotiate. The people involved in the conflict decide on a resolution strategy. Will the areas of conflict be discussed in hopes one person will change his or her mind? Will each person give up part of what is wanted? Will they toss a coin? Each person needs to agree on how to proceed.

5. Choose the best alternative. There is rarely a solution that makes everyone happy. Oftentimes, parties must make *concessions* (compromises) to agree on which alternative both can accept (**Figure 3.9**). Sometimes a compromise just is not possible. The two sides simply agree to disagree.

6. Solidify the agreement. The parties must accept and agree to implement the choice they have made.

7. Review and renegotiate. Review the issue to ensure compliance. If a person does not follow through on what he or she promised, renegotiate. Discuss the issue to try to come up with an agreeable compromise.

Figure 3.9 When there is no solution that makes everyone happy, the parties might choose to compromise. *Think about a time that you resolved a conflict by making a compromise. How did it make you feel?*

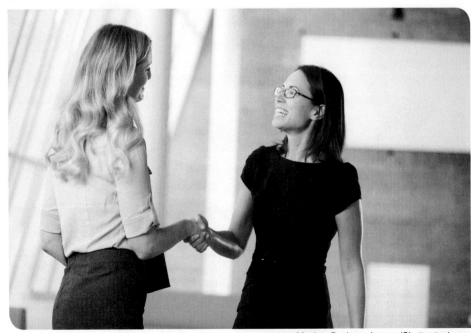

Monkey Business Images/Shutterstock.com

Copyright Goodheart-Willcox Co., Inc.

Of course, disagreements are not always easily solved. Often, the people involved are so emotional or convinced they are right that they will not negotiate. When this occurs, a third party who is neutral—a **mediator**—can often help the process. A mediator tries to help those in the dispute reach a peaceful agreement. When acting as mediators, human services workers play the role of an objective third party who is not directly involved. They help each participant move through the process of reaching a settlement or agreement. This process is called **mediation**.

Reading Recall

1. Identify two factors that increase the likelihood of conflict.
2. Name one effective approach human services workers often use to resolve conflict.
3. Define *mediation*.
4. What is the end goal of mediation?

Collaboration and Leadership Skills

Another important skill for any career in the human services field is the ability to *collaborate* (work together) with others. Human services workers often collaborate with other providers, their clients' families, and the extended community to meet the needs of their clients. Together, these people form a team that can work together to examine a problem, form a plan, and achieve the goal as a unit. When team members work together, they can accomplish projects and achieve goals efficiently.

Team members use many skills to work as part of a team. They use communication and cooperation skills to work with other team members. They do not cause conflict or spread gossip. Instead, team members are friendly toward fellow teammates. They recognize that team members are *diverse* (very different) and are able to understand and accept their opinions.

Team members have good interpersonal skills and can communicate effectively with others. They listen to others and speak clearly. They participate in the team by asking or answering questions. They may offer helpful information and accept help as needed. Team members accept responsibility for the progress of the team and actively work toward accomplishing the goal.

In addition to having good collaboration skills, human services workers also possess good leadership skills. **Leadership** is a quality that involves organizing, guiding, motivating, and taking responsibility for a team. Effective leaders demonstrate similar qualities and skills when leading a team (**Figure 3.10**). They encourage members to use their skills and talents. They are supportive, accommodating, and responsible.

Expert Insight

"Alone we can do so little; together we can do so much."

Helen Keller, writer and orator

Effective Leadership Qualities and Skills

- Communicates effectively with all group members.
- Maintains a positive attitude and motivates others.
- Models patience and persistence.
- Makes sound decisions and accepts responsibility for outcomes of decisions.
- Listens to others and is sensitive to the needs and wants of group members.
- Treats others with respect.
- Leads by example. Does not expect others to do what he or she would not do.
- Is knowledgeable about group goals and explains positions and reasons with others.
- Looks at the big picture and moves the group forward.
- Is ethical, honest, trustworthy, and does not take advantage of others.
- Possesses a good sense of humor.
- Empowers group members and recognizes their efforts. Acknowledges contributions from others on the team.
- Is organized and prepared for meetings and events.

Figure 3.10 This chart includes some of the qualities and skills of an effective leader. *Which of these qualities and skills do you already possess?*

Responsible team leaders acknowledge when there is a problem and work to solve the issue. They act as mediators when conflicts arise between team members. They acknowledge team member contributions and give credit to the team as a whole.

Joining a **Career and Technical Student Organization (CTSO)** is a great place to start developing and practicing both leadership and teamwork skills while still in school. CTSOs are usually run as nonprofit organizations, incorporated into Departments of Education at the state level, and eligible for funding at the national level. CTSOs are valuable assets to any educational program. There are a variety of organizations from which to choose, depending on the goals of educational programs (**Figure 3.11**). Participating in competitive events is a key aspect of membership in any CTSO. Participating in such competitions offers CTSO members an opportunity to expand their leadership and teamwork skills and develop skills necessary for life and career.

Reading Recall

1. Explain the importance of collaboration in the workplace.
2. Identify four skills and qualities of effective team members.
3. Define the term *leadership*.
4. List four qualities and skills of effective leaders.
5. What is a key aspect of membership in any CTSO?

Copyright Goodheart-Willcox Co., Inc.

Career and Technical Student Organizations		
Organization	**Purpose**	**Audience**
Business Professionals of America (BPA)	BPA prepares students for business and related fields by developing problem-solving, teamwork, and leadership skills.	Middle school, high school, and post-secondary students
Distributive Education Clubs of America (DECA)	DECA helps students develop leadership skills with a focus on marketing, business, hospitality services, finance, and entrepreneurship. DECA is an international organization.	High school and postsecondary students
Educators Rising	Educators Rising encourages leadership skills for students interested in education and related careers.	High school students
Family, Career and Community Leaders of America (FCCLA)	FCCLA encourages personal development, leadership, and teamwork skills, while focusing on family, community, and career topics.	Middle school and high school students
Future Business Leaders of America–Phi Beta Lambda (FBLA–PBL)	FBLA–PBL helps students develop leadership skills with a focus on business, management, and related career fields.	Middle school, high school, and post-secondary students
Health Occupations Students of America (HOSA)	HOSA helps prepare students for the health care industry with technical and interpersonal skills.	High school and postsecondary students
National FFA Organization (the letters FFA stand for Future Farmers of America)	The National FFA Organization prepares students for studies and careers in agriculture science, such as farming, food science, veterinarian studies, and engineering.	High school students
National Postsecondary Agricultural Student Organization (PAS)	Like the National FFA Organization, PAS focuses on career preparation and success in the agriculture industry, leadership, and personal growth.	Postsecondary students
National Young Farmer Educational Association (NYFEA)	NYFEA emphasizes integrating classroom learning and real life experiences in the food, fiber, business, agriculture production, and technology fields.	Postsecondary students
SkillsUSA	SkillsUSA is a career preparation CTSO for those enrolled in technical, skilled, and service occupations. It also includes health occupations.	High school and postsecondary students
Technology Student Association (TSA)	TSA focuses on using technology to develop leadership and teamwork skills and provide opportunities in Science, Technology, Engineering, and Mathematics (STEM).	Middle school and high school students

Figure 3.11 Each CTSO has different goals. *Which of these CTSOs are offered at your school? Are there any CTSOs you would like to join?*

Copyright Goodheart-Willcox Co., Inc.

Summary

- Communication involves being both a sender and receiver. To communicate effectively, words and nonverbal messages must match. When a discrepancy between the sender's verbal and nonverbal messages occurs, the receiver gets a mixed message.
- Communication must occur in the context of positive relationships and each form of communication—verbal, nonverbal, written, and electronic—depends on specific, but related skills.
- Decision-making skills are necessary at any level in the field of human services. Human services workers must make their own decisions, but they are also tasked with helping clients make decisions about opportunities presented to them. By using the decision-making process, human services workers and their clients can make responsible decisions based on their needs, wants, values, and priorities.
- In addition to helping their clients make decisions, human services workers also help

their clients solve problems. In doing so, they employ the problem-solving process, which includes defining and analyzing the problem, setting and implementing goals, and monitoring and evaluating the plan.
- Effective human services workers develop specific, measurable, attainable, relevant, and time-bound (S.M.A.R.T.) goals.
- Human services workers often work with people who are under stress and may routinely encounter situations in which disagreements or miscommunication lead to conflict. Effective human services workers can help those involved deal with their differences in constructive conflict management.
- Human services workers possess good collaboration and leadership skills. They collaborate by working well with others. Leadership is a quality that involves organizing, guiding, motivating, and taking responsibility for a team.

College and Career Portfolio

Organization

As you collect items for your portfolio, you will need a method to keep the items clean, safe, and organized for assembly at the appropriate time. A large manila envelope works well to keep hard copies of your documents, photos, awards, and other items. For certificates that are framed or already in scrapbooks, you may want to include photocopies of these items. Three-ring binders with sleeves are another good way to store your information. A box large enough for full-size documents will also work. Plan to keep like items together and label the categories. For example, store sample documents illustrating

your writing or computer skills together. Use notes clipped to the documents to identify each item and state why it is included in the portfolio. For example, a note might say, "Newsletter illustrating desktop publishing skills."

1. Select a method for storing hard copy items you will be collecting for your portfolio. (You will decide where to keep electronic copies in a later activity.)
2. Write a paragraph describing your plan for storing and labeling the items. Refer to this plan each time you add items to the portfolio.

Copyright Goodheart-Willcox Co., Inc.

Review and Reflect 📤

1. Describe two key components of effective communication.
2. Explain the difference between a *sender* and a *receiver*.
3. Good communication begins with positive relationships. Identify the three factors that go into building positive relationships. Give examples from your own life of using these three factors.
4. Differentiate among *assertive communicators*, *aggressive communicators*, and *passive communicators*.
5. Give one advantage and one disadvantage of the use of electronic communication by human services workers.
6. Give an example of a decision you would not want to make impulsively.
7. List and explain the steps in the decision-making process.
8. Give an example of a short-term goal that is set to help meet a long-term goal.
9. Compare and contrast *human resources*, *nonhuman resources*, and *community resources*.
10. Identify and explain the seven steps in constructive conflict management.
11. What is the role of a mediator?
12. Identify five CTSOs and describe their purposes.

Vocabulary Activities

13. **Key terms**   Use the Internet to locate images or videos that visually express the meaning of each key term. In small groups, take turns describing the visual meanings for each term.

active listening
aggressive communicators
assertive communicators
Career and Technical Student Organization (CTSO)
constructive conflict management
critical thinking
decision-making process
empathy
leadership
long-term goals
mediation
mediator
mixed message
passive communicators
problem-solving process
receiver
sender
short-term goals

14. **Academic terms**   Read the text passages that contain each of the following terms. Then write the definition of each term in your own words. Double-check your definitions by rereading the text and using the text glossary.

collaborate
concessions
diverse
impulsively
priorities
Standard English
validate
values

Self-Assessment Quiz 📤

Complete the self-assessment quiz online to help you practice and expand your knowledge and skills.

Critical Thinking

15. **Cause and effect**   The old saying "Think twice before you speak" is a wise one. Remember a time when you did not think before speaking. How did you feel afterward? What did you learn from this experience?
16. **Evaluate**   Keep a communication journal for a day. Take notes indicating who you communicated with and what messages were being conveyed. Also note if there were any troubles sending or receiving the messages. Evaluate your communications for the day. Were there any problems? If so, what caused the communication breakdown? How did you overcome any miscommunications?
17. **Draw conclusions**   Communicating via technology is commonplace in today's society. What would happen to a human services worker who sends sensitive data through a text message or e-mail that goes to someone other than the intended recipient? If you received an e-mail with someone else's information, what would you do?
18. **Compare and contrast**   Compare and contrast the decision-making process to the problem-solving process.
19. **Analyze**   Write a long-term goal you would like to accomplish for your professional life. Create short-term goals you will need to meet to

achieve your long-term goal. Analyze your goals to make sure they are specific, measurable, attainable, relevant, and time-bound.

20. **Make inferences** Certain situations increase the likelihood of conflict in relationships. What would you do if your best friend suddenly refuses to talk to you and you do not know why?

21. **Determine** How can you exhibit leadership skills in a group setting?

22. **Identify** Identify what CTSOs are available at your school.

Core Skills

23. **Listening and speaking** Try to improve your listening and speaking skills by practicing telephone etiquette. Identify correct and incorrect ways to answer a phone for a professional business, at your home, and at a friend's house. Identify correct and incorrect ways to end a conversation for a professional business, at your home, and at a friend's house.

24. **Writing** Select a topic relating to the field of human services. Write a two-page paper using the tips in Figure 3.6. After writing your paper, exchange papers with a partner. Read each other's papers. Answer the following questions: Does the *introduction* organize the whole paper? Is the *body* of the paper organized in a logical way? Does the *conclusion* help to summarize the whole paper? Together, discuss the answers to your questions.

25. **Writing, speaking, and listening** Create a poster listing tips on how to communicate effectively verbally, nonverbally, in writing, and electronically. Compare your poster with two others in the class. Did they list ideas that you did not? Discuss with your peers how to use these strategies to communicate with your parents when you are upset with them.

26. **Speaking and listening** In small groups, put together skits showing effective and ineffective communication of human services workers. Present your group skits to the class. Ask audience members to identify the communication blockers in the ineffective communication skits.

27. **Reading and speaking** As a class, contact local human services agencies or your state department of human services to request blank copies of forms they typically use. After

receiving the forms, divide into small groups. Review the forms to make sure you understand what information is required for each form. If your group does not understand something on the form, ask your teacher to explain it. Role-play how you would explain to someone who cannot read how to fill out the forms correctly.

28. **Math and speaking** Imagine you received the following amounts of money as gifts: $10, $25, $25, $30, $50, and $60. Total the amounts. How might this money be used to meet a need in your community? Use the decision-making process to decide what you would like to do with the money. Explain to the class how you used each step of the process to make a responsible decision consistent with your personal needs, wants, values, and priorities.

29. **Writing** Write four short-term S.M.A.R.T. goals you would like to accomplish in your personal life this semester that could help you work toward a personal long-term goal. Post your goals where you can see them daily. In a journal, keep track of your progress toward your goals, checking them off as you reach them. After you have achieved two of the four goals, write a journal entry explaining the ways you motivated yourself to reach these goals. Indicate what you will do to stay motivated to accomplish the rest of your goals.

30. **Research, reading, and speaking** Using online or print sources, find an article on effective problem solving in the workplace. Read the article to determine the main points the author is trying to communicate. How is the message being conveyed similar to the message in this text? How is it different? In what ways do you agree or disagree with the author's point of view? Discuss your findings with a partner.

31. **Technology** In small groups, create a video presentation to teach other students methods they can use to successfully resolve conflicts. Share your videos with the rest of the class.

32. **Reading and speaking** Read an autobiography of a person you think demonstrates strong leadership skills or who inspires you to be a leader. Give a five-minute verbal summary of the book in class. In your presentation, be sure to cite specific examples of leadership skills and qualities.

Copyright Goodheart-Willcox Co., Inc.

33. **Writing**   Create a list of the teamwork and leadership skills and qualities you already possess. What skills and qualities do you need to develop to become an effective team member and leader? Write a journal entry describing your plan of action or experience to improve your teamwork and leadership skills.

34. **CTE career readiness practice** Communication is an important part of the job for any employee. Individuals who are career ready understand the importance of communicating clearly both verbally and nonverbally. They listen carefully and consider their audience when sending a message.

Create a script you could use for a one-minute public service announcement about cyberbullying or another topic for which you are passionate. Present your script to a partner.

35. **CTE career readiness practice**   Successful employees model integrity. What role do you think ethics and integrity have in conflict resolution? Think of a conflict you have had with someone. Did you use ethical methods to resolve the conflict? How effective were your methods in resolving the conflict? In retrospect, do you think you used appropriate methods of conflict resolution? Would you have done anything differently?

Lend a Hand

Volunteering and Learning

Although one of the main reasons for volunteering is to help others, community service can also be a great opportunity for learning. *Service learning* is an educational experience combining academic or learning goals with community service. Service learning is associated with a course, so usually the activities are related to classroom learning. Service learning is different from an internship or volunteer experience that is completed after a course ends. It is meant to enhance the course material and connect it to real issues in the community. Service learning helps reinforce the ideas and theories learned in the classroom because it provides hands-on learning.

Successful service learning experiences should have a balance between academic goals and service goals. Students are able to apply in-class lessons to real issues in their communities. For example, one high school class created writing activities and materials to use in a writing lab they set up to help struggling students from a local elementary school.

Like other forms of volunteering, service learning can bring students closer to their communities. It can also bolster a feeling of unity and support teamwork within a class.

After a service learning experience, students are given the chance to reflect on their experiences. This reflection time provides the opportunity for students to think about the knowledge and skills they gained as a result of the service learning experience.

To learn more about service learning, complete the following:

1. Read about or talk with someone who has participated in a service learning project. What was the project? What did the person learn from being involved in the project? Share your findings with the class.

2. Research a possible service learning project you could complete with your class. Write a paper describing how the project ties into course learning and would benefit the students and community. Discuss your papers in class.

Copyright Goodheart-Willcox Co., Inc.

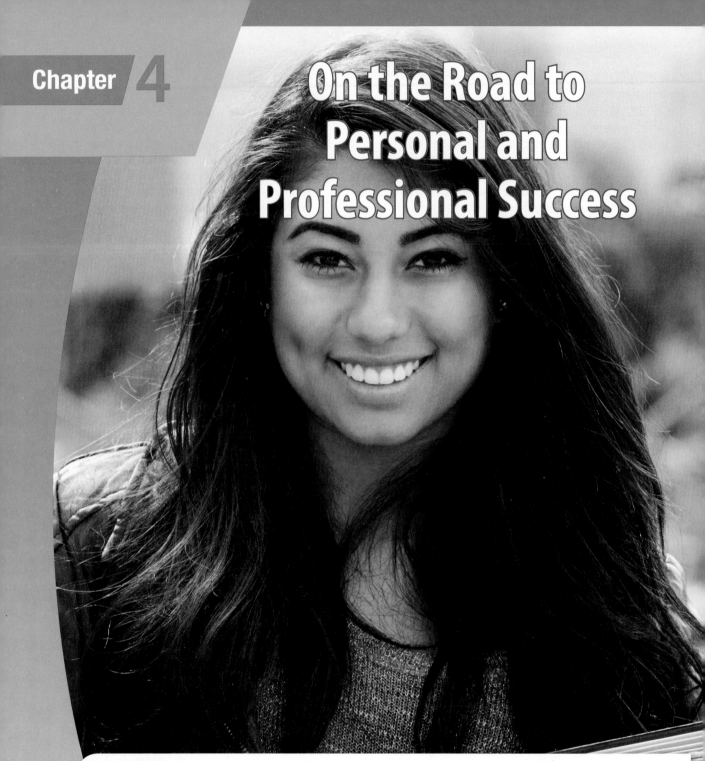

Chapter 4

On the Road to Personal and Professional Success

While studying, look for the activity icon  **to**

- **practice** key and academic terms with e-flash cards and matching activities;
- **assess** what you learn by completing self-assessment quizzes; and
- **reinforce** what you learn by mapping concepts and completing review and reflect questions.

www.g-wlearning.com/humanservices/

©Monkey Business Images/Shutterstock.com

Learning Outcomes

After studying this chapter, you will be able to

- **differentiate** between *health* and *wellness* and describe ways human services workers can promote wellness;
- **define** *maturity* and describe ways that human services workers can demonstrate characteristics of maturity to their clients;
- **explain** the importance of maintaining a work-life balance;
- **demonstrate** good time management skills;
- **recognize** causes and effects of stress and give examples of stress-coping techniques; and
- **apply** techniques for maintaining healthy relationships by identifying three ways that you can enhance your own personal relationships.

Reading Strategies

Before reading, arrange a study session with a classmate to read the chapter aloud. Take turns reading each section. As you are reading, stop at the end of each main heading to take notes about the main points. After you finish reading, answer the Reading Recall questions. Save any questions you cannot answer for a class discussion.

Mapping Concepts

In a mindmap like the one shown, organize your notes on the information presented in this chapter. Write *Best Practices* in the middle circle and fill in the surrounding circles in a way that will help you study the chapter material.

Key Terms

assimilation	prejudice
code of ethics	professional organizations
cultural competence	stereotypes
cultural diversity	stress
ethical decisions	substance abuse
ethics	time management
health	weight management
maturity	wellness
multiculturalism	work-life balance

Academic Terms

- acute
- audible
- dovetailing
- implicit
- leanings
- procrastinate
- proximity

Working in the human services field requires skill, knowledge, experience, and expertise. Within a caregiving, service-providing field of work, human services workers give a lot of themselves to their clients. They help their clients in solving problems, finding resources, and providing them with services to improve quality of life.

Human services workers must be at their best to provide high quality services. This involves using best practices. *Best practices* are methods that are recognized as being correct or most effective in producing a desired result. Best practices include promoting good personal health habits, demonstrating characteristics of maturity, and working to keep personal and work life in balance. Effective human services workers not only help their clients to adopt these practices, they model them, too.

Promote Good Personal Health Habits

Best practices, both personal and professional, include promoting good health and wellness. **Health** is an overall condition in reference to illness or disease. People in good health are free of illness or disease. **Wellness** involves making lifestyle choices that contribute to good physical, mental, and social well-being.

Physical, mental, and social health are all interrelated (**Figure 4.1**). For example, the way people look closely relates to the way they feel. In turn, this can have an effect on the way they interact with others. Good self-care habits help people maintain a neat appearance and look their best. When people look their best, they often feel their best, too. They are more confident in themselves. This feeling shows through in their personal interactions with family, friends, and coworkers.

In addition to maintaining a neat appearance, achieving and sustaining a healthy weight is important to promote wellness. Getting enough sleep and avoiding health hazards are also very important ways to promote wellness. Being in good health and living a healthy lifestyle gives people more energy to complete the tasks they need and want to do—both at home and at work.

When energy is boosted, increased productivity often follows. Of course, energy boosts can be used to pursue distractions, but for committed people, increased energy results in increased output of services. Those who commit to a healthy lifestyle practice good personal health habits and model good habits for others. When human services workers model good personal health habits to clients, the clients are more likely to adopt these behaviors themselves.

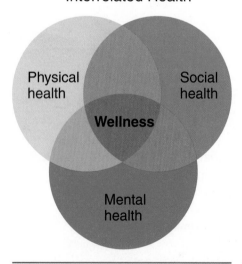

Interrelated Health

Figure 4.1 Physical, mental, and social health all contribute to a total sense of wellness. *How do you address each aspect of your own health?*

Copyright Goodheart-Willcox Co., Inc.

Maintain a Neat Appearance

Maintaining a neat appearance involves being well-groomed and wearing clean, well-fitting clothes that are in good condition (free of rips or tears). These personal habits are always important in both personal and professional settings. They are especially *acute* (critical) for human services workers. This is because they work so closely, both socially and often in physical *proximity* (nearness), with their clients. Neat appearance can increase trust and the perception of ability and confidence in a human services worker's skills and knowledge (**Figure 4.2**).

Grooming

Personal grooming involves taking care of one's body and general appearance. Good grooming is not an occasional practice. Rather, it is a daily ritual of good habits. First and foremost, grooming involves cleanliness and hygiene.

Regular bathing or showering is essential to good grooming and should occur daily when possible. Good grooming also includes brushing and flossing teeth after meals and applying deodorant to control body odor. Keeping hair well maintained is an important part of personal grooming. Good grooming also includes maintenance of hands and nails.

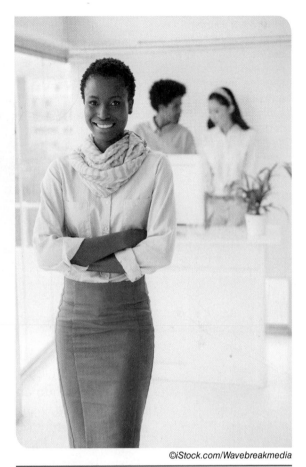

©iStock.com/Wavebreakmedia

Figure 4.2 Maintaining a neat appearance can play a critical role in establishing trust in a human service worker's skills and knowledge. *What steps do you take to maintain a neat appearance?*

Good grooming has many benefits. When people are well groomed, they generally feel better about themselves. Self-esteem and confidence are improved. Good grooming energizes a person. Well-groomed human services workers are generally better perceived by others, including their clients, as they appear more polished and competent (**Figure 4.3**). After all, when people show they can take care of themselves, they are more likely to be able to care for the needs of others at home and in the workplace.

Apparel Selection

Dressing appropriately for occasions is important. At home, people often dress casually. When going out for an evening, people may dress up more. When going to work, dressing in an appropriate manner is an important part of being prepared, and ultimately, performing well on the job.

Copyright Goodheart-Willcox Co., Inc.

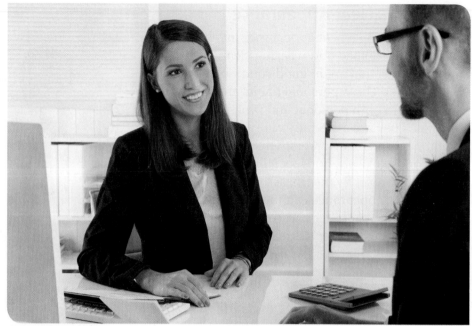

Figure 4.3 Human services workers who are well-groomed are perceived by clients as more competent and polished. *What are some other benefits of good grooming for human services workers?*

Jeanette Dietl/Shutterstock.com

For some human services workers, such as financial advisors, it is important to wear professional business dress. This includes suits and ties, jackets, and skirts or dresses. In these cases, dress should be conservative, of high quality, and not too trendy. For personal care assistants, comfortable clothing that allows the worker to move freely and provide physical help is important.

Clothing is a nonverbal way of communicating many messages. The clothes a person wears may communicate power, status, self-confidence, roles, and values. Clothing and appearance should match what a person communicates verbally. Just like spoken words, a person's appearance communication should be monitored and the message given understood.

Achieve and Sustain a Healthy Weight

Maintaining a healthy body weight through proper nutrition and physical activity positively affects people's physical and social well-being. People are less likely to suffer from chronic, avoidable health problems. They also feel good about themselves. This helps to create a positive self-image to family, friends, and coworkers.

Weight management is achieving and maintaining a healthy weight over time. Healthy body weight is determined by gender, height, and body frame. This means the weight amount will vary from person to person. To maintain a healthy body weight, people must be in energy balance. To have energy balance, the intake of calories must equal the output of calories.

Copyright Goodheart-Willcox Co., Inc.

In other words, the calories gained through foods consumed should equal calories burned through everyday movements and physical activities. Energy intake involves foods consumed. Energy output involves physical activity levels. When either side of this energy equation is unbalanced, body weight is affected. Ensuring the equation is balanced is a guide to maintaining healthy weight management.

Get Enough Sleep

The body needs sleep to relax and revitalize in preparation for the next day. Not getting enough sleep interferes with people's energy levels. This affects multiple aspects of well-being. For human services workers who get insufficient sleep, helping their clients to solve problems can become very difficult. Many human services workers are caring for critical needs. Inattention caused by lack of sleep can create serious problems.

Getting the right amount of sleep is important to maintaining a healthy lifestyle and optimum functioning at home, school, or work. Whenever possible, keeping a regular schedule can help save a set number of hours for sleeping. The environment in which people sleep can also affect the ease of sleeping (**Figure 4.4**). Mealtimes scheduled right before bedtime can interfere with sleep patterns. Scheduling meals earlier in the evening can reduce the impact food has on sleeping.

Avoid Health Hazards

At times, people choose to use tobacco, alcohol, and other drugs. These substances are dangerous, however. They can have harmful

Figure 4.4 A consistent lack of sleep can have significant short- and long-term effects. *How many hours of sleep do you get per night?*

ruigsantos/Shutterstock.com

Copyright Goodheart-Willcox Co., Inc.

effects on people's physical, social, and emotional health. They can cause problems in a person's ability to function at home and at work. They can also cause problems with personal relationships.

Substance abuse is the misuse of drugs to a toxic, dangerous level. Many drugs, such as nicotine, alcohol, and other substances, are addictive and can cause dependencies. A *physical dependency* develops when a person's body becomes reliant on the presence of a drug in the system to properly function. A *psychological dependency* develops when a person uses a drug for the feeling it causes. He or she may feel the drug is needed to be "normal."

Tobacco, which includes cigarettes, chewing tobacco, and snuff, contains *nicotine*, an addictive substance. Health risks associated with tobacco use include lung diseases, cancer, heart disease, and strokes. The use of tobacco can also cause complications for the throat, tongue, and teeth. In the US, tobacco use is the leading cause of premature and preventable death. To educate people about the health risks of tobacco use, health warnings must appear on all cigarette packages and advertisements (**Figure 4.5**).

Alcohol is another commonly abused drug. Alcohol is a *depressant*, which causes the body to have delayed reactions in the nervous system. Depressants interfere with the cognitive process, affecting speech, judgment, vision, coordination, and mobility. Health risks include liver disease and cancer, heart disease, and alcoholism.

Other commonly abused substances include marijuana, cocaine, heroin, PCP, LSD, and other hallucinogens. Even prescription and over-the-counter (OTC) medications can be misused. These types of drugs pose great risks to health, including

- cancer;

- heart, lung, and blood vessel damage;

- memory loss and other brain damage;

- delusional behavior;

Figure 4.5 By law, a Surgeon General's warnings must appear on all cigarette packages and advertisements. *Do you think these warnings are effective?*

Surgeon General's Warnings
• Cigarettes are addictive.
• Tobacco smoke can harm your children.
• Cigarettes cause fatal lung disease.
• Cigarettes cause cancer.
• Cigarettes cause strokes and heart disease.
• Smoking during pregnancy can harm your baby.
• Smoking can kill you.
• Tobacco smoke causes fatal lung disease in nonsmokers.
• Quitting smoking now greatly reduces serious risks to your health.

Copyright Goodheart-Willcox Co., Inc.

- violence; and

- death.

Some human services counselors and therapists are trained to recognize and treat substance abuse problems. Workers in health clinics, on hotlines, at support groups, and in other community services often have programs to help people cope with addictions and substance abuse. There are also many local and national campaigns that offer resources for substance abuse prevention.

Reading Recall

1. Differentiate between *health* and *wellness*.

2. Identify two reasons for human services workers to be concerned with maintaining a neat appearance.

3. Explain the importance of being in energy balance to maintain a healthy body weight.

4. Why is it so important for human services workers to get enough sleep each night?

5. Name three hazards that pose harmful effects on people's health and wellness and then give two examples of health risks associated with each of these substances.

Demonstrate Characteristics of Maturity

People grow and learn, families change, resources fluctuate, and bosses and coworkers come and go. Both life and work is about constant change. Even if it seems like life stays the same, people do not. Personal experiences, education, and aging will change people.

Maturity is the ability to adapt to the inevitable changes that happen in life, both personally and professionally. Specific characteristics of maturity include being dependable, responsible, respectful, ethical, and positive. Developing these characteristics can help people adjust to life's changes in constructive ways. Besides helping oneself, demonstrating characteristics of maturity builds client confidence in the abilities of a human services worker. These characteristics are viewed favorably, and are often noted as the signs of a qualified, proficient worker.

Be Dependable

Being dependable is an important characteristic of maturity. People who are dependable are willing to help where needed. They are reliable. They honor their commitments at home, at work, and in their communities. They show up on time and can be trusted to do what they say they will do. They are consistent in temperament and reactions to situations. People who have a reputation for being dependable set high standards for themselves, and others often view them as people they can go to and rely upon (**Figure 4.6**).

In the workplace, dependability is highly valued. People who are dependable are trustworthy, loyal, and faithful to their employers. For human services workers, being dependable is doubly important. Each workday, clients rely on human services workers to be available and ready to help them when needed. In turn, human services workers expect their clients to be dependable. They expect them to show up for appointments on time and do what they say they will do to be able to help themselves.

Think about what would happen if a human services worker fails to submit paperwork for services his or her client desperately needs. What might happen if a client repeatedly shows up late, or fails to show up at all, for counseling sessions? One person's lack of dependability can have far-reaching consequences. Demonstrating an ability to be dependable, however, can go a long way toward personal and professional success.

Be Responsible

Imagine you are a human services worker. You are gathering up your belongings to leave work on a Friday afternoon when you receive a call from one of your clients who is obviously upset. Your client tells you that her family has just been evicted from their home and she does not know if or where they will be able to find a place to stay.

You glance at the clock and realize you will be a bit late for dinner with friends if you stay to help. You view yourself as a responsible worker and are especially sensitive to the family's needs. You know you can help

Figure 4.6 Dependable employees are often viewed as trustworthy, loyal, and faithful. *What can you do to demonstrate an ability to be dependable?*

Andresr/Shutterstock.com

Copyright Goodheart-Willcox Co., Inc.

them, so you call your friends to tell them you will be late. Then you start tackling the problem at hand.

Because you took the time to follow through, the family has a place to stay at a shelter. Taking the time to aid this family is worth the minor inconvenience of getting together with your friends a little later than expected. You feel a responsibility for your clients that goes beyond the regular workday.

Being responsible means being committed in all activities, relationships, and actions—in both personal and professional settings (**Figure 4.7**). Responsibility means carrying a project through to the end whether or not the process is easy. When working on a team, responsibility means giving a best effort even if one team member does not do the same. Accepting responsibility means not making excuses for personal limitations or blaming someone else when things do not go exactly as planned.

Facing difficult challenges will earn respect from others and a reputation for accomplishment and trustworthiness. Those who handle responsibility well are usually asked to take on more. They find that facing difficult challenges can result in real personal satisfaction.

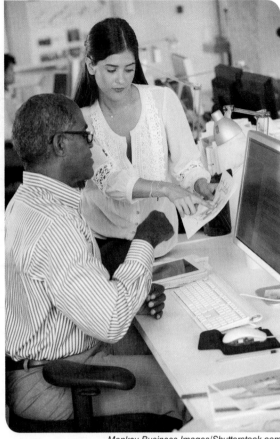

Monkey Business Images/Shutterstock.com

Figure 4.7 Handling job responsibilities well will usually result in an expanded role with greater opportunities to take on more tasks. *What does it mean to be considered responsible?*

Be Respectful

Whether in a personal or professional setting, people show respect through their attitudes, how they communicate, and the courtesy they show others. Being respectful involves showing regard for others' dignity, ideas, and expectations. It also involves treating others fairly and equally. Showing respect means listening to others and considering their needs, feelings, and potential (**Figure 4.8**). Treating others well, even when disagreeing with them, is another way of showing respect.

For human services workers, respecting people is an essential value. Human services workers see people at their best and worst. They frequently work with people of different cultures and ethnicities as clients, employers, customers, or coworkers. *Ethnicity* is a person's identity with a particular racial, national, or cultural group and support of that group's customs, beliefs, and language.

In past decades, minority individuals and families living in the US worked to fit in and become part of the majority culture. They learned

Copyright Goodheart-Willcox Co., Inc.

Monkey Business Images/Shutterstock.com

Figure 4.8 Listening attentively to others when they are speaking is one way of showing respect. *What are some other nonverbal ways of showing respect?*

the language, customs, and beliefs followed by the majority. The process of adapting to another culture's language, beliefs, and customs is called **assimilation**.

Many minority groups in the US also continued to practice their family customs and traditions while embracing the majority culture. The blending of many cultures and ethnicities is often referred to as a *melting pot*.

Today, a more appropriate description of the country's population is multicultural. **Multiculturalism** is based on the idea that cultural identities should not be ignored. Instead, they should be maintained, valued, and respected. Multiculturalism includes differences in race, ethnicity, religious beliefs, life experiences, values, and socioeconomic status. Human services workers honor this **cultural diversity** (different cultural and ethnic groups living in one society). They also respect and honor *lifestyle diversity* (personal lifestyle choices).

Multicultural individuals and families sometimes face unique challenges. Cultural stereotypes and prejudice can be difficult to overcome. **Stereotypes** are preconceived generalizations about certain groups of people. **Prejudice** involves opinions formed without sufficient knowledge.

Being knowledgeable about other cultures, called **cultural competence,** is especially important in human services. This knowledge enables human services workers to respectfully and effectively deliver services to people from different cultures and backgrounds. They

Copyright Goodheart-Willcox Co., Inc.

can respect and offer tools to the client for overcoming his or her situation. They can focus on positive changes that help their clients help themselves.

Be Ethical

Many aspects of ethics are based on common sense. **Ethics** refers to conduct based on moral principles. Being *ethical* involves acting in accordance with guidelines of good conduct. Examples of ethical practices include honesty, loyalty, and fairness. Even when conflicts occur, people should practice ethical behavior and treat others fairly and be honest in their attempts to resolve conflicts.

The term *unethical* is used to describe conduct that is morally wrong, such as lying, cheating, stealing, and harming others. For example, it would be unethical for a student to cheat on a test. It would also be unethical for a job applicant to provide inaccurate information about his or her educational background on a job application.

The field of human services involves more than helping clients meet their needs. Human services workers help to shape their clients' lives. They model the roles of professional and citizen. Because of this influence, human services workers are held to high ethical standards. Their behavior in the workplace and community must live up to that responsibility (**Figure 4.9**).

> ### Expert Insight
>
> *"Action indeed is the sole medium of expression for ethics."*
>
> Jane Addams, pioneer social worker

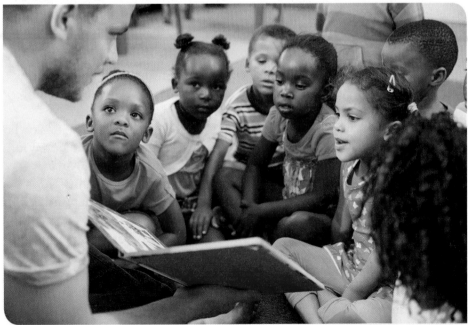

Monkey Business Images/Shutterstock.com

Figure 4.9 Because human services workers shape clients' lives, they are held to the highest ethical standards. *What are some examples of unethical behavior?*

Copyright Goodheart-Willcox Co., Inc.

Professional Ethical Standards

A **code of ethics** is a document that formally defines the moral principles that serve as rules for behavior, which are to be followed and upheld. Some people develop their own *personal code of ethics*. This identifies their beliefs and values and helps to guide them in their everyday lives. Most companies establish a *professional code of ethics* that employees are expected to follow. This professional code of ethics outlines acceptable behavior when interacting with coworkers, clients, customers, and other providers.

Many professional organizations also establish a professional code of ethics that members are to uphold. **Professional organizations** are recognized associations that are formed to unite people engaged in the same industry. These organizations provide opportunities for members to interact with others in similar professions. Professional development and advancement opportunities are also available. Another important role of professional organizations is to represent their industry's interests to the public and the government.

The professional organization that represents the broad field of human services is the *National Organization for Human Services (NOHS)*. In addition to NOHS, many other professional organizations also exist for human services occupations (**Figure 4.10**). Members of the NOHS follow the organization's code of ethics when making ethical decisions. The NOHS code of ethics contains guidelines that relate to human services workers' responsibilities to clients, the public and society, colleagues, employers, the profession, and to self and students. (See the *Appendix* in this text to view the NOHS code of ethics.)

Ethical Decision Making

Human services workers are constantly making ethical decisions that affect their clients, coworkers, and employers. **Ethical decisions** consider what is right or moral, not just what is most efficient, economic, or preferred. Sometimes making ethical decisions is easy. For example, when a law, rule, or regulation dictates appropriate behavior, an ethical decision may seem easy to make. Oftentimes, however, making ethical decisions is difficult and complex. Not all situations present clear-cut ethical issues. Instead, some situations may fall within "gray areas."

Ethical decision making for human services workers is often more complex than just choosing the right option, especially when dealing with the future of people. For example, human services workers have a responsibility to maintain client confidentiality. Sometimes, however, maintaining confidentiality can be tricky. It may present an ethical conflict for human services workers.

If clients are of age, they have the right to privacy. Human services workers must respect this right. It would be unethical for them to share

Copyright Goodheart-Willcox Co., Inc.

Professional Organizations for Human Services Occupations

Academy of Nutrition and Dietetics (AND)

American Association for Marriage and Family Therapy (AAMFT)

American Association of Cosmetology Schools (AACS)

American Association of Family and Consumer Sciences (AAFCS)

American Counseling Association (ACA)

American Culinary Federation (ACF)

American Mental Health Counselors Association (AMHCA)

American Nutrition Association (ANA)

American Psychological Association (APA)

American Public Health Association (APHA)

American Rehabilitation Counseling Association (ARCA)

American School Counselor Association (ASCA)

American Society of Interior Designers (ASID)

Association of Interior Design Professionals (AIDP)

Council of Fashion Designers of America (CFDA)

Fashion Industry Association (FIA)

International Association of Clothing Designers and Executives (IACDE)

International Interior Design Association (IIDA)

International Nanny Association (INA)

International Textile and Apparel Association (ITAA)

National Association for Family Child Care (NAFCC)

National Association for Home Care and Hospice (NAHCH)

National Association for the Education of Young Children (NAEYC)

National Association of Social Workers (NASW)

National Career Development Association (NCDA)

National Funeral Directors Association (NFDA)

National Organization for Human Services (NOHS)

National Recreation and Park Association (NRPA)

National Restaurant Association (NRA)

School Nutrition Association (SNA)

Figure 4.10 Many professional organizations exist for human services occupations. *Which of the listed organizations do you find interesting?*

Copyright Goodheart-Willcox Co., Inc.

information about their clients without the client's consent. If a client is at risk of causing him- or herself or others harm, however, a human services worker may need to consider breaking the confidentiality of the relationship. When making complex ethical decisions, a human services worker must use good judgment that keeps the best interests of clients in mind.

When working with clients, it is often advised that human services workers develop relationships with their professional peers for consultation and supervision (**Figure 4.11**). By including others, such as coworkers, in the decision-making process, human services workers can give better clarity between objective and subjective *leanings* (tendencies).

Have a Positive Attitude

Why do some people seem to love their lives while others do not? Two factors are usually involved. They have a positive attitude, and they get satisfaction from what they do. Having a positive attitude means having the optimism and energy to positively relate to others and to complete a job. People who have a positive attitude desire to make something happen.

Keeping a positive attitude has many benefits both personally and professionally. When people see the potential good in situations, those around them will be energized by their enthusiasm.

Expert Insight

"Whether you think you can, or you think you can't—you're right."

Henry Ford

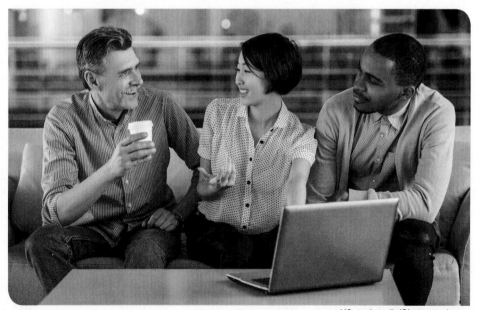

VGstockstudio/Shutterstock.com

Figure 4.11 Developing relationships with professional peers with whom they can consult gives human services workers clarity between any objective and subjective tendencies in their work. *What are some other possible benefits of including professional peers in the decision-making process?*

Law and Ethics   *Filtered Lenses*

Most communities are made up of various subgroups. These subgroups may vary in ethnicity, language, nationality, or lifestyles. Human services workers serve people from all walks of life. Many times, their clients' life experiences are very different from their own.

Regardless of these differences, human services workers have a responsibility to provide services without discrimination or preference. Age, lifestyle, socioeconomic status, ethnicity, race, religion, or gender cannot be used to determine whether or not they will provide services. These factors cannot be used to provide lower quality or inferior care.

In eliminating bias, human services workers should be knowledgeable and aware of their community's population makeup and its needs. For instance, there may be a large immigrant community from Ethiopia, South Korea, Trinidad, Romania, Brazil, or the Philippines. If the community has predominantly immigrated in the past generation or two, strong shared values may be present. Understanding these strengths and differences will help a human services worker provide best care practices.

Human services workers should be
- knowledgeable about their own culture and biases;
- knowledgeable about other cultures and ideologies represented in their communities;
- diligent in ensuring that their own biases or personal values are not forced upon their clients;
- interested in the commonalities between people;
- appreciative of differences among people; and
- nonjudgmental in their approach to providing services if safety and harm are not a concern.

Research Activity

Research the different ethnic groups that are represented in your community. Choose one group that emigrated from another country. Research the history of the group's immigration to your community. Choose one member, preferably someone that you know, to interview. Ask the person about what it was like when their family immigrated to your community. Also ask the interviewee about his perceived strengths and challenges of this subgroup. What might be helpful for a human services worker to know to provide good care? Write a one- to two-page summary of your interview.

Conversely, constantly complaining drags oneself and others down. People often have a tendency toward optimism or pessimism, but each person can make a conscious choice to try to keep a positive attitude.

Because the field of human services is in the people business, having a positive attitude is highly important and valued. Employers seek human services workers who are excited about helping their clients. Oftentimes, human services workers find themselves facing difficult situations when working with clients. Being proactive in finding solutions helps improve the attitudes of clients, coworkers, other providers, and community members. Focusing on the positive strides clients are making helps, too.

Think about the benefits of establishing these habits—thinking positively and improving difficult situations—now. They will help you through rough spots in school, work, and life. Most of all, you will enjoy life more and have a positive impact on others. You cannot control life, but you can control your reactions to it.

Copyright Goodheart-Willcox Co., Inc.

Reading Recall

1. Define *maturity*.
2. Why is being dependable such an important characteristic for human services workers to possess?
3. What is meant by the term *multiculturalism*?
4. How can human services workers help their clients assimilate into a new culture?
5. What is a *code of ethics*?
6. What are *professional organizations*? Name the professional organization that represents the broad field of human services.
7. Give an example of a complex ethical decision a human services worker may need to make.
8. Why is having a positive attitude so important for human services workers?

Keep Life in Balance

Like that challenging point of balance on a playground seesaw, it is often difficult to arrive at a balance in life. A balanced life is one in which there are no extremes. Rather, all components of life have a place, and a person's focus remains on his or her goals (**Figure 4.12**).

When life is in balance, people are happier, relaxed, and even more productive. When people are unable to achieve balance in their lives,

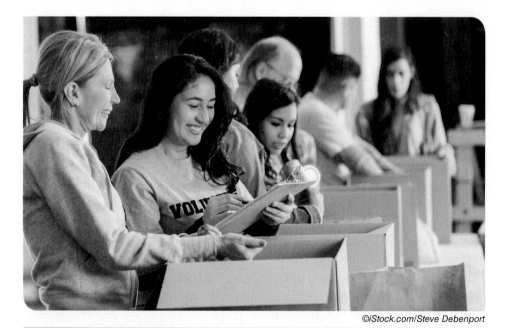

©iStock.com/Steve Debenport

Figure 4.12 A balanced life is often associated with a happier, relaxed, and even more productive person. *What does it mean to have a balanced life?*

Copyright Goodheart-Willcox Co., Inc.

their physical, mental, and social well-being are negatively impacted. To keep life in balance, people need to find a work-life balance, manage their stress, and maintain healthy relationships.

Find a Work-Life Balance

Work often takes more hours of a human services worker's day than any other activity, including sleep. Finding time to spend with family and friends and completing household chores can be difficult when too much time is devoted to work. When personal issues arise, however, more time may be spent at home than in the workplace. Leading a balanced life is important to promote wellness, but it is all too easy to get off track in one direction or another.

Juggling the many priorities between work and home life can be quite difficult and lead to spillover from one area to another. For example, feelings of frustration as a result of issues at work can carry into family relationships in the form of impatience, short temper, anxiety, or worry. In turn, problems and concerns at home can spillover into the workplace.

Work-life balance involves finding the right balance amid the many demands involving family and friends, career, and other interests or responsibilities. People are often concerned about more than just finding balance between their work and home lives, however. They also want to make a difference in the lives, organizations, and communities to which they contribute.

Work-life balance is a major cause of stress among workers and families today. It will likely continue to be so in the future. To help lessen some of this stress, many employers provide assistance to their employees in helping them maintain a work-life balance. Even with employer assistance, maintaining a work-life balance is not a simple task. Utilizing time management skills can help human services workers achieve a work-life balance.

> ### Expert Insight
>
> *"There are countless studies on the negative spillover of job pressures on family life, but few on how job satisfaction enhances the quality of family life."*
>
> Albert Bandura, psychologist

Employer Assistance in Maintaining Work-Life Balance

Many family and career transitions are made in early adulthood when the real challenges are in balancing competing demands. Traditionally, women transition in and out of the workforce more frequently than men in early adulthood due to parenting responsibilities. To assist employees during this transitional time, companies commonly provide maternity leave. They may also grant paternity leave to employees who are new parents.

Maternity leave is paid or unpaid time off women can take from work to care for a new child. *Paternity leave* is paid or unpaid time off from work that fathers may take after the birth or adoption of a child (**Figure 4.13**). In the US, the FMLA also allows for workers to take job-protected leave for certain family transitions.

Copyright Goodheart-Willcox Co., Inc.

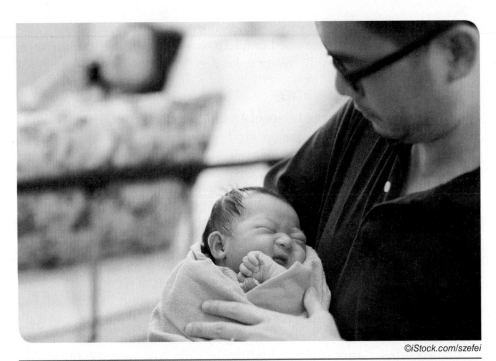

©iStock.com/szefei

Figure 4.13 Paternity leave allows a father to take paid or unpaid time off from work after the birth or adoption of a child. *What are other ways in which employers help their workers maintain work-life balance?*

Other ways in which employers may help workers maintain family-life balance is to offer family-friendly services and fringe benefits. An example of a family-friendly service is the provision of child care at the workplace. Several examples of fringe benefits include paid time off for vacations and holidays, sick leave, and health insurance.

Some employers also offer work programs that enable workers to set a flexible work schedule to accommodate their personal situations. This is called *flextime. Telecommuting* is yet another work program that allows workers to work from home rather than traveling to a central office.

Time Management

Time management plays a very important role in maintaining work-life balance. **Time management** is the method a person uses to manage or organize time. People with good time management skills are efficient and productive. They plan their time wisely so they can get everything done that they want to do—both at home and at work.

Human services workers need to possess good time management skills. They need to handle the many situations that occur throughout the workday so they can enjoy time at home as well. In addition to managing their own time, human services workers must also be able to teach their clients how they can develop time management skills to accomplish their

Copyright Goodheart-Willcox Co., Inc.

Pathway to Success

Manage Time and Increase Productivity

It's Tuesday morning, you are at work and your boss has just assigned you a project with a deadline of noon on Friday. What do you do next? Do you set the project aside until you are done with your current task? Do you take the time to skim through and see what you need to do to complete the project? Do you forget about the project until Friday morning and then rush to get it done?

Time is a limited resource that cannot be increased. Everyone has the same amount of time each day. Why is it then that some people seem to have plenty of time to do everything they want to do while other people seem to never have enough time? The difference is often in the way people are able to manage their time.

How well you manage your time can greatly affect your productivity, both personally and professionally. People who possess good time management skills know how to "work smart" to accomplish their goals. Working smart involves scheduling time wisely, prioritizing and keeping track of tasks, and avoiding *time wasters* (activities that stop productivity).

Time wasters can take up a little or a lot of time and prevent you from completing what needs to be done. Examples of time wasters at home, at school, and at work may include

- checking e-mail and social media sites;
- watching TV or videos;
- being interrupted by people stopping by to talk to about nonwork-related matters;
- talking on the phone or texting;
- attending an unexpected meeting that takes up half the day;
- procrastinating;
- being disorganized; and
- being fatigued.

So now that you know what time wasters are, take a closer look at this list. Which time wasters impact your productivity? Are there other time wasters you would add to this list?

Now that you have identified your time wasters, what strategies can you implement to stay on task? For example, perhaps you waste time by constantly checking e-mail or reading the latest updates on social media sites. In this case, you might want to schedule a few minutes each morning and afternoon to respond to messages and check social media accounts. At other times, keep the programs closed to avoid distractions. The same strategies you choose to use in your personal life can also be used in your professional life.

Role-Play Ways to Meet Deadlines

Review the scenario at the beginning of this feature. Write what you would normally do when a project assigned on Tuesday morning is due by noon on Friday. Then, explain what changes you would make to your normal routine to complete the job on or before the deadline.

Now, find a partner and share your two different approaches to the job assignment. As a team, make two different scenarios to act out in front of the class. The first scenario should show how time wasters can affect progress on the assignment. The second scenario should show a person using good time management skills to get the assignment done. In both scenarios, indicate whether or not the assignment is completed on or before the deadline, as well as your boss's reaction to your completed project.

Copyright Goodheart-Willcox Co., Inc.

goals. Following are some strategies human services workers may teach their clients:

- Make a schedule. Create to-do lists, use calendars, or use other organizational tools to remember important tasks and serve as a reminder to tackle them. Digital devices, such as computers, smartphones, and tablets, make scheduling quick and easy. They can also provide *audible* (hearable) reminders when tasks are due.

- Combine tasks. Save time and energy by *dovetailing* tasks, which involves doing several similar tasks at once.

- Designate priorities. Decide which tasks are essential, which are important, and which can be done if time allows. (Some people use *A*, *B*, *C* or *1*, *2*, *3* to designate priorities.)

- Avoid procrastination. To *procrastinate* is to put off starting a task until the last minute. Rather than procrastinating, start with the more difficult or complex tasks first. List all the steps that need to be completed to get a project done. Sometimes breaking a big project down into smaller pieces makes a project more manageable.

- Delegate tasks. By delegating tasks to other family or team members, friends, or coworkers, overwhelming tasks become manageable.

- Set limits and boundaries. Set personal physical, emotional, and mental limits or boundaries. These self-imposed limits help people realize they have rights and can say no to demands. By doing this, they can realize that their own needs are just as important as others' needs.

- Be flexible. Remember that unexpected things will happen from time to time. Schedule some time to deal with any emergencies that might arise. Reprioritize tasks, if necessary. Have a plan for spare time, too.

Expert Insight

"Many hands make light work."
John Heywood, playwright

Manage Stress

Stress is the body's response when faced with pressures and demands. Stress develops when the demands in life exceed the ability to cope with them easily. Something that causes stress is called a *stressor*. Oftentimes, stressors people experience make it difficult to lead a balanced life.

Typical stressors, which come from both inside and outside the home, can be negative or positive. For example, having financial or relationship problems are negative stressors. Getting married and starting a new job are examples of positive stressors. The negative stressors are usually more stressful. When there is pressure from a number of stressors, or a stressor is long lasting, stress levels often increase.

Everyone feels stressed from time to time. A bit of stress is not all bad. It can prompt a person to get tasks accomplished, even to think more

Copyright Goodheart-Willcox Co., Inc.

creatively. With too much stress, however, the body reacts as if it is facing a physical threat. The effects of stress may become evident in the body through physical and psychological reactions (**Figure 4.14**).

A person's physical or psychological reaction to stress depends on the stressor and how long the stressor may be an issue. For example, a short-term stressor, such as giving a presentation at work, may cause the employee to have sweaty palms and an upset stomach. These symptoms will most likely lessen once the presentation is complete.

The effects of stress may be long lasting if the situation is long term, such as dealing with a friend's addiction or the illness of a family member. In these cases, the stress can negatively impact wellness as the effects of stress can weaken the immune system and physically age a person when the stressor is ongoing.

To reduce the effects of stress, people must be able to effectively manage their stress. Human services workers help people manage their stress, but they must also be able to manage their own stress while dealing with many difficult situations. One of the best ways for human services workers to strengthen their ability to withstand stress is to stay in great physical shape. In doing so, they have more energy and are better able to cope with challenges. Adequate nutrition and regular physical activity are the building blocks of good health.

It is also important when working closely with people to learn to recognize when stress is building. Some people develop headaches, neck pain, or other physical problems. Others find themselves becoming short-tempered or eating more. When attuned to signals, appropriate action can be taken.

The first step is to figure out the true source of the stress. This can be difficult at times. Stress levels often rise when a person feels pressure from a number of competing situations. After identifying the source of

Physical and Psychological Reactions to Stress	
Physical Reactions	**Psychological Reactions**
• Sweaty palms	• Anger
• Increased heart rate	• Irritability
• Headaches	• Withdrawal
• Stomachaches	• Feeling sad or hopeless
• Fatigue	• Loss of focus
• Weakening of the immune system	• Inability to relax
• Worsening of preexisting health conditions	• Feelings of depression

Figure 4.14 Stress causes a number of psychological and physical reactions. *What two factors affect a person's psychological or physical reaction to stress?*

Copyright Goodheart-Willcox Co., Inc.

Case Study | *Coping and Hoping*

Haley loves her job as a health and wellness coordinator. She works with families looking for assisted living options either for themselves or for older family members. The clients she serves are often under stress, emotionally vulnerable, and in a crisis mode to find a living situation that could meet the needs of their loved ones.

For most people, locating assisted living options is a new experience. Haley helps her clients define their needs and discover their options. She helps them make decisions, understand state laws, and fill out necessary paperwork. She also finds resources for helping to make the move happen.

Although Haley likes her job, some days are intense. This is especially true when her clients want more counseling than problem-solving assistance. At the end of the day, however, Haley knows that she is making a difference in people's quality of life.

Andresr/Shutterstock.com

Recently, Haley and her boyfriend ended their relationship. It was a good decision and mutually agreed upon, but Haley missed her friendship with him. She was tired from all of the late night talk leading up to their decision to separate. She noticed that she was sometimes distracted when conversing with clients. As Haley processed the changes in her life, she sometimes felt sad. She began to journal those thoughts and shared some of her feelings with her sister, her mother, and her best friend.

Haley decided to put some of her own professional advice to good use. She realized that she needed to put more energy into connecting with other people outside of work. She also needed more activities that would distract her. Haley decided to take up running again. She even began to think of training for an upcoming 5K run that would benefit a charity. She asked a friend to join her in taking on the challenge. Haley's increased physical activity demanded that she get enough sleep and fuel herself with nutritious food.

Haley noticed that her own energy and attention were back to normal. It did not happen overnight, but soon Haley realized that she was enjoying her life once again. She was enjoying new friendships, spending time laughing and sharing. Her sister was now in a new relationship and she was excited for her. It had been a difficult period, but Haley knew that her life experiences would help her to better connect with her clients who were undergoing stressful life events.

For Discussion

1. Name at least four causes of stress in Haley's life.
2. Name some ways that Haley dealt with her own life stresses.
3. How did Haley's reactions affect her physically, emotionally, socially, and even spiritually?
4. How might you react in a similar situation?

Copyright Goodheart-Willcox Co., Inc.

the stress, human services workers can help their clients make changes to reduce pressure.

Stress develops when life demands exceed the ability to cope with them easily. Human services workers help their clients take control over how they react to stress by practicing ways to stay calm and by making alternative plans when things do not go as planned. They help their clients to consider long-term strategies for reducing stress. That way, when something unexpected happens, their client may be better able to cope.

Human services workers also help their clients find personal ways to deal with stress (**Figure 4.15**). For example, some people find that regular physical activity helps. Others find a friend to talk to when life seems overwhelming. Human services workers can help their clients to realize the importance of stress-relieving activities to their overall health and wellness and that of their family members. Human services workers encourage their clients to try several techniques and select the techniques that help them the most.

Maintain Healthy Relationships

People are social beings and need to have other people surrounding them. In fact, people needing people is really what human services is all about. This social interaction, however, is more than just the need to be around other people. It is a need for healthy relationships.

Stress-Coping Techniques
• Calling an old friend and catching up
• Dancing to favorite music
• Working around the house
• Exercising with a friend
• Discussing the situation with a close family member or friend
• Going for a walk, or walking a dog
• Greeting those who pass by
• Seeking counseling
• Listening to music
• Playing a video game with a friend
• Playing with a pet
• Reading a good book
• Running, bicycling, or other activity (consider training for an event)
• Spending time outside, and if possible, enjoying nature
• Starting or writing in a journal
• Taking a long bath
• Taking the stairs or walking further in the parking lot
• Watching a comedy

Figure 4.15 There are a variety of stress-relieving activities that promote overall health and wellness. *What is your favorite technique for coping with stress?*

Copyright Goodheart-Willcox Co., Inc.

Healthy relationships are critical to life. Having supportive relationships contributes to a person's physical, cognitive, social, and emotional well-being. Supportive relationships are healthy relationships that include give-and-take between those involved. Support may come from family members, friends, neighbors, or coworkers.

Human services workers are often surrounded by people during much of their working hours. These relationships may be strong, caring relationships. As caregivers, human services workers should be intentional about having relationships in their lives that are mutually supportive.

Human services workers can benefit from having friends outside of their work environment. They need friends whom they can share interests and hobbies that are unrelated to their work. This allows human services workers to leave the issues of their work at the office and "refuel their emotional tanks." It is especially helpful if these personal relationships are on equal footing rather than a helping relationship.

Although family relationships can provide support for human services workers, they, too, often involve healing relationships. This is especially true for parents, older siblings, and middle-age workers who may have responsibility to care for their own aging parents.

When dealing with new and challenging clients, human services workers may feel reluctant to ask for help from their colleagues. Professional peers, however, can offer support or reassurance and advice. Accepting help and support is important to well-being. Communicating with people who are supportive can create an understanding of new changes clients are experiencing.

When working with clients, human services workers may often find themselves in positions of unequal power. Clients may share very personal information or require delicate care. Maintaining a professional relationship is critical. Human services workers must be careful not to cross the line between professional and personal relationships with their clients. They cannot become so personally involved that they lose their professional objectivity. Trust must be *implicit* (unquestioning) in this helping relationship. Workers must use their best judgment in addressing their clients' needs.

Human services workers are often drawn to these careers because of their desire to work with people (**Figure 4.16**). They might cite the desire to help, to serve, or to make a real difference in people's lives. Although there are many rewards, dealing with people on a daily basis can be challenging and frustrating. It can be draining by the end of the day.

Human services workers can greatly benefit by maintaining their own health and well-being both personally and professionally. They do this by keeping positive relationships in their personal lives that do not cross over into their professional work. They also work to maintain their own health by eating nutritious foods, getting plenty of sleep, and being

Copyright Goodheart-Willcox Co., Inc.

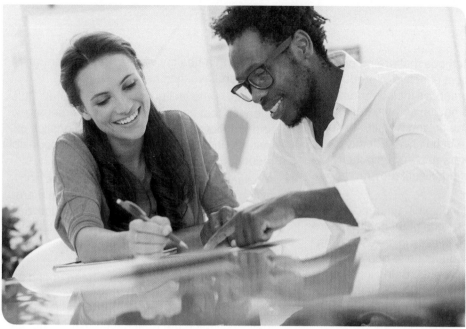

wavebreakmedia/Shutterstock.com

Figure 4.16 Many are drawn to a career in human services because they love working with people. *What are some ways in which human services workers can maintain their own health and well-being, both personally and professionally?*

physically active. By seeking balance between work and life, stress can be reduced and outlets are created for maintaining physical, emotional, and mental health.

Reading Recall

1. Why is leading a balanced life important to promote wellness?
2. Describe three ways that employers assist employees in maintaining a work-life balance.
3. List seven strategies human services workers may teach their clients to help them develop good time management skills.
4. What are *stressors*? Give an example of a negative stressor and an example of a positive stressor.
5. Name three physical and three psychological reactions to stress.
6. List six stress-coping techniques.
7. Why are healthy relationships important for human services workers?

Copyright Goodheart-Willcox Co., Inc.

Summary

- *Best practices* are methods that are recognized as being correct or most effective in producing a desired result. Best practices include promoting good personal health habits, demonstrating characteristics of maturity, and working to keep personal and work life in balance. Effective human services workers not only help their clients to adopt these practices, they model them, too.

- *Health* is an overall condition in reference to illness or disease. People in good health are free of illness or disease. *Wellness* involves making lifestyle choices that contribute to good physical, mental, and social well-being. Being in good health and living a healthy lifestyle gives people more energy to complete the tasks they need and want to do—both at home and at work.

- Important ways to promote wellness include maintaining a neat appearance, achieving and sustaining a healthy weight, getting enough sleep, and avoiding health hazards.

- *Maturity* is the ability to adapt to the inevitable changes that happen in life, both personally and professionally. Specific characteristics of maturity include being dependable, responsible, respectful, ethical, and positive.

- A balanced life is one in which there are no extremes. When life is in balance, people are happier, relaxed, and even more productive. When people are unable to achieve balance in their lives, their physical, mental, and social well-being is negatively impacted.

- To keep life in balance, people need to find a work-life balance, manage their stress, and maintain healthy relationships. *Work-life balance* involves finding the right balance amid the many demands involving family and friends, career, and other interests or responsibilities.

College and Career Portfolio

Portfolio Electronic Organization

You will create both a print portfolio and an e-Portfolio in this class. You have already decided how to store hard copy items for your print portfolio. Now you will create a plan for storing and organizing your e-Portfolio.

Ask your instructor where to save your documents. This could be on the school's network or a flash drive of your own. Think about how to organize related files into categories. For example, school transcripts and diplomas might be one category. Writing samples and statements of purpose might be another category, and so on. Next, consider how you will name the files. The names for folders and files should be descriptive, but not too long. You will decide in a later activity how to present your electronic files for viewers.

To begin organizing your e-Portfolio, complete the following activities:

1. Create a folder on the network drive or flash drive in which you will save your files.
2. Write a few sentences to describe how you will name the subfolders and files for your portfolio.
3. Create the subfolders to organize the files, using the naming system you created.

Copyright Goodheart-Willcox Co., Inc.

Review and Reflect ➦

1. Identify four ways you can promote wellness in your life.
2. What two personal habits are involved in maintaining a neat appearance?
3. Give an example of the type of clothing that would be appropriate to wear for a specific career in human services.
4. Define *weight management*.
5. What is *substance abuse*?
6. Explain the difference between a *physical dependency* and a *psychological dependency* on substances.
7. List five specific characteristics of maturity.
8. Identify two unique challenges multicultural individuals and families sometimes face.
9. Define *ethics*. Explain why human services workers would abide by a code of ethics.
10. List three ways to keep life in balance.
11. List four strategies human services workers may teach their clients to help them develop good time management skills.
12. What is one of the best ways for human services workers to strengthen their ability to withstand stress?

Vocabulary Activities

13. **Key terms**   On a separate sheet of paper, list words that relate to each of the following terms. Then, work with a partner to explain how these words are related.

assimilation	prejudice
code of ethics	professional
cultural competence	organizations
cultural diversity	stereotypes
ethical decisions	stress
ethics	substance abuse
health	time management
maturity	weight management
multiculturalism	wellness
	work-life balance

14. **Academic terms**   Individually or with a partner, create a T-chart on a sheet of paper and list each of the following terms in the left column. In the right column, list an *antonym* (a word of opposite meaning) for each term in the left column.

acute	leanings
audible	procrastinate
dovetailing	proximity
implicit	

Self-Assessment Quiz ➦

Complete the self-assessment quiz online to help you practice and expand your knowledge and skills.

Critical Thinking

15. **Compare and contrast**   Compare and contrast health and wellness using a Venn Diagram. Share your diagram with two of your classmates. Did they identify information that you did not?
16. **Make inferences**   You are in line at the store behind a woman who has body odor, greasy hair, and is wearing clothing that is old, stained, and torn. When she pays for the few items she has, she very carefully counts in change the money to pay for the items. Based on these observations, what can you infer about this person? What makes you believe this to be true?
17. **Draw conclusions**   It has been proven that when people look their best they feel their best. Look at your classmates and draw conclusions about their lives based on their appearance today. In a week, look at your classmates again and draw conclusions based on their appearance on that day. Has your conclusion about them changed? Why or why not?
18. **Evaluate**   You are on your way to a job interview. Do you spray a large amount of cologne or perfume on yourself or do you spritz just a small amount? Do you wear clothing with bright colors and flashy patterns or neutral tones? Explain your reasoning.
19. **Identify**   Look at pictures online or in magazines and identify pictures that show appropriate apparel selections for the following occasions: a job interview for a financial analyst position, a dinner with family at a casual dining restaurant, the first day on the

job as a child care worker at a preschool program, and the first day at a new school.

20. **Cause and effect** Eating habits formed early in life have far-reaching effects in people's lives. Look at your current eating habits. Infer what effect your current eating habits will have on you throughout your lifetime. Do you think your habits will change over time? Why or why not?

21. **Determine** You have helped a client fill out paperwork he needs to turn in to receive help. It is the end of the day and you leave the paperwork on your desk instead of filing it. When you come in the next day, the paperwork is missing off your desk. How will this affect your client? What are the consequences of your actions for yourself and your client?

22. **Analyze** Have you ever experienced prejudicial behavior toward yourself or someone close to you? Think about that event. What biases did the person showing the prejudice exhibit? How could you have educated them so they would understand your culture and its value to you?

Core Skills

23. **Research** Imagine you are preparing for your first job interview. You look into your wardrobe and realize you have very few items that could be used in a job interview to look professional. Find a pair of nice pants, a shirt, and a pair of shoes that you like and would feel confident to wear in a job interview. Get a picture, a price, and the location of where you can buy these items.

24. **Math** Using the information in number 23, create a budget over a three-month period where you can buy two of the three items (a pair of nice pants, a shirt, and a pair of shoes) to use for job interviews. You have a monthly income of $100.00 and monthly expenses of $80.00. Which items would you buy and why?

25. **Writing** In a journal, keep track of what you eat and how much physical activity you get for two weeks. Once a week, weigh yourself to see if you are maintaining your weight. Evaluate your results. Do you think you need to change any of your habits to achieve or maintain a healthy weight? Outline a plan of action you can take to manage your weight.

26. **Writing** Write a letter to a loved one explaining the effects of nicotine on the body and what he or she can do to overcome the addiction. Give reasons explaining why you are concerned about this person's health and how you can help.

27. **Research and technology** In small groups, use online or print sources to research the implications of alcohol or drug abuse on personal and professional success. How does substance abuse affect health and wellness? academic performance? relationships with family and friends? home life? employment? After researching, plan and shoot a public service announcement to educate others about the harmful effects of substance abuse.

28. **Research and technology** Research on the Internet different jobs' ethical policies. Compare at least two different companies' policies. Are there any similarities or differences? Create a scenario to present in class explaining one of the ethical policies you researched. Show how to follow the policy, as well as what not to do, and what would happen to the worker who did not follow ethical practices.

29. **Speaking** Think about Henry Ford's quote, "Whether you think you can, or you think you can't—you're right." With a partner, discuss your opinion of this quote. Allow each person to give his or her opinion without interruption using the communication skills you have learned in this class.

30. **Research, technology, and speaking** Look into the difference between flextime and telecommuting. How have these technological advances changed in the workforce? Identify any local businesses that offer these work options to their workers. Talk to a worker at one of the businesses to find out about the pros and cons of telecommuting or flextime.

31. **Writing** Everyone has stress in their lives at different times. How you deal with the stress can have an impact on your life. Imagine your best friend has become very snippy and angry when she talks to the people around her. Write a note you can give to your friend to help her cope with the stress in her life.

Copyright Goodheart-Willcox Co., Inc.

32. **CTE career readiness practice** Human services workers have a responsibility to be ethical. With a partner, create a role-play scenario in which a human services worker is using the constructive conflict management process to resolve a conflict. Practice different versions of the role-play to show ethical and appropriate methods of conflict resolution and unethical methods. Present your role-plays to the class and ask classmates to identify the ethical and unethical behaviors.

33. **CTE career readiness practice** Illustrate and label a time management document that you can use in your everyday life. Use the document to record how you spend your time for one week. After a week, review and evaluate how you spent your time. Write a one-page essay identifying any time wasters and steps you can take to manage your time more effectively and be more productive.

Lend a Hand

Volunteering: A Lifelong Habit

Community service is valuable no matter how often you participate, but the more you volunteer, the more impactful your work will be. Volunteering consistently maximizes the benefits to you and your community. If you work with the same group consistently, you spend less time learning the processes and more time doing the work that makes a difference. The more time you spend helping your community, the more you will feel like a part of it. As you spend more time with community members and fellow volunteers, you will feel more fulfilled and connected to them.

Many people find a volunteer opportunity they enjoy and stick with it for many years. Volunteering can become as habitual as exercising or spending time with friends. It is never too late to make a habit out of serving your community. Establishing a new habit is not always easy, but if you find something you enjoy and stick with it, you are likely to be successful.

To work toward the goal of making volunteering a habit, complete the following:

1. Set a goal for your volunteering habit. Determine how many hours a month you would like to spend on community service. Choose the place(s) you will volunteer. The more specific you are during the planning stage, the better.
2. Figure out how you will measure your goal. Use real numbers in your plan so you will know if you are on track.
3. Make sure your goal is achievable. You are more likely to establish a new habit of volunteering monthly than you are to start volunteering every day.
4. Choose volunteer opportunities that are relevant to your interests and skills. You are more likely to follow through with experiences if they seem worthwhile and important.
5. Identify a deadline for meeting your goal. After a certain amount of time, assess your progress. Has volunteering become a habit? Does your goal need to be adjusted to accommodate a new schedule?

Copyright Goodheart-Willcox Co., Inc.

Preparing for Career Success

america365/Shutterstock.com

Curriculum Director

Curtis Larkins

I have always loved working with children. Throughout high school, I babysat for several families to earn spending money. In college, I found that working as a nanny for a professional working family was both rewarding and allowed me the flexibility to earn a living while attending school. Through these experiences, I learned how important my work was in the lives of young children. Because I found the children to be utterly amazing, I quickly changed my major to early childhood education.

To add more practical experience to my education, I did an internship as part of my studies with an early childhood education center. During my internship, I learned about child-directed learning, the role of the teacher as a learning facilitator, and how to document childhood learning activities. I gained insight into the logistical and business aspects of the business of early childhood education. This is where I found my home and knew that this was the field in which I wanted to have a career.

eurobanks/
Shutterstock.com

After graduation, I first worked as an assistant teacher and then as a lead teacher. At our center, we take a whole family approach, involving children and their families in the joy of learning through play. Our classrooms are designed to feel like home with soft textures, warm lighting, plenty of art supplies, and opportunities for play and exploration. The children even have their own family photos displayed. We rely on natural and reused materials for artistic play, such as rocks, beans, and interesting recycled goods. The children paint, sculpt, draw, sing, and dance on a daily basis as a way of expressing their thoughts and ideas. We try to spend time outdoors each day, whenever possible. I take lots of photographs and record their intellectual, emotional, and social growth so I can share with and support their parents in facilitating their holistic growth.

Last year, I became the Curriculum Director for the center. This means that I lead teacher training, keeping them updated in the newest research about how young children learn. We brainstorm together about ways that we can best meet the needs of our children.

I know that this has been the right career path for me and that I am making a difference in the lives of young children. Someone once asked me, "What is it that you are really good at?" It seemed like a difficult question at the time, but now I know. I am good at creating learning environments where children can learn through play and discovery.

Research Activity

Conduct online research about different careers that would allow you to work with children. What common aptitudes, abilities, and skills are needed? What are the educational requirements? Would you be interested in this type of career?

Chapter 5

Looking Inward: Identifying Your Personal Brand

While studying, look for the activity icon ↗ **to**

- **practice** key and academic terms with e-flash cards and matching activities;
- **assess** what you learn by completing self-assessment quizzes; and
- **reinforce** what you learn by mapping concepts and completing review and reflect questions.

www.g-wlearning.com/humanservices/

©iStock.com/CREATISTA

Learning Outcomes

After studying this chapter, you will be able to

- **describe** ways to start a self-assessment and explain why it is a lifelong process;
- **summarize** your general experiences or accomplishments and personality characteristics;
- **recognize** your personal values and needs;
- **list** all of your assets and skills and determine which skills you want to develop;
- **assess** your personal preferences for health, physical ability, activity level, and tasks; and
- **identify** your own unique personal brand.

Reading Strategies

Before reading, skim the chapter and consider what each concept you learn might teach you about yourself. Write a list of these ideas, placing a star beside any concepts that especially interest you. As you are reading, take notes about information relating to these concepts. After reading this chapter, pick three of the ideas and write a few paragraphs reflecting on how these concepts have helped or will help you understand yourself.

Mapping Concepts

In the middle circle of a chart like the one shown, write *My Personal Brand*. Then, as you read this chapter and complete the activities of self-reflection, write your unique qualities in the surrounding boxes. After you have filled in the boxes, consider your personal brand. Next to each box, write any areas you would like to change or qualities you would like to develop.

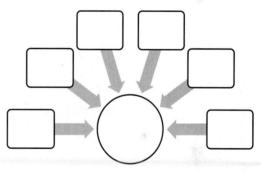

Key Terms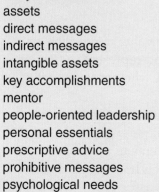

assets
direct messages
indirect messages
intangible assets
key accomplishments
mentor
people-oriented leadership
personal essentials
prescriptive advice
prohibitive messages
psychological needs

self-assessment
tangible assets
task-oriented leadership

Academic Terms

aspirations
commendation
haphazard
persona
repertoire
self-deprecating

Copyright Goodheart-Willcox Co., Inc.

Case Study *The Javier Brand*

Javier knows that he has a unique life story. At least he rarely meets anyone in his small town or high school who has lived a similar life story. Javier's mom was a single parent struggling to find steady work. Because of this, Javier and his mom had many financially challenging times. In the early years, they lived with his grandparents.

When Javier was two years old, his mom joined the United States Army. She loved her work and it gave them both more stability. It also meant that they relocated many times during his childhood. Javier's mom was even deployed overseas for a year. During this time, Javier returned to live with his grandparents.

When Javier was in fifth grade, his mom married William, a man he has grown to love and respect very much. William also served in the military. Together, the three of them, plus his two new younger siblings, moved to a base in Europe. Later, they returned to a small US town where they currently reside.

Javier often feels like his life experiences make it so that he does not fit in with this tight-knit community where people have known each other all their lives. Javier is a naturally quiet, reflective, and somewhat shy person. He knows a lot about movies, music, and computers as these were often his way of connecting with friends near and far. When he looks around him, it seems that most of his peers have friendships that have been in place since early childhood. He often wishes that he had a similar story. Lately, Javier's teacher has been talking about developing a personal brand. He wonders if he has one.

Volt Collection/Shutterstock.com

For Discussion

1. Make a list of Javier's most unique life experiences and qualities in descending order.

2. If Javier lived in your community, what would make him most unique?

3. How could Javier present his experiences as unique strengths to benefit future employers?

In the marketplace, brands communicate the value of products or services. This is called a *brand name*. When a brand represents a firm or organization, it is termed a *corporate brand*. In life, whether you want to admit it or not, you have a *personal brand*.

Much like a brand name, your brand or reputation speaks to your unique personality, temperament, talents, interests, and unique experiences—both positive and negative. These unique qualities differentiate you from others. Your personal brand is what you are known for—it is how people describe or know you. Over time, this personal brand becomes associated with a level of credibility, quality of work, and personal relationships.

Copyright Goodheart-Willcox Co., Inc.

Most people wish to project a certain vibe or *persona* (public image). Especially in adolescence, when your whole adult life lies ahead, you may have ideas about how you would like others to view you. Before you can develop your personal brand for tomorrow, however, you need to understand your brand today and what it is that makes you uniquely you.

As you study this chapter, complete the exercises within the sections. These activities of self-reflection will help you get to know yourself and understand your current brand. If, after careful and honest reflection, you realize you are unhappy with your personal brand, remember that you are not stuck with it. You have the ability to make the most of your uniqueness, making it a positive, marketable personal brand.

Starting a Self-Assessment

Self-assessment is a lifetime process that helps you reflect and identify your personal values, needs, resources, temperament or personality, skills, abilities, and dreams. In doing so, you can identify your own personal brand.

The best way to start a self-assessment is to ask the one who likely knows you best—you. Because self-assessment is often difficult to begin, you may want to devote 30 minutes each day for a couple of weeks to the process. Investing time at regular intervals will help you focus and complete the thought process.

While you are at it, ask others who know you well for their input. This input might come from family members, friends, coworkers, teachers, mentors, or counselors. These are the people who can be honest with you. They can openly share their opinions of your strengths and weaknesses, interests, and potential (**Figure 5.1**).

You can also use assessment tests to help you get to know yourself. Typical types of assessment tests include

- aptitude or ability tests;

- interest inventories;

- values assessments;

- personality inventories;

- leadership or management style assessments; and

- tests that identify personal strengths.

©iStock.com/digitalskillet

Figure 5.1 Asking someone you trust, such as a parent, to give his or her perception of your strengths and weaknesses, interests, and potential can help you with your self-assessment. *Who could you ask to help you with your self-assessment?*

Copyright Goodheart-Willcox Co., Inc.

Law and Ethics   *Self-Assess Your Personal Ethics*

As a student, you face many ethical dilemmas. How would you respond in these situations? How might your responses speak to your underlying motivations?

- You have been assigned a class group project. In the end, you will all share the same grade for your efforts. As a student athlete, you have a busy month filled with tryouts and hopefully, if you make the team, practices. Do you fully participate in the group project or slack off and let the other group members complete the work?

- You have seen a classmate disrespected on social media. Cruel and false statements were made about this person that quickly became the talk of the school. The victim was devastated and embarrassed. Will you ignore it, continue to spread the gossip, or report the cyberbullying incident? Does it matter whether or not the allegations were true?

- You are preparing for a big exam. Someone offers you the answers to the test. Do you take the answers or do you keep studying on your own? Do you let your teacher know? Why or why not?

- You are part of a group that planned a dance on campus. After the event, the place is a mess. It is littered with garbage, drink and food containers, and the aftermath of destroyed decorations and spills. One of your friends says, "Let's get out of here. The janitor will clean it up. That is what he is paid for." Do you agree and leave or begin helping with the cleanup?

How you respond to everyday ethical dilemmas speaks to your personal ethics. It also contributes toward your personal reputation as an ethical or unethical person. Ethical decisions often involve making difficult, time consuming, or unpopular decisions. They take into consideration the needs of others rather than just self. In the end, however, ethical behavior makes for a better living environment built on trust and care.

Writing Activity

Write a one-page paper describing some ethical decisions you faced this week. How did you respond? Based on your responses, how would you assess your personal ethics?

Although assessment tests can be helpful, use caution. First, avoid the tendency to be pigeon-holed or categorized by test results. Everyone is unique. For example, if a test describes you as "quick, impulsive, and decisive in decision making," do not generalize these characteristics in other areas. This description may reflect your management style. It is not, however, describing your personality or interpersonal interaction style. Remember, tests measure only one aspect of who you are. If you take one test, be sure you understand what is being tested and how to interpret the results.

Second, utilize many tests instead of relying on just one type of test. Some test formats will appeal to you more than others. For example, some people prefer forced-choice tests. Others prefer responding to open-ended questions. There is no one test that everyone loves or that works well. Taking multiple tests and properly interpreting the results will help paint a picture of you that is more accurate than taking just one as similarities will surface.

Lastly, the test-taking process and thoughtful self-evaluation of the results is often more valuable than the analysis. Test results may surprise

Copyright Goodheart-Willcox Co., Inc.

some people. This does not mean the results are wrong. Talk to friends and relatives about test results. Ask them if they agree with the analysis. The most important benefit of self-assessment tests is their ability to get you thinking.

There are several places you can find self-assessment tests. You can check the Internet as there are many online tests available. As a student, the best place to find good self-assessment tests is in your school counseling center. School guidance counselors are trained to help you select the most appropriate assessment test and to help you interpret the results. They can direct you toward tests that are reliable and relevant. Tests are frequently offered for free or at a discount price to students. Now is a great time to take advantage of these readily available services. Some commonly used free assessment tests include the following:

- Strong Campbell Interest Inventory®
- Myers-Briggs Type Indicator®
- Princeton Review Career Quiz®

Reading Recall

1. Define the term *self-assessment*.
2. Describe three ways to start a self-assessment.
3. Explain why self-assessment is a lifelong process.
4. Name three precautions to take when using assessment tests.
5. As a student, where is the best place to start finding good self-assessment tests?
6. Name one common and frequently used assessment test.

Getting to Know Yourself

In this first section of self-assessment, you will focus on your general experiences or accomplishments and personality characteristics. Understanding the experiences you are proud of and the characteristics of your personality and attitudes will help you identify your unique traits.

Personal Accomplishments

Identifying and focusing on positive past experiences is a good place to begin your self-assessment. These past experiences are your **key accomplishments**. Generally, these are the accomplishments for which you are most proud.

Accomplishments can include traditional achievements, such as being an employee of the month, earning a high grade on a school project, or receiving an honor. They may also be experiences for which you did not receive *commendation* (praise; congratulation) from others, but were important to you. If you recall your earliest memories, these are experiences where you said "I did it myself!" In later years, these may be experiences where you did something that you thought you could not do or perhaps you beat your personal best record.

Look at some examples of personal accomplishments in **Figure 5.2**. Then, think about all areas of your life—sports and exercise, volunteering, your job, community activities, family roles, cooking, or even pet ownership. Your personal accomplishments may include short- or long-term achievements. Develop a list of at least 15–20 accomplishments and then prioritize these into your top 5 achievements.

Personality Characteristics

Writing about your accomplishments can be a window into what makes you "tick." Your personality characteristics are evident through your key achievements. Experiences that you define as key achievements are those that bring you happiness and joy and through which you experience success.

After creating a list of accomplishments, you can identify your personality characteristics through each of your accomplishments. To do this, make a chart similar to the one in **Figure 5.3**. As you build your chart, keep in mind that Figure 5.3 only contains a sampling of personality characteristics. Feel free to add your own traits to the list.

Once you finish developing your chart, review your list of accomplishments. Then, on your chart, place a check mark next to any

Examples of Personal Accomplishments

- Making the honor roll for excellent grades.
- Being chosen for the school play.
- Creating a website for class.
- Earning money to go on a Spanish language trip to Spain.
- Giving a great speech in class.
- Getting an A on a test after studying all week.
- Being recognized by a teacher for working hard in class.
- Helping an older neighbor by organizing a neighborhood gardening service.
- Raising money for a cancer society walk.
- Running a six-minute mile.
- Learning how to play a difficult song on the guitar.
- Helping a younger sibling learn how to read.
- Coaching a youth summer soccer camp.
- Cooking a meal for the family without any help.

Figure 5.2 Personal accomplishments can be from any area of your life. *In what ways are your personal accomplishments similar to the ones shown here?*

Copyright Goodheart-Willcox Co., Inc.

Personality Characteristics

Characteristic	√	Characteristic	√	Characteristic	√	Characteristic	√
Accurate		Delightful		Inventive		Productive	
Adaptable		Demonstrative		Kind		Promoter	
Adventurous		Dependable		Leader		Proud	
Ambitious		Detailed		Listener		Refreshing	
Analytical		Diplomatic		Lively		Repetitious	
Animated		Disciplined		Logical		Resentful	
Assertive		Down-to-earth		Loyal		Reserved	
Athletic		Driving		Mediator		Resistant	
Balanced		Dry humor		Mixes easily		Resourceful	
Bashful		Efficient		Mover		Respectful	
Behaved		Emotional		Musical		Reticent	
Bold		Empathetic		Nonchalant		Rugged	
Bossy		Energetic		Obliging		Satisfied	
Bouncy		Enthusiastic		Optimistic		Scheduled	
Calm		Expressive		Orderly		Self-reliant	
Careful		Faithful		Original		Self-sacrificing	
Cheerful		Flexible		Outspoken		Sensitive	
Chief		Forceful		Patient		Shy	
Competitive		Forgiving		Peaceful		Sociable	
Confidant		Frank		Perfectionist		Spirited	
Conforming		Friendly		Permissive		Spontaneous	
Considerate		Funny		Persistent		Stable	
Consistent		Helpful		Persuasive		Strong-willed	
Contented		Idealistic		Pessimistic		Stubborn	
Controlled		Imaginative		Planner		Submissive	
Convincing		Impulsive		Playful		Sure	
Cooperative		Independent		Pleasant		Sympathetic	
Creative		Insecure		Popular		Tactful	

(Continued)

Figure 5.3 Use this chart to help you make your own list of personality characteristics. *What personality characteristics would you add to this list?*

Copyright Goodheart-Willcox Co., Inc.

Characteristic	√	Characteristic	√	Characteristic	√	Characteristic	√
Cultured		Insightful		Positive		Talkative	
Curious		Inspiring		Powerful		Thoughtful	
Daring		Intellectual		Practical		Tolerant	
Deep		Intuitive		Precise		Understanding	

Personality Characteristics 🔗 (Continued)

personality characteristics you demonstrated through your achievements. Be honest. Do not overstate or be too modest. If you have trouble identifying your personality characteristics, ask a close friend or family member to help you.

Reading Recall

1. What are *key accomplishments*?
2. What does *commendation* mean?

Understanding Your Motivations

What motivates you to try new activities, pursue goals, make decisions, or organize your time? Many choices you make are based on what is important to you. These are your values and needs.

Your values, or the beliefs you hold important, are the guideposts of your life. They are what motivate you and what you use to measure the success of your experiences. Even though values are basic to your operating in the world, oftentimes they are difficult to identify and articulate.

If you examine the stories of famous people, you can easily identify the values on which they base their actions. Many of your values are probably very evident to you. Other values, however, may be subtle and more difficult to identify.

Your needs closely relate to your values. Personal needs may include the need for status, belonging, respect, love, or other psychological benefits. The influence of your family and the sway of friends and mentors play an important role in the formation of your values and needs.

Identifying Personal Values

Every day you face life situations that call for thoughtful reflection, opinion formation, decision making, and action. Each opinion, decision, and action is based on your values. Values and motivations are intertwined as your values sometimes motivate you to tackle or complete a task. Because values are often difficult to define, understanding your motivations can sometimes get you started on defining your personal values. Personal values create beliefs, actions, and behaviors that are important in your personal life.

Despite school or career changes, most values remain constant. Use **Figure 5.4** to identify your values, adding additional values as you wish. Place a check mark next to the items you value highly or consider ideal for your personal life.

Personal Values Checklist

Value	√	Value	√	Value	√	Value	√
Accomplishment		Diversity		Joy		Rules	
Accountability		Education		Knowledge		Safety	
Accuracy		Efficiency		Leadership		Security	
Achievement		Equality		Learning		Selflessness	
Advancement		Excellence		Location		Self reliance	
Adventure		Excitement		Management		Seriousness	
Aesthetics		Fairness		Money		Service	
Aspiration		Faith		Moral fulfillment		Simplicity	
Balance		Family		Optimism		Sincerity	
Beauty		Fast pace		Orderliness		Skill	
Calm		Flair		Patriotism		Speed	
Challenge		Freedom		Personal growth		Spirituality	
Change		Friendship		Physical activity		Stability	
Cleanliness		Fun		Pleasure		Standardization	
Collaboration		Generosity		Positive attitude		Status	
Commitment		Global view		Power		Strength	
Communication		Goodness		Prosperity		Style	
Competence		Gratitude		Punctuality		Success	
Competition		Happiness		Purity		Systemization	
Concern		Hard work		Quality of work		Teamwork	
Cooperation		Harmony		Rationality		Timeliness	

(Continued)

Figure 5.4 Use this chart to help you make your own list of personal values. *Which of these values are the most important to you?*

Copyright Goodheart-Willcox Co., Inc.

Personal Values Checklist (Continued)							
Value	**√**	**Value**	**√**	**Value**	**√**	**Value**	**√**
Coordination		Health		Recognition		Tolerance	
Creativity		Helping		Regularity		Tradition	
Decisiveness		History		Reliability		Tranquility	
Democracy		Honesty		Resourcefulness		Truth	
Detail work		Honor		Respect		Unity	
Determination		Independence		Responsibility		Wealth	
Discipline		Inner peace		Results			
Discovery		Integrity		Risk			

Identifying Psychological Needs

Psychological needs are the fundamental desires you have that lead to self-satisfaction. Your needs are not the same as other people's needs. For example, you may feel satisfaction when you have the opportunity to lead a group in accomplishing a project. Another person may feel more satisfaction from working as a member of the team accomplishing the task. Many psychological needs overlap and, in the above example, both people may have the need to lead and to work collaboratively.

To identify your psychological needs, use **Figure 5.5**. Feel free to add items to your list. Place a check mark next to the psychological needs that are the most important to you.

Influences on Your Values and Needs Formation

The people you respect most influence your values and needs formation. These people often include family members, friends, or others you know and interact with daily. You may even respect people you have read about or admired from afar. Identifying the people you respect and admire is a helpful exercise in assessing your values and needs.

Family

Your family has a powerful influence on who you are and how you view the world. Family members can be powerful motivators. They often shape your values and needs. Your family, however, is not always a positive influence on your choices. In fact, the exact opposite may be true. Nevertheless, family plays a major role in many people's life decisions.

Families often impart many direct and indirect messages of advice. **Direct messages** are straightforward, whereas **indirect messages** are subtle and sometimes confusing. Direct messages are prescriptive or

Copyright Goodheart-Willcox Co., Inc.

Basic Psychological Needs							
Need to...	√	**Need to...**	√	**Need to...**	√	**Need to...**	√
achieve		belong		create		have status	
be alone		be responsible		earn a living		have structure	
be balanced		be social		ease boredom		have variety	
be competent		be useful		follow		influence	
be dependent		be with people		gain approval		lead	
be expressive		build		gain power		learn, grow	
be free		compete		have an identity		participate	
be independent		contribute		have security		serve	
be in unity		cooperate		have stability		work hard	

Figure 5.5 Use this chart to help you identify your psychological needs. *Which of these needs are already being met in your life?*

prohibitive words of advice. **Prescriptive advice** encourages you toward a certain decision or life path. **Prohibitive messages** or advice warn against a certain decision or life path. Look at the pieces of advice in **Figure 5.6** and determine whether they are prescriptive or prohibitive messages.

Think about the positive messages your family has conveyed to you and make a note of these messages. Next, record the negative messages you have received from your family. Negative messages can either motivate you to work harder or discourage you. For example, consider the negative message "you cannot afford to go to college." Hearing this may inspire you to find a way to finance your college *aspirations* (hopes; dreams) or it may discourage you from trying. Although family plays an important role, you are the only person who can decide what to do with their input.

Prescriptive or Prohibitive Messages

- Spending too much time looking at your computer or phone screen will strain your eyes.
- Leading an active lifestyle is good for your body and mind.
- A college degree does more than prepare you for a career.
- If you wait until the last minute to study, you will do poorly on the test.
- Make sure to get enough sleep each night.
- Choose your friends wisely.

Figure 5.6 Each of these pieces of advice is either prescriptive or prohibitive. *Determine whether each piece of advice is a prescriptive or prohibitive message.*

Copyright Goodheart-Willcox Co., Inc.

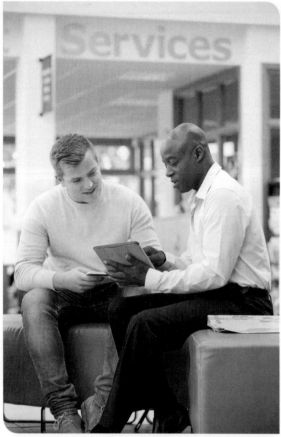

Monkey Business Images/Shutterstock.com

Figure 5.7 A teacher might become a mentor if you admire his personal values and his passion for the subject he teaches. *Is there anyone in your life that you consider a mentor? If so, what do you think attracted you to this person? If no, identify a person that could potentially become a mentor.*

Friends and Mentors

Friends and mentors are people you choose to have in your life. A **mentor** is an experienced person who provides support, guidance, and counsel to a less-experienced person. You may not consciously choose your friends and mentors. It may even be hard to trace their entrance into your life, but something attracted you to them. Friends and mentors have characteristics you admire and value (**Figure 5.7**). Because they are self-selected, reflecting on friends and mentors can give you valuable insight into your own personal characteristics and values.

Take a few minutes to write the names of your friends and mentors. Your friends may fall into different categories. These may include school friends, childhood friends, family friends, work friends, or friends from other experiences. Older adult friends, relatives, employers, and coworkers might be mentors. Of course, friends and other peers can also be mentors.

Perhaps someone in your life serves as an *official mentor*. This person guides you, models appropriate behaviors or attitudes, and takes an active role in your development. More likely, you have a number of people in your life who serve as unofficial mentors. An *unofficial mentor* serves as a model who is worthy of imitation, even though the person may not know it. For some reason you are drawn to them. Why? Only you can answer that question.

Reading Recall

1. Define *personal values*.
2. What are *psychological needs*?
3. Differentiate between *direct messages* and *indirect messages*.
4. What is a *mentor*? Name two possible sources of mentors.

Identifying Your Assets and Skills

Your **assets** are all the useful, valuable resources you possess that you can offer to others in exchange for something you want. Assets can be tangible or intangible. **Tangible assets** are physical, material possessions,

Copyright Goodheart-Willcox Co., Inc.

such as money, property, digital devices, vehicles, or furniture. **Intangible assets** are not physical in nature. Examples of intangible assets may include your knowledge, talents, and skills (**Figure 5.8**).

Assets are something you collect. Although you may learn more efficient and effective means of collecting assets, assets are generally not learned. An exception to this is your skills. These are all of the abilities you have learned over time, through experiences, practice, or instruction.

Most people possess hundreds of skills. Some of these are basic skills people have in common. Others are skills that are unique to you. To be successful in today's workplace, people are expected to have basic skills. These include skills in the areas of technology, communication, decision making, problem solving, conflict resolution, leadership, and time management. Because skill analysis often focuses on career skills, many people do not easily identify their full skill *repertoire* (collection). If they do, they may be modest in promoting them.

As you read the following sections, think about your skills in each of these areas. After you finish reading, take a few minutes to think about your other unique skills. Then, make a list of all of your assets and skills. Do not limit your list. Brainstorm and make the list as long as possible. Knowing what assets and skills you currently possess will help you identify assets you want to collect or skills you need or want to develop.

©iStock.com/Tomwang112

Figure 5.8 Each person has a unique collection of knowledge, talents, and skills. *What are some of your intangible assets?*

Copyright Goodheart-Willcox Co., Inc.

Technology Skills

There is clear and widespread agreement that technology skills are important in the workforce and daily living. People are expected to have basic technology literacy skills, such as sending e-mails or text messages, conducting an Internet search, or using social media. Technology is changing at an incredible speed, however. What it means to be technologically literate will continue to change over your lifetime.

Identify the technology skills you currently possess that go beyond the basic skills. For example, you might excel at using a specific software program, creating a graphic slide presentation, writing code, or designing a website. These are the skills that can set you apart from others.

Communication Skills

Communicating with others is an essential skill in business, families, friendships, and virtually any relationship. In fact, many employer surveys list communication skills as the top skill employers are looking for in employees (**Figure 5.9**). Think about your verbal, nonverbal, written, and electronic communication skills. Rate your ability by giving yourself a score of 1 to 10 for each skill, with 1 being the weakest and 10 being the strongest. Then, write a narrative summary of both your strongest and weakest communication skills. Do they vary by situation? Think of situations or experiences that could help you improve your weaker communication skills.

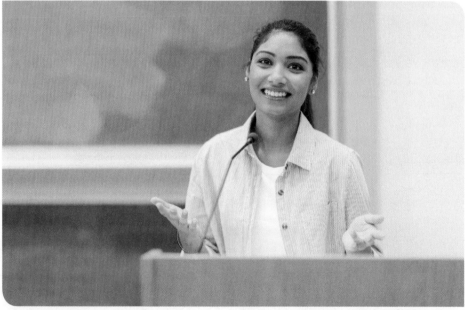

michaeljung/Shutterstock.com

Figure 5.9 Public speaking is a verbal communication skill with which many people struggle. You can practice this skill by giving presentations in class or by joining the speech or debate teams. *Do your public speaking skills need work?*

Copyright Goodheart-Willcox Co., Inc.

Decision-Making Skills

Decision making is the thought process of selecting a choice from the available options. Everyone has their own style of making decisions. Some people are thoughtful and thorough in evaluating their possibilities. Others are quick and decisive. Individual style in decision making is perfectly fine, but people tend to lean toward either more rational or emotional decision making. Although either type of decision-making style can get you to an end result, balance between the two is necessary for the most effective decision making.

Think about one of the best or perhaps the most difficult decisions you have ever made. Are you satisfied with your decision or did you second guess it later? Did you use a process to make the decision? If so, was that process *haphazard* (random; not following a set method) or did you conduct a detailed analysis, gathering facts and data before making your decision? Was your decision a rational choice or more of an emotional feeling that the choice "just felt right"?

Answering these questions can give you more insight into how you make decisions. If you are still unsure, review the steps of the decision-making process in **Figure 5.10**. Then, ask your family, friends, teachers, or other mentors to offer their insight about your decision-making abilities.

The Decision-Making Process

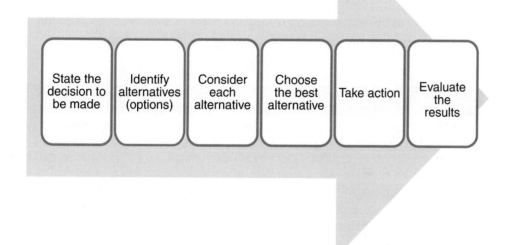

State the decision to be made → Identify alternatives (options) → Consider each alternative → Choose the best alternative → Take action → Evaluate the results

Figure 5.10 Following the steps in the decision-making process can help you make satisfying, rational decisions. *When making a decision, do you follow all of these steps? How can this process help you make better decisions?*

Copyright Goodheart-Willcox Co., Inc.

Problem-Solving Skills

As you may recall, the problem-solving process includes defining and analyzing the problem, setting and implementing goals, and monitoring and evaluating the plan. Problem solving is not always easy. Some people are either naturally better at solving problems or have learned and practiced effective problem-solving skills.

Think about the last challenging problem you faced. How did you approach solving the problem? Did you try to avoid the problem or hope someone else would solve it? Did you utilize the S.M.A.R.T. plan or did you "wing it" and hope for the best? Be honest with yourself when reflecting on and evaluating your problem-solving skills. Remember, through practice you can learn effective problem-solving skills.

Conflict Resolution Skills

Review the steps in the constructive conflict management process in Chapter 3. Following these steps helps people deal with their differences in a constructive way. Being able to handle conflicts constructively and ethically is an important skill to possess at home, at school, and in the workplace.

Throughout life, conflicts will inevitably occur. Avoiding conflict may lead to more issues down the road. Being proactive may be a way to turn a potentially negative situation into a situation with which both parties can live.

Think about how you typically handle conflicts. Do you avoid conflict or face it head on? Do you try to resolve conflicts ethically and treat others fairly and honestly? Read the two conflict resolution scenarios in **Figure 5.11**. How would you respond to these situations? Your responses may give you some insight about your conflict resolution skills or lack thereof. Like with other skills, asking others for their input may also prove helpful.

Conflict Resolution Scenarios

- Imagine you are working on a group project in class and several team members are disagreeing about how to best complete the project. Do you participate in solving the conflict among team members? If so, what would you do? If not, why not?
- Imagine a situation in which you need to reach an agreement with another person on an issue that is important to you. Unfortunately, you disagree on the issue. The other person is bossy, loud, and forceful. How might you go about resolving the conflict? Would you?

Figure 5.11 The scenarios in this chart describe common conflicts. *How would you respond to these conflict resolution scenarios? What do you think your responses say about your conflict resolution skills?*

Copyright Goodheart-Willcox Co., Inc.

Leadership Skills

The term *born leader* refers to someone who has personality characteristics and temperaments that make others want to follow him or her. You may know someone who is a born leader. You may even be a born leader yourself. Even if you are not a born leader, you can learn, practice, and improve your leadership skills.

Most leadership skills fall within two categories: people-oriented leadership and task-oriented leadership. **People-oriented leadership** involves motivating teams by utilizing team members' skills and talents while providing a supportive, accommodating, and responsible environment. **Task-oriented leadership** involves organizing and delegating tasks, guiding and motivating team members, and taking responsibility for completing a task. Both types of leadership skills are valued and needed.

Which leadership skills do you possess? Which skills you would like to develop? Review the list of leadership skills in Figure 3.10 of this text. Then, identify your leadership skills, including those you want to develop.

Time Management Skills

Life constantly involves managing priorities and deciding how to spend the hours in your day to meet your goals. Having good time management skills can make you more effective in your personal, school, and work life. Using time management techniques, such as scheduling, prioritizing, and delegating, can help you be more effective in meeting your goals, honoring your values, reducing stress, and subsequently, enjoying better relationships.

Think about how you would describe your time management skills. Are they an asset or a liability? Do they need a slight improvement or a major overhaul? As you assess your time management skills, consider how you would respond to the questions in **Figure 5.12**. If you are unsure, ask someone to help you assess your time management skills.

Time Management Questions

- How often do you turn homework in on time?
- How often do you feel prepared for an exam? Do you prepare over time or at the last minute?
- Do you plan tasks or are you often surprised by deadlines or responsibilities?
- Do you usually run late or are you often on time?
- When working on a project, how often are you distracted by online conversations or postings?
- How often do you put off responding to phone calls, text messages, or e-mails?
- How often do you feel that you do not have time for those things that are really important to you?
- How often do you end your day thinking that you did not accomplish much?

Figure 5.12 The questions in this chart can help you evaluate how well you manage your time. *How would you respond to these time management questions? How can you use your responses to improve your time management skills?*

Copyright Goodheart-Willcox Co., Inc.

Reading Recall

1. What are *assets*? List the two types of assets and give an example of each.

2. Give an example of a basic technology literacy skill.

3. List two types of decision-making styles. Which style allows for the most effective decision making?

4. How can you learn effective problem-solving skills?

5. Name three areas where conflict resolution skills are needed.

6. Differentiate between *people-oriented leadership* and *task-oriented leadership*.

Recognizing Personal Preferences

Everyone has individual preferences, aptitudes, and abilities. This is what makes people unique and interesting. Reflecting on, acknowledging, and understanding your personal preferences is important to finding meaningful and fulfilling work.

Although types and categories of preferences might be endless, those that strongly relate to career choices are health, physical ability, and activity level preferences. Task preferences are also important when considering career choices.

Health, Physical Ability, and Activity Level Preferences

"How much physical activity do you favor?" is not just a question of physical ability, but also a question of preference. In other words, sometimes physical ability and general health play a part, but more often than not your activity level preference overrides your ability (**Figure 5.13**). Can you change your physical ability and activity level preferences? For many people, the answer is yes. Increased physical activity and training can prepare you for a job that is more physically demanding than your current capabilities allow. The perception of health and activity can also play a part.

As you complete your self-assessment, think about your general health, physical abilities, and activity level preferences. How healthy are you? What are your physical abilities? What level of activity do you prefer? How does your general health and physical ability play a part in your activity level preferences? What conclusions can you draw about your physical ability and activity level preferences?

Task Preferences

What motivates you to complete a task? Your answer probably changes depending on the situation. You may be highly motivated in some situations and with some tasks and hardly ever motivated to do

Copyright Goodheart-Willcox Co., Inc.

©iStock.com/monkeybusinessimages

Figure 5.13 An interest in playing sports may positively affect your activity level preference. *How could you change your activity level preference?*

other tasks no matter what the situation. Reflecting on the tasks you want to pursue and involve yourself in can give you interesting data about yourself.

Think of a task you are usually motivated to do no matter what the situation. Many times this is an activity that brings you pleasure. If not, it may be a task that will reap pleasurable rewards, such as allowing you more time to pursue a hobby or spend with friends. Once you identify a task you are highly motivated to pursue, answer the questions in **Figure 5.14**.

Different people are drawn to different types of tasks and activities. The type of task or activity a person is drawn to is based on what the person values. Values form over time and are not constant. Determining what attracts and motivates you to certain types of tasks will help you to understand the type of values on which you base your beliefs, actions, and behaviors. In the following sections, you will have the opportunity to reflect and assess your personal and work values.

Reading Recall

1. Can a person change his or her physical ability and activity level preferences?
2. What determines the types of tasks or activities that a person might be drawn toward?

Copyright Goodheart-Willcox Co., Inc.

Figure 5.14 Answering the questions in this chart will help you evaluate your task preferences. *What can you learn about your task preferences by reviewing your answers to these questions?*

Evaluating Task Preferences
• What draws you to this task or activity?
• Do you enjoy the process of the task or the activity itself?
• Are you motivated by the end result more than the process of doing the task or activity?
• Will completing the task or activity result in a by-product that motivates you?
• Are there other similar tasks or activities you enjoy? What do the tasks or activities have in common?
• Does the task or activity involve working independently, with a few people, or with many people?
• Does the task or activity involve organizational skills or pure chance?
• Does the task or activity involve collaboration, leadership, or dependency on others to complete their tasks?

Reflecting on Life Satisfaction

Now that you have identified your values, needs, and skills, you need to figure out your wants and what will bring you the most satisfaction in life. Figuring out what your wants specifically look like will greatly improve your odds of achieving these wants in your life.

Take some time to dream about your future. This is not an exercise to complete in a few minutes. For many people, physical activities, such as walking, running, or biking, offer solitude and time to contemplate their dreams. For others, spending time with a close friend or relative sharing their dreams can help them identify what they desire in their future. Use the prompts in **Figure 5.15** to get your ideas flowing.

When you are finished dreaming, make a list of the things you hope will be a part of your future. This can include events, activities, people, values, experiences, or any number of items.

Personal Essentials

Personal essentials are the values, needs, and wants that are critical to you. These are the things you are not willing to sacrifice. To identify your personal essentials, first think about your self-assessment responses. Are there certain items or thoughts that appear frequently? Then, complete the following sentence: To feel happy and successful, I must have ___ (identify absolutely essential values, goals, needs, people, experiences, etc.) in my personal life and career.

Life Goals

Dreams rely on chance, whereas goals take determined effort. Life dreams, however, can become life goals. So how do you change your

Expert Insight

"They who dream by day are cognizant of many things which escape those who dream only by night."

Edgar Allan Poe, author

Copyright Goodheart-Willcox Co., Inc.

Envisioning the Future

- Where would you like to live?
- What type of lifestyle would you like to have?
- What would you like your future family and friendship circle to look like?
- What type of work will you be doing?
- What will be your hobbies?
- What would you like to accomplish?
- What would you like to be known for?
- What problems would you like to solve?

Figure 5.15 Spending time contemplating and dreaming about your future can help you identify what you desire in your future. *How much time do you spend thinking about your future?*

dreams into feasible goals? Begin by reviewing your list of dreams. Are some more important to you than others? Do any conflict with each other? Are some of your life dreams most appropriate for a certain stage of life? Rank in order the top three most important dreams in your life. Remember, to become a goal, your dream

- should be important to you personally;
- has to be feasible and reasonable;
- has to be clearly defined;
- needs a specific plan of action; and
- has to be something you have a reasonable chance of achieving.

Reading Recall

1. What are *personal essentials*?
2. What is the difference between life dreams and life goals?

Developing Your Brand

Everyone has positive characteristics, interests, skills, and motivations that contribute to their own unique personal brand (**Figure 5.16**). Thoughtfully and honestly reflect on your personal brand. Then, think about which characteristics you would like or need to develop. Which might you strive to change? Are you often late for events? Do you change plans, leaving others in the lurch if something better comes along? No one is perfect nor should you want to be, but by highlighting features that might need further refining, your personal brand becomes stronger and more authentic.

Developing your brand does not mean creating something that you are not. Instead, it means celebrating your uniqueness and positively marketing that brand. Personal brands should not be faked, but instead should be genuine and accurate. Just like in the marketing world, an inauthentic or falsely represented brand will eventually be discovered.

Copyright Goodheart-Willcox Co., Inc.

Monkey Business Images/Shutterstock.com

Figure 5.16 Your personal brand is made up of all of your interests, skills, characteristics, personal qualities, and motivations. *Describe your personal brand.*

Once you are clear on who you are, the next step is being able to communicate that to others. Doing so will give you confidence as you gain appreciation for your distinctive brand. Practice articulating your brand to others or alone in front of a mirror. Tell your brand story in a concise manner. Confidently say your name, your recent history and goals, and your unique interests, skills, and experiences. Keep practicing until you feel comfortable telling your own brand story.

As you practice communicating your personal brand, you may feel awkward talking about yourself at first. Remember not to be too modest or *self-deprecating* (undervaluing oneself). You can communicate your brand with a sense of humor, but do not make fun of yourself or put yourself down. Over time and with practice, you will feel less awkward. When you feel more comfortable, others will be, too.

Once you have identified your personal brand, the next step is to market it. The more consistent you are in being "you," the more powerful and desirable your personal brand becomes to others. Think about your communications with family, friends, teachers, and others in your daily life. Do these communications reflect your personal brand? Make sure your personal appearance also matches the image you want to project. Be vigilant in ensuring your online identity reinforces your brand.

Lastly, know that your personal brand does not stay the same. As you change and mature, develop new interests and motivations, learn new skills, and seek out new experiences, your brand will develop along with you. Your brand is your story, so enjoy it, celebrate it, and market it.

Reading Recall

1. What should a personal brand *not* represent?
2. What should your personal brand communicate?
3. What does *self-deprecation* mean?
4. What should be the next step after establishing a personal brand?

Copyright Goodheart-Willcox Co., Inc.

Pathway to Success

My Online Identity Versus My Brand

Your online reputation and personal brand is made up of what people can find about you when they put your name into a search. Your brand is reflected by any pictures, comments, blogs, or anything else you post. An awful lot of damage can be done in just a short time by behaving in an inappropriate manner online. This is why it is so important to think about what you want to communicate to others online. Consider that photos you post or words you say will still be accessible to others years from now.

Did you know that it is becoming more common for potential employers to look up your social media pages, as well as using search engines to see what you have posted? Some people have lost their jobs as a result of posting inappropriate pictures or comments on social media.

Just like establishing your personal brand, you need to establish and monitor your online identity to make sure you are presenting an appropriate image. Following are tips to help you boost and protect your online reputation:

- Set up your own reputation. Do not let someone else post pictures or comments about you without first obtaining your permission. Monitor to ensure that others are following this request. If you find information online that you have not approved, ask to have it removed.

- Think before you post something online. How would this affect your personal brand and message you want to convey?

- Use a search engine and look up your name every six months or so. Check to see what others might find when they look for you. Make sure there is more good information than bad information about you.

- Secure your personal information. Change passwords regularly to prevent hacking. Do not reveal full birth dates, addresses, or other personal information online.

- Look into free tools online that send notifications to you when there is a mention of your name online.

Looking into My Brand Online

Using the information above, search your name and any screen names that you have for what information is showing up online about you. Identify any information, pictures, or posts that need to be deleted. Create a list of what needs to be deleted by you and what needs to be deleted by others.

With a partner, practice how to ask someone politely to remove information that you do not want online. Then, contact the people who

have posted this information and ask them to remove it. After finishing this exercise, look at how much information was in cyberspace about you. How much was positive and how much was negative? What other steps can you take to ensure that your online identity showcases the personal brand you wish to project?

Copyright Goodheart-Willcox Co., Inc.

Summary

- Your personal brand is what you are known for—it is how people describe or know you.
- *Self-assessment* is a lifetime process that helps you reflect and identify your personal values, needs, resources, temperament or personality, skills, abilities, and dreams. In addition to your own reflections, you can also ask others for input or use assessment tests to help you get to know yourself. Self-assessment can be enlightening and enriching as you discover your personal brand.
- Understanding the experiences you are proud of and the characteristics of your personality and attitudes will help you identify your unique traits.
- Your *personal values* are the beliefs you hold important. They are guideposts that motivate you. They are used to measure the success of your experiences. The people you respect most in this world influence your values and needs formation.

- Assets are collected and skills are learned. Technology, communication, decision-making, problem-solving, conflict resolution, and time management skills are an important part of your skill set.
- Reflecting on, acknowledging, and understanding your personal preferences is important to finding meaningful and fulfilling work. Preferences that strongly relate to career choices are health, physical ability, and activity level preferences, along with preferable types of tasks.
- Understanding and developing your personal brand pays off in the long run as you consciously make choices that take you further away from or closer to your dreams.

College and Career Portfolio

Portfolio Checklist

Now that you know the purpose of and how you will organize your portfolio, consider what items you want to include. Having a checklist of components to include in your portfolio can help keep you organized. Your instructor may provide you with or guide you in developing a checklist. Make sure to create a checklist that works best for you and for the purpose of your portfolio.

After you create your checklist, identify *where* you will acquire these items. Also determine *how* you will acquire them and *what resources* you will need. Identify any items on your checklist which you will need outside help to acquire. Identifying these items early

will enable you to obtain them in a timely manner.

Complete the following steps to create your portfolio checklist:
1. Compile a checklist of items to include in your portfolio. If you need guidance, talk to your teacher or to a college or career counselor.
2. Determine how you will acquire the items on your checklist. Make note of any outside help you may need.
3. Save your checklist to an easy-to-access location in your e-Portfolio. Also, print a copy for easy reference.

Copyright Goodheart-Willcox Co., Inc.

Review and Reflect 📲

1. What is a *brand*? How do corporate and personal brands differ?
2. List three typical types of assessment tests.
3. How might you benefit from making a list of your personal accomplishments?
4. Identify the difference between a *value* and a *need*. Give an example of each.
5. Give an example of a psychological need that is important for you to feel satisfied.
6. Identify two possible influences on the formation of values and needs.
7. Differentiate between *prescriptive advice* and *prohibitive messages*.
8. Name four areas in which people are expected to have basic skills to be successful in today's workplace.
9. Give an example of a task you are highly motivated to pursue.
10. Name five factors that a dream should have to become an achievable goal.
11. What does developing your brand mean?
12. Once established, should a personal brand remain the same? Why or why not?

Vocabulary Activities

13. **Key terms**   In teams, play *picture charades* to identify each of the following terms. Write the terms on separate slips of paper and put the slips into a basket. Choose a team member to be the *sketcher*. The sketcher pulls a term from the basket and creates quick drawings or graphics to represent the term until the team guesses the term. Rotate turns as sketcher until the team identifies all terms.

assets	prescriptive advice
direct messages	prohibitive
indirect messages	messages
intangible assets	psychological needs
key accomplishments	self-assessment
mentor	tangible assets
people-oriented	task-oriented
leadership	leadership
personal essentials	

14. **Academic terms**   With a partner, create a T-chart. In the left column of the chart, write each of the following vocabulary terms. In the right column, write a *synonym* (a word that has the same or similar meaning) for each term. Discuss your synonyms with the class.

aspirations	persona
commendation	repertoire
haphazard	self-deprecating

Self-Assessment Quiz 📲

Complete the self-assessment quiz online to help you practice and expand your knowledge and skills.

Critical Thinking

15. **Evaluate**   Using your list of accomplishments that you completed from page 118, evaluate which ones you should include in your résumé. Explain why you chose these accomplishments. You will be using this information later to help you write your résumé.
16. **Make inferences**   Your family is a powerful motivator when it comes to your values and beliefs. Look at the values your parents have taught you. Do you agree with them or do you have a different opinion about a subject? Think about your future. Do you believe that your beliefs and values will change as you get older? Why or why not?
17. **Compare and contrast**   Compare and contrast *direct messages* and *indirect messages*. How are they similar and how are they different?
18. **Determine**   How do you determine that someone is a mentor or an unofficial mentor? Identify one of each type of mentor and explain why he or she fits into that category.
19. **Identify**   Identify people or places where you can find mentors. Make a list of people who you believe could be a mentor in your life.
20. **Analyze**   In small groups, identify a decision that teens make on a regular basis (dating, underage drinking, drugs, etc.). Use the decision-making process to analyze an answer

to the decision in the scenario. Present your scenario and the steps in the decision-making process that you used to arrive at a conclusion of what to do.

21. **Draw conclusions** There are five factors that dreams need to have to become life goals. Look at your list of dreams and choose two. Using the five factors, identify if those dreams can become a life goal. Why or why not?

22. **Cause and effect** Look at your online identity reflected on your social media sites. Is this the identity that you would like a future employer to see? Why or why not? If not, what can you do to change your online identity to make it portray the image that you have of yourself in your mind? If it is, what are some things that might have the potential to change your online identity to a negative perception?

Core Skills

23. **Research** Research online skills assessment tests. Are they free, do they cost, or does your district have a skills assessment that you can take? Choose one of the tests to complete. Based on the results of your skills assessment, what career is a good fit for you? Research what other careers use similar skills.

24. **Writing and speaking** Make a list of people you know that would give you a good reference for a job. Narrow your list to five people. Ask each person if he or she would be willing to be one of your references. You will be using this list later as you write your résumé.

25. **Writing** Create a list of your basic skills that can be transferred to any job. Then, add your unique skills. You will be using this list later to help you write your résumé.

26. **Writing and speaking** With a partner, write a script to use when calling a business to find out if they have any job openings. Present your script to the class and have them evaluate and critique your communication skills. What do you need to change before actually calling a local business to find out about openings?

27. **Speaking** Create several ethical scenarios to share with your class. Base your scenarios on decisions that you or people around you have made. Have your classmates act out the scenarios and what they would do. Analyze how many in the class agree and how many disagree with the outcome presented in the scenario.

28. **Technology** Create an electronic presentation on leadership skills. Include characteristics and examples of people-oriented and task-oriented leaders. Identify opportunities at school or in the community that are available for students to develop their leadership skills. Share your presentations with the class.

29. **Technology and math** Imagine you have been hired to create a new app that will revolutionize time management. In a small group, create a time management tool/app. Explain what it will do, how it will look, who you will sell it to, and what the cost will be. When figuring the cost, take into account the number of hours for a programmer to write the code for your app and a designer to create the look of your app. Also consider the cost to market your app to the general public.

30. **Writing and speaking** Using the app you created in number 29, develop an ad that you would place on TV, the Internet, or in a magazine to sell your app. Present your ad to the class. After your presentation, have classmates vote on whether or not they would buy your app.

31. **Writing** Everyone has preferences on what they like to do. Preferences related to your future career include health, physical ability, and activity level. Write a one-page essay detailing your preferences for your health, physical ability, and activity level. Explain what you want in your future career. You can also discuss things that you do not want.

32. **Writing, technology, and speaking** Different corporations have a brand that everyone recognizes as theirs. Create your own brand that speaks about your personality and talents.

Copyright Goodheart-Willcox Co., Inc.

Once you have a rough draft of what your brand would look like, use the computer and different software programs to create and print your brand. Present to the class explaining why this brand represents you.

33. **CTE career readiness practice** As a person who navigates life by firmly adhering to a strong code of ethics, you find yourself facing an ethical dilemma. A friend from school and work confides in you about her struggle with an eating disorder and makes you promise not to tell anyone. You have noticed over a period of time that your friend's productivity at work is declining, and she has stopped participating in class. You are concerned about her health and life. You wonder if you should talk with your friend's parents or the school counselor about your observations about her apparent symptoms of this condition. What should you do? What is the best way to practice integrity in this situation? What decision is best for your friend and those she interacts with daily?

Lend a Hand

Volunteering Based on Skills

Volunteering is a great way to enhance your current skills or gain new skills as you develop your personal brand. Thinking about what skills you already have or what skills you would like to possess can help you determine what types of service opportunities to explore. For example, if you want to improve your communication skills, consider a service project that includes interacting with the public or fellow volunteers. If you want to improve your writing, try to find a position where you can practice your writing skills, such as writing pet profiles for an animal shelter's website.

Not only can you learn job skills while volunteering, but you can also use the experience to work on your social skills. For some people, social interactions come easily. For others, social skills need to be practiced and improved just like any other skill. Volunteering in your community is a great way to learn how to interact effectively with others.

To explore how volunteering can help you improve your skills or gain new ones, complete the following:

1. Create a skills inventory or a list of your abilities. Think about any skills you have that might help define your personal brand. If you need help thinking of skills, ask your teacher or guidance counselor to recommend a skills inventory assessment you can take. You may also find a skills inventory assessment online that you can complete, but be sure the website is a reliable source.

2. With a partner, review your skills inventories. Help your partner think of skills he or she might have excluded from the list. Discuss and list possible volunteer positions that could help you improve the skills you have or gain new skills.

3. Using your list of volunteer positions, conduct an Internet search to locate service opportunities in your area.

Copyright Goodheart-Willcox Co., Inc.

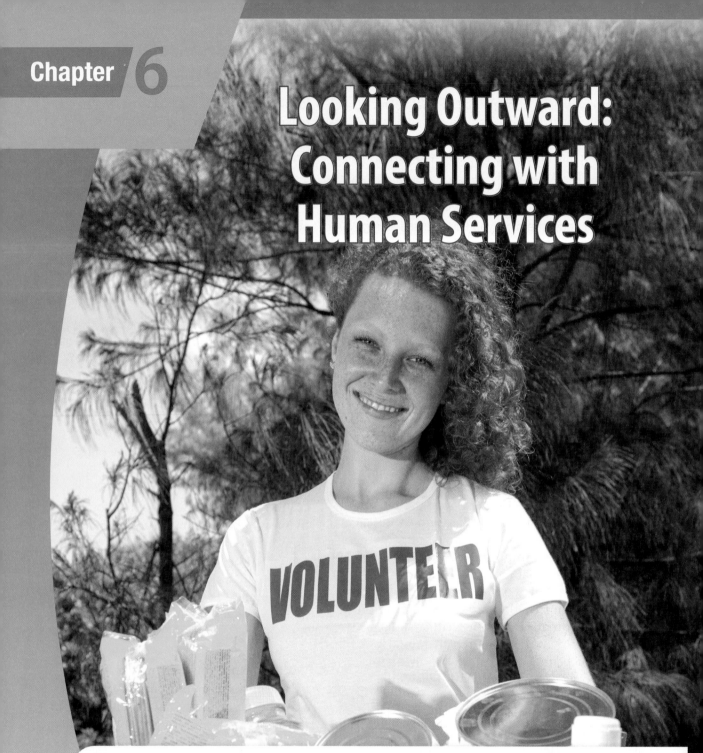

Chapter 6

Looking Outward: Connecting with Human Services

While studying, look for the activity icon  **to**

- **practice** key and academic terms with e-flash cards and matching activities;
- **assess** what you learn by completing self-assessment quizzes; and
- **reinforce** what you learn by mapping concepts and completing review and reflect questions.

www.g-wlearning.com/humanservices/

mangostock/shutterstock.com

Learning Outcomes

After studying this chapter, you will be able to

- **describe** various ways to gain firsthand knowledge about a career in human services;
- **use** the *Occupational Outlook Handbook* to investigate potential human services careers that interest you;
- **determine** ways to maximize your high school experience as you plan for your future;
- **identify** points to consider when evaluating possible higher education options; and
- **recognize** the importance of establishing goals and identifying steps to take to achieve them when developing a career plan.

Reading Strategies

Before reading, arrange to interview someone who works in a human services career you find interesting. Create a list of questions you would like to ask during the interview. As you are reading, take notes about items in the chapter that you would like to discuss with the person. After reading, look at your list of questions again and write any new questions you would like the person to answer based on what you learned.

Mapping Concepts

Create a KWL chart to organize what you already *know* (K), what you *want* (W) to know, and what you *learn* (L) as you read this chapter.

K What you already Know	W What you Want to know	L What you Learn

Key Terms

advanced placement courses
career goal
dual credit courses
higher education
informational interview

internship
job shadowing
program of study
volunteering

Academic Terms

attrition
erroneous
mean
median

In the previous chapter, you spent considerable time and effort looking inward, getting to know yourself better, and identifying your personal brand. In this chapter, the focus will be outward. You will be using your self-assessment as a basis for exploring human services careers that might best suit you based on your individual strengths and interests.

By carefully researching human services careers, you will be able to learn more about career realities, desired skills, and how to prepare for the job market. This information will enable you to make informed decisions about your future.

Today's workplace is highly competitive, which is why it is so important to begin planning for your future now while you are still in high school. This is a good time to determine what courses you will need to achieve your educational and career goals. If postsecondary education is part of your plan, then some of your time will involve researching schools to find the one that best fits your needs. Being involved in extended learning opportunities, such as joining student or professional organizations, will help you maximize your high school experience while sharpening your skills. Investing time in developing a career plan can help set you on the right path for future success.

Researching Human Services Careers

Imagine you have chosen early childhood education as a career area you think you want to pursue. You love children, their enthusiasm for learning, and the types of issues and questions educators often face. Loving children, however, does not necessarily mean that you will love working in this career field.

To identify your work passion, you must first discover if you truly enjoy doing the work. Unfortunately, many people make *erroneous* (incorrect; wrong) assumptions without conducting a thorough study of a career field. What seems like a good match, may not be a match at all. By conducting some background research, you will be able to determine whether a career field or occupation is a fit for or matches your interests. You will be better able to decide whether you are simply interested in a career field or you actually want to perform the job.

There are a number of ways to explore and investigate potential human services career areas. For example, reading this textbook is a good place to start. In later chapters, you will learn about many human services careers. The Internet also offers many valid and reliable resources for researching careers. You can find information about careers in the school career center, at the local library, from news sources, and in electronic databases. One of the best ways to learn about a certain career is to gain firsthand knowledge. Another way is to use the US Department of Labor's *Occupational Outlook Handbook* (OOH)—available in print or online formats.

Expert Insight

"Far and away the best prize that life offers is the chance to work hard at work worth doing."

Theodore Roosevelt, former US president

Copyright Goodheart-Willcox Co., Inc.

Case Study | *The End Goal*

Clemisha had always loved athletics. Volleyball, cheerleading, soccer, snow and wake boarding—she thrived on the challenge of learning and mastering. In high school, she settled in on one sport, soccer, and devoted much of her time to her school, club, and recreational teams.

By the time Clemisha reached her junior year of high school, she not only was playing year-round, but also coaching for a summer day camp for children. Everything changed this year, her senior year, when she injured her knee and broke her ankle. Clemisha required knee surgery and then physical therapy to repair the damage. It was a tough time, but Clemisha eventually recovered. After months of physical therapy, she was ready to play soccer again.

More and more, Clemisha's family and friends ask her what she plans to do after high school. The recurring question, "What would you like to be when you grow up?" seems daunting. She has no idea, but she does know that she

- is athletic and physically coordinated;
- has a positive attitude and a competitive spirit;
- likes most sports and athletic activities, especially soccer;
- likes being on a team and is often in a leadership position;
- has good time management skills;
- enjoys sharing what she knows with others; and
- appreciates, and is a bit fascinated by, the healing process of physical therapy, but even more so by the emotional therapy that accompanies physical recovery.

Clemisha's career counselor suggests looking into both healthcare and human services careers. She knows what healthcare careers might include, but what about human services careers?

Lopolo/Shutterstock.com

For Discussion

1. Do the personal attributes that Clemisha listed have anything in common? If so, what is the commonality between them?
2. How might Clemisha feel when her family and friends keep asking about her future plans? How could she use this question as a motivator?

Gaining Firsthand Knowledge

Getting hands-on experience in a career field of interest enables you to get a close-up look into what a person's job involves. Take advantage of opportunities to gain firsthand knowledge about careers. You can begin by scheduling short-term job shadowing experiences. **Job shadowing** is a short observation consisting of a few hours or a day. Although the observation is short, this opportunity can give you valuable insight into the daily tasks and activities of the job. You can also gain valuable insight into whether the job or career is of interest to you.

Copyright Goodheart-Willcox Co., Inc.

Job shadowing is a very short-term investment of time and energy. Sometimes a teacher or counselor can help you set up a job shadowing opportunity. You can also set up a job shadowing experience on your own. As long as safety, security, or job schedules are not an issue, most people are open to the idea of having a student shadow them for a few hours or a day.

Volunteer experiences are another way to gain firsthand knowledge about careers. **Volunteering** for an organization that is related to your career interests is valuable in several ways. First, volunteering provides an important free service for the organization. Second, volunteer opportunities give you experience to include on your résumé. Third, you can learn significant information about a career field by participating in the work. Finally, you can make key contacts with professionals in your field of interest.

Arranging an internship is another way you can learn firsthand about a career. An **internship** is similar to employment, but generally more informal with an emphasis placed on learning over performance. When an internship relationship is established, a company or organization agrees to provide students with an opportunity to gain exposure to an occupational area (**Figure 6.1**).

Internship positions differ from regular jobs in that they often offer a more in-depth look at management decision making and practices. For example, an internship in a child care center might provide an opportunity for a student to sit in on a budgeting session. As a child

Pressmaster/Shutterstock.com

Figure 6.1 An internship is a mutually beneficial arrangement for both the organization and the student. *What types of internships interest you?*

Copyright Goodheart-Willcox Co., Inc.

care worker, this opportunity may not be given. Internships often give students opportunities to see daily activities they would not have the opportunity to as a regular employee.

Conducting an **informational interview** is another great way to meet professionals and explore career options. By setting up an interview, you have the opportunity to talk with some of the key professionals in your field of interest. By asking questions, you can gain tremendous knowledge about the industry, career options, and how to enter the field. You can also find out about opportunities for advancement.

When conducting an informational interview, come prepared and dress appropriately. Bring a notepad and pen for note-taking and a list of questions to ask during the interview. For example, you might want to ask questions similar to the ones in **Figure 6.2**. Do not be discouraged if a professional cannot schedule time for an interview. Instead, try another person. When you do an informational interview, always leave a good impression. Write a thank-you note. You never know when you will see this person again.

Using the *Occupational Outlook Handbook* (OOH)

Using the *Occupational Outlook Handbook* (OOH) is an effective way to find out about careers. The OOH identifies the fastest growing occupations, as well as those with the most projected job openings. The OOH also includes information on the typical job duties and responsibilities, educational requirements, salary and wages, projected job outlook, and typical working environment for occupations (**Figure 6.3**). The US Department of Labor updates the OOH every two years. Taking time to study this information will give you a good idea whether a career field or specific occupation is right for you.

Job Duties and Responsibilities

Today, there is no reason to be surprised by the typical job duties and responsibilities of any occupation. Career and industry descriptions

Sample Informational Interview Questions
• How would you describe your typical day?
• What do you like (and dislike) about your job?
• What are some challenges of the job?
• How would you describe the work environment?
• How did you get into this field?
• What are the opportunities for career advancement?
• What advice do you have for me as a student?

Figure 6.2 Asking questions such as these during an informational interview is a great way to gain insight into a career field that might interest you. *What are some other questions that you might ask during an informational interview?*

Copyright Goodheart-Willcox Co., Inc.

Figure 6.3 The OOH is updated every two years and includes information on the typical job duties and responsibilities, educational requirements, salary and wages, projected job outlook, and typical working environment for occupations. *What careers would you like to explore on OOH?*

US Department of Labor

abound. Through the OOH, you can gain valuable knowledge about typical daily tasks and duties. You can find out about the skills and abilities you need for an occupation or industry. You can also learn about similar occupations with comparable job duties.

Do not let yourself be surprised about job duties and responsibilities. Remember, knowledge is power. Knowing about job duties and responsibilities will help you decide whether or not this is the kind of work you will enjoy doing every day.

Educational Requirements

Understanding the educational requirements of a given industry or career field is essential to making a career choice that is right for you. Only you know your educational needs, interests, and goals. What you need to figure out is how well your needs, interests, and goals match up with the requirements of a career or industry.

Today, many careers require higher education. **Higher education** refers to instruction and training that occurs postsecondary or after high school (**Figure 6.4**). The end result of higher education training can be a certificate, licensure, or a degree.

Educational requirements vary by occupation and state. For example, home health aides must complete training and pass a certification exam to work in the field. Cosmetologists are required to complete a training

Copyright Goodheart-Willcox Co., Inc.

Monkey Business Images/Shutterstock.com

Figure 6.4 Higher education is obtained through vocational schools, community colleges, and colleges and universities. *Are you interested in pursuing higher education? If so, which type of school interests you?*

program approved by their state and obtain a license. Massage therapists are also required by law to be licensed. Certification and licensure can be obtained though postsecondary vocational schools and career and technical education programs. Typically, these programs combine academics with job specific training and experience.

A two-year degree (often earned from a community college) is needed for a career in early childhood education, substance abuse counseling, career counseling, culinary arts, or community services. This degree may be appropriate for entering into the profession, but further education may be needed for career advancement. A four-year college or graduate degree is needed for careers in social services, social work, mental health counseling, finance, or teaching. Degrees may be sought in these specific areas or other related areas, such as psychology, human services, communications, or business.

Later in this text, you will read about different career opportunities in the vast field of human services. Within these descriptions, necessary postsecondary training requirements are highlighted. For some human services careers, such as a personal care aide, additional education is not required. Most other human services careers require a certificate, a degree, and/or licensure. High-wage jobs are generally linked to higher education requirements.

Salary and Wages

You may be strongly drawn to a career, but will the pay be that which you desire? Determining adequate pay is a personal decision based on desired lifestyle. Knowing your needs is an important consideration when

Expert Insight

"An investment in knowledge pays the best interest."

Benjamin Franklin, Founding Father of the US

Copyright Goodheart-Willcox Co., Inc.

researching monetary characteristics of a particular career. What level of financial income will meet your needs and help you achieve your goals?

Fortunately, you live in an era where a wide variety of salary and wage information is at your fingertips. For example, on the OOH website, you can view the *median* (middle value in a set of numbers) annual wage for occupations. You can also look up the *mean* (average of a set of numbers) hourly and annual wages for occupations by state.

There is more to consider, however, than just general salary and wage information. Also think about the geographic location and relative cost of living. The same salary in one city may have much less buying power than in another. Online resources exist that can help you use potential wage and salary figures to compare the cost of living in one city versus another. If you are considering relocating, be sure to look into specific costs in the new area, such as housing (**Figure 6.5**).

Be careful to view salary and wages in the right context. In some human services careers, there may be certain times of the year when there is less work to do. These slow times may be balanced by very busy times during the year. This is valuable information to obtain before you pursue a career in a particular field.

Projected Job Outlook

Researching the projected job outlook will help you determine if the occupation you are considering is highly competitive. You will also

CHRISTIAN DE ARAUJO /Shutterstock.com

Figure 6.5 Housing costs vary by location and are an important consideration when determining whether or not to relocate. *What cities do you think have the highest costs of living?*

Copyright Goodheart-Willcox Co., Inc.

be able to find out if the occupation is projected to grow much faster or slower than average or expected to decline over the years. You can also learn about which areas of the country may have better job prospects for certain occupations. You can research the fastest growing occupations or the occupations with the most projected job openings. In some cases, occupations may be growing, but little *attrition* (gradual reduction of workers) is expected. Other occupations may expect a large decrease in available workers.

If you want to get more specific in your research, you might look for the fastest growing occupations by education level. You can find out which occupations currently pay the most and which ones are predicted to pay the most in the future. You can explore industry trends and workforce statistics. You can even find out how many graduates are expected to enter the labor market by major. The more information you have about a particular job market, the more prepared you will be to successfully enter it. Again, knowledge is power.

As you are conducting your research, keep in mind that job markets change. What is considered a hot job market one year may be a very slow market five years later. Many career specialists advise their clients to pursue what they are passionate about and then find a way to make a living doing what they love. Whether or not this is a reasonable option for you depends on your lifestyle needs.

Working Environment

There are endless factors to consider when evaluating work environments (**Figure 6.6**). Human services professionals work in a variety of settings. Each industry and occupation has its own personality and culture. By learning about the work environment, you can discover which industries employ the most workers. You can also check out work schedules and travel demands.

As you evaluate work environments, you may begin to realize that there are certain aspects of a work environment that you love. There may also be other aspects that you do not like. When this occurs, consider looking for a segment of the same industry that would fit better with your needs.

Do not rule out a whole career field or industry based on broad generalizations. For example, imagine you love working with fashion, sales, and people, but do not like the long hours of retail sales. Perhaps a customer service position could offer the factors you love without the hours you dislike. Maybe you are passionate about caring for those with mobility and personal care needs, but do not wish to work in a medical facility. You might consider exploring a home healthcare career. You are still pursuing your passion and interests, but in a setting that is right for you.

Copyright Goodheart-Willcox Co., Inc.

Figure 6.6 When choosing a job, it is important to notice the company's organizational culture. Will you be working alone or with others? Is the working environment quiet or busy with coworkers talking all of the time? *Which type of work environment would you prefer?*

Monkey Business Images/Shutterstock.com

Reading Recall

1. Define *job shadowing*.
2. How does an internship differ from employment?
3. Name two benefits of conducting an informational interview.
4. What is *higher education*? Identify three end results of higher education training.
5. When looking at wage information for careers, what other two factors should you consider?
6. What factors would you consider when evaluating work environments?

Planning for Your Future

Do you already know what you want to do after high school? Maybe you want to begin working right away. Perhaps you want to attend a nearby vocational school or go to a university in another state. Whatever you choose to do, making the most of your remaining time in high school is vital to your future success. Your choices and performance in high school can make a difference in whether you get the job you want or gain admission into the school of your choice.

There is no time like the present to start maximizing your high school experience. Think about what you want to do and choose courses that will help you meet your goals. If you want to attend school after high school, start researching postsecondary options. Consider participating in a student organization. Join a professional association. Develop a career plan to keep track of your goals. Most importantly, stay focused on your plan for the future.

Copyright Goodheart-Willcox Co., Inc.

Choosing Courses

By taking this class, you are learning about career options in human services. If you want to pursue a career in this field, now would be a good time to make an appointment with your guidance counselor. Together, you can review your program of study.

A **program of study** is a guide that steps out the core and career-related courses you need to take to follow your career path. Your program of study meets your individual education and career needs. It includes the courses you will need to take to meet high school graduation requirements and many college entrance requirements. **Figure 6.7** shows a sample program of study. Keep in mind that your program of study will be much more detailed as it outlines everything you need to meet your academic and career goals.

If you plan to attend college, you may want to explore the possibility of including advanced placement or dual credit courses in your program of study, if available. **Advanced placement courses** are more difficult than regular high school courses. They include content similar to beginning-level college classes. At the end of the course, students take a standardized advanced placement test. A passing score on this test gives a student credit at the college level for having completed that college requirement.

With **dual credit courses**, a high school student actually enrolls in a college or university and takes one or more college classes while still attending high school. These may be taught in a high school or at a college or university. Successful completion gives the student college credits that can be transferred to another school after high school graduation. Both options require a high degree of dedication and maturity, but they give students a head start on college.

Researching Schools

Many careers in human services require additional education beyond a high school diploma. If you are interested in a career in human services, now is the time to take action to make a successful postsecondary educational experience a reality. Much like training for competition, getting yourself ready can increase your probability of success in higher education.

Choosing where you will go to school is a major decision, so you will want to allow plenty of time. There are deadlines for various aspects of the process—whether you are attending a vocational school, community college, or university. For example, college applications generally must be submitted in the fall of your senior year.

If you want to continue your education after graduation, begin to explore possible higher education options now. The goal is to find programs that will best match your needs and wants. Consider your

Sample Program of Study

Personal Care Services

	Grade 9	Grade 10	Grade 11	Grade 12
Core courses	• English I • Algebra I • Biology or earth science • World geography	• English II • Geometry • Chemistry • US history	• English III • Algebra II • Physics • World history	• English IV • Statistics or pre-calculus • Anatomy and physiology • Government and economics
Career-related courses	• Principles of human services	• Information technology • Human growth and development • Introduction to cosmetology • Information management	• Personal care services • Cosmetology I	• Practices in personal care services • Cosmetology II • Entrepreneurship • Accounting

Extracurricular Activities and Student Organizations

- Business Professionals of America
- Future Business Leaders of America
- Family, Career and Community Leaders of America
- SkillsUSA
- Student council
- School newspaper

Sample Occupations in This Pathway

- Barber, hairdresser, hairstylist
- Companion, caregiver, personal attendant, personal care aide
- Cosmetologist
- Electrologist
- Embalmer
- Esthetician, skin care specialist
- Exercise physiologist
- Funeral service worker or director
- Home health aide
- Massage therapist
- Nail technician, manicurist, pedicurist
- Personal assistant
- Personal fitness trainer
- Spa attendant

Figure 6.7 This program of study is just a sample. Your program of study should be customized to fit your individual needs and career goals and your local and state graduation requirements. Incorporate available career-preparation and work-based learning experiences into your program of study. *What would your program of study look like?*

expectations for higher education. Even if you are interested in only one vocational school, community college, or university, take time to evaluate others.

Following are some points to consider as you research various schools:

- Size. Would you prefer a large school environment or a smaller campus? There are advantages to both environments (**Figure 6.8**).

Copyright Goodheart-Willcox Co., Inc.

Tomasz Bidermann/Shutterstock.com

Figure 6.8 Large schools offer more options and resources while smaller schools have fewer students per class and more opportunities for involvement with faculty. *Do you have a preference for a large or small school?*

- Reputation. Look at a school's reputation in your area of study, not just its overall reputation. Ask your guidance counselor and teachers which schools have good programs in your interest areas.

- Location. Do you want to attend school in another part of the country or closer to home? Would you prefer a school in a large urban area or a small city or town?

- Admission requirements. Some schools are highly selective and accept a small percentage of applicants. Others accept a broad range of students. Check information from schools that interest you to see if you are likely to meet admission criteria.

- Cost. Tuition costs vary from school to school. Determine how much money you will need and plan accordingly. Explore all of your aid options. Look at what financial aid is available, as well as grants, loans, and scholarships. Consider other options to cut costs, such as living at home while taking classes. Higher education is a major expense, but also a long-term investment. The education you earn after high school improves your chances to make more money and have more job opportunities.

Late in your junior year or by early fall of your senior year, you should narrow your school choices. Continue your research on these schools. Try to visit your top choices. You can arrange for a guided tour through the school's admission's office. Plan to spend some time on your own as well. Ask if you can sit in on a class and eat in a dining hall. Walk around the campus to get a feel for the school's learning and social environment. Talk to a professor. Talk to students. Watch people. Ask questions. Visiting a campus is one of the best ways to assess what a school is like (**Figure 6.9**).

When the time comes to make your final choice, discuss your options with those people whose judgment you value. If you have done your homework, there is an excellent chance that the school you choose will be a good match. Often, there is no one right choice. Every school has advantages and disadvantages.

Remember, too, that you can get an excellent education at almost any school if you choose challenging courses, put effort into your classes, and take advantage of the many opportunities a school offers. Commit to make the most of what is available.

Participating in Student Organizations

Participating in student organizations at the high school level can be an excellent way to broaden your experiences and polish your skills. Commit to being actively involved in any organization you join. This will give you opportunities to practice teamwork, leadership, planning, organization, service, and other key skills. Such skills are linked to success in college, on the job, and in other aspects of adult life. Their importance is underscored by the role they play in the college admittance process. Most postsecondary schools evaluate applicants' involvement in activities and organizations, as well as their academic record and test scores. All of these help determine who will be accepted for enrollment.

Figure 6.9 Some universities will let you spend a couple of days on campus, including a dorm stay. *What factors are most important to you when looking at different colleges and universities?*

©iStock.com/Steve Debenport

Copyright Goodheart-Willcox Co., Inc.

Pathway to Success

The Cost of Higher Education

There are many options when it comes to obtaining higher education. When making a decision about postsecondary options, one major factor that everyone considers is the cost. The reality is that to receive a higher education, you will spend thousands of dollars.

Tuition costs vary from school to school. Vocational schools and community colleges cost less than four-year colleges. In general, state universities have lower tuition for in-state students than private colleges and universities. Students must also consider books and living expenses as part of education costs.

Students often rely on a combination of methods to meet their postsecondary education expenses. These include

- scholarships and grants (which do not have to be repaid);
- help from family;
- personal savings;
- loans; and
- part-time jobs.

Some financial aid is available directly from schools. There are also scholarships and grants available that are not linked to a particular school. If you need financial aid, your school guidance counselor can help you get started. There are also many websites and books to help guide your search.

Do not rule out schools immediately because of their tuition costs. Some may end up being more affordable than they appear. Scholarships from schools are usually not awarded until after you apply and are accepted. Apply to several schools and then compare your options.

Gathering information about higher education options can help you identify ones that seem to meet your needs and wants. Check schools' websites. Attend college fairs or similar events in your area. These give you an opportunity to talk to representatives of various schools. Contact the admissions offices of schools of interest and ask for informational packets. Talk to people about the schools they attended. Find out as much as you can. Remember, knowledge is power.

Investigating the Cost of Higher Education

Compare the advantages and disadvantages of attending vocational schools, community colleges, and universities. Think about where you might want to attend school. Then focus your research on that state or area of the country. Pay special attention to the cost of living in the area you choose. How do postsecondary education costs vary between the different types of schools? How might this research influence your choices for postsecondary education? Were you surprised by your findings? Explain.

Copyright Goodheart-Willcox Co., Inc.

Law and Ethics   *Does Robert Really Rule?*

Have you ever been in a group meeting when everyone is speaking at the same time and nothing seems to be accomplished? Meetings like this are often inefficient and can even be chaotic and frustrating. Tempers may flair and feelings may be hurt.

To avoid ineffective meetings, many groups often adopt rules of order (more commonly called *parliamentary procedure*). *Parliamentary procedure* is the practice groups use to keep their meetings orderly. Parliamentary procedure provides an opportunity for everyone's voice to be heard, for as long as it takes to do so. Parliamentary procedure uses voting to make decisions based on proposed ideas. Student groups, professional groups, and governing bodies use parliamentary procedure to accomplish their goals.

Meetings utilizing parliamentary procedure are led by an impartial chair or presiding officer. Proposals for discussions are called *motions*. A member first stands and addresses the chair. The chair acknowledges the member and invites the motion to be stated. The member states his or her motion. Another member must then "second" it, which is a way of expressing support for discussion of the motion. The chair then restates the motion so that the topic of discussion is clear to all the members. Discussion is then open. When the time is appropriate, the chair takes a vote and announces the result.

Robert's Rules of Order is the oldest standard by which the intricacies of parliamentary procedure are followed in more complex decision-making situations, including government legislation.

Parliamentary procedure is based on the following generalizations:

1. The simplest and most direct procedures or methods should be used.
2. All members of the group have equal rights, voice, and privilege.
3. Full and free discussion is a right of all members, but one must wait to be recognized or invited by the chair to speak.
4. Only one motion should be discussed at a time.
5. Members may speak only one time about a motion until all members have had a chance. Only then may a member make a second statement if the chair gives permission.
6. Member comments should never attack another member's character or statement.
7. Members may always ask the chair for clarification on the motion before them.

Observation and Writing Activity

Attend a meeting that uses parliamentary procedure, such as a school board meeting, local government meeting, or formal business meeting. If you cannot attend the meeting live, consider watching a broadcast version. Record the meeting's events, including all of the motions, discussions, voting, and outcomes. What were the advantages of using parliamentary procedure? the disadvantages?

Most school organizations provide opportunities to build key skills. Two are worth special consideration by students interested in the field of human services.

- Family, Career and Community Leaders of America (FCCLA) is an organization for high school and college students. FCCLA's goal is to promote personal growth and leadership development in students preparing to enter the adult world of work and family. In FCCLA, student groups complete projects that require them to apply

Copyright Goodheart-Willcox Co., Inc.

knowledge, interact with others, adapt to new technology, and logically think through problems. These have practical applications regardless of a person's specific career goals. For example, all adults must manage multiple roles, including being a family member, wage earner, and community member. FCCLA seeks to improve the quality of life for students and their families and to prepare students for the adult world.

- Educators Rising groups (formerly Future Educators Association, Future Teachers of America, and Future Educators of America) are active in many high schools and colleges. They bring together students who are interested in pursuing teaching or human services as a career.

Joining Professional Associations

One of the best ways to stay updated on human services career issues and practices is to join one or more professional organizations. There are many available for human services workers and some are available to students. If you have an opportunity to attend a professional meeting as a student, be sure to do so.

Professional associations vary in their purpose. Some focus broadly on a career field. Others concentrate on some aspect of it, such as personal investing. You can check the websites of associations to find out more about them. Look for information about the goals of the group. The site should give you a good overview of the activities, resources, and opportunities for members, as well as the costs of membership. Check whether the national organization has affiliated state or local groups.

Membership in a professional association can offer real opportunities for learning more about human services. Through newsletters, journals, online postings, and conferences, you can keep up with current events and future trends. Most associations hold conferences and meetings that provide opportunities for both formal and informal interactions, creating valuable networking contacts (**Figure 6.10**).

Developing a Career Plan

Dreams rely on chance whereas goals take concerted effort. How can you make your dream of becoming a human services professional a reality? Think seriously about what human need you would like to meet and who you would like to help. These are two important questions in understanding your desire to be a human services worker.

When you know what you want to achieve, you are more likely to achieve it. Use your personal answers to the "what" and "who" questions as a basis for writing a career goal. A **career goal** is a clear, concise statement of what you want to become in life. Write exactly what you want to accomplish in specific terms. Perhaps your goal is to be a social worker. Maybe you want to be a cosmetologist. How will you feel when

Copyright Goodheart-Willcox Co., Inc.

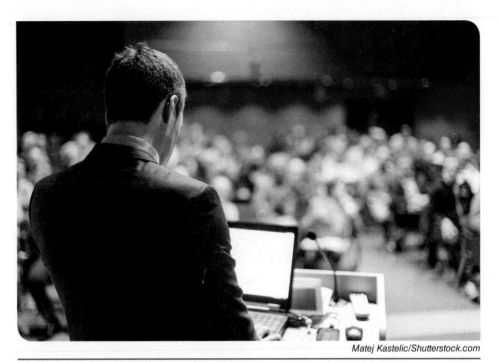

Matej Kastelic/Shutterstock.com

Figure 6.10 In addition to networking opportunities, professional association conferences offer sessions to keep professionals up-to-date in various aspects of their field. *Have you ever attended a conference?*

you accomplish this goal? Although you may modify your goal later, having a career goal will help you move ahead (**Figure 6.11**).

Your career goal forms the base for identifying interrelated goals that will help you achieve it. For example, to become that social worker, you might set the goal of being admitted to a particular university with an excellent social work program.

Think of the process like a tree. Your main career goal is the trunk. Your related goals, such as acceptance into the university of your choice, are the main branches. For each of those, you will identify the specific steps that will be needed to achieve them. These steps are like smaller branches off the main ones. You can identify even more specific ways to achieve those. In this way, you have a series of very specific goals to meet that will lead you to your main one. You have a path to follow.

Next, outline the steps you will take to complete each goal. If you want to get into a particular university with an excellent social work program, figure out what you need to do to get accepted and be able to attend. Perhaps you need to improve your grades, apply to the university early in your senior year, and develop a plan for paying for the cost of your education. Determine the specific things you will do to achieve each of these steps. For example, to improve your grades, you may commit to writing down each assignment, doing your homework as soon as you get home (with your cell phone off), and studying an extra hour each day. You

Copyright Goodheart-Willcox Co., Inc.

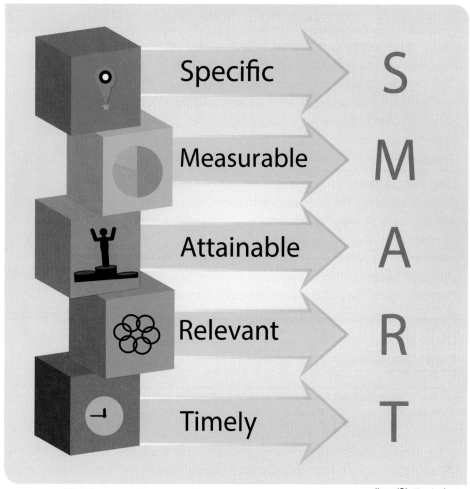

Specific **S**
Measurable **M**
Attainable **A**
Relevant **R**
Timely **T**

Figure 6.11 When writing your goals, follow the S.M.A.R.T. model by making sure your goals are Specific, Measurable, Attainable, Relevant, and have a Time frame. *Following the S.M.A.R.T. model, write a goal that you have for yourself.*

dinsor/Shutterstock.com

will reevaluate your strategy at the end of each month and modify it if your grades are not improving. Consider how you can deal with possible roadblocks or challenges to meeting your goal.

Career planning can seem overwhelming, but does not have to be. Begin your career planning today. Consider what you can do today, this week, this month, or this year to help you toward your goal. Perhaps you can begin by searching the Internet for information about college social work programs. Find a volunteer or paid work experience. Maybe you can have a conversation with a social worker about his or her career path. Now is a good time to set goals, enjoy your experiences, and be open to the changing world around you. See **Figure 6.12** for an example of one student's career plan. How will yours look?

Staying Focused

It is easy, as your time in high school winds down, to lose your focus. There is the distraction of choosing where to continue your education.

Copyright Goodheart-Willcox Co., Inc.

Sample Career Plan	
High school	• Take a career exploration course • Meet with guidance counselor to discuss interests • Gain experience participating in a student organization • Arrange a job shadowing experience with a social worker • Research college social work programs • Apply to colleges • Choose college social work program that best meets my needs
College	• Meet with guidance counselor and enroll in courses • Conduct informational interviews with social workers • Arrange a job shadowing experience with a social worker • Choose a social work specialty • Volunteer or complete an internship at a local human services organization • Complete necessary coursework to earn a bachelor's degree in social work • Complete necessary coursework to earn a master's degree
During last year or after college	• Earn the necessary certification or licensure • Obtain an entry-level job • Seek opportunities for advancement

Figure 6.12 Having a career plan can help you work toward and realize your goal, no matter how small of steps you take. *What does your career plan look like?*

Being excited about upcoming graduation and your future is natural. Spending time with friends may seem more important than classes and homework. Sometimes called "senior slump," this lack of focus begins even earlier for some students. The pattern is all too familiar and worrisome to veteran teachers. Along with lost learning, students' grades can drop significantly. This may leave some students unable to graduate and jeopardize others' class rank and even admission to college.

There is an added concern. An inability to stay focused indicates that some students are unable to handle the shift to more independence. That is a point where self-discipline and good personal decision making need to replace that imposed by parents and others.

Once out of high school and into college or the working world, those who cannot stay focused on their goals are unlikely to reach them. College professors do not issue constant reminders about homework and studying. Students having difficulty in a subject must seek help. Failure to keep up means failure of a course. Employers do not tolerate unreliable workers. They simply replace them.

When you keep your focus, regardless of what others are doing, you show the maturity you will need for life after high school (**Figure 6.13**). There, you will face more choices, distractions, and independence. Remember that reaching your goals is worth the effort.

Copyright Goodheart-Willcox Co., Inc.

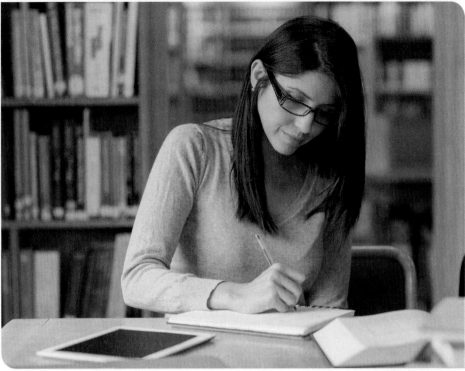

wavebreakmedia/Shutterstock.com

Figure 6.13 Keeping your focus on your schoolwork and minimizing distractions is necessary to be successful in college. *What steps can you take to minimize any potential distractions you may face at school?*

Reading Recall

1. What is a *program of study*?
2. What are *advanced placement courses* and what is their purpose?
3. Identify five aspects to consider when researching postsecondary schools.
4. Why might a student consider participating in a student organization or joining a professional association?
5. What is *parliamentary procedure*?
6. List three generalizations on which parliamentary procedure is based.
7. Define *career goal*.
8. Why is it so important to keep your focus on future goals during high school?

Copyright Goodheart-Willcox Co., Inc.

Summary

- Preparing for a career takes time and thought. Using your self-assessment as a basis for exploring human services careers will help you determine whether a career field or occupation is a fit for or matches your interests.

- Scheduling short-term job shadowing experiences, volunteering, becoming an intern, and conducting informational interviews with professionals are good ways to gain firsthand knowledge about a career in human services.

- Using the *Occupational Outlook Handbook* (OOH) is an effective way to find out about careers, including information on the typical job duties and responsibilities, educational requirements, salary and wages, projected job outlook, and typical working environment for occupations.

- Students can maximize their high school experience and plan for their future by establishing their program of study, choosing challenging courses, researching postsecondary educational options, participating in student organizations, joining professional associations, developing a career plan, and staying focused on their goals.

- A *program of study* is a guide that steps out the core and career-related courses you need to take to follow your career path. Your program of study meets your individual education and career needs.

- When evaluating possible higher education options, consider the size of the school environment, the school's reputation, the location of the school, admission requirements, and tuition costs.

- Developing a career plan involves identifying your goals and the steps you need to take to achieve them.

- When students keep their focus during high school, regardless of what others are doing, they show the maturity they will need for life after high school.

College and Career Portfolio

Certificates and Awards

After identifying the types of items you might place in your portfolio, you will be ready to begin adding items. As you continue this class, you will be able to complete activities that will help you add more items to your portfolio.

In this activity, you will be locating certificates and awards you have received. For example, a certificate might show that you have completed a training class. Another certificate might show that you can keyboard at a certain speed. Perhaps you received a special award for taking part in a community project. Be sure to include any certificates that show your skills, aptitudes, and abilities.

To add certificates and awards in your portfolio, complete the following:

1. Create a document that lists each certificate and when you received it. Briefly describe your activities, skills, or talents related to each certificate.

2. Scan or copy these documents to include in your e-Portfolio. Use the file format you selected in an earlier portfolio activity.

3. Using the naming system you created earlier, give each document an appropriate name. Place each certificate and the list in a subfolder for your e-Portfolio.

4. Place the hard-copy certificates and list in the container for your print portfolio.

Copyright Goodheart-Willcox Co., Inc.

Review and Reflect ↗

1. List three ways to explore and investigate potential human services career areas.
2. Differentiate between *job shadowing* and an *internship*.
3. Give three possible questions to ask during an informational interview.
4. List five types of information you can learn about a career from the *Occupational Outlook Handbook*.
5. How does knowing about job responsibilities and duties help you decide whether or not you will like a career?
6. How can you determine if the career you are considering has projected openings?
7. What are *dual credit courses* and what is their purpose?
8. Name three postsecondary educational options.
9. What is one of the best ways to assess what a postsecondary school is like?
10. Which two CTSOs are worth special consideration by students interested in the field of human services?
11. Give an example of a S.M.A.R.T. career goal.
12. How can you overcome the "senior slump"?

Vocabulary Activities

13. **Key terms**   With a partner, choose two words from the following list to compare. Create a Venn diagram to compare your words and identify differences. Write one term under the left circle and the other term under the right. Where the circles overlap, write two to three characteristics the terms have in common. For each term, write at least one difference of the term for each characteristic in its respective outer circle.

advanced placement courses	informational interview
career goal	internship
dual credit courses	job shadowing
higher education	program of study
	volunteering

14. **Academic terms**   Work with a partner to write the definitions of the following terms based on your current understanding before reading the chapter. Then, pair up with another team to discuss your definitions and any discrepancies. Finally, discuss the definitions with the class and ask your instructor for necessary correction or clarification.

attrition	mean
erroneous	median

Self-Assessment Quiz ↗

Complete the self-assessment quiz online to help you practice and expand your knowledge and skills.

Critical Thinking

15. **Compare and contrast**   Compare and contrast volunteering, job shadowing, informational interviews, and internships. Create a diagram showing the benefits and drawbacks of each.
16. **Make inferences**   Research the median and mean annual wages in your state for five human services careers that interest you. Based on your research, are you more or less likely to consider one of these career options?
17. **Draw conclusions**   Choose three human services careers from the *Occupational Outlook Handbook*. Create a chart to compare and contrast the three careers. Using the chart you create, draw a conclusion about which career would have more openings available by the time you graduate from a vocational school, community college, or university.
18. **Evaluate**   For many jobs, you may have to move to a different area to find employment. Evaluate how far you are willing to move from your present home to pursue your career goals.
19. **Determine**   Meet with your guidance counselor to determine or review your program of study. Then, research what advance placement and dual credit classes are available at your school. What are the prerequisites for getting into these classes?
20. **Identify**   Write a long-term S.M.A.R.T career goal for yourself. Identify short-term goals you would need to set to successfully meet your long-term career goal.

21. **Analyze**   Analyze what professional associations are available for you to join in your area. What is the cost for each of these? What benefits does each of these associations offer to you?

22. **Cause and effect**   Talk to your parents about how they decided on their career path. Did they stumble into their jobs or are they doing what they have always wanted to do? If they could go back in time, would they choose the same career pathway or would they choose something different? If choosing something different, what would they wish to do and why?

Core Skills

23. **Writing**   Schedule an informational interview with a human services worker. Before the interview, write a list of questions to ask during the interview. You can use the questions in figure 6.2 as a starting point. Try to have at least 25 questions that you can ask your interviewee about his or her career. Make sure you bring paper to the interview to record the person's responses.

24. **Writing**   Write a thank-you message to the person you interviewed in activity number 23. Be sure to use correct spelling, grammar, and punctuation. Send the message to your interviewee.

25. **Research and technology**   Choose three careers that interest you. Visit the OOH website and research these careers. Find out about the job duties and responsibilities, educational requirements, salary and wages, projected job outlook, and working environment. Using a software program of your choice, create an electronic presentation of your findings. Based on your research, are you more or less interested in these careers?

26. **Research and math**   Using the OOH website, research the median and mean salaries and wages for 10 human services careers. Create a chart of your findings to share with the class. Which occupations fit with your salary and wage needs?

27. **Research**   Research the different work environments that are available for people working in the human services career cluster. Use this information to make a list of your preferences of the environment in which you would like to work. Make a list of jobs that are in the human services career cluster that have this environment.

28. **Reading and writing**   Obtain a copy of a career-search book (such as the latest edition of *What Color Is Your Parachute?*). Read the book. Then, write a book report analyzing and identifying the important guidelines the author suggests for finding meaningful employment, including identifying your personal educational and career goals. Select two topics you found most valuable to share with the class. Give evidence from your reading to support your reasoning.

29. **Research and math**   Choose three postsecondary schools and research the cost of attending. Make sure you look at housing, books, and the cost for at least 15 hours for one semester. Evaluate the differences among the three schools. Which one is the most expensive? least expensive? How does this information impact your choice of attending that school?

30. **Research**   The cost of higher education is a major expense. Compile a list of scholarships in your local area for which you could apply. Include in your list the criteria they have for your application to be accepted. Next, begin putting together a list of other places where you can look for scholarships. Your school's guidance office might have scholarship resources. Remember to think outside of the box as well as think about your interests and hobbies as you compile this list.

31. **Writing and speaking**   Create a skit on how to run a meeting using parliamentary procedures. In the skit, make mistakes as well as follow the rules of parliamentary law. Have your classmates try and figure out which parts of the skit were incorrect and then have them explain what needed to be done instead.

32. **Writing**   Create a preliminary career goal by putting in writing the steps you are going to take to find out which career interests you. Share this career goal with your teacher. As you continue this course, check off the items in your career plan as you complete them.

33. **CTE career readiness practice**   Learning to use parliamentary procedure takes training

Copyright Goodheart-Willcox Co., Inc.

and practice. Volunteer to lead a group in your school or community in learning how to conduct a successful meeting using parliamentary procedure. How can using parliamentary procedure help individuals consistently act in ways that align to personal and community help ideals and principles? How might failure to use parliamentary procedure impact making decisions?

34. **CTE career readiness practice** Based on your research of human services careers, choose the human services career that interests you the most. Locate people in local companies or organizations who perform this job. Use these contacts to arrange a job shadowing experience to gain firsthand knowledge about the job. After your job shadowing experience, write an essay describing what you liked or did not like about the job. Share your essays with the class.

Lend a Hand

Volunteering and College Admissions

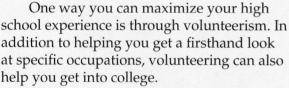

One way you can maximize your high school experience is through volunteerism. In addition to helping you get a firsthand look at specific occupations, volunteering can also help you get into college.

The college admissions process can be daunting and stressful. There is much competition to make your application stand out from the rest. College admissions boards expect to see volunteer experiences and involvement in extracurricular activities on college applications. So how can you make your volunteer experiences count and get admissions officers to take notice of your application over the others?

Your volunteer experience can really make you stand out from other applicants if you choose the types of organizations and causes about which you are passionate. Aligning volunteer experiences with your career goals is helpful, too. Volunteering in your field of interest shows that you are driven and already have some applicable experience. Another way to impress college admissions officers is to commit to one cause for an extended period of time. Not only does this demonstrate your dedication to an issue that is important to you, but can also speak volumes about your values, interests, goals, and passions.

Volunteer work provides an interesting topic for college essays and can make your writing feel more personal. Admissions officers are more likely to take notice when your essay sincerely expresses how you have grown and changed as a result of your volunteer experience.

Consider how your volunteerism can help you get into college by completing the following:

1. List the service projects or volunteer activities in which you have taken part. Identify which experiences would make you stand out the most. If you have many volunteer experiences, try to group them together under a larger issue, such as helping the underprivileged, or think about how they relate to your career goals.

2. Practice writing about your volunteer experiences. Create a draft of a college admissions essay that highlights a specific volunteer experience or your community service work as a whole.

Looking Ahead: Preparing for Workplace Success

While studying, look for the activity icon ⤴ **to**

- **practice** key and academic terms with e-flash cards and matching activities;
- **assess** what you learn by completing self-assessment quizzes; and
- **reinforce** what you learn by mapping concepts and completing review and reflect questions.

www.g-wlearning.com/humanservices/

Daxiao Productions/Shutterstock.com

Learning Outcomes

After studying this chapter, you will be able to

- **describe** three of the most common ways to find job openings;
- **demonstrate** how to complete a job application and résumé and write a cover message;
- **summarize** common features of effective portfolios;
- **demonstrate** how to interview for a job;
- **explain** what employees might expect to experience as they start a new job; and
- **describe** the proper way to resign from a job.

Reading Strategies

Before reading, look at the list of key terms for this chapter and, on a separate piece of paper, write what you think each term means. As you are reading the chapter, look carefully at the text definitions for the key terms. Are the text definitions similar to or different from the definitions you wrote? After you finish reading, make a list of any terms in which your definitions were different from the text definitions. Look these terms up in the dictionary and then rewrite your definitions based on what you learned.

Mapping Concepts

Draw two columns for taking notes. As you read, write main ideas in the left column and subtopics and detailed information in the right column. After reading this chapter, use your notes as a study guide. Cover the right column and use the left column to quiz yourself about the chapter content.

Main Ideas	Subtopics and Detailed Information
Job leads come from any number of sources	Some of the most common ways to find job openings include networking, searching online, and attending job fairs

Key Terms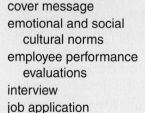

cover message
emotional and social cultural norms
employee performance evaluations
interview
job application
job fairs
networking
organizational culture
performance feedback
political culture
portfolio
references
résumé
work culture

Academic Terms

artifacts
exude
preempt

In previous chapters, you spent time looking inward getting to know yourself and identifying your personal brand. You also spent time looking outward learning how to explore human services careers that might best suit your individual strengths and interests. Next, it is time to learn about finding and landing a job in your field of interest. Through effective networking and searching for online job postings, you may find job opportunities that interest you.

In a competitive world, you need to know how to fill out a job application effectively. You also need to be able to write a good résumé and stand out from other candidates at job interviews. Strengthening your knowledge and skills today will help you be more prepared for your future job search.

Finding Job Openings

After investigating careers and developing a plan, the job search can begin. Job leads come from any number of sources. Help-wanted ads in the newspaper can be a resource when conducting a job search. Many of these ads are also available online. Some businesses post help-wanted signs where people passing by can see them. Some of the most common ways to find job openings include networking, searching online, and attending job fairs. People often use a combination of these methods to find job openings.

Networking

One of the best ways to find a job is through **networking**, which is the act of meeting and making contact with people. Networking can happen anywhere. It can occur at a family reunion, in the classroom, at a party, at a ballpark, or at any social event. Networking can take place in quiet conversations or in large group settings.

The key to networking is making connections between people. Because most employers are adults, networking can happen with your parent's friends, your teachers, extended family members, or those you meet in public places. When you meet people, let them know about your interests and passions. Remember, you are presenting your personal brand.

Referrals really do happen more casually than you might expect, but sometimes results can take a while. The more people you talk to, however, the faster you will make connections. If you are positive and upbeat, others will be more likely to feel comfortable recommending you to others. Sell your personal brand. If you are negative and demonstrate low energy, people will be more reluctant to give a referral. After all, people put their reputation on the line each time they give a referral.

Searching Online

In this digital age, there are many job opportunities online. Newspaper help-wanted ads are just one search option. When you know

Expert Insight

"Never lose an opportunity of urging a practical beginning, however small, for it is wonderful how often in such matters the mustard-seed germinates and roots itself."

Florence Nightingale, pioneer of modern nursing

of certain companies in which you would like to work, you can go directly to the company's website to check for current job openings. Sometimes local communities or cities post available jobs. Schools or places of worship may also post jobs.

Many employers like to use Internet job boards to spread the word about job openings (**Figure 7.1**). Searching Internet job boards is a quick and efficient way to look for jobs. On Internet job boards, you can search for many different types of jobs. You can also narrow the job search by identifying specific search criteria. For example, you may search for jobs within a specific region, industry or salary range, or by the amount of experience needed. Using certain keywords, such as a company name, an occupation, or a specific city, can help you refine your job search even further. By searching with keywords, you can indicate whether you want full-time, part-time, or temporary work.

Attending Job Fairs

Imagine dozens of potential employers in one place and at one time. This type of setting can be ideal for finding a job. **Job fairs** are events where employers network with potential employees. Sometimes they are referred to as *career fairs* or *employment fairs*.

Communities and schools often host job fairs for young workers. Job fairs offer the convenience of interacting with many employers at once, saving you both time and energy in making an initial contact (**Figure 7.2**). As good as job fairs sound, they can be overwhelming and ineffective if you are not prepared.

©iStock.com/Pixsooz

Figure 7.1 Companies are increasingly turning to Internet job boards to post any openings or opportunities. *What are some websites that you could search for job openings?*

Copyright Goodheart-Willcox Co., Inc.

©iStock.com/Steve Debenport

Figure 7.2 Job or career fairs are a great opportunity for job seekers to network with a large number of potential employers. *When and where is the next available job fair near you?*

To successfully navigate a job fair, find out which organizations will be represented. Research as many of these companies as possible before attending the job fair. Think of questions you might ask recruiters that will demonstrate your interest and preparedness. This will also help you show how you could fit in with the organization. Be prepared to discuss your career objectives and any relevant experiences, skills, and strengths. Practicing what to say before attending the job fair can be very helpful.

Spending time preparing for networking and job fairs can help you *exude* (show a lot of) confidence and personality in presenting your personal brand. Do not shortchange yourself. Instead, give yourself the best chance to make positive contacts with potential employers. To really set yourself apart, write a thank-you message to those you spent time talking with about your career interests. Let them know you enjoyed learning more about their organization. If you are interested, let them know what you can offer as an intern or employee.

Reading Recall

1. Name three common ways to find out about job openings.
2. Define *networking*.
3. List two ways that jobs can be found online.
4. What is one advantage of attending a job fair?
5. How can you make a good impression on potential employers after leaving the job fair?

Copyright Goodheart-Willcox Co., Inc.

Securing Employment

Many students desire or need to work while going to school. Others pursue employment before attending additional training. Still others *preempt* (forestall) postsecondary education and go straight into the job market. Whatever your life path, knowing how to secure employment is an important skill.

Once you find the job you would like to pursue, the real work begins. Most employers require job seekers to complete an application and submit a résumé. Creating a portfolio enables you to showcase your skills and abilities and make a good impression with potential employers. Almost all employers want to interview a potential candidate before making a decision to hire. If offered a position, you then have a decision to make whether or not this is the right job for you.

Completing an Application

A **job application** is a document that you fill out to give personal information about you and your eligibility to be an employee (**Figure 7.3**). Employers review applications to find potential employees who can meet their needs. Many times, the job application is the first objective piece of information an employer sees about a potential employee. For that reason, making a good first impression is highly important.

To apply for a position, first find out the preferred method of obtaining an application. Some companies have paper copies that you pick up in person, complete, and return. Others have online applications you submit electronically. Sometimes you can only apply for a specific position that is currently open. Other times, companies prefer to collect applications for both current and future openings. Whatever the case, be prepared with the necessary information to complete the application. Job applications often require the following information:

- Contact information—includes your full name, mailing and e-mail addresses, and phone number. Use an e-mail address that is professional and not offensive. If you do not have a phone number, leave a number where a message can be left for you.

- Educational history—includes schools attended and degrees received. Know the dates of attendance and graduation. Be prepared to also list any certifications as well as special skills or qualifications.

- Work history—includes current and previous positions. Be sure to know job titles and responsibilities, employer's contact information, supervisor's name and job title, salary, start and end dates of employment, and reason for leaving. Volunteer experiences may also be included. Typically, applications ask for the most recent employment or experiences first.

Copyright Goodheart-Willcox Co., Inc.

Job Application

Personal Information

Last Name		First Name		Middle Initial
Address	City		State	Zip
How long at present address?	Phone Number		Social Security Number	

What date will you be available for work?

Type of employment desired:

_____ Full-time only   _____ Part-time only   _____ Full- or part-time

If hired, can you furnish proof that you are legally entitled to work in the United States?

If hired, can you furnish proof of age?

What position are you applying for?	What are your salary requirements?

Hours you will be available to work:

Have you ever been convicted of a felony?

If yes, please explain

The XYZ Company is a drug-free employer and you will be required to pass a drug screening as a condition of employment. I understand and agree to participate in testing. (   ) initials

Educational Information

Name and Address of School	Course of Study	Diploma or Degree
High School		
College Education		
Graduate Education		
Other Education/ Training		

Figure 7.3 Be sure to read an application closely and carefully check your responses before submitting it to an employer. *Why is this step so important?*

Copyright Goodheart-Willcox Co., Inc.

- Availability—includes the days and hours you are available to work and whether you are looking for full- or part-time work.

- References—includes the names and contact information of three or four references. **References** are people other than relatives who know you and can attest to your work habits, skills, and abilities. Teachers, coaches, and former employers or coworkers can make good references (**Figure 7.4**). Before listing people as references, always check with them first and ask their permission. Employers will often contact an applicant's references and ask specific questions about the person's qualifications. Therefore, you will want to make sure that your references are willing to positively recommend you.

As you fill out an application, keep in mind that, on average, there are probably well over 100 people who are applying for the same job. To make sure your application does not get overlooked, follow directions exactly. Be sure to write clearly and legibly. Spell everything correctly, use correct grammar, and answer all questions completely. Do not leave any blank spaces unless instructed to do so. If something does not apply to you, simply state "not applicable" or "n/a." Remember that everything you state on your application must be true. If not, an employer has reason to fire you.

©iStock.com/monkeybusinessimages

Figure 7.4 Coaches can serve as good references, as they can speak to your work habits, skills, and abilities. *Who are three or four people whom you could list as your references?*

Submitting a Résumé

Many employers request that job applicants submit a résumé when they fill out an application. A **résumé** is a written or electronic document that lists your qualifications. Putting together a résumé is a great exercise for summarizing and organizing your education, work history, interests, and skills.

To write a good résumé, you need to know your target audience. Some industries value creativity. In other more conservative industries, creativity may decrease your chances of being taken seriously. Once you identify your audience, you can carefully construct and tailor your résumé to appeal to them. You will be able to highlight the aspects of your experiences which mean the most to your prospective employer.

Most career specialists agree that a résumé should be one page in length for an entry-level or first job. Because a résumé is short, make

Copyright Goodheart-Willcox Co., Inc.

Case Study *True or False?*

Justine was very excited about the idea of working as a recreation leader at the community sports camp this summer. As she prepared her résumé, she worried that she might get overlooked for the job because of her lack of experience. Justine debated about embellishing a few details. She thought, doesn't everybody embellish their résumés somewhat?

Maybe she could just make a few simple changes. So what if she was not really a student at the local university. She planned to apply this fall and hoped to get accepted. She had not ever coached before, but she did teach her younger sister how to pitch a softball. She didn't earn all A's in her classes this past year, but she could have if she hadn't missed turning in a few history assignments.

Justine wondered what could happen if she embellished or falsified her qualifications and was caught. She really wanted this job and felt that she could be good at it. She decided to search online for some answers. This is what she found:

1. The usual reaction of employers to falsification of credentials includes dismissal or firing. Employers can go further, however, and she could face criminal charges.

2. An employer can expect an employee to use skills that have been advertised on a résumé. For example, Justine could be asked to run a coaching program or clinic on softball pitching. With only the experience of helping her little sister, it would be much more difficult and humbling to ask for help after claiming expertise. She just may be in over her head.

3. Because Justine would be working with children, the employer would do a background check. Surely her dishonesty would be revealed then. If not, reference verifications could highlight dishonest claims. Dishonesty in reporting educational achievements are the easiest to uncover.

4. Employers hire based on the assumption of trust. Initiating a distrustful relationship does not set Justine up for success.

Justine thought about it more and decided to stay with the facts, but to find ways to highlight both her true experiences and most of all her eagerness and passion for sports and children. She got the job on honest terms and was enthusiastically mentored by others who shared their experience and knowledge. Overall, the job was a good fit.

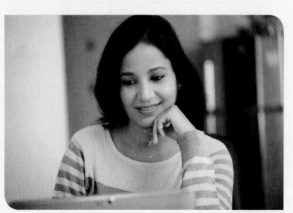
©iStock.com/SnowWhiteimages

For Discussion
1. Do you agree or disagree with Justine's decision?
2. What are the risks of overstating or exaggerating qualifications in your own life?

every word count. Résumés should list specific accomplishments and job experiences. If you have little or no work experience, focus on skills and abilities you possess from volunteer and extracurricular activities (**Figure 7.5**). Use active rather than passive verbs to communicate energy. Make sure there are no spelling or grammar errors. Have at least two people carefully edit your résumé to ensure accuracy.

Copyright Goodheart-Willcox Co., Inc.

Claire Johnson
1234 Stone Lane
Portland, OR 97212
333.555.4475
cjohnson@provider.com

Objective	To gain experience working with young children by assisting summer camp counselors.
Education	Portland High School, Portland, Oregon, 20XX to present.
	Focus on human services with an emphasis in child development courses. Proficient in Microsoft Word, Excel, and PowerPoint, and in Photoshop.
	Graduating in June 20XX.
Experience	Volunteer, Portland Grade School After-School Child Care Program, 20XX to present.
	Supervise craft activities, playtime, and games, and help with homework.
	Babysitter, 20XX to present.
	Provide child care for neighborhood children between the ages of 6 months and 12 years.
Honors and Activities	Portland High School honor roll, 20XX.
	Secretary, Family, Career and Community Leaders of America (FCCLA), Portland High School chapter, 20XX to present.
	Recreation Leader, Boys and Girls Club, Summer 20XX.
	Member, Portland High School yearbook committee, 20XX to present.

Figure 7.5 A résumé is a written or electronic document that summarizes and organizes your education, employment history, interests, and skills. *What does your résumé look like?*

There are many resources you can use to help you write a good résumé that "sells" you. High school counselors and teachers are great resources for helping students write résumés that enhance their skills, knowledge, and abilities. Résumé writing advice is also plentiful on the Internet.

The traditional way to submit a résumé is by mail or in person, but most people today submit their résumés online. Submitting a résumé online often involves sending your résumé as an e-mail attachment, uploading it to a website, or copying and pasting it into an online application form. Be aware that this process usually strips out formatting,

Copyright Goodheart-Willcox Co., Inc.

such as tabs, indentations, and bold type. You may need to make adjustments to the layout of your résumé after pasting it into an online application form.

Writing a Cover Message

Writing a cover message is an important part of the résumé writing process. A **cover message** is simply a letter of introduction that explains who you are and why you are sending your résumé to the reader. A cover message will give your résumé the proper introduction it deserves. Generally, three or four paragraphs will do the job. If you make the message too long, it will go unread. If you make the message too short, it may come across as hurried or careless.

Cover messages should show an employer which position you are applying for, how you learned about the job, why you are the right person for the job, and how you can be reached (**Figure 7.6**). If you do not have an abundance of work experience, focus on your career goals and what you hope to learn. You can also mention community service and volunteer projects. Before sending a cover message, make sure the presentation is perfect. Be sure to check for any spelling, grammar, and punctuation errors.

Developing a Personal Portfolio

A personal **portfolio** is a dynamic, ever-growing, and changing collection of *artifacts* (handmade objects) that illustrate your accomplishments, learning, strengths, and best works. Personal portfolios show what you have learned over time rather than just end products. You can adapt your personal portfolio to serve as a professional portfolio when you are ready to enter your career field. Your portfolio can be a great tool to use to highlight your skills and abilities when interviewing for a job. Portfolios can enhance anybody's marketability and serve as a source of personal reflection.

Effective portfolios share several common features. As you prepare and evaluate your own portfolio, keep the following in mind:

- Portfolios have a clear purpose. Remember that the purpose of your portfolio is to record and highlight your experiences and abilities. Your portfolio is not simply a scrapbook about your life.

- Portfolios reflect your uniqueness. Your abilities and experiences are not the same as anyone else's. Because of this, your portfolio should be original. You may choose to include different items from others. You might, for example, include photographs, certificates, descriptions of your work, and evidence of your personal leadership experiences.

- Portfolios show your progress. Your portfolio is not just a random collection of your works. Consider your portfolio as an opportunity to display your skills and abilities visually. Think carefully about

Copyright Goodheart-Willcox Co., Inc.

1234 Stone Lane
Portland, Oregon 97212
March 3, 20XX

Ms. Sandy Smith
Camp Director
Portland Summer Camp
Portland, OR 97212

Dear Ms. Smith:

I am interested in working as an assistant at Portland Summer Camp this summer. My Portland High School guidance counselor, Mr. Wilder, suggested I contact you about any entry-level positions you might have available.

This job would be an excellent learning experience for me. I also have much to offer as an employee. I have taken child and lifespan development courses in high school. As a volunteer at the Portland Grade School After-School Child Care Program, I work with over 30 children ages 5 through 12 each week. My duties are to supervise craft activities, playtime, games, and homework completion. As a babysitter for the past three years, I have provided care for children ages 6 months through 12 years. Last summer, I was the Recreation Leader at the Boys and Girls Club where I planned and supervised activities and crafts for 20 children of various ages. These experiences have confirmed my love for working with children. My long-term career goal is to eventually be a child care director after I graduate from college and gain enough experience.

Enclosed is my résumé. I would appreciate the opportunity to discuss how I could be of service to Portland Summer Camp. Please contact me at 333.555.4475 or at cjohnson@provider.com. Thank you for your time and consideration.

Sincerely,

Claire Johnson

Claire Johnson

Figure 7.6 A cover message should be tailored to the position and company to which you are applying. *What information would you include in a cover message?*

what to include (**Figure 7.7**). Identify and date each item. Write a thoughtful statement about why each item is meaningful and what it demonstrates. Remember, just like you, your portfolio is a work in progress. You can add or subtract items as you choose to keep your portfolio current.

- Portfolios reflect professionalism. An effective portfolio is well-organized, neat, and easy to understand. One of the most common methods of organizing a portfolio is to use a binder with tab dividers. Preparing your portfolio in an electronic format, such as creating a personal website, is an alternative to maintaining an actual physical

Copyright Goodheart-Willcox Co., Inc.

Common Items to Include in a Portfolio
• Basic information about yourself, including your name and year in school
• An essay focusing on your career goals and personal interests
• Documentation of any awards, honors, or honor society memberships
• Information on internships, apprenticeships, and special projects
• Information on independent learning (things you have learned on your own)
• A list of leadership positions held
• A list of hobbies or interests
• Journal entries about your volunteer experiences or other activities

Figure 7.7 A personal portfolio shows what you have learned over time and highlights your accomplishments, strengths, and best works. *What would you include in your own personal portfolio?*

portfolio. Whichever format you use, be sure the portfolio is interesting. Even the paper or webpage design you choose, the way you arrange items, and the lettering you use say something about you. Make sure that what you have written is accurate, clear to the reader, and grammatically correct. To be effective, a portfolio must be error-free.

Going on Job Interviews

Employers use applications, résumés, and cover messages to decide which candidates they think might be a good match for a job opening. If you seem like a potential match for a position, you will be asked for an interview. An **interview** is a conversation between an employer and a potential employee. **Figure 7.8** shows some of the different types of interviews you may go through. Even though the interview types may be different, they all serve the same purpose. The interview process gives employers a chance to assess your knowledge and skills and see if you would be a good fit for the company.

There are many factors that influence how you are perceived during a job interview. These might include how badly you need the job, your true interest in potential employment, and whether or not you see the company as a good fit for you. The more you interview, the more you will become comfortable with the process. No matter how much experience you have interviewing, however, preparation is the key to being successful.

Preparing for an Interview

Before you go to an interview, do your homework. Research the company and study the job description. Company websites provide much useful information to help you learn about the company. Pay special attention to the *About Us* section for an overview of the company.

Copyright Goodheart-Willcox Co., Inc.

Types of Job Interviews

- **Screening and phone interviews**—One of the first steps in the interview process. These normally take place over the phone with a member of the human resources department. The questions are direct and focus on your skills and experience.

- **One-on-one interviews**—The most common type of interview. These occur after it is decided that you have the necessary requirements, but the interviewer is looking to see how well you will fit into the company. The questions might test your listed skills and experience.

- **Candidate group interviews**—Two or more applicants are interviewed at the same time for the same position, sometimes by multiple interviewers. The interviewers are looking at your style, professionalism, leadership skills, and ability to function under pressure. It is important to show that you can handle yourself well in a group of peers and in stressful situations.

- **Panel or committee interviews**—An interview by several members of the company at the same time. These help the interviewers see how you perform under heightened pressure. It is important to connect with each interviewer, engaging with each member of the panel, even when you are addressing only one of them directly.

- **Mealtime interviews**—An interview that takes place outside of the office setting, often for breakfast or lunch. The interviewer will be paying attention to how you behave in a more relaxed environment, but you should still maintain your professionalism. Use this time to build common ground with the interviewer, but remember to mind your table manners.

- **Teleconferencing/web-conferencing interviews**—An interview done using a webcam online format due to distance. These should be treated the same way as face-to-face interviews, including professional attire and behavior. If you are taking this type of interview at home, be sure to eliminate any distractions before starting.

- **Behavioral interviews**—Often a part of any of the other types of interviews. The interviewer will ask how you have handled different situations in the past that relate to the available position. The idea is that you will repeat your past performance in the future. To prepare for these types of questions, think of challenges and issues you were faced with in the past and how you conquered them.

- **Stress interviews**—An interview to see how you react to unexpected situations and pressures. The interviewer might attempt to unnerve you by being sarcastic or argumentative, making you wait a while before starting the interview, or leaving long pauses between questions. Remember to stay calm, as you are being evaluated on how you act under pressure.

Figure 7.8 As you begin interviewing, you may go through different types of interviews such as these. *If you were in a group interview, what could you do to stand out from other candidates?*

In addition to researching the company website, use your network of friends and relatives to find people who are familiar with the employer. Get as much information from them as you can. You can also call the company's human resources department to find out more about working for the company.

Copyright Goodheart-Willcox Co., Inc.

As you are researching the company, make a list of questions you would like to ask during the interview. Keep in mind that the questions you ask reveal details about your personality. Asking questions can make a good impression. Questions show that you are interested and have done your homework. Good questions cover the duties and responsibilities of the position, to whom you will report, what a typical day is like, and how many people are in the department. Detailed questions about pay and working hours are usually discussed at the end of an interview or, more likely, at a later date.

During an interview, you will spend much of your time answering questions. To be prepared for this, think about how you will respond to typical interview questions, such as "Why do you want to work for the company?" Consider how you would answer this question. Be prepared for many other types of questions, too, especially open-ended questions, such as "Tell me about yourself." Many sample interview questions are available on the Internet to help you prepare for an interview.

Conducting several mock interviews with family members or friends is an excellent way to prepare for an interview. Practice answering and asking your interview questions. Although simple yes or no answers to questions are often not enough, find a balance between saying too much and saying too little. Tailor your answers to show how your skills, experiences, and passions match with the open position. Get feedback from your family and friends about your interview performance. Practice until you can give your planned responses naturally. The more prepared you are, the more relaxed, organized, competent, and professional you will appear to the interviewer.

During and After an Interview

On the day of your interview, be sure to have your paperwork in order. Carry a résumé, your reference list, and all other basic information required on job applications. Even if you have provided this information earlier, you may be asked for it again. Dress appropriately and be well-groomed. Clothes you choose should appear professional and respectful. Avoid wearing items that may cause you to fidget. Do not wear clothing, hairstyles, or accessories that will take the focus away from what you have to say. You want your interviewer to hear your words, not to be distracted by what you wear. Your appearance should be consistent with the company's culture.

Plan to arrive at your interview between 5 and 10 minutes before the scheduled time. Turn off your cell phone so you will not be interrupted. When you meet your interviewer, introduce yourself with a firm handshake and say something like, "I have been looking forward to meeting you." Use more formal language rather than the informal greetings you might use with friends.

Copyright Goodheart-Willcox Co., Inc.

Pathway to Success

Responding to Interview Questions

Wouldn't it be great if you knew what questions would be asked of you in an interview beforehand? As there are many different types of questions, there are some general questions that are asked more frequently than others.

Following are some common interview questions. After each question, there are points to consider as you draft your responses.

1. What can you tell me about yourself?

   Do not give your life story. Instead, give a concise and compelling answer that shows why you are a great fit for the job.

2. How did you hear about the position?

   This is a perfect opportunity to stand out and show your passion and connection to the company. Also, share what specifically caught your eye about the job.

3. Why should we hire you?

   This is a great question to highlight yourself and your skills to the hiring manager. Your answer needs to cover the following three things: that you can do the work, you can deliver great results, and you are a great fit for the company.

4. What are your strengths?

   Share your true strengths. Instead of saying people skills, choose persuasive communicator or relationship builder. Then, follow up with an example of how you have demonstrated this skill.

5. What are your weaknesses?

   With this question, interviewers are really trying to gauge your self-awareness and honesty. Tell about something you struggle with, but then give an example that shows how you are working on improving in this area. For example, if you have trouble with public speaking, you might mention that you recently volunteered to run some meeting to help you become comfortable when addressing a crowd.

Practice Interviewing Skills

Using the questions above as a reference, you can also research on the Internet other questions commonly asked during a job interview. Come up with a list of 15 common interview questions. Pair up with a partner and take turns interviewing each other using the list of questions you researched. Before doing the mock interview, think about what you want to say for each question. It may help you to write your thoughts down and look over your notes before going into the interview. Take turns critiquing each other's answers. Give suggestions on how to improve the answers to showcase your abilities, strengths, and weaknesses. Practice answering questions until you feel comfortable and happy with your responses.

Copyright Goodheart-Willcox Co., Inc.

Law and Ethics   *Federal Laws Protect Against Job Discrimination*

In the US, federal laws exist that prohibit job discrimination against a job applicant or employee. These laws ensure that people are not discriminated against based on their age, color, race, religion, sex, national origin, disability, or genetic information. The US Equal Employment Opportunity Commission (EEOC) is responsible for enforcing these laws.

One of these laws, the *Civil Rights Act*, prohibits employment discrimination based on race, color, religion, sex, or national origin. For both applications and interviews, any questions that hint at discrimination are considered illegal in the US. Examples of illegal questions may include the following:

- What nationality are you?
- What is your religion?
- Are you married?
- How did you get that disability (or scar, deformity, etc.)?
- Do you plan on having children? If so, when?
- Who will care for your children when you are working?
- Have you ever been arrested?

There are also several federal laws that protect specific groups of workers, such as women and older workers. For example, the *Equal Pay Act (EPA)* protects men and women who perform substantially equal work in the same place from sex-based wage discrimination. Age discrimination legislation protects individuals who are 40 years of age or older.

Employees also have a right to a *non-hostile work environment* that is free from harassment. It is unlawful to harass an employee because of his or her sex. *Sexual harassment* might include unwelcome sexual advances or requests for sexual favors. It can include any other verbal or physical harassment that has a sexual connotation or nature. In addition, offensive remarks about a person's sex, such as a derogatory comment about men or women in general, can also be deemed sexual harassment.

Americans with disabilities are also a protected group. The *Americans with Disabilities Act (ADA)* was enacted to prohibit employment discrimination against qualified individuals with disabilities. The ADA does not prohibit an employer from establishing job-related qualification standards. These standards are under the employer's authority, and employers may seek to hire the most qualified candidate. If candidates with disabilities meet the employment standards, reasonable accommodations must be made to enable employees to perform the job.

Writing Activity

Use online sources to learn more about federal laws that protect against discrimination. Choose one of these laws and write a one-page report about it to practice using a formal style of writing.

When you enter the interview room, wait to be offered a seat. Try to read the mood of the interviewer. If he or she is intense, offer decisive and clear answers. If the interviewer is more casual, mimic the casual tone while remaining courteous and professional. Use good posture and limit your body movements.

Interviewers understand that you are "on the spot" and probably a little nervous (**Figure 7.9**). If the interviewer is new or untrained at interviewing, he or she may be nervous, too. Even so, try to avoid appearing apprehensive. Steer clear of nervous habits, such as fidgeting, quick or jerky movements, and either staring or avoiding eye contact.

Copyright Goodheart-Willcox Co., Inc.

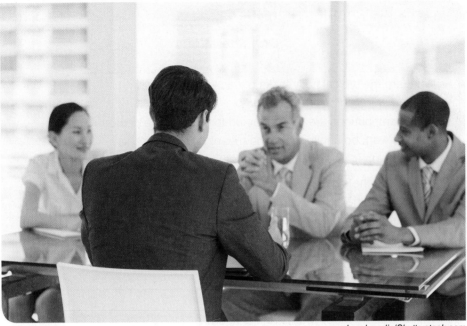

wavebreakmedia/Shutterstock.com

Figure 7.9 Interviews can be very stressful, and interviewers are often looking to see how well you can handle the stress. *What can you do to calm your nerves before and during an interview?*

Make it your goal to appear confident, but not arrogant. Think of the interview as a two-way conversation. The interviewer is trying to get to know you. Likewise, you are trying to get to know the interviewer and the company. Thinking of an interview as a conversation may make you feel more comfortable and the conversation less like a performance.

After interviewing, immediately write a thank-you message to every person who interviewed you. Either a handwritten letter or an e-mail to the interviewer is appropriate. Thank the interviewer for his or her time. Restate your interest in working for the company. Do not delay or procrastinate. Sometimes this is a deciding factor in the selection process.

Take some time to evaluate your performance after the interview. Even if you are not interested in the job, the interview process is a good opportunity to practice and develop your skills. Make a list of the things you feel you did right and things you would do differently next time.

Weighing Job Offers

If you do not receive a job offer right away, do not get discouraged; just keep trying. Many people must often apply for several jobs before experiencing success in receiving an offer. When you do receive a job offer, there are many considerations to make before you accept or reject the position (**Figure 7.10**). When weighing a job offer, it may be helpful to break your evaluation process into several categories for your review. These include job duties and responsibilities, the work environment,

Expert Insight

"Our greatest weakness lies in giving up. The most certain way to succeed is always to try just one more time."

Thomas Edison, inventor

Copyright Goodheart-Willcox Co., Inc.

Weighing Job Offers	
Categories to Evaluate	**Considerations**
Job duties and responsibilities	• What are the typical daily tasks of this job? • Will you enjoy doing this every day? • What contributions are you expected to make to the company? • Will this work be challenging and meaningful to you? • Does the job fit into your long-term career goals?
Work environment	• Do you like the setting and location of this job? • What are the personality and culture of this company? • What are the work schedules? • Are there any travel demands? • Are the people friendly? • What is the attire for this job?
Wages or salary	• Is the pay adequate? • Will this salary meet your financial needs? • Will this salary help you achieve your goals? • How does the pay compare to similar jobs? • Will your cost of living change with this job? • Is the pay consistent and stable throughout the year?
Benefits	• Does the company offer paid holidays, vacation, and sick days? • Is medical, dental, and vision insurance offered? • Is there a 401(k) or other retirement savings plan? • Do you have the option of telecommuting or flexible work hours? • Is subsidized training or education offered? • Does the company provide on-site child care?
Potential for advancement	• Can further training or education help you advance in this company over time? • Is it common to switch roles within this company? • What growth opportunities exist? • How often are salaries evaluated?
Transportation	• How long will your commute be? • What type of commute will be necessary? • Is public transportation a viable option? • Is there parking available? Does the parking cost or is it free?
Personal needs	• Can you see yourself fitting into this company? • Do you think you will enjoy spending every day with the boss and coworkers? • Does the company seem successful and stable? • Will you feel fulfilled and like you are making a difference in the world? • Are the company's values and beliefs compatible with yours?

Figure 7.10 Sample questions such as these can help you evaluate job offers. *What other factors might you consider when weighing a job offer?*

Copyright Goodheart-Willcox Co., Inc.

wages and benefits, potential for advancement, transportation, and your personal needs.

There is no one right answer, but thoughtfully evaluating the selection criteria will help you make an informed and rational decision. If you like the job, but are uncertain about whether accepting the job would be a good decision, ask your friends and family members for their input. Remember, jobs can act as stepping stones to learning new skills.

Reading Recall

1. What five pieces of information should you expect to be asked to provide on a job application?
2. Why do potential employers often ask for references?
3. What is the purpose of a résumé?
4. What is the purpose of a cover message?
5. What does a personal portfolio reflect?
6. Name three ways to prepare for a job interview.
7. Why do potential employers sometimes use group interviews?
8. What two things should be done after completing a job interview?

Starting a New Job

Your first day at a new job can be both overwhelming and exciting. You will probably spend the first day meeting coworkers and becoming familiar with the facility. There will be numerous employment forms to fill out, and new-hire training will begin. For the first few months on the job, you will be in a probationary period. During this time, you will have an opportunity to evaluate the work environment. In turn, your supervisors will be evaluating your work performance to make sure you are meeting job expectations.

Meeting Coworkers

Making a positive first impression with those you meet is important to get off to a good start. Greet each new coworker with a smile and pleasant conversation. Exhibit a positive attitude and your excitement to be part of the team. Your first impression sets the stage for your working career. When you meet with your new supervisor, convey your enthusiasm to be an asset to the company. Ask for guidance on your activities, people you should meet, and other information to make your first few days productive.

Filling Out Employment Forms

Whenever you begin a new job, come prepared with the personal information you will need to fill out a multitude of forms. This includes your Social Security number, contact information for emergencies, and other personal information. Several of the forms you will fill out include the I-9, W-4, and benefits forms.

Form I-9

The *Form I-9 Employment Eligibility Verification* is used to verify your identity and that you are authorized to work in the US. The Form I-9 is from the Department of Homeland Security of the US Citizenship and Immigration Services. **Figure 7.11** illustrates the portion of the form that shows citizenship status. Both citizens and noncitizens are required to complete this form.

You must complete and sign the Form I-9 in the presence of an authorized representative of the human resources department. You will need to present documentation of your identity when you sign the form. Acceptable documentation commonly includes a valid driver's license, a state-issued photo ID, or a passport. A list of acceptable documents is included on the form. The human resources department will explain this form and answer any questions you may have.

Employment Eligibility Verification

Department of Homeland Security

U.S. Citizenship and Immigration Services

USCIS
Form I-9
OMB No. 1615-0047
Expires 03/31/20XX

▶ **START HERE.**   Read instructions carefully before completing this form. The instructions must be available during completion of this form.
ANTI-DISCRIMINATION NOTICE.   It is illegal to discriminate against work-authorized individuals. Employers **CANNOT** specify which document(s) they will accept from an employee. The refusal to hire an individual because the documentation presented has a future expiration date may also constitute illegal discrimination.

Section 1. Employee Information and Attestation *(Employees must complete and sign Section 1 of Form I-9 no later than the **first day of employment**, but not before accepting a job offer)*

Last Name *(Family Name)*	First Name (Given Name)	Middle Initial	Other Names Used *(if any)*

Address *(Street Number and Name)*	Apt. Number	City or Town	State	Zip Code

Date of Birth *(mm/dd/yyyy)*	U.S. Social Security Number	E-mail Address	Telephone Number
	☐☐☐-☐☐-☐☐☐☐		

I am aware that federal law provides for imprisonment and/or fines for false statements or use of false documents in connection with the completion of this form.

I attest, under penalty of perjury, that I am (check one of the following):

☐ A citizen of the United States

☐ A noncitizen national of the United States *(See instructions)*

☐ A lawful permanent resident (Alien Registration Number/USCIS Number): _____

☐ An alien authorized to work until (expiration date, if applicable, mm/dd/yy) _____. Some aliens may write "NA" in this field.
(See instructions)

For aliens authorized to work, provide your Alien Registration Number/USCIS Number **OR** Form 1-94 Admission Number:

Figure 7.11 The *Form I-9 Employment Eligibility Verification* from the Department of Homeland Security of the US Citizenship and Immigration Services is used to verify your identity and that you are authorized to work in the US. *Have you ever completed one of these forms?*

Copyright Goodheart-Willcox Co., Inc.

Form W-4

The *Form W-4 Employee's Withholding Allowance Certificate* is used to indicate the appropriate amount of taxes to be withheld from your paycheck. Deductions are based on your marital status and the number of dependents you claim, including yourself. Based on your elections, the amounts withheld from your check are forwarded to the appropriate government agency. **Figure 7.12** shows a completed Form W-4.

At the end of the year, the employer sends the employee a *Form W-2 Wage and Tax Statement* to use when filing income tax returns. This form summarizes all wages and deductions for the year for an employee.

Benefits Forms

The human resources department will provide you with a variety of forms that are specific to the compensation package offered by the employer. You will complete forms indicating whether you elect to participate or decline participation in the various programs.

Undergoing New-Hire Training

As a new employee, you will be a part of an orientation for new hires. If you are one of several people hired at the same time, you may participate in group training. If you are the only individual hired at that time, your training may be one-on-one. Human resources, supervisors, and other senior employees typically conduct the training.

Figure 7.12 The *Form W-4 Employee's Withholding Allowance Certificate* indicates the appropriate amount of taxes to be withheld from your paycheck, which are based on marital status and the number of dependents claimed. *Would you claim any deductions when completing this form?*

Copyright Goodheart-Willcox Co., Inc.

Most companies have an employee handbook you will receive as part of the training materials. Topics such as the history of the company, its mission, and company policies will be introduced. Employee-related topics will also be covered, such as employee safety and security, compensation, attendance policies, and benefits.

After the company policies have been presented, your supervisor or someone on your team will train you on the processes and procedures for your specific job. Each team generally has specific guidelines for accomplishing tasks you will need to learn. This is an opportunity to start learning the expectations for your new position.

Evaluating the Work Environment

Each human services job has its own unique **work culture** or environment. Work culture includes the assumptions, values, behaviors, and actions of people as they interact with one another and complete their service or work. In larger work environments, work culture is referred to as **organizational culture** and is broadened to include group norms and other tangible signs of an organization. These tangible signs are easy to recognize. They might include the "look" of the space, the typical clothing worn, and which accomplishments are highlighted. The intangible signs of organizational culture are basically the personality traits of the organization.

Work culture includes emotional and social cultural norms. **Emotional and social cultural norms** include expectations of how workers interact with and respond to one another and clients (**Figure 7.13**). Just like it is often difficult to capture the personality of a person, it is

Figure 7.13 Work culture includes emotional and social cultural norms—that is, expectations of how workers interact with and respond to one another and clients. *What is a good way to understand organizational culture?*

©iStock.com/Cathy Yeulet

Copyright Goodheart-Willcox Co., Inc.

difficult to capture the personality of an organization. An organizational culture may be described as frugal, creative, reflective, or any number of ways. Sometimes organizations or employers describe their culture in ways that they hope to be perceived, but it does not play out in reality.

A good place to start figuring out work culture is with the systems, policies, rules, procedures, and structures. This is often referred to as **political culture**. It is about who holds and wields decision-making power. In human services work, the customer or client often holds the power. Policies, rules, and procedures are often set up with the client or service receiver in mind. Structures, such as caseworkers reporting to case managers, are often created to help and protect both the employees and their clients. Even the organization's company image that is promoted through sales techniques, advertising and marketing, and the product or service itself can be good indicators of work culture.

A subtle but important key to understanding organizational culture is to listen to the daily conversations and negotiations between the members of an organization. Just like in a family or classroom, these conversations are the emergent result of negotiations or ongoing agreements on the proper way to do things. Take the time to listen. Understanding and assessing work culture can mean the difference between success and failure in the workplace (**Figure 7.14**).

Finally, review the organization's published mission and goals. Although these should give an idea about the organization, in reality, there is often a disparity between the published and actual mission and goals of an organization.

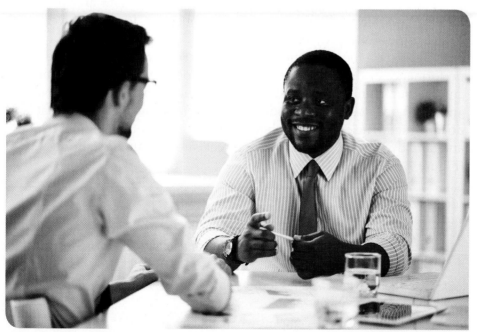

Figure 7.14 Success or failure in the workplace, to a certain extent, depends on understanding and assessing work culture. *Which type of work environment would appeal to you?*

Pressmaster/Shutterstock.com

Copyright Goodheart-Willcox Co., Inc.

Understanding work culture is critical to career success. Just like there are good matches between people, there are good matches between personalities of organizations, employers, and employees. When a good match is made, job stress is lower and employees are more productive.

Being Evaluated on Job Performance

As a student, you expect to receive grades that reflect your effort, commitment, engagement in learning, and meeting competence standards. As an employee, the same holds true. Instead of attending class, completing assignments, and taking tests to achieve grades, however, you are evaluated on your job performance. This, too, might include attendance, commitment, and meeting competency standards. It will likely also involve an evaluation of your customer and workplace relationships, leadership, and initiative. Employee reviews are often called *employee performance evaluations*.

Employee performance evaluations are used both to evaluate employees and as a means for managers or supervisors and their employees to formally communicate with one another. They also serve to protect employers and employees from legal action from disgruntled former employees. Evaluations can provide a systematic method of documenting negative behavior, failure to meet standards, or inability to perform the role with competence.

When employee performance evaluations are done well, better communication occurs. Sometimes good efforts are rewarded with acknowledgement and praise, pay raises, or added responsibilities, such as supervisory duties.

The most effective employee performance evaluations are based on the employer's overall mission or plan for business. If an employer's main business is to provide personal care services, employees should be evaluated on the care that they provide to clients. The employee performance evaluation process should include employee goal setting and measurements for evaluating performance in meeting these goals and standards. It should include regular **performance feedback** that is documented. The evaluation should be discussed between supervisor and employee using good listening, great care, and understanding (**Figure 7.15**).

Reading Recall

1. List three things you are likely to do your first day at a new job.
2. Are the terms *work culture* and *organizational culture* synonymous? Explain your answer.
3. Which cultural trait includes the systems, policies, rules, procedures, and structures of an organization?
4. Why do employers use employee performance reviews?

Copyright Goodheart-Willcox Co., Inc.

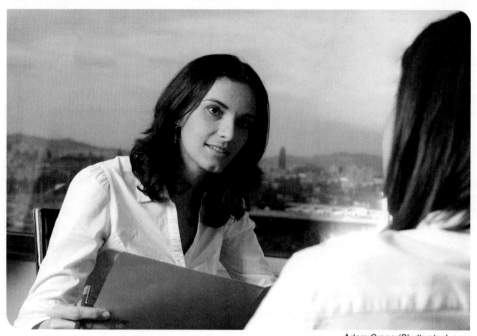

Adam Gregor/Shutterstock.com

Figure 7.15 Employee performance evaluations serve as a means for managers or supervisors and their employees to formally communicate with one another. *What types of items do you think are discussed during employee performance evaluations?*

Leaving a Job

There are many reasons for leaving a job. As a student, you need to focus more on your schoolwork. Maybe your commitment to a sports team or another activity now makes it difficult to find time to work. Maybe you have found a better job opportunity, or perhaps the job has not turned out to be what you had hoped it would be. In the professional world, leaving a job may be for many other reasons, such as the lack of "fit" between the job and your goals or even finding a better job opportunity.

The best way to leave a job is to write a letter of resignation to your supervisor. Just state the fact. "Please accept my resignation effective (date)." Sign your name and date it. There is no need to go into a long written explanation. Of course, you may want to let your supervisor know verbally why you are leaving.

It is considered good practice to give an employer at least two weeks' notice that you will be leaving. Longer is better. This allows your employer time to hire and train another employee. It will also serve to build your reputation as a good employee, especially when seeking job recommendations. Of course, if you are in an unsafe situation, you should leave immediately.

Reading Recall

1. What is the best way to leave a job?
2. How long is considered a reasonable notice of resignation?

Copyright Goodheart-Willcox Co., Inc.

Summary

- Three of the most common ways to find job openings include networking, searching online (through Internet job boards, classified ads, and company websites), and attending job fairs. *Networking* is the act of meeting and making contact with people. *Job fairs* are events where employers network with potential employees.

- Most employers require job seekers to complete an application and submit a résumé. A cover message accompanies a résumé and provides additional details about why a person is qualified for a job. Employers use these items to determine whom to invite for an interview.

- A personal portfolio can be a great tool to use to highlight skills and abilities when interviewing for a job or for personal reflection. An effective portfolio has a clear purpose, reflects uniqueness, shows progress, and reflects professionalism.

- Interviews serve as an opportunity for the employer and job seeker to evaluate whether or not they are a good match. Preparation and practice will lower anxiety and present applicants in the best possible light.

- Your first day at a new job will probably be spent meeting coworkers, filling out employment forms, and undergoing new-hire training.

- Each human services job has its own unique environment or *work culture*. In larger work environments, work culture is referred to as *organizational culture* and is broadened to include group norms and other tangible signs of an organization.

- When leaving a job, giving an employer at least two weeks' notice is considered a good practice.

College and Career Portfolio

Résumé and Cover Message

Whether your portfolio is for school or a job, you will need to include a résumé. A *résumé* is an outline of your education and relevant experience. It should be concise, detailed, and attractive and advertise why your chosen school or company needs *you*.

Many school and job applications require a cover message to accompany a portfolio or résumé. A *cover message* is an outline and explanation of your experiences. It should explain *why* and *how* your experiences have made you uniquely qualified for your desired school or job.

To create your résumé and cover message, complete the following activities.

1. Visit your school's career or writing center, or a local library to learn more about résumés and cover messages.
2. Write a draft résumé and cover message.
3. Ask a career counselor or teacher to review your documents. Edit your résumé and message according to his or her feedback.
4. Carefully proofread your résumé and cover message. Make sure you use proper spelling and grammar throughout the documents.

Copyright Goodheart-Willcox Co., Inc.

Review and Reflect ↪

1. What resources do you have in your town to find out who is hiring?
2. List three types of search criteria you might use when searching for jobs on Internet job boards.
3. Explain ways to successfully navigate a job fair.
4. Who is eligible to be a reference for you in your job search?
5. How long should a résumé be for an entry-level job?
6. What information should you include in a cover message?
7. What are the four common features that effective portfolios share?
8. What should you take with you when you go to an interview? Why?
9. What factors should you consider when weighing a job offer?
10. List three things to consider when evaluating a work environment.
11. What should be included in the employee performance evaluation process?
12. Why is it considered good practice to give an employer at least two weeks' notice that you will be leaving?

Vocabulary Activities

13. **Key terms** On a separate sheet of paper, list words that relate to each of the following terms. Then, work with a partner to explain how these words are related.

cover message
emotional and
  social cultural
  norms
employee
  performance
  evaluations
interview
job application
job fairs

networking
organizational
  culture
performance
  feedback
political culture
portfolio
references
résumé
work culture

14. **Academic terms** With a partner, create a T-chart. Write each of the following vocabulary terms in the left column. Write a *synonym* (a word that has the same or similar meaning) for each term in the right column. Discuss your synonyms with the class.

artifacts   preempt
exude

Self-Assessment Quiz ↪

Complete the self-assessment quiz online to help you practice and expand your knowledge and skills.

Critical Thinking

15. **Identify** Identify who you know that would be a good person to network with when you begin looking for a job.
16. **Evaluate** Check out several Internet job boards. Evaluate the types of information you can obtain from these sites. Which sites would you use to search for jobs?
17. **Determine** Think about all of the people other than relatives who you know that could attest to your work habits, skills, and abilities. Determine which of these people you would like to ask to be your references.
18. **Cause and effect** What would you do if you were an employer who found out that an employee you just hired had embellished and falsified qualifications on his or her résumé?
19. **Make inferences** Résumés are tailor made for the job you are applying for and may have different audiences. Why might you have more than one résumé for the same type of job?
20. **Compare and contrast** Compare and contrast a traditional portfolio with an electronic portfolio. Which would you use? Why?
21. **Determine** Explain in detail the type of outfit you would wear to the following interviews: fast-food restaurant worker, child care worker, sales associate at a retail store, high school teacher, chef, and night clerk at a hotel. Are there any similarities or differences in what you would wear?
22. **Analyze** Think about the considerations you would look at when evaluating a work environment. Why are these considerations necessary for workplace success?

Core Skills

23. **Writing and technology**   Use the lists of your basic skills, accomplishments, and contacts you completed in Chapter 5 to create a one-page résumé for a specific job in human services. To create your résumé, use a word processing program of your choice. Remember to highlight special skills and sell yourself for the job. Have two people edit your résumé to ensure accuracy. Fix any mistakes and then place the final version of your résumé in your portfolio.

24. **Writing and technology**   Cover messages generally have four paragraphs and are put together like a letter. Use a word processing program of your choice to write a cover message for an entry-level position in a human services career. If you need help, refer to Figure 7.6 in the text. Make sure you include your return address, the company's address, the name of the contact person at the company, as well as four paragraphs and a closing. Check for any spelling, grammar, and punctuation errors. Include this in your portfolio.

25. **Research and writing**   Research and write a list of questions to ask potential employers during an interview. Divide the questions into basic and advanced questions. Place this list in your portfolio.

26. **Speaking and writing**   In pairs, conduct a mock interview. Take turns being the interviewer and interviewee. After you both have had a chance to be interviewed, write a one-page summary on how you think this experience will help you when you actually attend an interview.

27. **Reading and speaking**   Read the Law and Ethics feature in this chapter titled *Federal Laws Protect Against Job Discrimination*. In small groups, discuss how the *Civil Rights Act* and the *Equal Pay Act* affect teens. Share your group's thoughts with the rest of the class.

28. **Writing and math**   Obtain two copies of *Form W-4 Employee's Withholding Allowance Certificate*. Fill out one copy of the form as a high school student, and then fill out the second form as an adult with two children. Explain the difference in the amount of money that will be withheld from a paycheck based on these two forms.

29. **Speaking and writing**   Each human services job has its own unique culture. Identify two people in two different fields to talk to and ask about their work environment, including typical clothing worn, expected behaviors, and assumptions that everyone has about the job. Do not forget to ask about emotional and social norms as well as political norms. After speaking with these two people, write a one-page paper explaining the differences between the two fields.

30. **Research and writing**   Using the Internet, choose a nonprofit organization and research its published mission and goals. Create a questionnaire you can share with your classmates to see if the reputation the nonprofit organization has actually reflects the published mission and goals. Write a letter to the CEO of the nonprofit explaining your findings. The questionnaire can be placed in your portfolio.

31. **Listening and speaking**   Interview a human resources director from a local company to find out about the organization's employee performance evaluation process. Be sure to have a list of questions prepared in advance that you can ask during the interview. Share your interview findings with the class.

32. **Technology and writing**   Use a word processing program to write a letter of resignation for the same human services job for which you wrote your cover message. Check for any spelling, grammar, and punctuation errors. A copy of this can be placed in your portfolio.

33. **CTE career readiness practice**   The Internet can provide opportunities to enhance the career search process and increase your productivity. There is much information available about how to make the job application process efficient. List five things you can do to improve your skills for completing a job application.

34. **CTE career readiness practice**   Most people use technology on a daily basis. Using technology in the workplace can help employees be more productive. In other instances, technology can be a distraction. Create a list of five types of technology, such as an app or computer program, and how people can use each to be more productive in the workplace.

   Copyright Goodheart-Willcox Co., Inc.

Lend a Hand

Volunteering for Your Future

When you think about your future, where do you see yourself in 10 years? How about in 20 years? Do you see volunteering as part of your future? If you haven't considered it, how might volunteering benefit your future career success?

As a student, the volunteer work you do now can help you learn what types of careers interest you. Through volunteering, you can discover what type of work suits your personality. You can find out about your skills and strengths and what areas you may need to improve upon to land your dream job. Volunteering can also provide an opportunity to try new things and explore new roles. You might even tap into a talent you would like to develop.

Searching and applying for volunteer work is great practice for your future college search and, eventually, your job search. You can also use your volunteer experience to bolster your college and career portfolio. The people you meet while volunteering may be willing to serve as a reference on college applications. They may even be willing to write a letter of recommendation for your portfolio. You can include in your portfolio photos and videos that encapsulate your volunteer experience. No matter what kind of volunteer work you participate in, these visual elements will enhance your portfolio and highlight your experience as meaningful.

As you join the workforce, volunteering can continue to create valuable opportunities to expand your network. If you become unhappy in a job, the contacts you make while volunteering may lead you to another job. The skills you develop or improve may be just what you need to boost your career.

To start compiling your volunteer experiences for use in your résumé, portfolio, or elsewhere, complete the following:

1. Locate and add to the list of service projects and volunteer activities you created in Chapter 6. If you received a certificate or award related to this service, mention it here. Locate photos and videos you already have from your volunteer work. Place the file in your e-Portfolio and physical portfolio that you are creating for this class.

2. Using the list you made, rate each experience on how much you enjoyed the work. Think about whether you would participate in these activities again, and consider whether you would enjoy a career in that field. Choose the activities you rated as the most enjoyable, and use the *Occupational Outlook Handbook* to search related careers.

Investigating Career Pathways in Human Services

america365/Shutterstock.com

Children's Domestic Violence Advocate

Crystal Johnson

As a children's domestic violence advocate, my job is to provide a 10-week in-home psycho-educational program for children who have witnessed domestic violence. I work with the nonviolent parent and his or her children to address issues that arise post-separation from an abusive partner.

The program focuses on fostering a healthy relationship between the nonviolent parent and his or her children. Research shows this is the number one predictor of resiliency in a child who has witnessed domestic violence. Each week of the program focuses on a different topic. Topics may include safety planning, counseling around why the violence is not the child's fault, coping skills, feelings identification, problem-solving skills, and anger education. I use tools, such as games, puppets, videos, and art for these topics.

Courtesy of Crystal Johnson, photo by Mary Campbell

Most of my job consists of direct service with clients. I am either meeting with clients for the program or conducting intakes on the phone with new clients. The indirect services include preparation for home visits, professional consultations (CPS, legal services, sexual assault centers, schools, etc.), paperwork, and community education about domestic violence. Every day looks different, so there are always new challenges to navigate. The clients I work with, however, do all of the hard work. I am there to offer support and expertise.

The greatest reward in my work is seeing a child's face when his or her parent is sitting on the ground playing silly games, singing a song, or talking about how he or she feels. Sometimes when we go through big transitions, we forget to take time with the people we love to be silly and laugh. It's great to see the families feel like they are able to do that again, and to be a part of that is something special. My goal in this work is to help families feel safe and whole again, and empower them to change the course of their children's lives.

Research Activity

Conduct online research to explore how to become a children's domestic violence advocate. What common aptitudes, abilities, and skills are needed? What are the educational and licensure requirements? What are the rewards and demands of working as a children's domestic violence advocate? What is the projected job outlook? After completing your research, determine whether or not you would be interested in pursuing this as a career. Why or why not?

Copyright Goodheart-Willcox Co., Inc.

Chapter 8

Consumer Services

While studying, look for the activity icon to

- **practice** key and academic terms with e-flash cards and matching activities;
- **assess** what you learn by completing self-assessment quizzes; and
- **reinforce** what you learn by mapping concepts and completing review and reflect questions.

www.g-wlearning.com/humanservices/

bikeriderlondon/Shutterstock.com

Learning Outcomes

After studying this chapter, you will be able to

- **compare and contrast** career opportunities for consumer services workers;
- **list** common aptitudes, attitudes, and skills of consumer services workers;
- **give examples** of postsecondary education, training, and experience required for several consumer services careers;
- **identify** consumer rights and responsibilities and consumer buying techniques;
- **develop** a personal budget and revise accordingly;
- **describe** various ways to save and invest money and use credit wisely; and
- **summarize** the rewards, demands, and future trends of careers in consumer services.

Reading Strategies

Before reading, use reliable online or print resources to research information about careers in consumer services. Record 10 facts you learn from conducting your research. As you are reading this chapter, look for any mention of the facts you identified. After reading, write an essay reflecting on your list in light of what you learned in this chapter.

Mapping Concepts

In small groups, create a photo collage depicting careers in consumer services. Write a two- to three-sentence summary about each career. Share your collage with another group.

Key Terms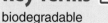

biodegradable
budget
comparison shopping
direct deposit
electronic banking
electronic funds transfer (EFT)
expenses
finance charges
income
installment credit
interest
investing

noninstallment credit
principal
revolving credit
saving
self-advocacy
social sustainability
sustainable
sustainable purchasing
warranty

Academic Terms

defaulted
gouging
intermediaries
just
penalize
redress
solvent

Copyright Goodheart-Willcox Co., Inc.

People often have problems managing their purchases and monetary resources. As some say, "money makes the world go around." Consumer services workers help their clients manage the details of being a consumer in today's complex world. *Consumers* are people who purchase goods and services. Consumer services workers help people solve financial and consumer problems and make good consumer decisions. They educate their clients on how to invest and plan financially. Consumer services workers must focus on the end goal of improving the quality of life for their clients.

Careers in Consumer Services

Career opportunities in consumer services are many, varied, and constantly expanding. Consumer services careers fall into four major tracks. These are consumer advocacy, financial services, customer service, and buying. Examples of careers in each of these areas are shown in **Figure 8.1**.

Figure 8.1 There are many different careers in consumer services. *Which area of consumer services interests you most?*

Examples of Consumer Services Careers	
Consumer advocacy	• Community consumer educator • Community organizer • Consumer advocate • Consumer journalist • Consumer litigation attorney • Consumer lobbyist • Nonprofit foundation manager • Policy analyst
Financial services	• Budget analyst • Credit counselor • Financial advisor • Financial analyst • Financial manager • Insurance sales agent • Insurance underwriter
Customer service	• Computer support specialist • Customer service representative • Retail sales manager • Retail sales worker • Sales manager • Sales worker
Buying	• Buyer • Purchasing agent • Purchasing manager • Retail buyer • Supply chain manager

Copyright Goodheart-Willcox Co., Inc.

Consumer Advocacy

Consumer advocacy involves speaking on behalf of or supporting consumers. *Consumer advocates* are human services workers who are on the side of consumers, looking out for their best interests. They listen to consumers' concerns. They provide information about consumer rights and offer guidance for **self-advocacy** (the action of speaking up for and representing oneself). They support actions to resolve a consumer-related conflict. Consumer advocates play an important role in today's business world. They often represent the "underdog" and seemingly powerless. Consumer advocates help them have a voice as consumers of goods and services.

Some consumer advocates work for consumer protection organizations (**Figure 8.2**). In these organizations, consumer advocates protect consumers by stopping unfair business practices so the impact on consumers is minimized. They may lead the charge to *penalize* (punish) those who carry out unfair business practices. Overall, their goals are to improve the quality of life for consumers and to enhance the quality of the marketplace by encouraging *just* (honest; fair) practices.

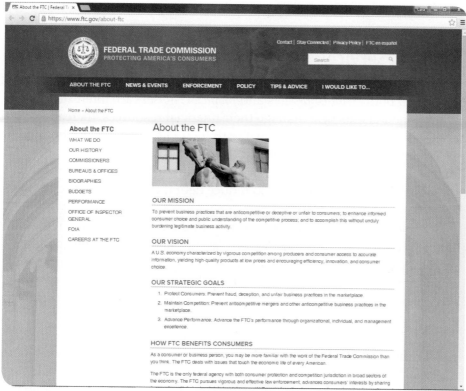

Source: Federal Trade Commission

Figure 8.2 The Federal Trade Commission (FTC) protects consumers by working to prevent unfair, anticompetitive, and deceptive business practices. *What are some other consumer protection organizations?*

Copyright Goodheart-Willcox Co., Inc.

In addition to consumer advocates, there are many other careers that fall into the category of consumer advocacy. Some of these include the following:

- *Community consumer educators* provide information and resources for consumers and the public in general.

- *Community organizers* recruit people to work together to raise awareness about an issue at the local, state, or federal level.

- *Consumer journalists* specialize in consumer matters, highlighting, advocating, or solving consumer issues. They may work in broadcast television, radio, print, or electronic media.

- *Consumer litigation attorneys* specialize in consumer issues or unjust practices, prosecuting those who fail to follow the law. They may specialize as *policy analysts*, carefully reviewing proposed or newly enacted laws or regulations for potential impact on consumers.

- *Consumer lobbyists* are also involved in regulations and laws. They are generally at the front end as campaigners for fair trade and consumer interest laws.

- *Nonprofit foundation managers* typically oversee the day-to-day operations and fundraising activities to support the foundation's cause.

Financial Services

In *financial services*, workers deal with money, investments, and insurance. Both *credit counselors* and *financial advisors* are interested in helping their clients best manage their financial resources, increase assets, and reduce debt. They meet with their clients to discuss financial situations in-depth. They use this information to assess each client's financial status. They review both income and debt and then propose a plan. This often involves a way to reduce debt through an agreed upon budget and spending plan.

Financial managers propose solutions to their clients on how to become financially *solvent* (secure), with more savings and investments to meet short- or long-term goals. *Financial analysts* specialize in researching and recommending stock performances as investments for their clients. *Budget analysts* work in the corporate world. They develop and review budget proposals and monitor organizational spending.

For the insurance area of financial services, *insurance sales agents* sell people and businesses different types of insurance to protect against financial loss resulting from accidents. Many insurance sales agents also provide financial planning services, such as retirement planning. *Insurance underwriters* review a person's financial situation to determine whether to insure an applicant. They also decide on insurance coverage amounts and premiums.

Copyright Goodheart-Willcox Co., Inc.

Case Study | *Money Matters*

Rona had dreams of becoming a midwife and returning to the Philippines, the country of her birth. She had not returned there since she was in high school. On her last visit, she worked with a nurse and a midwife in the poverty-stricken community outside the city of Manila. She returned home knowing that becoming a midwife was her dream. Now, she has found a college training program. A large debt that an unexpected visit to the hospital emergency room last year brought on, however, is thwarting her dream.

Rona had gone to the emergency room at the urging of the medics who responded to her at the scene of a car accident. She was uninsured at the time. The debt was huge, over $10,000. When she did not pay the bill, she could not get a car loan. The debt also prevented her from getting a credit card. Now she is concerned that she will not be awarded any student loans. As a result, she is not even trying. Frustrated and feeling stuck, Rona decided to ask for a free financial makeover from a credit counselor who was volunteering one Saturday morning at her community center.

The meeting with the credit counselor turned out to be very helpful. The credit counselor analyzed Rona's situation and then offered her some suggestions. The counselor helped Rona make some key decisions that resulted in cutting back her spending, lowering her housing costs, and making plans to invest in her future. Rona could feel her load lightening. The future felt much brighter.

Rona's credit counselor is just one example of a financial services worker. Financial services workers teach people how to use their financial resources wisely to meet their needs, wants, and goals and lead a higher quality of life.

R. Gino Santa Maria/Shutterstock.com

For Discussion

1. Which of Rona's decisions got her into financial distress?
2. Over which circumstances did Rona have control? Which did she not control?
3. What specific skills did Rona's financial counselor use to solve her financial struggles?

Customer Service

Customer service refers to taking care of customers' needs. *Customer service representatives* are the *intermediaries* (go-betweens) between a company and its customers. Their days are usually spent answering questions, quoting products and services, entering orders, and handling customer complaints. *Computer support specialists* solve customers' problems with computer software or equipment, satisfying both the customer and the supplier. They listen to and ask questions about the customer's problem and then provide solutions to fix the issue.

Copyright Goodheart-Willcox Co., Inc.

Law and Ethics   *Trust—The Cornerstone of Fiduciary Duty*

Financial services workers carry a huge responsibility to always keep the best interests of their clients and customers in the forefront. After all, the advice and service they offer their clients can have long-lasting effects on the clients' financial health and well-being. In this relationship, their clients are often vulnerable. Thus, financial services workers' loyalty must be undivided. Their clients must be confident that this is indeed the case.

Financial services workers who are placed in a position of trust to watch over the financial assets of others are called *fiduciaries*. Their responsibilities are termed *fiduciary duty*. Fiduciary duty is both an ethical and legal responsibility. Various state statutes and laws support this responsibility.

Examples of fiduciaries include investment bankers, financial counselors, asset managers, and managers of pension or retirement plans. It is important to know that not all financial planners or managers have fiduciary duty. Therefore, it is possible to get guidance that is designed to benefit the financial planner (in potential commissions earned) more than the client.

Fiduciary responsibility includes trust. It also includes loyalty and disclosure. Loyalty means outside forces will not sway the financial services worker. The worker will keep the best interests of his or her client in mind. Disclosure means transactions will be transparent. If the provider is benefitting from the services provided, this should be communicated openly. Loyalty and disclosure result in trust—the cornerstone of fiduciary duty.

Research Activity

Using online or print sources, research what the fiduciary laws or statutes are in your state. Who is considered a fiduciary? Share your findings with the rest of the class.

Customer service representatives are critical to positive business transactions. As purchasing interactions become less face-to-face and more dependent on technology, these representatives' skills become even more needed to smooth out frustrations that sometimes occur in the process (**Figure 8.3**). Overall, their goal is to mediate and support the purchase of the product or service so both the customer's and supplier's needs are met.

Sales workers, or *salespeople*, are needed in any industry involving sales of products or services. Sales workers help customers select and purchase or obtain goods and services. They often help their customers identify a need. They offer options. Finally, they close the sale. Other duties include managing stock, reviewing inventory and sales records, developing merchandising plans, and coordinating sales promotions. *Sales managers* supervise sales workers. They are often involved in incentive plans and forecasting future sales.

The retail industry provides fashion goods and services directly to customers. *Retail sales workers* work directly with customers to help them choose and purchase goods. *Retail sales managers* ensure customers get prompt service and quality goods. This means retail sales managers have total responsibility over all aspects of the store's daily functioning. They handle customer complaints and questions. They also oversee employees and are responsible for hiring, interviewing, training, and staffing.

Copyright Goodheart-Willcox Co., Inc.

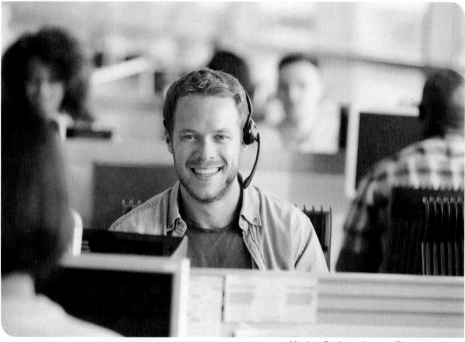

Monkey Business Images/Shutterstock.com

Figure 8.3 Effective customer service representatives have excellent speaking and active listening skills. *What other skills should a customer service representative possess?*

Buying

Buying involves choosing suppliers and merchandise for businesses and organizations. Typical positions in buying include buyers, retail buyers, purchasing agents, purchasing managers, and supply chain managers.

Buyers and *purchasing agents* purchase materials or services for their businesses and organizations. Some buyers focus on purchasing goods and services so the business can create higher-level products. Other buyers, such as *retail buyers*, purchase products to resell to consumers (**Figure 8.4**). Buyers of more complex products or product lines are *purchasing managers* or *supply chain managers*.

Buyers, of course, work with suppliers. Buyers evaluate suppliers to choose from whom they will purchase. They consider the price, performance, and quality of a needed product to get the best deal for their company. They look at the availability or time it will take to deliver the product. They also consider the reliability of the product and reputation of the supplier.

An important part of the buying process is negotiating with the supplier. Price and delivery must be agreed upon. A purchasing contract must be signed. Part of the contract includes expectations for any necessary corrective actions if a product arrives defective or does not perform as expected.

Copyright Goodheart-Willcox Co., Inc.

iofoto/Shutterstock.com

Figure 8.4 Anything that can be purchased in a retail store, such as kitchen dishes and utensils, was likely purchased by a retail buyer. The exception is if the retailer is also the manufacturer of the product. *What are some factors buyers must consider when evaluating suppliers?*

Buyers meet suppliers through a multitude of venues. These venues include trade shows, meetings, and conferences. This may involve frequent travel to these events. Depending on the industry, buyers may even travel abroad. Vendors may come to buyers trying to gain their business. Buyers and suppliers also connect through phone calls, as well as electronic and print media. Sometimes, buyers work with manufacturers to produce a specific desired product.

In addition to working with suppliers, buyers also study current inventory levels and determine when to order new items. Retail buyers may even determine which products to sell and when items will be marked down. They decide when to reorder products. Buyers play a huge role in the success of an organization. When the needed supplies for manufacturing, selling, or providing a service are made available, organizations may succeed.

Reading Recall

1. Describe the role of a consumer advocate.
2. In what ways do financial services workers help their clients?
3. Name three specific careers in financial services.
4. Describe the typical job duties of a customer service representative.
5. Name three types of buying careers.

Copyright Goodheart-Willcox Co., Inc.

Common Aptitudes, Attitudes, and Skills

Effective consumer services workers typically share common aptitudes, attitudes, and skills (**Figure 8.5**). For example, consumer services workers often possess strong interpersonal, verbal communication, and writing skills. Consumer services workers are skilled at solving their clients' personal consumer or financial problems. They resolve issues between conflicting parties through mediation, counseling, or strongly stated demands. They can read people's nonverbal cues, objectively listen, and show respect for those whose values are different from their own.

Consumer services workers know their content well. For example, consumer advocates know about consumer rights and responsibilities. Financial counselors are well-versed in financial knowledge, including investments and taxation. Customer service representatives understand order entry processes, consumer rights, the specifications of the product, and the expectations of the supplier. Buyers keep up-to-date in their field. They know the latest in product features, manufacturing processes, demands, and materials. They keep up with consumer trends and learn to forecast what might be coming next.

For many consumer services careers, workers must possess good analytical and math skills. Consumer services workers are focused, detail oriented, and good problem solvers. They are also very good at working with people. For example, customer service representatives are often called on to calm nerves and handle angry responses to solve consumer complaints and restore customer relations.

Common Aptitudes, Attitudes, and Skills of Consumer Services Workers

- Analytical
- Detail oriented
- Focused
- Patient
- Polite
- Socially perceptive
- Persuasive
- Fair
- Respectful
- Ethical
- Gets along well with others
- Active listener
- Conveys information effectively—verbally and in writing
- Establishes trust with clients
- Responds well to client's questions and concerns
- Explains complex financial concepts in understandable language
- Problem-solving skills
- Decision-making skills
- Conflict resolution skills
- Math skills

Figure 8.5 Consumer services workers share common aptitudes, attitudes, and skills. *What other aptitudes, attitudes, and skills would you add to this list?*

Copyright Goodheart-Willcox Co., Inc.

Having a good reputation and earning trust are particularly important traits for all consumer services workers (**Figure 8.6**). A reputation for being fair, respectful, and ethical is important in this field. People's financial futures are often at stake.

Reading Recall

1. Describe the common aptitudes, attitudes, and skills of consumer services workers.

2. List two careers in consumer services in which workers need to have knowledge about consumer rights.

Education, Training, and Experience

Most consumer services careers require postsecondary education, training, and experience. Consumer advocates in entry-level jobs often hold a bachelor's degree in a related field. They may have a degree in areas such as business, accounting, family and consumer sciences, political science, sociology, finance, or communications. Consumer educators typically hold related degrees. Some hold degrees in education. Consumer litigation attorneys need a law degree and regional certification to practice. Many times, they spend extra time specializing in a particular area of consumer advocacy.

oliveromg/Shutterstock.com

Figure 8.6 Consumer services workers can earn clients' trust by acting fairly, respectfully, and ethically. *Why is having a good reputation especially important for consumer services workers?*

Copyright Goodheart-Willcox Co., Inc.

For financial services, a bachelor's degree in either finance or accounting is preferred. Employers, and many states, may require financial counselors to earn the Certified Personal Finance Counselor (CPFC) certification, usually offered by their home state. Many financial services workers choose to earn a graduate degree, such as a master's of business administration (MBA). This helps them to further prepare for advancement and build their knowledge base or perceived expertise and credibility.

Customer service representatives, first and foremost, must be well-versed in their product and the company culture they represent. Some companies hire customer service representatives with minimal post–high school education, preferring to provide on-the-job training. Others, especially those in the technical fields, prefer or even require a college education. This may be a two-year associate's degree or a four-year bachelor's degree. Majors in business, as well as many other interdisciplinary majors, can provide good preparation for this career because customer service requires good communication skills.

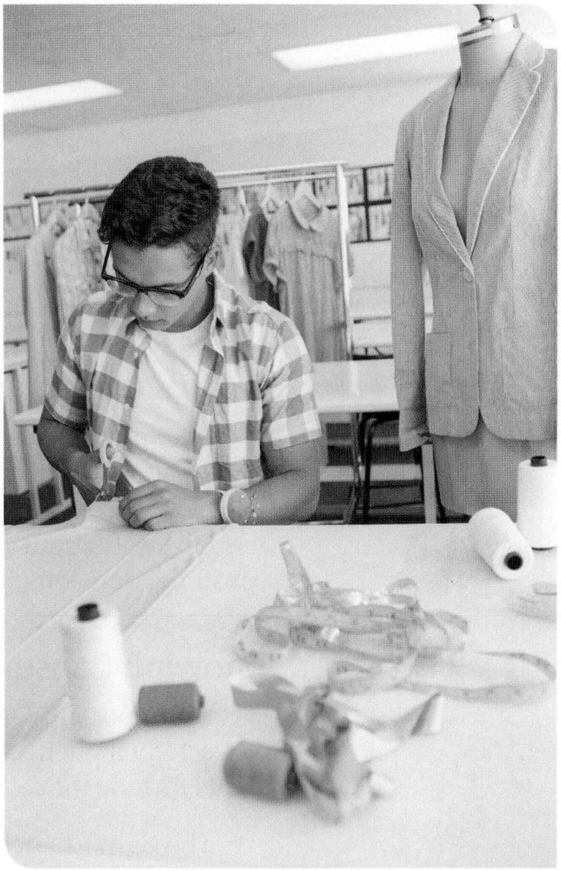

In buying careers, educational requirements vary greatly, depending on the industry and size of the organization. For some, a high school diploma with some training and experience is sufficient to enter the field. For most, however, a bachelor's degree is preferred or required. Business and accounting courses are desired, along with product knowledge. For example, in fashion retail buying, knowledge about apparel construction, sizing, textiles, and fashion trends is needed (**Figure 8.7**). In manufacturing firms, a four-year college degree is preferred or often required, especially in the technical field. Engineering, applied sciences, and business degrees are common. On-the-job training is a critical part of learning the expectations of buying in a chosen field.

wavebreakmedia/Shutterstock.com

Figure 8.7 A formal education in fashion merchandising or fashion design can help aspiring fashion retail buyers gain knowledge about the fashion industry. *Why is it important for buyers to be knowledgeable about the products they are purchasing?*

Overall, most careers in consumer services require at least a college education. Many consumer services careers also require certifications, based on specialization of expertise. Professionals who earn these certifications show they have the knowledge and skill to manage their clients' financial resources or give good advice.

Copyright Goodheart-Willcox Co., Inc.

Reading Recall

1. What information do customer service representatives need to know the best?

2. What level of education is needed for a career in buying?

3. What level of education do most consumer services workers possess?

Specialized Knowledge for Consumer Services Careers

Occupations in consumer services require workers to possess specialized knowledge. Many careers in consumer services involve helping people with consumer and financial problems. Consumer services workers need to know about consumer rights and responsibilities and understand consumer decisions. They also need to be able to manage finances.

Knowing Consumer Rights and Responsibilities

An important responsibility of many consumer services workers is to teach their clients and customers about their consumer rights. These rights include the following:

- The right to safety. The services or products should not harm clients and customers. This includes physical and emotional safety.

- The right to be informed. Consumers have the right to be informed with sufficient information to make intelligent decisions about services or products.

- The right to choose. Consumers have the right to choose which services or products they want (**Figure 8.8**). Consumer laws prohibit price *gouging* (overcharging) or cutting that makes for unfair advantage and fewer choices for consumers.

- The right to be heard. Consumers need to be provided with a way to voice their concerns or complaints about products and services.

- The right to redress. *Redress* refers to setting right something that is wrong. If an issue is not handled effectively, outside agencies exist to ensure action is taken to address consumer complaints. The Better Business Bureau, a national nongovernment organization, is one such agency that can act to help wronged consumers. Sometimes this may result in political or legal action.

- The right to consumer education. Consumer educators inform consumers about their consumer rights. Many publications and classes exist in schools and communities to provide this education.

Copyright Goodheart-Willcox Co., Inc.

fiphtoto/Shutterstock.com

Figure 8.8 Consumer laws that prevent price gouging or cutting prevent unfair advantages and ensure more choices for consumers. *What do you think would happen if these consumer laws did not exist?*

To enforce their basic rights, consumers have certain responsibilities they should uphold. These include the following:

- Use products properly. Products are manufactured to meet specifications. If a product is abused or used in a way that is not intended, the consumer may not have the right to ask for compensation.

- Utilize information. Most products, especially electrical products, come with user instructions and cautions or warnings. Consumers are responsible for following the usage instructions and safety warnings to prevent injury or other harm to people and property.

- Make careful choices. Consumers are responsible for making wise choices in products. One way to do this is to be a comparison shopper. **Comparison shopping** involves looking at different makes and models of a product at various stores (**Figure 8.9**).

- Speak up about likes and dislikes. Unless service providers or manufacturers get feedback, they have no way of making corrections or offering to redress. Consumers should speak to someone as soon as they notice the problem.

- Take action to have a wrong corrected. Usually, there are time limits for returning products or getting a warranty repair or replacement.

Copyright Goodheart-Willcox Co., Inc.

Dmitry Kalinovsky/Shutterstock.com

Figure 8.9 When comparison shopping, consumers should compare product features, quality, and price to identify the best choice for them. *Are you a comparison shopper?*

A **warranty** is a written guarantee from the manufacturer that a product is in good condition.

- Become educated about consumer rights. Although consumer rights exist, manufacturers are not required to direct consumers in taking action. Consumers need to learn about their rights.

Understanding Consumer Buying Techniques

Using finances wisely to make purchases requires careful planning and decision making. Comparison shopping is just one buying technique many consumers use to make good purchasing decisions. Wise consumers are also aware of all the places they can shop and choose the places that best meet their needs. They evaluate advertisements and determine whether or not they really need the product. They are also concerned about identifying sustainable products. Sometimes, consumers may have problems with goods and services they purchase and must take action to handle their complaints.

Deciding Where to Shop

Historically, consumers have purchased products in what are now known as *brick and mortar stores*. These stores have an actual presence in a location. Consumers get to examine what they want before buying it and then leave with the product in hand. Within this category, there are specialty stores that may charge a premium for having experts available

Copyright Goodheart-Willcox Co., Inc.

to guide customers' purchasing. There are also "box stores" that may offer better pricing, but provide less customer service and guidance. These types of stores may be labeled as *retail* and *warehouse stores*. One potential drawback of brick and mortar stores is that some items may be out of stock.

To avoid trips to the store only to find out the item is not in stock, many consumers like to shop online. *Online shopping* utilizes the Internet and virtual stores to make purchases (**Figure 8.10**). When shopping online, consumers are able to research the item before having it shipped directly to them. One advantage of online shopping is the convenience it provides. Another advantage is that prices may be lower than at brick and mortar stores. This is because the seller does not have to pay for retail space and may not carry as much inventory. One disadvantage of shopping online is that consumers do not have a chance to touch or try what they are buying. Other disadvantages include the cost and extra time required for shipping items.

Many times, consumers are able to try out a product in a brick and mortar store and then purchase it online. This raises an ethics question. The store owner has invested in providing consumers with a location and inventory to try out products. If a consumer buys the same product online, is this treating the store owner unfairly? Should consumers only research items online that they intend to buy online?

In some cases, items that consumers purchase may be available used. Some brick and mortar stores and several online sources sell used or rebuilt items. Consumers may save a lot of money buying a used product. On the other hand, the product will likely be sold "as-is," with no warranty or guarantee of being in working condition.

Bloomua/Shutterstock.com

Figure 8.10 Online shopping allows consumers to shop from home, work, or even on the go. *What are some advantages and disadvantages of online shopping?*

Evaluating Advertising Claims

Quite often, the only way consumers know a product exists is through advertising. Consumers are frequently being exposed to advertising. Advertising takes many forms (**Figure 8.11**). Online, there are banner ads on almost every webpage. Many online video

Figure 8.11 There are many ways that companies can reach consumers through advertisement media. *Which of these advertising media do you encounter most often?*

Kheng Guan Toh/Shutterstock.com

clips have trailers advertising products and services. There is advertising in print media—magazines, newspapers, mailers, and flyers. About 30 percent of network television time is dedicated to paid advertising.

Advertisements can be useful to help inform consumers about products and services. Consumers must be aware, however, that just because a product is advertised, it is not always good for them. An advertiser's goal is to try to get consumers to buy their product. As with all consumer decisions, consumers need to critically evaluate advertisements before making any purchasing decisions.

Identifying Sustainable Products

Many consumers are looking to buy sustainable products. **Sustainable** relates to a method of using a resource so it does not deplete or destroy the resource. In today's society, consumers have much more knowledge about the depletion or overuse of natural resources and the need to manage and reuse resources. This concern has led consumers to practice sustainable shopping (**Figure 8.12**). **Sustainable purchasing** involves buying products that benefit environmental, social, or human health.

Copyright Goodheart-Willcox Co., Inc.

Sustainable Shopping Techniques

- Learn about how a product is produced and how it can be disposed of before purchasing.
- Look for products that are reusable, not disposable. For example, use cloth napkins rather than paper napkins. Use a reusable stainless steel or aluminum water bottle filled with tap water rather than bottled water.
- Buy products in bulk to avoid single-packaged items. Store items in reusable glass containers rather than plastic ones.
- Take your own shopping bag with you to avoid using plastic bags.
- Buy used items or buy items to share with others.
- Take advantage of the local library or used book store.
- Look for products that use recycled materials or are energy efficient. Labels such as Energy Star or EPEAT help identify energy efficient products.
- Buy locally grown fruits and vegetables and organic foods.
- Choose *Marine Stewardship Council (MSC)-certified* seafood.
- Look for biodegradable cleaning products.

Figure 8.12 Consumers who practice sustainable shopping techniques help combat the depletion or destruction of resources. *Which of these sustainable shopping techniques do you practice? Can you think of other techniques to add to this list?*

In response to consumers' needs for sustainable products, many companies are changing their manufacturing processes. They are using more environmentally friendly and health conscious materials and packaging. They are also meeting environmental leadership standards to produce more sustainable products. These "greener" products typically include labels such as *energy efficient, made from recycled content,* or *biodegradable* (**Figure 8.13**). **Biodegradable** means that a product can break down or decompose naturally without harming the environment.

In addition to the sustainability of product materials and packaging, many consumers also care about a company's social sustainability. **Social sustainability** involves issues such as human rights; fair labor laws; community development; and health, safety, and wellness. Before purchasing items, consumers want to make sure the companies from which they are buying are being socially responsible.

Ye Liew/Shutterstock.com

Figure 8.13 Special labels such as this one enable consumers to identify products that are biodegradable. *Have you seen a label like this on any products you have purchased?*

Handling Consumer Complaints

To handle consumer problems with products, manufacturers and sellers often have policies for warranty repairs or replacements

Copyright Goodheart-Willcox Co., Inc.

and returns. Depending on the type of product, the manufacturer may warrant that the product is free from workmanship defects for a period of time, often ranging from months to years. If a product breaks while under warranty, consumers can follow the directions on the warranty to have the product repaired or replaced.

The seller usually sets policies that have to do with returns of products. Some sellers do not accept any product returns. Others allow returns if the product does not work. Some return policies may require that the product has not been used. A proof of purchase, or receipt, is often needed for returns. Return policies are usually similar whether consumers purchase the product in a store or online. In many cases, to promote online sales, merchants that sell both online and through stores will allow an online purchase to be returned to a brick and mortar store.

When returning an item to the seller, consumers may need to decide whether they want to exchange the item for another one or receive a refund. Refunds may be given in cash or store credit. For returns on credit card purchases, the refund is often credited to the consumer's credit card. When returning items, consumers need to remember to be fair in their expectations.

Sometimes, consumers are unable to get a satisfactory solution to their problem. When this occurs, there are many avenues consumers can pursue, going as far as working through the Better Business Bureau or taking legal action. Usually, there are less drastic actions consumers can take to achieve satisfactory results. For example, some complaints can be handled by calmly and politely expressing the issue to the customer service representative. If this person is unable to help, consumers can ask to speak to the store manager and then politely restate the problem. If this still does not work and the problem cannot be resolved at the store, consumers can write a complaint letter (**Figure 8.14**).

Managing Finances

Expert Insight

"A fool and his money are soon parted."

Thomas Tusser,
English poet

Many consumer services workers must possess a thorough knowledge of financial management. How people manage their finances can positively or negatively impact their lives. Many people develop a budget to manage their money. A **budget** is a written financial plan to manage income, expenses, and savings.

Budgeting

There are many benefits to creating a budget. By viewing a written list of planned **expenses** (goods and services requiring payment), people can see how they are spending their money. Through budgeting, people are able to determine when they can afford to purchase items. Using a budget can also help them plan and set money aside for future expenses.

Copyright Goodheart-Willcox Co., Inc.

7251 Autumn Lane
Peoria, IL 61604

May 23, 20XX

Ms. Ellie Smith
Director of Customer Service
ABC Company
481 Court Street
East Peoria, IL 61611

Dear Ms. Smith:

I recently purchased a bicycle from your ABC Company, and have enclosed a copy of my receipt. Overall, I am very pleased with the purchase. However, there is one problem that I am having for which I cannot get a fair resolution.

From the first day of delivery of the bicycle on May 18, both wheels have had a slight warp to them. When I returned the bicycle to the shop on May 22, I was told that this is not covered under warranty and that I would have to pay for the repair.

Because this is a new bicycle, I think you would agree that it should work as advertised. I am not asking for unreasonable compensation, I would just like to have the wheels in working order.

I am hoping that you will approve the needed repair at cost to ABC Company. If you are not authorized to approve this, please let me know whom I should escalate this situation to at ABC Company.

Thank you for your attention to this problem.

Sincerely,

Lena Zheng

Lena Zheng

Enclosure

Figure 8.14 Consumers can write a complaint letter to a store's corporate headquarters or the product manufacturer if their problem cannot be resolved at the store. *What can consumers do if the problem is not resolved after the letter of complaint?*

Copyright Goodheart-Willcox Co., Inc.

Following are five basic steps to creating a budget:

1. Gather information. Locate any available information about personal **income** (money earned) and expenses, such as bank statements or check stubs.

2. Determine income. Record the total amount of income available, including cash on hand. Use net income when taxes are being deducted from a paycheck (**Figure 8.15**).

3. Identify spending needs. List all fixed and discretionary expenses. *Fixed expenses* are costs that do not vary from time period to time period. Rent, car payments, and insurance premiums are examples of fixed expenses. *Discretionary expenses* are costs that vary in price and frequency. Entertainment and clothing purchases are examples of discretionary expenses. In addition to fixed and discretionary expenses, many budgets also include a *miscellaneous* category for unplanned expenses.

4. Total all income and then all expenses. If expenses are greater than income, overspending will result. If income is equal to expenses, overspending will not occur, but **saving** (setting money aside) will not be possible either. Saving money can occur only when income is greater than expenses (**Figure 8.16**).

5. Revise as needed. Make changes to the budget as necessary and remember that the budget needs to be flexible. Financial changes may include eliminating or reducing expenses. Prioritize to identify expenses that are needs and those that are wants.

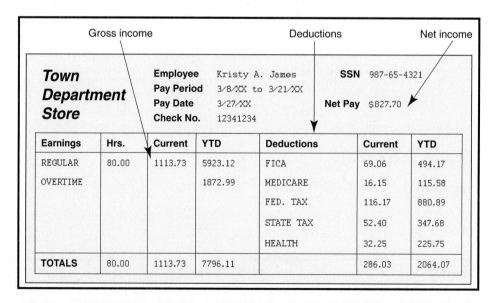

Gross income   Deductions   Net income

Town Department Store

Employee	Kristy A. James
Pay Period	3/8/XX to 3/21/XX
Pay Date	3/27/XX
Check No.	12341234

SSN 987-65-4321

Net Pay $827.70

Earnings	Hrs.	Current	YTD	Deductions	Current	YTD
REGULAR	80.00	1113.73	5923.12	FICA	69.06	494.17
OVERTIME			1872.99	MEDICARE	16.15	115.58
				FED. TAX	116.17	880.89
				STATE TAX	52.40	347.68
				HEALTH	32.25	225.75
TOTALS	80.00	1113.73	7796.11		286.03	2064.07

Figure 8.15 A paycheck stub shows how much gross income you earn and how much is taken out for deductions, which then equals your net income. *What other sources of income might you have?*

Copyright Goodheart-Willcox Co., Inc.

My Monthly Budget		
Income		
Part-time job	$150	
Babysitting	$50	
Gifts	$5	
Total income		$205
Expenses		
Fixed expenses		
Lunch	$30	
Flexible expenses		
Magazines	$5	
Snacks and eating out	$20	
Clothing and accessories	$20	
Transportation	$10	
Other flexible expenses	$10	
Total expenses		$95

Figure 8.16 When income is greater than expenses, saving money can occur. *How much money can be saved in this budget?*

Saving and Investing

Budgeting is not only about spending to meet needs and wants, but also about saving and investing for the future. **Investing** involves putting money into something to gain a financial return.

A common way to save money is to open a savings account that earns interest. **Interest** is a percentage of money the financial institution pays regularly for the use of the account holder's money. With an interest-bearing savings account, the interest rate is usually fairly low, but the **principal** (original amount invested) will grow over time. **Figure 8.17** shows other common ways to save and invest.

Banking Electronically

In times past, invoices or statements were mailed to purchasers of goods and services. The purchasers wrote checks and mailed them to the merchant. This took time and created a significant cost for transactions in printed paper, postage, and check processing.

Electronic banking has changed this process significantly (**Figure 8.18**). **Electronic banking** involves using the Internet to access banking services. Through the use of electronic banking, people can instantly check account balances and look at their statements. They can transfer money from one account to another, which is called **electronic funds transfer (EFT)**. They may even use *online bill pay* to electronically

Common Ways to Save and Invest	
Money market account	A type of savings account requiring a large minimum deposit. This account earns a higher rate of interest than a regular interest-bearing savings account. A money market account pays current interest rates. These rates change from day to day. A money market account is a relatively safe place to hold money between other investment transactions.
Certificate of deposit (CD)	Similar to a savings account. The financial institution issues a CD to a person for a minimum dollar amount and fixed time frame, such as $5,000 for one year. In exchange for the commitment, the financial institution will typically guarantee a higher rate of return than on a savings account.
Stocks, mutual funds, and bonds	*Stocks* represent part ownership in companies called *public companies*. *Mutual funds* are groupings of stocks. These groupings are managed by fund managers. Investments in mutual funds typically follow guidelines and levels of risk and represent a smaller ownership in many companies. *Bonds* are loans to companies or government entities at a fixed rate for a fixed period of time. When investors purchase bonds, they own a small share of the loan. Bonds offer a fixed income or interest rate return. There is some risk, however, in the borrower defaulting on the loan.
Retirement plans	A *401(k)* is an employer sponsored retirement plan. In a 401(k), the employee and/or employer make the investment. Anyone saving for retirement can start and invest in an *individual retirement account (IRA)* at a financial institution. There are three different types of IRAs. These are *Traditional*, *Roth*, and *Rollover*. Each type provides different tax benefits.

Figure 8.17 Sometimes, money will grow faster if invested. Investing carries some risk, however. *What might be a risk of investing?*

schedule and make a payment. Online bill pay is a service many financial institutions offer.

Today, written checks are almost a thing of the past. Most money transactions can now be done electronically. Many employers offer their employees the option of direct deposit. **Direct deposit** is an electronic payment from the employer's account to the employee's bank account. With direct deposit and online bill pay, no checks are written. Nothing is mailed. Even if a check is received, many financial institutions offer applications that allow photo deposit of checks into a personal checking or savings account. Another way to pay for a transaction or withdraw money from an account is to use a *debit card*. This card allows access to a checking account to pay for a purchase. A debit card can also be used to obtain cash through an automated teller machine (ATM).

As with all money transactions, security and the safety of consumers' assets are considerations. Banks and other companies are not flawless. There are regular reports of security breaches. In these breaches, individuals' identities are stolen. These identities may include financial

Copyright Goodheart-Willcox Co., Inc.

data. Anyone using electronic banking should take great care to keep account numbers, IDs, and passwords protected. Passwords should also be changed regularly.

Using Credit Wisely

Using credit involves buying or borrowing now and paying later. People use credit for many reasons. They might use credit to meet personal expenses, purchase a consumer good, finance an education, or buy a car or house. Several different types of credit are available, depending on a person's needs. These include installment credit, noninstallment credit, and revolving credit.

Installment credit is a cash loan repaid with interest in equal, regular payments. Installment credit may be obtained from a number of sources. These include financial institutions and mortgage and credit card companies. This type of credit is typically used for larger purchases, such as a car or home.

Student loans are another form of installment credit. These loans can offer students more affordable payments for higher education costs. Payments start immediately after the education is completed. This may come at a difficult time, when graduates are just starting to establish themselves or having trouble finding employment. These loans must be repaid, however, and cannot be *defaulted* (failed to pay). If a person defaults on a federal student loan (which is the most common form of student loan), there are serious consequences (**Figure 8.19**).

Bloomua/Shutterstock.com

Figure 8.18 Many banks now provide options for mobile banking, making electronic banking even more convenient. *Does your bank offer a mobile banking app?*

Similar to installment credit, in which payments are made and interest charges are assessed, **noninstallment credit** is offered by a financial institution or merchant to a consumer. The major difference is that, with noninstallment credit, the entire balance is expected to be paid at once on a short-term loan—generally in one month. Interest may or may not be charged on noninstallment credit.

Most credit cards are a form of **revolving credit**. The lender determines a credit line, or maximum amount of credit offered. The consumer uses the revolving credit line throughout a month to make purchases. A month-end statement is sent to the consumer. He or she must pay some or all of the balance. The loan amount at any moment, then, is not fixed. It revolves around the amount purchased and payments made.

Copyright Goodheart-Willcox Co., Inc.

wavebreakmedia/Shutterstock.com

Figure 8.19 Defaulting on a federal student loan can result in the government taking a portion of your earnings, suing you, or reducing payments on benefits (such as Social Security retirement or disability). The IRS can also take any tax refunds you receive. *If someone is struggling to pay a student loan, what should the person do?*

With revolving credit, lenders make money through **finance charges**, which are fees charged for buying on credit. In the case of credit cards, lenders may charge both the merchant a percentage of the purchase price and the purchaser for balances owed on the account. Although there are regulations governing the amount of finance charge that may be charged, there is a wide range of interest rates. These rates may range from 0 to 24+ percent Annual Percentage Rate (APR). The rate charged can depend on the credit-worthiness of the borrower, the type of loan, the amount and length of the loan, promotions, and any collateral property that may protect the loan.

Expert Insight

"Never spend your money before you have it."

Thomas Jefferson, former US president

Credit spending, for example, using credit cards rather than cash to make purchases, has become out of control in the last few decades. As a result, many people face huge debts. Credit card companies generally require borrowers to make a minimum monthly payment. Unfortunately, if only the minimum monthly payment is made, the majority of the payment goes toward interest. The debt remains for many years, until the loan is paid. This can turn into a vicious cycle of credit overuse and high interest costs. The best way to utilize credit card spending is to spend only as much as a person can budget to pay off each month. This allows for the use of a bank's money with no interest expense.

Copyright Goodheart-Willcox Co., Inc.

Pathway to Success

Using Credit Wisely

As soon as you turn 18 years old, many credit companies begin to send credit card offers in the mail. As you begin your journey into independence, getting your first credit card can be an exciting time. Learning to use that credit card wisely is an entirely different lesson.

Points to remember about credit cards include the following:

1. Credit cards are actually high-interest loans in disguise. The company loans you money and then gets their money back by charging interest. If you pay off your bill each month, you will not pay interest. If you carry a balance, however, the finance charges can be as much as 25 percent APR.

2. Companies record your payment history in your credit report. After college, you need a good credit history to rent an apartment, buy a car, or take out a loan. Many employers also check credit history before they hire.

3. If a credit card is in your name, you are responsible for paying the bill.

4. Read all application materials carefully, especially the fine print. Find out what happens after the introductory interest is over. What happens to your interest rate if you fail to make a payment?

5. Use a debit card or cash instead of credit, if possible. Save the credit card for emergencies.

6. Avoid buying items you do not need.

7. Pay bills on time to keep charges minimal. Pay the full balance every month if you can.

8. Federal law limits how credit card companies can do business with people younger than 21 years of age. Unless you have enough income to make monthly payments, you will need an adult cosigner to obtain a credit card.

Research Credit Cards

Gather credit card offers from the mail or online. Compare the credit applications from at least two different companies. Make sure to compare the following:

• Is there an introductory interest rate? If so, what is it?

• What is the annual percentage rate (APR)? Credit cards often charge different rates for purchases, cash advances, and balance transfers. What are the rates for each different use?

• Is the APR fixed or variable? Fixed rates remain constant while variable rates change depending on the prime rate.

• What is the billing cycle for the card?

• How long is the grace period?

• Is there an annual fee? If so, how much is it?

• What fees are associated with cash advances, balance transfers, and late payments?

• Does the credit card offer any rewards for use?

• Does the interest rate change after the introductory period?

Based on your research, which credit card offers the best deal? Why? Share your thoughts with the class.

Copyright Goodheart-Willcox Co., Inc.

Reading Recall

1. Name three consumer rights and three consumer responsibilities.
2. If you have a complaint about a product you purchased, what should you do?
3. List the five steps to creating a budget.
4. What do the terms *interest* and *principal* mean?
5. What form of credit is a student loan?

Rewards, Demands, and Future Trends

If you like solving problems, like working with money and people, and are detail oriented, a career in consumer services might be right for you. The consumer services field offers many opportunities for brainstorming and investigating creative solutions to problems. These solutions can make a huge difference in customers' or clients' lives.

Careers in consumer services are often salaried, and many workers are required to work long hours. Most require a relatively high level of education and training. These jobs demand brain power and can be very stressful. Careers in consumer services have a high level of responsibility. They are not physically demanding, but can be intellectually demanding and draining.

People will always need goods and services, help with navigating the consumer world, and assistance in managing their monetary resources. Many people cannot or do not personally perform the tasks that consumer services workers provide. For example, a consumer may not have the skills to effectively resolve a consumer complaint. A client may not know how to overcome debt or may not choose to take the time to manage investments. Corporations also need the help of consumer services workers. They hire and train customer service representatives to help their customers. They employ buyers to secure needed supplies and products for resale.

The future outlook for consumer services workers varies based on occupation (**Figure 8.20**). Some occupations, such as financial advisors and computer support specialists are projecting faster than average growth. Other occupations, such as consumer journalists and insurance underwriters, are expecting declines. Technology will continue to change the way consumer services workers share and communicate. The need for the information, however, will remain.

Reading Recall

1. What are some of the rewards and demands of careers in consumer services?
2. What is the future outlook for careers in consumer services?

Copyright Goodheart-Willcox Co., Inc.

Future Trends for Consumer Services Careers				
Occupation	**Projected Growth (2014–2024)**	**Projected Job Openings (2014–2024)**	**Median Wages (2014)**	**Education**
Budget analyst	Slower than average (2–4%)	16,700	$71,220	Bachelor's degree
Community consumer educator	Decline (–2% or lower)	800	$63,390	Master's degree
Computer support specialist	Faster than average (9–13%)	150,500	$47,610	Bachelor's degree
Consumer journalist	Decline (–2% or lower)	15,900	$36,000	Bachelor's degree
Consumer litigation attorney	Average (5–8%)	157,700	$114,970	Doctoral degree
Credit counselor	Much faster than average (14% or higher)	10,500	$42,110	Bachelor's degree
Customer service representative	Faster than average (9–13%)	888,700	$31,200	High school diploma
Financial advisor	Much faster than average (14% or higher)	136,400	$81,060	Bachelor's degree
Financial analyst	Faster than average (9–13%)	89,400	$78,620	Bachelor's degree
Financial manager	Average (5–8%)	169,300	$115,320	Bachelor's degree
Insurance sales agent	Faster than average (9–13%)	165,800	$47,860	Bachelor's degree
Insurance underwriter	Decline (–2% or lower)	19,500	$64,220	Bachelor's degree
Nonprofit foundation manager	Average (5–8%)	27,100	$101,510	Bachelor's degree
Policy analyst	Average (5–8%)	7,000	$95,710	Doctoral degree
Purchasing agent	Little or no change (–1–1%)	82,700	$60,980	Bachelor's degree
Purchasing manager	Little or no change (–1–1%)	17,900	$106,090	Bachelor's degree
Retail buyer	Average (5–8%)	49,100	$52,270	Bachelor's degree
Retail sales manager	Slower than average (2–4%)	411,300	$37,860	High school diploma
Retail sales worker	Average (5–8%)	1,917,200	$21,390	High school diploma
Sales manager	Average (5–8%)	108,000	$110,660	Bachelor's degree
Supply chain manager	Slower than average (2–4%)	255,400	$105,060	Bachelor's degree

Sources: O*NET and the *Occupational Outlook Handbook*

Figure 8.20 Learning as much as possible about careers can help you make informed career decisions. *According to the information in this chart, which consumer services careers are predicted to have the highest projected growth?*

Copyright Goodheart-Willcox Co., Inc.

Summary

- Consumer services careers fall into four major tracks: consumer advocacy, financial services, customer service, and buying. *Consumer advocacy* involves speaking on behalf of or supporting consumers. In *financial services*, workers deal with money, insurance, and investments. *Customer service* refers to taking care of customers' needs. *Buying* involves identifying products for purchase.

- Consumer services workers often possess strong interpersonal, verbal communication, writing, analytical, math, and conflict resolution skills. Having a good reputation for being fair, respectful, and ethical is important in consumer services.

- Most consumer services careers require at least a college education. Many consumer services careers also require certifications, based on specialization of expertise.

- Specialized knowledge for consumer services careers involves knowing consumer rights and responsibilities, understanding consumer buying techniques, and managing finances.

- *Sustainable purchasing* involves buying products that benefit environmental, social, or human health.

- A *budget* is a written financial plan to manage income, expenses, and savings. Using a budget can help consumers plan and save for future expenses.

- Common savings and investment tools include savings accounts, money market accounts, CDs, stocks, mutual funds, bonds, and IRAs.

- Three types of credit include installment, noninstallment, and revolving credit. Consumers can face enormous debt if they do not learn to use credit wisely.

- Many careers in consumer services are well paid, but can sometimes be stressful with a high level of responsibility. The future outlook for consumer services workers varies based on occupation.

College and Career Portfolio

Portfolio Samples

Portfolios for college or job applications often include *samples of work*. A sample of work might be an especially well-written paper, a persuasive presentation, or a hypothetical lesson plan.

Portfolio samples are examples of your best work, so it is important to read and edit them. Correct spelling and grammar are important in school and in the workplace, and your best work should display your grasp of language.

Before adding samples of your best work to your portfolio, complete the following:

1. Review samples of your work of which you are most proud. These samples might be from your schoolwork, participation in an extracurricular activity, or personal projects you have completed.

2. Consult with your teacher or college and career counselor about which samples of work would be best for your portfolio. Create a list of samples you want to use.

3. Proofread the samples for your portfolio. Check for correct spelling, grammar, and punctuation.

4. Partner with a trusted classmate to proofread each other's samples. Afterward, review and incorporate corrections your classmate made to your samples.

Copyright Goodheart-Willcox Co., Inc.

Review and Reflect

1. What are the four major tracks of consumer services careers?

2. What is the difference between a *financial advisor* and a *financial analyst*?

3. Overall, what is the goal of customer service representatives?

4. Where and how do buyers meet suppliers in the retail industry?

5. What are the two most important traits needed to be effective consumer services workers?

6. Explain the type of education and training requirements needed for a consumer services career that interests you.

7. Give an example for each consumer right and consumer responsibility.

8. Explain how a consumer can use comparison shopping.

9. Give step-by-step instructions on how to evaluate an advertising claim.

10. What does *sustainable* mean?

11. List three benefits to creating a budget.

12. What is *electronic banking*? Give an example of a transaction that can be made using electronic banking.

Vocabulary Activities

13. **Key terms** For each of the following terms, draw a cartoon bubble to express the meaning of each term as it relates to the chapter.

biodegradable	investing
budget	noninstallment credit
comparison shopping	principal
direct deposit	revolving credit
electronic banking	saving
electronic funds transfer (EFT)	self-advocacy
expenses	social sustainability
finance charges	sustainable
income	sustainable purchasing
installment credit	warranty
interest	

14. **Academic terms** Write each of the following terms on a separate sheet of paper. For each term, quickly write a word you think relates to the term. In small groups, exchange papers. Have each person in the group explain a term on the list. Take turns until all terms have been explained.

defaulted	penalize
gouging	redress
intermediaries	solvent
just	

Self-Assessment Quiz

Complete the self-assessment quiz online to help you practice and expand your knowledge and skills.

Critical Thinking

15. **Compare and contrast** Identify several consumer services careers that interest you. Compare and contrast employment opportunities for each of these careers.

16. **Analyze** Analyze some of the aptitudes, attitudes, and skills that effective consumer services workers typically share. How can you use these skills in your everyday life?

17. **Draw conclusions** Based on the six consumer responsibilities, draw conclusions about what a consumer should know before making a purchase.

18. **Determine** Determine the advantages and disadvantages of a brick and mortar store versus an online store.

19. **Identify** Identify the consumer protection organizations in your town. Make a list of their names and contact information. Use this information to create a flyer you can distribute in your neighborhood. Keep a copy for your portfolio.

20. **Evaluate** Evaluate any purchases you made in the last month. Are any of them sustainable purchases? If they are not sustainable, how can you change your purchasing practices to make them sustainable?

21. **Cause and effect** How has Internet use affected the banking industry? Cite specific examples. Explain in detail to the class.

22. **Make inferences** The level of risk the investor takes on usually determines the potential payback for an investment. Identify three stocks. Keep up with them for three weeks. If you had actually bought the stocks, would you have made or lost money? Why?

Core Skills

23. **Research and technology** Get copies of several different companies' advertisement flyers. Choose one product. Look into comparing the cost at each of the companies. Which company charges the most? Which company charges the least? Is the product exactly the same at each company? Are there differences? Create an electronic presentation describing how you compared the product from each of the different companies and determined which one would be the wisest purchase. Share your presentations with the class.

24. **Research, writing, and speaking** Choose a local company to research. Find out about its social sustainability. Look into issues involving fair labor laws, community development, safety, and wellness. Write a one-page paper explaining what you found out about the local business and its practices. Discuss your findings with the class.

25. **Speaking and listening** Pair up with a partner. One of you is the customer service manager for a retail store. The other person is an unhappy customer. Role-play how to handle a customer who is upset with the company due to a problem with a purchase or with a situation that occurred in the store, such as a rude salesperson. Take turns being the customer and the customer service representative.

26. **Writing** Using the information from this chapter, write a rough draft for a letter of complaint to a local business. Include what the problem is and how you would like it resolved. This can be put into your portfolio.

27. **Technology, writing, and math** Use a software program of your choice to keep track of your spending for two weeks. Then, create a chart with income and expenses listed into categories. Use this information to make a rough draft of a budget. Refer to the five basic steps of creating a budget identified in this chapter. As you are planning your budget, apply the decision-making process to determine how you will allocate and use your finances wisely. After completing your budget, follow it for one month. Adjust your plan as necessary and take notes about how well the plan works or about any challenges you may face. Why is following a budget a helpful habit to practice?

28. **Research and math** Identify local financial institutions. Research the types of interest available for home or car loans. Which place has the lowest interest rate? Which has the highest interest rate? Based on your research, which financial institution would you apply to for a loan? Explain.

29. **Research, math, and technology** Compare and contrast the rate of return between a certificate of deposit and a mutual fund. Which would help you grow your money faster?

30. **Technology** Financial institutions and other companies are not flawless. There are regular attempts at breaching security. Create an electronic public service announcement explaining these dangers, what you must do if your purse or wallet is stolen, and who you need to contact to get replacements for the items in your wallet. Share your presentations with other classes in your school.

31. **Writing and technology** In groups of three, work together to write and design a pamphlet explaining the differences among *installment credit*, *noninstallment credit*, and *revolving credit*. Describe how these different types of credit can affect a person's credit score. Be sure to check your pamphlet for correct grammar, spelling, and punctuation. Present your pamphlets in class.

Copyright Goodheart-Willcox Co., Inc.

32. **CTE career readiness practice** Everyone has a stake in protecting the environment. Taking steps as an individual to become more environmentally conscious is a behavior of responsible citizens. From a business standpoint, it may also help a company be more profitable. What actions can businesses take in the workplace to save energy or other resources?

33. **CTE career readiness practice** In the workplace, environmental awareness is important. Decisions that businesses make could have an impact on social and economic situations in the community. Give an example of a decision that a business might make that would have a positive impact on the community.

34. **CTE career readiness practice** Clean, pure drinking water is not available to many people in various parts of the world. Identify key areas where this is a problem. What are some cost effective ways to provide clean, pure drinking water? What are the social and economic impacts of countries failing to provide basic water purification for its citizens? Write a report of your findings to share with the class.

Lend a Hand

Volunteering and Fund-Raising

In the field of consumer services, workers help people solve financial and consumer problems. One of the main problems of many charities is that they lack funds or other resources for their cause. They rely on volunteers to help them meet their needs.

Think about different charities with which you are familiar. Some of these charities may send donation request cards or hold special events to raise funds for their cause. Other organizations may ask for donations of food, clothing, or other resources they need.

There are many ways you can get involved in fund-raising for a charity that interests you. One way you could get involved is to organize a donation drive. Find out what donated items an organization accepts and then set up a place for people to drop off items. Utilize social media to get the word out about your fund-raising efforts.

Another way you might help is to volunteer for a walk/run or other event to raise awareness about an issue. You could

even set up your own event to raise funds for a charity. For example, if you like to bake, you might run a bake sale. If you are good with math, you could start a tutoring service. Still another way you could help is by asking friends to donate to your cause instead of giving you gifts for your birthday.

To explore volunteering and fund-raising opportunities, complete the following:

1. Research at least five charities that interest you to find out how they handle fund-raising. How do they raise awareness for their cause? Do they have special events that you could participate in, such as a walk/run? Do they need donations of certain items?

2. Make note of any fund-raising opportunities that are of special interest to you. Who would you contact to learn more about getting involved? Find out as much information as you can. Then, take the next step and get involved.

Chapter 9

Counseling and Mental Health Services

G-WLEARNING.COM

While studying, look for the activity icon  to

- **practice** key and academic terms with e-flash cards and matching activities;
- **assess** what you learn by completing self-assessment quizzes; and
- **reinforce** what you learn by mapping concepts and completing review and reflect questions.

www.g-wlearning.com/humanservices/

©iStock.com/ ClarkandCompany

Learning Outcomes

After studying this chapter, you will be able to

- **compare and contrast** career opportunities for human services workers in the area of counseling and mental health services;
- **list** common aptitudes, attitudes, and skills of counselors and mental health services workers;
- **give examples** of postsecondary education, training, and experience required for several counseling and mental health services careers;
- **describe** the stages that typically occur in an individual's life cycle and in a family's life cycle;
- **identify** types of family-life crises and explain how each type of crisis affects individuals and families; and
- **summarize** the rewards, demands, and future trends of careers in counseling and mental health services.

Reading Strategies

Before reading, flip through the pages of this chapter. Look at the illustrations. For each photo, write a prediction about how the image illustrates a text concept. As you are reading, cite specific textual evidence to support the information in the illustrations. After reading the chapter, compare your predictions and the textual evidence you cited. How is this information similar? How is it different?

Mapping Concepts

Using a colored pen or pencil, write the key terms for this chapter on a piece of paper. Leave space around them for your notes. As you are reading, write your notes around the key term to which they most relate, until you have created a cloud of notes for each term.

family life cycle	family-life crisis	at risk

occurs when a stressor creates adversity disrupts family function

child custody court determination as to who is legally responsible for the child

joint custody	child support

Key Terms

addiction
advance directives
alcoholism
at risk
bipolar disorder
child custody
child support
clinical depression
domestic abuse

do not resuscitate (DNR) order
family-life crisis
family life cycle
grief
hospice care
joint custody
Last Will and Testament
living will

Academic Terms

adversity
mortality
resilient

Counseling and mental health services workers focus on people's psychological, social, intellectual, and/or spiritual well-being. They listen to their clients' problems and guide them to make good personal decisions and plan for the future.

Counseling and mental health services workers work with people of all ages to improve quality of life, mainly their mental health. They recognize crises people may face during various stages of the life cycle. They understand the effects these crises can have on their clients and work with them to improve their coping skills. Overall, counseling and mental health workers are compassionate and have a sincere desire to encourage people to be the best they can be.

Careers in Counseling and Mental Health Services

There are many career opportunities for human services workers in the area of counseling and mental health services. **Figure 9.1** shows some examples of careers in this field. You will be learning more about these careers in the following sections.

Counselors

A *counselor* or *therapist* encourages and guides clients through the process of overcoming problems and developing strategies to live an emotionally healthy and safe life. Counselors are good communicators who treat people individually and in groups. They often specialize in one area, such as working with people to overcome grief, eating disorders, mental or emotional issues, substance abuse, or relationship conflicts.

Examples of Counseling and Mental Health Services Careers

- Child life specialist
- Counselor (often specializes in one area, such as a substance abuse counselor)
- Marriage and family therapist
- Mental health counselor
- Psychiatrist
- Psychologist
- Rehabilitation counselor
- School counselor
- Therapist
- Vocational counselor

Figure 9.1 The field of counseling and mental health services offers many different career opportunities. *Which of these careers would you like to learn more about?*

Copyright Goodheart-Willcox Co., Inc.

Case Study *Real Life*

As soon as Eric arrived for his appointment, I knew something was up. Instead of being his upbeat self of recent weeks, he appeared quiet and serious. Eric has been a client of mine for the past year, ever since his parents separated and then divorced. This family crisis hit Eric hard, especially after losing his older brother in an alcohol-related auto accident three years earlier. Through his counseling sessions, Eric is learning ways to cope with his pain, loss, and grief and find happiness in his changed reality.

As Eric talked and shared about the events of the past week, he slowly started to reveal the reason for his recent mood change. His girlfriend of the past three months called off the relationship in a very public manner. He seemed more concerned about the way she had broken up with him than the breakup itself. Although he was not ready to talk about the issue further now, he would likely want some guidance to process his feelings later.

Eric would always mourn the loss of his brother and old family ways, but is well on his way to emotional healing. His relationship with both of his parents is improving. He is more connected at school. I am honored to walk alongside Eric as his counselor.

Alexander Raths/Shutterstock.com

For Discussion

1. What event(s) initially brought Eric to work with his counselor?
2. What treatment does Eric's counselor provide?
3. What does Eric's counselor hope for him as a result of their relationship?

They may focus on treating specific populations, such as children, teens, or older adults.

A *marriage and family therapist* works with individuals, couples, and families to improve personal relationships and resolve conflicts. Marriage and family therapists counsel couples preparing for marriage. They also address other concerns, such as separation, divorce, and grief over the loss of a loved one. They listen to clients and ask questions. They teach clients how to deal with their problems in positive ways, thereby improving their lives. As they work with clients, marriage and family therapists enhance communication and understanding among family members.

A *mental health counselor* assesses, addresses, and treats mental and emotional issues, such as anxiety, depression, trauma, stress, or grief. Mental health counselors often work closely with other mental health professionals, such as psychologists, psychiatrists, and social workers. After diagnosis of a mental health issue, counselors use a variety of techniques to improve clients' mental health. Likewise, *substance abuse*

Copyright Goodheart-Willcox Co., Inc.

counselors address people's problems with alcohol, drugs, or other substances. They also treat other behavioral disorders, such as gambling or eating disorders.

A *rehabilitation counselor* works with clients to overcome effects of physical and emotional disabilities and live as independently as possible. Rehabilitation counselors work in a variety of settings. These include rehabilitation agencies, independent living facilities, prisons, schools, or private practices. They develop programs to reduce the personal, social, and physical effects of the disabilities. They also provide vocational training, if necessary.

A *vocational counselor* assists people with finding a purpose or career path. Vocational counselors guide their clients through the process of finding and securing employment (**Figure 9.2**). Some vocational counselors work in educational settings. Others may work in private career counseling services or government job placement agencies.

School counselors work with students in educational settings. Generally, they are certified or licensed teachers who have completed additional graduate work in school counseling. Typically, school counselors focus either on academic counseling, including postgraduation planning, or social, relationship, or learning issues. In smaller schools, they may be responsible for both areas.

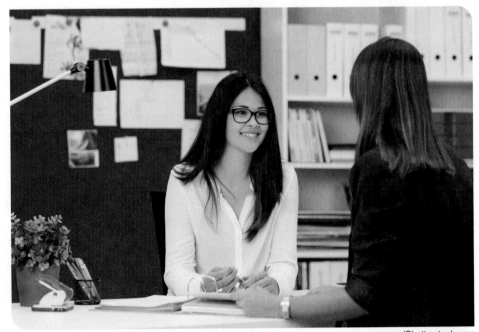

racorn/Shutterstock.com

Figure 9.2 Vocational counselors help people determine which careers suit their skills, talents, personality, job history and experience, and interests. *Have you ever spoken to a vocational counselor about your future employment?*

Copyright Goodheart-Willcox Co., Inc.

School counselors are often the links among students, school administrators, and parents or guardians. They assist administrators, especially with issues dealing with disciplinary actions. They may oversee learning resources, including finding services for learning challenges. School counselors are especially aware of any possible signs of abuse or neglect in their students, acting as their advocates.

Psychologists

A *psychologist* studies human behavior and mental processes and develops theories to explain why people behave the way they do. Psychologists conduct studies and research to understand and predict human emotions, feelings, and behaviors. They look for patterns of behavior or cause-and-effect relationships between events.

Psychologists work with people of all ages or they may choose to work with a specific age group (**Figure 9.3**). They commonly have certain areas in which they specialize. Some psychologists prefer to work directly with clients. Others prefer to conduct research. Some may work as part of a healthcare team to improve a person's overall health and well-being.

Psychiatrists

A *psychiatrist* is a medical doctor who specializes in mental disorders. Often, psychiatrists specialize in the diagnosis, treatment, and prevention of a particular mental illness or substance use disorder. As medical doctors, they understand and can distinguish between mental and physical suffering, and can prescribe medications as necessary.

Rob Marmion/Shutterstock.com

Figure 9.3 Some child psychologists work with a range of clients, including infants, toddlers, children, and teens. Others choose to work with a specific age group. *If you were a psychologist, would you choose to work with a specific age group? Why or why not?*

Copyright Goodheart-Willcox Co., Inc.

They tend to be utilized for more serious mental illness issues, such as bipolar disorder or schizophrenia. They often act as a consultant in criminal cases.

Child Life Specialists

A *child life specialist* works in a hospital or another medical setting serving children undergoing medical care. Child life specialists often use play to explain procedures or other medical care to children. For example, a child life specialist may demonstrate how a teddy bear would receive a shot, have a cast put on to set a bone, or wear an oxygen mask.

Child life specialists often create fun experiences for children, such as doing art projects, reading books, or playing games. These activities are meant to turn the child's attention away from serious or painful medical treatment and create a less scary setting (**Figure 9.4**). Child life specialists are trained to work with children, their families or caregivers, and other medical staff.

Reading Recall

1. Name three different types of counselors.
2. What is the difference between a *psychologist* and a *psychiatrist*?
3. What are *child life specialists*?
4. Why do child life specialists often use play in their work with a child?

gpointstudio/Shutterstock.com

Figure 9.4 A child life specialist makes children feel happier and more at ease during their medical treatment. *Why might a child feel less frightened by a medical procedure after seeing it demonstrated on a teddy bear?*

Copyright Goodheart-Willcox Co., Inc.

Common Aptitudes, Attitudes, and Skills

Effective counseling and mental health services workers typically share common aptitudes, attitudes, and skills (**Figure 9.5**). Counselors and mental health services workers possess good listening and speaking skills to communicate with clients effectively. They are good problem solvers and conflict mediators. They are patient and able to remain calm when their clients may be upset, angry, or distressed. They have high mental and physical energy to deal with stressful and difficult situations.

Content knowledge is critical to the success of counselors and mental health services workers. They need to understand changes people experience during their lives and identify issues that can negatively impact mental health. They need to know how to treat these issues and keep up-to-date on the latest treatments.

Counselors and mental health services workers must be compassionate and respectful of people. At the same time, they must be able to remain objective in difficult situations and not get caught up in emotions. They must be able to focus on the issue and help their client or patient move toward better mental health.

Reading Recall

1. Identify five aptitudes, attitudes, or skills of counselors and mental services workers.

2. How can counselors not get caught up in the emotions of their clients' problems or issues?

Education, Training, and Experience

Most counseling positions require both an undergraduate bachelor's degree and some form of licensure or certification to practice. Marriage and family therapists and substance abuse counselors are required in all

Common Aptitudes, Attitudes, and Skills of Counseling and Mental Health Services Workers	
• High mental and physical energy	• Focused
• Knowledge of human behavior and dynamics	• Socially perceptive
	• Reliable
• Keeps emotions under control	• Gets along well with others
• Compassionate	• Active listener
• Cares for others	• Conveys information effectively—verbally and in writing
• Respectful	
• Honest	• Problem-solving skills
• Ethical	• Conflict resolution skills

Figure 9.5 Counseling and mental health services workers share common aptitudes, attitudes, and skills. *What other aptitudes, attitudes, and skills would you add to this list?*

Copyright Goodheart-Willcox Co., Inc.

but a few states to hold some form of licensure or certification to practice. All states require school counselors to be certified. In addition, a master's degree is often required to be certified or licensed as a counselor.

Becoming a psychologist requires considerable time and commitment. Psychologists must earn a doctoral degree (**Figure 9.6**). Some graduate programs require completion of a master's degree before acceptance into a doctoral program. Other programs combine the master's and doctoral degrees. Graduate programs include required coursework, comprehensive examinations, and a thesis or project at the doctoral level.

Psychiatrists complete many years of schooling. This includes medical school after college. They then complete a four-year medical residency. Many continue to specialize in areas such as child, geriatric, pharmacology, or forensic psychiatry.

Child life specialists must complete a bachelor's degree with at least 10 credits in child life or a related subject, such as child development or child and family studies. If majoring in a related subject, at least one of the courses must be taught by a certified child life specialist. They must also complete 480 hours or more of clinical experience under the supervision of a certified child life specialist.

After completing educational requirements, child life specialists must pass a certification exam and then maintain their certification through annual continuing education. By 2022, to be eligible for certification, applicants will need to hold a master's degree from a program accredited by the Child Life Council (CLC).

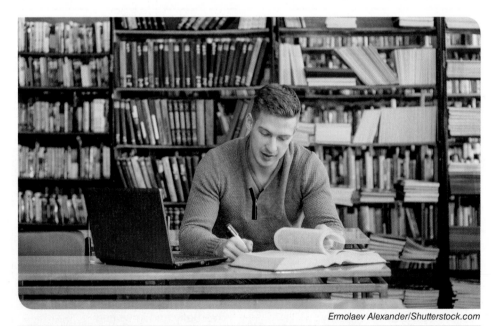

Ermolaev Alexander/Shutterstock.com

Figure 9.6 It usually takes between four and eight years of postsecondary full-time study to complete a Ph.D. *In your opinion, what are the pros and cons of earning an advanced degree?*

Copyright Goodheart-Willcox Co., Inc.

Reading Recall

1. What type of education do most human services counselors need?
2. What types of degrees do psychologists and psychiatrists hold?
3. Besides holding a bachelor's degree with at least 10 credits in child life, what else must child life specialists complete?

Specialized Knowledge for Counseling and Mental Health Services Careers

Counselors and mental health services workers guide their clients through all of life's transitions, challenges, and crises. To do so, they need specialized knowledge about individual and family life cycles. They must also recognize how family-life crises can affect their clients. Through all of life's stages, they teach their clients to make good decisions, cope with challenges, and improve mental health.

Understanding the Individual and Family Life Cycles

The term *lifespan* may seem like a synonym for *life cycle*. The two terms, however, have different meanings. *Lifespan* refers to the duration of life for a living organism. *Life cycle* refers to the developmental stages within the lifespan. The average human lifespan in the twenty-first century is 78 years of age. An individual's typical life cycle includes

- infancy (birth to 1 year);
- toddlerhood (1 to 3 years);
- early childhood (3 through 5 years);
- middle childhood (6 through 12 years);
- adolescence (13 through 18 years);
- early adulthood (19 through 39 years);
- middle adulthood (40 through 65 years); and
- older adulthood (66 years and older).

As individuals get married, they form a family. Just as individuals go through a life cycle, families also experience a life cycle. The **family life cycle** consists of six basic stages many families go through as a normal part of life (**Figure 9.7**). Each family, however, does not experience the family life cycle in the same way. Many times, families can be in more than one stage at a time.

The *beginning stage* is the first stage of the family life cycle. During this stage, a couple forms a bond and commits to a lasting relationship. They marry and start a home. The couple adjusts to life together and decides when, or if, they want to have children. Couples who choose to

The Family Life Cycle

Beginning stage

The couple marries and starts to build their life together. This stage lasts until the couple has a child.

Alan Bailey/Shutterstock.com

Launching stage

The couple's children leave home to live on their own. This stage ends when the last child moves out of the family home.

bikeriderlondon/Shutterstock.com

Childbearing stage

The couple has their first child. This stage ends when the couple has their last child.

wong yu liang/Shutterstock.com

Mid-years stage

The couple often faces an empty nest and may redefine their priorities. This stage lasts until retirement.

Monkey Business Images/Shutterstock.com

Parenting stage

The couple raises their children through the school-age and teen years. This stage continues until children begin to leave home.

Monkey Business Images/Shutterstock.com

Aging stage

The couple retires and focuses on their interests. This stage lasts through the eventual death of one and then the other spouse.

Pressmaster/Shutterstock.com

Figure 9.7 This chart illustrates the six basic stages of the family life cycle. Sometimes, families can be in more than one stage at the same time. *Give an example of a situation in which a family is in two stages of the family life cycle at the same time.*

Copyright Goodheart-Willcox Co., Inc.

never have children remain in the beginning stage of the family life cycle until they reach the mid-years stage.

When a couple decides to have their first child, they enter the *childbearing stage* of the family life cycle. The couple assumes the roles of parents and accepts many new responsibilities. Having a child is costly. Expenses increase a lot. Extra demands of time and energy are placed on the couple as they care for the child. Costs and demands may further increase if the couple adopts or has a child with special needs. The childbearing stage of the family life cycle continues until the couple decides to not have any more children.

A family enters the *parenting stage* of the family life cycle when the first child starts school. Oftentimes, the childbearing and parenting stages of the family life cycle overlap for couples who have several children. Navigating the school system and balancing work and family issues are often more difficult during the parenting stage. School activities can cause the family's schedule to change. Parents face new challenges as children enter the teen years and often seek more independence and less parental control.

The *launching stage* of the family life cycle occurs when the first child leaves home. Children may go to college or find jobs and move into their own places. Some may get married and start their own families. As children leave home, schedule demands may lessen. Parents often have more free time.

Next is the *mid-years stage* of the family life cycle. During this stage, many couples often face an empty nest when the last child leaves home. Couples may feel a void in their lives when the home is empty. Couples may develop new interests as they learn to accept the empty nest. As their grown children become parents, the couple welcomes grandchildren into the family (**Figure 9.8**). The couple also starts to focus on retirement.

Figure 9.8 During the mid-years stage of the family life cycle, many couples become grandparents. *In what ways do you think having grandchildren changes a couple's life?*

szefei/Shutterstock.com

Copyright Goodheart-Willcox Co., Inc.

The *aging stage* of the family life cycle lasts from retirement through the death of one and then the other spouse. During this stage, couples may experience the birth of grandchildren or great-grandchildren. They might travel or visit with family. Couples may even develop new hobbies. As a parent's health declines, a grown child may need to become a caregiver. When a spouse dies, the remaining spouse may need the support of a grief counselor to deal with the loss.

The family life cycle may seem familiar, but is not the reality for everyone. As society changes, the function of the family also changes. Some people choose to remain single and live alone. Others become single parents. Couples break up. Divorces and remarriages occur. New families are formed. Grown children may leave home, only to return later to live with their parents, perhaps bringing their children with them. At times, parents may raise their grandchildren. Other events can also cause the family to make many more changes.

Recognizing Family-Life Crises

Families exist in an ever-changing environment. The changes families go through often cause stress for family members. Some of these changes are common stressors most families face, such as the birth of a child or a change in employment. The effects of these types of stressors on families are often positive. Other stressors can have negative effects on families, resulting in a family-life crisis.

A **family-life crisis** occurs when a stressor creates *adversity* (hardships; difficulties) for the family, disrupting family function. Sometimes, families may go through a crisis that does not affect all family members. How significantly a family-life crisis affects family members depends on the family's ability to recognize and manage the crisis. Families with strong, healthy relationships and greater resources to draw upon are more *resilient* (capable of recovering from setbacks) in times of crisis than families with poor interpersonal relationships and fewer resources.

Counselors and mental health services workers recognize negative stressors that can create family-life crises. They work with families, teaching them the necessary coping skills to handle crises and develop resilience. Some of the types of crises counselors and mental health services workers deal with include poverty, addiction, domestic violence, divorce, depression and suicide, and death and grief.

Poverty

People who live below, at, or even near the poverty line often lack the resources to meet their basic needs for food, clothing, shelter, and healthcare. Living in poverty affects all family members, but can have profound effects on children's development and future prospects.

Children from families living in poverty are among those labeled as **at risk**. This means these children have characteristics that make

Expert Insight

"The ultimate measure of a man is not where he stands in moments of comfort and convenience, but where he stands at times of challenge and controversy."

Martin Luther King, Jr., social activist

Copyright Goodheart-Willcox Co., Inc.

Pathway to Success

Coping Skills in Crisis

When people go through a traumatic event, they often experience emotional and physical aftershocks. Sometimes, these symptoms appear right away. Other times, they may take hours, days, or even weeks to develop.

After a traumatic event, many people feel their sense of safety and security is shattered. They may express feelings of anger, shame, grief, or depression. Having flashbacks and nightmares is also common. All these symptoms can become evident in the body through aches and pains, headaches, weakness, dizziness, changes in sleeping patterns, digestive problems, and increased susceptibility to illness.

Following are some simple tips that can help you cope:

- Recognize that your feelings are normal. Talk about what is happening with someone you trust. Talking helps with healing.

- Keep a journal of your thoughts and feelings. This is very important if you do not have anyone with whom you can talk.

- Reach out to family and friends for support. Joining a support group can give you a chance to talk with others who have gone through similar situations. Group members can give you tips to cope that you may not have considered.

- Set small, realistic goals to tackle obstacles. Take one day at a time.

- Get as much physical activity as possible.

- Get plenty of sleep.

- Schedule breaks for yourself. Get involved in a hobby.

- Follow a daily routine as much as possible. Regular, normal activities can be comforting.

- Give someone a hug. Remember, touching is very important to healing.

- Avoid the use of alcohol and drugs.

- Create a place where you can go that makes you feel comfortable and safe.

- Use humor. Remember to laugh. Laughter is considered one of the best medicines for stress and crisis. Look for funny books, TV shows, movies, or life situations that will bring humor into your day.

Role-Play Activity

Imagine you have just found out that your best friend's sibling has committed suicide. What can you say to help your friend get through this crisis? Take turns role-playing how to help your friend cope with the changes in his or her life at the following times: right after the event, one month after the event, and one year later at the anniversary of the event. How can being supportive of what your friend is going through help you go through the grieving process as well?

Copyright Goodheart-Willcox Co., Inc.

them more likely to fail in school. Children become aware of social and economic status differences at a very young age. Students who are poor often struggle with emotional security and self-esteem issues. Learning is difficult when feelings of embarrassment, worry, anger, or fear prevent concentration. School may not feel like a welcoming environment.

Education provides the best chance to break the cycle of poverty (**Figure 9.9**). Today, a high school diploma is the minimum needed to find employment. Most jobs require more advanced education or training. Those who fail to finish school are unlikely to be able to provide adequately for themselves in the adult world.

Counselors and mental health services workers refer families living in poverty to the services they need. These services may range from job training to housing assistance to free meal programs for students. Counselors and mental health services workers may also act as mentors to students, committing to a long-term relationship to provide support and guidance.

Addiction

Addiction is a condition characterized by a compulsive physical and/or psychological dependence on a substance (such as alcohol) or behavior (such as gambling). When a person is addicted to something, he or she cannot cope without using the substance or engaging in the behavior. Common substances that can result in the development of an addiction include tobacco, alcohol, some prescription medications,

©iStock.com/Cathy Yeulet

Figure 9.9 For students living in poverty, education is a way to break the cycle of poverty. *Compared to his or her more affluent classmates, why might it be more difficult for a student living in poverty to succeed in school?*

Copyright Goodheart-Willcox Co., Inc.

and drugs. Examples of behaviors that can result in addictions include gambling, eating habits, using the Internet or playing computer games, shopping, exercising, and even working.

Addictions can cause serious problems for families. Some addictions, especially substance addictions, can result in serious physical problems. For example, drinking too much over time can lead to **alcoholism**, or the addiction of alcohol. Alcoholism can cause kidney and liver damage, various types of cancers, heart and nerve problems, and even death. In the workplace, alcoholism may put coworkers, customers, or the public in danger.

Addictions negatively affect personal relationships and work performance. Less time is spent with family members. More workplace absences occur. Great effort may be taken to cover up behaviors or consequences. As a result, trust is often broken. Even when people with addictions know their behavior is causing relationship or work performance problems and attempt to limit or stop the behavior, they often cannot. Treatment is needed for addicts and their families to repair relationships (**Figure 9.10**).

Addiction professionals, such as substance abuse counselors, teach their clients skills to stop the harmful behavior and instead make healthful choices. Support groups, such as Alcoholics Anonymous and Overeaters Anonymous, teach recovering addicts coping methods and healthful strategies. Family members and friends of addicts may also benefit from support groups, such as Al-Anon.

Expert Insight

"Always bear in mind that your own resolution to succeed is more important than any other one thing."

Abraham Lincoln,
former US president

wavebreakmedia/Shutterstock.com

Figure 9.10 Many people with addictions choose to attend meetings focused on treating their addiction and rehabilitating their lives. *Why do you think some people prefer to have the support of a group like this during their recovery?*

Domestic Violence

Ideally, home and family members should provide a place and relationships in which peace and comfort can be found amidst life's challenges. Unfortunately for many, this is not the case. Instead, home is a place of strife, fear for one's own safety, and threatened or actual violence.

Domestic violence takes many forms. Sometimes, domestic violence can be subtle—taking away a person's right to control his or her own life. For example, the victim of domestic violence may not be allowed to manage resources, hold a job, form outside friendships, or even have the freedom to leave home. Other times, domestic violence involves violent threats or abuse.

Domestic abuse involves threatening to or inflicting harm on another person with whom they are in a close relationship, such as a family member. Domestic abuse consists of physical, emotional, and sexual abuse (**Figure 9.11**). When domestic abuse is physical, signs such as bruises or broken bones may make the abuse easier to detect than emotional or sexual abuse. Signs of physical abuse, however, may not always be visible.

The effects of abuse are devastating to families. There can be physical harm and even death. Mental harm can be permanent. Trust is broken as relationships are damaged or severed. Often, victims do not report abuse. This may be due to the victim's feelings of shame and responsibility for the abuse. It may also be because the abuser promises that this is the last time it will happen. Threats and concerns for their safety or the safety of others, including children, sometimes keep victims from coming forward.

Causes

Although the causes for domestic abuse may vary, they still produce the same hurtful results. Often, domestic violence passes from generation to generation, as family relationship patterns are learned. Some people believe abuse is prevalent because of the amount of violence viewed in

---

Types of Domestic Abuse

- *Physical abuse* involves inflicting injury through beating, hitting, shaking, biting, punching, kicking, or by other means. Physical abuse often results in bruises and repeated injuries, such as broken bones, cuts, or scrapes.
- *Emotional abuse* includes constant criticism, threats, or rejection that harms a person's sense of self-worth and emotional development. Withholding love, support, or resources is also a part of emotional abuse.
- *Sexual abuse* includes engaging in sexual acts with other adult family members without their consent, or in the case of children or dependents, inappropriate behavior toward or with a child or dependent, including touching, sexual acts, and exposure to pornography.

Figure 9.11 Domestic abuse comes in different forms. *How would you respond to someone who claims that the only form of domestic abuse is physical abuse?*

Copyright Goodheart-Willcox Co., Inc.

society, especially within certain neighborhoods. Domestic abuse, however, can occur across all socio-economic, cultural, and ethnic groups. Often, causes are attributed to stress.

Economic distress brought on by unemployment, inadequate pay, or illness in the family is often associated with abuse. Lacking relationship skills plays a part. Personality issues, such as a need to control, low self-esteem, anger issues, social isolation, or difficulty coping with stress, are often factors. Depression and other mental health problems may be factors. Alcohol and substance abuse frequently play a part, too.

The presence of risk factors does not necessarily mean violence or abuse is taking place. Some adults may present certain risk factors, but they never engage in domestic violence. Identifying risk factors, however, can determine the type of support services or interventions that may benefit families.

iQoncept/Shutterstock.com

Figure 9.12 The cycle of domestic abuse might be broken by increasing public awareness, increasing education, and taking other steps to prevent domestic violence. *Why is it so important to break the cycle of domestic abuse?*

Prevention

Education and role modeling of healthy relationships are the best ways to break the cycle of domestic abuse, preventing it from repeating in the next generation. Individuals, families, communities, and society can all play a part in preventing domestic abuse (**Figure 9.12**). Raising public awareness of domestic abuse through public service announcements can promote healthy family relationships and safety.

Treatment

When cases of domestic abuse are confirmed, treatment for the abused can begin. In cases of physical abuse, immediate medical treatment for the victim may be needed. Crisis care programs, such as safe houses, offer temporary relief to the abused by providing a nonviolent place to live and receive services. Community resources that can lower family stress, including financial resources, child care, housing, and supplemental nutritional assistance, are also available because abusive behaviors are often linked to stress.

Treatment for sexual and emotional abuse often involves individual therapy. In some cases, group therapy is also encouraged. Qualified mental health professionals can assess the abused and the abuser to determine exactly what types of treatment would benefit them the most. Treatment programs can then be developed to promote safety and family education and reduce the risk of abuse recurring. Treatment for the abusers is also determined on a case-by-case basis. Because domestic abuse is illegal, adults may be convicted of a crime and ordered to receive therapy or jail time.

Copyright Goodheart-Willcox Co., Inc.

Domestic abuse comes from the abuser's need to control and manipulate. It often repeats itself in families through the generations. There is hope, however. If the cycle of abuse is broken and expectations of family and home life are altered, it can positively impact generations. Counselors and mental health services workers are trained to help abusers change their ways and victims heal from the trauma.

Divorce

Even in healthy marriages, conflicts are bound to arise. When conflicts occur, open communication can resolve an issue and relieve tension and stress. If couples have trouble communicating, attending counseling can be a way to resolve their conflicts. Counselors can create an open environment for both partners to discuss issues and understand the other person's position (**Figure 9.13**).

Sometimes, even with counseling and effort from both partners, the relationship is still dysfunctional. The couple may experience conflicts that are more difficult to resolve or cannot be resolved. They may no longer get along with and understand each other. Mistrust can arise. Partners in the relationship may then decide their differences are too great and would likely introduce more problems into the relationship. To prevent future issues and conflicts, they choose to divorce.

Breakups, separation, and divorce can feel tragic to everyone involved, especially children of the divorcing couples. All family members commonly experience emotional challenges, such as loneliness,

Photographee.eu/Shutterstock.com

Figure 9.13 The counselor's role is to guide the couple to a compromise or solution. *Do you think it is helpful to have a counselor serve as a mediator and provide guidance during conflicts? Why or why not?*

Copyright Goodheart-Willcox Co., Inc.

depression, and anxiety. In addition, children may feel anger or resentment toward one or both of their parents. They may even blame themselves for the breakup. Children may suffer academically and socially. Sometimes they may act out aggressively toward others. The emotional scars children suffer from divorce may last well into adulthood, affecting future relationships.

Divorce can have devastating financial effects, too. Income drops substantially. If children are involved, the financial impact can be long-standing. Often, the division of financial assets can be difficult. Child custody and support may be a source of heated disagreement for the couple.

Child custody is a court determination as to who retains legal responsibility for the child. In some cases, parents seek **joint custody** (a legal agreement in which both parents provide care and make decisions for the child). **Child support** is a legally binding agreement that determines the payments a noncustodial parent is to make to financially contribute toward the child's care. The term *noncustodial* refers to the parent whom the child does not live with most of the time. Usually, judgments concerning both child custody and child support involve lawyers and legally binding court decisions.

New issues of living situations and the frequency of visitation from either parent can be confusing and painful for children (**Figure 9.14**). Adults may experience difficulties adjusting to the many changes, too. During this time, parents and their children often need help coping with

Phonlawat_51/Shutterstock.com

Figure 9.14 Children may have trouble understanding and adjusting to the changes that occur as a result of divorce. *What are some sources of support for both parents and children coping with divorce?*

Copyright Goodheart-Willcox Co., Inc.

their feelings and adjusting to a new way of life after the divorce. Sources of support may include counseling services, support groups, and the love and encouragement of family members and friends.

Depression and Suicide

Sadness and *depression* are two words people may use interchangeably, but they are completely different in meaning and severity. Sadness is a normal emotion that people of all ages experience from time to time. Depression is an illness that cannot be easily overcome. Sadness is temporary. A person who feels sad may still experience moments of laughter. Depression, however, is much more serious and life-altering. Depression does not disappear in a few days and often requires medical intervention.

Clinical depression is a severe case of depression often caused by a combination of genetic and environmental influences. Signs of sadness and clinical depression can overlap. It is important to know the difference between these two conditions. With depression, strong, negative feelings from inside can develop and are not easy to ignore. Loneliness, stress, or feelings of failure or inadequacy are factors. Those who are depressed often feel as though there are few to no positive things in their life. They feel a sense of hopelessness about the present and future. **Figure 9.15** shows warning signs of clinical depression. These signs are more severe than feelings of sadness.

Periodic changes in the lifespan may trigger the effects of depression. The person may not be clinically depressed, however. For example, the loss of a family member or friend can cause similar symptoms of depression for days, weeks, or months.

In the latter teen years or early adulthood, **bipolar disorder** may be detected. Bipolar disorder is also called *manic depression*, but is not the same as clinical depression. Bipolar disorder affects social-emotional

Warning Signs of Depression

- Insomnia or oversleeping, accompanied by fatigue
- Loss of interest in life; indifference
- Concentration problems
- Feelings of hopelessness and worthlessness
- Feeling angry, irritable, or short-tempered
- Abuse of alcohol or drugs
- Changes in appetite; weight loss or gain
- Chronic aches and pains
- Suicidal thoughts

Figure 9.15 Depression is much more severe than common feelings of sadness. This chart includes some of the warning signs of clinical depression. *Who can you talk to if you are experiencing the symptoms of depression?*

Copyright Goodheart-Willcox Co., Inc.

health and is characterized by severe mood swings that range from manic to depressive. During manic phases, a person may exhibit high energy, irritability, and impulsive behavior. Depressive phases include fatigue, loss of interest in activities, and changes in eating or sleeping habits.

If in doubt about whether symptoms indicate sadness or depression, talking about concerns with a family member or friend may help. Professional counselors can determine the stressors and prescribe treatment to relieve symptoms of depression.

If left untreated, depression may lead to suicide, or the decision for a person to end his or her own life. Someone who is thinking about attempting suicide may show many of the same warning signs as for depression. The person may also show other warning signs, such as acting recklessly, giving away cherished possessions, or talking about not having a reason to live or killing oneself.

Suicide threats and attempts should always be taken seriously. They are a symptom of much deeper issues and a sign that a person needs immediate help. Talking with the person about his or her suicidal thoughts shows you care and want to help. Counselors can identify stressors and teach clients the necessary skills to cope with issues. Suicide prevention hotlines and local crisis centers have mental health services professionals on staff to help, too.

Death and Grief

Facing death is one of the most significant life events a person experiences. When people face their own *mortality* (eventual death), they reflect on their own life and accept that death is a part of their life. Facing another person's death means understanding that the person will no longer be there. Death can mean that one period in life may end, while a new one is beginning.

Preparing for Death

Adults will often plan for their passing in a rational and organized way. People may arrange their own funerals or memorial services in advance (**Figure 9.16**). They may seek burial plots or cremation holdings. They may prepare a **Last Will and Testament**, or will. This is a legally binding document giving directions on how to divide financial assets. Those who receive the financial assets are called *beneficiaries*.

For many, preparing for death also involves determining what medical care should be provided if a person is no longer able to make medical decisions for himself or herself. These decisions are called **advance directives**.

One type of advance directive is a living will. A **living will** is a legal document informing family and medical workers of preferences for being kept alive by artificial means, or letting them pass when there is no chance of recovery. Another type of advance directive is a **do not resuscitate (DNR) order**. A DNR order lets medical staff know that

Copyright Goodheart-Willcox Co., Inc.

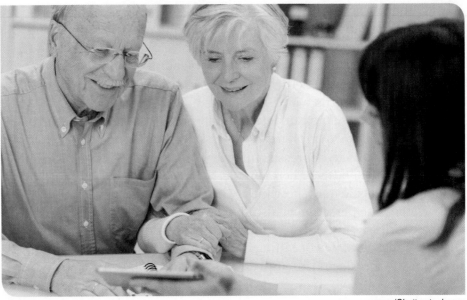

racorn/Shutterstock.com

Figure 9.16 Some people choose to plan their own funerals or memorial services in advance, choosing the service location, music, and even the guest list. *Why do you think some people choose to plan their own services?*

if a person's heart stops or the person stops breathing, he or she does not want CPR in order to be resuscitated. A DNR order may be included in a person's living will.

The Stages of Dying

Accepting the reality of one's own impending death is difficult. People often move through a process of acceptance as they face their own mortality. Learning to accept death is not an easy process. Many times, the rate of acceptance depends on the length of time people have left and the sense of control they feel.

Typically, there are five common stages people experience when learning to cope with their own death (**Figure 9.17**). Each person is different, however, and will not experience these stages in the same way. For some, one of these stages may last longer than another stage. The levels of severity can differ, too.

Importance of Support and Care

The process of dying is difficult for everyone involved, especially if the dying process is extended over time due to illness or disability. Caring for a loved one who is terminally ill is beyond what many people are capable of handling physically, emotionally, and financially. **Hospice care**, a form of care given by trained medical professionals, focuses on making a person comfortable in his or her last days and hours of life. Caregivers attempt to control their patient's pain while serving emotional and sometimes spiritual needs. Care can be provided either in the patient's

Copyright Goodheart-Willcox Co., Inc.

The Stages of Dying

1. Denial. In this first stage, individuals who learn they are terminally ill reject the idea of dying. They may ignore the concept of their own death and decide not to acknowledge it. They cannot believe that this could be happening to them.

2. Anger. During the second stage, feelings of negativity and resentment develop. Individuals may be angry at the illness or disease. They may be angry that they will experience death and possible pain, while others are still going to be alive and healthy.

3. Bargaining. In this stage, individuals realize their own death, but wish for more time. They may propose deals or exchanges in order to preserve their own life. Bargaining may be with doctors, family, friends, or a higher power. For example, an individual may offer to become a "better person" if his or her life is extended.

4. Depression. In the fourth stage, individuals struggle with the loss of life. They may think about people, activities, and events they will miss. They may become sad, withdrawn, and lose interest in activities. They may be afraid or feel they are not ready.

5. Acceptance. In the final stage, individuals understand and accept that the reality of their own death is near. They may no longer be afraid or resentful. This stage is usually calm, which can transition into a peaceful passing.

Figure 9.17 Accepting death is a process. Each person experiences it differently. *What factors might affect the rate of acceptance?*

home or in a hospice living center. Hospice caregivers focus not only on the patients, but also on the needs of the family and loved ones.

Having support and care from family, friends, and healthcare professionals is important to the well-being of the adult coping with dying. When an individual has a support group, he or she can more easily process and deal with the stages of dying than if facing these challenges alone (**Figure 9.18**). Accepting the process of dying also allows friends and family members to say goodbye, resolve any past conflicts, and organize personal and financial matters. Loved ones can care for the dying family member or friend while learning to cope with and acknowledge the death of the loved one.

The Stages of Grieving

Losing a loved one can be traumatic and often causes strong emotional reactions, even when it is believed to be the "right time." **Grief** describes the mental anguish or sorrow the person's death causes. Great distress, sadness, disbelief, numbness, anxiety, loneliness, and despair are all common when coping with the death of someone else. Experiencing grief is normal and healthy.

Copyright Goodheart-Willcox Co., Inc.

Figure 9.18 The support of family and friends can comfort an individual who is dying and make it easier for him or her to deal with the stages of dying. *What can happen once a person has accepted the process of dying?*

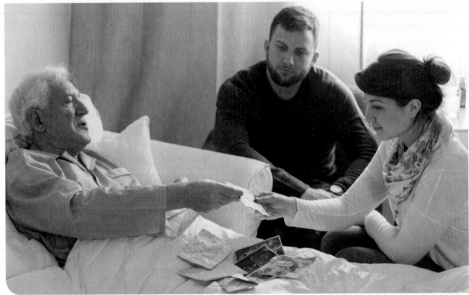

Photographee.eu/Shutterstock.com

Grieving is complex. Different people experience grieving differently. Similar to the stages of dying, there are also five stages of grieving. These stages are shown in **Figure 9.19**. As in the stages of dying, individuals may not experience these stages in order. They may skip stages or spend more time in one stage than another. There is no right or wrong amount of time to spend grieving. After experiencing a death, the survivor may continue to grieve for weeks, months, or years after the death. Some people may benefit from the support of grief counselors to be able to cope with the natural grieving process.

Celebrating the life, unique contributions, and personality of the one lost through death may ease the feeling of loss. This is especially important for adults who have lost a life partner. Death is inevitable. Although it is not always easy to accept, death is the final chapter of life.

Reading Recall

1. How do the definitions of the terms *lifespan* and *life cycle* differ?
2. Identify the six stages of the family life cycle.
3. Name four family-life crises.
4. Define *addiction*.
5. Describe three types of domestic abuse.
6. Describe the common emotional impacts of divorce on family members.
7. Name at least five common signs of clinical depression.
8. Describe how hospice care can help families deal with death and the loss of a loved one.

Copyright Goodheart-Willcox Co., Inc.

The Stages of Grieving
1. Denial. Survivors of the loved one may not believe or fully understand that the loved one passed away. They may ignore the death and continue in daily activities as if it did not happen.
2. Anger. After denial, feelings of anger may arise. The individual may be angry that he or she is left to deal with many new issues and possibly new roles. The individual may also be angry toward other family members, friends, and coworkers in the belief that others do not understand.
3. Bargaining. This stage occurs before the loved one dies. The individual may try to offer a deal or exchange to extend the life of a loved one.
4. Depression. Feelings of sadness, despair, withdrawal, and possibly loneliness may dominate now that the survivor understands the loved one will no longer be alive.
5. Acceptance. In the final stage, individuals begin to accept or feel comfortable with the loss of the loved one. They recognize that death is a normal part of the lifespan. They are able to move forward, without forgetting the loved one's death.

Figure 9.19 Each individual might experience the stages of grieving differently. *How long do survivors continue to grieve?*

Rewards, Demands, and Future Trends

There are significant rewards that come from helping people improve their lives. Counselors and mental health services workers play a part in seeing people improve their health, restore family relationships, recover from addictions, and overcome their grief. They receive great personal satisfaction in knowing they made a difference in someone's life.

Many counselors and mental health services workers find that the biggest challenge upon entering the field is finding the right balance between personal and professional roles. Clients often share serious issues from addiction to abuse or other violence. Counselors and mental health services workers see severely dysfunctional families. Many situations are sad, if not downright tragic. They see disappointing results when clients cannot or will not accept treatment.

Establishing appropriate personal boundaries is essential to long-term success in the field. The counselors' and therapists' jobs are to help their clients move beyond and past their current situations. Sometimes, it is difficult to not let personal emotions get in the way and "take on" the problems of clients, leading to stress and strife. Experienced professionals know this. Supervisors often work with those who are new to the field to teach them how to separate their own emotions from those of their clients.

Copyright Goodheart-Willcox Co., Inc.

Law and Ethics   *When Professional Care Becomes Personal*

Counseling and mental health services workers often develop close relationships with their clients. Clients may share their darkest secrets, fears, and concerns. They may disclose issues they are embarrassed about, such as facing financial crises, homelessness, medical issues, failed family relationships, or even criminal activities. They often share emotional highs and lows.

Although relationships can become very private, it is the responsibility of the counseling and mental health services workers to set and maintain professional boundaries. They should model these boundaries from the start. For example, expectations about how and when it is appropriate to contact the counseling and mental health services worker should be agreed on. Prohibiting sharing personal information about oneself that is not related to the client's condition or case also helps to set boundaries. Counseling and mental health services workers should avoid talking about their clients to others or discussing colleagues with their clients.

Although relationships may become very close, counseling and mental health services workers should always distinguish between professional service and personal friendship. When professional relationships become personal, objectivity is often compromised. Subjective feelings can cloud decision making. Personal friendships can ultimately harm relationships with clients, as boundaries and subsequent expectations blur.

Reading Activity

Find a nonfiction article or book about a case of inappropriate professional boundaries. In what ways was this relationship more personal than professional? Were there signs the professional relationship was becoming too personal? How did this cloud objectivity on the part of the counseling and mental health services worker? How did this cause harm to the client? How could this situation have been avoided?

Mental health is as important as physical health. Some might say it is even more important. By having good mental health, people can cope better with physical, financial, social, spiritual, and emotional woes. More than ever, employers, insurance companies, government, schools, and health providers understand the value of investing in the services of counselors and mental health services workers. As a result, counseling and mental health services is one of the fastest growing occupational fields. The future outlook for counseling and mental health services workers is very bright (**Figure 9.20**).

Reading Recall

1. What do many counselors and mental health services workers find to be the biggest challenge upon entering the field?
2. Why is it important for counselors and therapists to establish personal boundaries with their clients?
3. Describe future trends in counseling and mental health services careers.

Copyright Goodheart-Willcox Co., Inc.

Occupation	Projected Growth (2014–2024)	Projected Job Openings (2014–2024)	Median Wages (2014)	Education
Future Trends for Counseling and Mental Health Services Careers				
Child life specialist	Faster than average (9–13%)	6,600	$44,000	Bachelor's degree
Marriage and family therapist	Much faster than average (14% or higher)	12,100	$48,040	Master's degree
Mental health counselor	Much faster than average (14% or higher)	54,500	$40,850	Master's degree
Psychiatrist	Much faster than average (14% or higher)	11,800	$181,880	Post-doctoral training
Psychologist, clinical	Much faster than average (14% or higher)	63,800	$68,900	Post-doctoral training
Psychologist, counseling	Much faster than average (14% or higher)	63,800	$68,900	Post-doctoral training
Psychologist, school	Much faster than average (14% or higher)	63,800	$68,900	Master's degree
Rehabilitation counselor	Faster than average (9–13%)	36,000	$34,380	Master's degree
School counselor	Average (5–8%)	79,700	$53,370	Master's degree
Substance abuse counselor	Much faster than average (14% or higher)	41,100	$39,270	Master's degree
Therapist	Much faster than average (14% or higher)	63,800	$68,900	Post-doctoral training
Vocational counselor	Average (5–8%)	79,700	$53,370	Master's degree

Sources: O*NET and the *Occupational Outlook Handbook*

Figure 9.20 Many future opportunities are predicted for workers in the field of counseling and mental health services. *According to the information in this chart, which counseling and mental health services professional earned the most money in 2014?*

Copyright Goodheart-Willcox Co., Inc.

Summary

- Career opportunities in the counseling and mental health services field include counselors, psychologists, psychiatrists, and child life specialists.

- Counselors and other mental health services workers must be caring, communicative, and objective. They must be strong in content knowledge.

- Most career tracks in counseling and mental health services require postsecondary education and training. Undergraduate and graduate degrees, experience, and certification or licensure are common requirements for many positions.

- Specialized knowledge for counseling and mental health services careers involves understanding the individual and family life cycles and recognizing family-life crises. These

may include poverty, addiction, domestic violence, divorce, depression and suicide, and death and grief.

- How significantly a family-life crisis affects a family depends on the family's ability to recognize and manage the crisis. Counselors and mental health services workers work with families to teach them the necessary coping skills to handle crises and develop resilience.

- Counseling and mental health services workers receive great personal satisfaction in helping others. Many counselors and mental health services workers find that the biggest challenge upon entering the field is finding the right balance between personal and professional roles. The job outlook is bright for future career opportunities in counseling and mental health services.

College and Career Portfolio

Portfolio Personal Statement

Many portfolios require a *personal statement*. This is a short essay describing why you want to pursue a degree or job and what experiences have honed that vision. Whereas a cover message focuses primarily on experience, a personal statement includes your personal drive and interest in a career area.

When writing a personal statement, use this opportunity to write a short story with you as the main character. Talk about how your personal experiences and interests inspire you to pursue your academic or career goals. Be sure to write simply and clearly. Keep your personal statement brief and to the point. Essays that are too long can lose the reader's attention. Remember that your personal statement will continue to change as you change.

To write your own personal statement, complete the following:

1. Use online or print resources to see samples of other people's personal statements. Read these statements carefully. Which statements grab your attention? Are there similarities in the writing styles of these statements?

2. Draft a personal statement for your intended college or career.

3. Show your personal statement to a career counselor, teacher, or staff member in the school writing center to get his or her feedback.

4. Apply the feedback given. Proofread your personal statement carefully.

Copyright Goodheart-Willcox Co., Inc.

Review and Reflect ➦

1. Which type of therapist helps individuals, couples, and families resolve conflicts?
2. Which type of counselor works with students in an educational setting?
3. Give examples of how child life specialists would incorporate play into their dealings with clients.
4. Why is it important that counselors and mental health services workers have high mental and physical energy?
5. Choose one specific type of counselor position that interests you. Describe the education or training required for that job.
6. What are the eight stages in a typical individual's life cycle? Give an example of crises that could occur during various stages of the life cycle.
7. Give an example of a substance addiction and a behavioral addiction.
8. Describe the types of treatment for domestic abuse.
9. Are sadness and depression synonymous? Explain.
10. What is *child support*?
11. What is the difference between a *Last Will and Testament* (will) and a *living will*?
12. Define *advance directives* and identify two forms of advance directives.

Vocabulary Activities

13. **Key terms**   In teams, create categories for the following terms. Classify as many of the terms as possible. Share your ideas with the remainder of the class.

addiction	family-life crisis
advance directives	family life cycle
alcoholism	grief
at risk	hospice care
bipolar disorder	joint custody
child custody	Last Will and
child support	Testament
clinical depression	living will
domestic abuse	
do not resuscitate (DNR) order	

14. **Academic terms**   For each of the following terms, identify a word or group of words describing a quality of the term—an *attribute*. Pair up with a classmate. Discuss your list of attributes. Then, review your list of attributes with the whole class to increase understanding.

adversity   resilient
mortality

Self-Assessment Quiz ➦

Complete the self-assessment quiz online to help you practice and expand your knowledge and skills.

Critical Thinking

15. **Compare and contrast**   Identify several careers in counseling and mental health services that interest you. Compare and contrast employment opportunities for each of these careers.
16. **Make inferences**   In the past, having a GED or a high school diploma opened the doors to many entry-level positions. Today, most jobs require more advanced education or training. Explain how this change in the last 30 years is affecting families living at or below the poverty line. What predictions can you make about the educational requirements for future jobs based on this information?
17. **Analyze**   Identify a type of crisis. Determine the effects of this crisis on an individual and on a family.
18. **Determine**   Explain how a change in the family environment may cause stress which would lead to a family-life crisis. What advice would you give to someone going through this type of crisis?
19. **Evaluate**   Imagine you are working with a family whose income is below the poverty line. What management strategies would you suggest to help this family deal with the stress associated with living below the poverty line? What resources in your community would you suggest this family utilize? Why would these resources help this family?

20. **Cause and effect**   Some people believe domestic violence has become more prevalent due to the desensitization of society brought about by watching violent TV shows, movies, and video games. Create arguments for and against this statement that you can use in a debate in class.

21. **Identify**   There are five stages people experience when dealing with grief. Using Figure 9.19, name the stages. Give examples of how someone may react or act when dealing with each stage.

22. **Draw conclusions**   Identify some of the rewards and demands placed on the lives of counselors and mental health services workers. Determine ways these workers can balance the demands on their work and personal lives. How would your suggestions improve the lives of the workers?

Core Skills

23. **Writing**   Invite a school counselor or other type of mental health worker to come visit your classroom. Write a rough draft of the letter you would send to this person, along with a sample list of questions you would like answered during his or her presentation to your class. As a class, create a final letter and list of questions to send to the guest speaker.

24. **Writing and research**   Make a list of the types of family-life crises that can affect individuals and families. Give an example of how individuals and families are able to work through and overcome these crises. Choose one type of crisis from your list. Write a one-page paper on resources that can be used to deal with this crisis.

25. **Technology, research, and writing**   Using technology, create a list of resources families in crisis from your local area can use. List names, contact information, the services they provide, and the hours of operation. Compile this into an electronic presentation or flyer you can present to the local Chamber of Commerce. Keep a copy. Place it in your portfolio.

26. **Speaking and technology**   A public service announcement can be used on the radio or television and normally lasts about 15 to 30 seconds. Create a public service announcement about the prevention of domestic violence.

27. **Research**   Research the differences among and requirements for sole custody, joint custody, temporary managing conservatorship, permanent managing conservatorship, and joint managing conservatorship in your state. How are these beneficial to the family or child going through divorce or crises?

28. **Research**   Using online or print resources or informational interviews with professionals, investigate the causes, prevention, and treatment of domestic violence. Share your findings with the class.

29. **Research**   A friend comes to you and mentions he or she is feeling depressed and has thoughts of committing suicide. What advice would you give him or her? What resources in your town are available for suicide prevention? Using Figure 9.15, which lists the warning signs of clinical depression, how would you identify a friend you think may be feeling depressed and thinking of suicide? How can you let someone know you are worried about your friend committing suicide?

30. **Speaking and research**   Research the cost of a funeral. Ask what is included in the funeral home's services and what has to be paid for separately. Look at both a burial in a plot and cremation with an urn. Compare the two types of burials. Which type of burial would you like? Why?

31. **Research**   Explain how hospice care helps families dealing with the death process. What type of technology does hospice use? How does it help a dying person and his or her family deal with this difficult time?

32. **Research**   Many times, human services workers develop close relationships with their clients. How can human services workers set and maintain boundaries so they do not step out of line professionally and lose their licenses?

   Copyright Goodheart-Willcox Co., Inc.

33. **CTE career readiness practice**   Suppose you are interested in a career as a counselor or therapist in the counseling and mental health services career pathway. You have done your research in regard to educational requirements for such careers and think this fits with your personal and career goals. You feel, however, you are missing the first-hand experiential knowledge necessary to commit to such a career. Locate a person with a local company or organization who is an expert in your career of interest. Make arrangements to job shadow or work with this individual as a mentor, as you pursue your career. How can you benefit by having such a mentor in your life?

34. **CTE career readiness practice**   Maintaining a healthy lifestyle has an impact on how you function physically and mentally. What unhealthy behaviors could have an effect on how well you do your job? How do you think employers should deal with behaviors affecting the personal health of their employees?

Lend a Hand

Crisis Hotlines

As you have learned in this chapter, talking about a problem with an understanding person can be extremely helpful. Crisis hotlines are staffed by compassionate professionals and volunteers who are available to talk with anyone who needs help. Some hotlines have specific aims, such as preventing suicide and self-harm. Other hotlines are also available to anyone who needs someone to listen. For most hotlines, no problem is too small or insignificant. People may call in about depression, stress, anxiety, grief, bullying, abuse, trauma, and more.

If you have a desire to help people through crises, perhaps a volunteer opportunity on a crisis hotline might be right for you. On a crisis hotline, you would listen to callers and help them in whatever way you can. Crisis hotline workers receive extensive training in crisis intervention, risk assessment, and empathetic listening.

If you do not feel comfortable volunteering on the hotline, there are always other non-hotline opportunities. For example, you might be able to organize or participate in a fund-raiser for the crisis center or serve on a committee.

To discover how you can volunteer at a crisis hotline, complete the following:

1. Think about whether or not you are suited for a position on a crisis hotline. Reflect on a situation in which someone close to you was in a crisis situation. Were you able to keep a level head and help the person in need? Hotline work is not for everyone. It is important to know your limits before signing up.
2. Use online or print resources to locate crisis centers in your area. Make a list of the crisis centers that interest you. Find out what hotline and non-hotline volunteer opportunities are available.
3. Practice applying for one volunteer opportunity. Fill out the application. Answer any questionnaires as if you were ready to commit to the volunteer position.

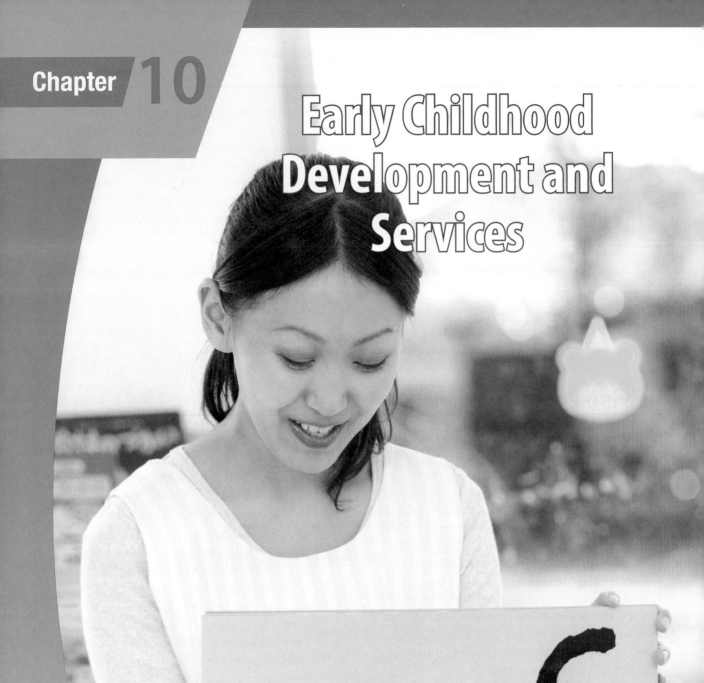

Chapter 10

Early Childhood Development and Services

While studying, look for the activity icon  **to**

- **practice** key and academic terms with e-flash cards and matching activities;
- **assess** what you learn by completing self-assessment quizzes; and
- **reinforce** what you learn by mapping concepts and completing review and reflect questions.

www.g-wlearning.com/humanservices/

KPG Payless2/Shutterstock.com

Learning Outcomes

After studying this chapter, you will be able to
- **compare and contrast** early childhood development and services careers;
- **list** common aptitudes, attitudes, and skills of early childhood development and services workers;
- **give examples** of education, training, and experience required for child-related careers;
- **recognize** developmental milestones and appropriate activities for children;
- **evaluate** guidance techniques that are developmentally appropriate for young children;
- **identify** ways to keep children safe, including protection from neglect and abuse; and
- **summarize** the rewards, demands, and future trends of careers in early childhood development and services.

Reading Strategies

Before reading, write the chapter headings on a separate piece of paper, leaving space between each heading. As you are reading, use the space under each heading to take notes. After reading, write a review question for material under each main heading. Exchange papers with a classmate and answer each other's questions.

Mapping Concepts

Organize your notes for this chapter by the following categories in a graph like the one shown: *Career options*; *Aptitudes, attitudes, and skills*; *Education and training*; *Specialized knowledge*; and *Rewards, demands, and future trends*.

Key Terms

authoritarian style
authoritative style
center-based child care programs
child abuse
child neglect
childproofing
developmentally appropriate practices (DAPs)
developmentally inappropriate practices (DIPs)
discipline

family child care centers
fine-motor skills
gross-motor skills
guidance
mandated reporters
permissive style
prekindergarten programs
preschool programs
work-related child care programs

Academic Terms

detrimental
exuberant
intuition
reciprocal

Do you love being with children? If so, a career in early childhood development and services might be right for you. Working with infants and young children is a world full of creativity and fun. Cuddles and first steps, building with blocks, storytelling and games, sandbox structures, and mixing paint are common activities as young children learn mainly through play and human interaction. Caregivers focus on nurturing and stimulating that interaction. They recognize the importance of exploration and play and build their programs around these activities. They teach children language skills, social skills, and science and math concepts. They provide a safe and nurturing setting that promotes interaction between people and the world around them.

Some early childhood development and services workers work with older preschool children, readying them for school. They generally use less structured approaches to teach preschool children than those used in the older grade levels (**Figure 10.1**). In some preschool settings, academics take priority. Letter recognition, phonics, numbers, and awareness of nature and science, traditionally taught in kindergarten and the elementary school years, may be stressed in preschool.

The first five years of a child's life may be the most important. Those years set the stage for physical, intellectual (also called *cognitive*), and social-emotional development. They impact a person's ability to attach to others in later life stages. They form the basis for a person's desire to explore and learn. They set the groundwork for a person to become independent and confident. Whether working with infants, toddlers, or young children, early childhood development and services workers perform a critical service.

Figure 10.1 Creative activities, such as art, dance, and music are frequently used to teach concepts to preschool children. *Why do you think such creative activities are used with children in this age group?*

Monkey Business Images/Shutterstock.com

Copyright Goodheart-Willcox Co., Inc.

Careers in Early Childhood Development and Services

There are many career opportunities for early childhood development and services workers. **Figure 10.2** shows some of these opportunities. In the following sections, you will learn much more about careers in early childhood development and services.

Child Care Workers

Child care workers provide care for children when parents are busy. They help meet children's basic needs—preparing meals and keeping them safe. They also plan activities that promote learning. Child care workers may work in private homes, their own homes, or in child care centers.

In-Home Care

Nannies and au pairs are child care workers who provide care in private homes. *Nannies* care for the children in one family and often develop close relationships with both the children and parents. They may work full- or part-time and may either live in the home or commute. Nannies can oversee outings, such as going to the zoo or park, and take children to other activities. Nannies may also help prepare meals for the children and travel with the family, if requested.

Au pairs provide child care services for a host family as part of a cultural exchange program. They live with the family and provide occasional child care as well as perform light household duties. Au pairs can expose children to another language and cultural traditions. Likewise, au pairs get to experience a new culture and sometimes learn a new language. Host families usually supervise au pairs and treat them as a member of the family.

Examples of Early Childhood Development and Services Careers

- Child care worker (opportunities to work with children in private homes, family child care centers, center-based child care programs, work-related child care programs, preschool and Pre-K programs, and Head Start programs)
- Nanny and Au pair
- Preschool teacher
- Teacher assistant
- Program director
- Assistant director
- Parent educator

Figure 10.2 The field of early childhood development and services offers many different career opportunities. *Which of these careers would you like to learn more about?*

Copyright Goodheart-Willcox Co., Inc.

Family Child Care Centers

Some child care workers provide child care services in their own homes. **Family child care centers** are operated in the child care worker's private home for a small number of children. Often, there is just one caregiver to watch the children. Using resources in the home, these child care workers provide nutritious meals and snacks, physical activity opportunities, and guidance for young children.

Some family child care centers are licensed and operate with written policies. Licensing requires in-home centers to meet certain standards set

Law and Ethics *Accreditation Affirmation*

When comparing child care centers, many differences can be found. Differences may include hours of operation, flexibility, religious affiliation, and types of discipline used. These are all preferences. Caregiver-to-child ratios and the number of children in each group or classroom also vary. To measure the quality of a child care program, people often check accreditation. Early childhood care and education programs can choose to obtain accreditation from a child care accrediting organization. Accreditation requires early child care providers to meet higher standards than state licensing regulations.

A good source of information about quality early childhood education programs can be found through the *National Association for the Education of Young Children (NAEYC)*. The NAEYC is a resource for parents and teachers. It offers accreditation to programs that meet their health, safety, and educational standards.

There are several resources for helping parents find quality child care options that are right for them. The *National Association of Child Care Resource and Referral Agencies (NACCRRA)* is a nonprofit group that helps make sure quality child care exists in most communities around the country. The NACCRRA trains child care workers, advocates for child care-friendly laws, and acts as a resource for parents seeking information.

Center-based child care centers must be licensed by the state in which they operate. Licensing standards vary by state, but voluntary national accreditation is available through the *National Association for Family Child Care*

(NAFCC). If a child care center is accredited by the NAFCC, it is a good indicator that the program is committed to quality care. It also indicates that employees are involved in ongoing training.

For in-home care, the *International Nanny Association* recommends asking for a criminal background check. Nanny placement or hiring agencies usually do this for families. If hiring an au pair or other in-home care worker, personal background checks and referrals should be used to gain more information about the prospective employee.

Many local child care referral services offer information about early childhood education programs in their area. This information often describes caregiver-to-child ratios and class sizes, caregiver or teacher qualifications, and mission of the organization. Information may also include descriptions of the facilities, extra services, or operating procedures.

Research Activity

When working with children and families, it is helpful to know of resources for finding child care. Use the Internet to research each of the following organizations. Give a description of what services each offers.
- NAEYC
- NACCRRA
- NAFCC
- International Nanny Association

Copyright Goodheart-Willcox Co., Inc.

forth by the state. Requirements vary from state to state, but often include regulations for

- a safe environment;

- a maximum number of children receiving care (including the caregiver's own children);

- child-caregiver interactions;

- the provision of age-appropriate activities; and

- the successful completion of background checks and safety inspections by accredited agencies.

Unfortunately, some family child care centers operate without licensing. A drawback to an unlicensed family child care center is that the care is unregulated by outside agencies. In other words, if caregivers do not register their family child care center with the state, they will not be inspected. They may not meet safety and other child care standards. Overcrowding, unsafe environments, and unqualified caregivers may be issues of concern with unregulated family child care centers. When seeking employment, be cautious of unlicensed centers.

Center-Based Child Care

Many jobs can be found for child care workers in center-based child care programs. **Center-based child care programs** are provided in a center and not in a home, and may serve a few or many children (**Figure 10.3**). They may be for-profit or not-for-profit programs.

Figure 10.3 Some center-based child care programs may care for 20 or fewer children while other programs may serve several hundred children. *What do you think are some advantages and disadvantages of having small center-based child care programs?*

Fh Photo/Shutterstock.com

Copyright Goodheart-Willcox Co., Inc.

For-profit programs are child care centers that make a profit or money like many other businesses. *Not-for-profit programs* are not set up to make money. They typically receive their funding from parents, community members, or corporate donors. Places of worship and other community centers are examples of not-for-profit programs. Some businesses may run not-for-profit programs for their employees' children. These programs are called **work-related child care programs**.

Both part- and full-time center-based programs are licensed as the result of meeting state standards and passing inspections. They also have clearly written policies for hours of operation, pick-up and drop-off times, disciplinary practices, and illness procedures. There are many part-time job prospects in center-based programs for students.

Preschool Teachers and Teacher Assistants

More and more children are enrolled in educational programs prior to kindergarten. Two such programs that have a stronger educational focus are preschool and prekindergarten programs. **Preschool programs** are for children two through four years of age. **Prekindergarten programs**, where available, are for children who will be in kindergarten the following year. Prekindergarten programs are often referred to as *Pre-K programs*. Preschool and Pre-K programs can be part- or full-time (**Figure 10.4**).

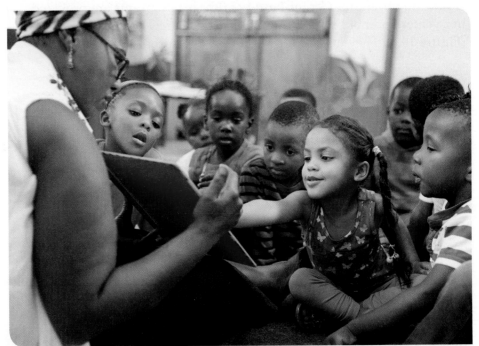

Monkey Business Images/Shutterstock.com

Figure 10.4 Part-time programs often run for partial day hours, such as morning or afternoon, or only on certain days of the week. *Why might you send a child to a part-time program?*

Copyright Goodheart-Willcox Co., Inc.

In preschool and Pre-K programs, *preschool* and *Pre-K teachers* plan activities that build on children's curiosity and interest in play. These activities are based on experience with children and a thorough knowledge of child development and learning. The activities help children develop the many skills they will need for kindergarten and beyond. *Teacher assistants* supervise children and reinforce educational lessons under the direct supervision of preschool teachers.

Some preschool teachers work in Head Start programs. Head Start is a government-funded program that helps prepare low-income three- and four-year-olds for school. In Head Start programs, teachers work with nutritionists, healthcare workers, and social workers to provide a broad range of services for economically disadvantaged children. Some Head Start programs are coordinated with other social programs to provide all-day child care. The result is children who are better prepared for their next level of schooling.

Program Directors and Assistant Directors

Program directors oversee the mission, goals, and programs of a center-based child care or preschool center (**Figure 10.5**). Program directors develop child care centers and organize how they are run. They evaluate the program's progress and success. They hire staff and provide orientation and training. Most program directors also work with state and federal agencies to secure grants and maintain health and safety regulations. Program directors need to stay up-to-date with current developments relating to their program.

Figure 10.5 A program director is a supervisory position that requires a combination of educational expertise and experience. *What sorts of qualities do you think make a program director successful?*

Milles Studio/Shutterstock.com

Because of the many responsibilities of program directors, they need direct support to oversee the day-to-day operations of the child care program. *Assistant directors* play this supporting role. They work under direct supervision of the program director. Assistant directors may perform a wide variety of duties to meet program standards.

Parent Educators

Parent educators teach parents the skills they need to meet their children's physical, intellectual, and social-emotional needs. Parent educators may organize a discussion among parents of newborns. They may also organize playgroups that focus on good parenting skills. They may offer classes on how to talk with teens. Parent educators can share knowledge and skills while offering encouragement and a community for parents to interact and ask questions. Some school districts, hospitals, places of worship, and other community organizations hire parent educators.

Reading Recall

1. Why are the first five years of life critically important?
2. Name the three main types of child care programs.
3. Compare and contrast *au pairs* and *nannies*.
4. What are the advantages of in-home child care?
5. What are the advantages of center-based child care?
6. How do *preschool programs* differ from *child care programs*?

Common Aptitudes, Attitudes, and Skills

In early childhood development and services positions, the qualities of the caregivers and their interactions with the children are important. Caregivers typically demonstrate characteristics reflecting quality child care (**Figure 10.6**). Caregivers who have a real interest in children and child development, who are patient, and who also enjoy the children they care for often tend to provide higher-quality care.

Characteristics of Quality Caregivers		
• Adaptable	• Encouraging	• Loving
• Committed to ongoing education	• Honest	• Nondiscriminatory
• Compassionate	• Interest in child development	• Patient
• Desire to be around children	• Kind and caring	• Reliable
• Empathetic	• Knowledgeable	• Responsible

Figure 10.6 There are many characteristics that caregivers can demonstrate to reflect quality child care. *Which characteristics in the table do you think are the most important indicators of quality child care?*

Copyright Goodheart-Willcox Co., Inc.

bikeriderlondon/Shutterstock.com

Figure 10.7 Through their interactions with the children, quality caregivers make children feel loved, accepted, and safe. *What are some actions that quality caregivers do to make children feel loved, accepted, and safe?*

Quality caregivers demonstrate positive, appropriate interactions with children (**Figure 10.7**). They have a thorough knowledge of child development, which they use to meet children's needs. For example, they know that infants are completely dependent and need to be held and supported in their efforts to roll over, crawl, stand, and walk. They provide a safe environment and the necessary guidance to toddlers as they explore the world around them. They patiently answer preschoolers' endless questions and support their efforts to learn new skills and gain independence. Throughout all stages of development, caregivers comfort children when they are upset.

In addition to working well with children, early childhood development and services workers interact well with adults, too. They have good listening and speaking skills to communicate effectively with parents and coworkers. They are good problem solvers and mediators. They work well as a team with parents and other professionals to meet the needs of the children they serve. They keep up-to-date on the latest information in the field of child development. They then implement this knowledge to improve children's quality of life.

Reading Recall

1. Name three characteristics of quality caregivers.
2. Why is it important that early childhood development and services workers interact well with adults?

Copyright Goodheart-Willcox Co., Inc.

Education, Training, and Experience

Early childhood postsecondary programs prepare students for careers in early childhood development and services. Along with formal education, experience is critical. Fortunately, part-time assistant jobs exist to help those interested in this field gain experience. Nanny services often require applicants to have child care training beyond high school or practical experience with good recommendations.

Licensing requirements for preschool teachers are not consistent, but vary state by state. Educational requirements range from an associate's degree in early childhood development to a bachelor's degree in a related area. Some states require certification by a nationally recognized authority, such as the Child Development Associate (CDA). The CDA requires a mix of classroom training and hands-on experience working with children (**Figure 10.8**).

Early childhood educators usually begin as assistant teachers. From there, most rise to teacher, then to lead teacher (who may be responsible for instruction of several classes), and finally to director of the center. Additional education is usually required at the director level. Many early childhood educators hold a bachelor's degree, which qualifies them to teach kindergarten through third grade. Teaching at these higher grades often results in higher pay.

Reading Recall

1. For what kinds of jobs do early childhood postsecondary programs prepare their graduates?
2. How are preschool teachers licensed?
3. What is a typical entry-level job for early childhood educators?

CDA Requirements

Age—18 years of age or older

Education level achieved—high school diploma or a GED

Working experience needed—480 hours of experience working with children within the five years prior to applying

Training in early childhood education—120 hours of documented and approved training within the last five years on the growth and development of children ages birth to five years and the eight CDA subject areas

Professional portfolio—includes documentation of hours logged in child care work environment, education and training, autobiography, and parent opinion questionnaires

Examination—computer-based examination that includes 65 questions

Verification visit—includes assessment observation, an oral interview, and a written assessment

Figure 10.8 Some states require preschool teachers obtain a Child Development Associate, which is issued by the Council of Professional Recognition. *Do you meet any of the requirements of the CDA?*

Copyright Goodheart-Willcox Co., Inc.

Specialized Knowledge for Early Childhood Development and Services Careers

Caregivers are responsible for promoting the development and safety of children. To do this, they must be able to identify and meet the basic needs of children. They also need to recognize that these needs change as children grow and develop. Therefore, early childhood development and services workers must have specialized knowledge in the developmental milestones children typically achieve in early childhood. Caregivers use this knowledge to provide developmentally appropriate activities that encourage physical, intellectual, and social-emotional development. They guide children's behavior and create a safe environment in which they can learn. They also recognize when children are in danger and take action to protect them from neglect and abuse.

Recognizing Developmental Milestones

Development during early childhood does not happen in the same way, at the same time, for all children. Some children will develop certain skills or abilities faster or slower than others. These differences are normal and expected. Even so, there are typical markers of development for each stage during the early childhood years. As you will see in the following sections, early childhood is a remarkable time of development.

During Infancy

When babies are born, they enter the stage in the life cycle known as *infancy*. This is the period from birth to the first birthday. Just after birth, babies are called *newborns*. This term refers to the time period from birth to 1 month of age. From 1 to 12 months, babies are known as *infants*. In these first 12 months of life, babies undergo great changes as they grow and learn at a rapid pace. The physical, intellectual, and social-emotional growth and development that occurs during infancy sets the foundation for a lifetime of growing and learning (**Figure 10.9**).

Physical qualities and changes during infancy are sequential and predictable. Babies grow significantly in both length and weight. Dramatic growth in the brain and nervous system occurs. There is speedy development in motor skills. Their improved **gross-motor skills** (those that involve large muscle movements) enable babies to crawl and eventually take their first steps. Development of their **fine-motor skills** (those that involve small muscle movements) help babies learn to pick up and grasp objects and self-feed.

Through the development of motor skills, babies explore their world, learning more and more as they organize their experiences. They learn to coordinate what they sense (see, hear, feel, taste) with motor

Copyright Goodheart-Willcox Co., Inc.

skills (actions). For example, babies love to put objects in their mouths, exploring the way they taste and feel. They touch, feel, and move objects around. With each new sensory exploration, intellectual development occurs (**Figure 10.10**).

Developmental Milestones During Infancy			
Age	**Physical**	**Intellectual**	**Social-Emotional**
1 month 	• Focuses on objects in close range, about 8 to 12 inches from eyes • Recognizes some sounds and voices • Has little control of arms • Lifts arms to mouth and eyes • Makes a tightly closed fist • Will turn to face sounds and noises • Dislikes strong smells	• Responds to mother's voice • Cries when wants a need addressed	• Prefers the attention and faces of people over toys and other objects
3 months  ©iStock.com/Jani Bryson	• Supports the upper body with arms when on stomach • Kicks legs • Uses leg muscles to resist flat surface at feet	• Follows objects in motion • Responds to sounds	• Focuses on faces and watches closely • Smiles • Expresses more emotions
4 to 7 months 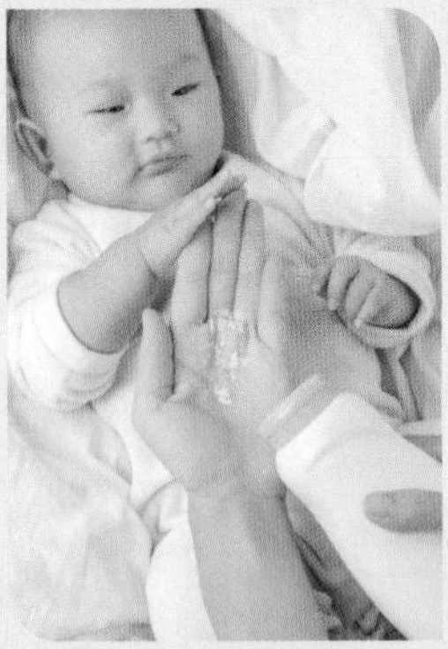 Aliwak/Shutterstock.com	• Reaches for objects • Moves object from one hand to the other • Strengthens ability to follow objects in motion	• Recognizes his or her name • Places objects in mouth to learn about them • Shows interest in and responds to mirrors	• Recognizes differences in emotions through changes in voice

(Continued)

Figure 10.9 Developmental milestones provide a general idea of when certain events will occur. *Around what age do babies start kicking?*

Copyright Goodheart-Willcox Co., Inc.

Developmental Milestones During Infancy (*Continued*)			
Age	**Physical**	**Intellectual**	**Social-Emotional**
8 to 12 months Bruno D'Andrea/ Shutterstock.com	• Sits up without any help • Supports body on hands and knees • Walks with assistance • Stands • Controls the release of an object from grasp • Brings objects together • Feeds self using fingers	• Understands *no* • Interacts with objects • Communicates with gestures • Imitates sounds such as tongue clicks	• Becomes shy around new people • Demonstrates separation anxiety and shows preference for regular caregiver • Shows disinterest in some objects and pushes away • Enjoys "peek-a-boo" and similar games

Babies' physical and intellectual growth and development are highly related to social-emotional growth. According to Erik Erikson's psychosocial theory, the stage for social-emotional development during infancy is termed *trust versus mistrust*. During this stage, caregivers and family members form the basis for babies to learn to develop trust relationships. Caregivers do this by responding to and meeting babies' needs. When babies cry, they need to be comforted. When their diapers are wet, they need to be changed. As caregivers meet their babies' needs, babies learn to trust their caregivers. This is only possible if babies are not hungry, in pain, or uncomfortable. The ability or inability to develop trust can have lifelong effects on personal relationships with others.

During the Toddler Years

When children reach their first birthday, they enter the *toddler years*, which last until the third birthday. Children who are between one and three years of age are known as *toddlers*. During this period, much growth and development occurs (**Figure 10.11**).

As toddlers develop physically, their bodily

Figure 10.10 Rolling, crawling, and reaching are all significant signs of intellectual growth. *What are some ways to facilitate a baby's intellectual development?*

proportions change and bodies mature. Height and weight continue to increase. More teeth develop, changing the look of toddlers' smiles and facial features. Children learn many new gross- and fine-motor skills.

Copyright Goodheart-Willcox Co., Inc.

Developmental Milestones During Toddlerhood

Age	Physical	Intellectual	Social-Emotional
12 months *Anetta/Shutterstock.com*	• Crawls on stomach • Moves from sitting to crawling position • Creeps up and down stairs • Attempts to self-feed using spoon and cup	• Follows simple instructions • Understands words have meanings • Understands simple requests • Shows interest in learning about objects and their names • Enjoys music and attempts to sing	• Shows favoritism and attachment to toys or objects • Begins responding with *no* • Watches caregivers for responses to actions
18 months *Anton Gvozdikov/ Shutterstock.com*	• Walks without assistance • Pushes or pulls objects while sitting • Dances in standing position for short periods	• Understands the purpose of everyday items • Identifies objects and body parts • Refuses food or toys by shaking head or using hands to push food away • Points to images or objects • Understands object permanence • Asks questions by raising voice at end of sentence	• Demonstrates desire to share object of interest with caregivers • Exhibits temper tantrums • Demonstrates comfort and affection toward familiar people
24 months *Felix Mizioznikov/ Shutterstock.com*	• Carries items while walking or pulls a toy behind • Runs short distances • Walks backward • Kicks a ball • Uses blocks to build • Stands on toes • Uses pincer grasp and a cup with handles to self-feed • Undresses self	• Identifies objects when prompted by caregivers • Tries to pronounce and repeat words in surrounding conversations • Begins to organize objects by color or shape • Uses discovery to solve problems	• Develops self-awareness • Mimics behavior of others • Shows interest in other children • Engages in parallel play

Figure 10.11 Although everyone develops at slightly different rates, caregivers should note difficulties in reaching developmental milestones. *Why do you think it is important to note such difficulties in reaching developmental milestones?*

Copyright Goodheart-Willcox Co., Inc.

They walk, kick, climb, run, hold a cup with handles, and can even begin scribbling. Toddlers are in constant motion.

Intellectually, toddlers are still discovering and learning by coordinating their senses and actions. As toddlers' brains mature and experiences increase, they develop more sophisticated thought processes. One easily recognizable sign of intellectual growth during the toddler years is the swift increase in language, both in understanding and using spoken words. At the beginning of the toddler years, children usually learn to say their first words. By the end of the toddler years, children can usually say several hundred words.

According to Erikson, toddlers are in the social-emotional stage of development known as *autonomy versus shame and doubt*. During this stage, toddlers begin to see themselves as separate from their caregivers, without feelings of embarrassment or uncertainty. As they learn how to control their bodies and develop new skills, toddlers gain self-confidence and become more independent. Relationships with others become more *reciprocal* (two-sided; mutual) as more two-way interaction occurs. Caregivers need to provide a stimulating environment to encourage learning and social-emotional development to help toddlers achieve autonomy.

During the Preschool Years

Children undergo major developmental changes during the preschool years. The *preschool years* begin at the third birthday and end at the sixth birthday. Children in this stage are called *preschoolers*. Although preschoolers develop in similar ways, each child is unique. Each represents a different time line for running, talking, toilet learning, and other milestones (**Figure 10.12**).

Individual differences in both height and weight become more apparent during the preschool years. Facial features are also somewhat slimmer when compared to the chubby faces of infants. Toothy smiles are common. As children reach the end of this stage, baby teeth fall out, causing gaps in their smiles. Bones are stronger and bodies are more muscular. This enables children to learn many gross- and fine-motor skills that require coordination. As young children develop their fine-motor skills, the preference for handedness (being left- or right-handed) becomes more apparent.

Young children are eager to learn and are often talkative, humorous, and imaginative. They love to play and interact with others. Preschoolers gradually move from using *intuition*, primitive reasoning based on feelings, to more rational and logical thinking. Their vocabulary grows rapidly as they talk with family and peers. Some experts estimate that a child learns a new word during every waking hour. This results in a vocabulary of over 14,000 words at the end of early childhood (**Figure 10.13**). That is, just in time to enter school.

Copyright Goodheart-Willcox Co., Inc.

Developmental Milestones During Preschool

Age	Physical	Intellectual	Social-Emotional
3 years *ziggy_mars/Shutterstock.com*	• Able to throw a ball overhand as hand and eye coordination increases • Catches a ball by trapping it in arms • Hops and jumps • Pedals a tricycle • Can draw a circle or an X	• Speaks in sentences between five and six words in length • Begins to put puzzles with large pieces together • Organizes items by color or shape • Begins to count • Follows more complex instructions	• Tells stories to others • Shows interest in new people, objects, or experiences • Shows affection for friends • Tries to comfort other children when sad or hurt • Engages in functional play • Understands possession (*mine*, *hers*, *yours*)
4 years *Vladimir Nikitin/ Shutterstock.com*	• Draws shapes and letters • Walks up and down stairs quickly • Uses flatware, such as a fork and spoon • Uses child scissors and follows cutting patterns • Self-dresses • Controls toilet needs and is progressing in toilet learning	• Remembers portions of stories • Identifies colors by name • Uses intuition to solve problems • Understands the concept of opposites • Counts to 10 or higher • Uses different tenses in language other than present tense • Understands and interacts with programs or websites on a computer	• Engages in cooperative and constructive play • Is increasingly self-aware of body, thoughts, emotions • Can feel embarrassment • May tell "tall tales" to protect self from consequences • Begins to express anger by yelling
5 years *Monkey Business Images/ Shutterstock.com*	• Climbs • Tumbles • Runs • Skips • Learns to ride a bike with training wheels	• Remembers his or her own name and address • Writes his or her name • Has a higher attention span • Recognizes some written words	• Seeks approval from adults • Is interested in other children and shows favoritism toward friends • Engages in pretend play • Desires to be like other children • Is able to distinguish right from wrong • Begins to understand the difference between reality and fantasy

Figure 10.12 If these milestones are missed or delayed, there may be a greater issue preventing the preschooler from reaching the milestone. *At what age do most children begin drawing shapes and letters?*

Copyright Goodheart-Willcox Co., Inc.

TAGSTOCK1/Shutterstock.com

Figure 10.13 One way that young children learn language and increase their vocabulary is by having adults and older children read books to them. *Do you recall being read to as a child?*

During the preschool years, children are very busy. They love to dance, run, tell stories, share secrets, and explore. They have a lot of energy, but are not very cautious. They can be *exuberant* (excited) about trying new activities. In their eagerness to do a task independently, they often fail. This failure can cause guilt, lowering their self-esteem. Erikson described this stage of social-emotional development as *initiative versus guilt*.

Providing Developmentally Appropriate Activities

Activities in early childhood education programs depend on the age and developmental milestones of each child. Quality child care workers will base activities on developmentally appropriate practices. **Developmentally appropriate practices (DAPs)** are age-appropriate activities and teaching methods that consider each child's strengths, interests, and culture.

DAPs take into consideration the developmental milestones of an age group as well as individual preferences, learning styles, and interests. Caregivers and teachers incorporate DAPs into activity plans to customize care to each child. DAPs also consider a child's culture for further insight into creating activities. Culture can affect many care aspects, such as language, foods, and play.

Activities that focus on young children as a group without considering developmentally appropriate activities or individual

Copyright Goodheart-Willcox Co., Inc.

preferences are called **developmentally inappropriate practices (DIPs)**. DIPs may utilize only one type of teaching or caregiving strategy without variation or adjustment for individual needs. For example, a DIP may allow children free time to play in a reading room. A DAP may allow free time in a room with various playing areas, such as blocks and toys, arts and crafts, a water station, and a reading area. Unlike DIPs, DAPs strive to add in all major types of development into activities (**Figure 10.14**). DAP activities also make adjustments for children with special needs.

Guiding Children's Behavior

Parents and caregivers use guidance and discipline to help teach children self-control, independence, safety, and forms of socially

DAPs Versus DIPs		
Age	**Examples of DAPs**	**Examples of DIPs**
Infants	• Guided movement activities, such as "patty cake" or "walking" • Tummy time for young infants • Safe exploration of room by crawling, scooting, or walking • Reading sturdy picture books with few words and lots of pictures • Clean, colorful toys that can be safely handled and mouthed • Holding, rocking, cuddling by caregiver • Lyrical and rhythmic music played, sung, motions	• Leaving child alone or with little caregiver interaction • Limiting physical exploration • Containing infant in small or limited space • Reading fragile books with more words and complex pictures • Toys with small parts or sharp edges, toxic finishes • Inadequate physical contact • An unstimulating sensory environment
Toddlers	• Child-size furniture • Moveable toy containers, such as baskets or carts • Play areas that promote gross-motor development • Sensory experiences, such as rice tables, soft toys, or toys that can be shaken, hammered, or wheeled	• Rigid schedules • Restrictive environments that minimize motor activity • Toys with small pieces • Time-out chair • Toys with just one specific use
Preschoolers	• Child-directed art activities • Dramatic play areas with props • Building materials, such as blocks • Outdoor areas for exploration • Play opportunities that utilize tools used in real life, such as cooking or cleaning	• Teacher-directed activities • Closely monitored activities, such as worksheets, coloring pages • Games and toys that can only be manipulated one way • Rigidity in schedules • Compliance with adult choices

Figure 10.14 It is important to focus on developmentally appropriate practices (DAPs) as opposed to developmentally inappropriate practices (DIPs). *What are some DAPs and DIPs for toddlers?*

Copyright Goodheart-Willcox Co., Inc.

acceptable actions and behavior. **Guidance** by its very definition means help, assistance, leadership, and regulation. **Discipline**, which is a part of guidance, refers to the techniques and methods caregivers use to teach children to behave acceptably.

There are three types of discipline parents and caregivers commonly use. As parents begin to use guidance and discipline, they develop a parenting style. They also apply common strategies to guide children's behavior in acceptable, age-appropriate ways.

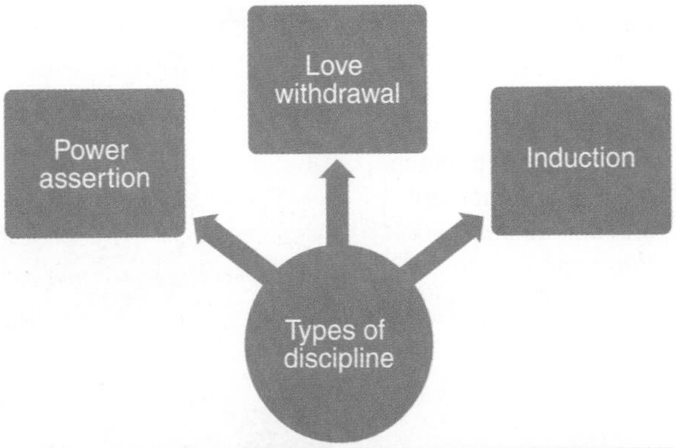

Figure 10.15 The three types of discipline are power assertion, love withdrawal, and induction. Some of these types are better than others. *Why might a parent use discipline against a child?*

Types of Discipline

Young children have active imaginations and are constantly exploring. They may test limits in unsafe or socially unacceptable ways. To guide children's behavior, parents and caregivers use various types of discipline (**Figure 10.15**).

Power Assertion

Power assertion involves using physical means to punish or deny children privileges. Also known as *corporal punishment*, this form of discipline can physically and emotionally harm a child. Spanking falls within this category of discipline. Views on spanking vary widely, but most experts advise against using spanking or power assertion as a form of discipline in the home. It should never be used in a caregiving situation.

Experts discourage power assertion mostly because it can be abusive. Power assertion also creates and relies on fear and demonstrates negative ways to handle emotions. Children who are disciplined with power assertion techniques are more likely to use power in their personal relationships, which creates a cycle of negativity.

Love Withdrawal

Love withdrawal includes threatening to remove love, even temporarily, from the caregiver-child relationship. Examples of love withdrawal include threatening to send the child away, telling the child he or she is not wanted or favored, ignoring the child, or giving the child the "silent treatment." Experts consider love withdrawal to be emotionally damaging (**Figure 10.16**). When caregivers threaten to take away love, they cause stress and instability within a child. Love withdrawal can send the wrong message that love is unsteady and can be used to gain power.

Induction

Induction is a form of discipline that uses logic and explanation to address a child's action or behavior. Induction involves listening to the child, understanding and acknowledging his or her emotions, and explaining the reasoning behind why an action or behavior is inappropriate

Copyright Goodheart-Willcox Co., Inc.

Figure 10.16 According to Maslow's *Hierarchy of Human Needs*, all people need to feel loved in order to reach optimal development and self-actualization. *What can you do to make children feel loved?*

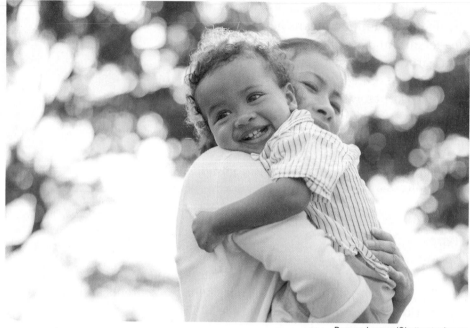

Dragon Images/Shutterstock.com

or unacceptable. For example, if a child is hitting other children during playtime, the caregiver will first remove the child from the group. The caregiver will then acknowledge the child's feelings by making statements such as, "I know you feel angry." Then the caregiver will explain why hitting other children is unacceptable. Once the child understands why hitting is wrong and calms down, he or she can return to the playgroup.

Induction teaches children through logic and reasoning that actions have consequences. Induction also opens two-way communication between the caregiver and child. The caregiver explains consequences in a logical and calm manner. This sends the message to children that they can talk with their caregivers about issues or problems in the future. Induction is ineffective for the first year of a child's life. After the first year, induction becomes increasingly effective (**Figure 10.17**).

Parenting Styles

The approach parents use when guiding and disciplining their children is known as their *parenting style*. Three common parenting styles include the following:

- Authoritarian style. An **authoritarian style** tends to be controlling and corrective. Caregivers who use this parenting style tend to be strict and expect obedience without discussion. Children with authoritarian caregivers may not understand why they are to behave a certain way.

- Permissive style. A **permissive style** tends to let children control situations, making the decisions with few limits or controls.

Copyright Goodheart-Willcox Co., Inc.

Marina Dyakonova/Shutterstock.com

Figure 10.17 Induction as a form of guidance can be utilized when the child is old enough to understand reasoning. *What is induction?*

Caregivers who use this style tend to be more like a friend than a parent. Children with few limits may have trouble getting along with others because they are only used to following their own rules.

- Authoritative style. Giving choices and encouraging children to practice decision making are common practices for caregivers using the **authoritative style** (also called *democratic style*). Caregivers who use this style offer support while setting clear limits. These limits may be strict, but they are set in a warm and responsive manner. Caregivers communicate their rationale for expectations in age-appropriate ways (**Figure 10.18**).

Although the authoritarian parenting style may be seen as less than ideal in Western cultures such as the United States, this style is used effectively in many cultures. Most experts agree that if combined with a sense of warmth, caring, and the best interests of the child, any type of involved parenting can be effective. A surrounding community that supports the parenting style is also important.

Parenting is culturally biased. Geographic location, local practices and customs, religious background, personal experiences, and education all influence parenting style. For most parents, styles or methods may vary based on the situation, emotional state of the child or parent, perceived threat to the child, or amount of energy a parent is willing to exert. It may vary day to day or hour to hour. Parenting that is consistent over time and situations is the most effective and provides the most stable, secure environment for a child.

Copyright Goodheart-Willcox Co., Inc.

©iStock.com/digitalskillet

Figure 10.18 An authoritative style can be used from early childhood through adolescence and into the transition years to young adulthood. *What are some characteristics of the authoritative parenting style?*

Guidance Strategies

Young children need support, encouragement, and instruction to become independent. They need to try new tasks on their own even though they may fail. Caregivers can provide this guidance and encouragement through the use of positive guidance techniques (**Figure 10.19**).

Guiding children boils down to treating them with respect. By treating even very young children with respect, children can learn to guide and conform their behaviors to appropriate cultural expectations. This involves speaking simply and clearly to young children.

Caregivers should let children know what they would like them to do more than what they do not want them to do. Caregivers should also keep rules simple and discuss them with children. They may want to ask children to help make rules, such as "be kind to each other" or "say please and thank you." Rules should be applied to the whole community, including caregivers and visitors.

Caregivers should provide positive examples of desired behavior. Modeling behavior is one of the most effective ways to guide children. Through modeling appropriate behaviors, children can even be examples to one another.

Like teens and adults, children prefer to have choices. Caregivers should find ways to offer positive choices for young children to practice making good decisions. To guide behavior, these choices should be clear and simple. "Would you like to sit in the red chair or the green

Expert Insight

"Example isn't another way to teach, it is the only way to teach."

Albert Einstein,
theoretical physicist

Copyright Goodheart-Willcox Co., Inc.

Early Childhood Guidance Techniques Checklist

- Respect and expect the best from children.
- Set clear, consistent rules that are easy for children to understand.
- Talk with children, not at them.
- Help children to see themselves as trustworthy, responsible, and cooperative.
- Make certain the environment is safe and worry-free for children.
- Provide children with developmentally appropriate and engaging activities and toys.
- Show interest in children's activities.
- Offer children simple choices whenever possible.
- Focus on the desired behavior, saying yes to children more often than no.
- Model positive behavior.
- Encourage and notice positive behavior in children.
- Use play to practice children's social skills, such as conflict resolution, kindness, sharing, friendliness, and good manners.
- Teach children how to self-correct inappropriate behavior.

Figure 10.19 There are several positive guidance techniques that can be used to help young children become independent. *Have you used any of the listed techniques?*

chair?" is an example of a choice that guides the child to the desired behavior of sitting down while offering a choice. When offering choices, communication is interactive rather than one-sided or directive, which offers another way of showing respect.

Encouraging play experiences is a good way for caregivers to give children a chance to practice their social skills. By using social skills, children can practice resolving conflicts, sharing, apologizing, and respecting others' feelings and needs. In the end, children learn how to adjust and self-guide their own behavior.

Creating a Safe Environment

As soon as children are able to crawl and walk, they are constantly on the go. **Childproofing**, the process of ensuring an environment is safe for children, is very important for young children. During early childhood, children are learning by exploring their world. As they explore, they may grab onto furniture or loose items to maintain balance. They are also curious and have enough motor skills to open cabinets and get into bottles or liquids that may be harmful. Monitoring the movement of young children is always important and necessary to ensure their safety.

Caregivers can use the following guidelines when childproofing an area for young children:

- Place sharp objects out of reach.
- Keep windows closed or open windows slightly and lock in place.

Copyright Goodheart-Willcox Co., Inc.

Case Study / *When the Holiday Unwraps*

When Ellie walked around her classroom the morning after the holiday, her three-year-olds were brimming with energy. Not all of that energy was being used in positive ways, however. Will and Claire were struggling over sharing a toy they both wanted to play with on their own. Ivy was refusing to move out of Paul's way as he was trying to get past her. Benjamin pulled down a box of building blocks, spilling them all over the floor, ignoring Ellie's request that he hold off on playing with them. Ellie heard few "please" and "thank you" messages, but saw a bit of pushing and shoving as the children began their day. Ellie knew that some guidance would be needed if this day was going to turn out positive for both her and the children.

oliveromg/Shutterstock.com

For Discussion

1. What do you think should be Ellie's goal for her class?
2. How might Ellie begin handling the situation?
3. What guidance techniques do you think Ellie should use to help the children interact in more pro-social ways?

- Ensure medicine, kitchen, and other cabinets have childproof locks.
- Use outlet and power strip covers.
- Install child protection gates at tops and bottoms of stairs.
- Set water heater at a low temperature (120°F or lower).
- Make sure toys are in good condition, are age appropriate, and do not have small or loose parts.
- Keep play areas tidy and free of hazardous items.
- Keep up-to-date on new safety regulations and product recalls for items such as cribs or certified child safety seats. This type of information can be found on the US Consumer Product Safety Commission (CPSC) website.

In early childhood education programs, both indoor and outdoor areas need to meet state safety regulations. Smoke and carbon monoxide detectors, fire extinguishers, and first-aid kits should all work and be present inside the center. Outdoor play areas should be in a safe location with no poisonous plants, bugs, or dangerous wildlife. Programs should have emergency plans in place and staff members who are trained in the execution of these plans. The child care center should also maintain appropriate sanitation and health practices, such as handwashing, food

Copyright Goodheart-Willcox Co., Inc.

Pathway to Success

Making an Emergency Response Plan

The prompt warning to employees to evacuate, take shelter, or lockdown can save lives. Having a plan in place when these actions occur ensures that everyone in a facility is on the same page. The first step when developing an emergency response plan is to identify potential emergency scenarios. An understanding of what can happen will help you to determine resource requirements and develop plans and procedures to prepare.

When an emergency occurs in an early childhood education program, the first priority is always to keep everyone safe. The second priority is stabilizing the incident. Protective actions to keep everyone safe include evacuation, sheltering, shelter-in-place, and lockdown. Any emergency plan should include these protective actions.

- Evacuation. Make sure there are sufficient exits available at all times. Identify a safe place away from the building where you can meet. Contact the fire department to develop a plan to evacuate persons with disabilities. Have a list of employees and children as well as maintaining a visitor log at the front desk. Use this list to account for everyone in the building.

- Sheltering. After a tornado warning has sounded, move everyone to the strongest part of the building. Conduct drills to ensure the space can hold everyone in the building.

- Shelter-in-place. Include a way to warn everyone to move away from windows and to the core of the building. Move everyone to upper floors in a multistory building. Close exterior doors and windows and shut down the building's air-handling system. Remain in place until it is safe to leave the building.

- Lockdown. Seek refuge in a room, close and lock the door, and barricade the door if it can be done quickly. Train everyone to hide under a desk, in the corner of a room, and away from the door or windows. Remain in place until the all-clear is given or emergency responders come and get you out of the room.

Creating an Emergency Response Plan for an Early Childhood Education Program

In small groups, obtain a copy of your school's emergency response plan as well as a copy of a local child care center's response plan. Compare the two plans, identifying differences and similarities. Then, using the information above, create an emergency response plan for an early childhood education program. Assume this is a one-story building with an office/reception area, kitchen/cafeteria area, and eight classrooms.

Draw a floor plan of the building, marking the emergency exits and indicating where to go for shelter-in-place. Also, write the policy for each of the four emergency situations, including what everyone should do step-by-step as well as where they should go. Do not forget to include a policy for picking up the children after evacuation and in the case of evacuation after a lockdown. Share your group's plan with the rest of the class and explain how this same information can be used at home.

Copyright Goodheart-Willcox Co., Inc.

preparation, and toileting. Licensed care centers go through periodic inspections to determine the program is meeting safety, health, and sanitation regulations and not endangering children's health and well-being.

Protecting Children from Neglect and Abuse

Children need care to have their needs met. They need food, clothing, and a place to call home. They need to receive nurturance and education. They also need protection from danger. Sadly, some children suffer from neglect or abuse by adults. Both neglect and abuse of children are illegal. **Child neglect** involves endangerment of or harm to a child caused by an adult's failure to provide for the child's basic needs. **Child abuse** involves threatening to or inflicting harm on a child. **Figure 10.20** shows types of child neglect and abuse.

Just as there are many types of child neglect and abuse, there are also many signs that may indicate neglect or abuse. **Figure 10.21** identifies a few signs of child neglect or abuse that a child may exhibit. Child neglect and abuse can also be detected through parents' actions. Refusing the child medical treatment for any reason can be *detrimental* (harmful) to the child's well-being. Failing to give the child proper schooling or education is another sign. A parent may also admit to disliking a child or to being indifferent toward the child.

Types of Child Neglect and Abuse
Types of Child Neglect
• *Physical neglect* refers to a failure to provide such basic needs as food, clothing, shelter, or appropriate supervision.
• *Medical neglect* involves a failure to provide necessary treatment for injuries, illnesses, or other health conditions.
• *Educational neglect* is a failure to conform to a state's legal requirements to provide for a child's education or special education needs.
• *Emotional neglect* involves a failure to meet a child's emotional needs or to provide psychological care, or to allow a child to use alcohol or drugs.
Types of Child Abuse
• *Physical abuse* involves inflicting injury through beating, hitting, shaking, biting, punching, kicking, or by other means. Physical abuse often results in bruises and repeated injuries, such as broken bones, cuts, or scrapes, but can also have no visual signs.
• *Emotional abuse* includes constant criticism, threats, or rejection that harms a child's sense of self-worth and emotional development. Withholding love, support, or guidance is also a part of emotional abuse.
• *Sexual abuse* includes inappropriate behavior toward or with a child, including touching, sexual acts, and exposure to pornography.

Figure 10.20 There are many different types of child neglect and abuse. *What is the difference between child neglect and child abuse?*

Copyright Goodheart-Willcox Co., Inc.

Signs of Child Neglect or Abuse
• Is malnourished
• Lacks basic physical items, such as clothing or shelter
• Has clothing that is ill-fitting, inappropriate for the weather, or that is used to cover physical marks
• Does not receive proper hygiene practices, such as bathing or dental care
• Is abandoned for long hours
• Has multiple, recurring bruises
• Does not feel cared for, secure, or loved
• Is withdrawn
• Fears parents and other adults
• Does not want to go home
• Shows a significant decrease in grades or extracurricular performance
• Has advanced or detailed sexual knowledge

Figure 10.21 There are many signs that indicate child neglect or child abuse. *What would you do if you saw signs of neglect or abuse in a child?*

Causes

You may often wonder why some adults neglect and abuse children. There is no one single cause of child neglect or abuse. The causes for neglect and abuse may vary, but they still produce the same hurtful results. Sometimes causes may pass from generation to generation as parenting is learned. When a child is a victim of abuse, he or she might think this is normal behavior. When the child grows up and has children, he or she may repeat the abusive behavior for lack of another known way.

Some people believe that abuse is prevalent because of the amount of violence viewed in society. Children who live in dangerous neighborhoods may be more likely to experience abuse. Adults who grew up in violent communities as children are also more likely to abuse their own children.

Neglect and abuse can occur across all socio-economic, cultural, and ethnic groups. There are certain risk factors that researchers commonly associate with neglect and abuse. These risk factors can be grouped into four types, which include parent or caregiver, family, child, and environmental factors (**Figure 10.22**). Although children are never responsible for the neglect or abuse, researchers have found some common factors shared among neglected and abused children.

Many of these risk factors relate to stressors. As some of the most vulnerable members of society, children become easy targets. They are the targets of anger and wrath from adults who are frustrated and stressed. Economic distress brought on by unemployment, inadequate pay, or illness in the family is often associated with abuse. Lacking parental skills plays a part. Parental personality issues such as a need to control, low self-esteem, anger issues, social isolation, or difficulty coping with

Copyright Goodheart-Willcox Co., Inc.

Risk Factors for Child Neglect and Abuse	
Type of Risk Factor	**Contributing Factors**
Parent or caregiver	• Low self-esteem • Impulsive • Depressed • Stressed • Antisocial behavior • Family history of abuse • Substance abuse • Mental illness • Lack of knowledge about child development • Unrealistic expectations that children are unable to meet • Focus is on children's negative actions and not on positive actions
Family	• Domestic abuse • Unemployment • Low-income/poverty—less care and opportunities available for children • Large family with many children • Single-parent household
*Child**	• Between birth and three years of age, children are most vulnerable, dependent, and defenseless • Has physical, intellectual, or social-emotional disabilities or special needs
Environmental	• Low-income neighborhoods • Violent neighborhoods • Lack of social support
*Children are not responsible for being victims of abuse or neglect. Research suggests children who have been abused or neglected may possess similar characteristics.	

Figure 10.22 Risk factors can be grouped into four types: parent or caregiver, family, child, and environmental factors. *Under which risk factor would unemployment be classified?*

stress are often factors. Depression and other mental health problems may be factors. Substance abuse frequently plays a part, too.

The presence of risk factors does not mean that neglect or abuse is taking place. Some adults may present certain risk factors, but never neglect or abuse their children. Identifying risk factors can help determine the type of support services or interventions that may benefit families.

Effects

The effects of both neglect and abuse are devastating to children. Physical neglect of children may cause them to fail to thrive. Growth and development may be severely impacted. Immediate health effects of physical abuse, such as bruises, burns, or broken bones may heal, but emotional scars remain. Some victims of physical abuse suffer long-term

Copyright Goodheart-Willcox Co., Inc.

effects, such as permanent brain damage or other disabilities. Some do not survive at all. Victims of sexual abuse may suffer internal and external injuries, contract sexually transmitted infections (STIs), or become pregnant. They also experience emotional trauma, which often results in depression that can continue long after the abuse stops.

Many times, physical and emotional abuse exist together. When physical and emotional abuse occurs together, the result often confirms questionable signs of physical injuries. Children who suffer from physical and emotional abuse are often withdrawn. They may have trouble making friends or they may be uncomfortable around adults. They may be hesitant to state their thoughts or needs. They often have low self-esteem and may suffer from depression. Some children who experience physical and emotional abuse demonstrate aggressiveness and uncontrolled anger toward others, especially younger children and animals.

Even after proper care is given and abuse stops, the effects can impact children well into their adult years. Most typically, long-term emotional problems follow. Without intervention, the cycle will likely continue to the next generation. Many parents who abuse children were often victims of abuse themselves.

Prevention

The cycle of child neglect and abuse does not have to repeat in the next generation. Individuals, families, communities, and society can all play a part in preventing child neglect and abuse. Raising public awareness of child neglect and abuse through public service announcements can promote healthy parent-child relationships and child safety. Many organizations provide educational materials that can inform individuals about child neglect and abuse (**Figure 10.23**).

Parent education is critical in stopping the neglect and abuse of children. Parent education should increase the parents' knowledge of children. Learning about developmental stages can give parents a better understanding of reasonable expectations for their children's behavior.

Child Mistreatment and Abuse Resources
• Administration for Children and Families (ACF)
• American Academy of Child and Adolescent Psychiatry
• American Humane Association
• American Professional Society on the Abuse of Children
• American Psychological Association
• Child Abuse Prevention Center
• Child Help
• Child Welfare Information Gateway
• National Center for Community-Based Child Abuse Prevention
• Prevent Child Abuse America

Figure 10.23 There are a number of organizations that provide materials to help inform the public about child neglect and abuse. *Have you ever seen material from any of the listed organizations? If so, which one(s)?*

Copyright Goodheart-Willcox Co., Inc.

Education should also include showing parents how to appropriately and effectively discipline their children. In addition to parent education, children need to learn safety and protection skills.

Recognizing risk factors often associated with child neglect and abuse is also important. When risk factors are present, families can be connected to social programs. Local government sources, doctors, religious organizations, schools, hospitals, health centers, and law enforcement agencies can provide referrals to support systems.

Home visitation is one example of a support service that can help new parents learn more about child development and healthy parenting. Professionals monitor families in their homes and provide one-on-one parent education. *Crisis care programs* are another example. These programs offer temporary relief to caregivers by providing care for children for a specified time. Because abusive behaviors are often linked to stress, community resources that can lower family stress, including financial resources, child care, housing, and supplemental nutritional assistance, are also available.

Parents who are stressed, frustrated, and struggling need to have a chance to discuss and find support from others who also struggle. Counselors and support groups can ease stress and the feeling of isolation for parents. Child abuse hotlines, provided through crisis intervention centers, can provide relief right away for parents who need someone to talk to during times of crisis.

Reporting

Although anyone can report child neglect or abuse, some people, called **mandated reporters**, must legally report suspected instances of child neglect and abuse. Mandated reporters include people in occupations that involve working with children (**Figure 10.24**).

Whether or not you are a mandated reporter, if you are in a situation where you suspect neglect or abuse of a child, you have a responsibility to report the situation. If you are a minor yourself, you need to contact a responsible adult and share your concerns. A parent, teacher, or school guidance counselor are some possible options. Be clear in your descriptions of what you have seen and heard. If you are employed as a child care worker, you should report the situation right away. If you are unaware of reporting procedures, speak to your employer about your concerns. He or she will know how to properly report the concern to legal authorities.

Treatment

When cases of neglect or abuse are confirmed, treatment for the children can begin. In cases of physical abuse or neglect, immediate medical treatment is needed. Doctors will examine the child, provide necessary care, and document their findings. Caseworkers from child protective services agencies often become involved to make decisions about the children's welfare. Referrals for necessary services children

Copyright Goodheart-Willcox Co., Inc.

Dave Clark Digital Photo/Shutterstock.com

Figure 10.24 Mandated reporters often include professionals such as teachers, caregivers, healthcare workers, and counselors. *Where can you check to see who is considered a mandated reporter?*

may need are determined on a case-by-case basis. Some commonly used services include foster care, counseling, and therapy.

Treatment for sexual and emotional abuse often involves individual therapy. In some cases, group therapy is encouraged. Qualified mental health professionals can assess the children to decide exactly what type of treatment will benefit them the most (**Figure 10.25**). Treatment programs can then be developed to address children's needs. Integrating family members into children's treatment often occurs with goals to promote child safety and family education, and to reduce the risk of abuse recurring.

Treatment for the abusers is also determined on a case-by-case basis. Depending on the severity of the abuse or neglect, some adults may not be allowed to see their children. They may have their parenting rights terminated. Because child neglect and abuse is illegal, adults may be convicted of a crime and ordered to receive therapy or go to jail.

Reading Recall

1. What are *DAPs*? Give an example of a DAP.
2. Describe the three parenting styles.
3. Why do caregivers often give young children choices?
4. Compare and contrast child neglect and child abuse.
5. Who should report child neglect or abuse?

Copyright Goodheart-Willcox Co., Inc.

Figure 10.25
Caseworkers act as advocates for the children and can help identify support systems that could benefit children and their families. *Why do you think it is important that a caseworker is an advocate specifically for the child? How might this differ from an advocate for the family as a whole?*

Olimpik/Shutterstock.com

Rewards, Demands, and Future Trends

Careers in early childhood development and services can be both rewarding and frustrating at the same time. Early childhood development and services workers can never truly know what to expect from day to day. Each day poses new challenges and the best laid plans often change. When working with children, one of the best rewards is seeing everyday victories. Early childhood development and services workers may soothe an anxious infant, help a toddler learn to go down a slide, or guide a young child to successfully handle a conflict on the playground.

Early childhood development and services workers take joy in seeing children grow, develop, and gain confidence as they learn new skills. They celebrate small successes and lend support and guidance to help children be the best they can be. In doing so, they develop quality caregiving relationships with the children they serve. They also develop relationships with parents, providing advice and support to promote their children's development. Early childhood development and services workers know they are making a difference in children's lives and take pride in the work they do.

Early childhood development and services workers also work very hard. The work is physically and emotionally demanding and requires much patience and persistence. They deal with swinging emotions and unexpected events daily. Children have different temperaments and behave differently. Learning how to handle these different temperaments and behaviors can be quite challenging. This is the same when dealing

Copyright Goodheart-Willcox Co., Inc.

with parents, too. Some parents may be easy to work with and others can be much more difficult. For many beginning their careers, the pay is low.

Many experienced people in this field will tell you that working with young children is inspiring, challenging, and as unique as each child. What makes working with young children truly different from many other professions is the potential long-term effect workers can have on the lives of others. Although the work requires energy, creativity, and patience, the results can be phenomenal.

Fortunately, there will always be a need for talented people in the field of early childhood development and services. The care and education of young children is the key to a successful society. Children need to be educated to be contributing members of society, and it begins far earlier than traditional school age. For working parents, child care and early education are necessary and desirable. Many people believe that having better early childhood education programs will impact the whole education system and workforce. As a result, the future outlook for early childhood development and services workers is bright (**Figure 10.26**).

Reading Recall

1. Describe the rewards of careers in early childhood development and services.
2. Describe the demands of careers in early childhood development and services.
3. Why are early childhood development and services workers so important to society?

Future Trends for Early Childhood Development and Services Careers				
Occupation	Projected Growth (2014–2024)	Projected Job Openings (2014–2024)	Median Wages (2014)	Education
Child care worker	Average (5–8%)	441,300	$19,730	High school diploma
Nanny	Average (5–8%)	441,300	$19,730	High school diploma
Preschool and Pre-K teacher	Average (5–8%)	158,700	$28,120	Some college, no degree
Teacher assistant	Average (5–8%)	374,500	$24,430	Some college, no degree
Program director	Average (5–8%)	22,900	$45,260	Bachelor's degree
Parent educator	Faster than average (9–13%)	19,500	$50,430	Bachelor's degree

Sources: O*NET and the *Occupational Outlook Handbook*

Figure 10.26 Projected growth is expected to be average or faster than average for careers in early childhood development and services. *According to this chart, which career has the most projected job openings?*

Copyright Goodheart-Willcox Co., Inc.

Summary

- Opportunities in early childhood development and services careers exist for child care workers, preschool teachers, teacher assistants, program directors, assistant directors, and parent educators.
- Quality caregivers share similar characteristics. They are compassionate, empathetic, encouraging, loving, patient, and adaptable. They know about child development and have a genuine interest in children. They work well as a team with parents and other professionals to meet the needs of the children they serve.
- Many early childhood development and services positions require experience and at least a two-year college education, preferably a four-year bachelor's degree. Some states may also require certification by a nationally recognized authority, such as the Child Development Associate (CDA).
- Effective early childhood development and services workers know the typical developmental stages and use DAPs. These are age-appropriate activities and teaching methods that consider each child's strengths, interests, and culture while respecting the milestones of the infants, toddlers, or young children who are under their care. They guide children's behavior and create a safe environment in which they can learn. They also recognize when children are in danger and take action to protect them from neglect and abuse.
- Careers in early childhood development and services can be both rewarding and frustrating at the same time. Employment opportunities in the field abound as parents find it more and more necessary to find quality child care and education for their infants and young children. As long as there are families, these careers will be vital.

College and Career Portfolio

Portfolio Letters of Recommendation

Whether for a college or job application, most schools and employers require applicants to provide letters of recommendation or references. These documents are often a part of your portfolio. When incorporating these into your portfolio, keep in mind that letters of recommendation and references can take time to acquire.

Consider which teachers, employers, or other adults can best speak about your skills and work. Then, decide on two to three individuals you want to ask to be your references, and complete the following activities.

1. Ask the individuals you chose if they would be willing to be your reference. Make sure to be polite and grateful and give them time to respond.
2. If the purpose of your portfolio requires a letter of recommendation, ask the individuals you chose to write a letter of recommendation for you. Be courteous, and make sure to communicate the deadline for your application.

Copyright Goodheart-Willcox Co., Inc.

Review and Reflect

1. What are the differences among *in-home child care*, *family child care centers*, and *center-based child care programs*?

2. What are some of the duties a preschool or Pre-K teacher performs on a daily basis?

3. Identify the roles various people play in the child care field. Give examples of some of the duties these people have on a day-to-day basis.

4. Why is it important that caregivers have a thorough knowledge of child development?

5. List four specifications of the CDA requirements.

6. What is the difference between *gross-motor skills* and *fine-motor skills*? Give an example of each.

7. By the end of the toddler years, how many words are usually in a child's vocabulary? By the end of preschool, how large is a typical child's vocabulary?

8. What does *DIP* mean?

9. How are *guidance* and *discipline* different?

10. Name the three types of discipline listed in the textbook. Give an example of each.

11. Identify the guidelines used in childproofing a home.

12. Describe the future trends for careers in early childhood development and services.

Vocabulary Activities

13. **Key terms**   With a partner, choose two words from the following list to compare. Create a Venn diagram to compare your words and identify differences. Write one term under the left circle and the other term under the right. Where the circles overlap, write two to three characteristics the terms have in common. For each term, write at least one difference of the term for each characteristic in its respective outer circle.

    authoritarian style
    authoritative style
    center-based child care programs

    child abuse
    child neglect
    childproofing

developmentally appropriate practices (DAPs)
developmentally inappropriate practices (DIPs)
discipline
family child care centers
fine-motor skills

gross-motor skills
guidance
mandated reporters
permissive style
prekindergarten programs
preschool programs
work-related child care programs

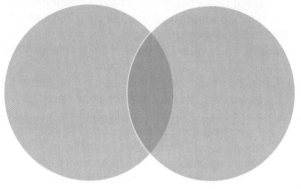

Term: _____   Term: _____

14. **Academic terms**   Individually or with a partner, create a T-chart on a sheet of paper and list each of the following terms in the left column. In the right column, list an *antonym* (a word of opposite meaning) for each term in the left column.

    detrimental   intuition
    exuberant   reciprocal

Self-Assessment Quiz

Complete the self-assessment quiz online to help you practice and expand your knowledge and skills.

Critical Thinking

15. **Evaluate**   Evaluate the training that a nanny and an au pair receive. How is it different from what a child care worker receives?

16. **Compare and contrast**   Explain the similarities and differences among the basic needs of infants, toddlers, and preschoolers.

17. **Determine**   Determine what licensing requirements are required in your state for in-home child care providers, preschool teachers, and center-based child care programs.

Copyright Goodheart-Willcox Co., Inc.

18. **Analyze** Create a chart depicting the typical milestone markers for each stage during the early childhood years. Include name; time period; and physical, intellectual, and social-emotional growth and development. Analyze the responsibilities of caregivers for promoting the development of children.

19. **Identify** Identify the three types of parenting styles. Based on the description of each, what type of parenting style do your parents use? What type of parenting style do you think you will use when you are raising children? Why?

20. **Make inferences** Explain why child care centers need to have emergency plans in place in which all staff members are trained. What would happen if someone was not trained in the emergency plan and there was an emergency?

21. **Cause and effect** Identify the four risk factor types commonly associated with neglect and abuse. Give an example of each type.

22. **Draw conclusions** What happens after someone reports suspected child abuse? What steps are taken to verify that abuse is occurring? When abuse is evident, what happens next? What are potential treatments of child abuse? You may need to talk to Child Protective Services, a lawyer, or even a judge to find out each step in the process. Create a presentation you can give in class, using technology to present your information.

Core Skills

23. **Research** Research the background of the Head Start program. Create a poster to hang in the classroom depicting your research findings. Be sure to include when and how the program started, who started it, and what laws affect the program.

24. **Technology and writing** Create a chart showcasing the theorists and their stages for birth to preschool-age children. Use technology to incorporate color, links, and pictures or graphs. Print a copy to place in your portfolio.

25. **Technology and speaking** Create a slide presentation explaining the developmental tasks of infants, toddlers, and preschoolers. Include captions and illustrations. Share your presentation with the rest of the class.

26. **Speaking and listening** With a partner, role play a preschool teacher and a preschooler who is acting up. Take turns using the three types of discipline. Which one were you most comfortable using? Why? Which one are you least likely to use? Why?

27. **Writing** Use Figure 10.19 and your own experiences to create a checklist that parents can use for guidance techniques in early childhood. Share this with the elementary parent/teacher organization (PTO) in your school district. Place a copy in your portfolio.

28. **Research and writing** Choose two different countries and research the guidance techniques used in each. Create a pamphlet explaining the similarities and differences, as well as the cultural biases about guidance and discipline in the two societies.

29. **Speaking** Looking at the contributing factors for the risk of child neglect and abuse found in Figure 10.22, discuss how many of the factors are economically related and what someone could to do to overcome the economic factor or take it out of the equation.

30. **Research and writing** Investigate the causes of child abuse. Research the long-term effects of both neglect and abuse from childhood. How can neglect and abuse impact a person's teen and adult years? Write a letter to an abuser explaining what you have found out and how neglect and abuse can impact his or her victims.

31. **Speaking and technology** Create a public service announcement on the prevention of child neglect and abuse. Remember that it needs to be between 15 and 30 seconds for a radio broadcast or 1 and 3 minutes for a TV broadcast. If possible, record your public service announcement and play it during your morning announcements. Save a copy of your announcement to a DVD and place it in your portfolio.

32. **Writing, listening, and speaking** Invite a court-appointed child advocate to come to class to discuss what he or she does for foster children. Create a list of questions to ask the person prior to the interview. Send a thank-you letter to this person after the interview.

33. **CTE career readiness practice** Identify several careers in early childhood development

Copyright Goodheart-Willcox Co., Inc.

and services that interest you. For each career, research the preparation requirements and employment opportunities.

34. **CTE career readiness practice** The ability to gather and analyze information with cultural relevance is an important workplace skill. Consider the following problem: As director for a child care center, it has come to your attention that foods served for snacks and lunch are not meeting cultural needs of all children.

Most child care centers serve a diverse population of families from many different ethnic backgrounds. You and your team need to make changes in some types of foods served, but need more information. With your team members, create a plan to gather and analyze the information you need with culture in mind. List culturally sensitive questions you need to ask about food needs and potential sources of reliable information.

Lend a Hand

Volunteering with Children

If you are interested in a career working with children or you are just hoping to make a difference in a child's life, you might consider focusing your community service on volunteering with children. Whether you are involved with a school club or service learning group or you want to get involved on your own, there are a variety of opportunities for volunteering with children.

Hospitals, especially children's hospitals, are a great place to volunteer. Many hospitals have volunteer programs in place, so applying is simple and straightforward. These volunteer positions usually involve an interview and a background check to ensure that children are getting the best support possible. Another option is volunteering at a summer or day camp. Volunteer camp counselors assist campers with activities and support them while they are away from home.

If you have a skill you would like to share, you might consider volunteering your time to teach children. You can teach children to play an instrument, tutor children in reading or

math, give swimming lessons, or volunteer to coach a sports team.

While there are programs in place to connect volunteers with children, this would be a good opportunity to start your own volunteer service. You can set up an after-school reading program or organize a clothing and toy drive for children in need. You have the opportunity to make a lasting impact on your community and on the lives of the children you serve.

To learn more about volunteering with children, complete the following:

1. Determine how you would like to volunteer to benefit children. Think about your skills, strengths, and interests when deciding on volunteer positions.
2. Use online or print resources to locate volunteer opportunities in your area. Make a list of the volunteer positions that interest you.
3. Find out the requirements for each position. Is there anything extra that you would have to do to apply, such as a background check?

Copyright Goodheart-Willcox Co., Inc.

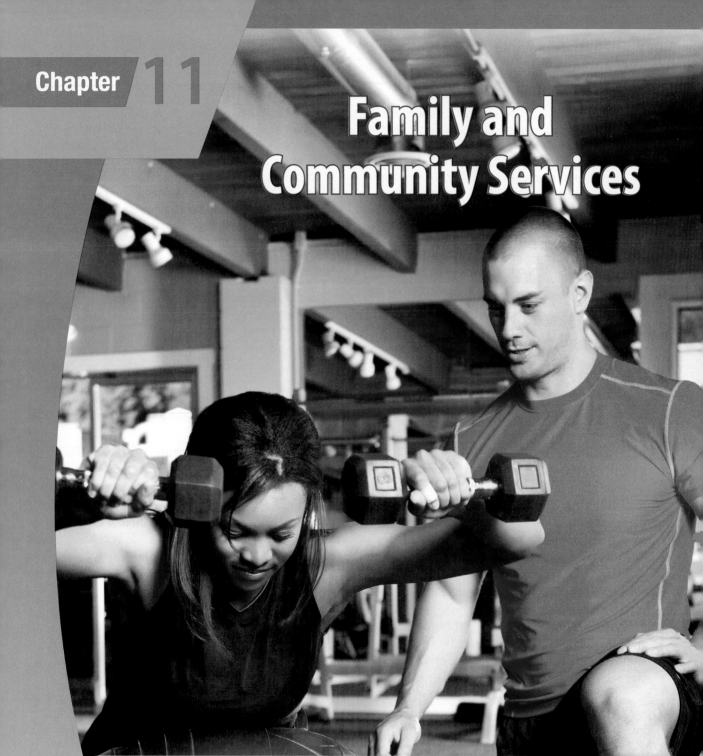

Chapter 11

Family and Community Services

G-WLEARNING.com

While studying, look for the activity icon ⤴ to

- **practice** key and academic terms with e-flash cards and matching activities;
- **assess** what you learn by completing self-assessment quizzes; and
- **reinforce** what you learn by mapping concepts and completing review and reflect questions.

www.g-wlearning.com/humanservices/

©iStock.com/arekmalang

Learning Outcomes

After studying this chapter, you will be able to

- **compare and contrast** career opportunities for family and community services workers;
- **list** common aptitudes, attitudes, and skills of family and community services workers;
- **give examples** of postsecondary education, training, and experience required for several family and community services careers;
- **identify** and describe the basic family functions, roles, and responsibilities;
- **describe** factors that affect the responsibilities of family members;
- **summarize** how public policy and civic engagement play a part in family and community services; and
- **summarize** the rewards, demands, and future trends of careers in family and community services.

Reading Strategies

Before reading, look at the summary at the end of the chapter. The summary highlights the most important concepts the author presents in the chapter. As you are reading the chapter, keep this information in mind. Make sure you understand these concepts. After reading, review the summary again. Do you agree or disagree with the author's identification of main points? Are there any concepts you would add to or delete from the list?

Mapping Concepts

For each type of family and community services career discussed in this chapter, draw a picture that represents the occupation. As you read the chapter, take notes in and around each picture.

Macrovector/Shutterstock.com

Key Terms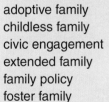

adoptive family
childless family
civic engagement
extended family
family policy
foster family

nuclear family
public policy
single-parent family
social system
stepfamily

Academic Terms

auxiliary
cognizant
dynamics
egalitarian
instrumental
liaisons
plethora

Copyright Goodheart-Willcox Co., Inc.

Look around you. People everywhere have needs. Family and community services workers work directly with all kinds of populations or people groups who have trouble meeting their own needs (**Figure 11.1**). Career options in family and community services may be available in government, for-profit, and not-for-profit agencies. Each different type of agency works with diverse clients. For example, some agencies work with infants or older adults. Other agencies focus on people who are homeless or have addictions. Still other agencies treat people with mental health conditions and disabilities.

Family and community services workers meet the needs of people in their neighborhoods, towns, cities, or counties. They find the resources their clients need to meet basic physical, psychological, and safety needs. A *plethora* (PLEH-tho-ruh), or large amount, of career opportunities await in the field of family and community services because people's needs are so different and vast.

Careers in Family and Community Services

There are many career opportunities for family and community services workers. **Figure 11.2** shows some of these opportunities. In the following sections, you will learn much more about careers in family and community services.

Monkey Business Images/Shutterstock.com

Figure 11.1 Family and community services workers help people find housing, food, clothing, mental health, social, and emergency or law enforcement resources. *Why do you think it might be difficult for people to locate these resources without assistance?*

Copyright Goodheart-Willcox Co., Inc.

Examples of Family and Community Services Careers
• Caseworker (also called *case coordinator* or *case manager*)
• Certified health coach
• Community health worker
• Development director
• Development officer
• Disaster relief worker
• Emergency and relief worker
• Executive director
• Firefighter
• Law enforcement officer
• Program director
• School social worker
• Social and human services assistant
• Social worker
• Volunteer coordinator
• Wellness coach

Figure 11.2 Family and community services workers' job titles and daily tasks may be very different, depending on the agency for which they work. *Which of the careers listed appeals to you the most?*

Social and Human Services Assistants

Social and human services assistants typically spend most of their time researching, finding, and obtaining available resources to meet their clients' needs. For example, they may find affordable child care for a single parent with a low income. They may also help a client with a disability complete the paperwork to apply for Social Security benefits. Social and human services assistants often specialize in one area, such as finding temporary housing.

Social and human services assistants are often in supportive roles. They are the frontline in dealing with people and interacting one-on-one with clients. In these positions, social and human services assistants identify the type of benefits or community services their clients need. They work with support professionals, such as caseworkers, counselors, and social workers, to develop a treatment plan. They then coordinate the services the client is to receive. Social and human services assistants are critical to the work of social services agencies. For many, working as a social and human services assistant opens the door for a lifetime career in human services.

Community Health Workers

Community health workers are part of a relatively new career field that focuses on guiding and coaching people in managing their own health and wellness. These workers are sometimes referred to as *wellness coaches* or *certified health coaches.* Community health workers assist their clients in making lifestyle changes as recommended by doctors, nurses, and other medical professionals. They may motivate their clients to make better nutrition choices, lose or gain weight, reduce stress, or be more physically active. Community health workers work with their clients to make lifestyle changes that improve overall health, fitness, and life outlook (**Figure 11.3**).

Emergency and Relief Workers

Emergency and relief workers can often be found helping people in emergencies or following natural disasters or other crises. They include the *firefighters*, *law enforcement officers*, and others who help people when most in need. They promote or restore order, rescue those in danger, and bring people to safety.

Some relief workers specialize in disaster relief. *Disaster relief workers* respond to disasters or crisis management needs. They offer disaster preparedness training. They also prepare emergency plans and procedures to use in natural, war-related, terrorist, or technological or chemical emergencies.

Like all human services workers, emergency and relief workers are people helpers (**Figure 11.4**). They are needed in every community around the world. They are employed by local, state, and federal governments.

racorn/Shutterstock.com

Figure 11.3 Community health workers work with their clients to make lifestyle changes by offering training, designing a physical fitness plan, or acting as an accountability coach. *In what ways would this type of career be rewarding?*

Copyright Goodheart-Willcox Co., Inc.

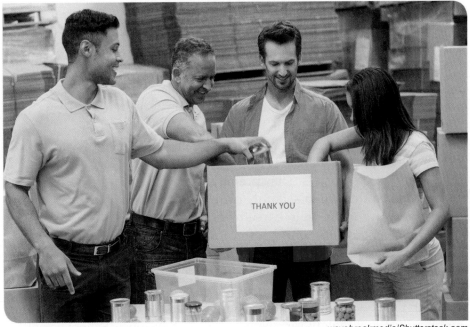

wavebreakmedia/Shutterstock.com

Figure 11.4 Following disasters, relief workers provide people with needed resources, including food, clothing, shelter, and counseling. *Have you ever donated to or volunteered for disaster relief efforts?*

For-profit, not-for-profit, and religious relief organizations also employ emergency and relief workers.

Caseworkers

Caseworkers assess their clients' needs, find them the necessary resources, and develop treatment plans. Typically, caseworkers have a fairly large caseload of clients whom they manage. They get to know their clients and their clients' family members. They find out about their clients' needs and the challenges and obstacles their clients face. Caseworkers are responsible for developing appropriate client care plans, while helping direct-care managers develop their own plans. Sometimes caseworkers are also called *case coordinators* or *case managers*.

Caseworkers work directly with clients in a variety of settings. For example, caseworkers may work in child protective services, government agencies, home healthcare agencies, substance abuse facilities, psychiatric clinics, and organizations serving older adults or people with disabilities. They usually work on a team that includes social workers and counselors or psychologists. Caseworkers do not provide counseling unless they have the required education, experience, and licensure. Instead, they identify the necessary professionals, such as mental health counselors and therapists, who can meet their clients' needs. These professionals depend on caseworkers to implement the treatment they recommend for the clients.

Social Workers

Social workers interview, coordinate, and plan programs and activities to meet their clients' social and emotional needs. Typically, social workers work with their clients to utilize community resources that meet the individualized needs of each client. Mostly, social workers are advocates for people who cannot or do not know how to help themselves (**Figure 11.5**).

Social workers interview clients and their family members to determine the clients' needs. They lead support groups and consult with other health professionals. They prepare treatment plans for their clients and work with their clients' family members. They monitor their clients' progress toward goals set in a treatment plan.

Social workers may work for the government, schools, private social services agencies, and healthcare organizations, such as hospitals and treatment centers. *School social workers* work with students and their families, assessing their educational, social, and basic needs. They are particularly *cognizant* (aware) of the safety needs of their students, clients, and families, looking out for suspected neglect or abuse. School social workers bridge home, school, and community assets to provide resources to meet the needs of students.

Coordinators and Directors

Volunteer coordinators recruit and organize volunteers for organizations. Volunteers are the people who are *instrumental* (necessary; helpful) in making family and community services organizations run

Figure 11.5 The people social workers help are often the least heard in society, such as people with a mental illness or those who are poor. *Why is it important for every member of society to have a voice?*

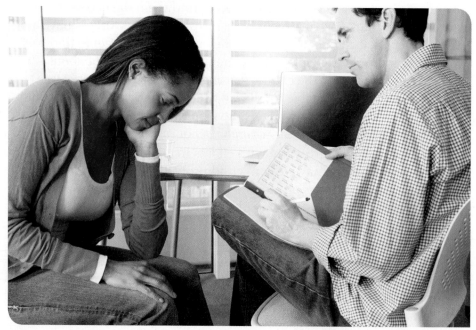

Monkey Business Images/Shutterstock.com

Copyright Goodheart-Willcox Co., Inc.

Case Study / *A Friend Through the Ages*

Camille loves her job as the volunteer coordinator at the Hilltop Senior Community Center. Her days are filled with planning events and activities. This includes coordinating classes, field trips, and many volunteers.

Camille first met Mary, an 86-year-old woman, when Mary was still living alone in her own home. Mary had come to the Hilltop Senior Community Center because she was lonely. She thought that becoming a volunteer would give her a chance to interact with others and be useful at the same time.

Mary told Camille a bit of her story. Her husband of 60 years had passed away this past year. Her only son lives in another state. Before her husband had become ill and later passed, they had enjoyed many community activities together, including playing cards at the center. Despite Mary's story, she was upbeat and happy and looking for purpose and socialization. She was also hoping to enjoy a hearty lunch each day she worked at the center.

As a volunteer, Mary was one of the most dedicated, reliable, and caring workers Camille had ever hired. Mary had a knack for getting others to talk and connect. Everyone at the center loved seeing Mary. Recently, however, Mary started missing some of her volunteer shifts. Camille became concerned about Mary's sudden absences and tried to call her, but Mary did not return any of her calls. When Camille couldn't get in touch with Mary, she decided to pay her a visit to make sure she was okay.

Upon arrival at Mary's home, Camille discovered that Mary had been in a minor "fender bender" with her car and was afraid to get behind the wheel again. She had a bruise over her right eye and a burn on her hand. She said she had fallen. When Camille offered to fix Mary lunch, she noticed outdated food and spoiled milk in Mary's refrigerator. Camille also noticed that Mary's pill box was full of medications she had not taken.

Camille was concerned for Mary's well-being. When she contacted Mary's son about her concerns, he thought it was because of his mother's age. Camille thought there might be more to the story. She arranged for Mary to be evaluated and a plan created to ensure Mary's needs were being met.

giorgiomtb/Shutterstock.com

For Discussion

1. Who should Camille talk with first about her concerns? Why?

2. What factors may be playing into the changes Mary is exhibiting?

3. Should Camille "fire" Mary from her volunteer position? Why or why not? What alternatives, if any, might Camille consider?

efficiently. In many organizations, they are often critical to the program's health and sustainability. For example, volunteer coordinators may prepare and serve meals, offer tutoring and skill training, or contribute to fund-raising projects. They plan and assign tasks and encourage their volunteers to contribute time, energy, and sometimes financial resources.

Copyright Goodheart-Willcox Co., Inc.

Program directors oversee an organization's mission, goals, and programs. They develop and implement agency programs and ensure programs meet the needs of clients and objectives of the organization. Program directors are supervisory positions that usually require a combination of education and experience. Most program directors spend a great deal of time working with state and federal agencies to secure grants, maintain compliance with regulations, and stay up-to-date with current developments. Program directors usually report to the agency's executive director.

Development officers implement strategies for securing funding to meet program goals and objectives. They write grant proposals, foster relationships with potential donors, and network with *auxiliary* (additional) support groups. The *development director* is a supervisory position within a development office. This person oversees the development officer's goals and giver relations. He or she ensures the success of special fund-raising events, such as charitable auctions. The development director is usually part of the senior staff, reporting directly to the executive director.

Executive directors are responsible for the overall management and leadership of an organization. They oversee the day-to-day functioning and operating procedures. They act as *liaisons* (people who aid communication) between the organization and the governing board. Successful executive directors are active in their community, serving as the face of the organization. They see the big picture and move the agency forward in meeting its goals.

Reading Recall

1. Name three common family and community services careers.
2. How do wellness coaches or certified health coaches help people?
3. List three examples of emergency and relief workers.
4. List a typical job duty of a caseworker.
5. Why is it important for a social worker to interview his or her clients before providing services?
6. Name three coordinator and director positions in family and community services.

Common Aptitudes, Attitudes, and Skills

Like counseling and mental health professionals, family and community services workers deal with people, both in good times and bad. Therefore, workers in these fields often share common aptitudes, attitudes, and skills (**Figure 11.6**). For example, family and community services workers possess good listening and speaking skills to communicate with clients effectively. They have good problem-solving,

Copyright Goodheart-Willcox Co., Inc.

Common Aptitudes, Attitudes, and Skills of Family and Community Services Workers

- High mental and physical energy
- Knowledge of family and group dynamics
- Knowledge of community programs
- Keeps emotions under control
- Advocates for others
- Gets along well with others
- Compassionate
- Respectful
- Honest

- Ethical
- Focused
- Nonjudgmental
- Reliable
- Resourceful
- Active listener
- Conveys information effectively—verbally and in writing
- Problem-solving skills
- Conflict resolution skills
- Critical thinking skills

Figure 11.6 Family and community services workers share common aptitudes, attitudes, and skills. *What other aptitudes, attitudes, and skills would you add to this list?*

conflict resolution, and critical thinking skills. They, too, possess high mental and physical energy to endure the stresses of working daily with people in difficult situations.

The issues family and community services workers deal with are often quite complex and many-layered. Sometimes, they do not have the luxury of time to solve difficult issues. Instead, they might need to intervene on behalf of clients to resolve emergency problems or conflicts. For example, imagine an elderly person enters a hospital with no known immediate family members and no known address. This person also shows signs of abuse and needs someone to make life-threatening medical decisions. The family and community services worker must uncover the layers of the problem at hand.

Family and community services workers need to understand family and group *dynamics* (pattern of change or growth over time). They must be resourceful to help people find the services that will enable them to lead fulfilling and better quality lives. They need to be well-connected within their communities, sharing ideas and resources with others in the field. They need to understand the organizations with which they directly work, such as the foster care, correctional, government assistance, or judicial systems. They also need to be willing to lobby and advocate for their clients.

Family and community services workers are compassionate and respectful of people. They work with people from a variety of ethnic, racial, religious, socio-economic, and cultural traditions. In doing so, they are open to diversity and nonjudgmental. They have a curiosity to learn and appreciate new customs or thinking that is different from their own.

Copyright Goodheart-Willcox Co., Inc.

Reading Recall

1. Why should family and community services workers be good communicators, be compassionate, and possess high mental and physical energy?
2. Give an example of a complex, many-layered issue a family and community services worker might need to solve.
3. Why do family and community services workers need to understand family and group dynamics?

Education, Training, and Experience

Many careers in the field of family and community services require a college degree. Some social and human services assistants might be able to obtain employment with only a high school diploma. Employers for most of these positions, however, want to hire people with a two- or four-year college degree. With a four-year degree, a social and human services assistant has a better opportunity for career advancement.

In many states, community health workers, and specifically, health coaches, must be certified (**Figure 11.7**). To become certified, workers need to complete a certain number of hours of supervised field experience. They must also earn a passing score on an exam. Although states generally oversee certification, there is current movement toward a national certification program for health or wellness coaches. The goals of certification are to protect consumers and better prepare community health workers. Some universities are now offering a combination of a four-year degree in a related field and certification.

Educational and training requirements for emergency and relief workers vary greatly based on employer, setting, and specific job requirements. To become a police officer or firefighter, the competition can be stiff. A high school diploma is a minimum requirement. A college degree is even better. Volunteer experience, excellent health and physical ability, and leadership skills can make a person a more competitive candidate. For some emergency and relief workers, a college degree and specialized training are preferred.

Monkey Business Images/Shutterstock.com

Figure 11.7 Community health is one of the quickest growing health-related employment trends. As the field becomes more understood and appreciated, specialized training and even a route to certification has developed. *Why are specialized training and certification important?*

Copyright Goodheart-Willcox Co., Inc.

Caseworker positions typically require a bachelor's degree. Many employers also prefer to hire someone with experience. Within family and community services college programs, internships are often available so students can gain experience in the field. Although internships are not required prior to employment, they do give students the chance to show potential employers their skills and abilities. Hiring a former intern may pose little risk to an employer because the employer is aware of how the worker performs in the role.

For a career as a social worker, a master's degree in social work, or MSW, and state licensure are necessary. Licensing requirements will vary from state to state. School social workers often need an MSW and two years of supervised social work experience. They also need a passing score on the social work component of the National Teaching Examination.

Family and community services workers must continue training to stay current in their professions, as legal regulations, therapeutic measures, and demographics constantly change (**Figure 11.8**). Those who are licensed must take courses to keep their certification current. Advanced on-the-job training is another important source of training for family and community services workers.

Reading Recall

1. What are the goals of certification of community health workers?

2. Compare and contrast the educational requirements for social and human services assistants and social workers.

3. Why is it important for family and community services workers to receive ongoing training after meeting educational requirements?

Figure 11.8 Seminars, workshops, and government training are important parts of most family and community services workers' career development. *What must licensed professionals do to keep their certification current?*

Dragon Images/Shutterstock.com

Copyright Goodheart-Willcox Co., Inc.

Specialized Knowledge for Family and Community Services Careers

Family and community services workers support families on a daily basis. In doing so, they need specialized knowledge on how families function. Understanding family dynamics and roles is critical. Beyond helping individual families, however, they also need to know how to effect positive change for all families in a given community. Understanding and participating in public policy is crucial for making a sustainable and long-lasting impact on families' well-being.

Understanding Family and Group Dynamics

To meet the needs of their clients, family and community services workers need to understand family and group dynamics. They need to know how families form and how they function. They also need to recognize how family members group together to meet each other's needs and the needs of society.

Expert Insight

"All happy families resemble one another, but each unhappy family is unhappy in its own way."

Leo Tolstoy, author,
Anna Karenina

Family Structure

According to the US Census Bureau, the traditional definition of *family* means two or more people living in the same household who are related by blood (birth), marriage, or adoption. In broader definitions, *family* might be defined as a group of people related by marriage. Family could also be a group of people who share common ancestors. A very close-knit group of unrelated people might even be viewed as a family. Sometimes, teachers and coaches talk about a class of students or a sports team as being a family.

Today, families form in a number of ways. Many people choose to marry and have children. Children may be a part of the family unit through biology or adoption. Couples, through choice or infertility, may remain childless. Children may be born to a single woman. Single fathers may parent children. Different family types often form as society changes. Following are some common family types in the US:

- A **nuclear family** consists of a husband and wife and their biological children. Parents of a nuclear family often share the responsibilities of raising their children, completing household chores, and supporting the family financially.

- A **single-parent family** includes a father or mother and his or her children. Single parents often face many challenges. Family and community services workers can provide great sources of support for single-parent families in need.

- An **extended family** includes several generations living under one roof. For example, an extended family might include parents and their children, grandparents, aunts, uncles, or cousins.

Copyright Goodheart-Willcox Co., Inc.

- A **stepfamily** forms when a single parent gets married. At times, the term *blended* is used to describe this type of family. Some people, however, believe this term is too simple. After all, two different family structures combine to form the new family unit, creating new role expectations to resolve. This is especially true when both parents have children from other marriages who will be living with them. Merging families requires many adjustments for everyone.

- An **adoptive family** forms when a state court legally grants permission to a married couple or single person to raise another person's child (**Figure 11.9**). The adopted child then becomes a permanent part of the family.

- A **foster family** forms when an adult provides a temporary home for a child who is unable to live with his or her biological parents because proper care is not provided. Caseworkers place children in foster homes until they can find a permanent home for the children. Sometimes, children can return to their original home if the parents can prove they are able to provide necessary care. In many states, children are no longer a part of the foster care system when they reach 18 years of age.

- A **childless family** exists when a married couple does not have children. Some couples may be unable to have children of their own and do not wish to adopt. Other couples may simply choose not to have children.

Figure 11.9 There are many reasons people choose to adopt a child. Perhaps they cannot have children of their own. They may want to add to their current family. Helping a child in need of a home may also be a reason to adopt. *What are some other reasons people may choose to adopt?*

©iStock.com/perkmeup

Copyright Goodheart-Willcox Co., Inc.

Family Functions

Families are fundamental to society, as they serve multiple important functions. One main function of the family is to socialize family members into their assigned roles. By being a member of a family, members assume assigned roles, such as wife, husband, spouse, child, daughter, or son. Roles become more complicated as family generations are considered. For example, a daughter may also be a sister, an aunt, a cousin, or eventually a wife, mother, or grandmother. She may be expected to act, think, or behave differently in each of these roles, as defined by the individual, family, and larger culture.

Another important family function is *procreation*, or generating a new generation. As the family life cycle repeats itself, new generations are added. As parents have children, they take on the legal responsibilities of socializing, educating, and meeting the needs of their children. Families also have a responsibility to provide economic support to individual family members.

The Family as a Social System

Families exist within a social system. A **social system** refers to the organization of individuals into groups based on characteristic patterned relationships (**Figure 11.10**). The family is a social system because its members group together to meet each other's needs and the needs of society.

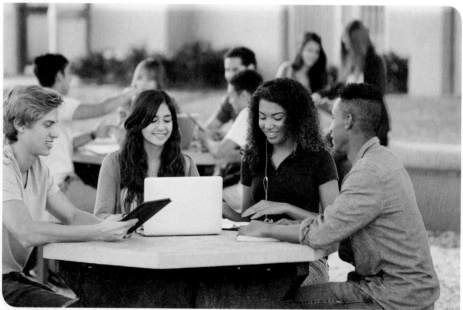

Monkey Business Images/Shutterstock.com

Figure 11.10 People often belong to several social systems at the same time. For example, in addition to your family, your high school is its own social system. *To what other social systems do you belong?*

Copyright Goodheart-Willcox Co., Inc.

Societal, cultural, demographic, and economic factors affect the roles and responsibilities of families and their members. As a social system, families will, in turn, affect the larger social system of society in which they operate. For family and community services workers, understanding the context is vital to providing appropriate services.

Societal Factors

The social environment affects the way people think about and value specific family characteristics. It also affects the way family characteristics are played out in everyday lives. For example, when more women entered the workforce in the 1970s, *egalitarian* (equal power) marital relationships became more common. Since then, increases in family diversity are more striking than during any time in previous history. This diversity is easy to spot in popular media today, as the media attempts to portray families that reflect what is happening in society.

Cultural Factors

Culture also plays a huge role in affecting how family identity, roles, and responsibilities are perceived. Parents decide with whom their children will play, where the family will shop, and where and with whom they will worship. They decide what the acceptable rules and boundaries are for family members, especially when children are young. These boundaries are constantly changing. As the tasks of the family unit change in a diverse society, cultural influences become more apparent, especially in regard to parenting styles and family role expectations.

Demographic Factors

Demographics affect family roles and responsibilities. When one age group increases in proportion to other age groups, especially those requiring care, such as infants or older adults, the impact can be great. For example, the older adult population will continue to grow over the next 50 years. An aging population raises several concerns for families, including healthcare management and costs, independence and housing solutions, and workforce participation and retirement. Another population boom is currently in young adulthood. Two large generations at opposite ends of the adult age spectrum can create resource distribution tensions.

Economic Factors

The economic environment influences families and the ability to provide resources. When adequate employment is available, family members can secure needed resources. Lack of adequate resources can cause stress, as can too much work. Work provides many things for families, the first of which is financial income and stability. Although financial motivation is primary, there are many other benefits to paid work such as social interaction and professional role identification and status.

Copyright Goodheart-Willcox Co., Inc.

Finding Community Resources for Clients

In many communities, resources abound for people who can pay for services and products. For those who cannot, resources are sometimes challenging and difficult to both find and access.

Family and community services workers must keep current with social services resources within their community. These resources may include food, shelter, clothing, financial relief, technology, government assistance, and any number of other amenities. Their job is to know what resources are available and how to obtain these resources for individuals and families in need.

Family and community services workers find community resources to meet their clients' needs. Through networking and experience, they go through a series of steps to match the potential resources with their clients (**Figure 11.11**).

The first step toward matching resources with the client is to examine the need. During this step, workers work with their clients to determine if the issue is a problem, an opportunity, or a goal, and whether or not outside resources are needed. For example, if affordable housing is needed, can finding housing be accomplished through budgeting? Is the need immediate? Will only emergency housing cover the need?

Family and community services workers help their clients analyze potential solutions. Usually, there is more than one possible way to

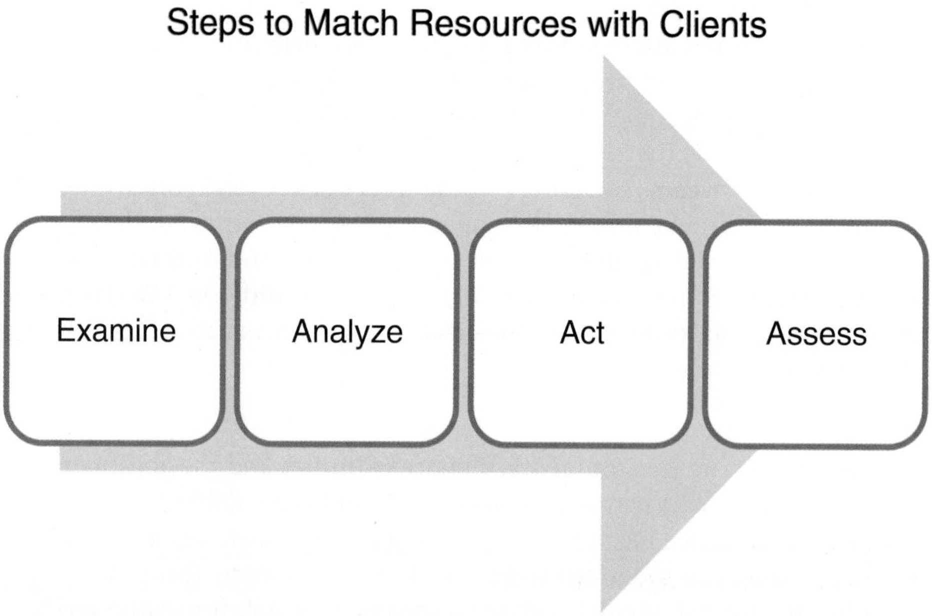

Steps to Match Resources with Clients

Examine Analyze Act Assess

Figure 11.11 Family and community services workers can use the Examine, Analyze, Act, Assess process to effectively help their clients and match them with the proper resources. *During which step does the worker come up with a list of potential solutions?*

Copyright Goodheart-Willcox Co., Inc.

Pathway to Success

Identifying Community Resources

Every community has resources unique to the area. Large cities, small towns, and communities with diverse ethnic backgrounds have different resources to identify and share. To discover your community's resources, look around your neighborhood and community with fresh eyes. Most communities have basic social services resources such as food pantries, shelters, and feeding programs, but there are many other resources to discover.

For example, some communities have resources for free or reduced price vision or dental care. You may also discover that your community has a youth outreach program. Your community may offer access to adaptive technology for people with disabilities. Some communities have resources for people

looking for employment. These programs help community members search for jobs, write résumés, and prepare for job interviews.

You may also discover that your community library has technology such as computers, WiFi, scanners, printers and copiers, and computer classes. In addition, the library may offer access to databases that can help you with research for your school assignments. Some libraries or community centers even have digital cameras available for rental. Most libraries offer audiobooks, which can be especially helpful for people with vision disabilities. You may find that your community library also has adaptive technology for people with disabilities. These might include magnifiers or ADA computer workstations.

Create a Community Resource Map

Complete the following steps to create a community resource map:

1. Get a copy of a map of your community.

2. Look at your community as if you were a visitor or someone who just moved to the area. Identify when and where people gather and what they do together. Include faith-based, social service, sporting entertainment, and other types of gatherings.

3. Next, look into what services are provided in the community and who provides them. Record all of this information.

4. Check with the different places you have identified to find out their hours of operation. Learn about what they do. Determine if there are any rules for

receiving services. Find out who to contact for more information.

5. Create a chart listing your findings, proximity to where you live and contact information if you have questions. In your chart, have a place for name, address, phone number, contact person's name, hours of operation, services provided, and the process for accessing services.

6. Pull out your map. Create icons for the different businesses. Mark these icons on your map. Create a legend identifying what each icon means.

7. Make copies. Share your community resource map with your local visitor's center.

Copyright Goodheart-Willcox Co., Inc.

address an issue. They then help their clients evaluate each alternative carefully. This may include thinking through the best- and worst-case scenarios.

Next, clients choose one alternative to act on after careful evaluation of all alternatives. Family and community services workers then assist their clients in carrying through with the alternative selected, if help is needed. Lastly, they help their clients assess if they made the right choice or if the situation should be handled differently next time.

Shaping Policies That Concern Families

Much work has been done in the past and is continuing in the present to create guidelines, laws, and regulations that will improve quality of life. Some family and community services workers concentrate on issues important to the family and carry out research suited to their particular strengths. For example, policy that improves the quality, affordability, and accessibility of child care ultimately improves the overall quality of family life. In the following section, you will learn what public policy is and how family and community services workers can effect change in public policy. You will also learn that, as an individual citizen, there are many ways to be actively involved in public policy change, including voting, campaigning, or otherwise supporting issues.

What Is Public Policy?

Public policy refers to the guidelines, regulations, and laws the government enacts to address a particular issue or problem. The area of public policy dealing with complex questions and issues affecting society and families is called **family policy**. Just as in the larger arena of creating public policy, in family policy, current government programs and policies are evaluated based on how they affect the family unit.

Family and community services workers are well qualified to contribute their expertise in public policy issues affecting the family. Joint research into various aspects of American politics and public policy has resulted in many changes that have led to improved quality of life. There are many examples of family and community services workers contributing their specialized knowledge to the conversation and participating in public policy formation. **Figure 11.12** shows a select list of public policy issues that include family and community services specific knowledge.

For many government programs to continue, politicians have to know if the programs are effective. They often call on family and community services workers to show evidence that the programs have effected change. They need personal stories and, more importantly, hard data. For example, when politicians evaluate the effectiveness of a preschool

Copyright Goodheart-Willcox Co., Inc.

Family and Community Services Public Policy Issues
• Financial literacy
• Affordable housing
• Homelessness
• Special Supplemental Program for Women, Infants, and Children (WIC)
• Head Start early childhood school preparation
• Food vouchers
• Child nutrition programs
• Child Care Development Block Grant (CCDBG)
• Dependent Care Tax Credit (DCTC)
• Right to privacy
• Private school vouchers

Figure 11.12 Family and community services workers can contribute their specialized knowledge to the public policy issues included in this list. *What kind of evidence can workers show to prove that programs have effected change in the community?*

education program, they want to know what effect the program has had on children, families, and the community. Did the program help prepare young children for kindergarten? Did it involve more parents in the learning process? Did it lower the incidence of early childhood hunger in the community? These are typical evaluative questions that must be addressed.

The Professional's Role in Shaping Public Policy

There are many ways family and community services workers can be involved in shaping public policy concerning families. First is to be well informed. For example, if concerned about affordable quality child care, they can find out what the issues and current standards or policies are in their city, county, or state. Shortages of affordable quality child care may stem from any number of factors unique to an area. Long-term and sustained unemployment could be an issue. Current guidelines and regulations concerning child care or a lack of educational programs preparing child care workers may be factors. Still other factors might be low wages for child care workers, high insurance premiums, or government funding limitations.

Voicing criticism or support for current programs and policies affecting families is one of the best ways to be involved. Working to educate others on the implications of current or proposed public policy is another way to be involved. Family and community services workers often carry the role of educators, leading discussions and explaining points of view of various groups. They can identify objectives and help decision makers sort through the details and data supporting or disputing a particular stance.

Copyright Goodheart-Willcox Co., Inc.

Law and Ethics   *It Is a Process: Public Policy*

Sometimes the process of changing public policy seems overwhelming and too complex for average citizens. It does not, however, have to be difficult. The American Association of Family and Consumer Sciences utilizes a policy analysis organizing tool developed by Braun and Bauer (2001) to explain the process of impacting public policy. This tool is built around five "I's" that represent stages in effecting public policy change. These include

- information. The *information* stage involves general fact-finding. This includes researching the current legislation on an issue, who needs information and when, the type of information needed, and the preferred media format for information delivery. During the information stage, fact-finding is on a very general level. Values and needs are assessed. Costs and benefits are weighed. Current legislation is evaluated based on needs.

- issues. In the second stage, the *issues* involved in the situation are analyzed. This is the stage when feelings, opinions, and attitudes of people who consider themselves stakeholders in the issue are considered.

- impact. In the third stage, the *impact* of the proposed legislation is assessed. The question is asked, "Who will the proposed legislation affect?" Some people will be affected intentionally by policy changes. Others will be affected unintentionally. There will be both long- and short-term effects with any public policy change. In this stage, these impacts are made clear.

- implications. In the fourth stage, the potential *implications* of the proposed legislation will be judged from the viewpoint of all who are directly and indirectly involved. How will the policy change the lives of those involved? Will the policy have a positive or negative effect? Will it affect the larger community, state, or federal requirements? How will nonprofit and faith-based groups react to the proposed legislation? Are there economic, social, political, or physical ramifications of the proposed legislation? In hotly debated issues, debates and discussions often take place through a number of media formats. The greater the impact of the proposed legislation, generally, the more media attention the proposed legislation receives.

- imperative. The last stage, the *imperative* stage, is evaluating the timeliness and urgency of the proposed legislation. This stage involves considering the impact of changing or not changing existing legislation.

Research and Writing Activity

To become more familiar with public policy, complete the following:

- Identify your US Congressional representatives in the House and Senate and your state governor and legislators in the House and Senate.

- Secure an electronic copy or a hard copy of your local newspaper. Read it thoroughly. As you do, look for public policy issues in your community that specifically impact families.

- Name one individual who has influenced public policy in the past year. This person could have influenced policy at the local, state, or federal level. Write a synopsis describing how he or she has participated in public policy formation.

An Individual Citizen's Role in Shaping Public Policy

Civic engagement is a process wherein different voices, opinions, or arguments are shared and oriented toward mutual understanding. In other words, it is a public conversation between individuals. It can include anyone—concerned citizens, experts in a related field, politicians, and government officials. Civic engagement works best when citizens involved

Copyright Goodheart-Willcox Co., Inc.

in the dialogue seek mutual understanding, rather than only furthering their own agenda.

Civic engagement offers individuals the chance to become involved in public policy formation at a local level. Although rules of order may be used in public forums, civic engagement is still considered an informal process. Individuals may participate in civic engagement as average citizens, policy educators, policy analysts, or policy advocates. Because public policies are undergoing continual change, civic engagement is appropriate and effective at many points during the public policy process.

For civic engagement to work effectively, participants must work together. *Collaboration* is the process of partnering with others to accomplish a goal. Collaborative learning has been the focus in schools for the past several years and social media has made civic engagement even more inviting. As a result, more and more adults feel comfortable with the collaborative process.

When people work together, more is accomplished. This is because unified efforts can utilize limited resources to their fullest extent. With different voices in the conversation, problems and goals can be more clearly defined. Public policies often involve very complex issues. Collaboration helps stakeholders to share the load.

Expert Insight

"Never doubt that a small group of thoughtful, committed citizens can change the world; indeed, it's the only thing that ever has."

Margaret Mead, anthropologist

Reading Recall

1. Name two functions of families in society.
2. Give an example from your own life of how the environment affects the family unit.
3. Name three public policy issues that include family and community services specific knowledge.
4. How can family and community services workers effect change in public policy?
5. How can individual citizens effect change in public policy?

Rewards, Demands, and Future Trends

Helping people meet their basic, social, medical, psychological, emotional, or spiritual needs is extremely gratifying work when there are successes. It can be extremely frustrating when there are not. Even so, family and community services workers often report they feel gratified. They are personally making a difference in the lives of their clients as well as in their communities (**Figure 11.13**).

Like counseling and mental health services, pay varies greatly. Entry-level positions, such as social and human services assistants, earn relatively low pay. Other positions, such as development officers

Copyright Goodheart-Willcox Co., Inc.

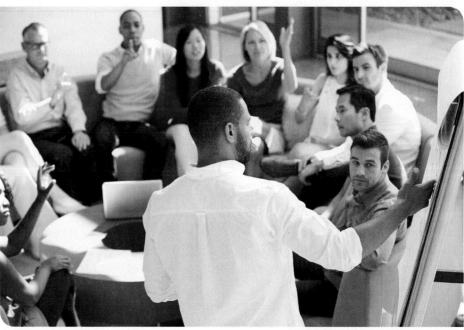

Monkey Business Images/Shutterstock.com

Figure 11.13 Family and community services workers are often the change agents in a community, proposing and implementing social change. *Do you think that a career in family and community services sounds rewarding?*

and executive directors, make a much higher wage. In family and community services, the lower-level jobs have much client interaction and the workload is often high. The higher-paying jobs tend to have less direct client contact. There is more interaction with other administrative colleagues within or outside of the organization or even business and government.

Family and community services workers often work long hours as people's problems or crises are not limited to certain hours of the day. The work can be very demanding and stressful. Family and community services workers have an emotional investment in their clients' well-being. Some workers in this field may have trouble learning to leave their work behind at the end of the day. If this occurs, work-life balance becomes very difficult.

The job outlook continues to be very good for family and community services workers (**Figure 11.14**). Projected growth for many positions is expected to occur much faster than average. The healthcare and social services areas are especially expected to grow based on population growth needs. As the older adult population continues to grow, services that reach older adults will be particularly needed in the coming decades. In addition, services for substance or alcohol addicted populations and children in crisis will continue to grow, opening up the need for more family and community services workers.

Copyright Goodheart-Willcox Co., Inc.

Future Trends for Family and Community Services Careers				
Occupation	**Projected Growth (2014–2024)**	**Projected Job Openings (2014–2024)**	**Median Wages (2014)**	**Education**
Caseworker	Faster than average (9–13%)	120,000	$29,790	Bachelor's degree
Certified health coach	Average (5–8%)	74,900	$34,980	Postsecondary certificate
Community health worker	Faster than average (9–13%)	19,500	$50,430	Bachelor's degree
Development officer	Average (5–8%)	27,100	$101,510	Bachelor's degree
Executive director	Little or no change (–1–1%)	58,400	$173,320	Master's degree
Firefighter	Average (5–8%)	112,300	$45,970	Postsecondary certificate
Law enforcement officer	Average (5–8%)	258,400	$56,810	High school diploma
Program director	Faster than average (9–13%)	50,500	$69,100	Bachelor's degree
School social worker	Average (5–8%)	92,500	$42,120	Master's degree
Social and human services assistant	Faster than average (9–13%)	120,000	$29,790	Bachelor's degree
Social worker	Much faster than average (14% or higher)	50,700	$41,380	Master's degree
Volunteer coordinator	Faster than average (9–13%)	49,800	$62,740	Bachelor's degree
Wellness coach	Average (5–8%)	74,900	$34,980	Postsecondary certificate

Sources: O*NET and the *Occupational Outlook Handbook*

Figure 11.14 Analyzing future career trends can help you decide on a career path. *According to the information in this chart, which family and community services professions require the highest level of education?*

Reading Recall

1. Describe rewards and demands of family and community services careers.
2. Describe future trends in family and community services careers.
3. How might an older adult population growth affect the field of family and community services in the coming decades?

Copyright Goodheart-Willcox Co., Inc.

Summary

- There are many job opportunities in the field of family and community services, including social and human services assistants, community health workers, emergency and relief workers, caseworkers, and social workers. Coordinator and director positions also exist. These include volunteer coordinators, program directors, development officers and directors, and executive directors.

- Family and community services workers are compassionate, respectful, caring, and nonjudgmental. They have good listening, speaking, problem-solving, conflict resolution, and critical thinking skills. They need to be resourceful to meet their clients' needs.

- Many positions in family and community services require some postsecondary education. Graduate degrees, experience, and certification or licensure is required in many career tracks and for advancement in others.

- Family and community services workers support families on a daily basis. Therefore, they need to be knowledgeable about how families form and how they function. They also need to understand how families exist as a social system and how societal, cultural, demographic, and economic factors affect family roles and responsibilities.

- Family and community services workers are often involved in organizing and promoting public policy legislation. Their voice is especially important in the public arena as they are acutely aware of needs and the obstacles that may keep people from attending to their needs.

- Family and community services workers must be diligent in staying connected and resourceful to most effectively help their clients. Although the field can be emotionally taxing, the rewards are great. The job outlook continues to be very good for family and community services workers.

College and Career Portfolio

Portfolio Transcripts

One of the most important elements of a portfolio—whether for college or for a first job—is a transcript. A *transcript* is an official record of a student's academic performance in courses, including final grades. As you complete your coursework during high school, keep in mind that college admission boards and future employers will want to view your transcript. How well you do in your classes can significantly impact your future.

Procedures for requesting a transcript vary depending on your school and the purpose of the transcript. If you need to request a transcript, it is best to do so well in advance, since they take time to generate. To include a transcript in your portfolio, complete the following steps:

1. Research how to request a transcript from your school. If you need help, ask your teacher or consult a career counselor. In a college or university, students' transcripts are available in the Office of the Registrar.

2. Follow the procedure to request your transcript in advance. Seek help if necessary.

Copyright Goodheart-Willcox Co., Inc.

Review and Reflect ↪

1. Name three duties of a social and human services assistant.
2. What is the primary focus of community health workers?
3. Compare and contrast the duties of a caseworker with those of a social worker.
4. Differentiate between the duties of a *development director* and an *executive director*.
5. List five common aptitudes, attitudes, and skills of family and community services workers.
6. Identify the preparation requirements needed for a family and community services career that interests you.
7. List two ways family and community services workers can continue to receive training after earning a college degree.
8. Compare the US Census Bureau's definition of *family* with your definition of *family*.
9. What is the difference between a *nuclear family* and an *extended family*?
10. Identify the roles that members assume in families. How do these roles change as you add in generations?
11. Explain the difference between *public policy* and *family policy*.
12. What do many family and community services workers say is the most rewarding part of their job?

Vocabulary Activities

13. **Key terms**   Working with a partner, locate a small image online that visually describes or explains each of the following terms. To create flash cards, write each term on a note card and paste the image that describes or explains the term on the opposite side.

adoptive family	nuclear family
childless family	public policy
civic engagement	single-parent family
extended family	social system
family policy	stepfamily
foster family	

14. **Academic terms**   Read the text passages that contain each of the following terms. Then write the definitions of each term in your own words. Double-check your definitions by rereading the text and using the text glossary.

auxiliary	instrumental
cognizant	liaisons
dynamics	plethora
egalitarian	

Self-Assessment Quiz ↪

Complete the self-assessment quiz online to help you practice and expand your knowledge and skills.

Critical Thinking

15. **Analyze**   Analyze the similarities and differences between the seven different family types discussed in this chapter. Create a diagram to help you explain the different types of families to someone who does not know. This diagram would be a good addition to your portfolio.
16. **Make inferences**   Based on your current family type, what type of family do you think you will be a part of within 20 years? What about in 40 years?
17. **Evaluate**   Evaluate why it is important to know the medical background of an adopted child. How would you react if you had no information on the birth parents and your adopted child became ill? What has changed about adoptions over the last 50 years to help in cases like this?
18. **Identify**   Draw, label, and illustrate a chart to show the functions of families in society in your own words.
19. **Cause and effect**   Public policy has led to the creation of several agencies that work with families. Identify three of these agencies and explain what they do and how they help families.
20. **Determine**   Determine ways that you as a teenager could effect or shape the role of public policy as it impacts the family. Write a one-page paper explaining what you can do

now, as well as in 10 and 20 years, to shape public policy.

21. **Compare and contrast**   Choose at least two careers in the family and community services field that interest you. Compare and contrast the pay, workloads, job outlooks, and education levels for these careers. Which career interests you the most? Why?

22. **Draw conclusions**   Identify several family and community services careers that are expected to grow faster than average over the next 10 years. Why are these careers growing so quickly? When might the growth rate for these careers decline?

Core Skills

23. **Research and technology**   Research the requirements to be a volunteer fireman or disaster relief volunteer in your community. What knowledge and experience do you need? Where can you get training? How old must you be? Create an electronic presentation to share this information with your classmates.

24. **Research and writing**   Create a family tree going back three generations (you and your siblings, your parents and their siblings, and your grandparents). On this family tree, identify any medical conditions, as well as each person's interests and abilities. Using this information, try to determine from whom in the family you have received your own interests and abilities. If you do not have access to this information for your own family, create a family tree for someone you know.

25. **Speaking**   In small groups, identify television programs that show the good and bad sides of various family types. Discuss examples from the TV programs that indicate how these families cope with adversity in the family. Share your group's examples with the rest of the class.

26. **Listening, speaking, and writing**   Find someone who has been adopted or has adopted a child. Talk to this person about his or her experience. Write a one-page paper explaining what you learned about adoption from your interview.

27. **Speaking and listening**   In small groups, discuss the basic functions of the family. Be sure to discuss the different roles family members assume. Identify specific examples of ways in which these roles can become more complicated as generations are added into the family. How do family members' responsibilities change as their roles change?

28. **Writing, speaking, and listening**   Make a list of 10 questions about family life in previous generations. Include questions about the multiple roles and responsibilities assumed by individuals within the family, and how these roles and responsibilities have changed throughout the years. Interview a member of your extended family or another older adult about growing up. Ask your 10 questions. Record the person's answers. Ask yourself the same 10 questions. How are the answers similar, and how are they different? In which time frame would you want to live? Why?

29. **Research and math**   An important family function is procreation. Research the cost of having a baby. Be sure to include the cost of prenatal care, birth and delivery, items needed to bring the baby home, as well as food and clothing for the first year of the child's life. Share your findings with the class.

30. **Speaking and listening**   In small groups, investigate the societal, cultural, demographic, and economic factors affecting the responsibilities of family members. Give examples of how each of these factors affect families. Then, discuss your group's examples with the rest of the class.

31. **Research and technology**   Using online resources or informational interviews with professionals, research different types of technology available to meet the diverse needs of individuals and families requiring assistance. Create an electronic presentation of your findings to share with the class.

32. **Research and reading**   Choose one of the public policy issues in Figure 11.12. Use online or print resources to find articles about the issue. Read the articles to find out how this policy impacts families. What are the current trends related to the issue? Based on your research, would you voice criticism or support for this issue? Explain.

Copyright Goodheart-Willcox Co., Inc.

33. **Research and speaking**   Research a list of volunteer activities you and your classmates could do to help families around the holidays. As a class, make a list of these volunteer activities. Choose one in which you can get involved. After your volunteer activity, discuss the experience with your classmates. Were there parts of the experience you particularly liked or disliked? Explain.

34. **CTE career readiness practice**   Imagine you are a social and human services assistant working with a client who has recently been laid off from work. The person's spouse has been diagnosed with cancer, and they have three children—ages 6 months, 5 years, and 15 years. As a professional trying to meet this family's needs, determine what you would say to the family. What strategies could you suggest to help the family meet their needs? What resources are available in your hometown that the family can benefit from until your client gets another job? Write a script describing how you, as a social and human services assistant, would handle this situation.

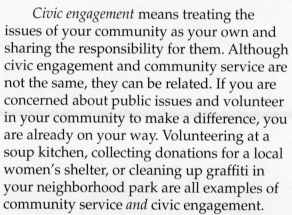

Lend a Hand

Civic Engagement: What Does It Mean?

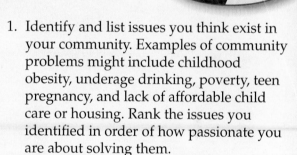

Civic engagement means treating the issues of your community as your own and sharing the responsibility for them. Although civic engagement and community service are not the same, they can be related. If you are concerned about public issues and volunteer in your community to make a difference, you are already on your way. Volunteering at a soup kitchen, collecting donations for a local women's shelter, or cleaning up graffiti in your neighborhood park are all examples of community service *and* civic engagement.

Beyond community service, there are other forms of civic engagement. For example, writing a letter to a local politician, attending a city council meeting, or getting involved with your neighborhood association are all ways to become civically engaged. Participation in local, state, and national elections is another example of civic engagement. The key to civic engagement is active participation in the community.

To discover how you can become more civically engaged, complete the following:

1. Identify and list issues you think exist in your community. Examples of community problems might include childhood obesity, underage drinking, poverty, teen pregnancy, and lack of affordable child care or housing. Rank the issues you identified in order of how passionate you are about solving them.

2. Research how you can get involved in solving the issues you listed. You may find resources online, but also visit your city or town hall, the local library, or community center for information. Find out if there are committees you can join or meetings you can attend. Is there an election approaching? Is there an issue you and your classmates could address? Consider how you can make a difference.

3. Choose one of the opportunities for civic engagement that you identified, and get involved. Attend a meeting, join a social media group, or participate in an event. Write a reflection paper about your experience.

Chapter 12

Personal Care Services

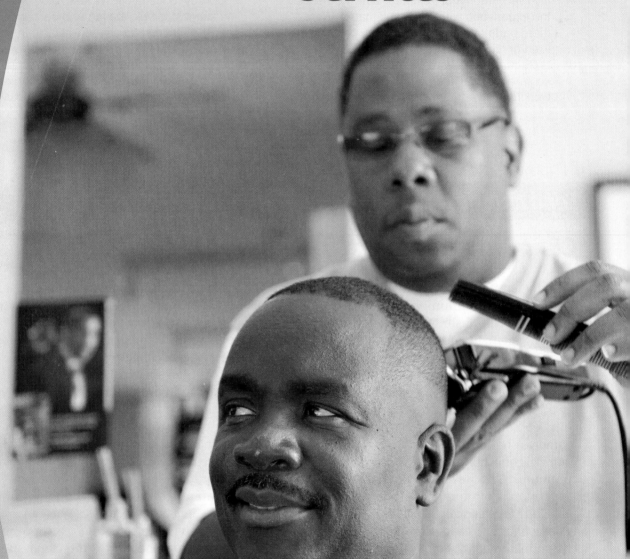

While studying, look for the activity icon  **to**

- **practice** key and academic terms with e-flash cards and matching activities;
- **assess** what you learn by completing self-assessment quizzes; and
- **reinforce** what you learn by mapping concepts and completing review and reflect questions.

www.g-wlearning.com/humanservices/

©iStock.com/EyeJoy

Learning Outcomes

After studying this chapter, you will be able to

- **compare and contrast** career opportunities for personal care services workers;
- **list** common aptitudes, attitudes, and skills of personal care services workers;
- **give examples** of postsecondary education, training, and experience required for several personal care services careers;
- **identify** ways in which to demonstrate good customer service;
- **describe** various ways to create and protect client records;
- **evaluate** different types of technology and explain the importance of using technology wisely to provide good personal care services;
- **summarize** the key physical, cognitive, social, and emotional characteristics and specialized health needs of older adults; and
- **summarize** the rewards, demands, and future trends of careers in personal care services.

Reading Strategies

Before reading, scan the chapter title. Write a paragraph describing what you know about this topic. As you are reading, compare and contrast the information in the chapter with the information you already know about careers in personal care services. After reading, consider how the information in this chapter supports or contradicts your understanding of the subject matter.

Mapping Concepts

As you read this chapter, use a tree diagram like the one shown to organize information about personal care services. Write *Personal Care Services* in the top circle. Record major categories and specific activities and notes in the circles below.

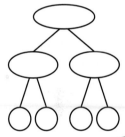

Key Terms

Alzheimer's disease
cosmetology
dementia
electrology
electrolysis

embalming
obituary
presbyopia
tinnitus

Academic Terms

acumen
dispense
precedence
riled

Personal care services workers hold a wide variety of jobs from flight attendant to theatrical makeup artist to animal care worker to gaming service worker. As you can see, the careers in personal care services are very diverse. The focus of these jobs is to provide a service to another person. Personal care services workers help people live their lives more effectively—sometimes in the most private and delicate ways.

Because personal care services occupations are so diverse, this chapter will only focus on some of the main career areas in the field. These areas include cosmetology, massage therapy, personal and home care, and funeral service occupations. Although the requirements for these jobs may vary greatly, the common factor involves working one-on-one with clients to provide a personal service. In general, personal care workers provide the most basic needs to their fellow humans. In so doing, they lend dignity and quality of life to those they serve.

Careers in Personal Care Services

Examples of Personal Care Services Careers
• Barber
• Caregiver
• Certified nursing assistant (CNA)
• Companion
• Cosmetologist
• Electrologist
• Embalmer
• Funeral attendant
• Funeral director
• Funeral service manager
• Hairdresser or hairstylist
• Home health aide
• Manicurist
• Massage therapist
• Nail technician
• Pedicurist
• Personal assistant
• Personal attendant
• Skin care specialist (also called *esthetician*)

Figure 12.1 The field of personal care services offers many different career opportunities. *Which of these careers would you like to learn more about?*

Personal care services careers include many diverse and wide-ranging professions (**Figure 12.1**). What these careers have in common is that the services provide needed personal care, usually in a one-on-one interaction. Those who enter this field tend to have a strong desire to help people in a personal way. In the following sections, you will learn much more about some of the main careers in personal care services.

Cosmetologists

Cosmetology is the study that involves enhancing a client's personal appearance through the treatment of hair, skin, and nails. *Cosmetologists* are licensed professionals who are trained in providing services in these different areas. In cosmetology, students may also choose to specialize in one specific area, such as hair care. Various specialized occupations in cosmetology include hairdressers, barbers, skin care specialists, electrologists, and nail technicians.

Hairdressers, or *hairstylists*, and *barbers* are licensed to provide hairstyling services. Hairdressers will shampoo, condition, cut, color, and style clients' hair. Hairdressers also offer advice on how clients can care for their hair at

Copyright Goodheart-Willcox Co., Inc.

home. Barbers mainly focus on men's grooming, so in addition to cutting and styling hair, they shave and trim facial hair. Depending on the state in which they are licensed, some barbers may also color hair.

Skin care specialists are licensed to assess their clients' skin condition and recommend products and treatments that will improve the health and appearance of the skin. Skin care specialists are also called *estheticians* (es-thi-TISH-uhns). They offer facials and full-body treatments, as well as other skin care treatments. They also apply makeup, give head and neck massages, and perform hair removal (which can be temporary or permanent).

Permanent hair removal is its own specialty area, which is known as **electrology**. With this service, *electrologists* are trained and licensed to use a process called *electrolysis*. The **electrolysis** process removes hair roots by applying heat through an electric current, which destroys the roots, thereby preventing further hair growth.

Another specialized area in cosmetology is nail care. *Nail technicians,* or *manicurists* and *pedicurists*, provide nail treatments and services to groom fingernails and toenails (**Figure 12.2**). Examples of services include trimming, painting, and polishing nails. Extending nails by applying acrylic or gel tips to the natural nail is also a common service nail technicians provide.

Massage Therapists

Massage therapists are licensed professionals who use physical touch to manipulate the muscles and other soft tissues of the body. Massage

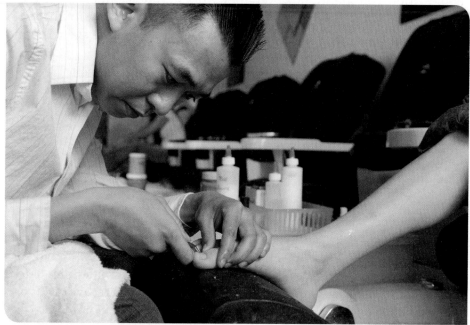

Figure 12.2 Pedicurists provide treatments and services to their clients' toenails, including trimming and grooming. *Have you ever received a manicure or pedicure?*

©iStock.com/Rich Legg

services are used to relieve stress, reduce pain, improve circulation, and encourage healing. These services also help clients relax and generally feel better. Massage therapists usually work at salons, health clubs, spas, hospitals, and treatment centers. Many massage therapists are self-employed.

Personal and Home Care Aides

Personal care aides help with daily tasks of people with special needs, such as older adults, people with disabilities, and those who have chronic illnesses. They can assist in short- or long-term recovery after an illness, injury, surgery, or accident. Other common job titles may include *companions, caregivers,* or *personal attendants.*

These aides often work in their clients' homes because they help with daily activities. The person needing care or his or her family most often directly hires them. Personal care aides help with grooming tasks, including bathing, showering, and dressing. They often perform light household duties, such as doing laundry, changing bed linens, and cooking. They might run errands for their clients. A large part of the job is simply being a companion—reading to clients, playing games, or chatting.

Home health aides perform many of the same duties as personal care aides, but have more medical training. Generally, home health aides are trained to *dispense* (give out) prescribed medications. They can also change bandages or perform other light wound care.

Certified nursing assistants (CNAs) are home health aides that have received formal training and passed a certification exam. CNAs, like personal care aides, may provide assistance with tasks in clients' private homes. More commonly, however, they work in care facilities under the supervision of nurses or other medical staff. These work environments include hospitals, nursing homes, adult care homes, hospice agencies, and other care facilities.

Personal assistants work with clients who are generally well. These clients need or want assistance with daily activities, often due to lack of time, interest, or energy. For example, a personal assistant may schedule appointments, run errands, act as a personal shopper, manage household maintenance, or answer correspondence. Personal assistants contribute to higher quality of life for their clients by relieving their clients' workloads and personal responsibilities.

Funeral Service Workers

Funeral service workers oversee the details of funerals. Funeral service jobs include funeral directors, funeral attendants, and funeral managers. *Funeral directors* assist families after a death occurs, and sometimes before, to help them plan a meaningful experience to remember their loved one. They help families plan burial, cremation, funeral, or memorial services. Funeral directors work with families to write an **obituary** (death notice,

Copyright Goodheart-Willcox Co., Inc.

Case Study *Living Life Together*

As Nadia drove to work this morning, she thought, "I am really one of the lucky ones. I got myself out of bed this morning, showered, dressed, fixed and ate breakfast, threw in a load of laundry, and even had time to fill my car with gas." This feeling did not weaken as Nadia reached work. In fact, it grew stronger.

Nadia is a personal care aide. She works to make life easier for her client, Mari, who has Multiple Sclerosis (MS). MS is a chronic disease affecting the immune system. It often results in a progressive loss of body functioning, such as walking. Due to her MS, Mari is confined to a wheelchair. She has also lost her ability to dress, prepare meals, and bathe or shower on her own. She can drive her modified car and transfer herself to a scooter when needed. Mari still feels like she leads a full and meaningful life. Much of that is due to the work of Nadia.

When Nadia arrives at work, she will be ready to help Mari with any personal grooming tasks. She will help her dress. Together, they will make breakfast and talk about any of Mari's current needs. Sometimes they go shopping together, if Mari needs groceries or other items. If Mari needs help planning her week or making plans for a special visit from her grandchildren, Nadia will help with these tasks, too. There are other times when Mari's needs are met and they just sit together to share a cup of tea or talk about a book they are both reading. The bond that has grown between Nadia and Mari goes beyond a professional relationship and has become a friendship.

michaeljung/Shutterstock.com

For Discussion

1. In what ways does Nadia help Mari lead an "abled" life?
2. Think of other ways Nadia may be asked to assist Mari in the future.
3. How might Nadia's help affect Mari's family?
4. How can Nadia ensure she maintains a professional role in caring for Mari, despite their friendship?

often in a newspaper). They also handle the media, condolence messages, and contributions or gifts.

Some funeral directors undergo training to embalm bodies. **Embalming** is a process through which a body is temporarily preserved for a viewing or visitation by family and friends. Funeral directors may also be called *morticians* or *undertakers*. Funeral directors who specialize in embalming bodies are known as *embalmers*.

Funeral attendants help funeral directors make sure their clients' wishes are carried out for funeral or memorial services. For example, funeral attendants may arrange rooms for visitations and funeral services. They may place the casket or set up the floral arrangements before services. They may also direct visitors to the room where services will be held.

Copyright Goodheart-Willcox Co., Inc.

Funeral service managers are the professionals who oversee the daily operations of a funeral home. This work involves many responsibilities. Funeral service managers handle the finances for the facility. They also take care of the marketing and public relations. Because this is a supervisory position, funeral service managers are responsible for the management of the staff.

Reading Recall

1. Name the four main career areas in personal care services.
2. What is *cosmetology*?
3. Describe the electrolysis process.
4. List four reasons people might want to use massage services.
5. What is a *CNA*?
6. What tasks might a personal assistant perform?
7. What is an *obituary*?
8. What do funeral directors do to help grieving families?

Common Aptitudes, Attitudes, and Skills

Workers in personal care services often share common aptitudes, attitudes, and skills (**Figure 12.3**). First and foremost, personal care services workers value and respect the people to whom they provide care services. They are empathetic and trustworthy, and keep the best interests of their clients in mind. This often demands that a sense of selflessness when caring for clients takes *precedence* (priority) over other demands and distractions.

Common Aptitudes, Attitudes, and Skills of Personal Care Services Workers	
• Empathetic	• Positive
• Selfless	• Creative
• Patient	• Energetic
• Respectful	• Compassionate
• Comforting	• Good listener
• Approachable	• Business sense
• Not easily riled	• Communication skills
• Trustworthy	• Time management skills
• Nonjudgmental	• Organizational skills

Figure 12.3 Personal care services workers share common aptitudes, attitudes, and skills. *What other aptitudes, attitudes, and skills would you add to this list?*

Copyright Goodheart-Willcox Co., Inc.

Cosmetologists and massage therapists have personal stamina, strength, and dexterity. They are creative and have good communication and time management skills. Personal care aides have energy, patience, and a sense of optimism. Having a sense of humor also helps when events or situations do not turn out exactly as planned. Personal care aides have excellent organizational skills. They need to know about their clients' stages of life and, if applicable, their clients' conditions. Funeral directors are compassionate and able to think clearly and offer support in times of stress. They are also good listeners, comforting, and nonjudgmental.

Large organizations within the personal care services industry attract employees with diverse skill levels; experience; and language, ethnic, and educational backgrounds. Workers in the industry value diversity in both their coworkers and customers. They must be energetic, approachable, and not easily *riled* (annoyed). They must have the attitude that the customer is already right, with the intent to serve his or her needs in the best way possible. At the same time, they should have business *acumen* (expertise). After all, personal care services is a service field.

Reading Recall

1. List three common aptitudes, attitudes, and skills of personal care services workers.

2. Why should personal care services workers be energetic, approachable, and not easily riled?

Education, Training, and Experience

The law requires cosmetologists, including those in hairstyling, skin care, and other personal appearance services, and massage therapists to be licensed (**Figure 12.4**). Cosmetologists and massage therapists are licensed by the state. Each state varies in its requirements for licensing.

In general, licensing requirements include at least a high school degree and completion of an approved training program. Each state requires a minimum number of hours of supervised experience and approved training. Many training programs are offered through postsecondary vocational schools that combine training and experience. Those who are interested in opening and running their own businesses would be well served to combine their cosmetology or massage therapy training with a business degree.

There is a wide range of educational requirements within the personal care services field. For example, personal care aides do not need an education beyond a high school diploma. Home health aides, however, need training and must pass a certification exam, such as the qualifying exam for CNAs. Many choose to obtain a college degree in an area, such

Monkey Business Images/Shutterstock.com

Figure 12.4 Hairdressers must be licensed, which usually requires at least a high school diploma, the completion of an approved training program, and a certain number of hours of supervised experience. *Why are specialized training and supervised experience important?*

as applied human biology or a nurse practitioner program, to become better qualified and more desirable in the marketplace. Training helps prepare caregivers to monitor vital signs, change bandages, safely move their clients, treat infections, or prepare specialized-diet meals. Home health aides are usually better paid than personal care aides because of their training (**Figure 12.5**).

Education and training requirements to become a funeral director vary by state. All states require at least a high school diploma and experience. Most require at least an associate's degree. Some require a bachelor's degree, usually in mortuary science. No matter what the educational requirement, most states require a one- or two-year apprenticeship, where skills are learned on-the-job. A passing score on the national board examination or individual state licensing exam is required in nearly all states.

Reading Recall

1. How are cosmetologists and massage therapists licensed?
2. What education and training do CNAs need?
3. What type of education is required to become a funeral director?

Copyright Goodheart-Willcox Co., Inc.

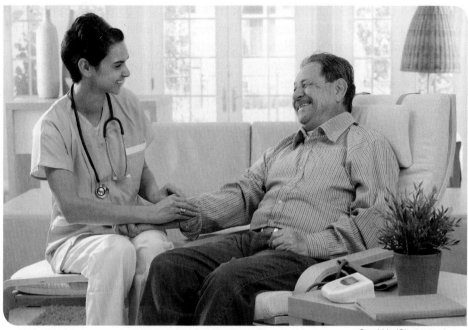

StockLite/Shutterstock.com

Figure 12.5 Home health aides are trained to monitor vital signs, such as blood pressure. *How can students interested in becoming home health aides gain experience in the field?*

Specialized Knowledge for Personal Care Services Careers

Specialized knowledge in personal care services is of utmost importance because these workers work so closely with their clients. Thus, specialized training, experience, and licensing are needed in most fields. Besides this technical knowledge, personal care services workers must also know their clients or customers. To be effective, they should demonstrate good customer service, use diligence in creating and protecting client records, and utilize technology to keep up-to-date in their fields. A large and growing segment of personal care services involves older adult care. Therefore, specialized knowledge in meeting the specific needs of older adults is required.

Demonstrating Good Customer Service

For personal care services workers, reputation is everything. A good reputation comes from providing skilled and knowledgeable services, while maintaining good relationships with customers or clients. This is known as good customer service. For example, when a customer asks a hairstylist to provide a new cut and color, the hairstylist will listen carefully to the client's description and desires. A personal care aide will accompany an older client to a medical check-up, listen carefully to the medical provider's instructions, take notes, and explain the information to the client.

Copyright Goodheart-Willcox Co., Inc.

Expert Insight

"One of the deep secrets of life is that all that is really worth doing is what we do for others."

Lewis Carroll, writer and mathematician

Good customer service comes in many forms. It comes from honest, ethical service provision. It comes from being reliable and trustworthy. It comes from listening to clients or customers so their needs can be effectively addressed. It comes from solving problems and resolving customer or client complaints. It means making the needs and desires of the customer or client a priority. These are all means of demonstrating good customer service using communication skills.

Professional image is another way to provide good customer service. Personal care services workers should appear appropriate for their work. Cosmetologists should appear stylish and fashion-forward (**Figure 12.6**). Personal care aides should be clean, well-groomed, and able to provide physical assistance, as they are often in close proximity to clients. Funeral directors should appear formal and respectful of their clients' needs during their grief and loss. Doing so builds a client's confidence in a personal care services worker's skills and abilities.

Lastly, professional behavior is critical to good customer service. Personal care services workers should always keep their relationships with customers and clients professional. Gossiping about other clients or customers, their family members and friends, or other coworkers is unacceptable and should always be avoided. Discussing political, religious, or other controversial topics should also be avoided unless the customer or client initiates it. Even in such cases, personal opinions or biases should be avoided, as relationships should be professional, not

antoniodiaz/Shutterstock.com

Figure 12.6 This barber projects a stylish professional image, which builds his clients' confidence in his skills and abilities. *What are some other ways personal care services workers can demonstrate good customer service?*

Copyright Goodheart-Willcox Co., Inc.

personal. Being unprofessional can break trust and damage the personal care services worker's reputation.

Although much of the communication between personal care services workers and their clients or customers happens face-to-face, services may also be provided over the phone or electronically via e-mail or social media. Extra care must be given to be friendly, helpful, and clear in communications because miscommunication may be more likely in these formats. The steps in **Figure 12.7** can help you demonstrate good customer service.

Creating and Protecting Client Records

When working with clients and customers, keeping accurate, up-to-date records is vital to effectively provide needed services. Cosmetologists and massage therapists keep records of their regular customers' wants, needs, and past treatments. Sometimes, therapeutic massage therapists may keep track of relevant medical conditions. Personal care aides use journals or notebooks for notes and symptom tracking and an organizer to keep track of appointments, medications, and medical conditions. Funeral service workers must also keep accurate and confidential records to meet the needs of their customers.

Some personal care services workers keep handwritten diaries or journals. Others use electronic devices to record and save important information. Documenting, saving, sharing, and retrieving records is crucial to providing effective personal care services.

Good recordkeeping can make the difference between a happy customer and an unhappy customer. For example, imagine how unhappy

Ten Steps to Good Customer Service

1. Be positive and friendly.
2. Remember, it is about the customer or client, not about you.
3. Calmly listen and restate the client's or customer's need, concern, or complaint.
4. Ask questions for clarification.
5. Read the client or customer to see what the underlying need or complaint might be.
6. Ask the customer or client how you can meet his or her needs or resolve the issue.
7. Offer your best solution, use your persuasion skills, and frequently communicate.
8. If the solution is not acceptable, patiently ask more clarifying questions and listen carefully.
9. Demonstrate tenacity in finding a solution and doing what needs to be done.
10. End the conversation with confirmed satisfaction (or as close to it as you can accomplish).

Figure 12.7 These steps can help personal care services workers demonstrate good customer service to their clients through all forms of communication. *What challenges might a personal care services worker face when communicating with a client?*

Copyright Goodheart-Willcox Co., Inc.

Pathway to Success

Greetings and Clients' First Impressions

First impressions are very important for businesses. The way you greet a potential or current client, whether it is on the phone or in person, makes a lasting impression. Many times, the first impression will be the deciding factor in whether a person will or will not want to do business with you.

How you greet clients will differ whether you are on the phone or talking face to face. The following are tips to use when greeting potential or current clients on the phone and in person.

On the phone, you want to be

- pleasant. Listeners tend to mirror the emotional state of speakers. If you are pleasant, the customer is likely to be pleasant, too. To help you be pleasant, smile, breathe deeply, pull your shoulders back, and look straight ahead. Simple body language creates emotional states.

- sincere and natural. Keep the greeting simple, like "XYZ Company, this is John. How may I direct your call?" Stating the company name lets customers know they contacted the right place.

- brief. Long greetings are not professional, and are more likely to waste the client's time.

In person, you want to

- project professionalism. You are in charge of giving the first impression to the client.

- greet all visitors loudly and clearly. Do not mumble so people have to ask what you said.

- ask for the visitor's name. Note the pronunciation so you will say the name correctly.

- ask visitors who their appointment is with. If there is a wait, keep the visitor informed. Say something, such as, "Mr. Fox will be with you shortly." Offering a glass of water or a cup of tea may help ease any frustration your waiting visitor may have.

- know the lay of the land. Be able to give clear and precise directions to clients so they can easily find restrooms, water fountains, and offices.

- keep your cool. Remaining calm keeps customers calm as well.

- know when to ask for help. One person cannot always get the job done, so ask for help when needed.

Role-Play Greeting Clients and Prospective Clients

With a partner, use the tips above to practice greeting clients on both the phone and in person. Take turns being the receptionist or business owner who answers the phone or greets the clients as they come into a business.

Decide before you start what type of business you will be representing, as well as the business name. As the client, come up with a list of questions you want to ask. These

may relate to hours of operation, location of and directions to the business, or cost of services.

After both you and your partner practice your greetings, discuss your performances. What type of impression were you giving? Consider what each one of you could do differently and what you would not change about each other's greetings.

Copyright Goodheart-Willcox Co., Inc.

a regular customer might be if a cosmetologist used the wrong hair color dye because the formula was recorded incorrectly (**Figure 12.8**). In some cases, inaccurate recordkeeping could prove fatal, such as in the case of a medication overdose. A grieving family may experience undue hardship if customer wants and needs are not recorded and followed correctly.

Personal care services workers must be especially careful in recordkeeping and should be aware of needed forms and processes. When taking on a new client, careful notes should be included on client intake forms so the personal care services worker can both understand and properly attend to the client's needs. Personal care services workers must maintain progress reports on client needs so other caregivers can step in and provide services. Examples of other forms workers fill out may include assisted living qualification, special needs assessment, insurance claim, and government assistance forms.

Keeping accurate and confidential records is just a good business practice. Sometimes, however, such as in the case of health or medical records, the law requires it. Personal care services providers are legally responsible to keep services provided and records confidential. Providers can share this information with others only if the client or customer explicitly gives permission in written form.

Using Technology to Provide Good Personal Care Services

Working with people, as personal care services workers do on a daily basis, requires a willingness to learn new techniques and improve

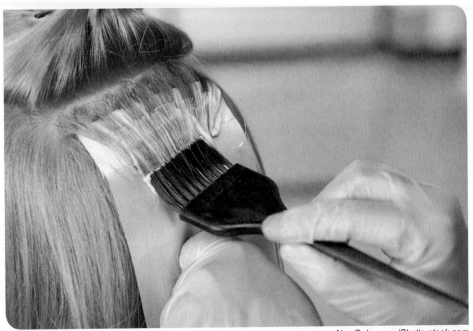

Figure 12.8 Good recordkeeping is important at a hair salon because the cosmetologist needs to know the correct coloring formula for his or her client. *How would you react if you went to your regular hairstylist and the wrong hair color was used because of poor recordkeeping?*

Alex Oakenman/Shutterstock.com

Law and Ethics   *Telling the Truth*

For personal care services workers, especially those who are running small businesses, marketing and advertising their services is key to business success. All forms of media, from telemarketing to websites to printed flyers, can be used to market and advertise offered services. Careful consideration, however, must be given to these marketing and advertising methods to ensure all claims are truthful, are not deceptive, and do not break the law.

In the US, the Federal Trade Commission (FTC) regulates and administers laws concerning the legal marketing and advertising of services and products. Although there are many aspects of the laws concerning fair trade, these particular knowledge points are especially useful to small personal care services businesses:

- Advertising must be truthful, accurate, and not misleading.
- Claims about services or products must be provable or verified.
- All marketing activities must be legal and not harmful.
- Products sold must be labeled correctly and accurately.
- Laws for telemarketing must be followed.
- Special care must be taken if advertising to children.
- Special promotions, including company donations to charities, must be completed.
- Service providers are responsible for carrying out their claims.
- Advertised or quoted prices must be honored and may not include hidden costs.

Research Activity

Using the FTC website, add five more points to those listed above. Use your research results to respond to the following questions:

1. According to the FTC, what makes an advertisement unfair?
2. According to guidelines the FTC issues, what makes an advertisement deceptive?
3. What should small business owners know about using SPAM in an e-mail campaign?
4. What should small business owners know about the Do Not Call Registry?

skills. Those who do not improve their skills fall behind and become less skilled and, subsequently, less sought out. For example, a cosmetologist should keep up with the latest hair dyes, treatments, and trends. Massage therapists should keep current in techniques and trends. Personal care aides should keep up-to-date with the various medications, treatments, mobility devices, or therapies recommended for their clients so they can serve as advocates. Funeral directors should keep current on available resources for grieving families.

Many of the changes in personal care services during the recent past decades have involved technology. Communications and data and record management are two areas technology impacts most. For example, hairstylists might provide a "virtual makeover" for a client before delivering an actual haircut. In this example, technology helps the customer and service provider better communicate with each other.

Technology continues to impact the quality and effectiveness of other services that personal care services workers provide, too. Robotics can help personal care aides provide care. Electronically timed pill dispensers can help older adults manage their medications and even notify caregivers

Copyright Goodheart-Willcox Co., Inc.

if a dosage is missed. Medical devices that improve mobility or lift clients physically can greatly improve the daily activities of personal care services workers (**Figure 12.9**). Digital communications can make face-to-face contact feasible, even when clients and personal care services workers are not physically near each other.

Technology can also help personal care services workers have a greater impact in their communities. For example, websites and other social media can be used to advertise and promote services offered, provide contact information, show a map or location, provide photographs of work done, or even offer online booking of services. Social media can be used to promote or highlight services available to potential customers or clients. Even though personal care services are very people-oriented careers, new and emerging technology can serve to enhance relationships and the services personal care services workers provide.

Understanding Special Needs in Older Adult Care

Older adults, especially those 80 years of age and older, often need personal care services workers to work with them. This is because people begin to "slow down" as they progress through older adulthood. Chronic illnesses may become debilitating. Health may decline dramatically. Older adults may need help with daily care. As for cognitive changes, forgetfulness and confusion may occur. Of course, not all older adults require personal care assistance. Some remain just as active and alert as

martin bowra/Shutterstock.com

Figure 12.9 This personal care services worker is operating special medical equipment that physically lifts her client, a child with disabilities, into a wheelchair. *What other ways can technology help personal care services workers provide good care?*

Copyright Goodheart-Willcox Co., Inc.

they were in previous years. Many, however, need personal care services workers to help them with grooming, relaxation, daily living, and end-of-life care (**Figure 12.10**). Understanding older adults' needs is important because this population is growing.

Physical Needs

Changes in physical appearance and functioning are common for many older adults. Older adults become shorter in stature or height, as they experience cartilage loss in their vertebrae. Muscle tissue and body weight decrease. Muscles give body firmness. As loss occurs, older bodies often sag. The loss also affects range of motion. Movements become slower. Physical activities, such as strengthening exercises, can slow this process, improving both physical appearance and abilities. Other signs of aging cannot be seen externally, as internal body organs age and lose some efficiency of their functions.

Sensory changes also continue throughout older adulthood. **Presbyopia**, a slow decrease in the eye's ability to see objects that are close, progressively worsens. Small print becomes difficult to read without holding a book at arm's length. Headaches and eye strain may occur. Other vision conditions also develop.

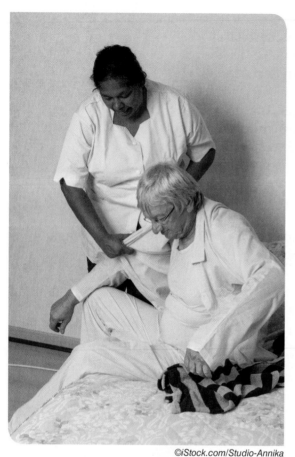

©iStock.com/Studio-Annika

Figure 12.10 Many older adults, such as this man, need personal care services workers to help with daily activities, including getting dressed. *What other types of support do personal care services workers provide to older adults?*

With age, hearing loss typically occurs, too. Many older adults complain of hearing a ringing sound in their ears, called **tinnitus**. Hearing changes can make communication difficult, as listening and deciphering messages from others become problematic. Hearing loss can also lead to increased feelings of isolation from family and friends. These feelings may then lead to depression. Other sensory changes include a decrease in the senses of taste and smell, along with less sensitivity to pain, touch, heat, and cold.

Nutrition and fitness remain important for promoting good health and slowing progression of muscle strength and bone loss. As in any other stage of life, proper nutrition is vital to maintaining health. The body's ability to absorb certain nutrients decreases in older adulthood. Older adults may need to take dietary supplements to ensure they are meeting nutritional needs. Physical fitness achieved through activity is also important to maintain health in any stage of life (**Figure 12.11**).

Copyright Goodheart-Willcox Co., Inc.

beeboys/Shutterstock.com

Figure 12.11 Walking is one way to achieve physical fitness, which is especially important throughout the lifespan. *In what kinds of physical fitness activities do you currently participate?*

Cognitive and Social Needs

How aging affects each person's cognitive abilities will, of course, vary among individuals. Brain processing is impacted because the brain is shrinking in older adulthood. As a result, older adults may have more trouble processing new information, recalling memories, and concentrating. Adults may also have more trouble moving from one task to the next. A decline in cognitive abilities can affect the ability to learn. The rate of cognitive decline, however, is much slower and less dramatic than previously thought, especially for active and healthy adults.

The need for love, acceptance, and companionship extends into older adulthood. Depression is common in older adults, as work and family roles change, and physical abilities decrease. These changes may be seen as losses. Intense sadness, pessimism, and hopelessness may follow. Loss of friends and family members increases these feelings. Feelings of depression can also increase if independence and control are lost, financial resources are scarce, or familial and social interactions are reduced.

Specialized Health Needs

Special needs in older adulthood vary. Many special needs are related to physical ailments, as the body is declining in ability. In addition to medications, adults may need to make other lifestyle adjustments to accommodate for changes. For example, adults with osteoporosis may need a walking aid. Cognitive changes require other treatments.

In older adulthood, dementia is common. **Dementia** is a term used to describe cognitive declines and memory loss. Damage to the brain causes the cognitive declines and memory loss. Dementia impairs a person's ability to perform everyday tasks, such as getting dressed, cleaning, eating, and remembering where items are placed. Not all older adults, however, suffer from dementia.

Copyright Goodheart-Willcox Co., Inc.

Memory loss for those with dementia differs from normal forgetfulness. Older adults can confuse words and meanings. This interferes with communication. As dementia continues, older adults can become frustrated. They may display irritability and even personality changes. A caregiver may need to help with daily functions and make changes to a living environment to improve safety.

Whereas dementia is a slow decline in abilities, **Alzheimer's disease** is a progressive brain disorder including, not only memory loss, but also progressively severe confusion. People with Alzheimer's disease may not be able to recall past life events. They may also forget where they are, how they got there, and how to leave. Eventually, they have trouble speaking or recognizing family and friends. Personal care services workers are critical to the health and well-being of those suffering from Alzheimer's disease.

Reading Recall

1. List at least 5 of the 10 steps to good customer service.
2. Describe the professional image that cosmetologists, personal care aides, and funeral directors should project.
3. What is one way technology can help a hairstylist better communicate with his or her client?
4. Name three outward physical changes that typically occur in older adulthood.
5. How does Alzheimer's disease differ from age-related dementia?

Rewards, Demands, and Future Trends

Careers as personal care services workers can be very rewarding. Providing personal care services can be exciting, fast-paced, and ever-changing. Strong and meaningful relationships can form between the personal care services worker and the client or customer. In many situations, help is offered to some of the most vulnerable humans. The work is meaningful. It is easy to see how efforts can make a difference on another person's quality of life on a daily, and even on an hourly, basis. In addition to being meaningful work, personal care services are greatly needed.

On the other hand, personal care services work can be quite demanding. Many jobs in the field are entry-level positions that do not pay a lot. Personal care services workers must often work long hours, many of which are standing on their feet. At times, they must deal with difficult clients or customers. Even so, many in the field report that one of the things they enjoy most about their job is the people interaction.

The job outlook continues to be very good for personal care services workers (**Figure 12.12**). Projected growth for many positions is expected to occur faster than average. Whether a person needs a haircut, a massage, help with daily living skills, or help when navigating end-of-life issues,

Copyright Goodheart-Willcox Co., Inc.

Future Trends for Personal Care Services Careers				
Occupation	**Projected Growth (2014–2024)**	**Projected Job Openings (2014–2024)**	**Median Wages (2014)**	**Education**
Certified nursing assistant (CNA)	Much faster than average (14% or higher)	599,000	$25,100	Postsecondary certificate
Cosmetologist	Faster than average (9–13%)	212,100	$23,120	Postsecondary certificate
Embalmer	Decline (–2% or lower)	800	$41,720	Associate's degree
Funeral attendant	Little or no change (–1–1%)	7,900	$23,080	High school diploma
Funeral director	Average (5–8%)	8,900	$47,250	Associate's degree
Funeral service manager	Slower than average (2–4%)	7,400	$68,870	Associate's degree
Home health aide	Much faster than average (14% or higher)	554,800	$21,380	High school diploma
Massage therapist	Much faster than average (14% or higher)	49,000	$37,180	Postsecondary certificate
Nail technician	Faster than average (9–13%)	20,600	$19,620	Unspecified
Personal assistant	Average (5–8%)	26,900	$21,500	High school diploma
Personal care aide	Much faster than average (14% or higher)	601,100	$20,440	High school diploma
Skin care specialist	Faster than average (9–13%)	10,900	$29,050	Postsecondary certificate

Sources: O*NET and the *Occupational Outlook Handbook*

Figure 12.12 Learning as much as possible about careers can help you make informed career decisions. *According to the information in this chart, which personal care services professions are predicted to have the most job openings in the near future?*

people will always need people. These needs will not go away. In fact, they may even continue to grow.

Reading Recall

1. Describe rewards of personal care services careers.
2. Describe demands of personal care services careers.
3. Describe future trends in personal care services.
4. Identify two careers in personal care services in which projected growth is expected to occur much faster than average.

Copyright Goodheart-Willcox Co., Inc.

Summary

- *Cosmetologists* enhance a client's appearance. *Massage therapists* manipulate muscles and soft tissues on clients. *Personal care aides* deal with the daily tasks of people with special needs, disabilities, and chronic illnesses. *Funeral service workers* oversee details pertaining to a person's death.
- Personal care services workers often possess good communication, time management, and organizational skills. Having a reputation for warmth, compassion, and a desire to serve is important in personal care services.
- The career opportunities in the personal care services field and the educational requirements vary greatly. Many personal care services careers require licenses or certifications.
- Specialized knowledge for personal care services is extremely important. Specialized training, experience, and licensing are needed in most fields. Personal care services workers also must know their clients or customers.
- Good customer service is providing skilled and knowledgeable services, while maintaining good relationships with customers or clients.
- Keeping accurate, up-to-date client records is vital to effectively provide needed services. Personal care services providers are legally responsible to keep services provided and records confidential.
- Technology impacts the quality and effectiveness of services that personal care services workers provide.
- Older adults have changes in physical appearance and functioning and more trouble processing information and concentrating. They need love, acceptance, and companionship. Many specialized health needs are related to physical ailments.
- In addition to being meaningful work, personal care services are greatly needed. The need for other people will not go away. It will continue to grow, however, as people have fewer extended family options.

College and Career Portfolio

Portfolio Standardized Test Scores

For college portfolios and some career portfolios, you may be asked to provide your standardized test scores. *Standardized tests* are national tests that assess your education level in general subjects, such as math, science, reading, and writing.

Standardized tests vary by state and region. They are administered and scored in a "standard" way. Types of standardized tests include the

- ACT;
- PSAT; and
- SAT.

To obtain your test scores, complete the following activities:

1. Determine which, if any, standardized test scores you need to include in your portfolio. If you are unsure, ask your teacher or a guidance counselor.
2. Research the steps for requesting your standardized test scores.
3. Submit the request or set a date to submit it, based on the deadline for your portfolio. Request your scores well in advance of when they are needed.

Copyright Goodheart-Willcox Co., Inc.

Review and Reflect

1. Personal care services careers include many diverse professions. What is the main factor these careers have in common?

2. Cosmetologists can specialize in fields. Name two of the specialties.

3. List three places massage therapists might work.

4. What is the difference between the duties of a *personal care aide* and those of a *home health aide*?

5. Explain some of the duties of funeral service workers and identify under which position these duties are performed.

6. Make a list of personal characteristics and skills found in people who work in personal care services careers.

7. Which job in the personal care services industry usually requires a one- or two-year apprenticeship? Why does it require this?

8. Explain why reputation is so important in the field of personal care services.

9. Why is it important to keep accurate and confidential records as a personal care services worker?

10. How can websites and social media be used to help personal care services workers have a greater impact in their communities?

11. Define *Alzheimer's disease*. List the signs and symptoms of someone with this disease.

12. Why are personal care services workers so important to society?

Vocabulary Activities

13. **Key terms**   With a partner, use the Internet to locate photos or graphics depicting the following terms. Print the graphics or use presentation software to show your graphics to the class, describing how they depict the meanings of the terms.

Alzheimer's disease	embalming
cosmetology	obituary
dementia	presbyopia
electrology	tinnitus
electrolysis	

14. **Academic terms**   Work with a partner to write the definitions of the following terms, based on your current understanding before reading the chapter. Team up with another pair to discuss your definitions and any discrepancies. Finally, discuss the definitions with the class. Ask your instructor for necessary correction or clarification.

acumen	precedence
dispense	riled

Self-Assessment Quiz

Complete the self-assessment quiz online to help you practice and expand your knowledge and skills.

Critical Thinking

15. **Draw conclusions**   Many people believe cosmetologists talk with their clients. What would happen if the cosmetologists took the information they learned and gossiped about it with other clients?

16. **Compare and contrast**   Compare and contrast the tasks a personal assistant might perform with the tasks a home health aide might perform. Explain which tasks are similar and which tasks are different.

17. **Make inferences**   Describe how funeral directors help grieving families through a difficult time in their lives. From what you know, do all funeral directors provide the same services, or do some give additional services, based on the towns in which they work? Explain.

18. **Determine**   When working with people, you also work with various attitudes and personalities. Determine what you would do if you were working with a client who was being rude and difficult. How would you maintain a professional attitude?

19. **Analyze**   Analyze the differences in the education or training required for a cosmetologist, a home health aide, and a funeral director.

20. **Identify**   Identify three examples of good customer service and three examples of bad customer service. Be specific in your details.

21. **Cause and effect**   Why do you need to protect clients' personal information? What would happen if your clients' information was compromised? How can you prevent this from happening?

Core Skills

22. **Research** Cosmetologists need to charge their clients for their services. The prices of their services are based on different factors. These may include the costs of their stalls, the towns in which they work, and the average prices others in the area charge. Taking this information into account, identify what you would charge for a haircut, a shampoo and style, and a haircut with a shampoo and style in a small town, a medium-sized town, and a large town. Justify your answers.

23. **Writing, speaking, and listening** Invite a funeral director to come to class to discuss what he or she does for grieving families. Create a list of questions to ask the speaker. Write a thank-you letter after the visit. Send it to the funeral director.

24. **Research and writing** Research what information is contained in an obituary. Write your personal obituary, as if you died in your late 90s. Be sure to include some of your accomplishments and who you are leaving behind.

25. **Research, listening, and speaking** Research personal care services careers to discover which careers in this field interest you. Select the career that interests you the most and arrange an informational interview to learn about the preparation requirements, job duties and responsibilities, and potential for advancement. Create a list of questions prior to the interview. Share your findings with the class.

26. **Reading, speaking, writing, and listening** Create a role-playing activity using the careers found in the chapter. Assign roles. Provide information each person might need to carry out his or her role successfully. These roles might include a specific career, a client, a bystander or an observer, and other people to fill in needed roles. Recruit four to five people who are willing to take the role-playing information cards and present a skit to the class. Have your classmates grade the role-play scenario as having all information needed to complete the project, or discuss what other information needs to be included.

27. **Research, writing, and technology** Create a TV or radio commercial for one of the careers listed in the chapter. You may need to research what information needs to go into a commercial and how long the commercial needs to be before writing the script for your commercial. Record your commercial and present it to the class.

28. **Research, reading, and writing** Locate in your local library a book on how to communicate or how to improve your communication skills. Read the book. Write a book report explaining what you learned and how you can implement it in your life.

29. **Research and writing** Research the specific requirements for licensure in your state for cosmetologists and massage therapists. Are there other personal care services careers that require licensure? If so, what are the requirements? Create a poster to share this information with your classmates.

30. **Writing** Identify some of the information a cosmetologist or massage therapist might keep in a client record. Using this information, create an electronic form a cosmetologist could use in his or her job. This could then be placed in your portfolio.

31. **Research** Research technological improvements being used in the personal care fields that have changed over the last 25 years. What improvements have been made? How have these advances helped workers in this field do their jobs?

32. **Writing, technology, speaking, and listening** Create a how-to demonstration relating to personal care services that you will present to the class. Create a list of supplies you will need, as well as any handouts. Make copies of the handouts for your audience. Present your how-to demonstration using step-by-step procedures. After the lesson, get feedback from your "students" on what went well about your lesson and what needs to be improved. After receiving your feedback, write a one-page summary describing what you did and how you would change your demonstration lesson the next time you presented it.

Copyright Goodheart-Willcox Co., Inc.

33. **CTE career readiness practice**   Search the Internet for new and emerging technologies that may affect personal care services. Choose one of interest. Determine the following: What are the benefits of using the technology to enhance productivity? What are some disadvantages or risks of using the new technology? What actions could you take to mitigate the disadvantages or risks? In your opinion, for what applications will this new technology most likely be used? Create a digital report to share your findings with the class.

34. **CTE career readiness practice**   Imagine you are a personal care aide. Your interpersonal skills—your ability to listen, speak, and empathize— are a great asset in working with clients. Lilly is your latest client. She was recently diagnosed with osteoporosis. Lilly now has several new medicines she has to take. Unfortunately, Lilly has trouble remembering when to take her medicines and how many she should take. What would you recommend Lilly do to help her remember to take the correct amount of medication at the right time?

Lend a Hand

Providing Personal Care

There are many opportunities to provide personal care to people in need. Nursing homes, residential care facilities, and hospitals have volunteer opportunities to provide residents and patients some friendly care and interaction. Some homeless shelters, women's shelters, and group homes may have similar opportunities.

Giving a manicure, washing and styling hair, applying makeup, or providing foot care are all great ways to make someone feel special. Sometimes residents in these facilities do not get many visitors, so simply providing them with companionship can be very meaningful.

If you are not comfortable with or skilled in providing personal care, there are still ways you can help. Most shelters are always in need of donations. You could organize a drive for personal care items. Sometimes facilities have a "wish list" for donations posted on their websites. Examples of items to collect might include shampoo and conditioner, lip balm, lotion, soap or body wash, toothpaste and toothbrushes, and deodorant. Remember that these donations should be new, unopened items.

To find out how you can assist in providing personal care to people in need, complete the following:

1. Think about how you can help provide personal care. Are you skilled at doing makeup? Would you like to give a manicure or brush someone's hair for them? Would you prefer just to talk and make a new friend? Are you skilled at organizing projects and getting others involved? Consider how to best apply your skills.

2. Research how you can get involved in your local community. Research nursing homes, group homes, residential care facilities, and shelters in your area. Use print and online resources to learn about the volunteer programs at these places or what types of donations they need.

3. Choose one of the opportunities for service. Try it out.

Unit 4

Exploring Human Services Related Careers

america365/Shutterstock.com

Registered Dietitian Nutritionist (RDN)

Mateo Villanueva

I am a registered dietitian nutritionist in a large university hospital. As a clinical dietitian, I am an expert in nutrition. My specialty is in the care and feeding of cancer patients.

On an average day, I usually begin by answering and sending e-mails and generally taking stock of the day ahead. I plan and organize my day by reviewing the patient charts and status. Then, I'm ready to start my "rounds." These are patient visits and consultations with medical staff. My pager keeps me moving from consult to consult. While on rounds, the pace can sometimes be hurried, but I always take time to keep thorough records of each patient.

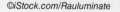
©iStock.com/Rauluminate

If any of my patients are being discharged, I need to allot extra time for consulting with the patient, his or her family, and the community dietitian who will be monitoring the patient after discharge. For example, one of my patients had surgery and chemotherapy for cancer of the stomach, can only manage liquids, and needs to be fed by tube. She is also diabetic. This further complicates matters. I need to make sure she fully understands her dietary needs because she lives alone. I'm currently working with a social worker to find a home health aide who can provide support services.

Another important aspect of my job involves participating in staff problem solving and consultations. A team of doctors, nurses, therapists, social workers, and other specialists reviews cases together. These sessions are invigorating. Our team works together to provide the best care and treatment for our patients. When a new patient health issue challenges one of us, another usually has some experience or insight to share.

I am really proud of my profession. Dietitians help people in a very tangible way. As a registered dietitian, I have many career options open to me. There are always new procedures to learn, research ideas to apply, drug therapies to explore, and patients who present new and unique challenges.

Research Activity

Conduct online research to find out more about a possible career as a registered dietitian. What are the educational requirements for becoming a dietitian? In what types of settings can dietitians work? What is the projected job outlook for this occupation? After completing your research, determine whether or not you would be interested in pursuing this as a career. Why or why not?

Copyright Goodheart-Willcox Co., Inc.

Chapter 13

Entrepreneurial Careers in Human Services

While studying, look for the activity icon ↗ to

- **practice** key and academic terms with e-flash cards and matching activities;
- **assess** what you learn by completing self-assessment quizzes; and
- **reinforce** what you learn by mapping concepts and completing review and reflect questions.

www.g-wlearning.com/humanservices/

©iStock.com/gpointstudio

Learning Outcomes

After studying this chapter, you will be able to

- **compare and contrast** career opportunities for entrepreneurial human services workers;
- **list** common aptitudes, attitudes, and skills of entrepreneurial human services workers;
- **give examples** of postsecondary education, training, and experience required for several entrepreneurial human services careers;
- **summarize** how a potential entrepreneur might analyze the potential strengths, weaknesses, opportunities, and threats for the prospective business;
- **describe** what to include in the different sections of a business plan; and
- **summarize** the rewards, demands, and future trends of careers in entrepreneurial human services.

Reading Strategies

Before reading, use online or print resources to find an article discussing entrepreneurial opportunities in the field of human services. Read the article and then this chapter. As you are reading, be sure to take notes. After reading, compare your notes about the article with your notes from the chapter. Assess how the article is similar to or different from this chapter. Do the article and this chapter contain similar information? Do the authors use different writing styles? Write a summary of your findings.

Mapping Concepts

As you are reading, arrange your notes into a list of considerations for entrepreneurial careers in human services. Your list should include all the major points covered in this chapter. Also, include annotations briefly describing why each consideration is important.

Considerations for Entrepreneurial Careers in Human Services

Key Terms

business license
business plan
competitive analysis
contractors
cooperative
corporation
cottage industry
entrepreneur
executive summary

freelancers
life coaching
limited liability company (LLC)
market analysis
partnership
S corporation
sole proprietorship
SWOT analysis
target market

Academic Terms

innovative
levy
replete

An **entrepreneur** is a person who starts and runs his or her own business. Human services careers readily lend themselves to self-run business opportunities. As entrepreneurs, self-employed human services workers decide which products or services to provide. They also decide how, when, and at what cost to provide them.

Entrepreneurs assume the responsibilities and risks for their own businesses. They generally work very hard, especially in the start-up phase. They also enjoy the flexibility of setting their own schedules. There can be great potential for financial reward. Entrepreneurship also has a potential for financial risk, however. For those who are willing to take the risk, all areas of human services are well-suited to self-run businesses because they offer services people need and want (**Figure 13.1**).

Careers in Entrepreneurial Human Services

The opportunities are endless for careers in entrepreneurial human services. **Figure 13.2** shows some examples of entrepreneurial opportunities in each of the career pathways in human services. There are also many other opportunities waiting to be conceived by those willing to take a risk and forge a new path.

One type of entrepreneurial work in the broad field of human services involves freelance or contract work. Freelancers and contractors offer services to employers. They are not, however, legally employees. **Freelancers** are small business owners who offer their services to larger

Monkey Business Images/Shutterstock.com

Figure 13.1 Entrepreneurs work very hard, but they can work when and where they want. *In what ways would you consider entrepreneurship to be rewarding?*

Copyright Goodheart-Willcox Co., Inc.

Examples of Entrepreneurial Human Services Careers	
Consumer services	• Broker • Consumer advocate • Mortgage lender • Personal financial planner • Personal shopper • Personal stylist • Undercover shopper
Counseling and mental health services	• Counselor • Life coach • Therapist
Early childhood development and services	• In-home child care provider • Parent educator • Self-employed nanny
Family and community services	• Camp director • Coach • Counselor • Instructor • Recreational specialist • Recreational therapist • Tour leader • Trainer
Personal care services	• Domestic worker • Household manager • Landscape designer • Landscape worker • Personal fitness trainer • Personal grooming services worker

Figure 13.2 There are many different entrepreneurial career opportunities in human services. *Which of these careers would you like to learn more about?*

organizations for a fee. Their product is the service they provide, such as a psychologist who provides consultant services for a group home. **Contractors** are temporary employees. They are independent and can experience the rewards of self-employment. At the same time, they enjoy stable pay and benefits for a set period of time. For example, a company might hire a grant writer as a contractor to prepare a specific grant. When the grant is finished, the job ends.

A company can benefit from using freelancers and contractors. By hiring a freelancer or contractor, the company does not have to hire a permanent employee and pay additional payroll burdens. Also, the company does not have to keep someone on the payroll longer than needed. Freelancers and contractors can provide professional services scaled to the needs of the company.

Copyright Goodheart-Willcox Co., Inc.

In addition to freelance and contract work, other creative human services self-run business ventures are common. There is often a better or more *innovative* (new; original) way of offering human services. Some of these prospects may have lower barriers to entry (cost). Therefore, the investment is minimal.

Consumer Services

Entrepreneurial careers in consumer services tend to focus on providing services, creating products that influence consumers, or educating consumers (**Figure 13.3**). Human services workers who are freelancers, consultants, and small business owners can be found in every area of consumer services. They support consumer needs from technology training to serving as consumer advocates. Most of these jobs can be found in corporations, government agencies, and sometimes even nonprofit organizations. Some consumer services careers lend themselves more readily to self-run businesses.

Personal financial planners may choose to work for themselves as consultants or self-employed advisors, rather than for large corporations. For many, after building relationships with clients in a corporate setting, they choose to venture out on their own. Sometimes, this is a more profitable endeavor. It may offer an opportunity to build deeper relationships and personalize service, with less emphasis on quantity of relationships.

Mortgage lenders and *brokers* often choose to be self-employed. Rather than working for one lending institution, they represent many. This

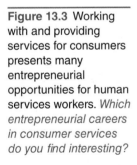

Figure 13.3 Working with and providing services for consumers presents many entrepreneurial opportunities for human services workers. *Which entrepreneurial careers in consumer services do you find interesting?*

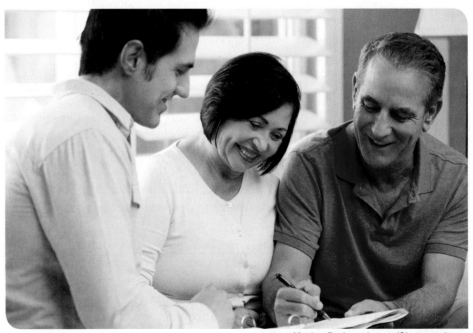

Monkey Business Images/Shutterstock.com

Copyright Goodheart-Willcox Co., Inc.

affords them the opportunity to find the best mortgage loans for their customers.

Personal shoppers and *personal stylists* help their clients create a personal fashion brand by purchasing fashion items meeting their needs. *Consumer advocates* may specialize in helping consumers make good car buying decisions. Others may work as consultants to evaluate customer service as *undercover shoppers*. They may write blogs, post video reviews, create trends, and influence buying through social media. Personal shoppers and consumer advocates work in every product and service industry.

Counseling and Mental Health Services

Counseling and mental health services workers often choose to offer their services as independent, self-employed counselors and therapists. Start-up costs are relatively low in this area. These workers mostly need private, professional space and, sometimes, administrative support. Some self-employed counselors and therapists may rely on word-of-mouth advertising. Many, however, choose to include advertising, promotion, and continuing education in their business budgets.

Life coaches are a relatively new career option. **Life coaching** is the practice of assisting clients to determine and achieve their life goals (**Figure 13.4**). Life coaches may help their clients overcome fears (for example, public speaking or travel), learn new skills (such as writing for social media), or find a job. Sometimes, life coaches focus on a specific personal area. This area might be weight management or healthy eating. Other life coaches may specialize in household organization, such as organizing closets and cabinets.

Figure 13.4 Life coaches might consult with their clients to help them learn new skills, such as using technology, or focus on other personal life goals. *What benefits can life coaches offer to their clients?*

Kinga/Shutterstock.com

Copyright Goodheart-Willcox Co., Inc.

Life coaches partner with clients to help them reach their goals and, ultimately, lead a fulfilling life through all the expected ups and downs. Life coaches do not focus on mental health issues and are not licensed therapists. Rather, their focus is on clients' personal and work-life issues and goals.

Early Childhood Development and Services

Entrepreneurial opportunities exist in all areas of early childhood development and services. These areas include preschools, child care centers, and nanny services. Most early childhood services began as small, self-run businesses—even those that are nationally known today.

One of the most common types of entrepreneurial careers in early childhood development and services is *in-home child care*. Many successful people have started in-home child care businesses. These businesses must be licensed and meet certain standards the state establishes. Entrepreneurs in early childhood care and education often develop close relationships with the children and parents they serve (**Figure 13.5**). As a business, in-home child care can be financially sound.

Another common type of entrepreneurial career in early childhood development and services is *self-employed nannies*. Self-employed nannies usually work for only one family. They are paid directly rather than through a nanny employment service. In many communities, nanny broker or referral services have been born from these small beginnings.

Duplass/Shutterstock.com

Figure 13.5 Entrepreneurs who start in-home child care businesses typically enjoy working with young children and often develop close relationships with their clients. *How can students interested in in-home child care gain experience in the field?*

Copyright Goodheart-Willcox Co., Inc.

Parent educators are also often self-employed. They may work as consultants. These educators might offer workshops and training to expectant parents, current parents, or guardians. Parent educators may offer their services to hospitals, community centers, places of worship, schools, or even to individuals as private coaches.

Family and Community Services

Family and community services range across all human needs and desires. One area in particular offers vast entrepreneurial opportunities. This area is *recreational services*. Many workers in this field are self-employed or small business owners. They offer their services to customers in creative ways.

All people are familiar with recreational activities. Hiking, swimming, reading, shopping, playing team sports, drawing, and dancing are just some of the endless recreational activities people pursue in their nonworking hours. Recreation is a fast-growing industry. As the population ages, more people may have time to commit to these activities. This is good news for *recreational services workers*. They base their careers on organizing and providing recreational activities for people.

Positions in recreational services include coaches, trainers, camp directors, tour leaders, and recreational specialists (**Figure 13.6**). These recreational services workers provide people with opportunities for leisure time enjoyment. They arrange recreational programs, offer coaching services, and provide or staff instructional workshops. They hold a variety of positions at different levels of responsibility. These positions include managers, directors, instructors, counselors, and even recreational therapists. Recreational services workers also work in a wide variety of settings. These settings include gyms, senior centers, community centers, schools, government agencies, hospitals, cruise ships, and camps.

Personal passions and hobbies often lead a person into a career in recreational services. Those who enjoy certain sports and activities may become experts and serve as instructors or tour event leaders. Mountain and water sports, such as climbing, hiking, SCUBA, and rafting, have created whole industries for entrepreneurs.

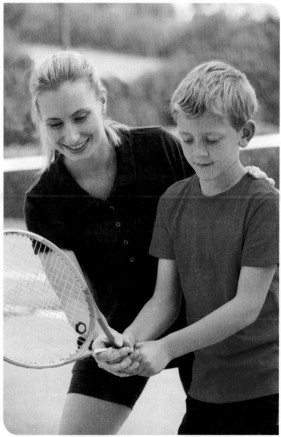

SpeedKingz/Shutterstock.com

Figure 13.6 This tennis coach is giving a lesson to a student. Recreational services workers can work at community centers, schools, or camps. *What are some other settings in which recreational services workers can work?*

Copyright Goodheart-Willcox Co., Inc.

Personal Care Services

There are many entrepreneurial opportunities in the personal care services career field. These are up close and personal services people need every day. For example, *personal grooming services workers* tend to focus their work on hair and skin care. These professionals often work independently as small business owners. They may lease space in salons, barbershops, cosmetic stores, department stores, and fitness clubs. They may choose, instead, to remain independent providers.

Personal fitness trainers may work in a number of corporate settings. They can also be self-employed. Personal fitness trainers work one-on-one with their clients to help them meet health and fitness goals (**Figure 13.7**). They devise physical activity plans based on their clients' needs, and then guide and motivate their clients to achieve their fitness goals. They also help their clients work on dietary goals. Personal fitness trainers usually work in a private gym or club, but may also provide services in their clients' homes.

Another opportunity for self-employment in personal care services involves domestic services. *Domestic workers* provide services within their employers' homes or places of business. Services primarily involve cleaning, de-cluttering, sanitizing, and overseeing of maintenance. In home environments, these workers may also provide cooking, shopping, laundry, or other domestic services. In large households, *household managers* are employed to oversee domestic workers. Their job is typically administrative.

©iStock.com/michaeljung

Figure 13.7 Personal fitness trainers help their clients achieve health, fitness, and dietary goals. *Where do personal fitness trainers usually work?*

Large businesses and corporations sometimes employ domestic workers. The field is *replete* (filled) with entrepreneurs. Home cleaning businesses abound. Domestic services do not always center on housecleaning and organization, however. They can also focus on the outdoors. For example, *landscape designers* create outdoor spaces. *Landscape workers* maintain these outdoor spaces.

Reading Recall

1. Differentiate between *freelancers* and *contractors*.
2. What is *life coaching*?
3. List three common job titles of recreational services workers.
4. Describe three opportunities for entrepreneurial careers in domestic services.
5. Give an example of an entrepreneurial opportunity in each of the five human services career pathways.

Common Aptitudes, Attitudes, and Skills

Think about people you know or have heard about who successfully run their own businesses. What do all these people have in common? What abilities and skills do they share? **Figure 13.8** shows some of the common aptitudes, attitudes, and skills of successful entrepreneurs.

First and foremost, human services entrepreneurs have good business sense. Knowledge of the many aspects of running a small business is very important for the business owner. This includes knowing about bookkeeping, tax preparation, payroll, and marketing. Business owners may hire others to perform these tasks, but without this necessary knowledge, business owners will have more difficulty making good business decisions.

Consumer services and counseling and mental health services workers work with people on a very personal, and often vulnerable, level. They are trustworthy and highly sensitive to confidential information. They are properly educated and licensed, enjoy interacting with people, and are nonjudgmental.

Entrepreneurs in early childhood development and services commonly possess the same aptitudes, attitudes, and skills of workers employed by early childhood education programs. They have a genuine interest in children and child development and demonstrate positive, appropriate interactions with children.

Common Aptitudes, Attitudes, and Skills of Entrepreneurial Human Services Workers

- Trustworthy
- Nonjudgmental
- Positive
- Dedicated
- Friendly
- Sensitive to confidential information
- Get along well with others
- Strong work ethic
- Business sense

Figure 13.8 Entrepreneurial human services workers share common aptitudes, attitudes, and skills. *What other aptitudes, attitudes, and skills would you add to this list?*

Copyright Goodheart-Willcox Co., Inc.

They have a thorough knowledge of child development and apply what they know to meet children's needs. As business owners, they are dedicated to training staff.

Recreational workers tend to be active, physically fit, and interested in promoting healthy choices. They are most effective when they are passionate about their work. These workers create inspiration for their clients. They are competent in their field, are confident in their knowledge, and exude leadership in their relationships with clients. Modeling behavior to clients requires energy, a positive outlook, and the ability to motivate others.

Domestic services workers need to have a strong work ethic and good organizational skills (**Figure 13.9**). They should be physically fit as moderate lifting is often involved in their labor. They must be willing to get dirty while getting things clean and have energy to get the job done. Workers are entering the most private areas of their clients' lives—their homes or office spaces. This means a trustworthy reputation and an ability to keep personal business confidential are highly important. A positive and friendly nature is important, too. These characteristics help build a solid business reputation.

Iakov Filimonov/Shutterstock.com

Figure 13.9 Domestic services workers work in homes and office spaces to help keep them clean. *What are some ways domestic services workers can build a solid business reputation?*

Copyright Goodheart-Willcox Co., Inc.

Reading Recall

1. What do entrepreneurs and self-employed human services workers need to have, first and foremost, to be prepared to run their own businesses?

2. List three common aptitudes, attitudes, and skills of a human services entrepreneur.

Education, Training, and Experience

There is a wide range of educational requirements within the entrepreneurial human services field. This field includes careers requiring no education beyond high school to careers requiring advanced degrees, certification, and licensure. Although the specific requirements vary greatly, business and product knowledge are highly important. This knowledge comes from education and experience.

Depending on the type of service or product provided, there may be licenses, permits, or guidelines that must be followed to be in legal compliance. These vary greatly by industry and state. In all states, a business license is required. A **business license** is a legal document allowing a business owner to conduct business through the city or county of residence (**Figure 13.10**). Some cities and counties require additional forms. If the business is selling a product, a *seller's permit* or *certificate of resale* is required in many states. This is not needed when selling a service.

Specific requirements vary by region and can usually be obtained through the federal and local small business sites. In some situations, government organizations *levy* (impose) strict requirements for training

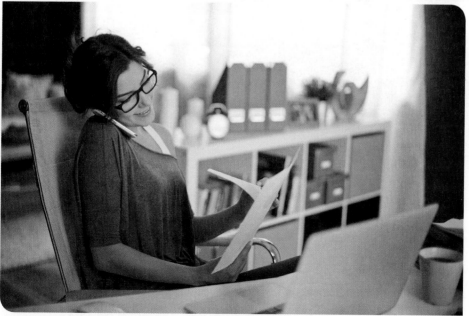

Figure 13.10 Many types of work require permits or compliance with specific guidelines, but all businesses require at least a business license. *When is a seller's permit or certificate of resale required?*

©iStock.com/gpointstudio

Copyright Goodheart-Willcox Co., Inc.

and licensing (in cosmetology and pharmaceuticals, for instance). In other situations, industries are governed by private organizations or self-regulated (sport and recreation instructors).

For recreation services entrepreneurs, specialized training in an area, such as early childhood education, dance, sports management, or a particular art, is often desired. Some jobs require teacher certification or management experience. A bachelor's degree and experience, along with certification, are preferred for personal fitness trainers. The field is not tightly monitored, however. As this field becomes more defined, having the right education, experience, and certification becomes more valuable, professionally and as a marketing tool.

As in most fields, the better a domestic services entrepreneur's credentials are, the more likely it is that customers will choose this person as a service provider. Therefore, although education, training, and experience beyond high school may not be required, they can be very important to future success. In specialized areas, such as landscape design, education and experience are highly valued (**Figure 13.11**).

Reading Recall

1. What legal document must a business owner have to conduct business?
2. What are the typical educational requirements for two entrepreneurial careers in human services?

Chaloemphan/Shutterstock.com

Figure 13.11 Landscape designers who are educated and experienced are more likely to be chosen as service providers than those with fewer credentials. *Why are education and experience important in specialized areas?*

Copyright Goodheart-Willcox Co., Inc.

Case Study / *Social Butterflies*

Damian had always been close to his grandmother and knew she thrived on social interaction with friends and family. To help her stay connected with people, he set her up on several social media sites. Before long, her friends wanted his help, and were willing to pay for his services. Damian liked providing a valuable service to his own grandmother and many others. He did not plan it, but his social media support business was booming. He even began wondering how he might keep up with all the requests for help.

Amy loves organizing things. Her closet, her backpack, her sister's bedroom—the bigger the disorganization and chaos are, the more pleasure she gets out of organizing and creating simplicity. Before long, Amy found herself helping her teachers and friends get organized. As she shared before and after photos on social media, requests for her services grew. Overwhelmed by requests, Amy started charging a fee for her services.

When Amy went to college in a nearby city, she thought her organization service days were over. Before long, however, she was helping her peers in her dorm and sorority create calm from disorder. She wondered if she could make this into a viable business.

Amy enrolled in a business program and, as a part of the program, registered for both accounting and entrepreneurship courses. In the accounting course, learning to organize numbers into assets and liabilities fascinated her. In the entrepreneurship course, her professor encouraged her to come up with an idea and flesh it out by drafting a potential business plan.

In the process of researching her idea, Amy learned that most consumers of organization services are middle-aged women who are relatively wealthy. Through her own experience, she found that many young adults also needed her services. Was there a potential unmet need for her services in younger, mobile, tighter-budget adults? If so, how could she provide services to them? Should she offer different, less costly services involving her customers' own physical labor? Would the use of social media to market and advertise, save costs? Perhaps Amy could blog about organizational skills to build interest and name recognition. That might even pay off in product advertisements. Could she expand to other markets, such as student housing, with the paying customer being the university rather than the individual students? Amy's mind was racing as her ideas blossomed.

Kekyalyaynen/Shutterstock.com

For Discussion

1. Do you think there could be potential unmet needs for Damian's or Amy's services in younger, mobile, tighter-budget adults? If so, how might Damian or Amy reach this new market?

2. How could Damian or Amy offer different, less costly services?

3. In what ways would you suggest Damian and Amy use social media to market and advertise to save costs?

4. Could Damian or Amy expand into other markets? Who would you recommend?

Copyright Goodheart-Willcox Co., Inc.

Specialized Knowledge for Entrepreneurial Careers

Expert Insight

"The value of an idea lies in the using of it."

Thomas Edison, inventor

An entrepreneur needs to offer a service for which there is a demand. When thinking about starting a business, it is easy to get caught up in the creativity of designing the product or service and choosing a name and marketing strategy. It is often less interesting and inviting to think through the "nuts and bolts" of making the business happen. These steps are critical, however, to starting a legal and viable business.

How can a potential entrepreneur evaluate whether or not a fun idea is a good business idea? Idea analysis involves determining whether or not a business idea will be feasible, successful, and profitable. After thinking about an idea and determining that it could work, there are many plans to make and steps to take to get the business off the ground.

Analyzing a Business Idea

Analyzing a business idea involves the ability to think critically about an issue or a problem to form a conclusion. Entrepreneurs need to be able to examine an issue from different points of view. They need to ask questions and think about the consequences of different options. With careful evaluation, they can make a more knowledgeable decision about whether or not a business idea will be worthwhile (**Figure 13.12**).

There are many reasons a business might fail. One of the most common is a failure to carefully think through whether or not the business idea is a good one. A tried and true method to analyze a business idea involves using **SWOT analysis**. This stands for strengths, weaknesses, opportunities, and threats. Using Amy's business idea from the Case Study in this chapter, think critically about potential SWOT of her organization services business venture.

To begin, analyze Amy's business idea for its strengths. This means looking for signs of the idea's uniqueness in relation to the potential marketplace. Strengths set the business apart from anything else currently available to potential customers. In offering a human service, what makes this service different from, and better than, the competition? Does it have competition? Keep in mind that competition may not be only "who." Consider all of a customer's potential alternatives. Can customers provide the service themselves? Can they do nothing? If there is competition, does the competition have an advantage? The advantages of your business are considered strengths. They are internal factors that make this idea distinctive.

Amy's business idea has several strengths. It appeals to younger adults and is priced accordingly. Amy herself is young, energetic, and in tune with the needs of a younger market. Amy is growing in her business knowledge and skilled at social media marketing. In addition, she is employed by Campus Housing. This gives her more contacts with

Questions to Ask Before Starting a Business

- What is my purpose for starting a business?
- What kind of business will I start?
- What services will my business provide?
- Do I have the time and money that will be needed to get this business started?
- How will my business and the services I provide be different from other similar businesses?
- Who are my target clients?
- Where will my business be physically located, if anywhere?
- Will I need any additional employees, and if so, how many?
- Will I need to find and secure any suppliers?
- How much money will I need to get this business started?
- Do I need to secure a loan?
- How long will it take before my services are available to clients?
- How soon will I be able to start making a profit?
- With what other businesses will my business be competing?
- How will I set up pricing for my services, and how does this compare with competing businesses?
- How will the legal structure of my business work?
- Will I need to pay taxes, and if so, which ones?
- Do I need any insurance, and if so, what kind?
- Do I have a plan for managing my business?
- What forms of advertisement will I use to promote my business?

Figure 13.12 These questions can be used to evaluate if your business idea is a good one. *Can you think of any other questions that would be useful to ask yourself before starting a business?*

decision-makers at her university. Her job also gives her the benefit of having a parking spot on campus. This is a privilege most students do not have.

After analyzing strengths, consider potential weaknesses of the business prospect. Just as strengths are internal advantages, weaknesses are internal disadvantages. Again, consider Amy's business. Amy is young. She does not have a lot of time or money to invest. She is devoted to finishing her education. Her education consumes much of her time. She has opportunity on her campus. Her time there is limited, however. In four years, she will graduate. Her university is the only one in town. She is not sure if this is what she wants to do for the rest of her life—or even for the next few years.

In a SWOT analysis, opportunities are assessed after strengths and weaknesses. Opportunities are positive external elements. Amy has external opportunities in that many of her friends go to other universities

Pathway to Success

Developing Critical Thinking Skills

Critical thinking is the skill of using reason to analyze ideas and explore questions about existing knowledge for issues not clearly defined. Critical thinking skills are really a combination of other thinking skills. For example, to develop and display critical thinking skills, you must have skills in interpreting or understanding the significance of data. This skill involves looking at evidence from multiple points of view and recognizing your own biases.

Analyzing is another important skill involved in critical thinking. To analyze information, you must be able to break it down and recombine it in new, meaningful ways. Reasoning skills are also a necessary part of critical thinking skills. You must be able to possess solid reasoning skills to create an argument through logical steps. Other important skills needed for critical thinking involve questioning and evaluating. Questioning allows you to actively engage with a subject, while evaluating enables you to judge the worth and credibility of the information presented.

In the twenty-first century, you are constantly bombarded with information. Critical thinking skills can help you engage with the world around you and evaluate the information from multiple sources. You can develop and practice your critical thinking skills by

- asking questions about your purpose for engaging with the information (why?);
- asking questions about the purpose of the information (why was it written or created?);
- asking questions about the context and relevance of the information (who? when? where?);
- asking questions about the arguments presented (are they fair? do they leave out perspectives of other groups?);
- asking questions about the evidence used (does it support your point of view? is it from an authority in the field? does it take into account different perspectives?);
- being fair (take into account accepted standards of judgment);
- conducting your own research using evidence from sources considered authoritative in the field; and
- considering viewpoints from a variety of perspectives (male, female, adult, child).

Essay Writing Activity

Use online or print sources to find an article about a current event. Refer to the information above on how to develop critical thinking skills as you read the article. After you finish reading, write an essay using critical thinking skills to answer the following three prompts.

1. Provide evidence to back up or challenge a point of view from the article.
2. Evaluate the validity and importance of the text/position.
3. Develop a reflective thought on the article you read.

Copyright Goodheart-Willcox Co., Inc.

outside her town. If she uses these contacts, she may be able to expand her business onto other campuses. At her school, two-person double rooms have been converted to three-person triple rooms because of a larger than usual freshman class. Her services will be needed even more in these smaller shared spaces. Even more exciting, a new retail outlet specializing in storage bins and other organizing supplies has just opened in town. This gives Amy the chance to pitch her business to sales associates who can spread the word.

Threats are factors in the external environment that could cause problems to the success of the business. The new retail outlet specializing in storage bins and other organizing supplies may actually encourage potential customers to do self-organizing rather than hiring Amy's services. The store might even offer how-to classes on self-organization. In addition, unemployment is climbing in the town, since the largest company was recently shut down.

It is impossible to predict whether or not an idea can translate into a successful business venture without first evaluating it from all angles. This includes an exhaustive look at all internal and external strengths, weaknesses, opportunities, and threats. A SWOT analysis achieves this in four straightforward steps. It is not difficult. This analysis does, however, take research, honesty, thoughtfulness, and critical thinking.

Creating a Business Plan

Utilizing a SWOT analysis helps potential entrepreneurs be realistic. If and when a person deems a business idea a good one, how should he or she begin to make it happen? An important beginning point is to organize ideas by drafting a business plan. A **business plan** is a document outlining the decisions and guidelines for the business. **Figure 13.13** shows the parts of a business plan.

> ### Expert Insight
>
> *"The way to get started is to quit talking and begin doing."*
>
> Walt Disney, founder
> Disney

The Executive Summary

A business plan usually starts with a brief summary of the business mission, products or services, financial information, and hopes for growth. This is called the **executive summary**. The executive summary describes the plan in broad strokes, almost like a view from the top, looking down. After reading the executive summary, the basic idea of the proposed business should be understood. The executive summary appears first in the business plan, but is usually written last. This is because the summary highlights the strengths of the entire plan. Therefore, the first part of the business plan a person usually completes is the company description.

The Parts of a Business Plan

- Title page
- Table of contents
- Executive summary
- Company description
- Market analysis
- Organizational and legal structures
- Service or product description
- Marketing and sales strategies
- Finances
- Appendix

Figure 13.13 A business plan is a useful tool for organizing your ideas about your business. *What information is typically included in the company description of a business plan?*

The Company Description

The company description includes the nature of the business and what needs the product or service is trying to satisfy. It also includes how the product or service will be provided, who will be providing it, and what materials will be needed. The description should also cover competitive advantages that will make for a successful business. After reading the company description, someone should be able to quickly understand the business goals and uniqueness of the proposal.

The Market Analysis

In a business plan, the market analysis usually follows the company description. A **market analysis** describes the desired customer base; competition; and methods for reaching the target market, or sales strategy. The **target market** is the specific customer base to which the business will aim to sell (**Figure 13.14**). A description of the target market usually includes any demographic data. This data includes average age, sex, race, education level, and income level.

Completing a market analysis involves doing a lot of research. This research includes a competitive analysis. A **competitive analysis** identifies the competition's strengths and weaknesses. It also shows any obstacles the business owner might face when trying to enter the market, such as a high investment cost. If there is a specific time that is better than another to enter the market, this is described as well.

antoniodiaz/Shutterstock.com

Figure 13.14 The target market for your business might be high school students who are planning on attending college and do not have much income. *If this is your target market, what opportunities do you have to sell your product or service? What challenges might this target market pose to your business?*

Copyright Goodheart-Willcox Co., Inc.

The Organizational and Legal Structures

Following the market analysis section of the business plan is a section describing the organizational and legal structures of the business. The organizational structure outlines who does what in the business and how they will be doing it. This section also includes the qualifications of the people who will be involved in the business, from employees to board members. If only one or two people will be involved in the business, it is still important to include this background information. It is also important to describe the benefits employees will receive, and any advancement opportunities.

The legal structure of the business refers to the ownership information. Ownership choices include the following:

- A **sole proprietorship** is owned by one person. The business may or may not have employees. The business owner is responsible for the business's financial successes and failures, assets, and liabilities (**Figure 13.15**). A sole proprietorship is the simplest legal structure.

- A **partnership** is shared ownership and responsibility among two or more people. In a partnership, the owners share the business's profits and losses. Partners are not always equal, however. Some may have more liability than others. Partnerships may also have employees.

- A **corporation** is a legal entity owned by shareholders. The shareholders are not legally responsible for the debts or actions of the business. A corporation is a much more complex legal structure to set up than a sole proprietorship or partnership because of all the tax and legal requirements it must meet. A corporation must pay federal,

bikeriderlondon/Shutterstock.com

Figure 13.15 This business owner is solely responsible for his business's success. *Would you like to own a sole proprietorship? Why or why not?*

Copyright Goodheart-Willcox Co., Inc.

state, and sometimes local taxes. Corporations must register with the IRS and obtain a *tax identification number*. When paying employees, an *employee identification number (EIN)* is needed.

- An **S corporation** is a type of corporation set up through an IRS tax election. The main difference between an S corporation and a corporation is that the personal liability varies for S corporations. Corporations and S corporations may include employees.

- A **limited liability company (LLC)** is a legal structure that combines the limited liability features of a corporation with the tax benefits and operational flexibility of a sole proprietorship or partnership. An LLC may include employees.

- A **cooperative** is a business providing a service or product for a collective need of a group of people. They are known as the *user-owners* (**Figure 13.16**). Any profits from the cooperative are shared among the user-owners. Tax and legal requirements are different for cooperatives, as compared to other types of legal business structures.

When starting a business, it is important to research the characteristics of legal business structures. People often seek legal counsel (hire an attorney) when deciding which structure would be the most appropriate. Many small businesses begin as sole proprietorships or partnerships. Sole proprietorships that produce a product and begin in a home are often referred to as part of a **cottage industry**, a non-legal term.

Figure 13.16 The profits from this cooperative food store are shared among the user-owners. *Are there any cooperative businesses in your community?*

Michaelpuche/Shutterstock.com

Copyright Goodheart-Willcox Co., Inc.

The Service or Product

After describing the organizational and legal structures, the next section of the business plan describes the service or product to be provided. This section outlines the benefits of the service or product to the target market. It describes how the product or service will meet the target market's needs. Be sure to describe any competitive advantages the product provides. If the product is still in the development phase or copyrighted, that information should be included in this section, too.

The Marketing and Sales Strategies

The marketing and sales strategies section of the business plan describes how the business owner will attract customers to the business. It also describes how the product or service will be sold. The marketing and sales strategies will vary from one business to the next, depending on which segment of the market the business is targeting.

The marketing strategy of the business plan should outline specific ways to reach the target market (**Figure 13.17**). Marketing a small business usually begins via word-of-mouth. Word-of-mouth is sharing information among family and friends, classmates, coworkers, or others in the business owner's personal circle of friends. Sometimes, word-of-mouth marketing can sustain a business. Often, however, it cannot. Social media is often used as a low-cost means of spreading information about a business. Advertising through social media or more traditional venues, such as newspaper ads, flyers, mailings, or other media forms, can also be used. Most businesses today invest time and resources into establishing

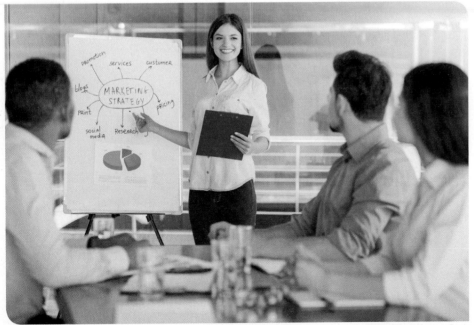

Figure 13.17 Marketing strategies can include word-of-mouth, social media, print media, websites, blogs, pricing, and promotions. *How can technology be used to improve a business's marketing strategies?*

©iStock.com/GeorgeRudy

Copyright Goodheart-Willcox Co., Inc.

and maintaining a website. Any marketing strategy that will be used should be described in the plan.

The overall sales strategy for the business should include how many people will be selling the product or service. These people are called the *sales force*. This part of the plan should also describe how the product or service will be sold. Include descriptions for each of the sales activities, as well as ways to increase sales over time.

The Financial Section

The financial part of the business plan usually follows the marketing and sales strategies section. For some business owners, the financial section may include a funding request. The funding request should identify the amount needed for the business now and in the future.

Financial projections are also an important part of this section. For a new business, most people reviewing the business plan will want to see projected income for the next five years. This is often shown monthly or quarterly for at least the first year. After that, projections may be shown annually. Many people often include a short analysis of the financial information in visual form, using graphs and charts, to quickly show financial trends (**Figure 13.18**).

The Appendix

The final portion of the business plan is the appendix. Not everyone who reviews the business plan will need to see the information in the appendix. This information, however, should be readily available for anyone who requests it.

Figure 13.18 Financial information can be communicated quickly with graphs and charts. *What else is typically included in the financial section?*

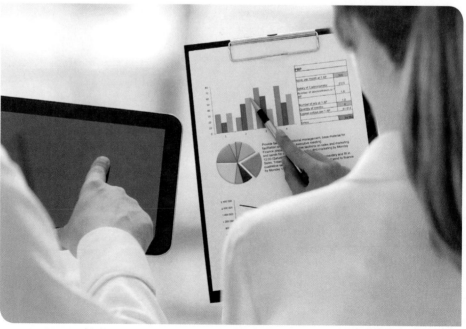

©iStock.com/Saklakova

Copyright Goodheart-Willcox Co., Inc.

The appendix typically includes

- résumés of key personnel;
- photos of the product;
- letters of reference;
- contracts;
- copies of leases;
- personal and business credit history reports;
- details of market studies; and
- copies of licenses or permits and any other legal documents.

Reading Recall

1. A tried and true method of determining whether an idea is worth starting a business or not is using SWOT analysis. What does the acronym *SWOT* mean?
2. What is an *executive summary*?
3. What is a *sole proprietorship*?

Rewards, Demands, and Future Trends

Entrepreneurial human services workers, whether contractors, freelancers, or self-employed workers, have the rewards and demands of leading their own career. In human services, self-employment can make a lot of sense, as a service is directly offered to a client. **Figure 13.19** shows some of the advantages and disadvantages of being an entrepreneur.

Self-employed human services workers have the potential to make a lot more money than their employed counterparts. There may be significant risk involved, however, and the potential to lose a lot of invested money. Most self-employed workers lose regular income as they build their business and forego benefits, such as insurance coverage, unless purchased on their own. There are also no benefits such as paid personal time off, sick leave, or a retirement plan. It is unreasonable to plan on generating immediate revenues and profits. The business plan should allow for several months, and perhaps much longer, before any income is derived.

Even with the risks, some people are drawn to the freedom of self-employment. They answer to themselves rather than to a boss. On the downside, they hold responsibility for making the business successful. Most work very long hours with little time off, until the business is established and running. When and how they work are under their own control.

People will always need human services. As a result, creative people will always come up with new services, ways of delivering them, or customers to serve. Entrepreneurship is a way of life in a competitive market economy, especially in human services. The innovation of entrepreneurs keeps human services an interesting and ever-changing field.

Copyright Goodheart-Willcox Co., Inc.

Figure 13.19 There are many pros and cons to entrepreneurship. *Can you think of additional advantages and disadvantages to entrepreneurship?*

Being an Entrepreneur	
Advantages	**Disadvantages**
• You reap all the financial benefits of your hard work. The earning potential is greater for an entrepreneur than an employee.	• There is no security of a set paycheck.
• You have control over your work schedule. You can take vacations and sick days whenever you want. You can work the days and hours you prefer.	• You often have to work very long hours, especially when first starting. Also, your schedule can be unpredictable, and you may have to deal with emergencies.
• You make all the decisions and have complete control over the business.	• Handling the responsibility of making all the business's decisions can be stressful and difficult.
• Seeing an idea turn into a realization is very exciting.	• There is great risk. The success or failure of the business is all up to you.
• You can hire your own employees, if needed.	• Your accounting and tax preparation are much more difficult.
• You will be doing what you love for your career.	• You will likely have to learn many new skills.
• You can achieve recognition from your family, friends, and community, and you can reach new levels of self-fulfillment.	• You have to understand every aspect of your business and be able to deal with all kinds of problems that may arise.
• You will have more job satisfaction because you will be doing work that makes the most of your strengths and skills.	• The workload is much greater because there is no one to delegate tasks to, at least initially.

Entrepreneurs and small business owners play a part in strengthening the US economy. Federal legislation, initiatives, and incentives can support or deter small businesses. They can act as external threats within a SWOT analysis of feasibility or continuing viability. These might include tax cuts or increases and access to capital or financial resources. With increased access to financial resources, including loans, small businesses can make potent new investments. These investments can include building new facilities and buying new equipment.

Growing and sustainable human services are the foundation of communities and the source of innovation and pride for small business owners. As long as there are new ways to serve human needs, there will be opportunities for entrepreneurs.

Many resources are available for human services workers who hope to launch their own small businesses. State and federal government

Copyright Goodheart-Willcox Co., Inc.

Law and Ethics *Laws for Small Businesses*

Did you know that small business owners and entrepreneurs are subject to many of the same laws as large businesses and corporations? It is often challenging for small business owners to stay abreast of all that is required because of the everyday challenges of keeping a small business up and running. Fortunately, there are many resources.

The Small Business Administration (SBA) is a part of the US federal government. It offers both online and printed legal information for small business owners, freelancers, consultants, and entrepreneurs. SBA counselors and mentors are available in many local district offices to train entrepreneurs and small business owners about their legal responsibilities. The SBA, along with state and local resources, can answer questions that entrepreneurs or small business owners may face.

SCORE is a nonprofit organization. The SBA and many corporations sponsor it. Volunteers who have successfully run businesses provide workshops, coaching, and mentoring to small business owners to launch and grow their businesses. To give a snapshot, following are a few of the areas in which small business owners must keep current:

- Privacy laws. By law, businesses must be extra vigilant with their clients' personal or financial information, with the intent of keeping them safe from harm, theft, or damage to personal reputation. Laws are even stricter for those working with children. It is not enough to just not share information. Business owners must be able to demonstrate that they make serious efforts to ensure privacy.
- Finance laws. Finance laws protect the small business owners, their competition, and any

investors or partners. They include bankruptcy laws and financial reporting obligations of the small business owner.

- Advertising and marketing laws. Small business owners must follow advertising and marketing laws when promoting their businesses. These laws include truth in marketing, laws specific to some industries (such as real estate or clothing), and acceptable ways of telemarketing or using SPAM.
- Workplace safety and health laws. All businesses must comply with the federal occupational safety and health laws, along with any additional requirements for their city, county, or state. These laws are meant to ensure that employees, products, and services are safe for workers, customers, clients, and the environment.

Depending on the type and size of a small business, environmental regulations, employment labor laws, intellectual property laws, or foreign worker laws might also apply. All these laws and more can be accessed through the US SBA.

Research Activity

Using the SBA website, find one article related to small business ownership laws. Give a verbal presentation of your finding in class.
- Summarize the article.
- What did you learn that you did not know before?
- Why is this information important for small business owners to know?

resources are especially valuable, and are readily available online. One excellent source of information for starting and operating a small business is the United States Small Business Administration (SBA).

Reading Recall

1. Name three creative entrepreneurial ventures that offer a better or more innovative way of offering human services and may have lower barriers to entry (cost), so the investment is minimal.
2. Name two rewards and demands of entrepreneurial careers in human services.

Copyright Goodheart-Willcox Co., Inc.

Summary

- There are endless possibilities for entrepreneurial careers in all of the human services pathways.
- Human services entrepreneurs must have good business acumen. They have bright and innovative ideas and a desire to meet the needs of their customers or clients.
- Entrepreneurial human services is a very people-oriented career field. It requires strong interpersonal skills.
- There is a wide range of educational requirements within the entrepreneurial human services field. Depending on the type of service or product provided, there may be licensing, permits, or guidelines that must be followed to be in legal compliance.
- An effective way to analyze the viability of a business idea is to conduct a SWOT analysis. It is impossible to predict whether or not an idea can translate into a successful business venture without first evaluating it from all angles.
- There are several necessary steps following the determination that it is a good idea to start a business. Crafting a business plan and securing legal documents are prudent steps. The parts of a business plan include the title page, table of contents, executive summary, company description, market analysis, organizational and legal structures, service or product description, marketing and sales strategies, finances, and appendix.
- Self-employed human services workers have the potential to make a lot more money than their employed counterparts. People will always come up with new services, ways of delivering them, or customers to service. As long as there are new ways to serve human needs, there will be opportunities for entrepreneurs.

College and Career Portfolio

Portfolio Website

Making your portfolio available electronically can make it easier for colleges and employers to review the portfolio's contents. Some professionals make their portfolios available through a website. There are many websites you can use to create an online portfolio. There are many user-friendly online platforms, even if you do not have any experience building websites. Some websites offer portfolio templates. Others offer the user complete freedom to design the page as he or she wishes. Some websites are free. Others, however, require users to pay a fee.

A strong portfolio uses technology to enhance its contents. Ways to use technology in your portfolio include adding a video to your portfolio samples or an audio recording narration to a presentation. Using technology in your portfolio enhances a sample in your portfolio, while demonstrating your creativity and ability to effectively utilize the tools to which you have access. To determine how you will use technology to enhance your portfolio, complete the following:

1. Research platforms for making your portfolio available online.
2. Use one platform to create a sample portfolio. Evaluate whether or not the platform is right for your portfolio.
3. Choose one portfolio sample you can improve using technology.
4. Use technology to enhance your portfolio sample. Present that sample to the class.

Copyright Goodheart-Willcox Co., Inc.

Review and Reflect

1. Define *entrepreneur* in your own words.
2. Identify the similarities between a *freelancer* and a *contractor*. Give an example of each.
3. Identify five activities you could turn into a job as a recreational services worker. Where would you work for each of these jobs?
4. Explain what entrepreneurs who are successful with their chosen career have in common.
5. Identify four skills an entrepreneur would need to have or have knowledge of that a worker in the same field would not necessarily know how to do.
6. Identify six questions to ask before starting a business.
7. Explore different reasons a business might fail.
8. Define *business license* and *business plan*. What are the differences between the two?
9. What is included in a business plan?
10. Why would you do a market analysis before starting a new business?
11. What information is found in the appendix of a business plan?
12. Explain some of the risks associated with owning your own business.

Vocabulary Activities

13. **Key terms**   In teams, create categories for the following terms. Classify as many of the terms as possible. Share your ideas with the remainder of the class.

business license
business plan
competitive analysis
contractors
cooperative
corporation
cottage industry
entrepreneur
executive summary
freelancers
life coaching
limited liability company (LLC)
market analysis
partnership
S corporation
sole proprietorship
SWOT analysis
target market

14. **Academic terms**   With a partner, create a T-chart. Write each of the following vocabulary terms in the left column. Write a *synonym* (a word that has the same or similar meaning) for each term in the right column. Discuss your synonyms with the class.

innovative   levy   replete

Self-Assessment Quiz

Complete the self-assessment quiz online to help you practice and expand your knowledge and skills.

Critical Thinking

15. **Cause and effect**   Explain what will happen if an entrepreneur does not assume the responsibility and risk for his or her own business.
16. **Make inferences**   What type of atmosphere would you expect for an office of a life coach? Describe in detail what the office should look like to help ensure clients feel comfortable hiring him or her.
17. **Draw conclusions**   One of the most common types of entrepreneurial careers in early childhood development and services is in-home child care. Use information about this career from the chapter. Draw conclusions explaining whether or not you would be interested in this as a career. Give specific examples for your reasoning.
18. **Determine**   Determine what type of specialized training you might need as an entrepreneur in the recreation services pathway versus the domestic services pathway.
19. **Evaluate**   All five of the human services career pathways have entrepreneurial opportunities. Identify entrepreneurial opportunities that interest you in each of the five human services career pathways. Evaluate what these jobs entail, how each worker interacts with clients, and how common each job is in your town. After evaluating this information, what are your thoughts about these entrepreneurial opportunities? Are you surprised by your findings?
20. **Identify**   Choose one of the entrepreneurial careers listed in the chapter. Identify and make

a list of different places in your town where this person could offer his or her services.

21. **Compare and contrast**   Create a chart comparing and contrasting the six different legal structure types of ownership.

22. **Analyze**   Research a local business. Find out about its business plan. Use the information found in this chapter about what should be in a business plan. Analyze the local business's plan to see what information the business included that was not talked about in the chapter and what information was in the chapter. Share your findings with he rest of the class.

Core Skills

23. **Writing, speaking, and listening**   Invite several different entrepreneurs in your community to come to class to discuss what they do in their respective jobs. Create a list of questions to ask them when they come. Write thank-you letters to the speakers after their visits. Be sure to send the thank-you notes.

24. **Research**   Identify different types of technology available for an entrepreneur to use to make his or her job easier. Explain how the technology makes the person's job easier.

25. **Research and writing**   Research the requirements for obtaining a business license in your city or state. Create a flyer or brochure explaining the steps needed to obtain a business license.

26. **Research and writing**   Research what postsecondary classes you could take to help with a job as an entrepreneur. Make a chart showing the names of these courses and what postsecondary schools in your state offer them. Share with your class.

27. **Speaking, listening, and math**   Identify a local entrepreneur to interview. As part of your interview, ask the person how he or she determined what to do in order to start the business, both skill-wise and monetary-wise. Be sure to include questions about how the person calculated what money was needed to start up the business and how many months' worth of expenses the person calculated would be needed before making a

profit. Create your list of questions prior to the interview. After the interview, send a thank-you letter to the interviewee,

28. **Writing, speaking, and listening**   Identify one product you would like to sell as an entrepreneur. Create a prototype of your product. List the cost of materials and the cost of marketing your product. Determine the target market and price at which you will sell your product. Have students critique your product and the price at which you are selling it. Have them give advice on any changes needed for your product or pricing.

29. **Reading and writing**   Use the information provided about a business plan in this chapter. Write your own company description that would be found in a business plan. Be sure to include the nature of the business and what needs the product or service you are selling will satisfy.

30. **Writing and speaking**   Come up with an idea for a new product you would like to sell. Identify the target market. Examine different types of media you can use to achieve maximum impact on your target market. Write your marketing strategy describing how you will sell your product. Share your marketing strategy with the rest of the class.

31. **Writing**   Create a chart showing the pros and cons of being an entrepreneur. Be sure to include hours, pay, challenges, and rewards in your chart. Hang the charts in your classroom.

32. **Research, reading, and writing**   Choose an article appearing on the SBA's website. Read the article. Create a memo to your employees about the information found in the article. Describe how this information could help your small business grow.

33. **CTE career readiness practice**   To be a successful employee requires creativity and innovation. Whether you see problems as challenges or opportunities, they often require critical thinking to solve them. Many new inventions are the result of attempting to solve a problem. Describe a problem you faced that led you to the creation of a new way of doing things or a new invention.

34. **CTE career readiness practice**   Becoming an entrepreneur in your community requires

   Copyright Goodheart-Willcox Co., Inc.

you to model integrity, ethical leadership, and effective management. Make a list of actions you could take to meet these requirements.

35. **CTE career readiness practice** The ability to read and interpret information is an important workplace skill. Presume you are starting a business. You will need to locate three reliable sources for financing. Research financing options that may be available to you at a local financial institution. Read and interpret the information you locate. Then, write a report summarizing your findings in an organized manner.

36. **CTE career readiness practice** Small business owners must behave in an ethical manner at all times. Misrepresentation of the company would put the business in jeopardy. Outline ways that a small business owner can be responsible and ethical when creating a promotional campaign for the business.

Lend a Hand

Entrepreneurial Volunteerism

There are many opportunities to join existing volunteer organizations and community service projects. You may prefer, however, to start your own instead. Starting a project on your own requires organization and dedication. Be sure to plan ahead and think of a mission for your volunteerism. Also, consider whether you want to work on your own or with a team, club, or group of friends. Remember that the more people who are involved, the more work it is to organize your efforts.

The possibilities for setting up a service project are endless. You could mow lawns or shovel snow for elderly or disabled adults in your neighborhood. You could offer computer or digital tablet training sessions to people who struggle to use technology. You and a group of friends could meet weekly at the local park to clean up trash. If you have a skill or talent, or simply some extra time, you could think of a way to use it for the good of your community.

To discover how you can be an entrepreneurial volunteer, complete the following:

1. Brainstorm a list of ideas for starting your own service project. Try to think of new ways you can help out in your neighborhood or local community. Is there anything not being done yet? Is there something more that could be done? Narrow your list down to your top three choices.

2. With your top three choices in mind, consider the details of your potential service projects. How many people would need to be involved? How much time would the project require? How often would you need to work on this project to accomplish your goal? Would you need any special permission to complete your project?

3. Choose the project you feel the most confident about. Try it!

Copyright Goodheart-Willcox Co., Inc.

Chapter 14

Food and Nutrition Related Human Services

While studying, look for the activity icon **to**

- **practice** key and academic terms with e-flash cards and matching activities;
- **assess** what you learn by completing self-assessment quizzes; and
- **reinforce** what you learn by mapping concepts and completing review and reflect questions.

www.g-wlearning.com/humanservices/

erwinova/Shutterstock.com

Learning Outcomes

After studying this chapter, you will be able to

- **compare and contrast** food and nutrition related career opportunities;
- **list** common aptitudes, attitudes, and skills of food and nutrition related human services workers;
- **give examples** of postsecondary education, training, and experience required for several food and nutrition related human services careers;
- **describe** unique nutrient needs during each stage of the life cycle, including special dietary needs based on certain lifestyle choices and conditions;
- **explain** the impact of physical activity and healthy eating patterns on physical health;
- **demonstrate** how to prepare healthy meals and snacks that contribute to wellness; and
- **summarize** the rewards, demands, and future trends of food and nutrition related careers.

Reading Strategies

Before reading, skim this chapter and place sticky notes next to sections of interest or where you have questions. Write your comments or questions on the sticky notes. As you are reading, pay special attention to these sections. After reading, find a partner and discuss your comments and questions.

Mapping Concepts

Two of the main topics covered in this chapter are food and nutrition. In a chart like the one shown, draw two circles, one labeled *food* and the other labeled *nutrition*. As you read, write information you learn around the circle to which it relates. If a piece of information relates to both topics, write it between the circles.

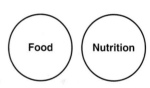

Key Terms ✍

anorexia nervosa	food allergy
binge-eating disorder	food intolerance
body composition	MyPlate
bulimia nervosa	nutrient-dense foods
catering	nutrition
diabetes	obesity
dietetics	overweight
eating disorder	recipe
fad diets	vegetarian

Academic Terms ✍

- aesthetic
- ingenuity
- lucrative
- palatable
- stringent

Food and nutrition careers are vast and varied. Opportunities are available in the agriculture, food, and natural resources; hospitality and tourism; and health sciences career clusters. Because food is a basic need and human services workers focus on meeting people's needs, many food and nutrition career opportunities relate to the human services field.

In the agriculture, food, and natural resources career cluster, examples of career opportunities in the food industry include farmers, produce buyers, and food scientists. In hospitality and tourism, jobs can range from a chef in a fine-dining restaurant to a beverage server at a concession stand (**Figure 14.1**). In health sciences, careers involve the science of nutrition. **Nutrition** is the study of how the body uses nutrients in foods and how these nutrients impact diet, productivity, health, and disease. Examples of careers in this area include dietitians and nutritionists.

Careers in food and nutrition related human services focus on the human side of food and nutrition. These careers involve

- preparing and serving foods to people;
- creating dietary plans to promote healthy lifestyles and meet people's health related needs;
- providing nutritional information to people; and
- developing new products and determining whether food products are healthy and safe for people to consume.

Figure 14.1 Many food careers in the hospitality industry involve working in restaurants and other foodservice establishments. *In addition to restaurants, what are some other foodservice establishments in your town?*

©iStock.com/monkeybusinessimages

Food and Nutrition Related Career Opportunities

There are many career opportunities for human services workers in the fields of food and nutrition. **Figure 14.2** shows some examples of careers in this field that relate to human services and helping people meet one of their most basic needs. You will be learning more about these careers in the following sections.

Food and Beverage Services Workers

The food and beverage services industry focuses on preparing, packaging, and selling food and beverages for people to eat and drink. Sometimes the product is served; other times it is simply sold to the customer. Generally, the food and beverage industry can be divided into commercial and institutional foodservice ventures.

Commercial foodservice ventures are food and beverage establishments that work directly with customers. For example, full-service restaurants prepare meals to serve to customers. Other commercial foodservice ventures include quick-service restaurants, specialty food providers, catering services, and food and beverage services provided by hotels, spas, and other recreational facilities.

Institutional foodservice ventures provide foodservice within an established organization, such as a school, hospital, or other venue (**Figure 14.3**). For example, a bookstore may have a coffee shop within the store that is run by another business entity. A sporting stadium may have several nonrelated food vendors offering food and beverage products within the stadium.

A *foodservice manager* directs and coordinates the operations of services that prepare and serve food. Opportunities for foodservice managers are vast and can be found in private, public, for-profit, and not-for-profit sectors. For example, the US military serves food to hundreds of thousands of military personnel each day. Restaurants, hotels, and cafeterias do so as well.

Foodservice managers are responsible for the daily operations of restaurants and other foodservice establishments. This includes all planning, organizing, and evaluating of foodservice functions. They also oversee the inventory and ordering of food, equipment, and supplies, and care for equipment and general facilities. Like managers of any

Examples of Food and Nutrition Related Human Services Careers

- Assistant manager of foodservice establishment
- Caterer
- Clinical dietitian and clinical nutritionist
- Community dietitian and community nutritionist
- Dietitian and nutritionist
- Executive chef
- Food and beverage serving worker
- Food scientist
- Foodservice manager
- General manager of foodservice establishment
- Management dietitian
- Nutrition educator
- Personal chef
- Registered dietetic technician (RDT)

Figure 14.2 The field of food and nutrition related human services offers many different career opportunities. *Which of these careers would you like to explore further?*

Copyright Goodheart-Willcox Co., Inc.

Figure 14.3 School cafeterias are good examples of institutional foodservice ventures. *What are some other examples of institutional foodservice ventures?*

Monkey Business Images/Shutterstock.com

large operation, the administrative and human resources duties are an important part of their work. This includes hiring new employees and monitoring employee performance and training. These tasks are important as restaurants tend to utilize entry-level, temporary workers.

In most full-service restaurants, the management team consists of a general manager, one or more assistant managers, and an executive chef. The *general manager* performs the administrative duties and provides general business oversight. Foodservice general managers perform a variety of administrative tasks. They maintain employee work records and handle payroll. They complete paperwork to comply with licensing laws; tax, wage and hour, and unemployment compensation; and Social Security laws. They also maintain, order, and pay for new equipment.

The *assistant manager* deals with the everyday running of the facility and often works on the dining floor. Assistant managers oversee the dining service and check in with customers to ensure their dining experience is pleasant. They handle any issues that may arise on the floor. They also work directly with food and beverage serving workers to make sure they are trained and can provide excellent customer service.

Food and beverage serving workers are the frontline of customer service in a restaurant or other foodservice establishment. They greet customers and set tables. They take food and drink orders and then serve the items to their customers. In some foodservice places, food and beverage serving workers may also prepare food and beverage items, such as sandwiches or coffee.

Copyright Goodheart-Willcox Co., Inc.

Case Study / *What Is It About Bob?*

Bob tells his story this way: While attending college, I discovered that I liked working in campus foodservice. I decided to combine my foodservice skills with my entrepreneurial spirit. I started a campus-wide concession operation, selling hot sandwiches I cooked on a camp stove at school football games. Through my efforts, I became known as the "campus food guy."

Upon graduation, I teamed up with my college buddy to open a taco-themed Mexican restaurant. Business was very good. We were serving over 800 dinners on Friday and Saturday nights. Our business even earned the highest sales volume of restaurants in the area.

A few years later, I opened a diner on my own. Unfortunately, I had to file for bankruptcy after only two years. This very tough experience taught me a great deal. I became very numbers oriented and learned how to become a people-mentoring coach.

My next venture into foodservice began when the general manager of a tennis club asked me to run the food and beverage side of the club. The club had not earned a profit in some 100 years in the food and beverage department. He was convinced, however, that I could turn around both the sales and operating numbers. After five years of growth in annual profits, I was asked to do the same at another club.

I went to work as general manager of The Lakeshore Club where I quickly learned why others had rejected the job. I was faced with my first payroll and our checking account was empty. What I failed to see was that in the week prior, the steam water boiler had blown and all cash went to repair the boiler. I began calling members, asking if I could collect their accounts we had just billed. Since that humble beginning, we have seen major growth in profits. Recently, we expanded our operation to serve more people. We also opened an employee cafeteria for a financial institution.

One of the things I love most about working in foodservice is that there is no typical day. As the general manager, my work day starts quite early. We are open for three meals a day. Much of my time is spent in meetings and coaching key direct report staff. As a coach and manager, I take great pride in putting together a team and then mentoring them with the goal of stretching and growing people's lives when possible. Eventually, I hope to send some of my team off to new opportunities. Thanks to my position, I feel that I touch many people's lives daily.

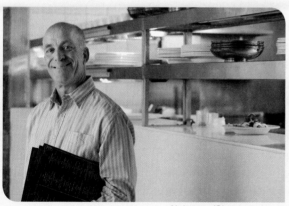

Air Images/Shutterstock.com

For Discussion

1. What is it about Bob that makes him successful in the food and beverage industry?
2. What kinds of specialized knowledge might he possess?

The *executive chef* is in charge of kitchen personnel and the food served in a restaurant or other facility, such as a group home or nursing home. Executive chefs are interested in the ingredients, *aesthetic* (pleasing in appearance) appeal of the food, and nutritional content of the menu (**Figure 14.4**). They direct the kitchen staff to make sure foods are

Copyright Goodheart-Willcox Co., Inc.

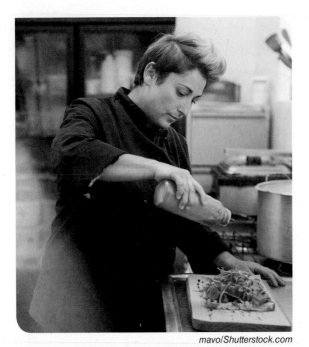

mavo/Shutterstock.com

Figure 14.4 Executive chefs select menu items that appeal to the customers' tastes and preferences. *What is your favorite casual dining restaurant? Is there a particular item on the menu that really appeals to you?*

prepared properly. They also work with the general manager to place food orders, check deliveries, and establish quality guidelines. A chef who performs the same duties for a client in a home setting is referred to as a *personal chef.*

Dietitians and Nutritionists

Dietitians and *nutritionists* help people apply and use knowledge to improve their health and wellness. The science of doing so is termed **dietetics**. These professionals work with people to modify their diets to achieve a healthy lifestyle or meet health-related goals. They assess clients' needs and then develop meal plans to promote better health. Meal plans may address goals to gain or lose weight, improve health, manage chronic illness, transition from hospital to home, extend the family's food budget, or prepare healthy meals.

Clinical dietitians and *clinical nutritionists* are healthcare professionals who earn the *Registered Dietitian Nutritionist (RDN)* credential.

Clinical dietitians and clinical nutritionists are vitally important in the medical industry as they assess patients' needs and plan dietetic therapy to improve health through nutrition. Clinical dietitians and clinical nutritionists may work in research institutions, hospitals, long-term care facilities, medical clinics and practices, public health agencies, or private practice. They may work directly with patients or at a policy level in which patients are rarely seen.

As the healthcare field has become more specialized, so has the field of nutrition. Clinical dietitians and clinical nutritionists often specialize in particular areas. Some of the specialized areas include pediatrics, public healthcare, critical care, and sports nutrition. Often, these specialty areas require advanced training and education. Although there is great diversity in career paths, clinical dietitians and clinical nutritionists share the common mission to provide nutritional healthcare for individuals and families.

Community dietitians and *community nutritionists* work with groups of people with varying needs (**Figure 14.5**). They identify food, health, and nutrition problems and develop programs to address the issues. They may also work as community educators and consultants, informing the public on related topics. Community dietitians and community nutritionists often work in government and nonprofit settings, public health clinics, health organizations, or as self-employed consultants.

Copyright Goodheart-Willcox Co., Inc.

Monkey Business Images/Shutterstock.com

Figure 14.5 Older adults are a special population with special dietary needs. *Do you know of anyone who has special dietary needs? What are the needs?*

Management dietitians plan food programs in institutions, such as schools, cafeterias, hospitals, and prisons. They are often in charge of developing the budget and buying food. They also oversee other kitchen workers or dietitians.

Registered Dietetic Technicians

A *registered dietetic technician (RDT)* works under the supervision of a registered dietitian nutritionist to provide health and nutrition care. Registered dietetic technicians may also work in partnership with a registered dietitian to provide specific nutrition information. They are often the frontline in patient care. They offer personalized service to clients, helping them to ensure a balanced diet and select nutritious foods. They work in the same settings as dietitians, and assist dietitians in their work in several ways. Typical work settings include hospitals, nursing homes, restaurants, college foodservices, and community organizations.

A registered dietetic technician could develop, implement, and review nutrition care plans established by a hospital clinical dietitian. Registered dietetic technicians talk with clients and learn their food preferences and diet histories. They assess their nutritional status and document the care in their medical records. Sometimes, they design specialized meal plans or work with families to apply specialized diet restrictions to their daily lives.

Registered dietetic technicians are involved in all aspects of food production and service. This includes quality service, safety standards, foodservice supervision, menu design, and food production. Registered

Copyright Goodheart-Willcox Co., Inc.

dietetic technicians serve in frontline and mid-level management positions, assisting clients and customers with food and nutrition decisions.

Nutrition Educators

Nutrition education is a large, growing specialty area that includes many routes to share nutrition information. Traditional *nutrition educators* provide nutrition information to students and foodservice workers in both public and private education, from child care centers through universities (**Figure 14.6**).

Nutrition educators may also follow the traditional teaching route. They may teach nutrition in a high school family and consumer sciences program or at a college or university. College and university nutrition educators must have highly specialized knowledge and, generally, must hold graduate degrees in nutrition. College and university nutrition educators, however, are not only employed in nutrition or family and consumer sciences fields. They may also teach in medical and other health-related programs, such as medical schools. Health organizations—hospitals, clinics, and health maintenance organizations (HMOs)—also employ nutrition educators.

Nutrition education does not always happen in a traditional setting. Private businesses, such as health clubs and spas, also offer classes on nutrition and healthy eating. Nutrition educators may also work for drug or sales companies. Through selling products, they serve as educators

SpeedKingz/Shutterstock.com

Figure 14.6 Students need to begin learning about nutrition at an early age. *When did you first begin to learn about nutrition?*

Copyright Goodheart-Willcox Co., Inc.

on the health benefits of the product sold. Because of their nutrition knowledge, sales are often through educational seminars and training sessions.

Media is another important tool for distributing nutrition information. Television news shows often carry food, nutrition, or health segments that feature nutrition educators. Newspapers and magazines may employ nutrition educators who write health and wellness features or columns. Newsletters distributed by HMOs, healthcare providers, and human resources departments may also carry articles written or edited by nutrition educators.

As technology continues to develop, so too will the desire for faster and more up-to-date nutrition information. Nutrition educators serve as the link between nutrition research, practice, and the sharing of nutrition knowledge.

Food Scientists

A *food scientist* develops new products and determines whether food products are healthy, safe, *palatable* (appetizing), and convenient. Food scientists apply knowledge of biochemistry, human biology, microbiology, toxicology, biotechnology, and other sciences to determine new or better ways to prepare, distribute, package, use, and store foods.

Sometimes, food scientists perform basic research. They may look at what food products are made of or they may focus on the nutritional composition of foods. Nutritional components include vitamins, minerals, protein, fat, and carbohydrates. Other times, food scientists look at the way food is processed to determine the healthiest and most tasteful, convenient, or efficient method of preparation.

Some food scientists are involved in enforcing government regulations, food inspection, sanitation, and other safety measures. Food scientists are often working on the forefront of the food industry, offering new and interesting food products for consumers. They usually work for food processing companies, government agencies, universities, or other research institutions.

There are numerous opportunities for food scientists, and their titles may include product development specialists, sensory scientists, and quality control specialists. In business related fields, they may be referred to as technical sales representatives.

Entrepreneurial Opportunities

There are many food and nutrition related human services entrepreneurial opportunities. Personal chefs often contract their services to a client. Dietitians and nutritionists may also work on a freelance or contract basis. One of the most common opportunities is providing field products and meals. Food is a basic need, but its preparation is a source of creative expression. Homemade breads, jams, salsas, and many other

Copyright Goodheart-Willcox Co., Inc.

Law and Ethics *Natural or Organic Food Labels*

Many consumers today show an interest in natural or organic foods. Some people think these two terms have the same meaning, but they do not. Although there is no legal definition for the term *natural*, it loosely means that no artificial ingredients or added colors were used during food processing. Whereas *natural* is not legally well-defined, the term *organic* is. *Organic* means that a food was produced by following strict guidelines established by the United States Department of Agriculture (USDA). Foods that are inspected and approved for meeting organic standards are certified by the USDA and carry an organic seal.

There are different levels of organic labeling, which include the following:

- *100 Percent Organic* contains only organically produced ingredients and may use the USDA organic seal of approval.
- *Organic* contains at least 95 percent organic ingredients and may use the USDA organic seal of approval.
- *Made with Organic Ingredients or Foods* contains at least 70 percent organic ingredients, but may not use the USDA seal.
- *Some Organic Ingredients* contains less than 70 percent organic ingredients. The ingredient panel on the package may only list the organic items. These products may not display the USDA seal.

People may show an interest in organic foods for several reasons. First, organic foods are free from artificial preservatives and chemicals. Second, no part of the food product may contain any genetically modified parts.

Genetically modified (GM) refers to a process of artificially altering genes to produce a desired trait. Third, organic foods often taste better—although this is not always the case. Many organic growers use "heirloom" or old-fashioned varieties of plants rather than the more modern overly bred plants. Over generations of plant life, flavors may be bred out of some plant varieties.

Whether organic foods are healthier—and safer—than conventional foods is an issue that experts commonly study and consumers frequently debate. One disadvantage of organic foods is the cost. Organic foods can cost significantly more than nonorganic food products. This seems to be a major obstacle that is keeping organic foods from being more widely consumed. Despite the added cost, the organic food market continues to grow. What used to be a market segment that was run by a handful of small farmers has now become a very large market both in restaurants and grocery stores.

Debate Activity

There is a long-standing debate among people as to whether organic foods are more nutritious (and safer) than conventional foods. As a class, divide into two teams. One team will debate the affirmative stance while the other team will debate the negative. Thoroughly research your topic to prepare for the debate. Read articles and talk to others about their opinions. As you debate, remember to keep your points clear and relevant.

products are sold online, at county fairs, farmers' markets, and in stores and restaurants.

Catering is another entrepreneurial opportunity for food and nutrition related human services workers. **Catering** is a part of the food and beverage industry that provides foodservice for social or business events, such as board meetings, conferences, and retreats.

Caterers work to provide food and beverages for special occasions, one-time or infrequent events, or regularly scheduled functions. Wedding

Copyright Goodheart-Willcox Co., Inc.

receptions, retirement parties, office lunches, and family events are just a few of the many occasions when caterers provide food for a gathering of people.

Caterers work closely with their clients to design, prepare, and serve menus for these events. For example, caterers provide menus and the clients choose their favorite dishes and work with the caterer to assemble a meal where each dish complements the others. They often work around a theme and always within budget constraints. Flower arrangements or other centerpieces and decorations, table linens, and serving pieces may also be a part of the total package offered by a caterer.

For people who love to prepare food and serve it in an artistic manner, catering can provide a *lucrative* (profitable) and creative outlet (**Figure 14.7**). There are some seasons of the year, such as summer weddings and winter holidays, that are busier than others.

A subset of the catering industry that has seen tremendous growth led by entrepreneurs is the food truck or mobile restaurant. Whole events or fairs may be planned around a gathering of these trucks, which offer a variety of food types. Although all of the health and business aspects of a restaurant must be adhered to, a food truck may be a less expensive way to enter the catering marketplace.

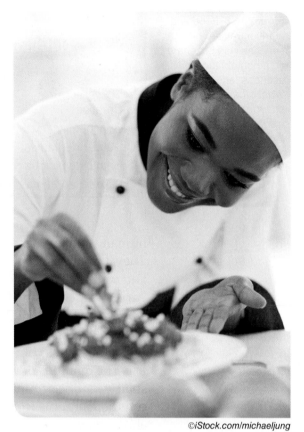

©iStock.com/michaeljung

Figure 14.7 Caterers often decorate their dishes so they are visually appealing, as well as tasty. *Have you ever been to a catered event? If so, what types of foods were served?*

Reading Recall

1. List and describe three food and nutrition related human services careers.
2. What is *dietetics*?
3. Describe the job of a food scientist.
4. List three possible sites where caterers might work to provide food and beverages for special occasions, one-time or infrequent events, or regularly scheduled functions.
5. Describe some daily tasks of a catering entrepreneur.

Common Aptitudes, Attitudes, and Skills

Workers in food and nutrition related human services share common aptitudes, attitudes, and skills (**Figure 14.8**). Food and nutrition related

Copyright Goodheart-Willcox Co., Inc.

Figure 14.8 Food and nutrition related human services workers share common aptitudes, attitudes, and skills. *What other aptitudes, attitudes, and skills would you add to this list?*

Common Aptitudes, Attitudes, and Skills of Food and Nutrition Related Human Services Workers

- Calm
- Precise
- Creative
- Confident
- Detail oriented
- Health conscious
- Flexible and adaptable

- Passionate about product or service
- Up-to-date in knowledge
- Get along well with others
- Willingness to be leaders
- Problem-solving skills
- People-helping skills

human services workers are calm, precise, and creative problem solvers. They are able to work through complex issues to ensure the overall health and well-being of their clients or customers. They work well with a variety of people and have well-honed interpersonal and people-helping skills. Because they act as resource people, they must be confident and up-to-date in their knowledge. They are able to apply what they know to a number of different settings.

The qualities of workers in the food and nutrition industry include solid scientific grounding, creativity, an eye for detail, and being health conscious. People in the food and nutrition industry must be passionate about the product or service they are offering, whether it entails nutritional advice or food products and services. All food and nutrition professionals must consider the needs of the end user, whether patient or consumer.

Making food taste and look great and delivering it in a timely manner are important tasks in the foodservice industry (**Figure 14.9**). Doing so takes a tremendous amount of *ingenuity* (cleverness; inventiveness), flexibility, and the ability to problem solve under time constraints when multiple issues arise and the pace is hectic. Foodservice managers must be creative, adaptable, and calm in the event of emergencies. They must be willing to be leaders of the personnel they supervise.

Reading Recall

1. List three common aptitudes, attitudes, and skills of food and nutrition related human services workers.
2. Describe two important tasks in the foodservice industry.

Education, Training, and Experience

Careers in food and nutrition are varied and vast. Thus, the education, training, and experience expectations are, too. A high school diploma is typically all the education required for entry-level positions as

Copyright Goodheart-Willcox Co., Inc.

bikeriderlondon/Shutterstock.com

Figure 14.9 Food and beverage serving workers must serve food to people in a timely manner, often at a hectic pace. *What are some other important tasks food and beverage serving workers must often perform?*

food and beverage serving workers. Most of these positions provide on-the-job training.

Educational requirements and training in foodservice management are highly dependent on the position. Some organizations require a degree in food science or even the registered dietitian credentials. Others require a degree in business administration or specialized culinary training. Because of the varying requirements, many seek advice from professionals in the foodservice management and hospitality field to determine desirable training and education.

For executive and personal chefs, postsecondary education is not required, but because of the competitiveness for these jobs, many attend culinary arts schools. The American Culinary Federation certifies certain culinary schools that meet their *stringent* (strict; rigorous) standards. Success in this field also requires one to pay his or her dues. That is, learning culinary skills through work experience. Executive chefs have often paid their dues by working as sous chefs, catering managers, kitchen or banquet managers, or as other support staff.

In the field of nutrition, a bachelor's degree from an approved program (designated by the Academy of Nutrition and Dietetics) is necessary to become a registered dietitian nutritionist. Candidates must also complete an accredited, supervised internship and receive a passing score on the national exam administered by the Commission on

Dietetic Registration. To maintain their credentials, registered dietitian nutritionists must complete continuing education requirements.

Registered dietetic technicians must complete a two-year associate's degree from an approved program and have supervised practical experience. Just like registered dietitian nutritionists, they must pass a national exam and complete continuing education requirements. Additional educational and training requirements for registered dietitian nutritionists and registered dietetic technicians may be obtained from the Academy of Nutrition and Dietetics.

Food scientists must have a minimum of a bachelor's degree in agricultural sciences. Many positions in this field, however, require an advanced degree in nutrition or dietetics. Graduate programs for food science place an emphasis on lab work and research. Certification from the Institute of Food Technologists (IFT) is not always necessary, but is helpful for career advancement as a food scientist.

For entrepreneurs selling food products and services, such as catering for special events, careful adherence to state standards and regulations is a must (**Figure 14.10**). Individual states enforce these food business laws. Some entrepreneurs must also adhere to additional laws. For example, people who sell food products online must also observe federal fair competition and tax laws. If shipping products internationally, then international laws apply, too. Food truck owners must adhere to standard foodservice laws and parking and business zoning regulations.

Dmitry Kalinovsky/Shutterstock.com

Figure 14.10 Most states require food handlers to take a class on food safety and/or pass a food handler's exam. *Where would someone go in your town to take a class on food safety?*

Copyright Goodheart-Willcox Co., Inc.

Reading Recall

1. What organization certifies culinary schools meeting its stringent standards?
2. What kind of certification is helpful for career advancement as a food scientist?

Specialized Knowledge for Food and Nutrition Related Human Services

Human services workers in the food and nutrition fields need specialized knowledge about the human side of food and nutrition. They understand that eating healthy across the life cycle and balancing food intake with physical activity will help maintain physical health. They also know how to plan and prepare healthy meals and snacks that contribute to wellness and provide the necessary energy to be productive throughout the lifespan.

Eating Healthy Across the Life Cycle

Food and nutrition related human services workers know that eating a well-balanced diet of healthful foods is important during every stage of life. They also know that establishing good eating behaviors early in life can help promote wellness. Healthful eating behaviors established at a young age are also likely to continue throughout adulthood. Likewise, poor nutrition choices established in childhood can have far-reaching effects. Nutritionists and dietitians work with their clients to develop menu plans that will promote eating healthy across the life cycle.

To help people ages two and older make healthful food choices, the USDA created a food guidance system called **MyPlate**. MyPlate divides foods into five groups: grains, vegetables, fruits, protein foods, and dairy (**Figure 14.11**). The MyPlate website offers information on nutritious food choices, healthy eating styles, and physical activity. Many online tools are available to keep track of food intake and activity levels, and much more.

During each stage of the life cycle, people have unique nutrient needs. These needs change as people age, which means people's eating patterns should change, too. Sometimes people have special dietary needs due to various lifestyle choices or health conditions.

Nutrition Before and During Pregnancy

A woman's well-balanced diet, healthy body weight, and physical fitness before pregnancy can provide the right setting for optimal development of a baby. Women who are at a healthy weight before pregnancy are more likely to have a healthy baby. Being overweight or underweight before pregnancy can increase the chances of problems occurring during the pregnancy.

Copyright Goodheart-Willcox Co., Inc.

The MyPlate Food Guidance System		
Food Groups	**Examples of Foods**	**Tips**
Grains *Scorpp/Shutterstock.com*	• Brown rice • Oatmeal • Popcorn • Quinoa • Whole-grain barley • Whole-grain cornmeal • Pasta • Whole-wheat bread, buns, and rolls • Tortillas • Grits • Breakfast cereals	• Substitute a whole-grain product for a refined product. • Experiment by substituting whole-wheat or oat flour for up to half of the flour in pancake, waffle, muffin, or other flour-based recipes. • Snack on ready-to-eat, whole-grain cereals, such as toasted oat cereal. • Add whole-grain flour or oatmeal when making cookies or other baked treats.
Vegetables *Stock Rocket/Shutterstock.com*	• Broccoli • Dark-green leafy lettuce • Acorn squash • Carrots • Corn • Cauliflower • Green beans • Artichokes • Kale • Potatoes • Asparagus	• Buy fresh vegetables in season. They cost less and are likely to be at their peak flavor. • Stock up on frozen vegetables for quick and easy cooking in the microwave. • Buy vegetables that are easy to prepare. Pick up pre-washed bags of salad greens, and add baby carrots or grape tomatoes for a salad in minutes. • Vary your veggie choices to keep meals interesting.
Fruits *leonori/Shutterstock.com*	• Melons • Berries • 100% fruit juice • Kiwi fruit • Tangerines • Lemons • Limes • Nectarines • Peaches • Bananas • Pears	• Keep a bowl of fruit on the table or in the refrigerator. • Refrigerate cut-up fruit to store for later. • Buy fresh fruits in season when they may be less expensive and at their peak flavor. • Buy dried, frozen, and canned fruit, as well as fresh, so you always have a supply on hand. • Try pre-cut packages of fruit for a healthy snack in seconds.

(Continued)

Figure 14.11 The MyPlate food guidance system offers many tips for choosing nutritious foods and eating healthy, incorporating a balanced diet of whole grains, vegetables, fruits, protein foods, and dairy products. *Which of these tips do you already follow? Which ones would you like to try?*

Copyright Goodheart-Willcox Co., Inc.

The MyPlate Food Guidance System (*Continued*)		
Food Groups	**Examples of Foods**	**Tips**
Protein foods *Africa Studio/Shutterstock.com*	• Almonds • Canned fish (anchovies, tuna, sardines) • Shellfish (lobster, shrimp, squid, clams) • Edamame • Hummus • Lean ground meats (beef, pork, sausage) • Lean luncheon meats (chicken, ham) • Duck • Ground chicken and turkey • Eggs • Tofu • Veggie burgers	• The leanest beef cuts include round steak and roasts, top loin, top sirloin, and chuck shoulder and arm roasts. • The leanest pork choices include pork loin, tenderloin, center loin, and ham. • Choose seafood at least twice a week as the main protein food. • Check the Nutrition Facts Label for the saturated fat, trans fat, cholesterol, and sodium content of packaged food. • Separate raw, cooked, and ready-to-eat foods.
Dairy *MaraZe/Shutterstock.com*	• Skim milk • Low-fat (1%) milk • Reduced-fat (2%) milk • Puddings • Frozen yogurt • Almond milk • Coconut milk • Yogurt • Kefir • Hard cheeses (cheddar, mozzarella) • Soft cheeses (ricotta, cottage cheese) • Ice cream • Rice milk	• Include fat-free milk as a beverage at meals. • If you drink whole milk, switch to fat-free milk to lower saturated fat and calories. • Avoid unpasteurized milk or any products made from unpasteurized milk. • Add fat-free or low-fat milk instead of water to oatmeal and hot cereals.

During pregnancy, each meal becomes a meal for mother and baby. Because so much growth and development is occurring for the baby, good nutrition is vital. To meet nutritional needs, women often need to eat an additional 300 calories daily beginning in the fourth month of their pregnancy. Women who are at a healthy weight before pregnancy should gain between 25 and 35 pounds while pregnant (**Figure 14.12**). Women who are overweight or underweight before pregnancy may be advised differently by their doctor.

Copyright Goodheart-Willcox Co., Inc.

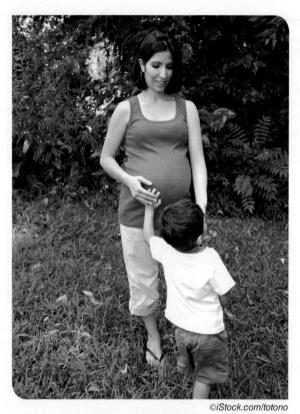
©iStock.com/totono

Figure 14.12 While women gain weight gradually during pregnancy, most of their weight is gained in the last three months. *Why do you think this is true?*

Pregnant women should strive to eat healthful foods. Even so, most doctors recommend additional vitamin and mineral supplements. *Prenatal vitamins*, made just for pregnancy, contain extra folic acid, calcium, and iron. The additional supplements have several benefits. *Folic acid* helps reduce brain and spinal cord birth defects. *Calcium* helps build strong bones and teeth. *Iron* helps to reduce the chance of babies being born at a low birthweight (less than 5.8 pounds).

Some foods should be avoided during pregnancy. These include some fish and shellfish that contain high levels of mercury. Undercooked meats, poultry (such as chicken), and eggs should be avoided. Milk products that are unpasteurized, such as cheese, should also not be eaten. All of these foods can cause food related illnesses that may affect the developing baby.

Nutrition During Infancy

Good nutrition is critical at any stage of development, but especially during infancy. Babies need well-balanced nutrition. Their needs are quite different from the nutritional needs of children or adults, however.

Because newborns are just learning to suck and swallow, their nutrition must come in liquid form. Breast milk is ideal food for babies for at least the first 6 months of life. Mothers, for a variety of reasons, may be unable to breast-feed and choose to feed their babies formula. In these cases, careful selection of a nutritious formula can meet the nutritional needs of the infant.

Between 6 and 12 months, caregivers often start feeding infants solids (**Figure 14.13**). A good way to do this is to introduce new foods to babies one at a time, and in small amounts. Caregivers should also try to wait several days before adding another new food to make sure the child does not have a bad reaction to the food.

Nutrition During the Toddler Years

During the toddler years, children no longer require baby foods. They are learning to feed themselves and use a cup. Toddlers can also eat foods that are prepared for the family. They are able to pick up bite-sized foods, chew, and swallow various solid foods.

Toddlers' stomachs are small and they prefer to eat small portions many times during the day. Long periods between meals do not sustain them, as their energy needs are high. Their taste buds are more sensitive

Copyright Goodheart-Willcox Co., Inc.

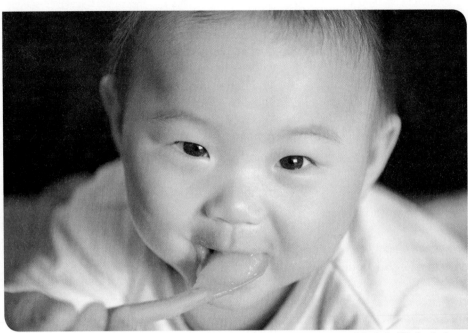

Figure 14.13 Solids for infants are semiliquid, mushy foods, such as commercially prepared baby foods or mashed, strained, or pureed table foods. *What are some examples of table foods that you could mash, strain, or puree for infants?*

totophotos/Shutterstock.com

than adults' and caregivers often interpret this as picky behavior. An assortment of flavors and textures can help toddlers enjoy a wider variety of foods.

To promote bone growth and strength, toddlers typically need to drink two cups of whole milk each day. Toddlers also need to eat a variety of nutritious foods, including plenty of fruits and vegetables. Toddlers who eat too many foods high in calories and low in nutritional value, such as junk foods, may gain too much weight. Physicians can help determine toddlers' nutritional needs based on their height, weight, and physical activity level.

Nutrition During Early Childhood

Because early childhood is such an important time for exploration, introducing a variety of nutritional food choices can have lasting positive effects on children. Providing well-balanced meals is important during this critical time of growth. Young children typically eat smaller amounts due to their smaller stomach size. Therefore, healthy snacks between meals are often necessary (**Figure 14.14**).

In early childhood, the eating habits of caregivers strongly influence the eating preferences of children. Eating meals on a regular schedule, decreasing distractions (such as television) and reducing stress from conflicts during meals, and offering healthy choices can have positive long-term effects. On the other hand, when meals are stressful or restrictive, the effects can be negative. For example, restricting food from a child's diet can result in the child overeating when the food becomes available. The child may eat the food even when he or she feels full.

Copyright Goodheart-Willcox Co., Inc.

Healthy Snacks for Children	
• Apple slices with string cheese or peanut butter • Baked potato with melted, reduced-fat cheese • Baked whole-grain crackers with almond butter and juice • Banana slices dipped in yogurt, rolled in cereal, and frozen • Canned salmon mixed with low-fat mayo • Crinkle-cut carrot "chips" with hummus • Edamame • Frozen no-sugar-added fruit bars with a glass of milk • Guacamole and baked snack chips • Instant oatmeal made with milk and topped with berries • Low-fat Greek yogurt • Low-fat yogurt smoothie • Low-fat ice cream or frozen yogurt topped with fresh fruit • Low-fat microwave popcorn tossed with Parmesan cheese	• Low-fat plain or chocolate milk and whole-wheat pretzels • Mini bagel spread with low-fat cream cheese and jam • Trail mix • Vegetables with low-fat ranch dressing • Whole-grain cereal and low-fat milk • Whole-grain crackers, string cheese, and mango slices • Whole-grain pretzels or rice cakes with a slice of cheese • Whole-grain tortilla chips topped with veggies and salsa • Whole-wheat pita bread triangles with melted cheese • Whole-wheat pretzels with peanut or almond butter • Whole-wheat tortilla chips with bean dip

Figure 14.14 These are some examples of healthy snacks children can eat between meals to keep them satisfied. *Which snacks on this list appeal to you the most? Are there other healthy snacks you would add to this list?*

Nutrition During Middle Childhood

Compared to early childhood, school-age children are less picky about food. Their taste buds are not as sensitive, and some children are willing to explore new foods. For other children, pickiness in food choices becomes a habit. Throughout middle childhood, children's appetites increase. Because their bodies are growing, frequent and nutritious meals and snacks are best.

During middle childhood, children are often making more of their own food choices at home, at school, and away from home. Poor nutrition may become an issue. Children should avoid junk foods high in calories and low in nutrients, such as cookies and cakes. Instead, they should make nutrient-dense food choices.

Nutrient-dense foods are rich in vitamins and minerals and contain relatively few calories. Examples of nutrient-dense foods include fruits, vegetables, whole-grain foods, seafood, eggs, beans, peas, and unsalted nuts. Fat-free and low-fat dairy products and meats and poultry that are lean or do not have much fat are also nutrient-dense choices (**Figure 14.15**). Foods that are *fortified*, or have added vitamins and minerals, may also be nutrient-dense food choices.

Copyright Goodheart-Willcox Co., Inc.

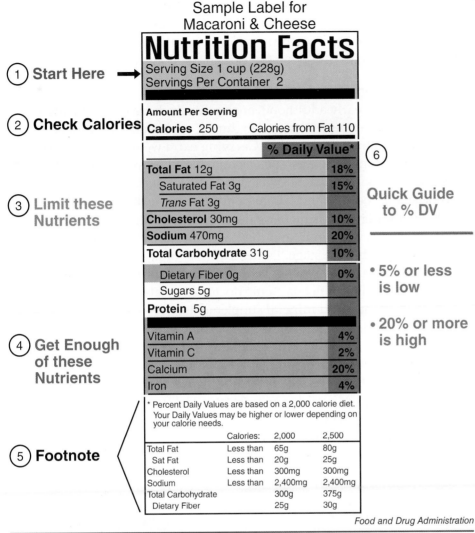

Sample Label for Macaroni & Cheese

Nutrition Facts

① **Start Here** →
Serving Size 1 cup (228g)
Servings Per Container 2

Amount Per Serving

② **Check Calories** | Calories 250 | Calories from Fat 110

	% Daily Value*	⑥
Total Fat 12g	18%	
Saturated Fat 3g	15%	
Trans Fat 3g		
Cholesterol 30mg	10%	
Sodium 470mg	20%	
Total Carbohydrate 31g	10%	
Dietary Fiber 0g	0%	
Sugars 5g		
Protein 5g		
Vitamin A	4%	
Vitamin C	2%	
Calcium	20%	
Iron	4%	

③ **Limit these Nutrients**

④ **Get Enough of these Nutrients**

Quick Guide to % DV

• **5% or less is low**

• **20% or more is high**

* Percent Daily Values are based on a 2,000 calorie diet. Your Daily Values may be higher or lower depending on your calorie needs.

⑤ **Footnote**

	Calories:	2,000	2,500
Total Fat	Less than	65g	80g
Sat Fat	Less than	20g	25g
Cholesterol	Less than	300mg	300mg
Sodium	Less than	2,400mg	2,400mg
Total Carbohydrate		300g	375g
Dietary Fiber		25g	30g

Food and Drug Administration

Figure 14.15 Check food labels to choose nutritious foods. *Which nutrients are the most important to limit in your diet?*

Nutrition During Adolescence

Adolescents are more responsible for their own food choices and meal preparation than in earlier stages of life. They also usually have very busy schedules. This may encourage unhealthy choices, such as skipping meals or grabbing unhealthy snacks. Their snack choices may be high in fat and sugar, which do not provide the body with the essential nutrients needed to fuel growth. As in other stages of the life cycle, adolescents should choose nutrient-dense foods at meal and snack times to meet their nutritional and energy needs.

As adolescents are making more of their own food choices, they can use the interactive tools and resources on the MyPlate website to create an eating style that promotes health and wellness now and into adulthood.

Copyright Goodheart-Willcox Co., Inc.

They can view sample menus and create their own to meet their personal nutrient needs. They can view many tips for making nutritious food choices (**Figure 14.16**). They can check out healthy recipes. They can even set weight loss goals and track their progress in meeting these goals.

Nutrition During Early Adulthood

Throughout early adulthood, energy needs decrease. Reducing food intake from the amounts consumed during adolescence is often necessary to avoid unhealthy weight gains. Carrying extra weight can increase the risk for chronic diseases, such as high blood pressure and high cholesterol. Making nutrient-dense food choices and avoiding foods high in cholesterol, sodium, and fat are important for health and wellness.

Some nutrient needs increase during early adulthood. Calcium, iron, potassium, zinc, vitamin D, and the B vitamins are nutrients that are often lacking during this life stage. Eating a variety of healthful, nutrient-dense foods, such as fruits, vegetables, seafood, whole grains, and low-fat dairy can help meet nutrient needs. Some doctors may also recommend that adults take vitamin and mineral supplements.

Culturally, dining at restaurants can be a main social activity during early adulthood. Adults can make healthful choices when dining out by selecting items from the menu that are low in fat, not fried, and have less sugar and salt. Selecting smaller portion sizes and food items with more fruits and vegetables can also help (**Figure 14.17**).

Nutrition During Middle Adulthood

During middle adulthood, energy needs continue to decrease and adults commonly gain one to two pounds per year. As in other stages

Healthy Tips for Choosing Foods

- Make half your plate fruits and vegetables.
- Make half your grains whole grains.
- Move to low-fat and fat-free dairy.
- Vary your protein routine.
- Compare the saturated fat, sodium, and added sugars in your foods and beverages.
- Eat and drink the right amount for you.
- Cook more often at home to control the ingredients in your food.
- Eat well when eating foods away from home.
- Be active your way.

Figure 14.16 These are some healthy tips from the MyPlate website that individuals can incorporate into their eating patterns to increase their health and wellness. *Which of these tips do you need to incorporate into your eating pattern?*

Copyright Goodheart-Willcox Co., Inc.

Dani Vincek/Shutterstock.com

Figure 14.17 While dining out, choosing meals with more vegetables often provides a healthier option. *What other tips can you use to make healthful choices when dining out?*

of the life cycle, weighing more than a healthy amount can increase the risk for certain chronic diseases. Carrying extra weight can also be hard on body joints, such as the knees. Knee joints may need to be replaced with artificial joints through surgical procedures. The risk of developing several different types of cancer also increases.

As physical abilities continue to decline throughout middle adulthood, good nutrition and regular physical activity are even more important to maintain in this stage of life. Maintaining a healthy weight helps to counteract many health problems. Physical activity helps to control weight and maintain muscle strength. Without some change in diet and activity level, the average middle-aged adult will gain 10 to 20 pounds throughout this stage of the life cycle (**Figure 14.18**).

Nutrition During Older Adulthood

Although nutritional needs change in older adulthood, adults still need to consume a variety of foods from the fruits, vegetables, grains, dairy, and protein food groups. Calories consumed should come from nutrient-dense, well-balanced sources that include protein, vitamins, and minerals.

During older adulthood, the body's ability to absorb certain nutrients decreases. Older adults may need to take dietary supplements to ensure they are meeting nutritional needs. The needs for calcium and vitamin D increase to help promote bone strength. Vitamin B_{12} and potassium needs also increase. By increasing fiber and water intake, older adults may prevent constipation. Sources for these additional nutritional needs

Copyright Goodheart-Willcox Co., Inc.

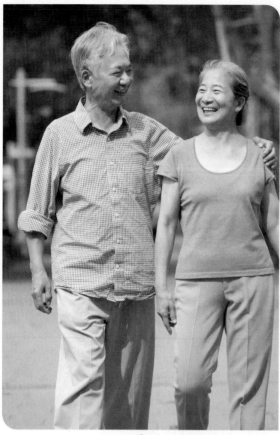

©iStock.com/monkeybusinessimages

Figure 14.18 Reducing calorie intake by just 100 calories a day and taking a daily walk can decrease the tendency for gradual weight increase over the years. *Why do caloric needs often decrease as people age?*

include milk, bananas, whole-grain foods, fortified foods, and dietary supplements.

As in other life stages, caloric needs vary depending on age, weight, height, and level of physical activity. Medications and state of health can have an effect on older adults' nutritional needs. Nutritionists or dietitians can create dietary plans that will meet older adults' nutritional needs. By making healthful changes in the diet, weight and chronic health issues may be controlled.

Special Dietary Needs

Regardless of the stage of the life cycle, certain choices and conditions result in some people having special dietary needs. For example, a competitive athlete is often much more physically active than a nonathlete. The level of activity is likely to be more strenuous, too. Therefore, competitive athletes may need more nutrients than a less active person of the same size and gender. Nutrient-dense food choices are important to maintain health and performance. Fluid intake is also highly important for athletes to avoid dehydration during training and competitive events. Drinking cool water before, during, and after training sessions or events can help athletes meet fluid needs.

Another lifestyle choice that involves special dietary needs is vegetarianism. A **vegetarian** is a person who excludes some or all animal products from his or her diet. There are several different types of vegetarian diets (**Figure 14.19**). Careful planning is essential to make sure that a vegetarian diet includes the necessary amounts of nutrients needed.

A condition that may require special dietary needs includes food intolerances and allergies. A **food intolerance** is an unpleasant reaction to a food, such as digestive or behavioral problems. A **food allergy** occurs when a food triggers a response by the body's immune system. A food allergy can cause a more severe reaction than a food intolerance, including breathing problems or death. Simply being around the food can cause reactions in some people. The most common causes of food allergies include milk, eggs, tree nuts, peanuts, soy, wheat, fish, and shellfish. To avoid foods that may trigger intolerances or allergies, it is important to read food labels and remove any offending foods from the diet.

Copyright Goodheart-Willcox Co., Inc.

Types of Vegetarians	
• Lacto-ovo vegetarians	• Eat milk products, eggs, and plant foods • Do not eat meat, fish, or poultry
• Lacto-vegetarians	• Eat milk products and plant foods • Do not eat meat, fish, poultry, or eggs
• Ovo-vegetarians	• Eat plant food and eggs • Do not eat milk products, meat, poultry, or fish
• Pescetarians	• Eat plant foods and fish • Do not eat meat or poultry
• Vegans	• Eat plant foods only • Also called *strict vegetarians*

Figure 14.19 Different types of vegetarians exclude different groups of animal products from their diets. *Which type of vegetarian excludes milk products, eggs, meat, fish, and poultry?*

Certain health conditions, such as diabetes, may also cause people to change their eating patterns. **Diabetes** is a disease in which the body is unable to produce *insulin* (a hormone), resulting in an inability to properly use energy from food. To manage diabetes, a healthy diet and regular physical activity are highly important. Prescription medication may also be recommended by the doctor. People with diabetes need controlled amounts of nutritious foods at meals, and often at about the same time each day (**Figure 14.20**). Other health conditions may also require special dietary needs. Nutritionists and dietitians can help people with medical conditions establish healthy eating patterns to meet their dietary needs.

Maintaining Physical Health

Being a healthy weight for your body build is an important sign of good health. Workers in food and nutrition fields, however, know that weight is not always the best gauge for determining a person's health. In fact, the amount of body fat a person carries has a much greater impact on health than total weight.

Body composition describes the proportion of body fat to lean mass (muscle, bone, and water) in a person's body. People who have a high amount of body fat in relation to lean body mass are characterized as **overweight**. **Obesity** is a condition characterized by an excessive amount of body fat. To maintain physical health, people need to get regular physical activity and avoid unhealthy eating patterns.

Getting Physical Activity

According to the *Physical Activity Guidelines for Americans*, children between 6–17 years of age should get 1 hour or more of moderate- or vigorous-intensity physical activity each day. Adults 18 years of age and

Copyright Goodheart-Willcox Co., Inc.

Martin Turzak/Shutterstock.com

Figure 14.20 Diabetic people are encouraged to eat a variety of healthful foods and watch portion sizes. *Why is it so important for people with diabetes to eat at about the same time each day?*

older should participate in 150 minutes of moderate or 75 minutes of vigorous physical activity per week. People may choose to divide this time for physical activities throughout the week (**Figure 14.21**).

Three types of activities that are important for maintaining physical health include aerobic, muscle-strengthening, and bone-strengthening activities. Aerobic activities, such as walking, biking, or swimming, help strengthen the heart and lungs. Muscle-strengthening activities, such as weightlifting, push-ups, or sit-ups, improve both large and small muscles. Bone-strengthening activities, such as jumping rope or playing basketball, create stronger bones to avoid bone-related diseases in the future.

In addition to physical activity promoting individual health, it can also be a social activity. Taking an aerobics class, visiting the local fitness center, walking with a friend, or playing a team sport are all social activities. Building or maintaining physical activity habits can positively impact a person's health in the future. Physical activity also helps to maintain a healthy body weight, lower stress, and reduce the occurrence of anxiety and depression.

Avoiding Unhealthy Eating Patterns

People who develop healthy eating patterns eat nutritious foods and in the right amounts to meet their nutrient needs. Unfortunately, some people develop eating patterns that are abnormal and potentially harmful to physical health. They may follow fad diets or develop an eating disorder.

Expert Insight

"Physical fitness is not only one of the most important keys to a healthy body, it is the basis of dynamic and creative intellectual activity."

John F. Kennedy, former US president

Copyright Goodheart-Willcox Co., Inc.

Physical Activity Guidelines for Americans

Children and adolescents (6–17 years)  *oliveromg/Shutterstock.com*	• Should do 1 hour or more of physical activity every day. • Most of the 1 hour or more of physical activity should be either moderate- or vigorous-intensity aerobic activity, and should include vigorous-intensity physical activity at least 3 days per week. • Part of the daily physical activity should include muscle-strengthening activity at least 3 days per week. • Part of the daily physical activity should include bone-strengthening activity at least 3 days per week.
Adults (18–64 years)  *Maridav/Shutterstock.com*	• Should do 2 hours and 30 minutes a week of moderate-intensity, or 1 hour and 15 minutes a week of vigorous-intensity aerobic physical activity. Aerobic activity should be performed in episodes of at least 10 minutes, preferably spread throughout the week. • Additional health benefits are provided by increasing to 5 hours a week of moderate-intensity aerobic physical activity, or 2 hours and 30 minutes a week of vigorous-intensity physical activity, or an equivalent combination of both. • Should also do muscle-strengthening activities that involve all major muscle groups performed on 2 or more days per week.
Older adults (65+ years)  *Monkey Business Images/Shutterstock.com*	• Older adults should follow the adult guidelines. If this is not possible due to limiting chronic conditions, older adults should be as physically active as their abilities allow. They should avoid inactivity. • Older adults should do exercises that maintain or improve balance if they are at risk of falling.

Figure 14.21 The *Physical Activity Guidelines for Americans* provides recommendations for weekly activity goals, according to age. *According to the guidelines, how much activity should you get each day?*

Fad Diets

Fad diets are diets promising quick and easy weight loss. Fad diets are often promoted in commercials or other advertising. They appear popular, successful, and may even be endorsed by celebrities. They are termed *fad* diets because they often do not last.

Copyright Goodheart-Willcox Co., Inc.

Fad dieting plans can be unsafe, and may especially be harmful to individuals with specific health needs. Fad diets may include pills, excluding a particular food group from the diet, or including only one food group in the diet. For example, a fad diet may claim a liquid-only diet can boost energy and promote rapid weight loss. An extreme dieting plan may involve fasting, or going lengthy periods without eating any meals.

The body requires essential nutrients from foods in all of the food groups to perform basic bodily functions, grow and develop, and maintain optimum health. When a diet excludes a food group or focuses on only one food group, the fad diet is likely unhealthy and should be avoided. Also, since these are short-term diets, they do nothing to promote long-term healthy eating habits needed for a lifetime of weight management.

Eating Disorders

An **eating disorder** is a serious condition that involves abnormal eating patterns that can cause severe or life-threatening physical problems. Eating disorders can cause significant concerns both physically and emotionally. They often develop from a combination of factors relating to self-esteem, personal body image, stress, and cultural views on the ideal body type. There are different types of eating disorders. These types include the following:

- **Anorexia nervosa** is the relentless pursuit of thinness through starvation. People who have anorexia have a fear of becoming overweight even though they are often underweight. Because anorexia involves self-starvation, the body does not get the essential nutrients needed to grow, develop, and function. Body processes must slow down to conserve energy. People who have anorexia may experience hair loss, fatigue, weakness, low blood pressure, and an abnormally slow heart rate. This increases the risk of heart failure.

- **Bulimia nervosa** involves consuming large amounts of food (*bingeing*) and then expelling the food from the system (*purging*), usually by means such as vomiting or using laxatives. Bulimia nervosa can cause serious health problems because of the bingeing and purging cycle. The entire digestive system can become damaged. Chemical imbalances in the body can lead to heart failure. Damage to other organs can cause them to not function properly. Bulimia is linked to both depression and low self-esteem.

- **Binge-eating disorder** involves eating large amounts of food without taking any actions to reduce the amount of food intake. Periods of bingeing are usually followed by feelings of shame or disgust and a lack of control over eating behaviors. People with this disorder are usually aware of their unhealthy eating habits, but feel they cannot

Expert Insight

"Too many people overvalue what they are not, and undervalue what they are."

Malcolm Forbes, entrepreneur

or do not know how to break the negative pattern. Health risks commonly associated with binge-eating disorder include high blood pressure, high cholesterol, diabetes, and heart disease.

People who have eating disorders need professional help to treat the condition. Psychologists, nutritionists, and doctors can provide support. Early diagnosis and intervention can help enhance recovery.

Preparing Healthy Meals

Preparing or offering healthy, well-balanced meals is the first order of business for food workers in human services. Food related human services workers, who by the very nature of their work, want to help people by providing food and services that will be beneficial to their customers and their clients. They prepare or serve nutritious meals or snacks that contribute to wellness and productivity through the lifespan. In preparing healthy meals, nutritional content should be considered. This consideration may be for one meal or snack or an entire meal plan. Nutritional knowledge is first and foremost in successful meal selection or preparation. Second is making the food appetizing.

A well-balanced meal is visually pleasing and does not duplicate tastes. It should offer contrast and variety in color, texture, flavor, and temperature, which contributes to an appetizing presentation and experience (**Figure 14.22**). For example, bland flavors found in pastas, potatoes, and breads should be contrasted with strong flavors, such as meats, condiments, or spicy vegetables.

For those workers who are preparing healthy meals, they need the critical knowledge of food safety and sanitation. Knowing how to prepare food properly in a safe manner is essential and can make or break a business.

Four Menu Planning Tips	
Create variety and contrast in:	**Methods:**
Color	Offer a variety of food colors, especially those that are bright, dark, and contrasting.
Texture	Offer both crunchy and smooth textures to add interest and promote the appetite.
Seasonings	Include both salty and sweet tastes as the first heightens the appetite and the other dulls it; contrast spicy with bland to build interest.
Temperature	Include a variety of temperatures from hot to cold.

Figure 14.22 Planning a menu requires choosing a combination of appetizing foods with visual appeal, contrast, and variety. *Give an example of a meal that incorporates all of these tips.*

Copyright Goodheart-Willcox Co., Inc.

Pathway to Success

Planning Healthy Meals

Planning meals in advance helps ensure you are getting the right amounts of foods from each of the food groups to meet your nutrient needs. Healthy meal planning takes time in advance, but the benefit of eating a healthy meal in the right portion size is worth the extra work. Eating healthy can positively impact wellness and even give you more energy to improve productivity.

The first step to planning healthy meals is to look at how many meals you need to plan for the week. Think about your budget and how much time you have to cook.

- Write the days of the week on the left side of a piece of paper and the meals you want to plan across the top.
- Sketch out with vague descriptions your weekly meals. Use phrases like quick dinner, leftover, or packable lunch.
- Tally up how many meals you will need, grouping similar ones like two quick dinners, three packable lunches.

Next, decide what you want to cook and look at recipes. Try to avoid selecting different recipes that do not fit together or you will be buying a lot of different ingredients.

Start a master recipe list of items you like and ones you would like to try. The following tips may help as you plan your meals:

- Organize meals using a calendar, recording meals once a week or month.
- Overlap ingredients by selecting recipes with like ingredients. This helps to minimize how much you have to buy.
- Look at grocery circulars for sales and specials. Jot down any deals of interest as a reminder to select recipes using those ingredients.
- Fill in your calendar, writing a grocery list as you do, including quantities for each ingredient. Look at the weather. You will probably not want soup if it is 90°F outside.
- Take stock of what you have on hand before heading to the store. Do not buy items you already have.
- Pick a time to shop. Use coupons and the circulars at the store for sales and specials.

Finally, prep your meals ahead of time, especially if you know you will be short on time the day you are cooking. Many people use Sunday afternoons to prep vegetables and other items for the week to help save time.

Writing a One-Week Meal Plan

Using the information and tips from above, create a healthy meal plan for you and your family for one week. Make sure your plan includes breakfasts, lunches, and dinners for the entire week. Take into consideration everyone's dietary needs when creating your meal plan. Type your meal plan and share with your family so everyone can implement the plan. After the week of meals, have your family critique how well you planned and executed the healthy meals you cooked. How did eating healthy meals all week affect your and your family members' wellness and productivity? Did you notice any differences?

Copyright Goodheart-Willcox Co., Inc.

Knowing how to read a recipe is essential to successful food preparation and minimizes loss. Lastly, knowing how to set a table and serve food is essential for food related human services workers' success in both running a business and meeting the needs of their clients and customers.

Food Safety and Sanitation

Each year, thousands of people become sick because of food that was not prepared or stored properly. Foodborne illness (also called *foodborne poisoning, disease,* or *infection*) is common, costly, preventable, and a huge public health problem. Several hundred different foodborne diseases have been identified, including infections caused by a variety of bacteria, viruses, and parasites that can be found in food (**Figure 14.23**). Sometimes harmful toxins or chemicals cause food related problems.

Symptoms related to foodborne illnesses vary. Because most foodborne illnesses enter the body through the mouth and pass through the intestinal tract, they often result in vomiting, nausea, abdominal cramps, and diarrhea. Sometimes they develop into much more serious diseases later. There are some basic food safety tips that those who work with food need to be aware of when purchasing, transporting, preparing, serving, and storing food.

When buying groceries, foods must be handled carefully and, if necessary, separated. For example, foods that are raw but need to be cooked, such as meats, must be separated from those that will be consumed raw, such as vegetables. If not separated, meat juices leak and contaminate other food items.

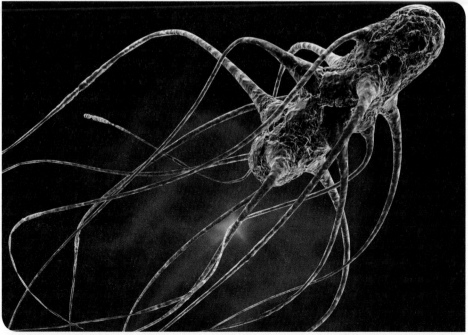

Figure 14.23 This salmonella bacterium is found in certain uncooked foods, and it can cause a serious infection if the food is not prepared or stored properly. *What are some of the symptoms related to foodborne illnesses?*

MichaelTaylor/Shutterstock.com

Copyright Goodheart-Willcox Co., Inc.

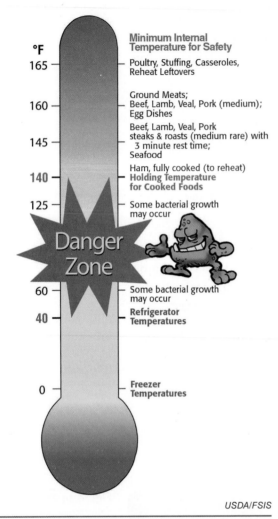

°F

165 — Minimum Internal
Temperature for Safety
Poultry, Stuffing, Casseroles,
Reheat Leftovers

160 — Ground Meats;
Beef, Lamb, Veal, Pork (medium);
Egg Dishes

145 — Beef, Lamb, Veal, Pork
steaks & roasts (medium rare) with
3 minute rest time;
Seafood

140 — Ham, fully cooked (to reheat)
Holding Temperature
for Cooked Foods

125 — Some bacterial growth
may occur

Danger Zone

60 — Some bacterial growth
may occur

40 — Refrigerator
Temperatures

0 — Freezer
Temperatures

USDA/FSIS

Figure 14.24 Use a food thermometer to check food temperatures. *What is the minimum internal temperature for a casserole?*

Hands should be washed thoroughly both before handling and during the process of preparing different ingredients. When handwashing, use hot water and antibacterial soap, scrubbing for at least 30 seconds. To dry your hands, use a disposable paper hand towel. Kitchen utensils should also be sanitized and clean. This is especially important for cutting boards, which should be cleaned and sanitized between each use. Meats should never be cut on the same cutting board as vegetables, fruits, or other raw food items. A good way to ensure that this is done is to use a bleach solution to sanitize and prevent the spread of harmful bacteria. There are color-coded cutting boards that can assist in keeping food types separate during processing.

When cooking meat, the internal temperature of the food needs to meet the minimum requirements (**Figure 14.24**). Beef and roasts should reach an internal temperature of at least 145°F. For ground meats, the internal temperature should reach at least 160°F, and for poultry 165°F. Some may choose to cook to a higher temperature according to taste and to ensure that it is safe to eat. It also helps to let meat sit for a minute, as it keeps cooking once it is out of the heat source. After cooking, meat should be refrigerated as soon as possible.

When serving, especially in buffet or reception settings, perishable food should not sit out on the table or counter for more than two hours. When hot perishable foods are set out, care should be taken to make sure they stay above 140° by using warming trays. Perishable food that is served at room temperature or below should be nestled in trays of ice. A good strategy is to use smaller serving trays or bowls that can be stored safely until needed, trading out empty containers when necessary. When the event is finished, all food should be refrigerated immediately.

Reading Recipes

The successful preparation of a meal or snack involves the ability to read and follow a **recipe** (a set of written instructions to prepare an item). Successfully using a recipe takes some preparation. Like any good story, the context and setting matter. This is why it is best to read through a whole recipe before beginning food preparation. **Figure 14.25** shows a sample recipe.

Copyright Goodheart-Willcox Co., Inc.

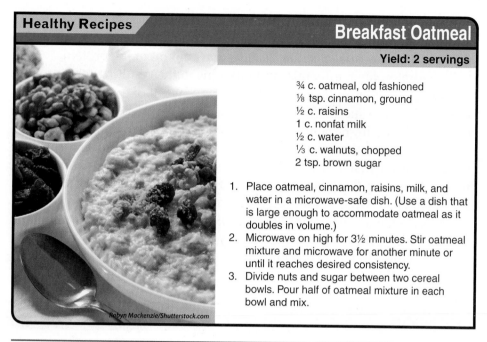

Healthy Recipes

Breakfast Oatmeal

Yield: 2 servings

¾ c. oatmeal, old fashioned
⅛ tsp. cinnamon, ground
½ c. raisins
1 c. nonfat milk
½ c. water
⅓ c. walnuts, chopped
2 tsp. brown sugar

1. Place oatmeal, cinnamon, raisins, milk, and water in a microwave-safe dish. (Use a dish that is large enough to accommodate oatmeal as it doubles in volume.)
2. Microwave on high for 3½ minutes. Stir oatmeal mixture and microwave for another minute or until it reaches desired consistency.
3. Divide nuts and sugar between two cereal bowls. Pour half of oatmeal mixture in each bowl and mix.

Robyn Mackenzie/Shutterstock.com

Figure 14.25 Reading through a recipe before beginning food preparation helps ensure you have everything you need and that you understand the directions. *How many servings does this recipe yield?*

First, when reading the recipe, the language must be understood. Recipes contain common food preparation terms. For example, how does the term "fold ingredients" differ from "mix ingredients" or "slice" differ from "cut," "chop," or "dice"? Just as when reading a book, if a word is not understood, a dictionary can help give meaning to the sentence or instructions.

The role of the ingredients must also be understood, too. That is, how ingredients chemically react to produce a successful food product. For example, in baked goods, a *leavening agent* might be used to make the product rise or expand and create the desired texture. A single leavening agent or a combination of ingredients can cause this effect. Examples of leavening agents may include yeast, baking powder, baking soda, or cream of tartar. For this reason, ingredients should be carefully measured and not substituted, if possible, if the expected results are desired (**Figure 14.26**).

Recipes can give a lot of useful information, including the expected number of servings and cooking equipment and utensils needed. Preparation time, including additional time

Abbreviations Used in Recipes	
Abbreviation	**Unit of Measure**
tsp. or t.	teaspoon
Tbsp. or T.	tablespoon
c. or C.	cup
pt.	pint
qt.	quart
gal.	gallon
oz.	ounce
lb. or #	pound

Figure 14.26 These are common measurements found in recipes. *Which of the following is larger: a teaspoon or a tablespoon?*

Copyright Goodheart-Willcox Co., Inc.

needed for resting, rising, refrigeration, or freezing during preparation, and cooking temperatures and times are also included. Recipes often give a nutritional analysis that includes the amount of fat, protein, carbohydrates, fiber, minerals, and vitamins in the resulting food product.

Recipes list ingredients and the correct amount of each ingredient that is needed to successfully prepare the item. It is a good practice to set out all required ingredients, measuring tools, and preparation equipment before beginning the assembly process. That way, the cook will be less likely to be surprised by a missing ingredient. It will also be easier to work when everything is within reach. **Figure 14.27** shows common kitchen utensils needed for food preparation tasks.

It is customary for recipes to be written so the ingredient is measured first and then processed second. For example, "one cup raisins, chopped" should be interpreted as one measured cup of raisins that is then

Common Kitchen Utensils

Measuring Tools	
 *Goodheart-Willcox*	• *Liquid measuring cup*—measure liquid ingredients, such as water, milk, or oil. • *Dry measuring cup*—measure dry ingredients, such as flour and sugar. • *Measuring spoon*—measure small amounts of liquid or dry ingredients, such as extracts and spices.
Mixing Tools	
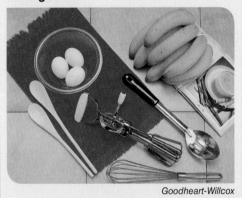 *Goodheart-Willcox*	• *Wooden spoon*—stir and mix ingredients. • *Rotary beater*—beat and blend ingredients. • *Slotted spoon*—remove pieces of food from liquid. • *Whisk*—incorporate air into foods.

(Continued)

Figure 14.27 Common kitchen utensils include measuring, mixing, baking, cutting, and other tools. *How many of the kitchen utensils in the photos are you able to match to the descriptions provided? Are there any tools you do not recognize?*

Copyright Goodheart-Willcox Co., Inc.

Common Kitchen Utensils *(Figure 14.27 Continued)*

Baking Tools  *Goodheart-Willcox*	• *Sifter*—blend dry ingredients and remove any lumps. • *Rubber spatula*—scrape foods from bowls and pans. • *Pastry blender*—blend shortening with flour or blend butter or cheese mixtures. • *Pastry brush*—apply butter or sauces on foods. • *Bent-edged spatula*—remove cookies from a baking tray or turn food items such as meats, pancakes, and eggs. • *Rolling pin*—roll dough or pastry. • *Pastry cloth*—keep dough from sticking to the counter while it is being kneaded or rolled. • *Straight-edged spatula*—spread icings and meringues and level ingredients in dry measures.
Cutting Tools  *Goodheart-Willcox*	• *Shredder-grater*—shred and grate vegetables and cheese. • *Peeler*—remove the peel or skin from fruits and vegetables. • *Kitchen shears*—cut herbs, vegetables, dough, pizza, poultry, and fish. • *Cutting board*—protect countertops and tabletops while cutting or chopping. • *Knives*—perform various tasks, such as cutting, dicing, chopping, or mincing.
Other Tools  *Goodheart-Willcox*	• *Colander*—drain foods or wash fruits and vegetables. • *Strainer*—separate liquid and solid foods. • *Ladle*—serve soups, sauces, stews, and punches. • *Kitchen fork*—turn heavy foods or transfer heavy meats and poultry. • *Tongs*—lift and turn foods or remove foods from hot liquid. • *Baster*—baste foods (cover foods with liquid) or skim fat from soups and gravies.

chopped. This also helps with more efficient assembly and reduces the possibility of cross-contamination of food ingredients and utensils.

When measuring, transparent measuring cups should be used for liquid ingredients. This allows the cook to accurately see the level of the liquid against the measurement line. Dry ingredients should be measured using cups that can be leveled off flat on the top.

Copyright Goodheart-Willcox Co., Inc.

When assembling ingredients in a recipe, it is important to follow instructions. The recipe author has likely carefully constructed the instructions to get the best result. Cooking and baking temperatures and times should be followed with consideration given to differences in cooking equipment, cookware, altitude, and relative humidity.

Setting the Table and Serving Food

In many food related human services scenarios, workers need to know how to set a table to offer their customers the best possible dining experience. Foodservice is as much about offering hospitality as it is about offering nourishment, and creating an environment is a large part of this. This is especially true in sit-down foodservice establishments.

Before guests are seated, the table must be prepared and set. First, it is customary to lay a tablecloth over the table in formal settings or placemats in less formal settings. For visual appeal, something of interest or beauty is often placed on the table. Flowers and candles are often chosen. Each guest's place setting is properly arranged (**Figure 14.28**).

Once meal service begins, food servers bring food to each guest. The server presents each guest's meal on the guest's left-hand side. In less formal food establishments, the server presents a serving dish to the host, who then passes it to the right. Each guest helps him- or herself as the serving dish moves around the table.

Figure 14.28 Setting a table properly requires several steps. *When setting the table, should the salad fork or the dinner fork be set closest to the plate?*

Setting a Table

Vibe Images/Shutterstock.com

- Set the knife and spoon to the right of the plate with the knife closest to the plate. The blade of the knife should face the plate.
- If needed, set the soupspoon to the right of the knife and spoon.
- Set the dinner fork and salad fork to the left of the plate with the dinner fork closest to the plate.
- If needed, set a dessert spoon or fork across the top of the plate.
- Set the beverage glass or cup above the upper-right corner of the plate.
- Set the bread plate above the upper left-corner of the plate.

Copyright Goodheart-Willcox Co., Inc.

Reading Recall

1. Give five examples of nutrient-dense foods.
2. Caloric intake depends on what factors?
3. Explain the difference between a *food intolerance* and a *food allergy*.
4. What are three benefits of physical activity?
5. What are three common types of eating disorders?
6. Identify common symptoms of foodborne illness.
7. Define *recipe.*
8. List six common kitchen utensils.
9. When setting a table, where should the knife and spoon be placed?
10. When setting a table, where should the beverage glass or cup be placed?

Rewards, Demands, and Future Trends

Workers in the food and nutrition field enjoy a fast-paced, dynamic, creative environment. Many like that every day is different, with new challenges. Food and nutrition workers often work long hours. They may be the first to arrive in the morning and the last to leave at night. Many workers spend the day on their feet, which can be physically demanding. For entry-level positions, the pay is considerably low, but opportunities for advancement are often possible.

Because people always have and always will have a need for food, the job outlook continues to be very good for food and nutrition related human services workers. Many job prospects in the food and nutrition industry are expected to grow at a faster rate than average (**Figure 14.29**). Career opportunities in clinical nutrition, nutrition education, community nutrition, public health, and research are just a few of the opportunities that exist in the field of nutrition. Foodservice management, food science, and food product development and marketing opportunities are available in the retail and marketing segments of the food industry.

Reading Recall

1. Give an example of a reward in the food and nutrition field.
2. Give an example of a demand in the food and nutrition field.
3. List five jobs in the food and nutrition industry that are expected to grow at a faster rate than average.
4. Identify at least three careers in Figure 14.29 that interest you. Based on the information in the chart, would you want to learn more about these careers?

Future Trends for Food and Nutrition Related Human Services Careers				
Occupation	**Projected Growth (2014–2024)**	**Projected Job Openings (2014–2024)**	**Median Wages (2014)**	**Education**
Caterer	Decline (–2% or lower)	48,000	$20,190	High school diploma
Clinical dietitian	Much faster than average (14% or higher)	16,000	$56,950	Post-baccalaureate certificate
Clinical nutritionist	Much faster than average (14% or higher)	16,000	$56,950	Post-baccalaureate certificate
Community consultant	Much faster than average (14% or higher)	18,800	$34,870	Unspecified
Community dietitian	Much faster than average (14% or higher)	18,800	$34,870	Unspecified
Community educator	Faster than average (9–13%)	19,500	$50,430	Unspecified
Community nutritionist	Much faster than average (14% or higher)	18,800	$34,870	Unspecified
Cook, institution and cafeteria	Average (5–8%)	136,800	$23,440	High school diploma
Dietitian	Much faster than average (14% or higher)	16,000	$56,950	Post-baccalaureate certificate
Executive chef	Faster than average (9–13%)	30,400	$41,610	Associate's degree
Food and beverage serving worker	Slower than average (2–4%)	1,255,000	$18,730	High school diploma
Food preparation worker	Average (5–8%)	298,300	$19,560	High school diploma
Food server, nonrestaurant	Faster than average (9–13%)	253,000	$19,900	High school diploma

(Continued)

Figure 14.29 Learning as much as possible about careers can help you make informed career decisions. *According to the information in this chart, which food and nutrition related human services careers are predicted to have the highest median wages?*

Copyright Goodheart-Willcox Co., Inc.

Future Trends for Food and Nutrition Related Human Services Careers *(Figure 14.29 Continued)*				
Occupation	**Projected Growth (2014–2024)**	**Projected Job Openings (2014–2024)**	**Median Wages (2014)**	**Education**
Food scientist	Slower than average (2–4%)	5,900	$61,480	Bachelor's degree
Foodservice assistant manager	Faster than average (9–13%)	352,900	$29,560	High school diploma
Foodservice general manager	Average (5–8%)	77,100	$48,560	Less than high school diploma
Kitchen worker	Average (5–8%)	298,300	$19,560	Less than high school diploma
Management dietitian	Much faster than average (14% or higher)	16,000	$56,950	Post-baccalaureate certificate
Nutrition educator	Much faster than average (14% or higher)	77,200	$90,210	Doctoral degree
Nutritionist	Much faster than average (14% or higher)	16,000	$56,950	Post-baccalaureate certificate
Personal chef	Little or no change (−1–1%)	9,700	$22,940	Postsecondary certificate
Product development specialist	Slower than average (2–4%)	5,900	$61,480	Bachelor's degree
Quality control specialist	Average (5–8%)	38,100	$44,650	Bachelor's degree
Registered dietetic technician (RDT)	Faster than average (9–13%)	6,800	$25,780	High school diploma
Registered dietitian nutritionist (RDN)	Much faster than average (14% or higher)	16,000	$56,950	Post-baccalaureate certificate
Sensory scientist	Average (5–8%)	12,400	$35,140	High school diploma
Technical sales representative	Average (5–8%)	95,400	$75,140	Bachelor's degree
Waiters and waitresses	Slower than average (2–4%)	1,255,000	$18,730	High school diploma

Sources: O*NET and the *Occupational Outlook Handbook*

Copyright Goodheart-Willcox Co., Inc.

Summary

- Careers in food and nutrition related human services focus on the human side of food and nutrition. Examples of careers in this field include food and beverage services workers, dietitians and nutritionists, registered dietetic technicians, nutrition educators, and food scientists. There are also many food and nutrition related human services entrepreneurial opportunities.

- The qualities of workers in the food and nutrition industry include solid scientific grounding, creativity, an eye for detail, and being health conscious. People in the food and nutrition industry must be passionate about the product or service they are offering whether it entails nutritional advice or food products and services.

- Education, training, and experience expectations are varied and vast for food and nutrition human services workers. A high school diploma is typically all the education required for entry-level positions as food and beverage serving workers. Other positions typically require a college degree and some require certification in addition to postsecondary education.

- Human services workers in the food and nutrition fields need specialized knowledge about the human side of food and nutrition. They understand that eating healthy across the life cycle and balancing food intake with physical activity will help maintain physical health. They also know how to plan and prepare healthy meals and snacks that contribute to wellness and provide the necessary energy to be productive throughout the lifespan.

- The job outlook continues to be very good for food and nutrition related human services workers. People always have and always will have a need for food.

College and Career Portfolio

Portfolio Review

Once you have selected, created, and compiled the elements of your portfolio, you can begin finalizing your work and preparing to present it. Now is a good time to have someone review your portfolio. The feedback you gain from a review can be extremely helpful.

Think about people you know who could review your portfolio and provide feedback. Perhaps you know someone working in your field of interest. Teachers and guidance counselors may also be good choices.

Complete the following to have someone review your portfolio:
1. Select one adult, such as a teacher or counselor, to review your portfolio. Ask the adult for honest feedback.
2. Listen to the adult's feedback and brainstorm how you can implement his or her advice at this stage.
3. Update your portfolio as needed.

Copyright Goodheart-Willcox Co., Inc.

Review and Reflect ↗

1. Define *nutrition*.
2. Careers focusing on food and nutrition in the human services involve working with what?
3. What is the difference between a *commercial foodservice venture* and an *institutional foodservice venture*?
4. What are some of the duties a food scientist performs on a daily basis?
5. Identify common attitudes and skills all workers in the food and nutrition related human services careers use.
6. List careers in the food and nutrition industry you can have while in high school, with a high school diploma, with a certification, and with a postsecondary degree.
7. What foods should be avoided during pregnancy? Why?
8. Define *body composition*, *overweight*, and *obesity*. What is the difference between overweight and obese?
9. What are fad diets, and why are they unsafe?
10. In a well-balanced meal, what would be some good contrasts with bland flavors, such as pastas, potatoes, and breads?
11. Draw the correct way to set a table.
12. What is the job outlook for food and nutrition related human services workers? Why?

Vocabulary Activities

13. **Key terms** In teams, create categories for the following terms and classify as many of the terms as possible. Then, share your ideas with the remainder of the class. How were your lists similar or different?

anorexia nervosa	eating disorder
binge-eating disorder	fad diets
	food allergy
body composition	food intolerance
bulimia nervosa	MyPlate
catering	nutrient-dense foods
diabetes	
dietetics	nutrition

obesity	recipe
overweight	vegetarian

14. **Academic terms** On a separate sheet of paper, list words that relate to each of the following terms. Then, work with a partner to explain how these words are related.

aesthetic	palatable
ingenuity	stringent
lucrative	

Self-Assessment Quiz ↗

Complete the self-assessment quiz online to help you practice and expand your knowledge and skills.

Critical Thinking

15. **Make inferences** Think about the impact of nutrition on development and wellness over the life cycle. What would happen if an infant did not receive the proper nutrition to promote growth and development? What might happen if a person had poor eating habits all throughout childhood? What effects might this have on the person's health, wellness, and productivity as an adult?
16. **Compare and contrast** Research and create a chart showing the nutritional needs across the lifespan. Start with infants, and end with older adulthood. How do nutritional needs change over the years? Which years need more portions or nutrients to help with development?
17. **Analyze** Analyze how certain health conditions affect people's eating patterns. Be sure to include diabetes, high blood pressure, and attention deficit hyperactivity disorder (ADHD).
18. **Draw conclusions** Based on the *Physical Activity Guidelines for Americans* and Figure 14.21, are you getting enough physical activity for your age group? Why or why not?
19. **Cause and effect** Examine the cause and effect of body image on teens and young adults based on the perceived ideal weight and body size.

20. **Identify**   Identify the different types of eating disorders and symptoms of someone who might have one of these disorders. What can you do to help someone exhibiting symptoms of an eating disorder?

21. **Evaluate**   Find a recipe and evaluate the different areas of the recipe to ensure you understand the instructions. Are there any terms with which you are unfamiliar? If you did not follow the directions as written, what would happen?

22. **Determine**   Using liquid and dry measuring cups and spoons, practice measuring different types of foods. Include water, oil, milk, vanilla extract, flour, sugar, brown sugar, salt, and nuts. Determine which type of measuring cup or spoon to use for each item and how to measure correctly.

Core Skills

23. **Speaking, listening, and writing**   Invite a caterer or an executive chef to come to class to discuss what he or she does for a living. Have this person explain the pathway he or she took to get to his or her current job. Create a list of questions to ask this person during the presentation. Write a thank-you note after the visit, and send it.

24. **Research**   Identify career opportunities in the food and nutrition industry that are available in your town and state. Choose the two career opportunities that interest you the most to compare and contrast the requirements for the job, what type of training or certification is needed, and what entry-level jobs are available that you could do with your current skill set.

25. **Reading and research**   Get several food labels from products you eat frequently. Read the labels. Compare the information about what one serving and the entire contents of the package provide nutritionally to what is recommended for a person your age to have daily. Are there certain ingredients that do not meet or that exceed the % Daily value (DV)? What happens to your body if you exceed the recommended nutrients daily over a long period of time? What about over a short period of time?

26. **Writing, research, and speaking**   Many people have dietary restrictions due to illness or disease. Your best friend has just been diagnosed with diabetes. Compile a one-day menu your friend could eat using the *Dietary Guidelines for Americans*, as well as information on what people who have diabetes should and should not eat. Present your menu to your classmates.

27. **Research and writing**   Using interactive tools on the MyPlate website, find out what a daily food plan should look like for someone your age, gender, height, and weight, and for the level of physical activity you engage in each day. View a sample plan and then develop your own healthy menu plan for one day. Be sure to plan for breakfast, lunch, dinner, and snacks. Make sure you have all the ingredients on hand to prepare your menu. Then, select a day to prepare your nutritious meals and snacks. After you have prepared all the items, write a journal entry describing the experience and how you felt. Which recipes did you really enjoy? Were there items you did not like? Were there certain foods that seemed to give you an energy boost after eating them?

28. **Writing**   Create a poster explaining step-by-step how to wash hands correctly when handling food and to prevent cross-contamination.

29. **Research and math**   Choose a recipe. Figure the cost of the meal for the recipe by finding out the total cost of all ingredients and dividing by the number of servings. Figure the costs of halving the recipe and doubling the recipe.

30. **Writing and research**   Create a worksheet of common kitchen equipment found in the home. Create a second worksheet of common kitchen equipment found in a commercial kitchen. Compare the two. Which pieces of equipment are found in both a home and commercial kitchen? Which pieces of equipment are exclusive to either a home kitchen or a commercial kitchen?

31. **Math and speaking**   It is the end of the month, and you have no groceries in the

Copyright Goodheart-Willcox Co., Inc.

house. You look around your living room and find change. This change adds up to $7.75. Go to the grocery store, and compile one meal that does not exceed $7.75. Tell what you bought and why, as well as how you could stretch your money to include a second meal using some of the same ingredients.

32. **Research and math** In years past, when eating out at a restaurant, you would leave a tip for service based on how good the service was. Over the years, the amount to tip has changed from 5% to 15% or more. Research what the current amount to tip a server is, based on good service, as well as mediocre service. Figure out how much the tips would be on bills totaling $25.79, $59.50, and $172.14, for both good service and mediocre service.

33. **CTE career readiness practice** Working in foodservice requires employees to adapt to diversity of the many individuals with whom they will come in contact. The interaction can be in formal or informal situations. Make a list of potential barriers that can evolve and solutions to eliminate those barriers.

Lend a Hand

Feeding the Community

Having enough food to eat is a necessity, but unfortunately, it is a struggle for many families and individuals. Most communities have food pantries and soup kitchens to help community members in need. Some areas also have food banks that store and distribute food to the surrounding communities. These organizations often rely on volunteers to operate.

Food pantries and food banks need help sorting through the donated food and grocery items and organizing them. This might involve stacking boxes, stocking shelves, or packing the food into emergency food boxes or backpacks. Sometimes help is also needed in more skilled areas, such as gardening, donor relations, or clerical work. Volunteers may also be needed to drive to grocery stores to pick up donations or to deliver donations to residential facilities in need. Volunteers at food pantries might also work directly with patrons, helping them select items and fill grocery bags.

Soup kitchens are also vital in providing food to those in need. Soup kitchens are places where people can go for a hot, nutritious meal. Some homeless shelters and women's shelters also offer meal service for their tenants. Volunteers help prepare the food, serve it to community members, and clean up. Some soup kitchens and shelters have age restrictions for volunteers.

To find out how you can assist in volunteering with food donation services, complete the following:

1. Research food banks, food pantries, soup kitchens, and meal preparation services in your community. Make note of the contact information for each opportunity.
2. Sign up to volunteer at one or two of the places you found in your research. Make sure you know what dates and times you will be able to volunteer.

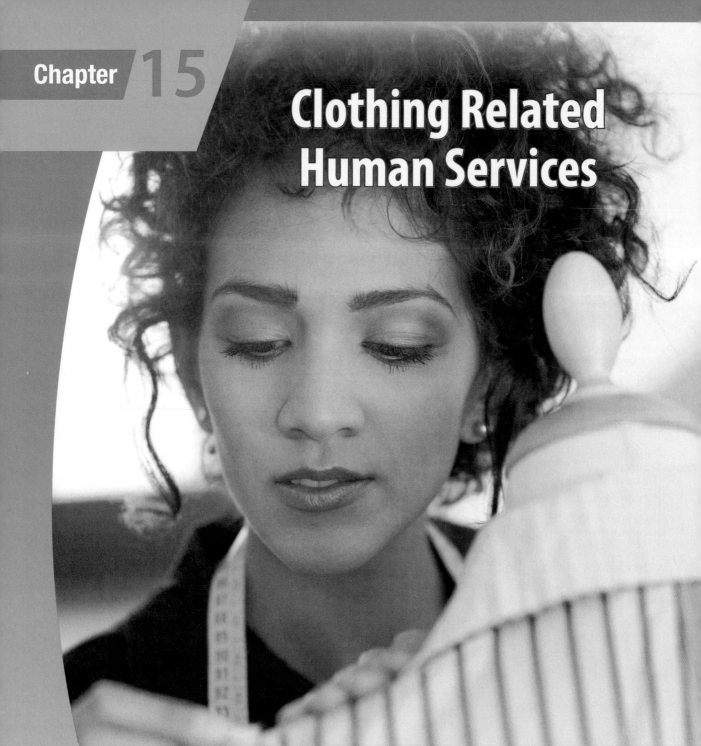

Chapter 15

Clothing Related Human Services

G-WLEARNING.com

While studying, look for the activity icon to

- **practice** key and academic terms with e-flash cards and matching activities;
- **assess** what you learn by completing self-assessment quizzes; and
- **reinforce** what you learn by mapping concepts and completing review and reflect questions.

www.g-wlearning.com/humanservices/

Diego Cervo/Shutterstock.com

Learning Outcomes

After studying this chapter, you will be able to

- **compare and contrast** career opportunities for clothing related human services workers;
- **list** common aptitudes, attitudes, and skills of clothing related human services workers;
- **give examples** of postsecondary education, training, and experience required for several clothing related human services careers;
- **identify** factors that influence apparel selection and analyze clothing needs across the life cycle;
- **recognize** and use information on care labels;
- **demonstrate** safety practices when using apparel construction tools and equipment; and
- **summarize** the rewards, demands, and future trends of clothing related careers.

Reading Strategies

Before reading, copy the terms from this chapter onto another piece of paper. Set a timer for three minutes and write as many facts or predictions about the meanings of these key terms as you can. As you are reading, review your paper and expand or correct your definitions as needed. After reading, write a summary paragraph of this chapter using all of the key terms.

Mapping Concepts

Draw and label a four-column chart like the one shown. As you read, organize your notes into these columns for each clothing related career.

Clothing Related Career	Aptitudes, Attitudes, and Abilities	Education and Specialized Knowledge	Rewards and Demands

Key Terms

adaptive clothing
buying plan
computer aided design (CAD)
design line
digital lookbooks
dry cleaning
ergonomics
fashion merchandising

forecast
ironing
natural fibers
niche markets
notions
synthetic fibers
visual merchandising

Academic Terms

agitation
circumference
collegiality
notorious

Like food, clothing is a basic need of families and individuals. Clothing, however, goes far beyond providing warmth and protection. In developed societies, clothing is *fashion*, an ever-evolving artifact of societal trends. The fashion industry is a multibillion dollar global industry that provides fashion products to meet the social, psychological, and physical needs of people. Because careers in the clothing industry focus on meeting a basic need of people, there are many opportunities in this field for human services workers. Whether creating, producing, or selling products, the business of providing clothing needs to people is an important part of human services.

Clothing Related Career Opportunities

Career opportunities in clothing related human services are many and varied. In the fashion industry, careers fall into three main categories. These categories include the textile industry, apparel design and production, and retail marketing and promotion. In addition to these areas, retail management, fashion forecasting, and entrepreneurial opportunities also exist. Examples of clothing related careers are shown in **Figure 15.1**.

Examples of Clothing Related Human Services Careers

- Apparel production manager
- Artist
- Fashion blogger
- Fashion designer
- Fashion forecaster
- Fashion journalist
- Hand cutter and trimmer
- Independent contractor
- Industrial engineer
- Patternmaker
- Personal shopper
- Personal stylist
- Production manager
- Retail buyer
- Retail fashion merchandiser
- Retail manager
- Scientist
- Textile cutting machine setter, operator, and tender
- Textile designer
- Visual merchandiser

Figure 15.1 These are just some of the careers in human services that are related to clothing. *Can you name some other clothing related careers?*

The Textile Industry

The textile industry involves the production of fibers and yarns used to make clothing. The textile industry is both an agricultural and a chemical industry. For example, cotton and flax (linen) are **natural fibers** that are grown and harvested from plants. Silk and wool are also natural fibers, but they come from animal sources (**Figure 15.2**). Polyester, acrylics, and nylon are just a few of the **synthetic fibers** produced in chemistry labs. The diverse nature of the agriculture and chemical industries cannot be understated.

The textile industry is a complex industry that includes both scientists and artists. *Scientists* work at the fiber stage, especially in synthetic fiber production. They also work in the agricultural sector when the highest and finest quality yield of natural fibers is desired. Scientists may be employed as *industrial engineers* in the manufacturing of textile goods. *Artists* are hired in the textile industry as *textile designers*. Finally, *production managers* are needed to oversee the manufacturing process of textiles.

Copyright Goodheart-Willcox Co., Inc.

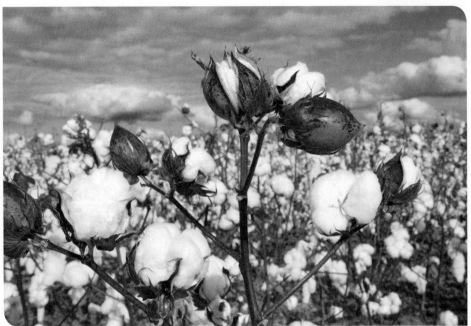

Steven Frame/Shutterstock.com

Figure 15.2 Cotton is grown as a plant, and silk is spun by a silkworm. *Do you prefer clothing made from natural or synthetic fibers? Why?*

fotohunter/Shutterstock.com

Apparel Design and Production

Clothing is one of the quickest changing design products. It involves the lowest monetary investment when compared to other design products in interiors, appliances, transportation, and housing. *Fashion designers* are the professionals who design clothing. Although a common assumption

Copyright Goodheart-Willcox Co., Inc.

Law and Ethics *The Real Fashion Police*

When making clothing purchases, some people consider moral issues. One potential moral issue involves *counterfeit* clothing. Counterfeit items are made to closely resemble another product already on the market, including the brand label or signature symbols. Designs that merely resemble another without the signature or registered trademark branding are considered to be a legal *knockoff* (copy or imitation). For the consumer, purchasing counterfeit goods may be a moral issue as it supports one company "stealing" the intellectual property of another.

Another potentially moral issue associated with clothing purchases involves global trade issues. Because so many countries participate in textile production, establishing trade issue agreement guidelines has been difficult. The textile industry is not only vast, but also varies greatly. For example, silk produced in China is a very labor intensive agricultural product. Nylon produced in the US, on the other hand, is a chemically derived product. These examples only involve fiber production. Yarn production, fabric construction, and fabric dyes and finishes are other large and varied segments of the textile industry.

Traditionally, textile trade was governed by various international agreements. These agreements established quotas limiting the import of textile products into countries whose textile trade was threatened by imports. For example, at one time, the US cotton industry was threatened by less expensive cotton fibers from other countries that had lower labor costs. Established quotas limited the amount of cotton fiber imported into the US, thus protecting the livelihood of cotton growers in the US.

The World Trade Organization (WTO) is an international organization that deals with the rules of trade between nations. As a global organization, the goal of WTO is to promote the export and import of goods in the global marketplace. They do this through lobbying for and establishing agreements between nations. The WTO helps producers, exporters, and importers of goods and services conduct their business.

Beginning in 2005, established quotas ended. Under WTO agreements, importing countries could no longer discriminate against some exporting countries. This move had a profound and far-reaching effect on textile trade. There are, of course, people who are both for and against the new agreements. Some believe this move unjustly discriminated against disadvantaged countries. Others believe the new agreement will offer more opportunities to developing countries. On either side, concerns about the preservation of domestic industry and economic effects are weighed against concerns for the global economy, economic equity, and human rights to livelihood.

Reflective Writing Activity

Think about how you would respond to the following questions and then record your responses on a separate piece of paper.

1. What factors do you consider when buying fashion goods?

2. Is there any harm in buying counterfeit goods? Why or why not?

3. When buying goods, do you take into consideration where the goods are produced, the salary and working conditions of those who produce the product, or the business practices of the manufacturer or service provider? Explain.

about fashion designers is that they spend their days sketching designs or draping fabric over dress forms until the perfect garment emerges, this is a simplistic view of their task. Today, designers use computers to draft their designs. Before any designing occurs, however, designers must keep up-to-date with fashion trends.

Copyright Goodheart-Willcox Co., Inc.

Watching fashion on the streets, shopping retail stores, keeping up with foreign fashion trends, and scanning tools from fashion forecasters are important activities for all designers. If a designer cannot predict what his or her customer will want to wear in the upcoming season, there is little chance for success. After all, the purpose of apparel design is to provide clothing to meet customers' needs.

Fashion designers are also involved in various other daily tasks. They may cut and sew sample garments as well as select fabrics, trimmings, and notions for their designs. **Notions** are items attached to a finished garment (**Figure 15.3**). Other activities include selling their **design line** (collection of related designs) to company merchandisers, working with manufacturing and production managers, and collecting sales data.

Most designers specialize in a particular type of clothing or accessory. For example, junior sportswear, children's sleepwear, misses' sweaters, or young men's jeans are just a few of the seemingly endless specialty markets. Generally, each specialization area becomes more defined with smaller and smaller **niche markets** (subsets of the larger market created to meet specific needs). Well-defined niche markets allow the designer to closely monitor the ever-changing needs of his or her target market.

After the design of a garment is complete, production begins. Skilled workers who specialize in cutting and marking fabric, pattern drafting, sewing, and quality control form the team to produce apparel products.

MskPhotoLife/Shutterstock.com

Figure 15.3 Threads, buttons, and zippers are all examples of notions. *Can you name other examples of notions?*

Copyright Goodheart-Willcox Co., Inc.

Case Study   *On Trend*

Rachel had a childhood dream. She would grow up, go to college, and become a wildly successful fashion designer. She would attend elegant parties every night. At the end of her Paris fashion show, she would walk down the runway to rave reviews.

Rachel did become a fashion designer and she is successful. Perhaps she is not successful in the way she fantasized about in the days of her youth, but she loves working with a great team of highly creative, talented people. Together, they produce some pretty amazing apparel for an upscale, trendy men's line. Her clothes may not be on Paris runways, but she does get to see her clothes on display in stores, or even worn by people at events. Last year, the company sales figures beat the previous year's record. Her company name has become synonymous with hip, trendy men.

As a fashion designer, Rachel is always coming up with new ideas. Even when walking down the street, she notices unique colors and textures, new ways of combining things, and interesting patterns. Seeing an interesting fabric can inspire a whole new line of apparel. Fashion design, however, is not just about coming up with great ideas. It is also about taking the idea to completion.

Rachel assists pattern drafters in making sample patterns. She also works with manufacturers, most outside of the US, in producing a sample design. She then fine-tunes the design and makes sure the fit is correct. When her team of designers, the company merchandisers, and company executives are satisfied, the design goes to production. As in other creative endeavors, there are often setbacks and adjustments.

©iStock.com/Ridofranz

For Discussion

1. How might Rachel's work as a fashion designer be considered a human service?
2. In addition to technical skills, what other skills does Rachel need to be successful?
3. How might Rachel use her skills to meet the needs of the underprivileged in her community?

Apparel production forms the largest segment of the fashion industry worldwide, and most developed countries have some apparel manufacturing industry (**Figure 15.4**). *Apparel production management* involves the administration of all aspects of the apparel manufacturing process from start to finish.

Retail Marketing and Promotion

Retail marketing and promotion includes the marketing, distribution, and selling of clothing. Traditionally, clothing manufacturers sell to retailers who, in turn, sell to customers. This is still the way that the majority of apparel is sold. Today, online retailing, outlet stores, catalog

Copyright Goodheart-Willcox Co., Inc.

michaeljung/Shutterstock.com

Figure 15.4 Workers who sew garments are a part of the apparel manufacturing industry. *What skills are required of a worker in apparel manufacturing?*

shopping, and television shopping also play a major role in the marketing, distribution, and promotion of fashion apparel.

Fashion merchandising is the umbrella term used for the business side of fashion. It involves the buying and selling of fashion, product development, retail management, and fashion marketing. Fashion merchandising is a fast-paced, energetic, and ever-changing field that offers many opportunities to hard working, creative people with good business sense.

Retail fashion merchandisers are the point people for ensuring that the correct apparel products are in the right store at the precise time. They know which trends are coming and how much of an impact a design trend may have on potential sales (**Figure 15.5**). Merchandisers plan inventory stock levels and monitor the sales performance of clothing lines and even individual items. They decide which design lines and how many items to buy. They monitor the delivery and distribution of stock. They decide when the merchandise will appear on the store sales floor. When a particular item does not sell well, the fashion merchandiser may choose to mark down the retail price to move the merchandise off the retail floor.

Retail buyers work with fashion merchandisers to select fashion apparel that will meet the needs of their target customer base and increase store revenue. Retail buyers follow a merchandise plan set by the retail fashion merchandiser to select and purchase apparel goods from manufacturing sales representatives. A description of the types, sizes, prices, and quantities of merchandise that the retail buyer is to select is called a **buying plan**.

Copyright Goodheart-Willcox Co., Inc.

Kzenon/Shutterstock.com

Figure 15.5 Retail fashion merchandisers are always thinking of the bottom line—how to maximize profits. *What is the result if a merchandiser buys too much stock of an item?*

Retail Management

The retail industry provides fashion goods and services directly to customers. *Retail managers* ensure that customers get prompt service and quality goods. This means they have total responsibility over all aspects of the store's daily functioning. Retail managers manage stock, review inventory and sales records, develop merchandising plans, and coordinate sales promotions. On a larger scale, they oversee the store's physical facilities, security and loss prevention programs, and general operating procedures. They handle customer complaints and questions. They also oversee employees and are responsible for hiring, interviewing, training, and staffing. In larger stores, they manage supervisors and department managers. In short, retail managers are responsible for the entire store's operations.

Managers are needed at all levels of the retail fashion industry from department managers to regional and division managers. At all levels, managers are responsible for the daily functioning as well as the long-range planning of their group. Most importantly, the manager is ultimately responsible for the sales profit margin of his or her group.

Visual merchandising includes window and interior store displays, placement of posters, signage on clothing racks, wall displays, seasonal store displays, and media used to capture attention (**Figure 15.6**). *Visual merchandisers* are always thinking and planning ahead to upcoming seasons and promotional events. They must be very artistic and

Copyright Goodheart-Willcox Co., Inc.

Gaieva Tetiana/Shutterstock.com

Figure 15.6 Window displays are designed to catch a shopper's attention and show a product to its advantage. *What personal characteristics are beneficial to a visual merchandiser?*

conceptual. They must also have well-honed communication skills to convey their artistic vision to those who will implement it.

Fashion Forecasting

Have you ever wondered who decides which new fashions are around the corner? *Fashion forecasters* are the "they" who **forecast** (predict a future trend), not dictate, the upcoming fashion trends. They are the eyes and ears of the fashion industry. Which colors and fabrics will attract consumers next year? What styles will interest them? These are questions that fashion forecasters answer for the textile and apparel manufacturing industry.

Fashion forecasters review significant social developments, political events, economic trends, and weather changes to determine consumers' future clothing demands. They convey trends through forecasting publications, subscription websites, and training seminars. In many ways, they must step out on a limb and take a risk. When fashion forecasters are good at what they do, they provide an extremely valuable service to textile manufacturers, apparel producers, and retailers. Manufacturers and retailers must put a considerable investment into their decisions.

Copyright Goodheart-Willcox Co., Inc.

If a forecaster can help them to invest in the right trends, the financial payoff is huge (**Figure 15.7**).

Consumers also want to know the trends in beauty and fashion. *Fashion journalism* involves the spreading of information about beauty and fashion trends for consumers. Because fashion is an artifact of societal trends, fashion journalists act, in a sense, as "contemporary archaeologists." They tell people what is in, what is out, what to expect, and what is appropriate or not appropriate in beauty and fashion.

Today, fashion journalists use Internet, television, and video mediums to relay fashion and beauty trends and advice. On the Internet, fashion journalists write articles to post on websites. They use e-mail and e-bulletins, blogs and vlogs, as well as social media platforms. They can also use **digital lookbooks**, which are a collection of fashion related photos.

Entrepreneurial Opportunities

The fashion field lends itself well to entrepreneurial careers. In both fashion design and merchandising, some clothing related human services workers get their experience in the corporate setting and then begin freelancing or running their own business. For example, a designer may begin designing and manufacturing his or her own apparel line (**Figure 15.8**). A merchandiser might begin offering his or her services as an independent contractor. Visual merchandising or personal stylists and

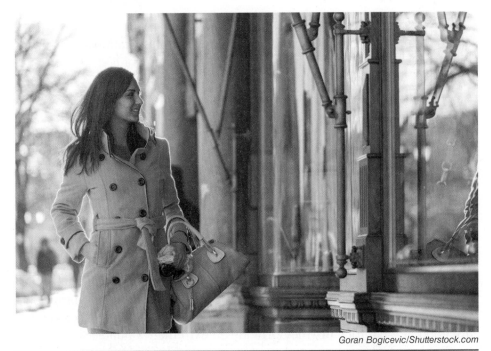

Goran Bogicevic/Shutterstock.com

Figure 15.7 Promoting current trends to consumers can result in big sales. *How do trends figure into your purchasing decisions?*

Copyright Goodheart-Willcox Co., Inc.

©iStock.com/Berc

Figure 15.8 Designers are one example of entrepreneurs in the fashion field. *What experience would most benefit designers who want to start their own business?*

shoppers are two examples. Likewise, fashion journalists may freelance for fashion magazines. Fashion bloggers may use social media as a small business forum. Overall, fashion is a highly creative field that, by its very nature, is always changing. Such an environment is prime for those with an entrepreneurial spirit.

Reading Recall

1. Name three jobs found in the textile industry.
2. What is the purpose of apparel design?
3. Name three specialty or niche markets of apparel designers.
4. What is *apparel production management*?
5. What is *fashion merchandising*?
6. What is *visual merchandising*?
7. What is the main role of a fashion journalist?
8. Identify an entrepreneurial opportunity in the fashion field that interests you.

Common Aptitudes, Attitudes, and Skills

Human services workers in the clothing field share common aptitudes, attitudes, and skills (**Figure 15.9**). Fashion designers are creative people who can turn their imaginative ideas into actual products. They need technical skills to produce designs through hand-sketching or using computers, create technical specifications, and understand the techniques

Figure 15.9 Workers in different areas of the clothing industry are likely to share these characteristics. *Which of these characteristics best describe you?*

Common Aptitudes, Attitudes, and Skills of Clothing Related Human Services Workers	
• Artistic	• Passionate about product
• Creative	• Get along well with others
• Energetic	• Business sense
• Confident	• People-helping skills
• Savvy	• Technical skills
• Fashion oriented	• Problem-solving skills
• Up-to-date in knowledge	

and tools necessary to produce a garment. They must possess knowledge of textiles to select the most serviceable materials for the garments they design. Lastly, they must be able to communicate their ideas to others.

In addition to creative and technical skills, fashion designers must have good business sense. Creative designs that do not sell well cannot be tolerated over the long term if a designer is to be successful in the fashion field. Understanding price points, supply and demand, fashion timing and cycles, and wholesale and retail accounting practices are some of the business skills fashion apparel designers need.

The fashion industry demands workers who are creative, savvy, and fashion-oriented, as well as good problem solvers. They must be passionate about the product they are marketing. All fashion industry workers, whether designing textiles or selling on a retail floor, must consider the needs of the end user—the consumer. Because fashion is by nature always changing, the field requires the ability to explore and apply new ideas and concepts (**Figure 15.10**).

Reading Recall

1. List three common aptitudes, attitudes, and skills of human services workers in the clothing field.
2. Identify two tasks for which fashion designers need technical skills.
3. List three business skills fashion apparel designers need.

Education, Training, and Experience

Careers in clothing are varied and vast. Thus, the education, training, and experience expectations are, too. Many aspects of the fashion industry require professionals who possess a creative flair combined with business acumen. A creative flair and good business sense can get you started, but in today's highly competitive market, a college or university degree combined with natural talent and industry experience create an unbeatable combination. Specific training needed depends on the job.

Copyright Goodheart-Willcox Co., Inc.

wavebreakmedia/Shutterstock.com

Figure 15.10 Fashion is a fast-paced industry that requires its workers to explore and adapt. *How has fashion changed in the last two years? ten years? fifty years?*

In general, the fashion industry requires no licensure or particular specialized degree. Due to the diverse and complex nature of the industry, however, strong technical skills, problem-solving and analytical skills, and industry knowledge are needed to effectively compete. As the global fashion industry becomes more reliant on technology and more complex problems are addressed, a solid education, a college degree, and experience will be desired by employers.

Reading Recall

1. Possessing what two things can get you started in the fashion industry?
2. What are the general educational requirements to work in the fashion industry?
3. How might educational requirements change as the global fashion industry becomes more reliant on technology and more complex problems are addressed?

Specialized Knowledge for Clothing Related Human Services

The way people dress and present themselves through clothing is a powerful form of nonverbal communication. Clothing protects the body from the elements and often helps human performance. Fashion relates

Copyright Goodheart-Willcox Co., Inc.

to the social aspects of clothing, including status, roles, and self-esteem. Fashion is also something about which people often have strong opinions. Those who work in the clothing related human services field may need specialized knowledge about the human side of clothing and fashion, including selection factors, clothing needs across the life cycle, and the mechanics of caring for and maintaining clothing.

Identifying Factors That Influence Apparel Selection

Clothing is a necessity, and people's choices are often determined by the climate and weather (**Figure 15.11**). Clothing, however, can be trendy, fashionable, and fun, too. It can make a person feel confident, a part of a group, or even powerful.

When purchasing clothing, people often consider needs, trends, price, quality, and fit. A person's age, lifestyle, cultural norms, and values impact clothing choices as well. Special occasions, the desire to show status, and organizational expectations all affect clothing choices when selecting what to wear or not to wear in daily life. Individual abilities associated with age and activities are also an important part of clothing choices.

Selecting Clothing Across the Life Cycle

Clothing related human services workers know that as individuals change throughout the lifespan, so will their clothing needs. As growth occurs, people need different sizes of clothing. As people age, physical needs and individual styles change and develop. When lifestyle changes occur, clothing needs often change, too. By understanding clothing needs at different stages of the life cycle, clothing related human services workers can meet people's basic need for clothing.

Infants

Infants need soft, warm, comfortable clothes. Ideally, infant's clothes will have plenty of "give" or stretch for maximum comfort while sleeping and playing (**Figure 15.12**). Because caregivers must change infant's diapers many times in a day, infant clothing often features snaps that allow caregivers to easily unfasten and remove items.

Babies are naturally messy. Between diaper changes and feedings, burping, and spit-ups, infant clothing needs to be easy to care for through machine wash and drying. Designs

©iStock.com/XiXinXing

Figure 15.11 People in colder climates must invest in winter wear such as coats and gloves. *How does your home's climate influence your clothing choices?*

Copyright Goodheart-Willcox Co., Inc.

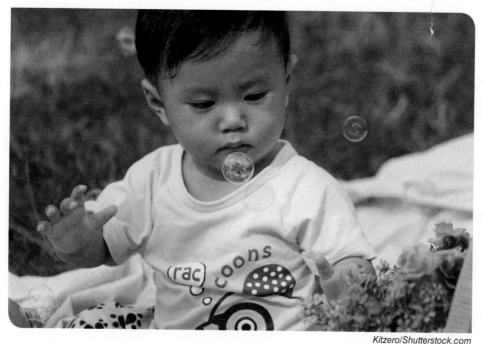

Kitzero/Shutterstock.com

Figure 15.12 Soft, knit fabrics enable babies to move freely while playing. *What type of adult clothing is likely to feature knit fabrics?*

should be simple without a lot of ornamentation or small buttons or other closures that if swallowed could cause the baby to choke. Inexpensive items are a good choice as babies grow and develop rapidly, thereby outgrowing clothing items quickly. By law, all clothing made for infants, toddlers, and children must be flame resistant.

Toddlers

Toddlers are busy exploring their world. As such, they need clothing that freely allows them to move and play. Crawling, walking, reaching, and rolling should all be possible in the clothes they wear. Clothing that is soft, durable, and colorful works well. Because toddlers can be fairly hard on their clothing, reinforcement in the knees, elbows, and other points of contact are important.

As toddlers are learning to self-feed, toilet learn, and master motor skills, clothing often becomes stained or dirty. Toddler clothing should be easy to care for through machine wash and drying. Because toddlers are learning to self-dress, many clothing options include self-help features, such as snaps and elastic waistbands (**Figure 15.13**).

Preschoolers

Preschoolers continue to grow and have much more mobility as their gross-motor skills develop. They run, jump, skip, hop, climb, and enjoy other active movements. As such, they have an even greater need for clothing that allows them to move freely.

Copyright Goodheart-Willcox Co., Inc.

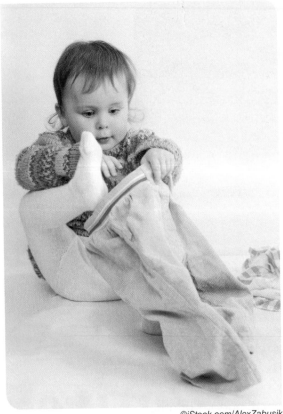

©iStock.com/AlexZabusik

Figure 15.13 Clothing for toddlers include features that help them learn to dress themselves. *What self-help features can you identify in this toddler's clothing?*

During the preschool years, children may enjoy selecting their own clothing and demonstrating self-help abilities. Clothing with zippers, Velcro®, and buttons allow preschoolers to dress themselves. Shoes that use Velcro® closures over laces give preschoolers the freedom and independence to put on and take off their own shoes. Growing independence is an important social trait for preschool children.

School-Age Children

School-age children are active and on the go. They need school clothes as well as play clothes. If they participate in school clubs or sports teams, they may need uniforms or special clothing. They may also need clothes for special occasions. Clothing choices for school-age children should be comfortable and relatively inexpensive as children this age quickly outgrow their clothes.

During middle childhood, school-age children think more about their own clothing preferences. They care more about fashion and clothing styles and what peers think about their appearance. Their increased desire to fit in with peers will often cause school-age children to want clothing items that match what their friends are wearing (**Figure 15.14**).

Figure 15.14 School-age children want clothing that allows them to be active and fit in with their classmates. *What common elements can you identify among these children's clothing?*

wavebreakmedia/Shutterstock.com

Copyright Goodheart-Willcox Co., Inc.

Adolescents

Adolescents need clothing for school and various school or community activities. They need comfortable clothes when spending time at home or with friends. They also need clothes for special events, such as school dances. They may need clothing for work.

During adolescence, teens develop a personal sense of style. They care a lot about the way they look and how others perceive them. Many have a strong interest in fashion trends. Teens are attempting to figure out who they are and clothing is a great way for them to express themselves. Teens decide which type of clothing best fits their personality and select clothing accordingly. Their choice of clothes sends a message about who they are.

Young Adults

Young adult clothing needs also change as they explore new adult life roles. College and university students often develop a particular style based on their school culture. Some young adults enter military service where uniforms are necessary. As young adults go on interviews and begin to work and develop their careers, many integrate business attire into their wardrobes (**Figure 15.15**).

During young adulthood, clothing needs may also develop for other life changes. These might include maternity wear needs during pregnancy, travel clothing, or new clothing after relocation to a different climate. As young adults' lifestyles and interests change, their clothing

> ### Expert Insight
>
> *"Don't be into trends. Don't make fashion own you, but you decide what you are, what you want to express by the way you dress and the way to live."*
>
> Gianni Versace, fashion designer

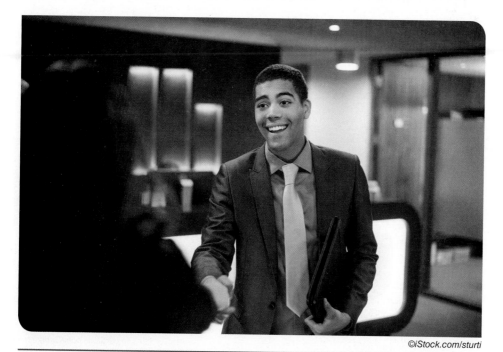

©iStock.com/sturti

Figure 15.15 A person's clothing needs for work will vary depending on the occupation. *What type of clothing do you expect to wear for your future occupation?*

Copyright Goodheart-Willcox Co., Inc.

needs may change, too. Special occasions, such as weddings, religious ceremonies, and other special events occur more frequently, thereby influencing new clothing needs. At this stage in the life cycle, young adults are typically responsible for meeting all of their own clothing needs. Therefore, many clothing choices depend on the person's budget.

Middle-Aged Adults

Middle-aged adults continue to select clothing that reflects lifestyle choices. Work attire, comfort, and personal style remain important factors. Middle-aged adults often have focused interests, such as golfing, hiking, or gardening, that require specific clothing. Although adults are no longer growing, weight may fluctuate. Trying on garments before completing a purchase can ensure clothing fits properly.

Older Adults

Clothing needs for older adults depend on the needs of each person (**Figure 15.16**). Some older adults may continue to wear clothing items from middle adulthood. Others may need new clothes to help ease changes related to aging. For example, clothing with snaps and buttons can become painful and frustrating for adults with arthritis. Clothing with elastic waistbands may be easier and more comfortable to wear. Nonrestrictive clothing that allows for movement and comfort are important considerations. Sometimes, poor blood circulation in older adults makes warm clothing desirable. For example, sweaters, robes, slippers, and thick socks may be worn more frequently.

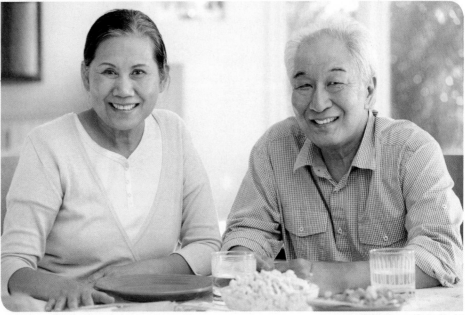

©iStock.com/Cathy Yeulet

Figure 15.16 Many older adults prefer clothing that is comfortable, yet attractive. *What attributes do you notice about this couple's clothing?*

Copyright Goodheart-Willcox Co., Inc.

Pathway to Success

Planning a Professional Wardrobe on a Budget

A basic professional wardrobe includes the clothing items you own that are easy to adapt into multiple outfits for work. These basic items are best bought in neutral colors like black, brown, gray, navy, and taupe. You can then add splashes of color in scarves, ties, jewelry, or in other accessory choices.

Basic pieces to include in a professional wardrobe are trousers/pants, dress suit, skirts, blouses, and sweater sets. All of these can be changed around, mixed, and matched by adding accessories like pumps and flats or dress shoes, handbags/wallets, scarves or ties, and jewelry to make multiple outfits.

Planning a professional wardrobe on a budget ensures you have to think outside the box to get the best deals on pieces that are highly valuable to your satisfaction and appearance. Knowing where to shop, how much money you have to spend, and how to spend it wisely will help you get the most for your money while shopping.

When planning a professional wardrobe on a budget, consider the following:

- Look at daily deal sites, clearance racks, or thrift shops. Remember, you may not always find what you are looking for and may have to save up to buy a key piece of jewelry or a high-end piece of clothing like a trench coat.

- Ask for the item as a gift or request gift cards to help you get the pieces you cannot afford at this time.

- Take notes before you shop for essentials. Put a note on your phone when you are struggling to piece together an outfit at home and you wish you had a specific something to go with it. This will help you remember what to look for when you are out shopping—without wasting money or time.

- Ask the following questions while shopping and before buying: How many outfits will this make? What outfit will this item complete? If the item will not help you, then do not buy it at this time. You can always go back later and spend 30 dollars each season to get a few seasonal pieces to go with your basics.

- Be patient. You may not find everything in one trip.

Planning Your First Professional Wardrobe

Using the information above, plan what you need for your first professional wardrobe. First, take stock of what is in your closet already. Once you know what you have in your wardrobe, make a list of what you need to complete your wardrobe.

Plan to have enough clothes for six days. This will help you get you through the week,

plus give you an extra outfit just in case. Remember that items can be mixed and matched to make multiple outfits. You have a budget of 300 dollars to complete your wardrobe. Compile pictures of what you would choose. Include where you will purchase the item and how much it will cost. Do not forget your accessories.

Copyright Goodheart-Willcox Co., Inc.

People with Special Needs

People with special needs, such as children or adults with physical disabilities, have the same interests and desires when selecting clothing as others. At times, people may develop special clothing needs throughout the life cycle. For example, a person recovering from surgery or rehabilitating from an accident may need special clothing for a period of time. As you just read, older adults may also have special clothing needs due to changes related to aging. Depending on the special need or disability, clothing needs may vary. In general, people with special needs should be able to select clothing that is comfortable, easy to care for, durable, and functional, too. Clothing items should also be appropriate for the person's age, the occasion, and his or her peer group.

Adaptive clothing refers to clothing items that are designed specifically to provide easy access for people with special needs. Adaptive clothing can also be called *easy access clothing*. Examples of adaptive clothing may include open back clothing, garments with snap closures instead of buttons, side-opening pants, wrap-around skirts, and other special designs that make it easier for people with limited mobility to change or remove clothing. In short, adaptive clothing should promote independence, confidence, and a sense of self-respect for the person with special needs.

Caring for Clothing

Wearing clothes that are clean and in good repair enhances a person's appearance and conveys a message to others. For example, what would you think about someone who is wearing ripped and wrinkled clothing to school or work? Would you get the impression that this person does not care about his or her appearance? The ability to properly care for and maintain clothing enhances appearance in personal and professional settings.

Clothing care begins with reading care labels. In the US, it is required by law that all clothing labels suggest methods of care. This includes type of washing, bleaching, drying, and dry-cleaning instructions. Ironing instructions also appear on care labels to prevent damage to clothing. **Ironing** is the process of using heat to remove wrinkles from clothing. **Figure 15.17** shows the international signs for laundry care.

Pretreating Stains and Sorting

Before laundering clothing, the first step is to check items for any stains. If stains are visible, pretreatment is needed. Many stain removal products and pretreatments are available on the market. When using pretreatments, test them in an area on the clothing that is not visible to make sure no damage occurs.

After the pretreatment of any stains, the next step is to sort clothing items into like colors. For example, put dark colors together and launder

Copyright Goodheart-Willcox Co., Inc.

Melica/Shutterstock.com

Figure 15.17 Laundry care icons provide suggested methods of care and are required on all clothing labels. *What are the six categories that comprise the international signs for laundry care?*

light colors separately. Likewise, sort and separate clothing by laundering method and fiber type. Natural fibers, such as cotton, may need to be laundered separately from clothing made of synthetic fibers, such as nylon or polyester. Sorting by fiber content is especially important during drying as dry times can vary greatly, and excessive heat can damage some fibers.

Washing and Drying Clothes

The most common way to launder clothing is using an automatic washer and dryer. When using an automatic washer, the "normal" cycle includes warm water, moderate *agitation* (the movement of water, detergent, and clothes), and warm water rinse. For more delicate items, cold temperatures and gentle agitation are often recommended. For sturdy or extra dirty items, hot water and more aggressive agitation may be needed. Bleach can be added to the laundry cycle to

Copyright Goodheart-Willcox Co., Inc.

whiten or sanitize, but should not be used on synthetic fibers as it can damage or yellow garments. Clothing care labels will indicate how to wash items and whether bleach should or should not be used. Failure to read the clothing care label may result in damaging or ruining clothing.

Care labels also indicate whether an item can be safely dried and on what temperature. For more delicate items that might shrink or be damaged by automatic washing or drying, handwashing and air-drying might be recommended instead. Air-drying can be done by laying the item flat to dry or by hanging from a clothesline.

Some clothing should not be laundered in a washer or dryer or even by hand. Instead, the clothing label indicates the item should be dry-cleaned only. **Dry cleaning** involves the use of a chemical solvent to clean clothes rather than water. Common items that require dry cleaning often include suits, coats, and certain business attire. Clothes that need to be dry cleaned are often taken to a dry cleaner, but home dry-cleaning kits are also available.

Ironing

Using hangers or folding and stacking, as appropriate, can extend the life and maintain the appearance of clothing over time. It can also help to prevent wrinkling. When wrinkling does occur, ironing will remove the wrinkles from clothing. Clothing care labels show whether an item can or cannot be ironed, and at what temperature. If an item is ironed at too high a temperature, the item can be scorched and ruined. As with any appliance, carefully read the instruction manual and follow all safety precautions to avoid injury.

Using Apparel Construction Tools and Equipment

Apparel is the main product of clothing related human services workers. As a product, clothing or apparel items are designed, manufactured, sold, and purchased. As such, those who work in this field should know how to use the construction tools and equipment needed to construct and produce clothing. Although the end product is the same, tools and equipment vary depending on whether clothing is constructed one-by-one or in mass production.

Construction Tools

To construct individual clothing items, common tools people use consist of measuring, marking, cutting, and sewing tools (**Figure 15.18**). When clothing is constructed in mass production, workers commonly use computerized machines and equipment. For example, clothing related human services workers may use **computer aided design (CAD)** software to create, mark, and modify design patterns. To cut fabric into garment piece shapes during mass production, workers may use

Copyright Goodheart-Willcox Co., Inc.

Construction Tools

Measuring Tools
- Use a *tape measure* to take accurate body measurements or to measure fabric and pattern pieces.
- Use a *sewing gauge* when measuring short distances, such as hems.

Marking Tools
- Use a *tracing wheel*, *dressmaker's carbon paper*, *tailor's chalk*, and a *tailor's pencil* to mark pattern shapes or transfer pattern markings onto fabric before cutting. Be sure to use a color similar to the color of the fabric, yet still visible.

Julia Ardaran/Shutterstock.com

Cutting Tools
- Use a *seam ripper* to undo mistakes or remove stitches.
- *Pinking shears* are used to produce a decorative look on some fabric, but may also be used to give seam edges a finished look.
- *Shears* are used to cut fabric pattern pieces from fabric.
- *Scissors* are used to trim seams, open buttonholes, or cut around curves. Use caution with cutting tools as they are very sharp.

Sewing Tools
- Before sewing, use *pins* to hold the fabric together.
- When making stitches, wear a *thimble* to protect the finger when pushing the *needle* through the fabric.
- Keep pins and needles in a *pincushion* while sewing.
- Use the *emery bag* as needed to sharpen the pins and needles.

Figure 15.18 These tools are commonly used for measuring, marking, cutting, and sewing. *Which of these construction tools can you identify?*

manually operated cutting equipment or computerized cutting machines that cut fabric using either blades or laser beams.

Construction Equipment

The primary piece of equipment used in clothing manufacturing is the sewing machine. *Home sewing machines* are used by single users. *Commercial sewing machines* are typically used when mass-producing clothing. Commercial sewing machines are faster, larger, and can usually handle heavier fabrics than home sewing machines. To understand how a sewing machine works, it is important to know the names of the parts and their functions. **Figure 15.19** shows the parts and functions of a home sewing machine. Sewing machines are complex. Therefore, reading the user's manual and following the safety instructions are important steps before using the sewing machine.

Copyright Goodheart-Willcox Co., Inc.

The Parts of a Sewing Machine

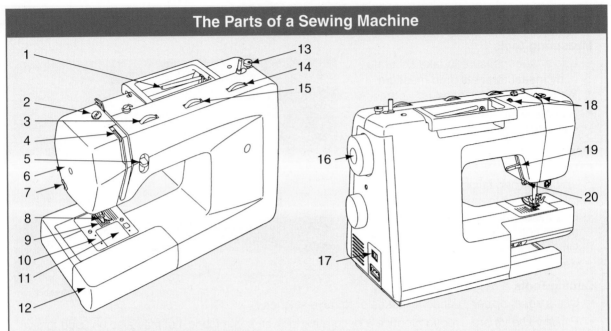

1. *Spool pin*—holds the spool of thread.
2. *Presser foot pressure adjustment*—controls the amount of pressure placed against the feed system.
3. *Needle thread tension dial*—lets you set the tension for your particular project.
4. *Take-up lever*—controls the flow of needle thread.
5. *Reverse-stitch button*—lets you stitch backward.
6. *Face plate*—swings open for access to the movable parts and the light.
7. *Thread cutter*—cuts the thread. It is on the back of the presser bar for convenience.
8. *Presser foot*—holds fabric against the feed system teeth.
9. *Feed dog*—moves fabric under the presser foot.
10. *Needle plate*—helps you sew straight, even seams with its guidelines. Supports fabric during sewing.
11. *Bobbin plate cover*—covers the bobbin and bobbin case.
12. *Removable extension table*—lets you change from flat bed to free arm; convenient for circular projects.
13. *Bobbin winder*—guides the thread when filling the bobbin with thread.
14. *Stitch length dial*—controls the length of the stitches.
15. *Stitch width dial*—controls width of zigzag stitching. Also positions the needle for straight stitching.
16. *Handwheel*—controls the movement of the take-up lever and needle.
17. *Power and light switch*—turns on the machine and sewing light at the same time.
18. *Thread guide*—leads the thread to the needle.
19. *Presser foot lifter*—allows you to raise and lower the presser foot.
20. *Needle clamp*—holds the needle in place.

Figure 15.19 Knowing the parts of a sewing machine will help users operate it correctly. *How familiar are you with sewing machines?*

Copyright Goodheart-Willcox Co., Inc.

Safety Practices

Some safety practices when using and caring for construction tools and equipment include the following:

- Place pins and needles in pincushions. Do not leave them on a table or by the sewing machine. Also, do not hold pins or needles in your mouth. You could swallow them.

- Store scissors and shears in a safe place and keep blades closed when not in use.

- Hand scissors and other sharp objects to people with the handle turned toward them.

- Test the temperature of an iron on a scrap of fabric. Never touch the iron with your hand. You may burn yourself.

- Rest the iron on its heel. Never rest it face down.

- Turn off the iron when not in use. If left on, the iron might overheat and start a fire.

- Read the user's manual before operating a sewing machine. Follow instructions carefully. Do not operate a sewing machine if it is jammed or making unusual sounds.

- When machine sewing, keep fingers away from the presser foot and needle while holding the fabric securely (**Figure 15.20**). If the machine has a finger guard attachment, use it for safety. Do not lean too close to the machine while stitching.

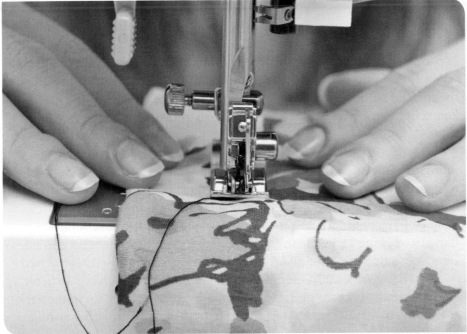

Figure 15.20 When sewing, hold the fabric securely to help keep your stitches straight. *What parts of the sewing machine can you identify in this image?*

Djem/Shutterstock.com

- Unplug all electrical equipment when not in use. Make sure cords are wrapped around equipment and not hanging loose.

- Do not sew over straight pins. The pins could break and end up in your finger.

- Do not force your machine to sew through thick or tough material. You could cause injury to yourself.

- Consider the **ergonomics** (equipment design to promote efficiency and reduce work-related injury) of your sewing table and chair. If your sewing machine is too high, it can cause strain on your back.

Making Simple Repairs

Keeping clothes well-maintained and in good repair involves checking clothing items regularly to make sure there are no rips or tears. Closures (such as buttons and snaps) and hems should be checked and if not properly secured, should be repaired. Knowing how to perform simple repairs can save a lot of time and money. Simple directions for performing the most basic repairs are provided in **Figure 15.21**.

Making Simple Alterations

Understanding how to make simple alternations to clothing items is critical for clothing related human services workers as clients' bodies are different. Typically, simple alterations include either taking width or *circumference* (distance around something) in or out—depending on whether more or less room is desired—or changing the length. Alterations are easiest to perform while a garment is being constructed. Garment patterns are graded to different sizes. Lengths are shortened or lengthened depending on need. During construction, patterns are expanded or shortened within the body of the pattern piece. For example, when shortening pant length, the extra fabric is typically eliminated from the middle of the leg prior to cutting the pattern. This method better keeps the shape of the pant legs, especially those with curve or bell-shaped bottoms.

Once garments are constructed, making alterations becomes more challenging. For example, shortening a pair of pants is done by re-hemming to a shorter length. When pants have shaping, such as bell-bottoms, these changes may slightly alter the silhouette of the pants. When a garment is too big in circumference, simple alterations can be done by making larger seams. For waistbands, the waistband can be removed, side seams made larger, and the waistband then reattached to a smaller garment. In menswear, waistbands are often constructed so that circumference can be eliminated by sewing up the center back seam. **Figure 15.22** shows step-by-step directions for making simple alterations.

Copyright Goodheart-Willcox Co., Inc.

Performing Basic Repairs

Replacing a Button (two or four hole)

1. Thread a hand sewing needle and secure the thread ends with a knot.
2. Mark the spot where the button should be located. To do this, start at the back of the fabric and bring the needle up to the front and through one buttonhole. Bring threaded needle down through other buttonhole.
3. Put a toothpick between the fabric and button, centered between the two buttonholes. Bring the needle up through the fabric and button. Bring the thread over the toothpick and back down through the button.
4. Repeat Step 3 to make about six stitches over the button. Too many stitches can weaken or tear the fabric.
5. Remove toothpick. Pull the button up and bring needle between fabric and button. Make a shank by winding thread around stitches several times. This will add space between the button and fabric, which makes the button stay on longer and also makes buttoning easier.
6. For a button with four holes, repeat the above steps for the other two holes.
7. Bring the needle and thread to the back of the fabric and knot the thread. Repeat the knot for extra security. Then cut the thread.

Repairing a Torn Seam

1. Turn the garment inside out and examine the seam.
2. If necessary/possible, press the seam together flat to prevent bunching when sewn.
3. Thread a hand sewing needle and secure the thread ends with a knot.
4. Bring the threaded needle through the seam just below the rip or tear. Push the needle through to other side of seam.
5. Repeat stitching along length of rip or tear. Allow some overlap with the unbroken seam on each end of the repair to give a smoother and more secure finish.
6. To finish, sew several small stitches in the same place on the fabric. Pull thread and cut end as close to fabric as possible.

Patching a Hole

1. Check if the hole or rip can be repaired by incorporating it into a seam and following seam repair instructions. Make sure that doing so does not result in pulling, puckering, or changing the fit of the garment.
2. If the hole or rip needs to be covered with a patch, choose a compatible fabric to use to make the patch. The fabric can match in color or act as a decorative contrast.
3. Cut the patch to cover the hole plus extend beyond at least ¼ inch on all sides.
4. Using fusible web, adhere the patch in place using a hot iron following product instructions. *Fusible web* is an adhesive that melts when heated to bond fabrics together without sewing.
5. If desired, machine sew or hand sew to reinforce.

Figure 15.21 Performing basic clothing repairs can save you from costly professional repairs or replacement items. *Have you performed any of these tasks? If so, which ones?*

Copyright Goodheart-Willcox Co., Inc.

Making Simple Alterations

Adjusting Pattern Length During Construction

Altering a pattern during construction is much easier than altering a finished garment. In fact, some pattern pieces have labels that indicate where to cut to lengthen or shorten the pattern. Use the following directions to shorten and add length in sleeves, pants, skirts, tops, and bodice:

1. Using a ruler and pencil, carefully mark a horizontal line across the front and back pattern pieces at mid-section. An alternative method for fitted women's bodices that have darts is to increase or decrease the dart size. By doing so, it adds or reduces the bust line curvature/shaping.
2. Carefully cut across the marked line.
3. Overlap or extend both the front and back pattern pieces the desired amount, measuring carefully. The front and back should be increased or decreased the same amount and then taped in place. Be careful to keep the pattern pieces flat.
4. Using the altered pattern piece, cut the fabric pieces. Then continue constructing the garment as per instructions.

Adjusting Pattern Width During Construction

Use the following directions to decrease or add width in pattern pieces:

1. Using a ruler and pencil, carefully mark a vertical line across the pattern piece at mid-section.
2. Carefully cut across the marked line.
3. Overlap or extend the desired amount, measuring carefully and then taping in place. Be careful to keep the pattern piece flat.
4. When altering a front piece, be sure to do the same to the back piece to ensure equal distribution around the garment.
5. Using the altered pattern piece, cut the fabric pieces. Then continue constructing the garment as per instructions.

Shortening and Adding Length on Finished Garments

1. Carefully pull out the original hem thread.
2. Using a steam iron, press the skirt or pant leg flat.
3. Put on the skirt or pants, securing fasteners, and donning appropriate shoes.
4. While standing straight in front of a full-length mirror, have a friend or assistant pin the hem in place.
5. After removing the garment, turn it inside out and place on an ironing board. Press the new hemline up as indicated by the pins, which should be removed as the hem is pressed.
6. For shortening, the new hem may need to be trimmed so that it is not too wide. If lengthening, allow at least ½ inch for new hem. If needed, add a strip of hem tape to the bottom to increase hem width.
7. Once new hemline is determined, finish the raw edge of the hem by stitching with a sewing machine.
8. Press the hem in place once again.
9. Using a hand sewing needle, stitch the hem in place.
10. Turn right side out and press.

(Continued)

Figure 15.22 Simple alterations can be done quickly and easily. *Would you want a career as an alterationist? Why or why not?*

Copyright Goodheart-Willcox Co., Inc.

Making Simple Alterations *(Continued)*
Taking in Side Seams on Finished Garments
1. If possible, put on the garment inside out, securing fasteners and donning appropriate shoes.
2. While standing straight in front of a full-length mirror, have a friend or assistant pin the garment in place along the seam lines, determining how much the seam needs to be taken in. Taking in the seam will make the garment smaller after altering.
3. Remove the garment and place on an ironing board. Press the seams flat so the stitching can be easily accessed. Mark with pins or tailor's chalk where the new seam line will be.
4. Resew the seam. Press.
5. Carefully pull out the original seam thread.
6. Turn the garment right side out and press seams. If seams are too bulky, trim and finish raw edges with a zigzag machine stitch to help prevent raveling.
Letting Out Side Seams on Finished Garments
1. If possible, put on the garment inside out, securing fasteners and donning appropriate shoes.
2. While standing straight in front of a full-length mirror, have a friend or assistant pin the garment in place along the seam lines, determining how much the seam can be let out, at least ¼ inch. Letting out the seam will make the garment larger after altering.
3. Remove the garment and place on an ironing board. Press the seams flat so the stitching can be easily accessed. Mark with pins or tailor's chalk where the new seam line will be.
4. Resew the seam. Press.
5. Carefully pull out the original seam thread.
6. Turn the garment right side out and press seams.

Reading Recall

1. What should you look for when buying clothing for toddlers and preschoolers?
2. What are some clothing needs that might be unique to older adults?
3. Why is it important to read clothing care labels when laundering clothes?
4. Define *ergonomics*.
5. Explain how to safely make a simple alteration of your choice.

Rewards, Demands, and Future Trends

The fashion industry is known for both its *collegiality* (cooperative relationship) among coworkers and its fierce rivalry among industry competitors (**Figure 15.23**). It demands creative, forward-thinking people who are not afraid to take a risk. It is an industry known for long working hours that vary by demand. For example, November and December are months *notorious* (well-known; famous) for long, frantic employee working hours due to the increase in sales around the holiday

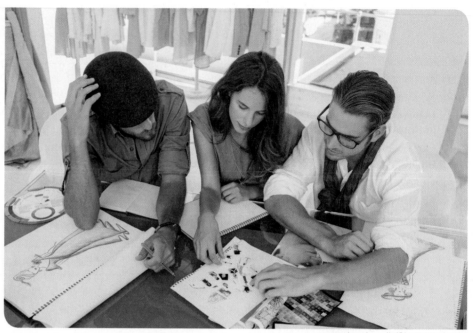

wavebreakmedia/Shutterstock.com

Figure 15.23 Careers in the fashion industry are often highly collaborative, requiring teamwork among coworkers. *Do you prefer working alone or with a group?*

season. Likewise, apparel manufacturers face preseason fluxes when long working hours are expected.

The fashion industry continually offers new opportunities and new ideas and the creative nature of the environment is stimulating. People who thrive in this environment are attracted to the pace and energy. Industry professionals are always on the lookout for fresh new recruits who can breathe new life into an ever-changing industry.

People always have and always will have a need for clothing. The clothing and fashion industry represents a vast global industry. Clothing materials may be sourced in one country, constructed in another, and sold all over the world. Fashion trends change faster than ever as communication happens instantaneously. Career opportunities in clothing related areas of human services will not only always exist, but they are also always changing. As a result, the future outlook for clothing related human services workers is bright (**Figure 15.24**).

Reading Recall

1. What months are notorious for long, frantic employee working hours in the fashion industry?

2. What is the future outlook for clothing related human services workers? Why?

Copyright Goodheart-Willcox Co., Inc.

Future Trends for Clothing Related Human Services Careers				
Occupation	**Projected Growth (2014–2024)**	**Projected Job Openings (2014–2024)**	**Median Wages (2014)**	**Education**
Apparel production manager	Decline (–2% or lower)	95,900	$55,520	High school diploma
Artist	Little or no change (–1–1%)	2,000	$31,080	High school diploma
Fashion blogger	Decline (–2% or lower)	15,900	$36,000	Bachelor's degree
Fashion designer	Slower than average (2–4%)	6,200	$64,030	Associate's degree
Fashion forecaster	Much faster than average (14% or higher)	151,400	$61,290	Bachelor's degree
Fashion journalist	Decline (–2% or lower)	15,900	$36,000	Bachelor's degree
Industrial engineer	Little or no change (–1–1%)	72,800	$81,490	Bachelor's degree
Personal shopper	Average (5–8%)	26,900	$21,500	Unspecified
Production manager	Decline (–2% or lower)	49,100	$92,470	Bachelor's degree
Retail buyer	Average (5–8%)	49,100	$52,270	Bachelor's degree
Retail fashion merchandiser	Faster than average (9–13%)	64,200	$127,130	Bachelor's degree
Retail manager	Slower than average (2–4%)	411,300	$37,860	High school diploma
Scientist	Slower than average (2–4%)	1,800	$91,980	Bachelor's degree
Textile designer	Slower than average (2–4%)	9,900	$64,620	Bachelor's degree
Visual merchandiser	Slower than average (2–4%)	32,100	$26,590	High school diploma

Sources: O*NET and the *Occupational Outlook Handbook*

Figure 15.24 These trends could help you narrow down career choices in clothing related human services. *Which of these careers would you like to explore further? Why?*

Copyright Goodheart-Willcox Co., Inc.

Summary

- Career opportunities in clothing related human services are many and varied. Clothing related human services careers include the textile industry, apparel design and production, retail marketing and promotion, retail management, fashion forecasting, and entrepreneurial opportunities.

- Clothing related human services workers must have good interpersonal and people-helping skills. They are creative, savvy, and fashion-oriented, and have a desire to meet the needs of the end user. Clothing related human services requires strong problem-solving skills.

- There is a wide range of educational requirements within the clothing related human services field. The fashion industry requires no licensure or particular specialized degree, but employers often desire a college or university degree, combined with natural talent and industry experience. Strong technical, problem-solving, and analytical skills, along with industry knowledge, will help you compete in this field.

- Those who work in the clothing related human services fields may need specialized knowledge about the human side of clothing and fashion, including selection factors, clothing needs across the life cycle, the mechanics of caring for and maintaining clothing, and how to use apparel construction tools and equipment.

- The fashion industry is known for both its collegiality among coworkers and its fierce rivalry among industry competitors. It demands creative, forward-thinking people who are not afraid to take a risk. Career opportunities in clothing related areas of human services will not only always exist, but they are also always changing. As a result, creative people will come up with new services, new ways of delivering them, or new customers to serve.

College and Career Portfolio

Portfolio Presentation Preparation

Depending on the purpose of your portfolio, the way in which you present the portfolio may vary. For example, schools may expect you to submit your portfolio electronically. Employers may expect you to walk an interviewer through the portfolio's highlights.

Presenting your portfolio well requires a great deal of preparation. At a job or school interview, you likely will not have time to present your entire portfolio. It is important, therefore, to highlight special achievements you want your audience to see. As you prepare to present your portfolio, it is wise to prepare notes that you can quickly reference before or during the presentation. These notes will ensure that you do not forget anything important.

To determine how you will present your portfolio, complete the following:

1. Talk to a college or career counselor or search online to find out how portfolios in your field are generally presented.

2. Identify two or three components of your portfolio of which you are especially proud. Brainstorm ways to make these components the first and most important items a potential employer or school would see.

3. Identify the highlights of your portfolio presentation. Create notes you can use as a reference before or during the presentation.

Copyright Goodheart-Willcox Co., Inc.

Review and Reflect ➡

1. Identify three employment opportunities in the fashion industry that interest you.
2. Define *natural fibers* and *synthetic fibers*. Identify three examples of each type of fiber.
3. Explain what types of job duties a fashion designer performs on a daily basis.
4. What forms of media might a fashion journalist use to share information with consumers?
5. Why does the fashion field require the ability to explore and apply new ideas and concepts?
6. In today's highly competitive market, what would be the ideal combination of qualifications for a career in the fashion industry?
7. What factors should be considered when purchasing clothing?
8. Explain the clothing needs of four stages of the life cycle. Give specific examples of clothing options during each stage, and describe how to care for these items.
9. Explain the difference between laundering clothes by machine washing and dry cleaning.
10. Using Figure 15.19, explain three parts and functions of a home sewing machine.
11. Identify some of the safety practices that should be followed when using and caring for clothing construction tools and equipment.
12. Describe rewards and demands of working in fashion design.

Vocabulary Activities

13. **Key terms** Write each of the following terms on a separate sheet of paper. For each term, quickly write a word you think relates to the term. In small groups, exchange papers. Have each person in the group explain a term on the list. Take turns until all terms have complete explanations.

adaptive clothing
buying plan
computer aided design (CAD)
design line
digital lookbooks
dry cleaning
ergonomics
fashion merchandising
forecast
ironing
natural fibers
niche markets
notions
synthetic fibers
visual merchandising

14. **Academic terms** With a partner, create a T-chart. In the left column, write each of the following terms. In the right column, write a *synonym* (a word that has the same or similar meaning) for each term. Discuss your synonyms with the class.

agitation
circumference
collegiality
notorious

Self-Assessment Quiz ➡

Complete the self-assessment quiz online to help you practice and expand your knowledge and skills.

Critical Thinking

15. **Compare and contrast** Compare and contrast the job of a retail fashion merchandiser and the job of a retail buyer.
16. **Evaluate** Toddlers need soft, durable, and colorful clothing due to the types of activities in which they engage. Why is this important? What other traits are important for toddler clothing?
17. **Make inferences** During adolescence, teens develop a personal sense of style. Looking at the clothes you are wearing right now, make inferences about your style choice and why these clothes express your personality, as well as what message you are sending to others.
18. **Identify** Create a chart showing common clothing care symbols found on clothing labels. Be sure to draw and label the symbols on your chart.
19. **Cause and effect** Describe future trends in fashion design. How might these trends affect workers entering the fashion industry?
20. **Determine** Using a measuring tape, determine your actual clothing size. For men, measure the neck, chest, sleeve, waist, hip, and inseam. For women, measure the bust, waist, and hips. Are the measurements you took the same as the size you buy? Why or why not?

21. **Analyze** Using Figure 15.22, explain why altering a pattern during construction is easier than altering a finished garment.

22. **Draw conclusions** The clothing and fashion industry represents a vast global industry. Clothing materials might be sourced in one country, constructed in another, and sold all over the world. Draw conclusions about what would happen if any one of those sources was unable to deliver its product. How would this affect the fashion industry over the short term, as well as over the long term? How would this affect the price of clothing?

Core Skills

23. **Research** Obtain unlabeled fabric samples. Using the identifiable traits of natural and synthetic fibers, separate the samples into the two categories. Using information you know about the fabrics, identify what types of fiber they each are.

24. **Writing and math** Imagine you have been hired as the new retail buyer for a local clothing store. You have to turn in the buying plan for the spring order in three days. Your spring order consists of 1,000 pieces of clothing. Identify the types, sizes, prices, and quantities of each item in your buying plan.

25. **Technology** Create a window display that could be used for a local store. Be sure to think about placement, signage, wall displays, and mannequin placement, as well as clothing and accessories, as you create your display. Take a picture, and place it in your portfolio.

26. **Writing and research** Pretend you are doing a fashion critique at a runway show. Write an article giving your opinion about the runway show and the styles being presented in the designer's line. Research fashion critiques if you need help writing your article.

27. **Research and writing** Research the degrees offered at colleges and universities in your area that have an emphasis on fashion design. What classes would you need to take? How long would it take you to finish a degree? Are there other options, such as taking some of the classes at a community college or while still in high school? Using the information you gather,

create a degree plan for yourself to receive a degree in fashion design. Include what classes you will take and where you will take them.

28. **Technology, writing, speaking, and listening** Take pictures of the clothing other people around you wear, without the peoples' heads in the pictures. Put together an electronic presentation using these pictures, explaining where these outfits would be appropriate to wear in everyday life. Try to find outfits that could be worn on a date, at work, at home, exercising, shopping, and eating out. Identify which outfits demonstrate apparel maintenance and care that enhances appearance in personal and professional settings. Share your presentation with your classmates. Have them agree or disagree with your clothing choices for each event.

29. **Research and math** Maternity clothes can be an expensive investment, especially if you work in an office with a dress code. Research the cost of maternity clothes in your town. Figure out how much money you would need to spend on a basic wardrobe with interchangeable outfits. Be sure to include sales tax for your local area when adding the total cost.

30. **Research and writing** In small groups, research places where people with special needs can purchase adaptive clothing. As you are looking, select adaptive clothing items for the following people with special needs: a 7-year-old girl in a wheelchair, a 23-year-old man who was in an accident and his arm is in a cast, a 56-year-old woman with severe arthritis in her hands, and an 80-year-old man who had a stroke and has lost mobility and functioning in the left side of his body. Create a pamphlet that shows a picture of each item you selected. Under each item, include where it can be purchased, sizes that are available for purchase, and how much the item costs. Also include a brief description for each piece of adaptive clothing. Indicate how each article of clothing can promote independence, confidence, and a sense of self-respect for the person with special needs. Share your group's findings with the rest of the class.

31. **Reading and speaking** Look at a piece of clothing and read the instructions on the care label. Using this information, explain to

Copyright Goodheart-Willcox Co., Inc.

someone who cannot read the instructions how to care for the clothing item.

32. **Technology, speaking, and listening** With a partner, create a how-to video on clothing care, giving step-by-step instructions for cleaning, maintaining, and storing clothes properly. Base your video around reading and following the instructions on clothing care labels. Present your video in class. As a class, analyze the videos to determine if the instructions are clear and accurate.

33. **Technology, speaking, and listening** Create a presentation to deliver in class that shows your classmates how to perform a basic clothing repair (such as replacing a button) and an alteration (such as adjusting

pattern length during construction). In your presentation, clearly demonstrate each step to teach someone who does not know how to perform these tasks. Be sure to also demonstrate how to safely and correctly use and care for the construction tools and equipment necessary to complete your project. As a class, analyze the presentation to determine if the instructions are clear and accurate.

34. **CTE career readiness practice** Think of one trend in fashion that is relevant today. Analyze the possibility of this trend continuing. Do you think it will ever be predominant? What evidence supports your view? Share your findings with the class.

Lend a Hand

Clothing Donations

Clothing is a basic necessity, but not everyone can afford to purchase new clothes at a retail store when they need them. Thrift stores and resale shops offer new and gently used clothing at discounted prices. People can buy seasonally appropriate clothing without worrying too much about the cost. Many of these stores receive all of their merchandise as donations from stores and individuals. Some communities also have "clothing closets," which are like food pantries for clothing. People who qualify for this assistance can shop for clothing a couple times a month.

Schools, places of worship, clubs and teams, or other organizations will sometimes hold clothing drives to collect new clothing to donate to people in need. For example, a theater club might offer a discounted play admission if theatergoers bring new hats, gloves, or scarves to donate.

To find out how you can help donate clothing, complete the following:

1. Go through your closet and determine if there is anything that you would like to donate. (Make sure you have parent or guardian permission first!) Perhaps there are clothes that you have grown out of or that you never wear. Gather these clothing items together.

2. Assess your chosen clothing items. Are all of the clothes clean and free of odors? Are there any repairs that need to be made? If so, wash or repair the clothing accordingly. If there is any clothing beyond repair, do not donate it. Only donate quality items.

3. Ask your family and friends if they would like to participate in your clothing drive. Offer to launder clothes or help perform basic clothing repairs.

4. Research organizations in your area that take clothing donations. Read mission statements for these organizations to find out how your donation will be used. Choose an organization and make arrangements to donate the clothing.

Copyright Goodheart-Willcox Co., Inc.

Chapter 16

Housing Related Human Services

While studying, look for the activity icon ➦ to

- **practice** key and academic terms with e-flash cards and matching activities;
- **assess** what you learn by completing self-assessment quizzes; and
- **reinforce** what you learn by mapping concepts and completing review and reflect questions.

www.g-wlearning.com/humanservices/

Tyler Olson/Shutterstock.com

Learning Outcomes

After studying this chapter, you will be able to
- **compare and contrast** career opportunities for housing related human services workers;
- **list** common aptitudes, attitudes, and skills of housing related human services workers;
- **give examples** of postsecondary education, training, and experience required for several housing related human services careers;
- **describe** priorities and needs that affect housing decisions throughout the lifespan;
- **explain** ways to keep the home clean and safe;
- **describe** the elements and principles of design used to create interior spaces;
- **identify** factors that influence interior design trends; and
- **summarize** the rewards, demands, and future trends of housing related careers.

Reading Strategies

Before reading, imagine you are an interior designer and your client wants to redesign her kitchen. What would you tell her about the factors that might affect her design choices? Write two paragraphs explaining these factors. As you are reading the chapter, consider what you wrote. After reading, make changes to your paragraphs based on what you learned.

Mapping Concepts

Create a fishbone map to organize your notes while reading this chapter. In the body of the map, write a short topic sentence that summarizes the main point of the chapter. In the surrounding scales, write your specific notes.

Key Terms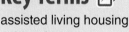

assisted living housing
color schemes
color wheel
elements of design
focal point
hues
human scale
independent living communities
interior design

nursing homes
principles of design
proxemics
shades
tints
tones
universal design
value

Academic Terms

contours
downsizing
geometric shapes
opulent
paramount
tactile

Like food and clothing, housing is a basic need of individuals and families. Throughout history, people have constructed buildings as shelter to keep out the natural elements. Buildings offer protection to people from the heat, cold, rain, sun, and any creatures that could cause harm. Buildings can also provide a feeling of safety and security for people. Because human services workers focus on meeting people's needs, many careers in the housing industry relate to the human services field.

The housing industry focuses on the behavioral, social, economic, functional, and aesthetic aspects of housing, interiors, and other constructed environments. The housing industry includes diverse careers in the architecture and construction; hospitality and tourism; and marketing, sales, and services career clusters. Specifically in the human services career cluster, housing specialists work with people to find housing that will meet their needs.

In the architecture and construction career cluster, examples of careers include architects, building inspectors, and construction workers. Interior designers are also in this cluster. **Interior design** is the process of shaping the experience of interior space through the manipulation of space, the application of the elements and principles of design, and the use of materials (**Figure 16.1**).

In the hospitality and tourism career cluster, jobs can range from housekeeping and janitorial workers and maids to hotel lodging

Zastolskiy Victor/Shutterstock.com

Figure 16.1 An interior designer may specialize in designing a residential space such as this or a commercial (business) space. *Which type of space would you be more interested in designing?*

Copyright Goodheart-Willcox Co., Inc.

managers. In marketing, sales, and services, examples of careers include real estate brokers and sales agents and property managers.

For human services workers who enjoy working closely with people, certain careers in the housing field are ideal. Job duties revolve around the development of personal and professional relationships with others. There are significant intangible rewards in helping people secure housing.

Housing Related Career Opportunities

There are many career opportunities for human services workers in the housing industry. **Figure 16.2** shows some examples of careers in this field that relate to human services and helping people meet one of their most basic needs. In the following sections, you will learn more about each of these careers.

Housing Specialists

A *housing specialist* finds available resources to meet special populations' unique housing needs. For example, housing specialists may assist people going through home foreclosure. They may find placement in group homes for people with special needs. Some may find housing for military families who are relocating. Housing specialists may also act as advocates for their clients in dealing with public housing authorities.

Housing specialists plan, organize, and direct activities relating to affordable and market-priced housing. They often work with community groups, government and nonprofit agencies, developers, and the public to identify county and regional housing needs and objectives. They then formulate plans to meet the housing needs of their community. At times, housing specialists act as consultants to mortgage lenders, real estate agents, property developers, and property management companies. Government housing specialists may provide community resource information or pretrial mediation in landlord/tenant cases.

Examples of Housing Related Human Services Careers	
• Commercial interior designer	• Real estate broker
• Fashion blogger	• Real estate sales agent
• Fashion journalist	• Residential interior designer
• Housing specialist	• Retail buyer
• Kitchen and bathroom designer	• Retail fashion merchandiser
• Lighting designer	• Retail manager
• Production manager	• Space planner
• Property manager	• Visual merchandiser

Figure 16.2 These are just some of the careers in human services that are related to the housing industry. *Can you name some other housing related careers?*

Copyright Goodheart-Willcox Co., Inc.

Real Estate Brokers and Sales Agents

Real estate brokers and *real estate sales agents* perform similar duties. They help their clients buy, sell, and lease properties (**Figure 16.3**). They may offer their expertise in listing, advertising, and selling properties. They may also assist buyers in obtaining financing and completing and filing proper paperwork. Real estate brokers and sales agents primarily work in offices, but are often busy in the field. At other times, they visit homes to keep abreast of other properties on the market.

The primary difference between a real estate broker and a sales agent involves licensing. In every state, both real estate brokers and sales agents must have a license to sell property. Real estate brokers, however, have additional licensing. Real estate brokers are licensed to manage their own businesses, whereas sales agents must work with a broker.

Property Managers

A *property manager* manages housing properties when the owner is not present. This may include rental properties and multifamily units, such as apartments or condominiums. Property managers act as the go-between for the owner and renters. They oversee property maintenance, monitor rent payments, and meet with owners or show properties to potential renters. They typically work in an office setting, but spend time walking the property to ensure proper upkeep.

©iStock.com/andresr

Figure 16.3 Real estate sales agents spend a great deal of time meeting at clients' homes and showing potential buyers homes that are for sale. *What other duties might real estate sales agents perform?*

Copyright Goodheart-Willcox Co., Inc.

Law and Ethics / *Landlord and Tenant Rights*

Landlords own rental housing properties and *tenants* rent them. Types of properties that landlords lease or rent may include single-family homes, apartments, condominiums, and even group living environments. *Leases* refer to long-term arrangements, often year by year. *Rentals* are frequently month to month. These terms are often used interchangeably, however.

Landlord and tenant relationships can be tricky. There are dozens of laws that landlords and tenants must observe. Both parties have responsibilities and expectations to follow according to federal and individual state laws.

Federal laws prohibit landlords from discriminating against potential tenants, especially on the basis of race, color, religion, national origin, family status, disability, age, or gender. Although the federal Fair Housing Act of 1968 and the federal Fair Housing Amendments Act of 1988 prohibit discrimination, there are exceptions. Some states have landlord and tenant laws that include many exceptions, usually in favor of landlords more than tenants.

State laws cover dozens of specific components of the landlord and tenant relationship. Laws may address issues involving security deposits and refunds, late payment fees, and nontoxic and safe conditions. Other laws may relate to the landlord's rights in accessing the property. Still other laws exist regarding landlord and tenant rights in ending the relationship. In some states, laws appear to favor landlords. In other states, laws seem to favor tenants. In most states, landlord and tenant laws are highly political.

Understanding landlord and tenant laws for the state is critical for landlords and tenants. Not only does it help both parties to be prepared and reach agreement, but also to be satisfied in their arrangement. A lack of understanding of landlord and tenant legal rights and responsibilities can end in costly legal battles, loss of time and money, and even unsafe conditions.

Research Activity

Imagine you are ready to rent an apartment. Research your rights as a tenant in your state. Choose one of the following ways to share your findings with the rest of the class:
- Write a blog post that shares important tenant rights information in your state.
- Make a brochure on tenant rights to share with others.
- Create an electronic presentation that focuses on tenant rights laws.

Home Furnishings Sales and Marketing Staff

Home furnishings sales and marketing is the segment of the housing industry that focuses on getting products to consumers. Workers in this field design, produce, market, and sell home furnishings to wholesalers or retailers who then merchandise and sell the products to consumers. The home furnishings market has many segments that focus on very specific niche markets. In fact, it is difficult to convey the number of career opportunities available in the home furnishings industry.

Because apparel and home furnishings are both fashion products, these areas share similar career opportunities in sales and marketing. For example, both the apparel and home furnishing industries hire *production managers, retail buyers, retail managers, retail fashion merchandisers,* and *visual merchandisers.* Career opportunities are also available for *fashion journalists* and *fashion bloggers,* as well as careers in other promotional marketing (**Figure 16.4**). Retail stores often employ

Copyright Goodheart-Willcox Co., Inc.

Figure 16.4 Because home furnishings are fashion-oriented products, advertising and promotions play a large part in sales. *What types of advertising and promotions have you seen recently for home furnishing products?*

©iStock.com/ideabug

interior designers as consultants for their consumers, especially when selling high-end home furnishings.

Designers

The job of the *residential interior designer* is to create environments that are safe, functional, aesthetically pleasing, and feel like home. Residential interior designers focus on the design needs of individuals and families in their home living environments. This often means single-family homes, but may also include apartments, condominiums, and townhouses. Residential interior designers select furnishings, colors, textures, and materials that make an existing interior feel like home and perform functionally for the user.

In addition to working in existing homes, residential interior designers may work in newly built housing developments. Their role is to create model interiors for showing homes during sales. In the planning stage, residential interior designers create plans for lighting and electrical, kitchen surfaces and equipment, bathroom fixtures, wall treatments, flooring, and window treatments. In the sales stage, residential interior designers "set the stage." They make a home look lived in, inspiring potential homeowners or renters to imagine living in the space.

A *commercial interior designer* creates safe, efficient, functional, and aesthetically pleasing interior spaces for businesses. Rather than focusing on one individual or family, commercial interior designers must design for the functional needs of many users. Commercial interiors differ from residential interiors in the level of safety regulations and the end use.

Expert Insight

"We shape our buildings, and afterwards our buildings shape us."

Winston Churchill, former British Prime Minister

Copyright Goodheart-Willcox Co., Inc.

Case Study | *Home Is Where the Heart Is*

Andrea designs the interiors of homes in which people live, sleep, play, cook, build relationships, and feel safe. Andrea is a residential interior designer. She specializes in designing and creating home spaces for transitional housing apartments. These apartments are for people facing tough issues who are now "getting on their feet." Andrea finds her work to be creative, rewarding, and meaningful.

During high school, Andrea thought she might want to become an architect so she could work together with her father, who is a builder. To see what the job would be like, Andrea set up a job shadowing experience to follow a local architect for a day. Although the work was interesting, it did not quite capture her curiosity. What did interest her was the design of the interior environment of the building.

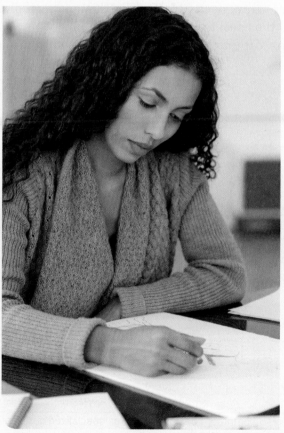

racom/Shutterstock.com

After earning a degree in interior design and completing an internship with a residential interior design firm, Andrea was ready to apply for an interior design position. For the next 10 years, she worked her way toward specialization in designing transitional housing spaces. Andrea realizes that she really has the best of both worlds as she works closely with architects and builders. She speaks their language and understands building codes, but her focus is on her passion, the interior.

Now, Andrea has a team of designers she works with to create pleasing environments for her clients. Her team achieves this through the use of lighting, color, interior space planning, texture, flooring, furniture, drapery and fabric, and many other highly inventive materials. As far as creativity goes, the sky is the limit.

Today will be an interesting day because Andrea is planning to meet with a new client. This client wants Andrea to design a "safe" temporary group home for women and children who are victims of domestic violence. Once Andrea fully understands her new client's goals, she will then come up with a strategy. Andrea wants to think outside the box to create an environment that affords privacy, comfort, and a sense of community. By taking the time to really listen to her client's needs, Andrea is confident that her team will implement the best visual and functional design solution for her new client.

For Discussion

1. What types of spaces might the future residents of the temporary group home find most desirable?

2. How might Andrea use colors, textures, and space to contribute to these desires?

3. What questions could Andrea ask her client to get a better feel for the client's design needs and wants? Who else might Andrea ask? What other information might Andrea be able to gather?

Copyright Goodheart-Willcox Co., Inc.

Commercial interiors must also be accessible to people with varying physical abilities.

Commercial interior designers tend to specialize in one area. For example, one commercial interior designer may concentrate on upscale retail stores for the youth market. Other specialty areas may include office spaces, hotels, restaurants, places of worship, department stores, libraries, educational facilities, medical facilities, and government buildings.

A *kitchen and bathroom designer* specializes in designing kitchens and bathrooms (**Figure 16.5**). These designers need to know about kitchen and bathroom features, such as kitchen appliances, bathroom fixtures, countertop materials, flooring, lighting, windows, and plumbing. They also require specialized knowledge in installation, electrical wiring, lighting, plumbing, and control systems. Training and continuing education is necessary to safely utilize the newest features for kitchen and bathroom spaces.

Creating an interior space that reflects a given attitude is not just about the right colors, textures, and furniture. Effectively lighting the space is also very important to the overall design. A *lighting designer* knows how to combine light intensities and direct and use different light colors to create a functional, pleasing environment. Lighting designers understand architectural needs, electrical codes, energy issues, maintenance concerns, and the latest technological advancements in lighting and control systems. Although all lighting designers are not

MR. INTERIOR/Shutterstock.com

Figure 16.5 To become a kitchen and bathroom designer requires specialized certification. *Are there any postsecondary programs in your town that offer specialized certification in kitchen and bath design?*

Copyright Goodheart-Willcox Co., Inc.

interior designers, most interior designers must possess a basic level of knowledge and skill related to lighting.

A *space planner* creatively solves complex problems that involve the organization and layout of interior spaces. A space planner is concerned about space efficiency and function, making the space the most usable for end users. Typically, space planners work closely with architects and interior designers. Their work is highly specialized. Because the problems space planners solve are usually complex, they most often work in the commercial design field. Many specialize in lighting design within a certain type of commercial space planning, such as retail boutiques, places of worship, amusement parks, or community buildings, such as senior service centers.

Entrepreneurial Opportunities

Parts of the housing related human services field lend well to entrepreneurial careers. For example, many real estate brokers run their own businesses. Interior design, in particular, is often run as a small business. Many interior designers also act as consultants.

Like entrepreneurs in the fashion design and merchandising fields, some housing related human services workers get their experience in the corporate setting and then begin freelancing or running their own business. For example, a designer may begin offering services as an independent contractor. Overall, interior design is a highly creative field that, by its very nature, is always changing. Such an environment is prime for those with an entrepreneurial spirit.

Reading Recall
1. Give an example of how a housing specialist might meet a person's housing need.
2. What is the primary difference between a *real estate broker* and a *real estate sales agent*?
3. List two daily tasks of property managers.
4. Name the industry focusing on getting home decorating and furnishings products to consumers.
5. List three interior design specialty areas.

Common Aptitudes, Attitudes, and Skills

Human services workers in the housing industry share common aptitudes, attitudes, and skills (**Figure 16.6**). They must be resourceful to find the resources that will enable clients to meet their housing needs. They must be compassionate, respectful, and nonjudgmental as they work with a variety of different people. Housing related human services workers must also have excellent listening and speaking skills. They need

Copyright Goodheart-Willcox Co., Inc.

Common Aptitudes, Attitudes, and Skills of Housing Related Human Services Workers

• Resourceful	• Math skills
• Compassionate	• Negotiation skills
• Creative	• Listening and speaking skills
• Respectful	• Up-to-date in knowledge
• Nonjudgmental	• Teamwork skills
• Artistic	• Technical skills
• Detail oriented	• Problem-solving skills

Figure 16.6 Workers in human services housing related careers are likely to share common aptitudes, attitudes, and skills. *Which of these characteristics best describe you?*

to be able to quickly address client concerns and be negotiators when necessary.

People working in the housing industry often possess artistic ability and are very creative. They are detail oriented and knowledgeable about state and local building laws and codes. Interior designers have a strong sense of visual awareness to be able to see how designs fit together.

Because the housing industry deals with complex issues, workers must demonstrate problem-solving and technical skills. The field requires the ability to explore and apply new ideas and concepts. Housing careers promote collaborative working teams that share a common purpose. Working with like-minded colleagues in a collaborative effort is gratifying.

Reading Recall

1. Give an example of an occupation in the housing industry requiring workers to be knowledgeable about state and local building laws and codes.

2. Why must human services workers in the housing industry demonstrate problem-solving and technical skills?

Education, Training, and Experience

Education, training, and experience expectations vary for careers in housing related human services. A bachelor's degree in housing, family services, business or public administration, finance, economics, or a related field is desired for a career as a housing specialist. Housing specialists need knowledge of housing laws, regulations, ordinances, programs, and resources. They must also understand current social and economic issues and practices affecting housing and community development. A combination of educational background and experience provides the best preparation for a career in this field.

Copyright Goodheart-Willcox Co., Inc.

Real estate brokers and sales agents must be licensed by the state. Each state differs in the number of hours of real estate training courses needed. The licensing exam also varies. For each state, candidates must be at least 18 or 19 years old and have completed high school.

Many property managers hold college degrees and some also hold a real estate license. Some entry-level property manager positions require just a high school diploma, but to move into higher-level management positions, a college degree is preferred. Experience ranging from one to five years is generally required for many of these positions (**Figure 16.7**). Some degree programs provide internship opportunities that enable students to gain experience.

The interior design industry requires professionals who possess a creative flair combined with scientific knowledge and business and technical skills. To be called an *interior designer*, there are specific training requirements. An interior designer is defined by the American Society of Interior Designers (ASID) as a professional who is trained to create both functional and quality environments.

An interior designer is qualified through education, training, experience, and professional examination. In some states, interior designers are required to be licensed or registered. States may require that practicing interior designers pass the National Council for Interior Design Qualification (NCIDQ) certificate exam. Successful completion of this

Robert Crum/Shutterstock.com

Figure 16.7 Many larger apartment complexes may provide opportunities for college graduates to work as assistant property managers to gain the experience needed to become a property manager. *How else might someone gain experience to become a property manager?*

Copyright Goodheart-Willcox Co., Inc.

exam demonstrates the designer has the appropriate knowledge, skill, and experience to solve complex problems related to interior design.

Reading Recall

1. List the educational and training requirements for two housing related human services careers.
2. How does the ASID define an interior designer?
3. What does successful completion of the NCIDQ certificate exam demonstrate?

Specialized Knowledge for Housing Related Human Services

Those who work in housing related human services need specialized knowledge about the human side of the housing industry. They need to know how people meet their needs through housing across the family life cycle. They also understand the importance of keeping a home clean and safe. To create pleasing interiors, they use the elements and principles of design. They also keep informed about factors that influence interior design trends.

Meeting Needs Through Housing

Housing is a need that when filled may offer protection from the elements, privacy, and safety. Once these basic needs are met, housing may become a means of self-expression, creativity, and beauty (**Figure 16.8**). People may consider family values, attitudes, composition, income, and the housing market when making housing choices.

Housing needs change over the lifespan as people grow and change in the roles they play and the values they hold dear. This is all a part of the family life cycle. Housing related human services workers are aware of these changes.

Housing Needs Across the Family Life Cycle

In the *beginning stage* of the family life cycle, a married couple establishes a home for their family. In many cultures, this home is independent from their parents. As a newly established couple, finding affordable housing is often *paramount* (most important) in their selection process. They often seek housing that communicates their desired lifestyle and is close to friends or employment.

When a couple enters the *childbearing stage* of the family life cycle, their housing needs may change. The family may desire a bigger house or a house in a different location, such as closer to extended family or certain schools. Housing needs often change again during the *launching* and *mid-years stages* of the family life cycle. As children leave home and

Copyright Goodheart-Willcox Co., Inc.

Podsolnukh/Shutterstock.com

Figure 16.8 Designing a personal space offers a creative outlet to express your personality. *In what ways do you express your personality through design?*

get places of their own, the family home becomes empty. Extra room is suddenly not as important. When this occurs, people may look into *downsizing* (reducing the size or cost of their housing).

During the *aging stage* of the family life cycle, many older adults want to remain independent and grow old in their own homes. As health declines, however, this may not be possible. For some older adults, special housing modifications may enable them to continue living independently. Other older adults may have to move in with a family member or make other housing decisions.

Special Housing Needs for Older Adults

Three main types of living communities offer different levels of support for older adults. These types include the following:

- **Independent living communities** provide housing for older adults who can care for themselves, but desire the community support of those of similar age (**Figure 16.9**).

- **Assisted living housing** environments provide gradually expanded oversight and help with daily activities. Medical care is available when necessary.

- **Nursing homes** offer more intense nursing care for residents, usually provided by medical staff.

Although some older adults are optimistic about new living arrangements, others struggle with the transition. They may be resentful of losing the independence they had when living alone or with a loved

Copyright Goodheart-Willcox Co., Inc.

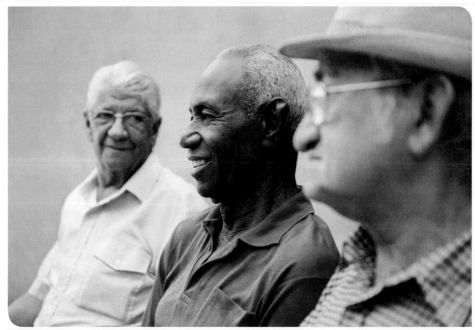

Diego Cervo/Shutterstock.com

Figure 16.9 Independent living communities provide good socialization opportunities for older adults. *What types of housing are available for older adults in your community?*

one. Like any major transition, change can be emotionally difficult. If the move requires parting with some possessions, older adults may feel additional loss for objects representing a past stage in life.

Other Special Housing Needs

During any stage of life, accessibility is important. Sometimes special circumstances, such as an accident or special need, warrant consideration. Depending on the type of accident, a person with a physical disability may also need new housing accommodations to make getting around less challenging.

Universal design is housing design that meets the physical needs of people of all ages and abilities. Universal design includes adjusting countertop height, creating a wheelchair accessible ramp, and widening the hallways for adults in wheelchairs. Features are also added, such as handrails for safety and convenience, wooden floors for wheelchairs and walking aids, and waterproof seats in the shower. The main purposes of universal design are safety, convenience, and accessibility. During the mid-years and beyond, universal design becomes a high priority that influences people's design decisions.

Keeping the Home Clean and Safe

Housing related human services workers understand the importance of keeping a home clean and safe. Taking care of the home's housing systems, surfaces, and appliances can prolong the life of these components

Copyright Goodheart-Willcox Co., Inc.

in the home. Periodically inspecting roofs and foundations can prevent costly repair fees. Following a cleaning and maintenance schedule can also help keep the home clean and safe.

Care of Housing Systems

To keep a home safe, housing related human services workers have a general knowledge of the systems that make a home run. Housing systems include the electrical, heating and cooling, plumbing, and physical components (**Figure 16.10**). Maintaining the housing systems is necessary to keep a home running efficiently and safely.

Reading instruction and safety manuals is important to ensure proper, safe use and maintenance of housing systems. Instruction manuals provide directions for stopping, starting, or shutting down equipment and systems, if necessary. Routine inspection and maintenance schedules are also available in instruction manuals. As a precaution, store instructions in a safe place and review periodically.

Care of Surfaces and Appliances

In addition to maintaining housing systems, care of surfaces and appliances inside the home is also necessary. These include flooring, walls, kitchen and bathroom surfaces, glass, and appliances. For all surfaces, frequent cleaning keeps the surfaces clean and sanitary and prolongs the surface's life. By preserving the life of the surface, replacement is necessary less often than for poorly maintained surfaces. As with housing systems, reading and following the instruction manuals is also necessary to ensure safe use and maintenance of surfaces and appliances. **Figure 16.11** lists common methods for cleaning surfaces in the home, including using both commercial and common household products.

Housing Systems	
System	**Description**
Electrical system	Keeps lights on and appliances running. May also keep the heating and cooling running by powering the furnace, air conditioner, and water heater. Some housing utilizes other forms of energy, such as natural gas.
Heating and cooling system	Includes the furnace, water heater, ventilation, and air conditioner.
Plumbing system	Provides water supply and drainage.
Physical components	Includes the foundation, walls, roof, and other physical parts of the house.

Figure 16.10 Housing related human services workers must be knowledgeable about these housing systems. *With which of these systems are you most familiar? least familiar?*

Copyright Goodheart-Willcox Co., Inc.

Figure 16.11 As you can see in this chart, different materials in the home require different cleaning methods. *What cleaning methods do you use when cleaning your home?*

Common Methods for Cleaning Surfaces	
Material	**Cleaning Method**
Ceramic appliances and fixtures	• Vinegar and water • Bleach solution to kill mildew • Nonabrasive commercial cleaners
Ceramic tile	• Damp cloth or mop • 50/50 solution of hydrogen peroxide and water for grout
Copper	• Damp cloth • Lemon and salt mixture
Glass	• Ammonia and water solution • Commercial glass cleaners
Granite	• Damp cloth • Mild soap and water, vinegar
Marble	• Damp cloth • Mild soap and water
Plastic-coated laminates	• Vinegar and water • Commercial nonabrasive all-purpose cleaners
Quartz, engineered stone	• Damp cloth • Mild soap and water, vinegar • Commercial nonabrasive all-purpose cleaners
Solid surface	• Damp cloth • Mild soap and water, vinegar • Commercial nonabrasive all-purpose cleaners
Stainless steel	• Commercial stainless steel cleaners
Wood	• Damp cloth with vinegar and water

Flooring

Flooring surfaces commonly include carpeting, laminate, wood, concrete, and tile. To prolong the life of carpeting, vacuum regularly and clean up any stains or spills immediately. Periodic deep cleaning can further preserve the life of carpeting. For other flooring types, regularly sweep, dust, wash, clean, or polish, depending on manufacturer recommendations. Check seams as necessary.

Walls

Walls in a home require care less often than floors. This is because there is typically less interaction with the human body. Depending on the age of people in the home, fingerprints, spills, and other surface soil

Copyright Goodheart-Willcox Co., Inc.

may need to be removed from the walls periodically. Washing with a damp cloth may be a cleaning option with certain types of paints. This is especially true if paint has a gloss or semi-gloss finish.

Kitchen and Bathroom Surfaces

Kitchen and bathroom countertop surfaces are often made from many materials, including plastic-coated laminate, engineered stone (such as quartz), and solid stone surfaces. Each type of surface has its advantages and disadvantages, including cost, use, and maintenance (**Figure 16.12**). Follow manufacturer or vendor instructions when cleaning, sealing, cutting, or placing hot items on the surface.

Glass

Glass surfaces can be found in windows, skylights, mirrors, and appliances. Proper care of glass surfaces involves cleaning and protecting

Popular Countertop Materials		
Material	**Advantages**	**Disadvantages**
Butcher-block wood	• Warm appearance • Variety of choices • Noise absorbent • Easy to clean	• Can scratch, mar • Easily stained • Damaged by heat • Damaged by water if unsealed • Needs periodic sealing
Ceramic tile	• Affordable material • Color • Heat resistant	• Labor-intensive construction • Uneven surface • Difficult to clean grout
Concrete	• Many colors and textures • Inexpensive material • Resists scratches • Tolerates heat	• Heavy • Expensive installation • Industrial looking
Copper	• Unique color and appearance • Cleans with soap and water • Antimicrobial	• Expensive to fabricate • Dents • Shows marks • Needs sealing to protect from color change
Granite	• Elegance and beauty • Durable • Heat resistant	• Expensive • Needs periodic sealing • Stains • Cracks • Limited colors and sizes

(Continued)

Figure 16.12 Countertop materials have different advantages and disadvantages. *Which of these countertop materials are found in your home?*

Copyright Goodheart-Willcox Co., Inc.

Popular Countertop Materials (*Continued*)		
Material	**Advantages**	**Disadvantages**
Marble	• Elegance and beauty • Durable • Heat resistant	• Very expensive • Needs periodic sealing • Stains • Porous • Limited colors and sizes
Plastic-coated laminates	• Easy to clean • Smooth surface • Affordable • Many colors/patterns	• Seams visible • Can scratch and tear
Quartz, engineered stone	• Looks like granite • Many colors and patterns • Resists scratches, stains • Nonporous • No sealing needed	• Expensive • Damaged by heat
Solid surface	• Custom fabricated to size • Seamless • Stain resistant • Scratches repairable	• Expensive • Heat intolerance
Stainless steel	• Durable • Hygienic • Seamless • Heat resistant • Easy to clean	• Expensive to fabricate • Dents • Shows marks • Smudges easily • Noisy

the glass from hard hits and nicks. To prevent windows and skylights from leaking, periodically check seals.

Appliances

Care of appliances is dependent on the type of appliance, manufacturer instructions, and source of power. Careful consideration of care and maintenance required, along with cost and efficiency, should be an important part of any appliance purchase decision. The ENERGY STAR program provides efficiency ratings for electrical appliances and other household equipment.

Inspection of Roofs and Foundations

Over the life of a home, roofs and foundations wear and tear and require inspection. Roofs wear out or are damaged over time. Because replacing a roof can be very costly, regular cleaning and maintenance can catch or prevent leaks, prolong the life of the roof, and lengthen

Copyright Goodheart-Willcox Co., Inc.

time between replacements. Foundations are usually not replaced, but sometimes cracks or settling makes repairs necessary.

Schedules for Cleaning and Maintenance

Home cleaning and maintenance is best done on a schedule (**Figure 16.13**). In that way, repairs involving significant damage and cost may be avoided by utilizing preventive maintenance. Some repairs, especially repairs involving water leakage, need to be dealt with immediately to prevent large scale and costly repairs from potential flooding. Simple cleaning and organizing help the resident or caretaker keep current with the state of the home.

Using the Elements of Design

Interior designers create pleasing environments for their clients, both for residential home environments and commercial spaces. To create a

Example Cleaning Schedule	
Time Period	**Tasks**
Daily	• Straightening and tidying • Cleaning countertops • Washing dishes • Filing papers
Bi-weekly	• Removing garbage to outside • Dusting surfaces • Doing laundry (depending on resident needs)
Weekly	• Changing bed linens • Cleaning bathrooms • Sweeping and vacuuming • Cleaning stovetop, microwave, sink
Bi-monthly	• Dusting ceilings and light fixtures
Monthly	• Dusting ceiling fans and air vents • Cleaning walls and windows • Spot cleaning carpet • Checking fire alarms • Dusting intensively • Vacuuming inside furniture
Quarterly	• Organizing closets by season
Yearly	• Cleaning out storage drawers and units • Polishing, waxing, and sealing surfaces, if needed • Cleaning out garage and storage spaces

Figure 16.13
Establishing a schedule for cleaning can help you keep track of when tasks need to be done around the home. *Are there other tasks you would add to this schedule?*

Copyright Goodheart-Willcox Co., Inc.

Expert Insight

"The details are not the details. They make the design."

Charles Eames, designer

space that is both functional and aesthetically pleasing, designers use the elements of design.

The **elements of design** include line, shape, form, space, texture, pattern, color, and light. Designers use each of the elements of design as they alter, modify, and create visually pleasing interiors for their clients.

Line

Line is the most basic element of design, as it connects two points to create a defined space or shape (two other elements). Line can enclose a space into a two- or three-dimensional form. It can indicate direction, creating a sense of rhythm or movement. Line can also create a mood or emotional reaction (**Figure 16.14**). For example, diagonal, jagged lines communicate tension. Curved lines communicate serenity. Vertical lines indicate strength and stability. Horizontal lines indicate calm.

Shape and Form

Shape is the measurable, identifiable *contours* (outline) of an object. Common, recognizable shapes in design include circles, ovals, squares, rectangles, and triangles. These shapes are *geometric shapes*. When a two-dimensional shape becomes three dimensional, having volume or mass, it becomes a *form*. For example, a two-dimensional square shape may become a three-dimensional cube form. A triangle may become a pyramid form. Like lines in design, shape and form communicate an emotion to the viewer.

karamysh/Shutterstock.com

Figure 16.14 This photo shows how a designer uses various types of lines in design. *What kind of mood or emotional reaction does this design communicate to you?*

Copyright Goodheart-Willcox Co., Inc.

Space

Space is a basic element of design that must be defined. In a house, space is defined by walls, ceilings, and floors. Furniture and accessories within a room can further shape the space. Interior designers manipulate the space in rooms depending on how their clients want to use the space. Interior designers may choose to capitalize on a small space or manipulate the design elements to make the space appear larger. **Proxemics** is the study of how people create the space around them. In interior design, proxemics standards exist. These include standards for doorway widths, counter heights, and traffic or walkway widths. Cultural expectations of space needs vary, especially differences in acceptable personal and social space needs.

Texture and Pattern

Texture is the feel or appearance of a surface. It can be *tactile* (felt) or visual. Texture can be inherent to the design, such as velvet fabric, or applied, such as on a printed fabric. *Pattern*, which is often used with texture, is the orderly repetition of a specific design. Like other elements, texture and pattern communicate various moods (**Figure 16.15**).

Color and Light

Color and light are two interrelated elements of design. *Color* is visible light. The visible spectrum of light that is known as color ranges from red to orange, yellow, green, blue, and violet. *Light* not only creates visible

ben bryant/Shutterstock.com

Figure 16.15 Different textures and patterns are often used in design to communicate various moods. *What type of mood do these textures and patterns communicate to you?*

Copyright Goodheart-Willcox Co., Inc.

Pathway to Success

Designing Small Spaces

Using the elements of design, you can make a space appear large or small, regardless of its actual size. Suppose, for example, you want to make a small, cramped space appear larger and more airy. The following interior design tips could help you use the elements of design to create the illusion of space:

- Reduce clutter by using storage containers and storing items in furniture. For example, a chest can be used as a seat, but can also be used to store blankets.
- Choose pieces of furniture that can be used for many functions. For example, you could purchase an ottoman that doubles as a table.
- Display artwork and notes on bulletin or magnetic boards to draw the eye upward toward the ceiling, making the room appear taller.
- Hang curtains high above the windows to give the illusion of high ceilings.
- Consider using stripes to visually expand the space. A striped rug can make a space appear wider. Stripes on a wall can make a space appear taller.

- Do not center artwork on the wall. Instead, hang pictures off center to focus the eyes on something other than the size of the space.
- Use mirrors and glass furniture to fool the eye into perceiving more space than there actually is.
- Go bold with some colors. Bold colors or patterns can make objects and furniture appear larger. They can make a small room feel more spacious.
- Consider using cool colors for walls. Cool colors will visually recede from the eye, making walls appear further away.
- Arrange the space so maximum light enters it. Use sheer curtains instead of colored or patterned ones. An abundance of natural light makes a space appear larger.

These tips are just a few of the ways you can make a small room appear spacious and organized. There are many more steps you can take, too. Just remember that each space is unique. What works in one space may not work as well in another.

Redesigning a Small Space

Choose a small space, such as a closet or bedroom, in your house. Take a picture of the space and analyze how certain elements of design make the space appear small or cluttered. Summarize your analysis and then create a plan for redesigning the room to make it look more spacious. Choose aspects of the room you can realistically change.

Execute your plan for redesigning the room and take notes about how each change you

make affects the appearance of the space. After you are done, take a picture of the redesigned space. Bring both pictures—from before redesigning and after redesigning—to class. In small groups, share your pictures and discuss what you learned. Offer one another suggestions about other steps you could take to redesign the space.

Copyright Goodheart-Willcox Co., Inc.

color, it impacts the way people view color. Other factors that impact how colors are perceived include the way the object absorbs and reflects color. For example, a thick carpet absorbs and reflects light differently than a shiny satin drapery fabric.

The type of light used to view an object can also change how color is perceived. For example, the color beige may look very different under daylight versus lamplight. Background material and the way that it reflects light also impacts how color is perceived. A green chair on a pink carpet will look very different from a green chair on a brown carpet, as the light from one surface will impact the light reflected on the other surface. Finally, depending on the physical condition of the viewer's eyes, light can drastically affect how a space or an object is perceived.

The Color Wheel

Because color is the element that viewers often notice first, it is important to understand its impact. *Color theory* helps designers understand color and its power on observers. The easiest way to discuss color is in the form of the color wheel. The **color wheel** shows the relationships between primary, secondary, and tertiary colors (**Figure 16.16**).

The Color Wheel

Outer ring = *shades* of hues

Middle ring = *normal values* of hues

Inner circle = *tints* of hues

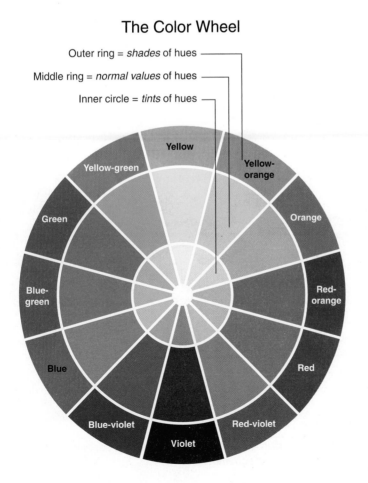

Figure 16.16 A color wheel is a common system that shows the primary, secondary, and tertiary colors. *How are secondary and tertiary colors formed?*

Copyright Goodheart-Willcox Co., Inc.

- The *primary colors* are red, blue, and yellow.
- *Secondary colors*—orange, purple, and green—are created from mixing the primary colors. For example, mixing red and yellow creates orange.
- The *tertiary colors* fall in between and are formed by mixing the primary and secondary colors together. Yellow-orange, red-orange, red-violet, blue-violet, blue-green, and yellow-green are tertiary colors.

Hues (colors) found on the color wheel are in their purest form or highest intensity. These, of course, can be changed or altered. **Value** is the lightness or darkness of a color that is produced by adding white or black. To create lighter values or **tints**, add white to the hue. For example, adding white to the color red produces a pink tint. To create darker values or **shades**, add black. For example, adding black to red produces maroon. Create **tones** by adding grey, which lowers the intensity of the color.

Intensity can also be changed by adding another color. For example, mixing a small amount of green to red will lower the intensity. Combining green and red in equal proportion will produce brown. Through the blending of colors, creating different values and intensities, color options expand to seemingly endless possibilities.

Color is perceived as either warm or cool. Warm colors include those colors that are on the red, orange, or yellow side of the color wheel (**Figure 16.17**). These colors remind people of heat and sunlight. Warm

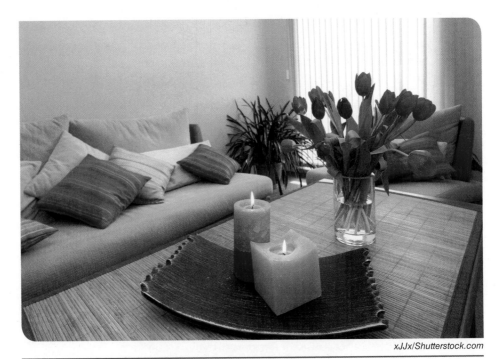

xJJx/Shutterstock.com

Figure 16.17 Warm colors in a room can make the space seem inviting. *What rooms in your home have a warm color scheme?*

Copyright Goodheart-Willcox Co., Inc.

colors can make spaces seem inviting and cozy. Cool colors are on the blue, violet, and green side of the color wheel. These colors remind people of water or the sky. Cool colors tend to be calming, stable, or relaxing.

Color Schemes

Designers create **color schemes** or color combinations to communicate the desired message for the design space. Designers create these color schemes by combining different colors in various tints, shades, and intensities on the color wheel.

A *monochromatic color scheme* is created by taking one hue and changing the intensity and value. A monochromatic color scheme could include orange, peach, and rust—all variants of the single hue orange. An *analogous* (uh-NAH-luh-gus) *color scheme* uses variants of colors next to each other on the color wheel. For example, orange, peach, and rust, all variants of the single hue orange, may be combined with variants of the yellow hue. Both monochromatic and analogous color schemes can be predictable, calming, sometimes subdued, and easy on the eyes.

Triad color schemes use variants of hues that are an equal distance apart on the color wheel. Use of the primary colors—red, yellow, and blue—is the most common triad used. When a stronger impact is desired, designers often use *complementary color schemes*. Complementary color schemes utilize variants of hues that are opposite each other on the color wheel. By their very nature, complementary colors or hues complement each other, creating the perception of increased intensity (**Figure 16.18**). For example, pink, a variation of red, appears more vibrant when used with green, a complementary hue. Complementary color schemes have impact. For example, green and red, the colors of the Italian flag, can carry not only cultural meaning, but also psychological impact through color. Together, they appear brighter and are perceived as more energetic, especially than when green is viewed separately.

Expert Insight

"All fine architectural values are human values, else not valuable."

Frank Lloyd Wright, architect

Using the Principles of Design

The **principles of design** are the guidelines for effectively using the elements of design. Utilizing the principles of design creates pleasing and interesting compositions or spaces. The principles of design include harmony, emphasis, rhythm, balance, and proportion.

Harmony

Harmony involves using the elements of design to create both unity and variety among parts of the design. For example, color may be

Pablo Scapinachis/Shutterstock.com

Figure 16.18 This yellow and violet room has a striking complementary color scheme. *What other combination of colors could be used to make a complementary color scheme?*

Copyright Goodheart-Willcox Co., Inc.

repeated to create unity, but altered to create interesting variety. Unity is achieved through repetitive use of one or more elements of design. Variety is achieved through creating contrast or breaking repetition.

Emphasis

Good design utilizes the need for a **focal point** by creating an *emphasis* (**Figure 16.19**). Strong lines, interesting textures, and bright colors are some ways that interior designers create emphasis. Other ways include using repetition, neutral backgrounds, or creating contrast through size, texture, color, or shape.

Rhythm

Rhythm keeps the human eye moving throughout the design or space. Rhythm creates organized visual movement through the design. Designers achieve rhythm through repetitive use of a design element. For example, they may achieve rhythm in a design by repeating a dominant shape. Alternating design elements, such as alternating round and square shapes, is another way designers may achieve rhythm in a design.

Balance

Balance offers equal distribution of visual weight. Visual weight differs from actual weight. Visual weight is determined by design

Natalia Kashina/Shutterstock.com

Figure 16.19 The human eye naturally seeks a place to rest or focus. *What is the focal point of this design?*

Copyright Goodheart-Willcox Co., Inc.

elements that capture the eye, creating more visual weight. For example, a heavily textured rug may appear heavier than a smooth wood bookshelf even though the actual weight of the bookshelf may be heavier. Balance offers visual equilibrium in design.

Proportion

Proportion is the relative size and scale of the various elements in a design. The human body is the most universal standard for determining size and scale. This is often referred to as **human scale**. By altering the scale of a design, it can seem very small or dainty or grand and intimidating, depending on its relative scale. For example, smaller scaled furnishings can create a sense of intimacy. High ceilings and large scaled furnishings can create an air of grandness (**Figure 16.20**).

Identifying Factors That Influence Interior Design Trends

There are many factors that influence interior design trends. The factors that influence people's interior design decisions the most are their priorities. Two main influences are cultural and societal. *Cultural influences* on design choices and interior design trends take into consideration people's beliefs, traditions, customs, values, and religion. For example, in many Asian homes, it is customary for people to sit on cushions or mats rather than on furniture. Other cultural influences include people's attitudes toward community, privacy, nature, and security. Some people prefer a lot of privacy and, therefore, their priority may be to have a fenced-in yard with lots of land. Others, however, may prefer a city environment, their priority might be to have neighbors living very close.

Societal influences on interior design trends involve demographic and economic factors. *Demographic factors* take into consideration family structures, ages and roles of family members, and populations of age groups. For example, in societies where extended families often live in one home, homes are commonly designed with this family type in mind. In other communities, single-parent families may be more prevalent, and smaller houses are more common. An increase in the population of older adults may lead to many houses that are specially designed to meet the need of an aging population.

Economic factors on housing and interior design trends affect the sizes and furnishings of

yampi/Shutterstock.com

Figure 16.20 This photo depicts how high ceilings in a design can help create an air of grandness. *Do you think the furnishings in this picture are the appropriate size for the room? Why or why not?*

Copyright Goodheart-Willcox Co., Inc.

homes. Unemployment, high interest rates, and a poor housing market all affect design trends. For example, during the 1970s, an economic downturn resulted in design trends that focused on earthy colors and "homey" simple designs. In the 1980s, a vibrant economy influenced large homes and *opulent* (rich, luxurious) furnishing trends. In the 2000s, design trends turned toward smaller spaces and sustainable materials.

Reading Recall

1. Define *universal design*. Give examples of universal design in a home and in an office building.
2. Name four types of surfaces and a common method of cleaning each.
3. Draw and label a color wheel.
4. Identify two influences on interior design trends. Give an example of each.
5. Describe the priorities that would influence your interior design decisions.

Rewards, Demands, and Future Trends

Like the fashion industry, the housing and interior design industry is known for both its collegiality (cooperative relationship) among coworkers and its fierce rivalry among industry competitors. This field demands creative, forward-thinking people who are not afraid to take a risk.

Housing and interior design is an industry known for long working hours that vary by demand. For example, housing workers often work with people during times of crisis, and crises are rarely planned or well-timed. Those who deal with construction and sourcing of materials are often on short timelines and must heed budget constraints. Sometimes things do not go as planned and clear-headedness is needed to solve problems in a crunch.

People will always need housing. As a result, the future outlook for housing related human services workers is bright (**Figure 16.21**). The housing field is stimulating as a problem-solving endeavor. The housing related human services field continually offers new opportunities and new ideas, and many people find the creative nature of the environment highly rewarding. People who thrive in this environment are attracted to the pace and energy.

Reading Recall

1. What are some rewards of a career in the housing and interior design industry?
2. What is the future outlook for housing related human services workers? Why?

Future Trends for Housing Related Human Services Careers				
Occupation	**Projected Growth (2014–2024)**	**Projected Job Openings (2014–2024)**	**Median Wages (2014)**	**Education**
Commercial interior designer	Slower than average (2–4%)	16,200	$48,400	Bachelor's degree
Consultant	Average (5–8%)	1,917,200	$21,390	High school diploma
Fashion blogger	Decline (–2% or lower)	15,900	$36,000	Bachelor's degree
Fashion journalist	Decline (–2% or lower)	15,900	$36,000	Bachelor's degree
Housing specialist	Faster than average (9–13%)	120,000	$29,790	Bachelor's degree
Interior designer	Slower than average (2–4%)	16,200	$48,400	Bachelor's degree
Kitchen and bathroom designer	Slower than average (2–4%)	16,200	$48,400	Bachelor's degree
Production manager	Decline (–2% or lower)	49,100	$92,470	Bachelor's degree
Property manager	Average (5–8%)	79,900	$54,270	Bachelor's degree
Real estate broker	Slower than average (2–4%)	7,300	$57,360	Bachelor's degree
Real estate sales agent	Slower than average (2–4%)	33,000	$40,990	High school diploma
Residential interior designer	Slower than average (2–4%)	16,200	$48,400	Bachelor's degree
Retail buyer	Average (5–8%)	49,100	$52,270	Bachelor's degree
Retail fashion merchandiser	Faster than average (9–13%)	64,200	$127,130	Bachelor's degree
Retail manager	Slower than average (2–4%)	411,300	$37,860	High school diploma
Space planner	Average (5–8%)	2,700	$49,310	Unspecified
Visual merchandiser	Slower than average (2–4%)	32,100	$26,590	High school diploma

Sources: O*NET and the *Occupational Outlook Handbook*

Figure 16.21 Learning as much as possible about careers can help you make informed career decisions. *According to the information in this chart, which housing related human services career is predicted to have the most projected job openings?*

Copyright Goodheart-Willcox Co., Inc.

Summary

- The housing industry focuses on the behavioral, social, economic, functional, and aesthetic aspects of housing, interiors, and other constructed environments. Examples of career opportunities for human services workers in the housing industry include housing specialists, real estate brokers and sales agents, property managers, home furnishings sales and marketing staff, and designers. Parts of the housing related human services field also lend well to entrepreneurial careers.

- People working in the housing industry must be compassionate, respectful, and nonjudgmental as they work with a variety of different people. These professionals often possess artistic ability and are very creative. They are detail oriented and demonstrate excellent problem-solving and technical skills.

- Education, training, and experience expectations vary for careers in housing related human services. A bachelor's degree is desired for a career as a housing specialist. Real estate brokers and sales agents must be licensed by the state. Many property managers hold college degrees and some also hold a real estate license. In some states, interior designers are required to be licensed or registered.

- Those who work in housing related human services need to know how people meet their needs through housing across the family life cycle. They also understand the importance of keeping a home clean and safe. To create pleasing interiors, they use the elements and principles of design. They also keep informed about factors that influence interior design trends.

- People will always need housing. As a result, the future outlook for housing related human services workers is bright.

College and Career Portfolio

Portfolio Presentation

The portfolio you have been creating over the course of this text may now be ready to present. Before presenting your portfolio, however, you will want to practice. Practicing can help you remain calm during a presentation. Practicing also gives you a chance to select the right words that will best communicate your skills and experiences.

As you practice presenting your portfolio, time your presentation and pay attention to your body language and enunciation. Ask a trusted adult or friend to watch your presentation and give you feedback about your presentation delivery. Practice until you feel comfortable with your presentation.

Review your notes for your presentation, and in small groups of three, practice presenting your portfolios.

1. Present your portfolio as if to a college admissions officer or employer.
2. Ask your peers for feedback on your presentation. Also give feedback on your peers' presentations.

Copyright Goodheart-Willcox Co., Inc.

Review and Reflect ↗

1. Define *interior design*.
2. Residential interior designers work with newly built housing developments in two stages. Identify the two stages and what the residential interior designer's job entails in each stage.
3. Identify at least three entrepreneurial opportunities in housing related careers.
4. Identify the common attitudes and skills human services workers in the housing industry need. Why are these attitudes and skills important?
5. Name a housing related human services career that requires licensure.
6. What are the requirements to become an interior designer?
7. Explain the housing needs across the family life cycle.
8. What are the four housing systems that must be cared for in order to keep a home running efficiently and safely?
9. Identify the elements and principles of design. Give examples of each.
10. Define a *focal point*, and give an example.
11. Make a list of factors impacting or influencing housing and design trends. Choose one of these factors. Give an example of its impact or influence on housing and design trends.
12. What are some of the demands of the housing and interior design industry?

Vocabulary Activities

13. **Key terms**   With a partner, choose two of the following terms. Use the Internet to locate photos or graphics that show the meaning of these two terms. Print the photos or graphics and show them to the class. Explain how the photos show the meaning of the terms.

assisted living housing	hues
color schemes	human scale
color wheel	independent living communities
elements of design	interior design
focal point	nursing homes
principles of design	tones
proxemics	universal design
shades	value
tints	

14. **Academic terms**   Write each of the following terms on a separate sheet of paper. For each term, quickly write a word you think relates to the term. In small groups, exchange papers. Have each person in the group explain a term on the list. Take turns until all terms have been explained.

contours	opulent
downsizing	paramount
geometric shapes	tactile

Self-Assessment Quiz ↗

Complete the self-assessment quiz online to help you practice and expand your knowledge and skills.

Critical Thinking

15. **Identify**   Identify several employment opportunities in housing related careers that interest you. What are the preparation requirements for these careers?
16. **Make inferences**   What does it mean when an interior designer makes a home aesthetically pleasing?
17. **Determine**   Research how you could become a real estate agent in your state. Determine whether or not there are any additional criteria for becoming a real estate broker in your local area.
18. **Draw conclusions**   As the family life cycle changes, many people find they have to downsize their homes. A family gets a divorce, and one spouse moves out of state. Draw conclusions based on this information about how this will affect the housing choices of the remaining spouse and children.
19. **Compare and contrast**   Compare and contrast the housing choices for older adults. Be sure to include independent living communities, assisted living housing, and nursing homes in your comparison.
20. **Cause and effect**   Using Figure 16.11, identify surfaces that need to be maintained

in the home and how to safely clean them. Identify additional cleaning products you might use for these surfaces that are not listed in the chart. What effect might using the wrong product have on a surface?

21. **Analyze**   Get three pictures of the interiors of homes and commercial buildings. Identify the elements and principles of design in the pictures. Analyze how well the elements and principles are used in the spaces. What would you change to make the space more pleasing?

22. **Evaluate**   Evaluate the rewards and demands of working in the housing industry. Be sure to include multiple jobs as you make your lists. Using your information, make a Venn diagram showing the unique rewards and demands, as well as the common rewards and demands, of two different careers in this field.

Core Skills

23. **Research, speaking, listening, and writing**   Find out if a housing specialist works in your area. If so, interview the person about job duties, responsibilities, and any special skills needed for the job. Find out how many hours he or she spends working with a client. Write a report, and present your findings to the class.

24. **Writing**   List the interior furnishings and equipment in each room of your home. Review any safety instructions available for these items. For each item, write a description indicating how to safely use and care for it. Use this information to create a cleaning and maintenance schedule that will enable you to keep your home clean and safe.

25. **Writing, listening, and speaking**   Invite an interior designer or a building contractor to come to class to discuss what it is like to have this job. Have the speaker explain the pathway he or she took to get to the current job. Create a list of questions to ask the speaker prior to the presentation. Write a thank-you letter after the visit, and send it to him or her.

26. **Writing and math**   Create a brochure explaining how to figure square footage for walls and floors. Do not forget to take into account doors and windows and how to

remove those calculations from the square footage needed for paint or wallpaper. Also, include how to figure out how many quarts of paint or rolls of wallpaper to buy.

27. **Reading and math**   Using the brochure you created in question 26, complete the following. You have a 12 x 14 foot room. Figure out the total square footage for the walls. You are looking at three different ways to fix the walls. Two are wallpaper options (a single roll will cover 25 square feet), and one is a paint option. The first wallpaper option is $2.25 a roll with a repeat pattern. (You will need to match up the pattern.) The second wallpaper option is $10.95 a roll. The paint costs $8.50 a quart. Figure the cost of all three options. Then, determine the best value for your money.

28. **Reading, math, and research**   Using the brochure you created in question 26, complete the following. You have a 10 x 12 foot room. Figure out the total square footage for this room. Now, look into the cost of wood floors, laminate floors, and carpet for this room. What would be the total cost of materials for each type of flooring? Which would you choose, and why?

29. **Research**   Identify interior design career opportunities in your town and state. Choose two options to compare and contrast the job requirements, the types of training or certification needed for the jobs, and the entry-level jobs available that you could do with your current skill set. What are the future trends for interior design careers? Do any of these opportunities interest you?

30. **Writing**   You have been hired to redecorate and repurpose a one-room apartment attached to a home. Inside this one-room apartment, you will need to arrange walls to create a small living room, kitchen, bedroom, and bathroom that will accommodate a wheelchair-bound, 70-year-old man. After drawing the outline of what the finished rooms will look like, list the accommodations you will add to help the 70-year-old man move about and adapt to his living space.

31. **Research**   Research proxemics standards for doorway widths, counter heights, and traffic or walkway widths. Research what

Copyright Goodheart-Willcox Co., Inc.

additional standards are needed in homes that need to be adapted for special needs. What are the differences in these standards?

32. **Writing**   Find four pictures showcasing color schemes. Be sure to include a monochromatic, an analogous, a triad, and a complementary color scheme. Write a paragraph explaining how each picture showcases a particular color scheme and why.

33. **CTE career readiness practice**   Create a one-act play for two persons that depicts a positive interaction between an interior designer and his or her client. Be sure to include notes to the actors about body language and facial expressions. Do the same to illustrate a negative interaction on the same topic. What is the essential difference between the two plays/interactions? How does the way you say something influence whether it will be received negatively or positively?

34. **CTE career readiness practice**   As a student, you use technology skills every day to enhance your productivity. As an employee, you may be required to travel as part of your job responsibilities. Describe the technology methods you would use to enhance your productivity while you are traveling.

Lend a Hand

Community Housing Needs

A safe, comfortable place to live is important to the well-being of all people. As a volunteer, you can help improve homes in your community and neighboring communities. Both national and local organizations work to provide and improve housing for homeless, low-income, and disabled people. These organizations need volunteers to paint, make basic repairs, or even offer cleaning services. Some organizations like Habitat for Humanity build and renovate homes for people in need. There are also many local housing organizations that support their communities by transforming and improving houses.

Keep in mind that many of these organizations require volunteers who help on building sites to be at least 16 years old. There are still many other opportunities to get involved. Some organizations have a specific program dedicated to youth volunteers. You could also raise funds to donate to your local organization. Some organizations need volunteers to help out with special events or different committees or projects.

To find out how you can assist in volunteering with housing services, complete the following:

1. Think about how you could best volunteer your time to a housing organization. Are you good at painting rooms? Can you make basic home repairs? Do you have any experience with home improvement? Are you good at organizing information or talking to people? Are you willing to learn? Thinking about how you can best lend your time will help you locate the best opportunities for you.

2. Research housing organizations with volunteer opportunities in your area. Make note of the contact information and any age requirements for each opportunity.

3. Sign up to volunteer at one of the places you found in your research. Make sure you know what dates and times you will be able to volunteer.

Ethical Standards for Human Service Professionals

National Organization for Human Services Adopted 2015

Preamble

Human services is a profession developed in response to the direction of human needs and human problems in the 1960s. Characterized by an appreciation of human beings in all of their diversity, human services offers assistance to its clients within the context of their communities and environments. Human service professionals and those who educate them promote and encourage the unique values and characteristics of human services. In so doing, human service professionals uphold the integrity and ethics of the profession, promote client and community well-being, and enhance their own professional growth.

The fundamental values of the human services profession include respecting the dignity and welfare of all people; promoting self-determination; honoring cultural diversity; advocating for social justice; and acting with integrity, honesty, genuineness, and objectivity.

Human service professionals consider these standards in ethical and professional decision making. Conflicts may exist between this code and laws, workplace policies, cultural practices, credentialing boards, and personal beliefs. Ethical decision-making processes should be employed to assure careful choices. Although ethical codes are not legal documents, they may be used to address issues related to the behavior of human service professionals.

Persons who use this code include members of the National Organization for Human Services, students in relevant academic degree programs, faculty in those same programs, researchers, administrators, and professionals in community agencies who identify with the profession of human services. The ethical standards are organized in sections around those persons to whom ethical practice should be applied.

Copyright Goodheart-Willcox Co., Inc.

Responsibility to Clients

STANDARD 1

Human service professionals recognize and build on client and community strengths.

STANDARD 2

Human service professionals obtain informed consent to provide services to clients at the beginning of the helping relationship. Clients should be informed that they may withdraw consent at any time except where denied by court order and should be able to ask questions before agreeing to the services. Clients who are unable to give consent should have those who are legally able to give consent for them review an informed consent statement and provide appropriate consent.

STANDARD 3

Human service professionals protect the client's right to privacy and confidentiality except when such confidentiality would cause serious harm to the client or others, when agency guidelines state otherwise, or under other stated conditions (e.g., local, state, or federal laws). Human service professionals inform clients of the limits of confidentiality prior to the onset of the helping relationship.

STANDARD 4

If it is suspected that danger or harm may occur to the client or to others as a result of a client's behavior, the human service professional acts in an appropriate and professional manner to protect the safety of those individuals. This may involve, but is not limited to, seeking consultation, supervision, and/or breaking the confidentiality of the relationship.

STANDARD 5

Human service professionals recognize that multiple relationships may increase the risk of harm to or exploitation of clients and may impair their professional judgment. When it is not feasible to avoid dual or multiple relationships, human service professionals should consider whether the professional relationship should be avoided or curtailed.

STANDARD 6

Sexual or romantic relationships with current clients are prohibited. Before engaging in sexual or romantic relationships with former clients, friends, or family members of former clients, human service professionals carefully evaluate potential exploitation or harm and refrain from entering into such a relationship.

STANDARD 7

Human service professionals ensure that their values or biases are not imposed upon their clients.

STANDARD 8

Human service professionals protect the integrity, safety, and security of client records. Client information in written or electronic form that is shared with other professionals must have the client's prior written consent except in the course of professional supervision or when legally obliged or permitted to share such information.

STANDARD 9

When providing services through the use of technology, human service professionals take precautions to ensure and maintain confidentiality and comply with all relevant laws and requirements regarding storing, transmitting, and retrieving data. In addition, human service professionals ensure that clients are aware of any issues and concerns related to confidentiality, service issues, and how technology might negatively or positively impact the helping relationship.

Responsibility to the Public and Society

STANDARD 10

Human service professionals provide services without discrimination or preference in regards to age, ethnicity, culture, race, ability, gender, language preference, religion, sexual orientation, socioeconomic status, nationality, or other historically oppressed groups.

STANDARD 11

Human service professionals are knowledgeable about their cultures and communities within which they practice. They are aware of multiculturalism in society and its impact on the community as well as individuals within the community. They respect the cultures and beliefs of individuals and groups.

STANDARD 12

Human service professionals are aware of local, state, and federal laws. They advocate for change in regulations and statutes when such legislation conflicts with ethical guidelines and/or client rights. Where laws are harmful to individuals, groups, or communities, human service professionals consider the conflict between the values of obeying the law and the values of serving people and may decide to initiate social action.

Copyright Goodheart-Willcox Co., Inc.

STANDARD 13

Human service professionals stay informed about current social issues as they affect clients and communities. If appropriate to the helping relationship, they share this information with clients, groups, and communities as part of their work.

STANDARD 14

Human service professionals are aware of social and political issues that differentially affect clients from diverse backgrounds.

STANDARD 15

Human service professionals provide a mechanism for identifying client needs and assets, calling attention to these needs and assets, and assisting in planning and mobilizing to advocate for those needs at the individual, community, and societal levels when appropriate to the goals of the relationship.

STANDARD 16

Human service professionals advocate for social justice and seek to eliminate oppression. They raise awareness of underserved populations in their communities and with the legislative system.

STANDARD 17

Human service professionals accurately represent their qualifications to the public. This includes, but is not limited to, their abilities, training, education, credentials, academic endeavors, and areas of expertise. They avoid the appearance of misrepresentation or impropriety and take immediate steps to correct it if it occurs.

STANDARD 18

Human service professionals accurately describe the effectiveness of treatment programs, interventions and treatments, and/or techniques, supported by data whenever possible.

Responsibility to Colleagues
STANDARD 19

Human service professionals avoid duplicating another professional's helping relationship with a client. They consult with other professionals who are assisting the client in a different type of relationship when it is in the best interest of the client to do so. In addition, human service professionals seek ways to actively collaborate and coordinate with other professionals when appropriate.

Copyright Goodheart-Willcox Co., Inc.

STANDARD 20

When human service professionals have a conflict with a colleague, they first seek out the colleague in an attempt to manage the problem. If this effort fails, the professional then seeks the assistance of supervisors, consultants, or other professionals in efforts to address the conflict.

STANDARD 21

Human service professionals respond appropriately to unethical and problematic behavior of colleagues. Usually this means initially talking directly with the colleague, and, if no satisfactory resolution is achieved, reporting the colleague's behavior to supervisory or administrative staff.

STANDARD 22

All consultations between human service professionals are kept private, unless to do so would result in harm to clients or communities.

Responsibility to Employers

STANDARD 23

To the extent possible, human service professionals adhere to commitments made to their employers.

STANDARD 24

Human service professionals participate in efforts to establish and maintain employment conditions which are conducive to high quality client services. Whenever possible, they assist in evaluating the effectiveness of the agency through reliable and valid assessment measures.

STANDARD 25

When a conflict arises between fulfilling the responsibility to the employer and the responsibility to the client, human service professionals work with all involved to manage the conflict.

Responsibility to the Profession

STANDARD 26

Human service professionals seek the training, experience, education, and supervision necessary to ensure their effectiveness in working with culturally diverse individuals based on age, ethnicity, culture, race, ability, gender, language preference, religion, sexual orientation, socioeconomic status, nationality, or other historically oppressed groups. In addition, they will strive to increase their competence in methods which are known to be the best fit for the population(s) with whom they work.

Copyright Goodheart-Willcox Co., Inc.

STANDARD 27

Human service professionals know the limit and scope of their professional knowledge and offer services only within their knowledge, skill base, and scope of practice.

STANDARD 28

Human service professionals seek appropriate consultation and supervision to assist in decision making when there are legal, ethical, or other dilemmas.

STANDARD 29

Human service professionals promote cooperation among related disciplines to foster professional growth and to optimize the impact of inter-professional collaboration on clients at all levels.

STANDARD 30

Human service professionals promote the continuing development of their profession. They encourage membership in professional associations, support research endeavors, foster educational advancement, advocate for appropriate legislative actions, and participate in other related professional activities.

STANDARD 31

Human service professionals continually seek out new and effective approaches to enhance their professional abilities and use techniques that are conceptually or evidence based. When practicing techniques that are experimental or new, they inform clients of the status of such techniques as well as the possible risks.

STANDARD 32

Human service professionals conduct research that adheres to all ethical principles, institutional standards, and scientific rigor. Such research takes into consideration cross-cultural bias and is reported in a manner that addresses any limitations.

STANDARD 33

Human service professionals make careful decisions about disclosing personal information while using social media, knowing that they reflect the profession of human services. In addition, they consider how their public conduct may reflect on themselves and their profession.

Copyright Goodheart-Willcox Co., Inc.

Responsibility to Self
STANDARD 34
Human service professionals are aware of their own cultural backgrounds, beliefs, values, and biases. They recognize the potential impact of their backgrounds on their relationships with others and work diligently to provide culturally competent service to all of their clients.

STANDARD 35
Human service professionals strive to develop and maintain healthy personal growth to ensure that they are capable of giving optimal services to clients. When they find that they are physically, emotionally, psychologically, or otherwise not able to offer such services, they identify alternative services for clients.

STANDARD 36
Human service professionals hold a commitment to lifelong learning and continually advance their knowledge and skills to serve clients more effectively.

Responsibility to Students
STANDARD 37
Human service educators develop and implement culturally sensitive knowledge, awareness, and teaching methodologies.

STANDARD 38
Human service educators are committed to the principles of access and inclusion and take all available and applicable steps to make education available to differently-abled students.

STANDARD 39
Human service educators demonstrate high standards of scholarship in their scholarship, pedagogy, and professional service and stay current in the field by being members of their professional associations, attending workshops and conferences, and reviewing and/or conducting research.

STANDARD 40
Human service educators recognize and acknowledge the contributions of students to the work of the educator in such activities as case material, grants, workshops, research, publications, and other related activities.

Copyright Goodheart-Willcox Co., Inc.

STANDARD 41

Human service educators monitor students' field experiences to ensure the quality of the placement site, supervisory experience, and learning experience toward the goals of personal, professional, academic, career, and civic development. When students experience potentially harmful events during field placements, educators provide reasonable investigation and response as necessary to safeguard the student.

STANDARD 42

Human service educators establish and uphold appropriate guidelines concerning student disclosure of sensitive/personal information, which includes letting students have fair warning of any self-disclosure activities, allowing students to opt-out of in-depth self-disclosure activities when feasible, and ensuring that a mechanism is available to discuss and process such activities as needed.

STANDARD 43

Human service educators are aware that in their relationships with students, power and status are unequal. Human service educators are responsible to clearly define and maintain ethical and professional relationships with students; avoid conduct that is demeaning, embarrassing or exploitative of students; and always strive to treat students fairly, equally, and without discrimination.

STANDARD 44

Human service educators ensure students are familiar with, informed by, and accountable to the ethical standards and policies put forth by their program/department, the course syllabus/instructor, their advisor(s), and the Ethical Standards of Human Service Professionals.

Copyright Goodheart-Willcox Co., Inc.

Glossary

A

active listening: Asking questions and restating ideas to discover the true message of the sender. (3)

acumen: Expertise. (12)

acute: Critical. (4)

adaptive clothing: Garments that are designed specifically to provide easy access for people with special needs. (15)

addiction: Condition characterized by a compulsive physical and/or psychological dependence on a substance or behavior. (9)

adoptive family: Family that forms when a state court legally grants permission to a married couple or single person to raise another person's child. (11)

advance directives: Person's decisions involving what medical care should be provided in the event the person is no longer able to make medical decisions for him- or herself. (9)

advanced placement courses: High school classes that offer college level content and exams; students receive college credit for successful completion. (6)

adversity: Hardships; difficulties. (9)

aesthetic: Pleasing in appearance. (14)

aggressive communicators: People who aim to hurt or put down other people and show disrespect. (3)

agitation: Movement of water, detergent, and clothes. (15)

alcoholism: Addiction of alcohol. (9)

allocate: Distribute. (1)

Alzheimer's disease: Progressive brain disorder that includes not only memory loss, but also progressively severe confusion. (12)

anorexia nervosa: Eating disorder that involves the relentless pursuit of thinness through starvation. (14)

apprenticeship: Training opportunity that involves working for a qualified professional to learn a skilled trade. (1)

aptitudes: Natural abilities. (1)

artifacts: Handmade objects. (7)

aspirations: Hopes; dreams. (5)

assertive communicators: People who freely express their thoughts, ideas, and feelings respectfully and allow others to do the same. (3)

assets: Useful, valuable resources a person possesses that can be offered to others in exchange for something else. (5)

assimilation: Process of adapting to another culture's language, beliefs, and customs. (4)

assisted living housing: Environments for older adults that provide gradually expanded oversight and help with daily activities. (16)

associate's degree: Two-year degree earned through community college. (1)

at risk: Children who have characteristics that make them more likely to fail in school. (9)

attitudes: Set ways of thinking or feeling about someone or something. (1)

attrition: Gradual reduction of workers. (6)

audible: Hearable. (4)

authoritarian style: Parenting style that tends to be controlling and corrective. (10)

authoritative style: Parenting style that tends to offer support while setting clear limits; also called *democratic style*. (10)

auxiliary: Additional. (11)

The numbers in parentheses following definitions represent the chapter in which the terms appear.

Copyright Goodheart-Willcox Co., Inc.

B

bachelor's degree: Four-year degree earned through colleges and universities. (1)

behaviorism: Theory based on the belief that people's behavior is determined by forces in the environment that are beyond their control. (2)

binge-eating disorder: Eating disorder that involves eating large amounts of food without taking any actions to reduce the amount of food intake. (14)

biodegradable: Type of product that can break down or decompose naturally without harming the environment. (8)

bipolar disorder: Condition that affects social-emotional health and is characterized by severe mood swings that range from manic to depressive; also called *manic depression*. (9)

body composition: Proportion of body fat to lean mass (muscle, bone, and water) in a person's body. (14)

budget: Written financial plan to manage income, expenses, and savings. (8)

bulimia nervosa: Eating disorder that involves consuming large amounts of food and then expelling the food from the system, usually by means such as vomiting or using laxatives. (14)

business license: Legal document allowing a business owner to conduct business through the city or county of residence. (13)

business plan: Document outlining the decisions and guidelines for the business. (13)

buying plan: Description of the types, sizes, prices, and quantities of merchandise that a retail buyer is to select. (15)

C

career and technical program: Course of study that prepares students for careers in specific trades and occupations that need skilled workers. (1)

Career and Technical Student Organization (CTSO): Group that provides students with opportunities to develop and practice both leadership and teamwork skills while still in school. (3)

career goal: Clear, concise statement of what a person wants to become in life. (6)

catering: Part of the food and beverage industry that provides foodservice for social or business events, such as board meetings, conferences, and retreats. (14)

center-based child care programs: Programs provided in a center and not in a home, and may serve a few or many children. (10)

child abuse: Threatening to or inflicting harm on a child. (10)

child custody: Court determination as to which parent in a divorce retains legal responsibility for the child. (9)

childless family: Married couple who does not have children. (11)

child neglect: Endangerment of or harm to a child caused by an adult's failure to provide for the child's basic needs. (10)

childproofing: Process of ensuring an environment is safe for children. (10)

child support: Legally binding agreement that determines the payments a noncustodial parent is to make to financially contribute toward the child's care. (9)

circumference: Distance around something. (15)

civic engagement: Process wherein different voices, opinions, or arguments are shared and oriented toward mutual understanding. (11)

classical conditioning: Behaviors associated with emotional responses. (2)

clinical depression: Severe case of depression often caused by a combination of genetic and environmental influences. (9)

code of ethics: Document that formally defines the moral principles that serve as rules for behavior, which are to be followed and upheld. (4)

cognitive theories: Ideas about how people process information, think, and learn. (2)

cognizant: Aware. (11)

collaborate: Work together. (3)

collegiality: Cooperative relationship. (15)

color schemes: Combinations of different colors in various tints, shades, and intensities. (16)

color wheel: Diagram that shows the relationships between primary, secondary, and tertiary colors. (16)

commendation: Praise; congratulation. (5)

comparison shopping: Looking at different makes and models of a product at various stores to make a wise choice in purchasing products. (8)

competencies: Abilities; skills. (1)

competitive analysis: Part of the market analysis in the business plan that identifies the competition's strengths and weaknesses. (13)

computer aided design (CAD): Computerized software used to create, mark, and modify design patterns. (15)

concessions: Compromises. (3)

constructive conflict management: Step-by-step method to resolve a disagreement. (3)

consumer services: Employment category in the field of human services in which workers help people budget, solve financial problems, and make good consumer decisions. (1)

contours: Outline. (16)

contractors: Temporary employees. (13)

cooperative: Business providing a service or product for a collective need of a group of people who are known as the *user-owners*. (13)

corporation: Legal entity owned by shareholders. (13)

cosmetology: Study that involves enhancing a client's personal appearance through the treatment of hair, skin, and nails. (12)

cottage industry: Non-legal term referring to sole proprietorships that produce a product and begin in a home. (13)

counseling and mental health services: Employment category in the field of human services that involves helping people maintain healthy, productive lives through therapy, counseling, and education or training. (1)

cover message: Letter of introduction that accompanies a résumé and provides additional details about why a person is qualified for a job. (7)

critical thinking: Way of looking closely at a situation and weighing possible outcomes before determining a solution. (3)

cultural competence: Being knowledgeable about other cultures. (4)

cultural diversity: Different cultural and ethnic groups living in one society. (4)

D

decision-making process: Series of six steps that involves examining an issue, analyzing alternatives, and acting based on careful evaluation. (3)

defaulted: Failure to pay a loan. (8)

dementia: Brain disorder involving cognitive declines and memory loss. (12)

Copyright Goodheart-Willcox Co., Inc.

design line: Designer's collection of related designs. (15)

detrimental: Harmful. (10)

developmentally appropriate practices (DAPs): Age-appropriate activities and teaching methods that consider each child's strengths, interests, and culture. (10)

developmentally inappropriate practices (DIPs): Activities that utilize only one type of teaching or caregiving strategy without variation or adjustment for a child's individual needs. (10)

developmental theories: Comprehensive explanations about why people act and behave the way they do and how they change over time. (2)

diabetes: Disease in which the body is unable to produce insulin, resulting in an inability to properly use energy from food. (14)

dietetics: Science of helping people apply and use knowledge to improve their health and wellness. (14)

digital lookbooks: Collection of fashion related photos used to relay fashion and beauty trends. (15)

direct deposit: Electronic payment from the employer's bank account to the employee's bank account. (8)

direct messages: Communications that are straightforward. (5)

discipline: Techniques and methods caregivers use to teach children to behave acceptably. (10)

dispense: Give out. (12)

diverse: Very different. (3)

doctorate degree: Highest degree a person can earn; also called a *PhD*. (1)

domestic abuse: Threatening to or inflicting harm on another person within a close relationship, such as a family member; consists of physical, emotional, and sexual abuse. (9)

do not resuscitate (DNR) order: Type of advance directive letting medical staff know that if a person's heart stops or the person stops breathing, he or she does not want CPR in order to be resuscitated. (9)

dovetailing: Doing several similar tasks at once. (4)

downsizing: Reducing the size or cost of one's housing. (16)

dry cleaning: Laundering process that involves the use of a chemical solvent to clean clothes rather than water. (15)

dual credit courses: College or university classes that students take while still attending high school; students receive college credit for successful completion. (6)

dynamics: Pattern of change or growth over time. (11)

E

early childhood development and services: Employment category in the field of human services that involves understanding and meeting the needs of infants, toddlers, and young children. (1)

eating disorder: Serious condition that involves abnormal eating patterns that can cause severe or life-threatening physical problems. (14)

egalitarian: Equal power. (11)

electrology: Specialty area of cosmetology that involves permanent hair removal. (12)

electrolysis: Permanent hair removal process that involves applying heat through an electric current to destroy the hair roots, thereby preventing further hair growth. (12)

Copyright Goodheart-Willcox Co., Inc.

electronic banking: Using the Internet to access banking services. (8)

electronic funds transfer (EFT): Transferring money from one account to another through the use of electronic banking. (8)

elements: Weather conditions. (2)

elements of design: Line, shape, form, space, texture, pattern, color, and light. (16)

embalming: Process through which a body is temporarily preserved for a viewing or visitation by family and friends. (12)

emotional and social cultural norms: Expectations of how workers interact with and respond to one another and clients. (7)

empathy: Ability to identify with and share another person's feelings. (3)

employee performance evaluations: Management or supervisory reviews of an employee's job performance. (7)

entrepreneur: Person who starts and runs his or her own business. (13)

entrepreneurial careers: Employment opportunity that involves establishing and running one's own business. (1)

environment: All of a person's surroundings and the people in them. (2)

ergonomics: Equipment design to promote efficiency and reduce work-related injury. (15)

erroneous: Incorrect; wrong. (6)

esteem: Respect; admiration. (2)

ethical decisions: Considerations about what is right or moral, not just what is most efficient, economic, or preferred. (4)

ethics: Conduct based on moral principles. (4)

executive summary: Part of the business plan that includes a brief summary of the business mission, products or services, financial information, and hopes for growth. (13)

expansion mode: When the economy accelerates and increases. (2)

expenses: Goods and services requiring payment. (8)

extended family: Several generations, such as parents and their children, grandparents, aunts, uncles, or cousins, living under one roof. (11)

exuberant: Excited. (10)

exude: Show a lot of. (7)

F

fad diets: Dieting plans that promise quick and easy weight loss. (14)

family and community services: Employment category in the field of human services that involves offering advice and assistance to people at all stages of life. (1)

Family and Medical Leave Act (FMLA): Law that allows full-time employees to take unpaid job-protected leave for family transitions involving close family members, such as spouses, children, and parents. (1)

family child care centers: Programs operated in the child care worker's private home for a small number of children. (10)

family-life crisis: Event that occurs when a stressor creates adversity for the family, disrupting family function. (9)

family life cycle: Six basic stages many families go through as a normal part of life; includes the beginning, childbearing, parenting, launching, mid-years, and aging stages. (9)

family policy: Area of public policy dealing with complex questions and issues affecting society and families. (11)

fashion merchandising: Field that involves the buying and selling of fashion, product

Copyright Goodheart-Willcox Co., Inc.

development, retail management, and fashion marketing. (15)

finance charges: Fees lenders charge consumers for buying on credit. (8)

fine-motor skills: Physical tasks involving small muscle movements. (10)

focal point: Something that attracts the eye. (16)

food allergy: Severe reaction that occurs when a food triggers a response by the body's immune system. (14)

food intolerance: Unpleasant reaction to a food, such as digestive or behavioral problems. (14)

forecast: Predict a future trend. (15)

foster family: Family that forms when an adult provides a temporary home for a child who is unable to live with his or her biological parents because proper care is not provided. (11)

freelancers: Small business owners who offer their services to larger organizations for a fee. (13)

G

geometric shapes: Circles, ovals, squares, rectangles, and triangles. (16)

gouging: Overcharging. (8)

grief: Mental anguish or sorrow a person experiences when losing a loved one. (9)

gross-motor skills: Physical tasks involving large muscle movements. (10)

guidance: Help, assistance, leadership, and regulation provided for children learning to behave acceptably. (10)

H

haphazard: Random; not following a set method. (5)

Head Start: Government-funded preschool program that focuses on preparing disadvantaged children for school. (1)

health: Overall condition in reference to illness or disease. (4)

heredity: Traits with which people are born. (2)

hierarchy: Arrangement of something according to importance. (2)

higher education: Instruction and training that occurs postsecondary or after high school. (6)

hospice care: Form of care given by trained medical professionals, focusing on making a person comfortable in his or her last days and hours of life. (9)

hues: Colors. (16)

human development: Gradual process in which people change from birth through adulthood. (2)

human scale: Universal standard for determining size and scale of a design. (16)

human services: Generic term that describes a career field providing for the needs of people. (1)

I

ideology: System of beliefs and ideals important to a society. (1)

implicit: Unquestioning. (4)

impoverished: Poor. (1)

impulsively: Acting without thinking something through. (3)

income: Money earned. (8)

independent living communities: Housing for older adults who can care for themselves, but desire the community support of those of similar age. (16)

Copyright Goodheart-Willcox Co., Inc.

indirect messages: Communications that are often subtle and sometimes confusing. (5)

Industrial Revolution: Time in history of rapid industrial growth. (1)

inferiority: Person's belief that he or she is not as good as other people. (2)

informational interview: Way to explore career options by talking with key professionals in a person's field of interest. (6)

ingenuity: Cleverness; inventiveness. (14)

innovative: New; original. (13)

installment credit: Cash loan repaid with interest in equal, regular payments. (8)

instrumental: Necessary; helpful. (11)

intangible assets: Resources that are not physical in nature, such as knowledge, talents, and skills. (5)

interdisciplinary: Relating to more than one branch of knowledge. (1)

interest: Percentage of money a financial institution pays regularly for the use of the account holder's money. (8)

interior design: Process of shaping the experience of interior space through the manipulation of space, the application of the elements and principles of design, and the use of materials. (16)

intermediaries: People who act as go-betweens among parties to bring about a resolution. (8)

internship: Program in which a company or organization agrees to provide students with an opportunity to gain exposure to an occupational area. (6)

interview: Conversation between an employer and a potential employee. (7)

intuition: Primitive reasoning based on feelings. (10)

investing: Putting money into something to gain a financial return. (8)

ironing: Process of using heat to remove wrinkles from clothing. (15)

J

job application: Document a potential employee fills out to give an employer personal information about employment qualifications and eligibility. (7)

job fairs: Events where employers network with potential employees; also called *career fairs* or *employment fairs*. (7)

job shadowing: Gaining insight into a career of interest through short observation consisting of a few hours or a day. (6)

joint custody: In divorce, legal agreement in which both parents provide care and make decisions for the child. (9)

just: Honest; fair. (8)

K

key accomplishments: Positive past experiences for which a person is proud. (5)

L

Last Will and Testament: Legally binding document giving directions on how to divide financial assets when a person dies. (9)

leadership: Quality that involves organizing, guiding, motivating, and taking responsibility for a team. (3)

leanings: Tendencies. (4)

levy: Impose. (13)

liaisons: People who aid communication between groups of people or organizations. (11)

Copyright Goodheart-Willcox Co., Inc.

life coaching: Practice of assisting clients to determine and achieve their life goals. (13)

limited liability company (LLC): Legal structure that combines the limited liability features of a corporation with the tax benefits and operational flexibility of a sole proprietorship or partnership. (13)

living will: Legal document informing family and medical workers of preferences for being kept alive by artificial means, or letting them pass when there is no chance of recovery. (9)

long-term goals: Goals that may take months or even years to achieve. (3)

lucrative: Profitable. (14)

M

mandated reporters: People who must legally report suspected instances of child neglect and abuse. (10)

market analysis: Part of the business plan that describes the desired customer base; competition; and methods for reaching the target market, or sales strategy. (13)

master's degree: Earned after completing at least one year of study beyond a bachelor's degree. (1)

maturity: Ability to adapt to the inevitable changes that happen in life, both personally and professionally. (4)

mean: Average of a set of numbers. (6)

median: Middle value in a set of numbers. (6)

mediation: Process in which a mediator tries to help those in a dispute reach a peaceful agreement. (3)

mediator: A neutral third party. (3)

mentor: Experienced person who provides support, guidance, and counsel to a less-experienced person. (5)

mixed message: A discrepancy between verbal and nonverbal messages. (3)

moral issues: Matters that deal with what a person judges to be right or wrong. (2)

mortality: Eventual death. (9)

multiculturalism: Idea that cultural identities should not be ignored, but instead should be maintained, valued, and respected. (4)

MyPlate: Food guidance system created by the USDA to help people ages two and older make healthful food choices. (14)

N

natural fibers: Fibers that come from plant and animal sources. (15)

networking: Act of meeting and making contact with people. (7)

niche markets: Subsets of the larger market created to meet specific target market's needs. (15)

noninstallment credit: Type of short-term loan in which the entire balance is expected to be paid at once. (8)

notions: Items, such as threads, buttons, and zippers, that are attached to a finished garment. (15)

notorious: Well-known; famous. (15)

nuclear family: Husband and wife and their biological children. (11)

nursing homes: Special housing for older adults that offers more intense nursing care, usually provided by medical staff. (16)

nutrient-dense foods: Foods that are rich in vitamins and minerals and contain relatively few calories. (14)

nutrition: Study of how the body uses nutrients in foods and how these nutrients impact diet, productivity, health, and disease. (14)

Copyright Goodheart-Willcox Co., Inc.

O

obesity: Condition characterized by an excessive amount of body fat. (14)

obituary: Death notice. (12)

operant conditioning: Repetition of behaviors when reinforced. (2)

opulent: Rich; luxurious. (16)

organizational culture: Refers to work culture in larger work environments, and is broadened to include group norms and other tangible signs of an organization. (7)

overweight: Condition that results from having a high amount of body fat in relation to lean body mass. (14)

P

palatable: Appetizing. (14)

paramount: Most important. (16)

paraprofessionals: Trained workers who assist qualified professionals. (1)

partnership: Business that has shared ownership and responsibility among two or more people. (13)

passive communicators: People who are unwilling to say what they feel, think, or desire and want to avoid all conflict. (3)

penalize: Punish. (8)

people-oriented leadership: Motivating teams by utilizing team members' skills and talents while providing a supportive, accommodating, and responsible environment. (5)

performance feedback: Part of the employee performance evaluation process that includes documentation on how an employee is doing on the job. (7)

permissive style: Parenting style that tends to let children control situations, making the decisions with few limits or controls. (10)

persona: Public image. (5)

personal care services: Employment category in the field of human services that involves providing personal services for people. (1)

personal essentials: Values, needs, and wants that are critical to a person. (5)

plethora (PLEH-tho-ruh): Large amount of something. (11)

political culture: Refers to the systems, policies, rules, procedures, and structures of a work culture. (7)

portable: Easily transferrable from one job to another. (1)

portfolio: Dynamic, ever-growing and changing collection of artifacts that illustrate personal accomplishments, learning, strengths, and best works. (7)

precedence: Priority. (12)

preempt: Forestall. (7)

prejudice: Opinions formed without sufficient knowledge. (4)

prekindergarten programs: Educational programs for children who will be in kindergarten the following year; also called *Pre-K*. (10)

presbyopia: Slow decrease in the eye's ability to focus on nearby objects. (12)

preschool programs: Educational programs for children two through four years of age. (10)

prescriptive advice: Messages that encourage a person toward a certain decision or life path. (5)

principal: Original amount of money invested. (8)

principles of design: Harmony, emphasis, rhythm, balance, and proportion. (16)

priorities: Things that are most important to a person. (3)

problem-solving process: Strategy that includes defining and analyzing a

Copyright Goodheart-Willcox Co., Inc.

problem, setting and implementing goals, and monitoring and evaluating the plan. (3)

procrastinate: Put off starting a task until the last minute. (4)

professional organizations: Recognized associations that are formed to unite people engaged in the same industry. (4)

program of study: Guide that steps out the core and career-related courses a person needs to take to follow his or her career path. (6)

prohibitive messages: Advice that warns against a certain decision or life path. (5)

proxemics: Study of how people create the space around them. (16)

proximity: Nearness. (4)

psychoanalytic theories: Ideas that analyze the symbolic meaning behind behaviors. (2)

psychological needs: Person's fundamental desires that lead to self-satisfaction. (5)

public policy: Guidelines, regulations, and laws the government enacts to address a particular issue or problem. (11)

R

receiver: In communication, the person who accepts a message. (3)

recession mode: Slowing and decline in the economy. (2)

recipe: Set of written instructions to prepare a food item. (14)

reciprocal: Two-sided; mutual. (10)

recovery mode: When the economy begins to accelerate or look hopeful. (2)

redress: Setting right something that is wrong. (8)

references: People other than relatives who know a person and can attest to his or her work habits, skills, and abilities. (7)

repertoire: Collection. (5)

replete: Filled. (13)

resilient: Capable of recovering from setbacks. (9)

resources: Supply of assets that can be used when needed. (2)

résumé: Written or electronic document that summarizes a person's education, qualifications, and work experience. (7)

revolving credit: Type of loan that is repeatedly available as long as regular payments are made each month. (8)

riled: Annoyed. (12)

S

saving: Setting money aside. (8)

S corporation: Type of corporation set up through an IRS tax election. (13)

self-actualization: Fully realize one's own potential. (2)

self-advocacy: Action of speaking up for and representing oneself. (8)

self-assessment: Lifetime process that helps a person reflect and identify his or her personal values, needs, resources, temperament or personality, skills, abilities, and dreams. (5)

self-deprecating: Undervaluing oneself. (5)

sender: In communication, the person who transmits a message or messages. (3)

shades: Darker values created by adding black to the hue. (16)

short-term goals: Goals that are achievable in the immediate to near future. (3)

single-parent family: Father or mother and his or her children. (11)

skills: Developed talents or abilities. (1)

Copyright Goodheart-Willcox Co., Inc.

social cognitive theory: Theory based on the assumption that people are affected by rewards and punishments, but their reactions to rewards and punishments are filtered by their own perceptions, thoughts, and motivations. (2)

social sustainability: Company's or society's consideration of issues such as human rights; fair labor laws; community development; and health, safety, and wellness. (8)

social system: Organization of individuals into groups based on characteristic patterned relationships. (11)

sole proprietorship: Business that is owned by one person. (13)

solvent: Secure. (8)

Standard English: Most widely accepted form of the English language. (3)

standard of living: Person or family's measure of the wealth, comforts, and material goods available to them. (2)

stepfamily: Forms when a single parent gets married; also called *blended family*. (11)

stereotypes: Preconceived generalizations about certain groups of people. (4)

stress: Body's response when faced with pressures and demands. (4)

stringent: Strict; rigorous. (14)

substance abuse: Misuse of drugs to a toxic, dangerous level. (4)

sustainable: Method of using a resource so it does not deplete or destroy the resource. (8)

sustainable purchasing: Buying products that benefit environmental, social, or human health. (8)

SWOT analysis: Method used to evaluate a business idea for its strengths, weaknesses, opportunities, and threats. (13)

synthetic fibers: Fibers that are produced in chemistry labs. (15)

T

tactile: Perceived by touch. (16)

tangible assets: Resources that are physical, material possessions, such as money, property, digital devices, vehicles, or furniture. (5)

target market: Specific customer base to which a business will aim to sell. (13)

task-oriented leadership: Organizing and delegating duties, guiding and motivating team members, and taking responsibility for completing a job. (5)

time management: Method a person uses to manage or organize time. (4)

tinnitus: Ringing sound in a person's ears. (12)

tints: Lighter values created by adding white to the hue. (16)

tones: Colors created by adding grey, which lowers the intensity of the colors. (16)

U

universal design: Housing design that meets the physical needs of people of all ages and abilities. (16)

V

validate: Confirm. (3)

value: Lightness or darkness of a color that is produced by adding white or black. (16)

values: Things a person considers to be important in life. (3)

vegetarian: Person who excludes some or all animal products from his or her diet. (14)

visual merchandising: Field that involves capturing consumers' attention through window and interior store displays, placement of posters, signage on clothing racks, wall displays, seasonal store displays, and media. (15)

Copyright Goodheart-Willcox Co., Inc.

volunteering: Providing an important free service for a person or an organization. (6)

W

warranty: Written guarantee from the manufacturer that a product is in good condition. (8)

weight management: Achieving and maintaining a healthy weight over time. (4)

wellness: Process that involves making lifestyle choices that contribute to good physical, mental, and social well-being. (4)

work culture: Environment that includes the assumptions, values, behaviors, and actions of people as they interact with one another and complete their service or work. (7)

work-life balance: Concept that involves finding the right balance amid the many demands involving family and friends, career, and other interests or responsibilities. (4)

work-related child care programs: Not-for-profit programs businesses may run for their employees' children. (10)

Index

Copyright Goodheart-Willcox Co., Inc.

binge-eating disorder, 412–413
bingeing, 412
biodegradable, 215
bipolar disorder, 250
blended family, 313
body composition, 409
brick and mortar stores, 212
brokers, 358
budget analyst, 202
budgeting, 45, 216, 218, 447
    creating, 45, 218
    definition, 216
    planning a professional wardrobe, 447
bulimia nervosa, 412
business license, 365
business plans, 371–377
    appendix, 376–377
    company description, 372
    definition, 371
    executive summary, 371
    financial section, 376
    market analysis, 372
    marketing and sales strategies, 375–376
    organizational and legal structures, 373–374
    parts of, 371
    service or product description, 375
business structures, 373–374
buying, careers, 205, 212–216, 435
buying plan, 435

C

CAD, 450
calcium, 402
career and technical program, 19
Career and Technical Student Organizations
    (CTSOs), 74–75
career counselor, 234
career fairs, 169
career goal, 157
career plan, 157–159
career portfolio. *See* portfolio
careers. *See also* employment
    clothing related, 16, 430–439
    consumer services, 12–13, 198–225

counseling and mental health services, 13,
    232–236
early childhood development and services,
    13, 15, 265–270
entrepreneurial, 15–16, 354–379
family and community services, 15,
    302–308
food and nutrition, 16, 387–395
housing related, 16, 467–473
overview of human services, 11–17
personal care services, 15, 330–334
planning, 150–161
researching, 142–165
workplace success, 166–195
caregivers, 332
case coordinators, 305
case managers, 305
caseworkers, 305
catering, 394
CDA, 272
center-based child care programs, 267–268
certificate of resale, 365
certified hospital child life specialist, 3
certified nursing assistants (CNAs), 332
Certified Personal Finance Counselor (CPFC)
    certification, 209
Charitable Organization Society (COS), 9
child abuse and neglect, 288–293
    causes, 289–290
    definition, 288
    effects, 290–291
    prevention, 291–292
    reporting, 292
    treatment, 292–293
    types, 288
childbearing stage, 240–241
child care workers, 265–268
    center-based child care, 267–268
    family child care centers, 266–267
    in-home, 265
child custody, 249
Child Development Associate (CDA), 272
childhood development and services. *See* early
    childhood development and services
childless family, 313

Copyright Goodheart-Willcox Co., Inc.

Copyright Goodheart-Willcox Co., Inc.

Copyright Goodheart-Willcox Co., Inc.

Copyright Goodheart-Willcox Co., Inc.

Copyright Goodheart-Willcox Co., Inc.

Copyright Goodheart-Willcox Co., Inc.

Copyright Goodheart-Willcox Co., Inc.

Copyright Goodheart-Willcox Co., Inc.

Copyright Goodheart-Willcox Co., Inc.

Copyright Goodheart-Willcox Co., Inc.

Copyright Goodheart-Willcox Co., Inc.

Copyright Goodheart-Willcox Co., Inc.

Copyright Goodheart-Willcox Co., Inc.